Achieving the Sustainable Development Goals Punctually

Achieving the Sustainable Development Goals Punctually:

An Impossible Remit?

By

Graeme Baber

Cambridge Scholars Publishing

Achieving the Sustainable Development Goals Punctually:
An Impossible Remit?

By Graeme Baber

This book first published 2021

Cambridge Scholars Publishing

Lady Stephenson Library, Newcastle upon Tyne, NE6 2PA, UK

British Library Cataloguing in Publication Data
A catalogue record for this book is available from the British Library

ISBN (10): 1-5275-6150-X
ISBN (13): 978-1-5275-6150-2

To my Mum for her support, and my Dad for his company,
in the endeavour to research and write this monograph.

CONTENTS

LIST OF TABLES

PREFACE

In 'Development, the European Union and the financial crisis: assessing the picture', *Journal of Financial Crime*, 23(2), 441-464, I create a sustainable development index – Baber's Sustainable Development Index (BSDI), which I then apply to selected countries including all those in the European Union. One interesting observation there is the unexpectedly low value of the BSDI that the United Kingdom obtained and also that of France. These countries are the backbone of the world – traditional, civilized, prosperous, educated. But, they both only just qualified as developed states. Why? Because they were being neglected by the European Union in large part because the supranational organization had been concentrating on integration and enlargement simultaneously, stretching funds – many of which were destined for the newer Member States. What happened next? The United Kingdom went one way – voting by 51.9% to 48.1% to leave the European Union in June 2016 – a vote that was subsequently endorsed in the General Election of December 2019. France went the other way, voting in the internationalist and centrist candidate Mr. Emmanuel Macron as the President of France in May 2017 and subsequently endorsing Mr. Macron's new political party *La République En Marche !* as the ruling entity. These changes were reactionary, showing a shifting world order of which sustainable development was an integral part.

So, I decided that the Sustainable Development Goals should be studied – they were enormous, new, ambitious, and, if successful, would change the world. This book is the product of that decision, taken a few years ago. It builds on my earlier books entitled *Essays on International Law* and *The United Nations System: A Synopsis*, which are also published by Cambridge Scholars Publishing. It comprises two microstudies and two macrostudies, which between them cover all seventeen of the Sustainable Development Goals, and it concentrates on whether, and the extent to which, these Goals and their targets will be punctually accomplished.

Graeme Baber,
September 2020.

CHAPTER ONE

THE CONTEXT OF THE SUSTAINABLE DEVELOPMENT GOALS

Sustainable Development

'Sustainable development' is "[e]conomic development that is conducted without depletion of natural resources".[1] Thus, conservation of the *environment* is a necessary element of this process. The World Commission on Environment and Development provides a more detailed definition of the term 'sustainable development', as follows.

> Sustainable development is development that meets the needs of the present without compromising the ability of future generations to meet their own needs. It contains within it two key concepts: – the concept of 'needs', in particular the essential needs of the world's poor, to which overriding priority should be given; and – the idea of limitations imposed by the state of technology and social organization on the environment's ability to meet present and future needs.[2]

Human needs are essential to sustainable development, as the Commission emphasizes.

> [S]ustainable development is a process of change in which the exploitation of resources, the direction of investments, the orientation of technological development; and institutional change are all in harmony and enhance both current and future potential to meet human needs and aspirations.[3]

---

[1] "Sustainable development", Lexico, accessed January 9, 2020, https://www.lexico.com/definition/sustainable_development.
[2] World Commission on Environment and Development, Report: Our Common Future (New York, 1987), 41.
[3] World Commission on Environment and Development, Report: Our Common Future (New York, 1987), 43.

One classic model of human needs is that proposed by Dr. Abraham Maslow[4] in 1943, in which he envisaged a five-layer hierarchy as follows.

> (1) There are at least five sets of goals, which we may call basic needs. These are briefly physiological, safety, love, [self-]esteem, and self-actualization. In addition, we are motivated by the desire to achieve or maintain the various conditions upon which these basic satisfactions rest and by certain more intellectual desires. (2) These basic goals are related to each other, being arranged in a hierarchy of prepotency. This means that the most prepotent goal will monopolize consciousness and will tend of itself to organize the recruitment of the various capacities of the organism. The less prepotent needs are minimized, even forgotten or denied. But when a need is fairly well satisfied, the next prepotent ('higher') need emerges, in turn to dominate the conscious life and to serve as the center of organization of behavior, since gratified needs are not active motivators.[5]

On the assumption that Maslow's hierarchy of needs is acceptable as a simple working model of human needs, it is submitted that the physiological and safety needs correspond to *economic* aspect of sustainable development, and that the need for love and for esteem correlate with the *social* dimension of sustainable development.[6] As stated above,[7] conservation of the *environment* – i.e., the third element of sustainable development – is a necessary part of the concept of sustainable development. Thus, the three-dimensional model of sustainable development – upon which the SDGs are based, fits with the definition of that term.

Furthermore, not only is sustainable development considered to comprise economic, social and environmental dimensions, but these aspects are integrated into the whole. As Dr. Rachel Emas[8] illustrates, it is

---

[4] Dr. Maslow was Professor of Psychology at Brandeis University from 1951 until 1969 ("Abraham Maslow: American Psychologist", Encyclopaedia Britannica, accessed January 10, 2020, https://www.britannica.com/biography/Abraham-H-Maslow).

[5] Abraham Maslow, "A Theory of Human Motivation", *Psychological Review*, 1943, 50(4), 370-396, 394-395.

[6] The three dimensions of sustainable development, i.e., economic development, social development and environmental protection, are considered in relation to the SDGs at pages 66-74 of Graeme Baber, *The United Nations System: A Synopsis* (Newcastle-upon-Tyne: Cambridge Scholars Publishing, 2019).

[7] This reference is to the second sentence of the first paragraph of this section, i.e., that entitled 'Sustainable Development'.

[8] Dr. Emas is an Assistant Teaching Professor at Rutgers University ("Rachel Emas, PhD", Rutgers School of Public Affairs and Administration, accessed January 11, 2020, https://spaa.newark.rutgers.edu/about).

that blending which drives the process of sustainable development from a worse state to a better condition.

> The key principle of sustainable development underlying all others is the integration of environmental, social, and economic concerns into all aspects of decision making. … It is this deeply fixed concept of integration that distinguishes sustainability from other forms of policy. … [S]ustainable development requires the integration of economic, environmental, and social objectives across sectors, territories, and generations. [E]nvironmental, social, and economic concerns must be integrated throughout decision making processes in order to move towards development that is truly sustainable.[9]

The Launch of the Sustainable Development Goals

From inception to Rio+20

The idea for the SDGs was that of Ms. Paula Caballero[10] in January 2011, when stating in a brainstorming meeting with colleagues from the Government of Colombia which she had convoked, that Colombia "propose a new set of goals [i.e., other than the MDGs] that would encompass the many dimensions of development".[11] Having promptly gained the backing of Dr. Patti Londoño,[12] who was then Vice Minister of Foreign Affairs in the Government of Colombia,[13] Ms. Caballero, together with Dr. Londoño and other supportive ministers/officials from Colombia and those from other countries, publicised the draft SDGs at international

---

[9] Rachel Emas, "The Concept of Sustainable Development: Definition and Defining Principles", *Brief for Global Sustainable Development Report 2015*, 1-3, 3.

[10] Ms. Caballero is Managing Director, Lands for Life, at Rare ("We are Rare", Rare, accessed January 13, 2020, https://rare.org/we-are-rare/).

[11] Paula Caballero, *A Short History of the SDGS*, available at https://web.archive.org/web/20171118221940/http://deliver2030.org/wp%2Dcontent/uploads/2016/04/A%2Dshort%2Dhistory%2Dof%2Dthe%2DSDGs%2DPaula%2DCaballero.pdf, accessed January 13, 2020, 1. *The United Nations System: A Synopsis* contains a fuller version of Ms. Caballero's recollections of the initiation of the SDGs, at page 61 therein.

[12] Dr. Londoño is Senior Policy Adviser at Cepei ("Patti Londoño", Cepei, accessed January 13, 2020, http://cepei.org/unds_staff/patti-londono-2/).

[13] Paula Caballero, *A Short History of the SDGS*, available at https://web.archive.org/web/20171118221940/http://deliver2030.org/wp%2Dcontent/uploads/2016/04/A%2Dshort%2Dhistory%2Dof%2Dthe%2DSDGs%2DPaula%2DCaballero.pdf, accessed January 13, 2020, 1.

meetings.[14] The participants at Rio+20[15] approved the Goals in principle, requiring the refinement of these SDGs through the establishment of an open working group – which would later submit a proposal for SDGs to the General Assembly of the UN for its consideration.[16] The outcome document from Rio+20[17] states the following.

> … The goals [for sustainable development] should address and incorporate in a balanced way all three dimensions of sustainable development [i.e., economic, social and environmental] and their interlinkages. They should be coherent with and integrated into the United Nations development agenda beyond 2015, thus contributing to the achievement of sustainable development and serving as a driver for implementation and mainstreaming of sustainable development in the United Nations system as a whole. …[18]

From Rio+20 to the UN Sustainable Development Summit

On 27th July 2012, the General Assembly of the UN endorsed the outcome document from Rio+20.[19] The General Assembly founded the Open Working Group on Sustainable Development Goals,[20] which comprised 30 representatives from 70 states – 24 of those 30 places being shared between two, three or four countries.[21] At its first session, which was

---

[14] Baber, *The United Nations System: A Synopsis*, 62.

[15] Rio+20 took place from 20th to 22nd June 2012 (United Nations, Resolution 66/288 adopted by the General Assembly on 27 July 2012, Annex, para.1).

[16] Baber, *The United Nations System: A Synopsis*, 62-63.

[17] The outcome document from Rio+20 is titled 'The future we want' (United Nations, Resolution 66/288 adopted by the General Assembly on 27 July 2012, art.2).

[18] Resolution 66/288 adopted by the General Assembly on 27 July 2012, Annex, para.246.

[19] Resolution 66/288 adopted by the General Assembly on 27 July 2012, art.2.

[20] United Nations, Decision 67/555 of the General Assembly dated 22 January 2013, art.(a).

[21] The 30 places on the Open Working Group on Sustainable Development Goals were allotted/shared as follows: 1 Algeria-Egypt-Morocco-Tunisia, 2 Ghana, 3 Benin, 4 Kenya, 5 Tanzania, 6 the Republic of the Congo, 7 Zambia-Zimbabwe, 8 Nauru-Palau-Papua New Guinea 10 India-Pakistan-Sri Lanka 11 China-Indonesia-Kazakhstan 12 Cyprus-Singapore-the United Arab Emirates 13 Bangladesh-the Republic of Korea-Saudi Arabia 14 Iran-Japan-Nepal 15 Colombia-Guatemala 16 the Bahamas-Barbados 17 Guyana-Haiti-Trinidad and Tobago 18 Mexico-Peru 19 Brazil-Nicaragua 20 Argentina-Bolivia-Ecuador 21 Australia-the Netherlands-the UK 22 Canada-Israel-the USA 23 Denmark-Ireland-Norway 24 France-Germany-Switzerland 25 Italy-Spain-Turkey 26 Hungary 27 Belarus-Serbia 28 Bulgaria-

convened on 14th and 15th March 2013,[22] the Open Working Group on Sustainable Development Goals appointed Messrs. Macharia Kamau[23] and Csaba Kőrösi [24] as its co-chairs – these gentlemen then being the Permanent Representative of Kenya to the UN and the Permanent Representative of Hungary to the UN, respectively.[25] Whilst this meeting included general and interactive discussions on the SDGs,[26] the second to eighth sessions were each dedicated to pre-specified topics and the ninth to thirteenth sessions were devoted to developing a proposal on SDGs –

Croatia 29 Montenegro-Slovenia 30 Poland-Romania (Decision 67/555 of the General Assembly dated 22 January 2013, Annex). Whilst the Annex to Decision 67/255 of the General Assembly names the state at number 6 as "Congo", an inquiry to the UN over which of the two countries named 'The Congo' was that selected to be a Member of the Open Working Group on Sustainable Development Goals yielded the reply that, in the UN's diplomatic language, 'Congo' refers to the Republic of the Congo and 'DRC' refers to the Democratic Republic of the Congo ("Open Working Group on Sustainable Development Goals (reference #203333)", United Nations Sustainable Development Knowledge Platform, accessed January 15, 2020, https://sustainabledevelopment.un.org/account.php?page=view&nr=751&type=12 &msg=203333&menu=1457). Consequently, number 6 on the list above in this note is deemed to equate to the Republic of the Congo.

[22] "First session of the Open Working Group on Sustainable Development Goals", United Nations Sustainable Development Knowledge Platform, accessed January 14, 2020, https://sustainabledevelopment.un.org/owg1.html.

[23] Mr. Kamau is Principal Secretary in the Ministry of Foreign Affairs in the Government of Kenya ("Ambassador Kamau Macharia", Ministry of Foreign Affairs in the Government of Kenya, accessed January 14, 2020, http://www.mfa.go.ke/?page_id=2224).

[24] Mr. Kőrösi is Director of Environmental Sustainability at the Office of the President of the Republic of Hungary ("Csaba Kőrösi", Vienna Energy Forum, accessed January 14, 2020, https://www.viennaenergyforum.org/content/csaba-k%C5%91r%C3%B6si).

[25] "Open Working Group on Sustainable Development Goals", United Nations Sustainable Development Knowledge Platform, accessed January 14, 2020, https://sustainabledevelopment.un.org/owg.html. Kenya and Hungary each had an exclusive place on the Open Working Group on Sustainable Development Goals (i.e., numbers 4 and 26, respectively, in the list in note 21).

[26] United Nations, Sixty-eighth session of the General Assembly: Agenda items 14, 19(a) and 118, A/68/970, 12 August 2014 – Report of the Open Working Group of the General Assembly on Sustainable Development Goals (New York, 2014), III.F.9, 4.

which would constitute most of its final report.[27] The programme for the second to eighth sessions were as follows.

Table 1.1: The topics considered at the second to eighth sessions of the Open Working Group on Sustainable Development Goals[28]

Session of Open Working Group	Dates on which the session was held	Topics considered
Second	17th to 19th April 2013	(i) Conceptualizing the SDGs (ii) The eradication of poverty (iii) Universality (iv) Key lessons from the MDGs (v) Alternative measures of poverty
Third	22nd to 24th May 2013	(i) Food security and nutrition (ii) Sustainable agriculture (iii) Desertification (iv) Land degradation and drought (v) Water and sanitation

[27] Report of the Open Working Group of the General Assembly on Sustainable Development Goals, III.F.11, 5; "Open Working Group on Sustainable Development", United Nations Sustainable Development 2015, accessed January 15, 2020, https://www.sustainabledevelopment2015.org/index.php/intergovernmental-processes/sustainable-development-goals/open-working-group/. The ninth to thirteenth sessions of the Open Working Group on Sustainable Development Goals were held from 3rd to 7th March, 31st March to 7th April, 5th to 9th May, 2nd to 6th June, and 14th to 18th July, respectively, of 2014; the Open Working Group's final report was finished in July 2014 ("Open Working Group on Sustainable Development", United Nations Sustainable Development 2015, accessed January 16, 2020, https://www.sustainabledevelopment2015.org/index.php/intergovernmental-processes/sustainable-development-goals/open-working-group/).

[28] Report of the Open Working Group of the General Assembly on Sustainable Development Goals, III.F.10, 4-5; "Open Working Group on Sustainable Development", United Nations Sustainable Development 2015, accessed January 16, 2020, https://www.sustainabledevelopment2015.org/index.php/intergovernmental-processes/sustainable-development-goals/open-working-group/.

Fourth	17th to 19th June 2013	(i) Employment and decent work for all (ii) Social protection (iii) Youth (iv) Education (v) Culture (vi) Health (vii) Population dynamics
Fifth	25th to 27th November 2013	(i) Sustainable and inclusive economic growth (ii) Macroeconomic policy questions (iii) Infrastructure development and industrialization
Sixth	9th to 13th December 2013	(i) Means of implementation (ii) Global partnership for accomplishing sustainable development (iii) Needs of countries in special situations – African states, LDCs, LLDCs, SIDS, and specific challenges that the middle-income countries face (iv) Human rights (v) The right to development (vi) Global governance
Seventh	6th to 10th January 2014	(i) Sustainable cities and human settlements (ii) Sustainable transport (iii) Sustainable energy (iv) Sustainable consumption and production (v) Climate change and disaster risk reduction
Eighth	3rd to 7th February 2014	(i) Oceans and seas (ii) Forests (iii) Biodiversity (iv) Promoting equality, including social equity, gender equality, and women's empowerment (v) The prevention of conflict (vi) Peace and security – peacebuilding after conflict and the promotion of durable peace (vii) The rule of law and governance

At the second meeting of the thirteenth session of the Open Working Group on Sustainable Development Goals – on 19th July 2014[29] – the Open Working Group: (i) discussed a proposal on SDGs,[30] (ii) heard statements – including both reservations and positional explanations from many states,[31] and (iii) pursuant to Paragraph 248 of 'The Future We Want'[32] – i.e., the outcome document from Rio+20,[33] agreed to submit this plan to the General Assembly at its sixty-eighth session for consideration and suitable action.[34] The 17 SDGs that the Open Working Group's proposal for Sustainable Development Goals contains are the same as those which the General Assembly later adopted on 25th September 2015 in Resolution 70/1,[35] and are as follows.

---

[29] The thirteenth session of the Open Working Group on Sustainable Development took place from 14th to 18th July 2014 (note 27). The documents associated with this session include one entitled 'Final Compilation of Amendments to Goals and Targets By Major Groups and other stakeholders including citizen's responses to MY World 6 priorities', which is available at https://sustainabledevelopment.un.org/content/documents/4438mgscompilationowg13.pdf (accessed January 17, 2020), another titled 'Introduction and Proposed Goals and Targets on Sustainable Development for the Post2015 Development Agenda, which is available at https://sustainabledevelopment.un.org/content/documents/4523zerodraft.pdf (accessed January 17, 2020), and the main outcome document – labelled 'Introduction to the Proposal of the Open Working Group for Sustainable Development Goals' and dated 'Sat 19 July 1:20 pm' – in which both the preliminary paragraphs and the targets of the SDGs differ slightly from those of the final report (which is entitled 'Open Working Group proposal for Sustainable Development Goals' and which is contained in the General Assembly's document A/68/970 (note 26) as item IV on pages 6-24 of that paper under the heading 'Proposal of the Open Working Group on sustainable development goals); the SDGs are identical in both these latter documents.

[30] Report of the Open Working Group of the General Assembly on Sustainable Development Goals, III.G.12, 5.

[31] Report of the Open Working Group of the General Assembly on Sustainable Development Goals, III.G.13, 5-6.

[32] This Paragraph is contained in the Annex to Resolution 66/288 adopted by the General Assembly on 27 July 2012, and is quoted in its entity at pages 62-63 of Baber, *The United Nations System: A Synopsis*.

[33] Note 17.

[34] Report of the Open Working Group of the General Assembly on Sustainable Development Goals, III.G.14, 6.

[35] The *presentation* of these two sources of the 17 SDGs differs – in particular, the former refers to the 'global partnership for sustainable development' in SDG 17 whilst the latter mentions the 'Global Partnership for Sustainable Development'.

Goal 1[:] End poverty in all its forms everywhere
Goal 2[:] End hunger, achieve food security and improved nutrition and promote sustainable agriculture
Goal 3[:] Ensure healthy lives and promote well-being for all at all ages
Goal 4[:] Ensure inclusive and equitable quality education and promote lifelong learning opportunities for all
Goal 5[:] Achieve gender equality and empower all women and girls
Goal 6[:] Ensure availability and sustainable management of water and sanitation for all
Goal 7[:] Ensure access to affordable, reliable, sustainable and modern energy for all
Goal 8[:] Promote sustained, inclusive and sustainable economic growth, full and productive employment and decent work for all
Goal 9[:] Build resilient infrastructure, promote inclusive and sustainable industrialization and foster innovation
Goal 10[:] Reduce inequality within and among countries
Goal 11[:] Make cities and human settlements inclusive, safe, resilient and sustainable
Goal 12[:] Ensure sustainable consumption and production patterns
Goal 13[:] Take urgent action to combat climate change and its impacts
Goal 14[:] Conserve and sustainably use the oceans, seas and marine resources for sustainable development
Goal 15[:] Protect, restore and promote sustainable use of terrestrial ecosystems, sustainably manage forests, combat desertification, and halt and reverse land degradation and halt biodiversity loss
Goal 16[:] Promote peaceful and inclusive societies for sustainable development, provide access to justice for all and build effective, accountable and inclusive institutions at all levels
Goal 17[:] Strengthen the means of implementation and revitalize the Global Partnership for Sustainable Development[36]

These SDGs are accompanied by 169 targets, which the General Assembly also adopted on 25th September 2015.[37] Prior to the UN Sustainable

Notwithstanding this, the *content* of each and every SDG is identical in the two documents.

[36] United Nations, Open Working Group Proposal for Sustainable Development Goals (New York, 2014), 6; United Nations, Resolution 70/1 adopted by the General Assembly on 25 September 2015, Transforming our world: the 2030 Agenda for Sustainable Development, 14.

[37] Resolution 70/1 adopted by the General Assembly on 25 September 2015, Transforming our world: the 2030 Agenda for Sustainable Development, 1.

Development Summit in September 2015[38] – of which 'Transforming our world: the 2030 Agenda for Sustainable Development' – which the General Assembly adopted in Resolution 70/1 – is the outcome document,[39] the UN held its Third International Conference on Financing for Development in Addis Ababa from 13th to 16th July 2015.[40] The main outcome paper from the latter symposium is the Addis Ababa Action Agenda,[41] which the General Assembly endorsed in its Resolution dated 27th July 2015.[42]

Addis Ababa Action Agenda: The Agenda declares the goal of the Heads of Government and High Representatives to be "to end poverty and hunger and to achieve sustainable development in its three dimensions [i.e., economic, social and environmental[43]] through inclusive economic growth, protecting the environment and promoting social inclusion".[44] Whilst "each country has primary responsibility for its own economic and social development …, national development efforts need to be supported by an enabling international economic environment".[45] The "global partnership for sustainable development, led by Governments … should reflect the fact that the post-2015 development agenda, including the sustainable development goals, is global in nature and universally

---

[38] The UN Sustainable Development Summit was held at the Headquarters of the UN in New York from 25th to 27th September 2015 ("Sustainable Development Goals", United Nations, accessed January 27, 2020, https://www.un.org/sustainabledevelopment/summit/).

[39] Resolution 70/1 adopted by the General Assembly on 25 September 2015, 1.

[40] "Third International Conference: Financing for Development", United Nations, accessed January 27, 2020, https://www.un.org/esa/ffd/ffd3/index.html.

[41] Two other documents relating to the Third International Conference on Financing for Development are one entitled 'Declaration from the Addis Ababa Civil Society Forum on Financing for Development' and dated 12th July 2015 – which is available at https://csoforffd.files.wordpress.com/2015/07/addis-ababa-cso-ffd-forum-declaration-12-july-2015.pdf (accessed January 27, 2020), and another titled 'International Business Forum: Third International Conference on Financing for Development' and dated 14th July 2015 – which is available at https://www.un.org/esa/ffd/ffd3/wp-content/uploads/sites/2/2015/04/Business-Forum-Summary.pdf (accessed January 27, 2020).

[42] United Nations, Resolution 69/313 adopted by the General Assembly on 27 July 2015, art.1.

[43] The section above entitled 'Sustainable Development' establishes and contextualizes these three dimensions of sustainable development.

[44] Resolution 69/313 adopted by the General Assembly on 27 July 2015, Annex, para.1.

[45] Resolution 69/313 adopted by the General Assembly on 27 July 2015, Annex, para.9.

applicable to all countries whilst taking into account different national realities, capacities, needs and levels of development and respecting national policies and priorities".[46] The many financial promises of the Heads of Government and High Representatives include those to "encourage both international and domestic development banks to promote finance for micro, small and medium-sized enterprises … through the creation of credit lines targeting those enterprises, as well as technical assistance",[47] "work towards developing domestic capital markets, particularly long-term bond and insurance markets where appropriate, including crop insurance on non-distortive terms [and] to strengthen supervision, clearing, settlement and risk management",[48] and "build capacity to enter into public-private partnerships, including with regard to planning, contract negotiation, management, accounting and budgeting for contingent liabilities".[49] Although "many countries still fall short of their ODA commitments and … the fulfilment of all ODA commitments remains crucial[,] ODA providers reaffirm their respective ODA commitments, including the commitment by many developed countries to achieve the target of 0.7 per cent of gross national income for official development assistance (ODA/GNI) and 0.15 to 0.20 per cent of ODA/GNI to least developed countries".[50] The Heads of Government and High Representatives "recognize that funding from all sources, including public and private, bilateral and multilateral, as well as alternative sources of finance, will need to be stepped up for investments in many areas, including for low-carbon and climate resilient development".[51] They "will step up [their] efforts to assist countries in accessing financing for peacebuilding and development in the post-conflict context[,] recogniz[ing] the need for aid to be delivered efficiently through simplified mechanisms".[52] In respect of "innovative sources and

[46] Resolution 69/313 adopted by the General Assembly on 27 July 2015, Annex, para.10.
[47] Resolution 69/313 adopted by the General Assembly on 27 July 2015, Annex, para.43.
[48] Resolution 69/313 adopted by the General Assembly on 27 July 2015, Annex, para.44.
[49] Resolution 69/313 adopted by the General Assembly on 27 July 2015, Annex, para.48.
[50] Resolution 69/313 adopted by the General Assembly on 27 July 2015, Annex, para.51.
[51] Resolution 69/313 adopted by the General Assembly on 27 July 2015, Annex, para.60.
[52] Resolution 69/313 adopted by the General Assembly on 27 July 2015, Annex, para.67.

mechanisms of additional financing, [the Heads of Government and High Representatives] encourage [(i)] consideration of how existing mechanisms, such as the International Finance Facility for Immunization,[53] might be replicated to address broader development needs[, and (ii)] exploring additional innovative mechanisms based on models combining public and private resources such as green bonds,[54] vaccine bonds,[55] triangular loans[56] and pull mechanisms[57] and carbon pricing mechanisms[58]".[59]

---

[53] The IFFIm was established in 2006 in order to raise and expedite the joint effect of government donors and private investors on worldwide health; it provides an example of how its vaccine bonds work, as follows: "[A] sovereign donor pledges US$ 200 million paid in US$ 10 million tranches annually over 20 years. Without IFFIm, Gavi [i.e., the Global Alliance for Vaccines and Immunization] would be limited to spending this US$ 10 million each year and would have to wait 20 years before seeing its full impact. But, backed by these pledges, IFFIm issues its Vaccine Bonds on the international capital markets. Capital market investors buy these bonds for an attractive rate of return, which makes funds immediately available to IFFIm[.] Gavi uses the proceeds of these bond issuances to purchase more vaccines to immunise more children in the world's poorest countries. In order to ensure investors of its ability to pay back interest and principal, IFFIm only raises bonds against a percentage of their overall pledge. IFFIm uses the remainder as a reserve to make sure that there will always be more than sufficient funds to pay bondholders when the bonds mature. Donors' annual payments to IFFIm – or proceeds from new bond issues – go toward repayments to bondholders. … At the end of the donor payment period and after all bonds are redeemed, IFFIm can transfer to Gavi any outstanding reserve … . ("About IFFIm", International Finance Facility for Immunisation, accessed January 28, 2020, https://iffim.org/about-iffim)".

[54] A 'green bond' is one "specifically earmarked to be used for climate and environmental projects. These bonds are typically asset-linked and backed by the issuer's balance sheet, and are also referred to as climate bonds" ("Green bond", Investopedia, accessed January 28, 2020,
https://www.investopedia.com/terms/g/green-bond.asp).

[55] The IFFIm issues vaccine bonds (note 53).

[56] Triangular' means "shaped like a triangle; having three sides and three corners[;] *involving three people or parties*" (Oxford University Press, *The New Oxford Dictionary of English* (Oxford: Oxford University Press, 1998), 1977; emphasis added). Whilst a definition of 'triangular loan' was not found, the ECOSOC's Development Cooperation Forum has provided a definition of 'triangular co-operation', as follows: "Triangular cooperation involves three partners that can be described as "enabler", "provider/contributor" and "associate". The partners can be a public entity, civil society or academic organization, private enterprise or an international organization. Specific roles played by each partner can be interchangeable in different development cooperation arrangements and initiatives." (United Nations, ECOSOC Development Cooperation Forum: Promoting Sustainable

The 2030 Agenda for Sustainable Development: Ten weeks after its Third International Conference on Financing for Development,[60] the UN held its Sustainable Development Summit.[61] Many world leaders attended this historic event.[62] The Summit endorsed a document entitled 'Transforming

---

Development through Triangular Cooperation, DCF Policy Briefs, September 2017, No. 19 (New York, 2017), 1). Based on this definition, and on the relevant ordinary meaning of the word 'triangular' (italicized above), it is submitted that a 'triangular loan' would be one involving three parties, possibly a lender, a guarantor and a borrower.

[57] 'Pull mechanisms' are "designed to overcome market failures and promote innovation by rewarding successful innovations ex post. By providing assured public funding for goods that embody socially beneficial technologies for which private demand is inadequate (for example, vaccines, pharmaceuticals and renewable energy technologies), they aim to turn notional into effective demand, thus allowing investors to capture more fully the social value of their research and investments. … [One example of a pull mechanism comprises s]tandard prizes, which reward achievements in a technology development contest." (United Nations, Department of Economic and Social Affairs: World Economic and Social Survey 2012 – In Search of New Development Finance, E/2012/50/Rev.1, ST/ESA/341 (New York, 2012), 60). The phrase '*ex post*' is from modern Latin – from '*ex*' (from) and '*post*' (after); it means "based on actual results rather than forecasts" (*The New Oxford Dictionary of English*, 649).

[58] 'Carbon pricing' "captures the external costs of greenhouse gas (GHG) emissions – the costs of emissions that the public pays for, such as damage to crops, health care costs from heat waves and droughts, and loss of property from flooding and sea level rise – and ties them to their sources through a price, usually in the form of a price on the carbon dioxide (CO_2) emitted. A price on carbon helps [to] shift the burden for the damage from GHG emissions back to those who are responsible for it and who can avoid it. … Placing an adequate price on GHG emissions is of fundamental relevance to internalize the external cost of climate change in the broadest possible range of economic decision making and in setting economic incentives for clean development. It can help to mobilize the financial investment required to stimulate clean technology and market innovation, fueling new, low-carbon drivers of economic growth." ("Carbon Pricing Dashboard: What is Carbon Pricing?", World Bank, accessed January 28, 2020, https://carbonpricingdashboard.worldbank.org/what-carbon-pricing).

[59] Resolution 69/313 adopted by the General Assembly on 27 July 2015, Annex, para.69.

[60] The UN's Third International Conference on Financing for Development was held from 13th to 16th July 2015 (text to note 40).

[61] The UN's Sustainable Development Summit was held from 25th to 27th September 2015 (note 38).

[62] "Sustainable Development Goals", United Nations, accessed January 29, 2020, https://www.un.org/sustainabledevelopment/summit/.

our world: the 2030 Agenda for Sustainable Development', which was quickly adopted by the General Assembly in Resolution 70/1.[63] In addition to containing the 17 SDGs[64] and their targets,[65] the 2030 Agenda for Sustainable Development contains a Preamble,[66] a Declaration,[67] an introduction to the SDGs and their targets titled 'Sustainable Development Goals and targets',[68] a section headed 'Means of implementation and Global Partnership',[69] and a section denominated 'Follow-up and review'.[70] The Preamble re-emphasizes the aim of ending poverty in Paragraph 1 of the Addis Ababa Action Agenda[71] by "recogniz[ing] that eradicating poverty in all its forms and dimensions, including extreme poverty, is the greatest global challenge and an indispensable requirement for sustainable development".[72] It states, among other things, that the SDGs and their targets "demonstrate the scale and ambition of this new universal [2030] Agenda [for Sustainable Development, and] "are integrated and indivisible and balance the three dimensions of sustainable development: the economic, social and environmental".[73] The Declaration includes, among other things: (i) a recognition that the elimination of

---

[63] Note 39 and accompanying text.

[64] Text to note 35. The text to note 36 lists the SDGs.

[65] Note 37 and accompanying text.

[66] Resolution 70/1 adopted by the General Assembly on 25 September 2015, Transforming our world: the 2030 Agenda for Sustainable Development, 1-2.

[67] The Declaration comprises Paragraphs 1-53 of the 2030 Agenda for Sustainable Development (Resolution 70/1 adopted by the General Assembly on 25 September 2015, Transforming our world: the 2030 Agenda for Sustainable Development, 3-12).

[68] The section entitled 'Sustainable Development Goals and targets' contains Paragraphs 54-59 of the 2030 Agenda for Sustainable Development (Resolution 70/1 adopted by the General Assembly on 25 September 2015, Transforming our world: the 2030 Agenda for Sustainable Development, 13).

[69] The section titled 'Means of implementation and Global Partnership' consists of Paragraphs 60-71 of the 2030 Agenda for Sustainable Development (Resolution 70/1 adopted by the General Assembly on 25 September 2015, Transforming our world: the 2030 Agenda for Sustainable Development, 28-31).

[70] The section entitled 'Follow-up and review' is composed of Paragraphs 72-91 of the 2030 Agenda for Sustainable Development (Resolution 70/1 adopted by the General Assembly on 25 September 2015, Transforming our world: the 2030 Agenda for Sustainable Development, 31-35).

[71] Text to note 44.

[72] Resolution 70/1 adopted by the General Assembly on 25 September 2015, Transforming our world: the 2030 Agenda for Sustainable Development, 1.

[73] Resolution 70/1 adopted by the General Assembly on 25 September 2015, Transforming our world: the 2030 Agenda for Sustainable Development, 1.

poverty is the largest worldwide challenge and an essential requisite for sustainable development,[74] (ii) a commitment to accomplish sustainable development in its economic, social and environmental dimensions in an even-handed and unified way,[75] (iii) an assertion that the 2030 Agenda for Sustainable Development is accepted by, and applicable to, all states,[76] (iv) a declaration that the Agenda is directed by the UN Charter's principles and purposes,[77] (v) a confirmation of the commitment of the Heads of State and High Representatives to international law,[78] (vi) an affirmation that the 2030 Agenda for Sustainable Development is to be carried out in a way that is compatible with countries' rights and responsibilities under international law,[79] (vi) a resolution of the Heads of State and High Representatives to take additional, efficacious actions and measures, in accordance with international law, to eliminate impediments and constraints in respect of assistance to, increase support to, and satisfy the special needs of, people who live in areas that are affected by terrorism and/or complicated humanitarian crises,[80] (vii) a claim that the 2030 Agenda for Sustainable Development – including the SDGs – can be fulfilled within the framework of a reinvigorated Global Partnership for Sustainable Development, supported by the policies and actions that the Addis Ababa Action Agenda summarizes,[81] (viii) a recognition that each

---

[74] Resolution 70/1 adopted by the General Assembly on 25 September 2015, Transforming our world: the 2030 Agenda for Sustainable Development, para.2. This statement is repeated from the Preamble (text to note 72).

[75] Resolution 70/1 adopted by the General Assembly on 25 September 2015, Transforming our world: the 2030 Agenda for Sustainable Development, para.2. The section above entitled 'Sustainable Development' establishes and contextualizes the economic, social and environmental dimensions of sustainable development.

[76] Resolution 70/1 adopted by the General Assembly on 25 September 2015, Transforming our world: the 2030 Agenda for Sustainable Development, para.5.

[77] Resolution 70/1 adopted by the General Assembly on 25 September 2015, Transforming our world: the 2030 Agenda for Sustainable Development, para.10.

[78] Resolution 70/1 adopted by the General Assembly on 25 September 2015, Transforming our world: the 2030 Agenda for Sustainable Development, paras.18 and 1.

[79] Resolution 70/1 adopted by the General Assembly on 25 September 2015, Transforming our world: the 2030 Agenda for Sustainable Development, para.18.

[80] Resolution 70/1 adopted by the General Assembly on 25 September 2015, Transforming our world: the 2030 Agenda for Sustainable Development, paras.18 and 23.

[81] Resolution 70/1 adopted by the General Assembly on 25 September 2015, Transforming our world: the 2030 Agenda for Sustainable Development, para.40. The immediately-preceding paragraph in the text, i.e., that headed '*Addis Ababa Action Agenda*', synopsizes the Addis Ababa Action Agenda.

state has prime responsibility for its economic and social development, and (ix) a reaffirmation by providers of ODA of their separate commitments regarding ODA – which include those by many advanced countries to reach the target of 0.7% of GNI (i.e., ODA/GNI = 0.007) to developing countries, and 0.15% to 0.2% of GNI (i.e., ODA/GNI = 0.0015-0.002) to LDCs. [82] The 'Sustainable Development Goals and targets' section, states, among other things, that the Heads of State and High Representatives recognize that different visions, approaches, models and tools are to hand for each country to attain sustainable development in line with its domestic priorities and circumstances;[83] this part also makes the following comments.

> The Sustainable Development Goals and targets are integrated and indivisible, global in nature and universally applicable, taking into account different national realities, capacities and levels of development and respecting national policies and priorities. Targets are defined as aspirational and global, with each Government setting its own national targets guided by the global level of ambition but taking into account national circumstances. Each Government will also decide how these aspirational and global targets should be incorporated into national planning processes, policies and strategies. It is important to recognize the link between sustainable development and other relevant ongoing processes in the economic, social and environmental fields.[84]

The section entitled 'Means of implementation and the Global Partnership', specifies that the Global Partnership for Sustainable Development is to facilitate worldwide participation to support implementation of all the SDGs and their targets, assembling different parties and mobilizing all resources that are available.[85] It also announces the launch by the Heads of State and High Representatives of a Technology Facilitation Mechanism, which comprises: (i) a UN inter-agency task force on science, technology and innovation for the SDGs, (ii) a multi-stakeholder forum on these areas

---

[82] Resolution 70/1 adopted by the General Assembly on 25 September 2015, Transforming our world: the 2030 Agenda for Sustainable Development, para.43. Providers of ODA also made this reaffirmation in the Addis Ababa Action Agenda (text to note 50). Note 125 of Chapter Two lists all 47 LDCs.

[83] Resolution 70/1 adopted by the General Assembly on 25 September 2015, Transforming our world: the 2030 Agenda for Sustainable Development, paras.59 and 1.

[84] Resolution 70/1 adopted by the General Assembly on 25 September 2015, Transforming our world: the 2030 Agenda for Sustainable Development, para.55.

[85] Resolution 70/1 adopted by the General Assembly on 25 September 2015, Transforming our world: the 2030 Agenda for Sustainable Development, para.60.

– which will convene annually for two days to discuss co-operation on issues of science, technology and innovation around themes for the fulfilment of the SDGs, and (iii) an on-line platform which will be a point of access for information concerning current schemes in science, technology and innovation, both within and beyond the UN System.[86] The section named 'Follow-up and review': (i) lays down the following principles regarding follow-up and review processes – (a) they will be voluntary and led by states, (b) they will follow progress in the implementation of the SDGs and their targets in a way that respects their global, interrelated and integrated nature and the three dimensions of sustainable development,[87] (c) they will maintain a long-term orientation, (d) they will be transparent, inclusive and participatory, (e) they will centre on people, take account of gender, take cognizance of human rights, and focus on the poor, vulnerable and disadvantaged, (f) they will augment existing processes and platforms, eschew duplication, and respond to domestic needs, priorities, capacities and circumstances, (g) they will be scrupulous, founded on evidence, and informed by high-quality data and country-led evaluations, (h) they will necessitate help in building capacity for developing countries – such as strengthening national systems for data collection and evaluation, and (i) they will be supported by multilateral institutions – including the UN System.[88] A set of worldwide indicators – to be complemented by indicators at the national level which states are to develop – will be used to follow-up and review the SDGs and their targets.[89] There will be regular, inclusive reviews of progress at global, regional, domestic and sub-national levels.[90] Working harmoniously with the General Assembly and the ECOSOC (among others) in conformity with existing mandates, the high-level political forum will oversee a system of follow-up and review processes at the international level.[91]

[86] Resolution 70/1 adopted by the General Assembly on 25 September 2015, Transforming our world: the 2030 Agenda for Sustainable Development, paras.70 and 1.

[87] The section above entitled 'Sustainable Development' establishes and contextualizes the three dimensions of sustainable development, i.e., economic, social and environmental facets.

[88] Resolution 70/1 adopted by the General Assembly on 25 September 2015, Transforming our world: the 2030 Agenda for Sustainable Development, para.74.

[89] Resolution 70/1 adopted by the General Assembly on 25 September 2015, Transforming our world: the 2030 Agenda for Sustainable Development, para.75.

[90] Resolution 70/1 adopted by the General Assembly on 25 September 2015, Transforming our world: the 2030 Agenda for Sustainable Development, para.77.

[91] Resolution 70/1 adopted by the General Assembly on 25 September 2015, Transforming our world: the 2030 Agenda for Sustainable Development, para.82.

Under the auspices of the ECOSOC, the high-level political forum shall conduct reviews in compliance with Resolution 67/290 of the General Assembly.[92] Meeting quadrennially under the auspices of the General Assembly,[93] the high-level political forum will supply high-level political

---

[92] Resolution 70/1 adopted by the General Assembly on 25 September 2015, Transforming our world: the 2030 Agenda for Sustainable Development, para.84. Articles 3, 7 and 8 of Resolution 67/290 adopted by the General Assembly on 9 July 2013 state, in part: "*The General Assembly* ... 3. *Also decides* that the meetings of the [high-level political] forum shall be convened under the auspices of the General Assembly and of the Economic and Social Council; ... 7. *Further decides* that the meetings of the forum under the auspices of the Economic and Social Council: (a) Shall be convened annually by the President of the [Economic and Social] Council for a period of eight days ... ; (b) Shall be chaired by the President of the Council; (c) Shall have a thematic focus reflecting the integration of the three dimensions of sustainable development, in line with the thematic focus of the activities of the Council and consistent with the post-2015 development agenda; (d) Shall follow up and review progress in the implementation of all the outcomes of the major United Nations conferences and summits in the economic, social and environmental fields ... ; (e) Shall take into account the work of the Development Cooperation Forum, as well as other activities of the Council relating to the integration and implementation of sustainable development; (f) Shall benefit from regional preparatory processes; (g) Shall result in a negotiated ministerial decision for the inclusion in the report of the Council to the General Assembly; 8. *Decides* that the [high-level political] forum, under the auspices of the Economic and Social Council, shall conduct regular reviews, starting in 2016, on the follow-up and implementation of sustainable development commitments and objectives, including those related to the means of implementation, within the context of the post-2015 development agenda, and further decides that those reviews: (a) shall be voluntary ... ; (b) shall be State-led ... ; (c) shall provide a platform for partnerships ... ; (d) shall replace the national voluntary presentations held in the context of the annual ministerial-level substantive reviews of the Council ... ;" (emphasis original).

[93] Article 6 of Resolution 67/290 adopted by the General Assembly on 9 July 2013 specifies: "*The General Assembly* ... 6. *Also decides* that the meetings of the forum under the auspices of the General Assembly: (a) Shall be convened at the levels of the Heads of State and Government; (b) Shall be convened every four years by the President of the Assembly for a period of two days, at the beginning of the session of Assembly, as well as on other occasions, on an exceptional basis, upon a decision by the Assembly; (c) Shall be chaired by the President of the Assembly; (d) Shall result in a concise negotiated political declaration to be submitted for the consideration of the Assembly;" (emphasis original). The most recent quadrennial meeting of the high-level political forum on sustainable development convened under the auspices of the General Assembly was on 24th and 25th September 2019

guidance on the 2030 Agenda for Sustainable Development and its implementation, pinpoint progress and emerging difficulties, and initiate further actions to quicken implementation.[94]

Mapping the Millennium Development Goals to the Sustainable Development Goals

A prerequisite for writing Chapters Four and Five, i.e., respectively the Continuation and New Ground Macrostudies, is to distinguish between those SDGs that follow from the MDGs and those SDGs that are new. In order to satisfy this prior condition, the paragraphs below map the MDGs and their targets onto the SDGs and their targets. Based on the results to this operation, the SDGs are divided into those that proceed from the MDGs and those that are fresh. This separation of SDGs enables the prompt allocation of Goals as subject-matter for the forthcoming Chapters, which is the last function that this section contains. To an extent, the mapping is a subjective exercise. Thus, it is open to the possibility of error. It is submitted that approximations of this type are inevitable when real-world conditions are simplified by the use of a model, which the binary process of deciding whether or not an MDG or its target is precursory to an SDG or its target performs. However, it is opined that the gains from this procedure in the form of generating discrete material for analysis in next Chapters are worth more than the approximations that it engenders.

MDG 1[95] maps to SDG 1[96] and to SDG 2.[97] MDG Target 1.A[98] maps to SDG Target 1.1.[99] MDG Target 1.B[100] maps to SDG Target 8.5.[101] MDG Target 1.C[102] maps to SDG Target 2.1.[103]

(United Nations, Resolution 74/4 adopted by the General assembly on 15 October 2019, Annex, para.1).

[94] Resolution 70/1 adopted by the General Assembly on 25 September 2015, Transforming our world: the 2030 Agenda for Sustainable Development, para.87.

[95] MDG 1: "Eradicate extreme poverty and hunger" ("Goals, targets and indicators", International Telecommunication Union, accessed February 16, 2020, http://www.itu.int/ITU-D/ict/mdg/goals.html#fa).

[96] SDG 1: "End poverty in all its forms everywhere" (text to note 36).

[97] SDG 2: "End hunger, achieve food security and improved nutrition and promote sustainable agriculture" (text to note 36).

[98] MDG Target 1.A: "Halve, between 1990 and 2015, the proportion of people whose income is less than one dollar a day" ("Goals, targets and indicators", International Telecommunication Union, accessed February 16, 2020, http://www.itu.int/ITU-D/ict/mdg/goals.html#fa).

[99] SDG Target 1.1: "By 2030, eradicate extreme poverty for all people everywhere, currently measured as people living on less than $1.25 a day" (Resolution 70/1

MDG 2[104] maps to SDG 4.[105] MDG Target 2.A[106] maps to SDG Target 4.1.[107]

MDG 3[108] maps to SDG 5.[109] MDG Target 3.A[110] maps to SDG Target 4.5.[111]

---

adopted by the General Assembly on 25 September 2015, Transforming our world: the 2030 Agenda for Sustainable Development, 15).

100 MDG Target 1.B: "Achieve full and productive employment and decent work for all, including women and young people" ("Goals, targets and indicators", International Telecommunication Union, accessed February 16, 2020, http://www.itu.int/ITU-D/ict/mdg/goals.html#fa).

101 SDG Target 8.5: "By 2030, achieve full and productive employment and decent work for all women and men, including for young people and persons with disabilities, and equal pay for work of equal value" (Resolution 70/1 adopted by the General Assembly on 25 September 2015, Transforming our world: the 2030 Agenda for Sustainable Development, 19).

102 MDG Target 1.C: "Halve, between 1990 and 2015, the proportion of people who suffer from hunger" ("Goals, targets and indicators", International Telecommunication Union, accessed February 16, 2020, http://www.itu.int/ITU-D/ict/mdg/goals.html#fa).

103 SDG Target 2.1: "By 2030, end hunger and ensure access by all people, in particular the poor and people in vulnerable situations, including infants, to safe, nutritious and sufficient food all year round" (Resolution 70/1 adopted by the General Assembly on 25 September 2015, Transforming our world: the 2030 Agenda for Sustainable Development, 15).

104 MDG 2: "Achieve universal primary education" ("Goals, targets and indicators", International Telecommunication Union, accessed February 16, 2020, http://www.itu.int/ITU-D/ict/mdg/goals.html#fa).

105 SDG 4: "Ensure inclusive and equitable quality education and promote lifelong learning opportunities for all" (text to note 36).

106 MDG Target 2.A: "Ensure that, by 2015, children everywhere, boys and girls alike, will be able to complete a full course of primary schooling" ("Goals, targets and indicators", International Telecommunication Union, accessed February 16, 2020, http://www.itu.int/ITU-D/ict/mdg/goals.html#fa).

107 SDG Target 4.1: "By 2030, ensure that all girls and boys complete free, equitable and quality primary and secondary education leading to relevant and effective learning outcomes" (Resolution 70/1 adopted by the General Assembly on 25 September 2015, Transforming our world: the 2030 Agenda for Sustainable Development, 17).

108 MDG 3: "Promote gender equality and empower women" ("Goals, targets and indicators", International Telecommunication Union, accessed February 16, 2020, http://www.itu.int/ITU-D/ict/mdg/goals.html#fa).

109 SDG 5: "Achieve gender equality and empower all women and girls" (text to note 36).

MDG 4[112] maps to SDG 3.[113] MDG Target 4.A[114] maps to SDG Target 3.2.[115]

MDG 5[116] maps to SDG 3[117] and to SDG 5.[118] MDG Target 5.A[119] maps to SDG Target 3.1.[120] MDG Target 5.B[121] maps to SDG Target 5.6.[122]

---

110 MDG Target 3.A: "Eliminate gender disparity in primary and secondary education, preferably by 2005, and in all levels of education no later than 2015" ("Goals, targets and indicators", International Telecommunication Union, accessed February 17, 2020, http://www.itu.int/ITU-D/ict/mdg/goals.html#fa).

111 SDG Target 4.5: "By 2030, eliminate gender disparities in education and ensure equal access to all levels of education and vocational training for the vulnerable, including persons with disabilities, indigenous peoples and children in vulnerable situations" (Resolution 70/1 adopted by the General Assembly on 25 September 2015, Transforming our world: the 2030 Agenda for Sustainable Development, 17).

112 MDG 4: "Reduce child mortality" ("Goals, targets and indicators", International Telecommunication Union, accessed February 17, 2020, http://www.itu.int/ITU-D/ict/mdg/goals.html#fa).

113 SDG 3: "Ensure healthy lives and promote well-being for all at all ages" (text to note 36).

114 MDG Target 4.A: "Reduce by two-thirds, between 1990 and 2015, the under-five mortality rate" ("Goals, targets and indicators", International Telecommunication Union, accessed February 17, 2020, http://www.itu.int/ITU-D/ict/mdg/goals.html#fa).

115 SDG Target 3.2: "By 2030, end preventable deaths of newborns and children under 5 years of age, with all countries aiming to reduce neonatal mortality to at least as low as 12 per 1,000 live births and under-5 mortality to at least as low as 25 per 1,000 live births" (Resolution 70/1 adopted by the General Assembly on 25 September 2015, Transforming our world: the 2030 Agenda for Sustainable Development, 16).

116 MDG 5: "Improve maternal health" ("Goals, targets and indicators", International Telecommunication Union, accessed February 17, 2020, http://www.itu.int/ITU-D/ict/mdg/goals.html#fa).

117 Note 113 specifies SDG 3.

118 Note 109 states SDG 5.

119 MDG Target 5.A: "Reduce by three quarters, between 1990 and 2015, the maternal mortality ratio" ("Goals, targets and indicators", International Telecommunication Union, accessed February 17, 2020, http://www.itu.int/ITU-D/ict/mdg/goals.html#fa).

120 SDG Target 3.1: "By 2030, reduce the global maternal mortality ratio to less than 70 per 100,000 live births" (Resolution 70/1 adopted by the General Assembly on 25 September 2015, Transforming our world: the 2030 Agenda for Sustainable Development, 16).

MDG 6[123] maps to SDG 3.[124] MDG Target 6.A[125] maps to SDG Target 3.3.[126] MDG Target 6.B[127] maps to SDG Target 3.3[128] and to SDG Target 3.8.[129] MDG Target 6.C[130] maps to SDG Target 3.3.[131]

MDG 7[132] maps to SDG 6,[133] to SDG 11,[134] to SDG 14[135] and to SDG 15.[136] MDG Target 7.A[137] maps to SDG Target 6.4,[138] to SDG Target

---

121 MDG Target 5.B: "Achieve, by 2015, universal access to reproductive health" ("Goals, targets and indicators", International Telecommunication Union, accessed February 17, 2020, http://www.itu.int/ITU-D/ict/mdg/goals.html#fa).

122 SDG Target 5.6. "Ensure universal access to sexual and reproductive health and reproductive rights as agreed in accordance with the Programme of Action of the International Conference on Population and Development and the Beijing Platform for Action and the outcome documents of their review conferences" (Resolution 70/1 adopted by the General Assembly on 25 September 2015, Transforming our world: the 2030 Agenda for Sustainable Development, 18).

123 MDG 6: "Combat HIV/AIDS, malaria and other diseases" ("Goals, targets and indicators", International Telecommunication Union, accessed February 17, 2020, http://www.itu.int/ITU-D/ict/mdg/goals.html#fa).

124 Note 113 states SDG 3.

125 MDG Target 6.A: "Have halted by 2015 and begun to reverse the spread of HIV/AIDS" ("Goals, targets and indicators", International Telecommunication Union, accessed February 17, 2020, http://www.itu.int/ITU-D/ict/mdg/goals.html#fa).

126 SDG Target 3.3: "By 2030, end the epidemics of AIDS, tuberculosis, malaria and neglected tropical diseases and combat hepatitis, water-borne diseases and other communicable diseases" (Resolution 70/1 adopted by the General Assembly on 25 September 2015, Transforming our world: the 2030 Agenda for Sustainable Development, 16).

127 MDG Target 6.B: "Achieve, by 2010, universal access to treatment for HIV/AIDS for all those who need it" ("Goals, targets and indicators", International Telecommunication Union, accessed February 17, 2020, http://www.itu.int/ITU-D/ict/mdg/goals.html#fa).

128 Note 126 specifies SDG Target 3.3.

129 SDG Target 3.8: "Achieve universal health coverage, including financial risk protection, access to quality essential health-care services and access to safe, effective, quality and affordable essential medicines and vaccines for all" (Resolution 70/1 adopted by the General Assembly on 25 September 2015, Transforming our world: the 2030 Agenda for Sustainable Development, 16).

130 MDG Target 6.C: "Have halted by 2015 and begun to reverse the incidence of malaria and other major diseases" ("Goals, targets and indicators", International Telecommunication Union, accessed February 17, 2020, http://www.itu.int/ITU-D/ict/mdg/goals.html#fa).

131 Note 126 states SDG Target 3.3.

132 MDG 7: "Ensure environmental sustainability" ("Goals, targets and indicators", International Telecommunication Union, accessed February 17, 2020,

11.3,[139] to SDG Target 14.2,[140] to SDG Target 14.4,[141] to SDG Target 15.2,[142] to SDG Target 15.3[143] and to SDG Target 15.9.[144] MDG Target

---

http://www.itu.int/ITU-D/ict/mdg/goals.html#fa).

133 SDG 6: "Ensure availability and sustainable management of water and sanitation for all" (text to note 36).

134 SDG 11: "Make cities and human settlements inclusive, safe, resilient and sustainable" (text to note 36).

135 SDG 14: "Conserve and sustainably use the oceans, seas and marine resources for sustainable development" (text to note 36).

136 SDG 15 "Protect, restore and promote sustainable use of territorial ecosystems, sustainably manage forests, combat desertification, and halt and reverse land degradation and halt biodiversity loss" (text to note 36).

137 MDG Target 7.A: "Integrate the principles of sustainable development into country policies and programmes and reverse the loss of environmental resources" ("Goals, targets and indicators", International Telecommunication Union, accessed February 17, 2020, http://www.itu.int/ITU-D/ict/mdg/goals.html#fa).

138 SDG Target 6.4: "By 2030, substantially increase water-use efficiency across all sectors and ensure sustainable withdrawals and supply of freshwater to address water scarcity and substantially reduce the number of people suffering from water scarcity" (Resolution 70/1 adopted by the General Assembly on 25 September 2015, Transforming our world: the 2030 Agenda for Sustainable Development, 18).

139 SDG Target 11.3: "By 2030, enhance inclusive and sustainable urbanization and capacity for participatory, integrated and sustainable human settlement planning and management in all countries" (Resolution 70/1 adopted by the General Assembly on 25 September 2015, Transforming our world: the 2030 Agenda for Sustainable Development, 21).

140 SDG Target 14.2: "By 2020, sustainably manage and protect marine and coastal ecosystems to avoid significant adverse impacts, including by strengthening their resilience, and take action for their restoration in order to achieve healthy and productive oceans" (Resolution 70/1 adopted by the General Assembly on 25 September 2015, Transforming our world: the 2030 Agenda for Sustainable Development, 23).

141 SDG Target 14.4: "By 2020, effectively regulate harvesting and end overfishing, illegal, unreported and unregulated fishing and destructive fishing practices and implement science-based management plans, in order to restore fish stocks in the shortest time feasible, at least to levels that can produce maximum sustainable yield as determined by their biological characteristics" (Resolution 70/1 adopted by the General Assembly on 25 September 2015, Transforming our world: the 2030 Agenda for Sustainable Development, 24).

142 SDG Target 15.2: "By 2020, promote the implementation of sustainable management of all types of forests, halt deforestation, restore degraded forests and substantially increase afforestation and reforestation globally" (Resolution 70/1 adopted by the General Assembly on 25 September 2015, Transforming our world: the 2030 Agenda for Sustainable Development, 24).

7.B[145] maps to SDG Target 6.6,[146] to SDG Target 14.2,[147] to SDG Target 14.5,[148] to SDG Target 14.c,[149] to SDG Target 15.4[150] and to SDG Target 15.5.[151] MDG Target 7.C[152] maps to SDG Target 6.1[153] and to SDG Target 6.2.[154] MDG Target 7.D[155] maps to SDG Target 11.1.[156]

---

143 SDG Target 15.3: "By 2030, combat desertification, restore degraded land and soil, including land affected by desertification, drought and floods, and strive to achieve a land degradation-neutral world" (Resolution 70/1 adopted by the General Assembly on 25 September 2015, Transforming our world: the 2030 Agenda for Sustainable Development, 24).

144 SDG Target 15.9: "By 2020, integrate ecosystem and biodiversity values into national and local planning, development processes, poverty reduction strategies and accounts" (Resolution 70/1 adopted by the General Assembly on 25 September 2015, Transforming our world: the 2030 Agenda for Sustainable Development, 25).

145 MDG Target 7.B: "Reduce biodiversity loss, achieving, by 2010, a significant reduction in the rate of loss" ("Goals, targets and indicators", International Telecommunication Union, accessed February 17, 2020, http://www.itu.int/ITU-D/ict/mdg/goals.html#fa).

146 SDG Target 6.6: "By 2020, protect and restore water-related ecosystems, including mountains, forests, wetlands, rivers, aquifers and lakes" (Resolution 70/1 adopted by the General Assembly on 25 September 2015, Transforming our world: the 2030 Agenda for Sustainable Development, 18).

147 Note 140 specifies SDG Target 14.2.

148 SDG Target 14.5: "By 2020, conserve at least 10 per cent of coastal and marine areas, consistent with national and international law and based on the best available scientific information" (Resolution 70/1 adopted by the General Assembly on 25 September 2015, Transforming our world: the 2030 Agenda for Sustainable Development, 24).

149 SDG Target 14.c: "Enhance the conservation and sustainable use of oceans and their resources by implementing international law as reflected in the United Nations Convention on the Law of the Sea, which provides the legal framework for the conservation and sustainable use of oceans and their resources …" (Resolution 70/1 adopted by the General Assembly on 25 September 2015, Transforming our world: the 2030 Agenda for Sustainable Development, 24).

150 SDG Target 15.4: "By 2030, ensure the conservation of mountain ecosystems, including their biodiversity, in order to enhance their capacity to provide benefits that are essential for sustainable development" (Resolution 70/1 adopted by the General Assembly on 25 September 2015, Transforming our world: the 2030 Agenda for Sustainable Development, 25).

151 SDG Target 15.5: "Take urgent and significant action to reduce the degradation of natural habitats, halt the loss of biodiversity and, by 2020, protect and prevent the extinction of threatened species" (Resolution 70/1 adopted by the General Assembly on 25 September 2015, Transforming our world: the 2030 Agenda for Sustainable Development, 25).

MDG 8[157] maps to SDG 17.[158] MDG Target 8.A[159] maps to SDG 17.10.[160] MDG Target 8.B[161] maps to SDG Target 17.5,[162] to SDG Target

---

[152] MDG Target 7.C: "Halve, by 2015, the proportion of people without sustainable access to safe drinking water and basic sanitation" ("Goals, targets and indicators", International Telecommunication Union, accessed February 17, 2020, http://www.itu.int/ITU-D/ict/mdg/goals.html#fa).

[153] SDG Target 6.1: "By 2030, achieve universal and equitable access to safe and affordable drinking water for all" (Resolution 70/1 adopted by the General Assembly on 25 September 2015, Transforming our world: the 2030 Agenda for Sustainable Development, 18).

[154] SDG Target 6.2: "By 2030, achieve access to adequate and equitable sanitation and hygiene for all and end open defecation, paying special attention to the needs of women and girls and those in vulnerable situations" (Resolution 70/1 adopted by the General Assembly on 25 September 2015, Transforming our world: the 2030 Agenda for Sustainable Development, 18).

[155] MDG Target 7.D: "By 2020, to have achieved a significant improvement in the lives of at least 100 million slum dwellers" ("Goals, targets and indicators", International Telecommunication Union, accessed February 17, 2020, http://www.itu.int/ITU-D/ict/mdg/goals.html#fa).

[156] SDG Target 11.1: "By 2030, ensure access for all to adequate, safe and affordable housing and basic services and upgrade slums" (Resolution 70/1 adopted by the General Assembly on 25 September 2015, Transforming our world: the 2030 Agenda for Sustainable Development, 21).

[157] MDG 8: "Develop a global partnership for development" ("Goals, targets and indicators", International Telecommunication Union, accessed February 17, 2020, http://www.itu.int/ITU-D/ict/mdg/goals.html#fa).

[158] SDG 17: "Strengthen the means of implementation and revitalize the Global Partnership for Sustainable Development" (text to note 36).

[159] MDG Target 8.A: "Develop further an open, rule-based, predictable, non-discriminatory trading and financial system" ("Goals, targets and indicators", International Telecommunication Union, accessed February 17, 2020, http://www.itu.int/ITU-D/ict/mdg/goals.html#fa).

[160] SDG Target 17.10: "Promote a universal, rules-based, open, non-discriminatory and equitable multilateral trading system under the World Trade Organization, including through the conclusion of negotiations under its Doha Development Agenda" (Resolution 70/1 adopted by the General Assembly on 25 September 2015, Transforming our world: the 2030 Agenda for Sustainable Development, 27).

[161] MDG Target 8.B: "Address the special needs of the least developed countries" ("Goals, targets and indicators", International Telecommunication Union, accessed February 17, 2020, http://www.itu.int/ITU-D/ict/mdg/goals.html#fa).

[162] SDG Target 17.5: "Adopt and implement investment promotion regimes for least developed countries" (Resolution 70/1 adopted by the General Assembly on 25 September 2015, Transforming our world: the 2030 Agenda for Sustainable Development, 26).

17.8,[163] to SDG Target 17.12[164] and to SDG Target 17.18.[165] MDG Target 8.C[166] maps to SDG Target 17.18.[167] MDG Target 8.D[168] maps to SDG Target 17.4.[169] MDG Target 8.E[170] maps to SDG Target 3.8.[171] MDG

---

[163] SDG Target 17.8: "Fully operationalize the technology bank and science, technology and innovation capacity-building mechanism for least developed countries by 2017 and enhance the use of enabling technology, in particular information and communications technology" (Resolution 70/1 adopted by the General Assembly on 25 September 2015, Transforming our world: the 2030 Agenda for Sustainable Development, 26).

[164] SDG Target 17.12: "Realize timely implementation of duty-free and quota-free market access on a lasting basis for all least developed countries, consistent with World Trade Organization decisions, including by ensuring that preferential rules of origin applicable to imports from least developed countries are transparent and simple, and contribute to facilitating market access" (Resolution 70/1 adopted by the General Assembly on 25 September 2015, Transforming our world: the 2030 Agenda for Sustainable Development, 27).

[165] SDG Target 17.18: "By 2020, enhance capacity-building support to developing countries, including for least developed countries and small island developing States, to increase significantly the availability of high-quality, timely and reliable data disaggregated by income, gender, age, race, ethnicity, migratory status, disability, geographical location and other characteristics relevant in national contexts" (Resolution 70/1 adopted by the General Assembly on 25 September 2015, Transforming our world: the 2030 Agenda for Sustainable Development, 27).

[166] MDG Target 8.C: "Address the special needs of landlocked developing countries and small island developing States ..." ("Goals, targets and indicators", International Telecommunication Union, accessed February 17, 2020, http://www.itu.int/ITU-D/ict/mdg/goals.html#fa).

[167] Note 165 specifies SDG Target 17.18.

[168] MDG Target 8.D: "Deal comprehensively with the debt problems of developing countries through national and international measures in order to make debt sustainable in the long term" ("Goals, targets and indicators", International Telecommunication Union, accessed February 17, 2020, http://www.itu.int/ITU-D/ict/mdg/goals.html#fa).

[169] SDG Target 17.4: "Assist developing countries in attaining long-term debt sustainability through coordinated policies aimed at fostering debt financing, debt relief and debt restructuring, as appropriate, and address the external debt of highly indebted poor countries to reduce debt distress" (Resolution 70/1 adopted by the General Assembly on 25 September 2015, Transforming our world: the 2030 Agenda for Sustainable Development, 26).

[170] MDG Target 8.E: "In cooperation with pharmaceutical companies, provide access to affordable essential drugs in developing countries" ("Goals, targets and indicators", International Telecommunication Union, accessed February 17, 2020, http://www.itu.int/ITU-D/ict/mdg/goals.html#fa).

Target 8.F[172] maps to SDG Target 17.6,[173] to SDG Target 17.7[174] and to SDG Target 17.8.[175]

Table 1.2: The number of mappings to each SDG and its targets

SDG Number	***Number of mappings from MDGs to the relevant SDG***	**Total number of targets of the relevant SDG**	***Number of these SDG Targets to which MDG Targets are mapped***	***Total number of mappings to the targets of the relevant SDG***
1	*1*	7[176]	*1*	*1*
2	*1*	8[177]	*1*	*1*
3	*3*	13[178]	*4*	*7*

---

[171] Note 129 states SDG Target 3.8.

[172] MDG Target 8.F: "In cooperation with the private sector, make available the benefits of new technologies, especially information and communications" ("Goals, targets and indicators", International Telecommunication Union, accessed February 17, 2020, http://www.itu.int/ITU-D/ict/mdg/goals.html#fa).

[173] SDG Target 17.6: "Enhance North-South, South-South and triangular regional and international cooperation on and access to science, technology and innovation and enhance knowledge sharing on mutually agreed terms, including through improved coordination among existing mechanisms, in particular at United Nations level, and through a global technology facilitation mechanism" (Resolution 70/1 adopted by the General Assembly on 25 September 2015, Transforming our world: the 2030 Agenda for Sustainable Development, 26). 'North' represents advanced economies and 'South' less-developed countries, because the former states constitute a greater part of the northern hemisphere and the latter a larger portion of the southern hemisphere (Graeme Baber, *Essays on International Law* (Newcastle-upon-Tyne: Cambridge Scholars Publishing, 2017), 25; Baber, *The United Nations System: A Synopsis*, 152).

[174] SDG Target 17.7: "Promote the development, transfer, dissemination and diffusion of environmentally sound techniques to developing countries on favourable terms, including on concessional and preferential terms, as mutually agreed" (Resolution 70/1 adopted by the General Assembly on 25 September 2015, Transforming our world: the 2030 Agenda for Sustainable Development, 26).

[175] Note 163 specifies SDG Target 17.8.

[176] The targets of SDG 1 comprise 1.1-1.5 and 1.a-1.b (Resolution 70/1 adopted by the General Assembly on 25 September 2015, Transforming our world: the 2030 Agenda for Sustainable Development, 15).

[177] The targets of SDG 2 comprise 2.1-2.5 and 2.a-2.c (Resolution 70/1 adopted by the General Assembly on 25 September 2015, Transforming our world: the 2030 Agenda for Sustainable Development, 15-16).

4	*1*	10[179]	*2*	*2*
5	*2*	9[180]	*1*	*1*
6	*1*	8[181]	*4*	*4*
7	*0*	5[182]	*0*	*0*
8	*0*	12[183]	*1*	*1*
9	*0*	8[184]	*0*	*0*
10	*0*	10[185]	*0*	*0*
11	*1*	10[186]	*2*	*2*
12	*0*	11[187]	*0*	*0*
13	*0*	5[188]	*0*	*0*

[178] The targets of SDG 3 comprise 3.1-3.9 and 3.a-3.d (Resolution 70/1 adopted by the General Assembly on 25 September 2015, Transforming our world: the 2030 Agenda for Sustainable Development, 16-17).
[179] The targets of SDG 4 comprise 4.1-4.7 and 4.a-4.c (Resolution 70/1 adopted by the General Assembly on 25 September 2015, Transforming our world: the 2030 Agenda for Sustainable Development, 17).
[180] The targets of SDG 5 comprise 5.1-5.6 and 5.a-5.c (Resolution 70/1 adopted by the General Assembly on 25 September 2015, Transforming our world: the 2030 Agenda for Sustainable Development, 18).
[181] The targets of SDG 6 comprise 6.1-6.6 and 6.a-6.b (Resolution 70/1 adopted by the General Assembly on 25 September 2015, Transforming our world: the 2030 Agenda for Sustainable Development, 18-19).
[182] The targets of SDG 7 comprise 7.1-7.3 and 7.a-7.b (Resolution 70/1 adopted by the General Assembly on 25 September 2015, Transforming our world: the 2030 Agenda for Sustainable Development, 19).
[183] The targets of SDG 8 comprise 8.1-8.10 and 8.a-8.b (Resolution 70/1 adopted by the General Assembly on 25 September 2015, Transforming our world: the 2030 Agenda for Sustainable Development, 19-20).
[184] The targets of SDG 9 comprise 9.1-9.5 and 9.a-9.c (Resolution 70/1 adopted by the General Assembly on 25 September 2015, Transforming our world: the 2030 Agenda for Sustainable Development, 20-21).
[185] The targets of SDG 10 comprise 10.1-10.7 and 10.a-10.c (Resolution 70/1 adopted by the General Assembly on 25 September 2015, Transforming our world: the 2030 Agenda for Sustainable Development, 21).
[186] The targets of SDG 11 comprise 11.1-11.7 and 11.a-11.c (Resolution 70/1 adopted by the General Assembly on 25 September 2015, Transforming our world: the 2030 Agenda for Sustainable Development, 21-22).
[187] The targets of SDG 12 comprise 12.1-12.8 and 12.a-12.c (Resolution 70/1 adopted by the General Assembly on 25 September 2015, Transforming our world: the 2030 Agenda for Sustainable Development, 22-23).
[188] The targets of SDG 13 comprise 13.1-13.3 and 13.a-13.b (Resolution 70/1 adopted by the General Assembly on 25 September 2015, Transforming our world: the 2030 Agenda for Sustainable Development, 23).

14	*1*	10[189]	*4*	*5*
15	*1*	12[190]	*5*	*5*
16	*0*	12[191]	*0*	*0*
17	*1*	19[192]	*8*	*10*

The next step is to use the data from Table 1.2 to help to classify each of the 17 SDGs as either continuing from the MDGs or new. As SDGs 7, 9, 10, 12, 13 and 16 receive no mappings from MDGs, they are categorized as new Goals.

SDG 3 receives three mappings from MDGs; four of its thirteen targets receive mappings from MDG Targets, with a total of seven mappings received. SDG 3 is classed as a continuation goal.

SDG 5 receives two mappings from MDGs; one of its nine targets receives a single mapping from an MDG Target. At the level of the Goals, SDG 5 is a continuation Goal. However, at the level of the targets, SDG 5 is a new goal. Therefore, for now, SDG 5 is unclassified.

Similarly, whilst SDGs 1 and 2 each receive one mapping from an MDG,[193] one of the seven/eight (respectively) targets of each receives a single mapping from an MDG Target. At the level of the Goals, SDGs 1 and 2 are both continuation Goals. At the level of the targets, both these SDGs are new Goals. Consequently, for the moment, SDGs 1 and 2 are unclassified.

Whilst one of the twelve targets of SDG 8 receives a single mapping from an MDG Target, SDG 8 receives no mappings from MDGs. One mapping to a target of an SDG is insufficient to render that SDG a continuation Goal. Therefore, SDG 8 is categorized as a new Goal.

---

189 The targets of SDG 14 comprise 14.1-14.7 and 14.a-14.c (Resolution 70/1 adopted by the General Assembly on 25 September 2015, Transforming our world: the 2030 Agenda for Sustainable Development, 23-24).

190 The targets of SDG 15 comprise 15.1-15.9 and 15.a-15.c (Resolution 70/1 adopted by the General Assembly on 25 September 2015, Transforming our world: the 2030 Agenda for Sustainable Development, 24-25).

191 The targets of SDG 16 comprise 16.1-16.10 and 16.a-16.b (Resolution 70/1 adopted by the General Assembly on 25 September 2015, Transforming our world: the 2030 Agenda for Sustainable Development, 25-26).

192 The targets of SDG 17 comprise 17.1-17.19 (Resolution 70/1 adopted by the General Assembly on 25 September 2015, Transforming our world: the 2030 Agenda for Sustainable Development, 26-27).

193 Both SDG 1 and SDG 2 receive a mapping from MDG 1 (text to notes 95-97).

SDGs 6, 14, 15 and 17 each receive one mapping from an MDG.[194] Four of the eight targets of SDG 6 receive a mapping from the MDG Targets. Three of the ten targets of SDG 14 receive one mapping from the MDG Targets, and one of the targets of SDG 14 receives two mappings from the MDG Targets. Five of the ten targets of SDG 15 receive a mapping from the MDG Targets. Six of the nineteen targets of SDG 17 receive one mapping from the MDG Targets, and two of the targets of SDG 17 each receives two mappings from the MDG Targets. This combination of one mapping from an MDG and almost half its targets receiving at least one mapping from the MDG Targets, is enough to make each of these SDGs a continuation Goal.

SDGs 4 and 11 each receive one mapping from an MDG.[195] Both these SDGs have ten targets, two of which – in each case – receive a mapping from an MDG Target. At the level of the Goals, SDGs 4 and 11 are both continuation Goals. At the level of the targets, two mappings from MDG Targets to two SDG Targets out of ten SDG Targets comprises a fairly small link between the MDGs and the SDGs. Consequently, for now, SDGs 4 and 11 are unclassified. Table 1.3 shows the interim categorization of the SDGs into continuation Goals, unclassified, and new Goals, based on the above reasoning.

Table 1.3: Interim classification of the SDGs

SDGs proceeding from the MDGs	Unclassified SDGs	SDGs that are new Goals
3, 6, 14, 15, 17	1, 2, 4, 5, 11	7, 8, 9, 10, 12, 13, 16

With regard to classifying SDGs 1, 2, 4, 5 and 11 – which Table 1.3 shows to be currently unclassified, it is appropriate for a similar number of SDGs to be assessed as continuation Goals as those to be evaluated as new Goals. Thus, there should either be nine SDGs that are grouped as continuation Goals and eight SDGs that are categorized as new Goals – in which case four of the five unclassified SDGs are to be transferred to the class of continuation Goals and the other one to the new Goals, or there should be eight SDGs that are classed as continuation Goals and nine SDGs that are grouped as new Goals – which requires three of the five

[194] SDG 6, SDG 14 and SDG 15 – as well as SDG 11 – each receive a mapping from MDG 7 (text to notes 132-136). SDG 17 receives a mapping from MDG 8 (text to notes 157 and 158).

[195] SDG 4 receives a mapping from MDG 2 (text to notes 104 and 105). For SDG 11, see note 194.

unclassified SDGs to be moved to the group of continuation Goals and the other two to the new Goals.

In the book entitled *Transforming Multilateral Diplomacy: The Inside Story of the Sustainable Development Goals*, Mr. Kamau[196] and two co-authors[197] hold that SDGs 1 to 6 are continuations of the MDGs.[198] Accepting this as true, SDGs 1, 2, 4 and 5 are moved from the category in Table 1.3 entitled 'Unclassified SDGs' to the class therein titled 'SDGs proceeding from the MDGs'. Consequent to this, there are nine SDGs in the latter group. In order to achieve the most similar number of SDGs in the continuation and new categories in accordance with the immediately-preceding paragraph, SDG 11 is transferred from the class in Table 1.3 named 'Unclassified SDGs' to the group therein headed 'SDGs that are new Goals'. Following this final allocation, there are nine SDGs in the continuation category and eight SDGs in the new class. Table 1.4 shows the final categorization of the SDGs.

Table 1.4: Final classification of the SDGs

SDGs proceeding from the MDGs	SDGs that are new Goals
1, 2, 3, 4, 5, 6, 14, 15, 17	7, 8, 9, 10, 11, 12, 13, 16

Chapter Two, entitled 'Continuation Microstudy', discusses the progression of SDG 1, which proceeds from MDG 1 based on the mappings that it receives.[199] The remaining SDGs in the class in Table 1.4 titled 'SDGs proceeding from the MDGs' are considered in Chapter Four, which is named 'Continuation Macrostudy'. The word 'macro' is used in the title to Chapter Four, because the study therein extends the 'micro'

[196] Note 23 and the text to note 25 provide information concerning Mr. Kamau.

[197] Mr. Kamau's two co-authors are Dr. Pamela Chasek, who is presently the Chair of the Department of Political Science at Manhattan College ("Pamela Chasek", Manhattan College, accessed February 21, 2020, https://manhattan.edu/campus-directory/pamela.chasek), and Dr. David O'Connor, who currently works in the Sustainable Development Goals' Delivery Team at the World Resources Institute, and who is the Permanent Observer of the International Union for Conservation of Nature to the UN ("David O'Connor: Sustainable Economist", World Resources Institute, accessed February 21, 2020, https://www.wri.org/profile/david-oconnor).

[198] Macharia Kamau, Pamela Chasek, and David O'Connor, *Transforming Multilateral Diplomacy: The Inside Story of the Sustainable Development Goals* (Abingdon: Routledge, 2018), vi.

[199] Text to notes 95-96 and 98-99.

analysis in Chapter Two to the whole group of SDGs that proceed from the MDGs.

Chapter Three, headed 'New Ground Microstudy', appraises the progression of SDG 10, which is a new SDG that receives no mappings from the MDGs.[200] The remaining SDGs in the category in Table 1.4 entitled 'SDGs that are new Goals' are covered in Chapter Five, which is titled 'New Ground Macrostudy'. Similarly to Chapters Two and Four, the word 'macro' is used in the title to Chapter Five because the deliberations therein enlarge the 'micro' examination in Chapter Three to the entire class of SDGs that are new Goals.

Conclusion

This Chapter defines the term 'sustainable development'. It ascertains that sustainable development comprises economic, social and environmental dimensions which are integrated into the totality of this concept. The Chapter describes the creation of the sustainable goals from their inception in January 2011 to their launch at the UN Sustainable Development Summit in September 2015. It maps the MDGs and their targets to the SDGs and their targets and, based on the outcome to this mapping, classifies the SDGs into those that continue from the MDGs – which form the content of Chapters Two and Four, and those that are new – which constitute the subject matter of Chapters Three and Five.

The next Chapter traces the process made towards achieving SDG 1 – i.e., "End poverty in all its forms everywhere".[201] Whilst this Goal proceeds from MDG 1[202] and, in particular, whilst its Target 1.1[203] is a continuation of MDG Target 1.A,[204] it includes new targets – which are discussed.

---

[200] Table 1.2 shows that: (i) SDG 10 receives no mappings from any MDG, and (ii) none of the ten targets of SDG 10 receive a mapping from an MDG Target.

[201] Text to note 36.

[202] Text to notes 95 and 96. Note 95 states MDG 1.

[203] Note 99 specifies SDG Target 1.1.

[204] Text to notes 98 and 99. Note 98 sets out MDG Target 1.A.

CHAPTER TWO

CONTINUATION MICROSTUDY: DEVELOPMENT AND REALIZATION OF GOAL 1 – END POVERTY

Introduction

SDG 1 requires all states[1] to "[e]nd poverty in all its forms everywhere".[2] As determined by the mapping operation in Chapter One,[3] this SDG receives a single mapping from the MDGs, i.e., MDG 1 – which is to "[e]radicate extreme poverty and hunger".[4] Furthermore, as Chapter One determines,[5] SDG Target 1.1 – i.e., "By 2030, eradicate extreme poverty for all people everywhere, currently measured as people living on less than $1.25 a day"[6] – is a follow-up to MDG Target 1.A – i.e., "Halve, between 1990 and 2015, the proportion of people whose income is less than one dollar a day".[7] In addition to Target 1.1, SDG 1 comprises six other targets,[8] none of which receive mappings from the targets of the MDGs.[9]

---

[1] The post-2015 development agenda, including the SDGs, applies to all countries (text to note 46 of Chapter One).

[2] Note 96 of Chapter One. The text to note 36 of Chapter One specifies all 17 SDGs.

[3] The section entitled 'Mapping the Millennium Development Goals to the Sustainable Development Goals', in Chapter One, maps the MDGs to SDGs and the targets of the MDGs to targets of the SDGs and, based on the results of this mapping exercise, allocates SDGs to a class entitled 'SDGs proceeding from the MDGs' or to an alternative category titled 'SDGs that are new Goals' (Tables 1.3 and 1.4).

[4] Note 95 of Chapter One.

[5] Text to notes 98 and 99 of Chapter One.

[6] Note 99 of Chapter One.

[7] Note 98 of Chapter One.

[8] Note 176 of Chapter One.

[9] In Table 1.2, one target for SDG 1 – i.e., SDG Target 1.1 – receives a single mapping from an MDG Target – i.e., MDG Target 1.A (text to notes 98 and 99 of Chapter One). Therefore, none of the six other targets of SDG 1 receive such a mapping.

This Chapter devotes a section to MDG 1, which contains general comments on that Goal, reflection on the international poverty line and inferences from this – resulting in modifications to MDG Target 1.A and SDG Target 1.1, followed by an assessment as to the extent to which MDG Target 1.A has been achieved and a comment on the progression from MDG Target 1.A to SDG Target 1.1. The next section investigates the progress made in the accomplishment of SDG Target 1.1, and opines whether this target will be met on time. The third section explores headway made towards the attainment of the other targets of SDG 1, and posits whether this Goal will be fulfilled punctually. The final section concludes the Chapter.

MDG 1

General comments concerning the accomplishment of MDG 1

The UN's MDG Report of 2015 synopsizes the situation concerning MDG 1 thus.

> Although the MDG targets of halving the proportion of people living in extreme poverty[10] and hunger[11] have been met[12] or almost met,[13] the world is still far from reaching the MDG goal of eradicating extreme poverty and hunger.[14] In 2015, an estimated 825 million people still live in extreme

[10] This is MDG Target 1.A (note 98 of Chapter One, and text to note 7).
[11] This is MDG Target 1.C (note 102 of Chapter One).
[12] The number of people worldwide living in extreme poverty was halved from its 1990 level in 2010 (United Nations, The Millennium Development Goals Report 2015 (New York, 2015), 15; "MDG 1: Eradicate extreme poverty and hunger", MDG Monitor, accessed February 29, 2020, https://www.mdgmonitor.org/mdg-1-eradicate-poverty-hunger/).
[13] The percentage of the population in developing countries who were undernourished almost halved between 1990-1992 and 2014-2016 (The Millennium Development Goals Report 2015, 20; MDG Monitor, accessed February 29, 2020, https://www.mdgmonitor.org/mdg-1-eradicate-poverty-hunger/). The Millennium Development Report 2015 states: "*Projections indicate* a drop of almost half in the proportion of undernourished people in the developing regions, from 23.3 per cent in 1990-1992 to 12.9 per cent in 2014-2016." (The Millennium Development Goals Report 2015, 20; emphasis added). It is submitted that the 2014-2016 figure of 12.9% is partly or wholly based on estimates, as *The Millennium Development Goals Report 2015* would have been finalized and published before all the data upon which this percentage relies were available.
[14] This MDG is MDG 1 (note 95 of Chapter One, and text to note 4).

poverty and 800 million still suffer from hunger. Eradicating poverty[15] and hunger[16] remains at the core of the post-2015 development agenda.[17]

Whilst MDG Target 1.A has been fulfilled,[18] and MDG Target 1.C almost satisfied,[19] MDG Target 1.B, – i.e., "Achieve full and productive employment and decent work for all, including women and young people",[20] has not been met.[21] MDG Target 1.B has been updated and repackaged as SDG Target 8.5, i.e., "By 2030, achieve full and productive employment and decent work for all women and men, including for young people and persons with disabilities, and equal pay for work of equal value".[22] It is submitted that this is an unrealistic objective, as full employment is very difficult to achieve even in ideal conditions; for instance, some workers need to translocate when their jobs terminate, and others move in order to seek promotion and/or better work conditions. Thus, given progress regarding MDG Targets 1.A and 1.C, and noting the unlikelihood of accomplishing Target 1.B, the outcome in 2015 in respect of

---

[15] SDG 1 (note 96 of Chapter One, and text to note 2), and SDG Targets 1.1 (note 99 of Chapter One, and text to note 6) and 1.2, concern the eradication of poverty. SDG Target 1.2 states: "By 2030, reduce at least by half the proportion of men, women and children of all ages living in poverty in all its dimensions according to national definitions" (United Nations, Resolution 70/1 adopted by the General Assembly on 25 September 2015, Transforming our world: the 2030 Agenda for Sustainable Development, 15).

[16] SDG 2 (note 97 of Chapter One), and SDG Targets 2.1 (note 103 of Chapter One) and 2.2, relate to the extirpation of hunger. SDG Target 2.2 declares: "By 2030, end all forms of malnutrition, including achieving, by 2025, the internationally agreed targets on stunting and wasting in children under 5 years of age, and address the nutritional needs of adolescent girls, pregnant and lactating women and older persons" (Resolution 70/1 adopted by the General Assembly on 25 September 2015, Transforming our world: the 2030 Agenda for Sustainable Development, 15).

[17] The Millennium Development Goals Report 2015, 23.

[18] Notes 10 and 12, and accompanying text.

[19] Notes 11 and 13, and accompanying text.

[20] Note 100 of Chapter One.

[21] The UN's MDG Report states: "As the global economy has entered a new period combining slower growth, widening inequalities and turbulence, employment is not expanding fast enough to keep up with the growing labour force. The global employment-to-population ratio – the proportion of the working-age population that is employed – has fallen from 62 per cent in 1991 to 60 per cent in 2015, with an especially significant downturn during the global economic crisis of 2008/2009." (The Millennium Development Goals Report 2015, 17).

[22] Note 101 of Chapter One.

MDG 1 is successful given comparable conditions over the areas of its targets 25 years earlier.

The international poverty line and inferences from it

The international poverty line: Readers may have observed that MDG Target 1.A refers to people whose income is less than USD 1.00 per day[23] and that SDG Target 1.1 mentions individuals living on less than USD 1.25 per day.[24] Both these figures refer to the international poverty line.[25] MDG Target 1.A was set in the UN's Millennium Declaration,[26] in which Heads of State and Government[27] – meeting at the Millennium Summit of the UN from 6th to 8th September 2000[28] – resolved "[t]o halve, by the year

---

[23] Text to note 7.

[24] Text to note 6.

[25] Bauer *et al.* state the following: "How does one go about setting an international poverty line? Researchers at the World Bank came up with a simple approach to tackle this question in 1990. [T]hey argued that the national poverty line of low income countries provided a natural benchmark for comparing the incidence of extreme poverty globally and across countries. Based on national poverty lines for a sample of 33 countries, the World Bank researchers found that a poverty line of $1-a-day per person was "representative" of the national poverty lines employed in 10 low-income countries. Accordingly, they proposed it as a common benchmark against which internationally comparable estimates of extreme poverty could be obtained. The '$1-a-day poverty line was thus born and introduced in the *World Bank's World Development Report 1990*. … The latest update [by World Bank researchers to the $1-a-day international poverty line], announced in March 2008, is $1.25 per day in 2005 prices." (Armin Bauer, Rana Hasan, Rhoda Magsombol, and Guanghua Wan, "The World Bank's New Poverty Data: Implications for the Asian Development Bank", *ADB Sustainable Development Working Paper Series*, No. 2, November 2008, 2-3; emphasis original).

[26] The UN's website notes: "The world leaders who gathered at the [Millennium] Summit [of the UN] committed their nations to a new global partnership to reduce extreme poverty, and set out a series of time-bound targets, with a deadline of 2015, that have become known, since the Millennium Summit, as the Millennium Development Goals." ("Conferences, Meetings and Events: Millennium Summit (6-8 September 2000)", United Nations, accessed February 24, 2020, https://www.un.org/en/events/pastevents/millennium_summit.shtml).

[27] United Nations, Resolution 55/2 adopted by the General Assembly on 8 September 2000, art.1.

[28] Resolution 55/2 adopted by the General Assembly on 8 September 2000, art.1; "Conferences, Meetings and Events: Millennium Summit (6-8 September 2000)", United Nations, accessed February 24, 2020, https://www.un.org/en/events/pastevents/millennium_summit.shtml.

2015, the proportion of the world's people whose income is less than one dollar per day.[29] Based on the updated figure from the World Bank,[30] the UN adjusted MDG Target 1.A to read "Halve, between 1990 and 2015, the proportion of people whose income is less than *$1.25* a day".[31] As this income of USD 1.25 per day persists from the later version of MDG Target 1.A into the initial version of SDG Target 1.1,[32] a direct comparison can be made between readings regarding the former and those concerning the latter. However, from October 2015 the World Bank altered its estimate of the international poverty line to USD 1.90 per day.[33] The changes in the international poverty line are to compensate for rises in prices, so that the line measures a constant level of poverty; thus, whilst the USD 1.00 per day poverty line (or USD 370 per person per year) was measured in constant *1985* PPP prices),[34] the USD 1.25 per day poverty line was based on the latest available worldwide comparisons of PPP prices for *2005*,[35] and the USD 1.90 per day poverty line was measured in *2011* PPP USD.[36]

Rephrasing of MDG Target 1.A and SDG Target 1.1 in the light of the changes to the international poverty line: Given the periodic upgrading that the World Bank makes to its estimates of the international poverty line – as discussed in the immediately-preceding paragraph, it would facilitate the analyses in this Chapter to treat the level of the international poverty line as an exogenous factor for which an adjustment does not have to be made. Accordingly, MDG Target 1.A[37] is modified to read the following.

> Halve, between 1990 and 2015, the proportion of people whose income is *below the international poverty line*.

---

[29] Resolution 55/2 adopted by the General Assembly on 8 September 2000, art.1.
[30] This 'updated figure' is $1.25 per day – see the last quoted sentence in note 25.
[31] "We can end poverty: Millennium Development Goals and Beyond 2015 – Goal 1: Eradicate extreme poverty & hunger", United Nations, accessed February 24, 2020, https://www.un.org/millenniumgoals/poverty.shtml; emphasis added.
[32] Note 99 of Chapter One.
[33] "FAQs: Global Poverty Line Update", World Bank, accessed February 28, 2020, https://www.worldbank.org/en/topic/poverty/brief/global-poverty-line-faq.
[34] World Bank, World Development Report 1990: Poverty – World Development Indicators, PUB8507 (Oxford: Oxford University Press, 1990), 27.
[35] Bauer *et al.*, "The World Bank's New Poverty Data: Implications for the Asian Development Bank", *ADB Sustainable Development Working Paper Series*, No. 2, November 2008, 3.
[36] World Bank, Poverty and Shared Prosperity 2018: Piecing Together the Poverty Puzzle (Washington, D.C., 2018), 19.
[37] Note 98 of Chapter One, and text to note 7.

Similarly, SDG Target 1.1[38] is altered thus.

> By 2030, eradicate extreme poverty for all people everywhere, *as measured by the international poverty line.*[39]

These general versions of MDG Target 1.A and SDG Target 1.1 are the basis of the deliberations in the remainder of this section and in the next.[40]

Progress in the accomplishment of MDG Target 1.A

Notwithstanding the attainment globally of MDG Target 1.A in 2010,[41] there are regional differences as to the extent of the decline in extreme poverty between 1990 and 2015. The proportion of individuals living on USD 1.25 per day fell by 94%, 84%, 81%, 77%, 66%, 66%, 46% and 28% over those 25 years in China, South-East Asia, North Africa, the Caucasus and Central Asia, South Asia,[42] Latin America and the Caribbean, West Asia, and Sub-Saharan Africa, respectively.[43] Thus, six out of eight developing regions meet MDG Target 1.A.[44] Sub-Saharan Africa's 28%

---

[38] Note 99 of Chapter One, and text to note 6.

[39] Expressing SDG Target 1.1 in this way suits the wording of its Indicator – i.e., SDG Indicator 1.1.1, which reads: "Proportion of population below the international poverty line, by sex, age, employment status and geographical location (urban/rural)" ("Sustainable Development Goal 1: End poverty in all its forms everywhere – Targets & Indicators", United Nations Sustainable Development Knowledge Platform, accessed March 24, 2020, https://sustainabledevelopment.un.org/sdg1#targets). Note 239 specifies the refinement of SDG Indicator 1.1.1 that the UNStC approved and adopted in March 2020.

[40] This is especially relevant to the subsection below entitled 'From MDG Target 1.A to SDG Target 1.1'.

[41] Note 98 of Chapter One, and the text to note 7, both state MDG Target 1.A. Note 12 records the accomplishment of this MDG Target in 2010.

[42] Whilst the proportion of persons living on USD 1.25 per day in South Asia fell 66% between 1990 and 2015, this statistic for South Asia *excluding India* dropped 73% in the same period (The Millennium Development Goals Report 2015, 14).

[43] The Millennium Development Goals Report 2015, 17. Whilst the 2015 figures are projected, the data for 2011 show all the listed developing regions other than Sub-Saharan Africa achieving the target of halving from 1990 the percentage of individuals living on USD 1.25 per day (The Millennium Development Goals Report 2015, 14-15).

[44] There is insufficient data for Oceania to include a percentage for its decline in extreme poverty between 1990 and 2015 (The Millennium Development Goals Report 2015, 15).

drop in the proportion of persons living in extreme poverty occurred wholly between 2002 and 2015, with 41%[45] of the population in that region continuing to live in those conditions in the latter year.[46]

In 2011, almost 60% of the world's extremely poor people – i.e., those living on less than USD 1.25 per day, resided (from the most to the least) in India, Nigeria, China, Bangladesh and the Democratic Republic of the Congo.[47] In that year, 1.011 billion individuals worldwide were below the international poverty line – which was then[48] USD 1.25 per day.[49]

From MDG Target 1.A to SDG Target 1.1

The progression from MDG Target 1.A to SDG Target 1.1 is from halving the level of extreme poverty – measured as the percentage of people whose income is below the international poverty line – to eliminating extreme poverty; i.e., for SDG Target 1.1 to be wholly successful, no-one's income must be below the international poverty line at the date of assessment – which is currently scheduled to take place no later than on 31st December 2030.[50] Whilst it has been practicable to *halve* extreme poverty,[51] it is

---

45 This 41% is an estimate (note 43).

46 The Millennium Development Goals Report 2015, 14-15.

47 The Millennium Development Goals Report 2015, 15.

48 The World Bank raised its estimate of the international poverty line to USD 1.25 per day in March 2008 (note 25), and to USD 1.90 per day in October 2015 (text to note 33).

49 The Millennium Development Goals Report 2015, 15.

50 Note 40 and accompanying text. The date 31st December 2030 is introduced pursuant to the use of the phrase 'by 2030' in SDG Target 1.1. Even if SDG Target 1.1 is fulfilled at 11.55 p.m. on 31st December 2030, there remain five minutes of 2030 – which would mean that the target is attained 'by 2030'. Pedantically, it is submitted that (i) SDG Target 1.1 would be achieved even if this accomplishment took place at 11.55 p.m. on 31st December 2030 in American Samoa – which is eleven hours behind Greenwich Mean Time ("Time Zone in American Samoa", Time and Date AS, accessed March 16, 2020, https://www.timeanddate.com/time/zone/american-samoa), but (ii) would *not* be met if the accomplishment occurred five minutes or more beyond that moment – even though Baker Island and Howland Island – which are *uninhabited* territories belonging to the USA – are *twelve* hours behind Greenwich Mean Time ("GMT-12 Offset: Countries and Regions", Greenwich 2000 Limited, accessed March 16, 2020, https://greenwichmeantime.com/time-zone/gmt-12/), and (iii) at 11.55 p.m. on 31st December 2030, Samoa Standard Time, it will be 10.55 a.m. on 1st January 2031 in London (i.e., Greenwich Mean Time) and 12.55 a.m. on *2nd* January 2031 in the Line Islands (Kiribati) – which are *fourteen* hours *ahead* of Greenwich Mean Time ("GMT+14 Offset: Countries and Regions", Greenwich 2000 Limited,

submitted that it is impossible to *eradicate* extreme poverty because individual, local or national circumstances may preclude a 100% success rate in raising incomes above the international poverty line.[52] For example, whilst it is too early at the time of writing to predict the global profile of the COVID-19 pandemic,[53] this may adversely affect some developing states and LDCs to such an extent that the income of some of their citizens is held under, or pushed below, the international poverty line.[54] Consequently, the ensuing discussion considers the *extent to which* SDG Target 1.1 might be achieved by 31st December 2030.

---

accessed March 16, 2020, https://greenwichmeantime.com/time-zone/gmt-plus-14/). As both American Samoa and the Line Islands are inhabited territories, for one hour each day people situated on the latter experience a date which is two calendar days ahead of that encountered by individuals located in the former, and these two places do not at any moment *simultaneously* experience the same calendar day.

[51] Note 12, and text to note 41.

[52] The UN may set a numerical target that allows for this difficulty – although such an objective would not amount to *eradicating* extreme poverty (note 56 and accompanying text). Note 60 of Chapter Four defines 'eradicate'. Notes 59 and 60 of Chapter Four and their accompanying text apply a literal interpretation to the *prima facie* requirements of MDG 1. Note 59 of Chapter Four defines the phrase '*prima facie*'.

[53] The WHO classified the outbreak and spread of COVID-19 as a pandemic on 11th March 2020 ("WHO Director-General's opening remarks at the media briefing on COVID-19", World Health Organization, accessed March 16 2020, https://www.who.int/dg/speeches/detail/who-director-general-s-opening-remarks-at-the-media-briefing-on-covid-19---11-march-2020). A 'pandemic' is "an outbreak of … a disease [that is] prevalent over a whole country or the world" (Oxford University Press, *The New Oxford Dictionary of English* (Oxford: Oxford University Press, 1998), 1339. The meaning of 'pandemic' can be compared to, and contrasted with, the definition of 'epidemic'. An 'epidemic' is "a widespread occurrence of an infectious disease in a community at a particular time (*The New Oxford Dictionary of English*, 619).

[54] Italy, which is already substantially prejudiced by the COVID-19 pandemic, was predicted on 3rd March 2020 to have an economic growth rate of 0.2% in 2020 – which is lower than the estimated economic growth rate the previous month of 0.4% in 2020 when fewer Italians had tested positive for coronavirus than on 3rd March 2020 ("Italy Economic Outlook: March 3, 2020", FocusEconomics, accessed March 16, 2020, https://www.focus-economics.com/countries/italy#; "Italy: Coronavirus Cases", Worldometer, accessed March 16 2020, https://www.worldometers.info/coronavirus/country/italy/).

SDG Target 1.1

Progress to date in the accomplishment of SDG Target 1.1

In May 2019, the high-level political forum on sustainable development convened under the auspices of the ECOSOC[55] published a Report of the Secretary-General as part of its commentary on progress towards the SDGs, which made the following remarks concerning the accomplishment of SDG Target 1.1.

> The decline of global extreme poverty continues, but has slowed. The deceleration indicates that the world is not on track to achieve the target of less than 3 per cent of the world living in extreme poverty by 2030.[56] … The share of the world population living in extreme poverty declined to 10 per cent in 2015, down from 16 per cent in 2010 and 36 per cent in 1990. However, the pace of poverty reduction is decelerating, with a "nowcast" of 8.6 per cent in 2018. Moreover, baseline projections suggest that 6 per cent of the world population will still be living in extreme poverty in 2030, missing the target of ending poverty.[57] Despite having a job, 8 per cent of the world's workers and their families still lived in extreme poverty in 2018. This situation remains particularly alarming in sub-Saharan Africa, where the share of the working poor stood at 38 per cent in 2018. …[58]

The 'working poor' refers to the extreme working poverty rate, which the ILO calculates as [(employed persons living on less than USD 1.90 per day/total employment)*100%].[59] The ILO's figures and estimates give the

---

[55] Note 92 of Chapter One, and accompanying text.

[56] Neither SDG Target 1.1 (note 99 of Chapter One, and text to note 6), nor SDG 1 (note 96 of Chapter One, and text to note 2) refers to a target of reducing extreme poverty to less than 3% of the global population; SDG Target 1.1 aims to *eradicate* extreme poverty; SDG 1 seeks to *end* poverty. Note 52 and its accompanying text opine on this theme.

[57] There is no target, as such, of ending poverty. There is a *Goal* to end poverty, i.e., SDG 1 (note 96 of Chapter One, and text to note 2). There is a target to end *extreme* poverty, i.e., SDG Target 1.1 (note 99 of Chapter One, and text to note 6). There is a target to *halve* poverty, i.e., SDG Target 1.2 (note 15).

[58] United Nations, Economic and Social Council: High-level political forum on sustainable development, convened under the auspices of the Economic and Social Council – Special edition: progress towards the Sustainable Development Goals: Report of the Secretary-General, E/2019/68, 8 May 2019 (New York, 2019), para.22.

[59] United Nations, Department of Economic and Social Affairs – Statistics Division: Metadata for Target 1.1 – Indicator 1.1.1: ILO – Last updated: March 2019 (New York, 2019), 2.

extreme working poverty rate as 8.3%, 8.0%, 7.7%, 7.4%, 7.1%, 6.9%, 6.6%, 6.4%, 6.3% and 6.1% in 2015, 2016, 2017, 2018, 2019, 2020, 2021, 2022, 2023 and 2024, respectively.[60] Whilst these percentages are reducing, they are set to remain above 5% by the target date, i.e., 31st December 2030,[61] on the basis of the trend.

The World Bank provides data on its PovcalNet database for the following 166 economies: Albania, Algeria, Angola, Argentina – Urban,[62] Armenia, Australia, Austria, Azerbaijan, Bangladesh, Belarus, Belgium, Belize, Benin, Bhutan, Bolivia,[63] Bosnia and Herzegovina, Botswana, Brazil, Bulgaria, Burkina Faso, Burundi, Cabo Verde, Cameroon, Canada, Central African Republic, Chad, Chile, China,[64] Colombia,[65] Comoros, Costa Rica, Côte d'Ivoire, Croatia, Cyprus, the Czech Republic, the Democratic Republic of the Congo, Denmark, Djibouti, the Dominican Republic, Ecuador,[66] Egypt, El Salvador, Estonia, Eswatini, Ethiopia,[67]

---

[60] International Labour Organization, World Employment and Social Outlook – Trends 2020 (Geneva, 2020), 90-91; "ILOSTAT: 1.1.1 Working poverty rate", International Labour Organization, accessed March 25, 2020.
https://www.ilo.org/ilostat/faces/oracle/webcenter/portalapp/pagehierarchy/Page33.jspx;ILOSTATCOOKIE=4iYG0WpxcNKkwq_7OKV65n0AL_7kXm8QDqnc6720zRNb0WXMYQo2!-1102363596?locale=EN&MBI_ID=530&_afrLoop=9945026141909335&_afrWindowMode=0&_afrWindowId=null#!%40%40%3F_afrWindowId%3Dnull%26locale%3DEN%26_afrLoop%3D9945026141909335%26MBI_ID%3D530%26_afrWindowMode%3D0%26_adf.ctrl-state%3Dk8au5er2e_4.

[61] Note 50 and accompanying text.

[62] The PovcalNet database provides only urban data on poverty for Argentina ("PovcalNet: Choose economies/aggregates", World Bank, accessed March 26, 2020, http://iresearch.worldbank.org/PovcalNet/povOnDemand.aspx).

[63] The PovcalNet database supplies country-wide and urban data on poverty for Bolivia ("PovcalNet: Choose economies/aggregates", World Bank, accessed March 26, 2020, http://iresearch.worldbank.org/PovcalNet/povOnDemand.aspx).

[64] The PovcalNet database supplies country-wide, urban and rural data on poverty for China ("PovcalNet: Choose economies/aggregates", World Bank, accessed March 26, 2020, http://iresearch.worldbank.org/PovcalNet/povOnDemand.aspx).

[65] The PovcalNet database supplies country-wide and urban data on poverty for Colombia ("PovcalNet: Choose economies/aggregates", World Bank, accessed March 26, 2020, http://iresearch.worldbank.org/PovcalNet/povOnDemand.aspx).

[66] The PovcalNet database supplies country-wide and urban data on poverty for Ecuador ("PovcalNet: Choose economies/aggregates", World Bank, accessed March 26, 2020, http://iresearch.worldbank.org/PovcalNet/povOnDemand.aspx).

[67] The PovcalNet database supplies country-wide and rural data on poverty for Ethiopia ("PovcalNet: Choose economies/aggregates", World Bank, accessed March 26, 2020, http://iresearch.worldbank.org/PovcalNet/povOnDemand.aspx).

Fiji, Finland, France, Gabon, the Gambia, Georgia, Germany, Ghana, Greece, Guatemala, Guinea, Guinea-Bissau, Guyana, Haiti, Honduras,[68] Hungary, Iceland, India,[69] Indonesia,[70] Iran, Iraq, Ireland, Israel, Italy, Jamaica, Japan, Jordan, Kazakhstan, Kenya, Kiribati, Kosovo, Kyrgyzstan, Laos, Latvia, Lebanon, Lesotho, Liberia, Lithuania, Luxembourg, Madagascar, Malawi, Malaysia, the Maldives, Mali, Malta, Mauritania, Mauritius, Mexico, Micronesia,[71] Moldova, Mongolia, Montenegro, Morocco, Mozambique, Myanmar, Namibia, Nepal, the Netherlands, Nicaragua, Niger, Nigeria, North Macedonia, Norway, Pakistan, Panama, Papua New Guinea, Paraguay, Peru, the Philippines, Poland, Portugal, the Republic of the Congo, the Republic of Korea, Romania, Russia, Rwanda,[72] Saint Lucia, Samoa, São Tomé and Príncipe, Senegal, Serbia, the Seychelles, Sierra Leone, Slovakia, Slovenia, the Solomon Islands, South Africa, South Sudan, Spain, Sri Lanka, Sudan, Suriname, Sweden, Switzerland, Syria, Taiwan, Tajikistan, Tanzania, Thailand, Timor-Leste, Togo, Tonga, Trinidad and Tobago, Tunisia, Turkey, Turkmenistan, Tuvalu, Uganda, the UK, Ukraine, the United Arab Emirates, Uruguay,[73] the USA, Uzbekistan, Vanuatu, Venezuela, Vietnam, West Bank and Gaza, Yemen, Zambia, and Zimbabwe.[74] Aggregating the data on extreme poverty for these countries reveals a headcount[75] below the international

---

68 The PovcalNet database supplies country-wide and urban data on poverty for Honduras ("PovcalNet: Choose economies/aggregates", World Bank, accessed March 26, 2020, http://iresearch.worldbank.org/PovcalNet/povOnDemand.aspx).

69 The PovcalNet database supplies country-wide, urban and rural data on poverty for India ("PovcalNet: Choose economies/aggregates", World Bank, accessed March 26, 2020, http://iresearch.worldbank.org/PovcalNet/povOnDemand.aspx).

70 The PovcalNet database supplies country-wide, urban and rural data on poverty for Indonesia ("PovcalNet: Choose economies/aggregates", World Bank, accessed March 26, 2020, http://iresearch.worldbank.org/PovcalNet/povOnDemand.aspx).

71 The PovcalNet database supplies country-wide and urban data on poverty for Micronesia ("PovcalNet: Choose economies/aggregates", World Bank, accessed March 26, 2020, http://iresearch.worldbank.org/PovcalNet/povOnDemand.aspx).

72 The PovcalNet database supplies country-wide and rural data on poverty for Rwanda ("PovcalNet: Choose economies/aggregates", World Bank, accessed March 26, 2020, http://iresearch.worldbank.org/PovcalNet/povOnDemand.aspx).

73 The PovcalNet database supplies country-wide and urban data on poverty for Uruguay ("PovcalNet: Choose economies/aggregates", World Bank, accessed March 26, 2020, http://iresearch.worldbank.org/PovcalNet/povOnDemand.aspx).

74 "PovcalNet: Choose economies/aggregates", World Bank, accessed March 26, 2020, http://iresearch.worldbank.org/PovcalNet/povOnDemand.aspx.

75 'Headcount' means "% of population living in households with consumption or income per person below the [relevant] poverty line" ("PovcalNet: Choose economies/aggregates", World Bank, accessed March 26, 2020,

poverty line[76] of 10.11% in 2015 and of 8.50% in 2018, and a poverty gap[77] of 3.12% in 2015 and of 2.90% in 2018.[78] The PovcalNet data are based on the following facts, assumptions and methods: (i) the international poverty line of USD 1.90 per day at 2011 PPP, was calculated as the average of the national poverty lines for Chad, Ethiopia, the Gambia, Ghana, Guinea-Bissau, Malawi, Mali, Mozambique, Nepal, Niger, Rwanda, Sierra Leone, Tajikistan, Tanzania and Uganda,[79] which had also been used to compute the immediately-preceding international poverty line of USD 1.25 per day at 2005 PPP; (ii) to calculate regional aggregates, the national estimates of poverty are calibrated to a common reference year, interpolating and extrapolating for economies in which data are unavailable in that year but are obtainable before and/or after;[80]

http://iresearch.worldbank.org/PovcalNet/povOnDemand.aspx).

[76] The current international poverty line is USD 1.90 per day (text to note 33), which is a monthly poverty line measured in 2011 consumption PPP USD (PovcalNet: Choose economies/aggregates", World Bank, accessed March 26, 2020, http://iresearch.worldbank.org/PovcalNet/povOnDemand.aspx; text to note 36).

[77] 'Poverty gap' means the "mean distance below the [international] poverty line as a percentage of the [international] poverty line" (PovcalNet: Choose economies/aggregates", World Bank, accessed March 26, 2020, http://iresearch.worldbank.org/PovcalNet/povOnDemand.aspx).

[78] "PovcalNet: Choose economies/aggregates", World Bank, accessed March 26, 2020, http://iresearch.worldbank.org/PovcalNet/povOnDemand.aspx. These percentages are given to two decimal places.

[79] Francisco Ferreira, Shaohua Chen, Andrew Dabalen, Yuri Dikhanov, Nada Hamadeh, Dean Jolliffe, Ambar Narayan, Espen Prydz, Ana Revenga, Prem Sangraula, Umar Serajuddin, and Nobuo Yoshida, "A global count of the extreme poor in 2012: data issues, methodology and initial results", *Journal of Economic Inequality*, 14 (2016): 141-172, 145.

[80] This process of interpolation and extrapolation "requires adjusting the mean income or expenditure observed in the survey year by a growth factor to infer the unobserved level in the reference year. Thus, *two assumptions* are required to implement this process: *distribution-neutral growth* and *a real rate of growth between the survey and reference year. Distribution-neutral growth* implies that income or expenditure levels are adjusted for growth assuming that the underlying relative distribution of income or expenditure observed in survey years remains unchanged [– i.e.,] the growth rate is the same along the distribution. Under this assumption, it is straightforward to interpolate the poverty estimate in a given reference year implied by a given rate of growth in income or expenditure. Rates of change in real consumption per capita should be based on the change in real consumption measured by comparing survey data across different years. In practice, however, survey data in most economies are not available on an annual

(iii) each region's aggregate headcount index is the population-weighted mean of the headcount indices across the economies in that area; (iv) the number of poor in each region is the region's headcount index multiplied by total regional population;[81] (v) the distributional data are taken from nationally-representative household surveys, and are acquired from governmental statistical offices and functional departments within the World Bank Group, (vi) the 'What is new' note that is provided with every update to PovcalNet gives the source of each CPI series that is used in the estimates of poverty,[82] (vii) if available, household-level data are used to estimate poverty; other estimates depend upon grouped tabulations combined with a parametric Lorenz curve, (viii) with three exceptions,[83]

---

basis. Therefore, the change in private consumption per capita as measured from the national accounts is used instead. While there can be no guarantee that the survey-based measure of income or consumption changes at exactly the same rate as private consumption in the national accounts, this appears to be the best available option. When the reference year falls between two survey years, an estimate of mean consumption at the reference year is constructed by extrapolating the means obtained from the surveys forward and backward to the reference year. The second step is to compute the headcount poverty rate at the reference year after normalizing the distributions observed in the two survey years by the reference year mean. This yields two estimates of the headcount poverty rates in the reference year. The final reported poverty headcount rate for the reference years is the linear interpolation of the two. When data from only one survey year are available, the reference year mean is based on the survey mean by applying the growth rate in private consumption per capita from the national accounts. The reference year poverty estimate is then based on this mean and on the distribution observed in the one survey year." ("PovcalNet Methodology", World Bank, accessed March 27, 2020, http://iresearch.worldbank.org/PovcalNet/methodology.aspx).

[81] This assumes that the poverty rate for a country without a household survey is the regional mean ("PovcalNet Methodology", World Bank, accessed March 28, 2020, http://iresearch.worldbank.org/PovcalNet/methodology.aspx).

[82] This 'What is new' page, and the links thereon to information that it supplies, is accessible on the World Bank's website at http://iresearch.worldbank.org/PovcalNet/WhatIsNew.aspx.

[83] These exceptions are China, India and Indonesia, for which national PPPs from the World Bank's International Comparison Program "are disaggregated into rural and urban PPPs that are constructed to reflect cost-of-living differences between rural and urban areas. [T]his adjustment requires rural and urban poverty lines (which are used to capture differences in the cost of living) as well as information on the rural and urban shares of the ICP [i.e., International Comparison Program] price collection ("PovcalNet Methodology", World Bank, accessed March 28, 2020, http://iresearch.worldbank.org/PovcalNet/methodology.aspx). The International Comparison Program "is a worldwide statistical initiative led by the World Bank

the same data on PPP are used to convert international poverty lines to local currency units,[84] (ix) observations showing negative incomes are omitted from those household surveys in which income (rather than consumption)[85] is the measure of welfare,[86] (x) PovcalNet uses income per

---

under the auspices of the United Nations Statistical Commission, with the main objective of providing comparable price and volume measures of gross domestic product (GDP) and its expenditure aggregates among countries within and across regions. Through a partnership with international, regional, sub-regional and national agencies, the ICP collects and compares price data and GDP expenditures to estimate and publish purchasing power parities (PPPs) of the world's economies." ("International Comparison Program (ICP): Overview", World Bank, accessed March 28, 2020, https://www.worldbank.org/en/programs/icp#1).

[84] Besides China, India and Indonesia (note 83), "[i]n several other economies, the welfare aggregate has also been adjusted for within-economy spatial price differences" ("PovcalNet Methodology", World Bank, accessed March 28, 2020, http://iresearch.worldbank.org/PovcalNet/methodology.aspx).

[85] The data used for welfare in the PovcalNet database are either measures of income or of consumption; for Mexico and Poland, measures of consumption were used for the 2015 dataset and measures of income for the 2018 dataset; for Argentina, Australia, Austria, Belgium, Belize, Bolivia, Brazil, Bulgaria, Canada, Chile, Colombia, Costa Rica, Croatia, Cyprus, the Czech Republic, Denmark, the Dominican Republic, Ecuador, El Salvador, Estonia, Finland, France, Germany, Greece, Guatemala, Guyana, Honduras, Hungary, Iceland, Ireland, Israel, Italy, Japan, Latvia, Lithuania, Luxembourg, Malaysia, Malta, Montenegro, the Netherlands, Nicaragua, North Macedonia, Norway, Panama, Paraguay, Peru, Portugal, the Republic of Korea, Romania, Saint Lucia, the Seychelles, Slovakia, Slovenia, Spain, Suriname, Sweden, Switzerland, Taiwan, Trinidad and Tobago, the UK, the United Arab Emirates, Uruguay, the USA, and Venezuela, measures of income were used for both 2015 and 2018 datasets; for Albania, Algeria, Angola, Armenia, Azerbaijan, Bangladesh, Belarus, Benin, Bhutan, Bosnia and Herzegovina, Botswana, Burkina Faso, Burundi, Cabo Verde, Cameroon, Central African Republic, Chad, China, Comoros, Côte d'Ivoire, the Democratic Republic of the Congo, Djibouti, Egypt, Eswatini, Ethiopia, Fiji, Gabon, the Gambia, Georgia, Ghana, Guinea, Guinea-Bissau, Haiti, India, Indonesia, Iran, Iraq, Jamaica, Jordan, Kazakhstan, Kenya, Kiribati, Kosovo, Kyrgyzstan, Laos, Lebanon, Lesotho, Liberia, Madagascar, Malawi, the Maldives, Mali, Mauritania, Mauritius, Micronesia, Moldova, Mongolia, Morocco, Mozambique, Myanmar, Namibia, Nepal, Niger, Nigeria, Pakistan, Papua New Guinea, the Philippines, the Republic of the Congo, Russia, Rwanda, Samoa, São Tomé and Príncipe, Senegal Serbia, Sierra Leone, the Solomon Islands, South Africa, South Sudan, Sri Lanka, Sudan, Syria, Tajikistan, Tanzania, Thailand, Timor-Leste, Togo, Tonga, Tunisia, Turkey, Turkmenistan, Tuvalu, Uganda, Ukraine, Uzbekistan, Vanuatu, Vietnam, West Bank and Gaza, Yemen, Zambia, and Zimbabwe, measures of consumption

person, or consumption expenditure per person – each member of a household is allotted an equal portion of household income or expenditure, (xi) non-representative surveys are omitted from the computation of international poverty rates, (xii) whilst data coverage is improving everywhere, Africa and the Middle East lag behind, (xiii) poverty rates for a region are only reported when the available surveys cover at least 40% of the population in that area, (xiv) the lag between the reference year and when the estimates of poverty become available depends upon the accessibility and reliability of household surveys for each country,[87] (xv) there are limitations in using PPP to construct the international poverty line,[88] (xvi) discrepancies between household surveys and national

---

were used for both 2015 and 2018 datasets (PovcalNet: Choose economies/aggregates", World Bank, accessed March 28, 2020, http://iresearch.worldbank.org/PovcalNet/povOnDemand.aspx).

[86] From October 2017, this approach has been followed in all surveys of income; before this, it was only observed in Latin America and the Caribbean ("PovcalNet Methodology", World Bank, accessed March 28, 2020, http://iresearch.worldbank.org/PovcalNet/methodology.aspx). The entry for October 2017 on the 'What is new' page (note 82 and accompanying text) states: "The data for the "other high income" countries, as well as some of the income surveys in Europe and Central Asia, have a small number of observations with negative incomes, which we have dropped from the underlying database. These observations are typically the result of negative profits for self-employed individuals. The observed negative income is unlikely to reflect the permanent income of the household. It also does not reflect household consumption for this year, since households smooth their consumption from one year to the next, and consumption expenditure by definition cannot be negative. [F]or those negative income households, we do not observe a level of income or consumption expenditure that would be a good predictor of their welfare in this year, so we exclude them from the analysis. This is consistent with our approach adopted for economies in Latin America and the Caribbean. … We view this as a temporary fix until we can develop a better method to impute a more meaningful level of income or consumption for these observations." ("PovcalNet: What is new", World Bank, accessed March 28. 2020, http://iresearch.worldbank.org/PovcalNet/WhatIsNew.aspx).

[87] This lag is approximately two years; for instance, the World Bank released its poverty estimates for reference year 2018 in 2020 ("PovcalNet Methodology", World Bank, accessed March 28, 2020, http://iresearch.worldbank.org/PovcalNet/methodology.aspx).

[88] The PovcalNet webpage encapsulating the World Bank's methodology for its poverty estimates states: "An important step in the process of compiling global poverty estimates is the conversion of the $1.90 a day International Poverty Line into respective national currency units. PPP exchange rates … are used because they take into account the local prices of goods and services not traded

accounts render difficult the estimation of poverty,[89] (xvii) there are problems comparing the surveys underlying the welfare distributions that PovcalNet uses, both across economies and over time,[90] and (xviii) incomplete reporting of income and/or other required input data is a source of errors in measurement.[91] The global headcount below the international poverty line[92] and worldwide poverty gap,[93] together with the results in the succeeding paragraphs, are subject to the following constraints: (i) the World Bank advises that aggregated poverty data which include those for China,[94] India[95] and/or Indonesia[96] should incorporate these countries' urban and rural results;[97] for each of these states, the population datum for

---

internationally. Since PPP rates were designed for comparing national accounts aggregates, they were not intended for making international poverty comparisons. PPPs are based on prices of goods and services that may not be representative of the consumption baskets of the poor, so they may not fully reflect the relative price level faced by very poor consumers. As a result, there is no certainty that an international poverty line measures exactly the same degree of deprivation across economies. Similarly, the poverty line may need to be adjusted for different locations (such as urban and rural areas) within the economy, if prices or access to goods and services differs. [F]or most … economies, this information is not available." ("PovcalNet Methodology", World Bank, accessed March 28, 2020, http://iresearch.worldbank.org/PovcalNet/methodology.aspx).

[89] As household surveys and national accounts "are not strictly measuring the same thing[,] there is no reason why these sources would agree closely on consumption[; b]ut large discrepancies are still of concern, as they may reflect measurement errors in either number ("PovcalNet Methodology", World Bank, accessed March 28, 2020, http://iresearch.worldbank.org/PovcalNet/methodology.aspx).

[90] These surveys "are carried out by national statistical offices, central banks, or other national agencies, so they are designed to serve the specific needs and interests of each particular economy. Household survey questionnaires can differ widely, and similar surveys may not be strictly comparable because of differences in quality. … These problems are diminishing as survey methods improve and become more standardized, but achieving strict comparability is still impossible." ("PovcalNet Methodology", World Bank, accessed March 28, 2020, http://iresearch.worldbank.org/PovcalNet/methodology.aspx).

[91] "PovcalNet Methodology", World Bank, accessed March 28, 2020, http://iresearch.worldbank.org/PovcalNet/methodology.aspx.

[92] Notes 75 and 76, and accompanying text.

[93] Note 77 and accompanying text.

[94] Note 64 specifies the three types of data on poverty that are available for China.

[95] Note 69 indicates the three types of data on poverty that are available for India.

[96] Note 70 identifies the three types of data on poverty that are available for Indonesia.

[97] The note for each of these three countries on the relevant PovcalNet webpage reads: "National distribution is based on aggregated Lorenz curve from original

the country in the relevant year is the sum of the population datum for the rural areas of the country and the population datum for the urban areas of the country;[98] pursuant to this, as each region's aggregate headcount index is the population-weighted mean of the headcount indices for the economies in that area,[99] and as the percentages for the headcount below the international poverty line and the poverty gap for the whole of China, India and Indonesia, respectively, are the population-weighted mean of those for the rural and the urban parts of the same country,[100] the *country-*

---

rural and urban distribution. Rural and urban distributions must be included when aggregating poverty measures from a group of economies (PovcalNet: Choose economies/aggregates", World Bank, accessed March 29, 2020, http://iresearch.worldbank.org/PovcalNet/povOnDemand.aspx). Note 83 provides information on the disaggregation of China's, India's and Indonesia's national values for PPP into rural and urban values for PPP.

[98] Thus, for 2015, (i) China's country-wide population [1,371,220,000 people] = China' s rural population [610,190,000 people] + China's urban population [761,030,000 people], (ii) India's country-wide population [1,310,150,000 people] = India's rural population [880,720,000 people] + India's urban population [429,430,000 people], and (iii) Indonesia's country-wide population [258,380,000 people] = Indonesia's rural population [120,630,000 people] + Indonesia's urban population [137,750,000 people]; for 2018, (i) China's country-wide population [1,392,730,000 people] = China's rural population [568,900,000 people] + China's urban population [823,830,000 people], (ii) India's country-wide population [1,352,620,000 people] = India's rural population [892,320,000 people] + India's Urban population [460,300,000 people], and (iii) Indonesia's country-wide population [267,660,000 people] = Indonesia's rural population [119,580,000 people] + Indonesia's urban population [148,080,000 people] (PovcalNet: Choose economies/aggregates", World Bank, accessed March 30, 2020, http://iresearch.worldbank.org/PovcalNet/povOnDemand.aspx). These numbers are given to five significant figures – except for the four data that exceed one billion, which are given to six significant figures.

[99] Point (iii) in the immediately-preceding list in the text makes this statement.

[100] The headcount (note 75) below the international poverty line (i.e., USD 1.90 per day) for: (i) China, China – Rural, and China – Urban, respectively, is 0.73%, 1.25% and 0.31% in 2015, and 0.27%, 0.51% and 0.10% in 2018, (ii) India, India – Rural, and India – Urban, respectively, is 13.35%, 15.25% and 9.45% in 2015, and n/a, n/a and n/a in 2018, and (iii) Indonesia, Indonesia – Rural, and Indonesia – Urban, respectively, is 7.18%, 7.38% and 7.00% in 2015, and 4.64%, 4.93% and 4.40% in 2018; the poverty gap (note 77) for (i) China, China – Rural, and China – Urban, respectively, is 0.16%, 0.23% and 0.10% in 2015, and 0.07%, 0.12% and 0.04% in 2018, (ii) India, India – Rural, and India – Urban, respectively, is 2.36%, 2.71% and 1.65% in 2015, and n/a, n/a and n/a in 2018, and (iii) Indonesia, Indonesia – Rural, and Indonesia – Urban, respectively, is 1.19%, 1.16% and

1.21% in 2015, and 0.67%, 0.68% and 0.66% in 2018 (PovcalNet: Choose economies/aggregates", World Bank, accessed March 29, 2020, http://iresearch.worldbank.org/PovcalNet/povOnDemand.aspx). These percentages are given to two decimal places. It is submitted that the 'n/a' entries for India, India – Rural, and India – Urban in 2018 result from the data on poverty for India being unavailable at the date of the latest update to the PovcalNet database, which, at the time of writing, was 17th March 2020 – see note 87 and its accompanying text ("PovcalNet: What is new", World Bank, accessed March 28. 2020, http://iresearch.worldbank.org/PovcalNet/WhatIsNew.aspx). To verify the truth of the following statement in the text: "the percentages for the headcount below the international poverty line and the poverty gap for the whole of China, India and Indonesia, respectively, are the population-weighted mean of those for the rural and the urban parts of the same country", the following equivalences are demonstrated for these percentages – which the first sentence of the current footnote (i.e., note 100) specifies – using the relevant population figures – which note 98 contains: (a) *Headcount below the international poverty line:* (i) Headcount in 2015 (China) * Population in 2015 (China) ≡ [Headcount in 2015 (China – Rural) * Population in 2015 (China – Rural)] + [Headcount in 2015 (China – Urban) * Population in 2015 (China – Urban)], → [0.73% * 1,371,220,000 people] ≡ [1.25% * 610,190,000 people] + [0.31% * 761,030,000 people], → 1,000,990,600 %people ≡ 762,737,500 %people + 235,919,300 %people, → 1,000,990,600 %people ≡ 998,656,800 %people, → 0.73% ≡ 998,656,800 %people / 1,371,220,000 people; → *0.73% ≡ 0.73%*; (ii) Headcount in 2018 (China) * Population in 2018 (China) ≡ [Headcount in 2018 (China – Rural) * Population in 2018 (China – Rural)] + [Headcount in 2018 (China – Urban) * Population in 2018 (China – Urban)], → [0.27% * 1,392,730,000 people] ≡ [0.51% * 568,900,000 people] + [0.10% * 823,830,000 people], → 376,037,100 %people ≡ 290,139,000 %people + 82,383,000 %people, → 376,037,100 %people ≡ 372,522,000 %people, → 0.27% ≡ 372,522,000 %people / 1,392,730,000 people; → *0.27% ≡ 0.27%*; (iii) Headcount in 2015 (India) * Population in 2015 (India) ≡ [Headcount in 2015 (India – Rural) * Population in 2015 (India – Rural)] + [Headcount in 2015 (India – Urban) * Population in 2015 (India – Urban)], → [13.35% * 1,310,150,000 people] ≡ [15.25% * 880,720,000 people] + [9.45% * 429,430,000 people], → 17,490,502,500 %people ≡ 13,430,980,000 %people + 4,058,113,500 %people, → 17,490,502,500 %people ≡ 17,489,093,500 %people, → 0.73% ≡ 17,489,093,500 %people / 1,310,150,000 people; → *13.35% ≡ 13.35%*; (iv) Headcount in 2015 (Indonesia) * Population in 2015 (Indonesia) ≡ [Headcount in 2015 (Indonesia – Rural) * Population in 2015 (Indonesia – Rural)] + [Headcount in 2015 (Indonesia – Urban) * Population in 2015 (Indonesia – Urban)], → [7.18% * 258,380,000 people] ≡ [7.38% * 120,630,000 people] + [7.00% * 137,750,000 people], → 1,855,168,400 %people ≡ 890,249,400 %people + 964,250,000 %people, → 1,855,168,400 %people ≡ 1,854,499,400 %people, → 7.18% ≡ 1,854,499,400 %people / 258,380,000 people; → *7.18% ≡ 7.18%*; (v) Headcount in 2018 (Indonesia) * Population in 2018 (Indonesia) ≡ [Headcount in 2018 (Indonesia – Rural) * Population in 2018 (Indonesia – Rural)] + [Headcount in 2018 (Indonesia – Urban) * Population in 2018 (Indonesia – Urban)], → [4.64% * 267,660,000 people] ≡ [4.93% * 119,580,000 people] + [4.40% * 148,080,000 people], → 1,241,942,400 %people ≡ 589,529,400 %people + 651,552,000 %people, → 1,241,942,400 %people ≡ 1,241,081,400 %people, → 4.64% ≡ 1,241,081,400 %people / 267,660,000 people; → *4.64% ≡ 4.64%*; (b) *Poverty gap:* (i) Poverty gap in 2015 (China) * Population in 2015 (China) ≡ [Poverty gap in 2015 (China – Rural) * Population in 2015 (China – Rural)] + [Poverty gap in 2015 (China – Urban) * Population in 2015 (China – Urban)], → [0.16% * 1,371,220,000 people] ≡ [0.23% * 610,190,000 people] + [0.10% * 761,030,000 people], → 219,395,200 %people ≡ 140,343,700 %people + 76,103,000 %people, → 219,395,200 %people ≡ 216,446,700 %people, → 0.16% ≡ 216,446,700 %people / 1,371,220,000 people; → *0.16% ≡ 0.16%*; (ii) Poverty gap in 2018 (China) * Population in 2018 (China) ≡ [Poverty gap in 2018 (China – Rural) * Population in 2018 (China – Rural)] + [Poverty gap in 2018 (China – Urban) * Population in 2018 (China – Urban)], → [0.07% * 1,392,730,000 people] ≡ [0.12% * 568,900,000 people] + [0.04% * 823,830,000 people], → 97,491,100 %people ≡ 68,268,000 %people + 32,953,200 %people, → 97,491,100 %people ≡ 101,221,200 %people, → 0.07% ≡ 101,221,200 %people / 1,392,730,000 people; → *0.07% ≡ 0.07%*; (iii) Poverty gap in 2015 (India) * Population in 2015 (India) ≡ [Poverty gap in 2015 (India – Rural) * Population in 2015 (India – Rural)] + [Poverty gap in 2015 (India – Urban) * Population in 2015 (India – Urban)], → [2.36% * 1,310,150,000 people] ≡ [2.71% * 880,720,000 people] + [1.65% * 429,430,000 people], → 3,091,954,000 %people ≡ 2,386,751,200 %people + 708,559,500 %people, → 3,091,954,000 %people ≡ 3,095,310,700 %people, → 2.36% ≡ 3,095,310,700 %people / 1,310,150,000 people; → *2.36% ≡ 2.36%*; (iv) Poverty gap in 2015 (Indonesia) * Population in 2015 (Indonesia) ≡ [Poverty gap in 2015 (Indonesia – Rural) * Population in 2015 (Indonesia – Rural)] + [Poverty gap in 2015 (Indonesia – Urban) * Population in 2015 (Indonesia – Urban)], → [1.19% * 258,380,000 people] ≡ [1.16% * 120,630,000 people] + [1.21% * 137,750,000 people], → 307,472,200 %people ≡ 139,930,800 %people + 166,677,500 %people, → 307,472,200 %people ≡ 306,608,300 %people, → 1.19% ≡ 306,608,300 %people / 258,380,000 people; → *1.19% ≡ 1.19%*; (v) Poverty gap in 2018 (Indonesia) * Population in 2018 (Indonesia) ≡ [Poverty gap in 2018 (Indonesia – Rural) * Population in 2018 (Indonesia – Rural)] + [Poverty gap in 2018 (Indonesia – Urban) * Population in 2018 (Indonesia – Urban)], → [0.67% * 267,660,000 people] ≡ [0.68% * 119,580,000 people] + [0.66% * 148,080,000 people], → 179,332,200 %people ≡ 81,314,400 %people + 97,732,800 %people, → 179,332,200 %people ≡ 179,047,200 %people, → 0.67% ≡ 179,047,200 %people / 267,660,000 people; → *0.67% ≡ 0.67%*. It is submitted that, although there are slight inequalities when the equivalences are expressed in '%people' units, these are due at least in part to numerical approximations caused by the difference in the number of significant figures between the population numbers and the headcount/poverty gap percentages – the former having more significant figures than the latter. All ten equivalences in headcount/poverty gap percentages (i.e., (a)(i)-(v) and (b)(i)-(v), above in this footnote) are successfully *wide data* for each of these three states are included in the global and regional poverty aggregates to which that country contributes – having been shown to comprise the data for its rural areas and the data for its urban areas, (ii) the data for 'Argentina – Urban' is used in the poverty aggregates to which Argentina contributes, because PovcalNet does not provide country-wide data for that state,[101] and (iii) the data for Bolivia,[102] Columbia,[103] Ecuador,[104] Ethiopia,[105] Honduras,[106] Micronesia,[107] Rwanda,[108] and Uruguay[109] include *only* the country-wide data in the poverty aggregates to which these countries contribute.[110]

The aggregated data for high-income countries[111] yield a headcount[112] below the international poverty line[113] of 0.71% in 2015 and of 0.67% in

---

demonstrated, which substantiates the accuracy of the following statement in the text: "the percentages for the headcount below the international poverty line and the poverty gap for the whole of China, India and Indonesia, respectively, are the population-weighted mean of those for the rural and the urban parts of the same country".

[101] Note 62.

[102] Note 63.

[103] Note 65.

[104] Note 66.

[105] Note 67.

[106] Note 68.

[107] Note 71.

[108] Note 72.

[109] Note 73.

[110] Thus, *166 economies* contribute to the global figures on extreme poverty provided above (text to note 78) – those of the 166 countries listed above (text to note 74) plus *but excluding* Bolivia – Urban, China – Rural, China – Urban, Colombia – Urban, Ecuador – Urban, Ethiopia – Rural, Honduras – Urban, India – Rural, India – Urban, Indonesia – Rural, Indonesia – Urban, Micronesia – Urban, Rwanda – Rural, and Uruguay – Urban – whose inclusion would amount to all 180 economies that the PovcalNet database provides being utilized in the global aggregate (PovcalNet: Choose economies/aggregates", World Bank, accessed March 29, 2020,
http://iresearch.worldbank.org/PovcalNet/povOnDemand.aspx).

[111] These 'high-income countries' comprise the following 28 economies: Australia, Austria, Belgium, Canada, Cyprus, Denmark, Finland, France, Germany, Greece, Iceland, Ireland, Israel, Italy, Japan, Luxembourg, Malta, the Netherlands, Norway, Portugal, the Republic of Korea, Spain, Sweden, Switzerland, Taiwan, the UK, the United Arab Emirates, and the USA ("PovcalNet: Choose economies/aggregates", World Bank, accessed April 1, 2020,
http://iresearch.worldbank.org/PovcalNet/povOnDemand.aspx).

[112] Note 75 defines 'headcount'.

[113] Note 76 specifies the current international poverty line.

2018, and a poverty gap[114] of 0.48% in 2015 and of 0.45% in 2018.[115] Thus, from a very low level of extreme poverty in 2015 for which the poverty gap is small, there is a minor reduction in both the headcount and the poverty gap to the level noted in 2018. Among these high-income economies,[116] Greece,[117] Italy,[118] Spain[119] and the USA[120] each have a raised headcount and poverty gap – and Germany,[121] Taiwan[122] and the United Arab Emirates[123] each have a headcount and poverty gap of zero – in both 2015 and 2018.[124]

---

[114] Note 77 defines 'poverty gap'.

[115] "PovcalNet: Choose economies/aggregates", World Bank, accessed April 1, 2020, http://iresearch.worldbank.org/PovcalNet/povOnDemand.aspx. These percentages are given to two decimal places.

[116] Note 111 lists these high-income countries.

[117] Greece has a headcount of 1.38% in 2015, and of 0.87% in 2018; it has a poverty gap of 0.79 in 2015, and of 0.42% in 2018; Greece's survey years are 2015 and 2017 ("PovcalNet: Choose economies/aggregates", World Bank, accessed April 1, 2020, http://iresearch.worldbank.org/PovcalNet/povOnDemand.aspx).

[118] Italy has a headcount of 1.96% in 2015, and of 1.42% in 2018; it has a poverty gap of 1.41% in 2015, and of 1.11% in 2018; Italy's survey years are 2015 and 2017 ("PovcalNet: Choose economies/aggregates", World Bank, accessed April 1, 2020, http://iresearch.worldbank.org/PovcalNet/povOnDemand.aspx).

[119] Spain has a headcount of 0.94% in 2015, and of 0.68% in 2018; it has a poverty gap of 0.64% in 2015, and of 0.54% in 2018; Spain's survey years are 2015 and 2017 ("PovcalNet: Choose economies/aggregates", World Bank, accessed April 1, 2020, http://iresearch.worldbank.org/PovcalNet/povOnDemand.aspx).

[120] The USA has a headcount of 1.17% in 2015, and of 1.25% in 2018; it has a poverty gap of 0.93% in 2015, and of 0.96% in 2018; the USA's results for 2015 are interpolated, and its most-recent survey year is 2016 ("PovcalNet: Choose economies/aggregates", World Bank, accessed April 1, 2020, http://iresearch.worldbank.org/PovcalNet/povOnDemand.aspx).

[121] Germany's survey years are 2015 and 2016 (("PovcalNet: Choose economies/aggregates", World Bank, accessed April 1, 2020, http://iresearch.worldbank.org/PovcalNet/povOnDemand.aspx).

[122] Taiwan's results for 2015 are interpolated, and its most-recent survey year is 2016 ("PovcalNet: Choose economies/aggregates", World Bank, accessed April 1, 2020, http://iresearch.worldbank.org/PovcalNet/povOnDemand.aspx).

[123] The United Arab Emirates' most recent survey year is 2014. It is submitted that this state's headcount and poverty gap were found to be zero in the survey of that year.

[124] "PovcalNet: Choose economies/aggregates", World Bank, accessed April 1, 2020, http://iresearch.worldbank.org/PovcalNet/povOnDemand.aspx.

The aggregated data for LDCs[125] produce a headcount[126] below the international poverty line[127] of 36.47% in 2015 and of 34.59% in 2018, and a poverty gap[128] of 13.47% in 2015 and of 13.25% in 2018.[129] It is opined that these figures are both high and persistent, i.e., the poorest countries in the world continue to contain citizens who are deprived, and this is only improving very slowly. 33 of the 47 LDCs are in Sub-Saharan Africa.[130] Thus, it appears that this region is prospering only slowly.[131]

---

[125] At present, the LDCs are the following 47 states: Afghanistan, Angola (scheduled by UN General Assembly Resolution A/RES/70/253 adopted on 12th February 2016 to graduate from the LDC category on 12th February 2021), Bangladesh, Benin, Bhutan (scheduled by UN General Assembly Resolution A/73/L.40/Rev.1 adopted on 13th December 2018 to graduate from the LDC class on 13th December 2023), Burkina Faso, Burundi, Cambodia, Central African Republic, Chad, Comoros, the Democratic Republic of the Congo, Djibouti, Eritrea, Ethiopia, the Gambia, Guinea, Guinea-Bissau, Haiti, Kiribati, Laos, Lesotho, Liberia, Madagascar, Malawi, Mali, Mauritania, Mozambique, Myanmar, Nepal, Niger, Rwanda, São Tomé and Príncipe (scheduled by UN General Assembly Resolution A/73/L.40/Rev.1 adopted on 13th December 2018 to graduate from the LDC group on 13th December 2024), Senegal, Sierra Leone, the Solomon Islands (scheduled by UN General Assembly Resolution A/73/L.40/Rev.1 adopted on 13th December 2018 to graduate from the LDC division on 13th December 2024), Somalia, South Sudan, Sudan, Tanzania, Timor-Leste, Togo, Tuvalu, Uganda, Vanuatu (scheduled by UN General Assembly Resolution A/RES/70/78 adopted on 9th December 2015 to graduate from the LDC bracket on 4th December 2020), Yemen, and Zambia (United Nations, United Nations Committee for Development Policy: List of Least Developed Countries (as of December 2018). New York, 2018). The PovcalNet database contains data for 43 of these 47 economies – data for Afghanistan, Cambodia, Eritrea, and Somalia, are unavailable ("PovcalNet: Choose economies/aggregates", World Bank, accessed April 1, 2020, http://iresearch.worldbank.org/PovcalNet/povOnDemand.aspx).

[126] Note 75 defines 'headcount'.

[127] Note 76 specifies the current international poverty line.

[128] Note 77 defines 'poverty gap'.

[129] "PovcalNet: Choose economies/aggregates", World Bank, accessed April 1, 2020, http://iresearch.worldbank.org/PovcalNet/povOnDemand.aspx. These percentages are given to two decimal places.

[130] The LDCs that are located in Sub-Saharan Africa (note 153) are Angola, Benin, Burkina Faso, Burundi, Central African Republic, Chad, Comoros, the Democratic Republic of the Congo, Djibouti, Eritrea, Ethiopia, the Gambia, Guinea, Guinea-Bissau, Lesotho, Liberia, Madagascar, Malawi, Mali, Mauritania, Mozambique, Niger, Rwanda, São Tomé and Príncipe, Senegal, Sierra Leone, Somalia, South Sudan, Sudan, Tanzania, Togo, Uganda, and Zambia. Note 125 lists all 47 of the LDCs.

[131] The next paragraph considers extreme poverty in Sub-Saharan Africa.

There is much variation among the LDCs as to headcount and poverty gap: the five countries that the data show to have the greatest extent of severe poverty – all exceeding a headcount of 70% in both 2015 and 2018 – are Burundi,[132] Central African Republic,[133] the Democratic Republic of the Congo,[134] Madagascar,[135] and South Sudan,[136] whilst the five states that the data to show to have the lowest level of extreme poverty – all with a headcount of less than 7% in both 2015 and 2018 – are Bhutan,[137]

---

[132] Burundi has a headcount of 74.87% in 2015, and of 78.19% in 2018; it has a poverty gap of 33.12% in 2015, and of 36.46% in 2018; Burundi's most recent survey year is 2013 ("PovcalNet: Choose economies/aggregates", World Bank, accessed April 2, 2020, http://iresearch.worldbank.org/PovcalNet/povOnDemand.aspx). It is submitted that the lack of survey data for Burundi beyond 2013 renders these percentages – especially those for 2018 – imprecise.

[133] Central African Republic has a headcount of 74.78% in 2015, and of 71.65% in 2018; it has a poverty gap of 41.18% in 2015, and of 38.14% in 2018; Central African Republic's most recent survey year is 2008 ("PovcalNet: Choose economies/aggregates", World Bank, accessed April 2, 2020, http://iresearch.worldbank.org/PovcalNet/povOnDemand.aspx). It is opined that the lack of survey data for Central African Republic beyond 2008 renders these percentages very inexact.

[134] The Democratic Republic of the Congo has a headcount of 71.74% in 2015, and of 70.73% in 2018; it has a poverty gap of 34.12% in 2015, and of 33.42% in 2018; the Democratic Republic of the Congo's most recent survey year is 2012 ("PovcalNet: Choose economies/aggregates", World Bank, accessed April 2, 2020, http://iresearch.worldbank.org/PovcalNet/povOnDemand.aspx). It is suggested that the lack of survey data for the Democratic Republic of the Congo beyond 2012 renders these percentages – particularly those for 2018 – approximate.

[135] Madagascar has a headcount of 77.45% in 2015, and of 75.94% in 2018; it has a poverty gap of 38.79% in 2015, and of 37.16% in 2018; Madagascar's most recent survey year is 2012 ("PovcalNet: Choose economies/aggregates", World Bank, accessed April 3, 2020, http://iresearch.worldbank.org/PovcalNet/povOnDemand.aspx). It is submitted that the lack of survey data for Madagascar beyond 2012 renders these percentages – especially those for 2018 – imprecise.

[136] South Sudan has a headcount of 73.26% in 2015, and of 84.82% in 2018; it has a poverty gap of 39.98% in 2015, and of 51.42% in 2018. South Sudan's most recent survey year is 2009 ("PovcalNet: Choose economies/aggregates", World Bank, accessed April 3, 2020, http://iresearch.worldbank.org/PovcalNet/povOnDemand.aspx). It is opined that the lack of survey data for South Sudan beyond 2009 renders these percentages very inexact.

[137] Bhutan has a headcount of 0.86% in 2015, and of 0.75% in 2018; it has a poverty gap of 0.13% in 2015, and of 0.12% in 2018; Bhutan's results for 2015 are

Mauritania,[138] Myanmar,[139] Nepal,[140] and Tuvalu.[141] Whilst the infrequency of surveys within all these states[142] bar Myanmar[143] and, possibly, Bhutan,[144] casts doubt upon the reliability of the corresponding data on extreme poverty reported in this paragraph,[145] it is noteworthy that: (i) the headcount and, especially, the poverty gap, for the latter five LDCs[146] is more consistent with those for the four high-income countries with raised headcount and poverty gap reported in the immediately-preceding paragraph[147] than with the headcount and poverty gap for the former five

---

interpolated, and its most-recent survey year is 2017 ("PovcalNet: Choose economies/aggregates", World Bank, accessed April 3, 2020, http://iresearch.worldbank.org/PovcalNet/povOnDemand.aspx).

[138] Mauritania has a headcount of 6.44% in both 2015 and 2018; it has a poverty gap of 1.53% in 2015, and of 1.54% in 2018; Mauritania's most recent survey year is 2014 ("PovcalNet: Choose economies/aggregates", World Bank, accessed April 3, 2020, http://iresearch.worldbank.org/PovcalNet/povOnDemand.aspx). It is suggested that the lack of survey data for Mauritania beyond 2014 renders the percentages for its headcount and poverty gap in 2018 approximate.

[139] Myanmar has a headcount of 6.22% in 2015, and of 1.52% in 2018; it has a poverty gap of 1.45% in 2015, and of 0.24% in 2018; Myanmar's survey years are 2015 and 2017 ("PovcalNet: Choose economies/aggregates", World Bank, accessed April 3, 2020, http://iresearch.worldbank.org/PovcalNet/povOnDemand.aspx).

[140] Nepal has a headcount of 5.88% in 2015, and of 5.81% in 2018; it has a poverty gap of 1.09% in 2015, and of 1.07% in 2018; Nepal's most recent survey year is 2010 ("PovcalNet: Choose economies/aggregates", World Bank, accessed April 3, 2020, http://iresearch.worldbank.org/PovcalNet/povOnDemand.aspx). It is submitted that the lack of survey data for Nepal beyond 2010 renders these percentages imprecise.

[141] Tuvalu has a headcount of 1.62% in 2015, and of 0.58% in 2018; it has a poverty gap of 0.12% in 2015, and of 0.06% in 2018; Tuvalu's most recent survey year is 2010 ("PovcalNet: Choose economies/aggregates", World Bank, accessed April 3, 2020, http://iresearch.worldbank.org/PovcalNet/povOnDemand.aspx). It is opined that the lack of survey data for Tuvalu beyond 2010 renders these percentages inexact.

[142] Notes 132-141.

[143] Note 139.

[144] Note 137.

[145] Notes 132-136, 138, and 140-141.

[146] These are Bhutan, Mauritania, Myanmar, Nepal and Tuvalu (notes 137-141 and accompanying text).

[147] These are Greece, Italy, Spain and the USA (notes 117-120, and accompanying text).

LDCs,[148] and (ii) the five LDCs with the greatest degree of extreme poverty[149] are all Sub-Saharan African states,[150] whilst the five LDCs with the least extent of severe poverty[151] comprise three South-East Asian countries, one Oceanic state, and only one Sub-Saharan African country – i.e., Mauritania.[152] Thus, a hypothesis emerges that extreme poverty preponderates over better conditions in Sub-Saharan Africa, which is tested by inspection of the region's data in the next paragraph. There is a corresponding proposition that extreme poverty does not predominate in the other regions, which is examined in the paragraphs following that.

The aggregated data for Sub-Saharan Africa[153] supply a headcount[154] below the international poverty line[155] of 42.29% in 2015 and of 41.58% in 2018, and a poverty gap[156] of 16.16% in 2015 and of 16.13% in 2018.[157] These vary from the sky-high headcount and poverty gap for each of Burundi,[158] Central African Republic,[159] the Democratic Republic of the

---

148 These are Burundi, Central African Republic, the Democratic Republic of the Congo, Madagascar and South Sudan (notes 132-136, and accompanying text).

149 Note 148.

150 Note 130 lists the LDCs that are situated in Sub-Saharan Africa.

151 Note 146.

152 Notes 150 and 153.

153 PovcalNet data are available for the following 46 states in Sub-Saharan Africa: Angola, Benin, Botswana, Burkina Faso, Burundi, Cabo Verde, Cameroon, Central African Republic, Chad, Comoros, Côte d'Ivoire, the Democratic Republic of the Congo, Djibouti, Eswatini, Ethiopia, Gabon, the Gambia, Ghana, Guinea, Guinea-Bissau, Kenya, Lesotho, Liberia, Madagascar, Malawi, Mali, Mauritania, Mauritius, Mozambique, Namibia, Niger, Nigeria, the Republic of the Congo, Rwanda, São Tomé and Príncipe, Senegal, the Seychelles, Sierra Leone, South Africa, South Sudan, Sudan, Tanzania, Togo, Uganda, Zambia, and Zimbabwe ("PovcalNet: Choose economies/aggregates", World Bank, accessed April 4, 2020, http://iresearch.worldbank.org/PovcalNet/povOnDemand.aspx). Thus, PovcalNet data are unavailable for Equatorial Guinea, Eritrea, and Somalia. Within this book, all 54 of the UN Member States that are located in Africa are considered to be within Sub-Saharan Africa *except for* Algeria, Egypt, Libya, Morocco and Tunisia – i.e., Chad, Eritrea, Mali, Mauritania, Niger, and Sudan are *included* in this region.

154 Note 75 defines 'headcount'.

155 Note 76 specifies the current international poverty line.

156 Note 77 defines 'poverty gap'.

157 "PovcalNet: Choose economies/aggregates", World Bank, accessed April 4, 2020, http://iresearch.worldbank.org/PovcalNet/povOnDemand.aspx.
These percentages are given to two decimal places.

158 Note 132 states the headcount and poverty gap for Burundi in 2015 and in 2018.

Congo,[160] Madagascar,[161] and South Sudan[162] to the low headcount and poverty gap – i.e., under 7% and 2%, respectively – for Cabo Verde,[163] Gabon[164], Mauritania,[165] Mauritius[166] and the Seychelles.[167] Whilst the headcount and poverty gap for the highest five countries[168] and the lowest five states[169] in the aggregated data for Sub-Saharan Africa are the same and similar, respectively, as the headcount and poverty gap for the highest five states[170] and the lowest five countries[171] in the aggregated data for the

---

[159] Note 133 specifies the headcount and poverty gap for Central African Republic in 2015 and in 2018.

[160] Note 134 declares the headcount and poverty gap for the Democratic Republic of the Congo in 2015 and in 2018.

[161] Note 135 proclaims the headcount and poverty gap for Madagascar in 2015 and in 2018.

[162] Note 136 pronounces the headcount and poverty gap for South Sudan in 2015 and 2018.

[163] Cabo Verde has a headcount of 3.23% in 2015, and of 2.36% in 2018; it has a poverty gap of 0.69% in 2015, and of 0.47% in 2018; Cabo Verde's most recent survey year is 2015 ("PovcalNet: Choose economies/aggregates", World Bank, accessed April 4, 2020, http://iresearch.worldbank.org/PovcalNet/povOnDemand.aspx).

[164] Gabon has a headcount of 3.99% in 2015, and of 3.47% in 2018; it has a poverty gap of 0.96% in 2015, and of 0.88% in 2018; Gabon's results for 2015 are interpolated, and its most-recent survey year is 2017 ("PovcalNet: Choose economies/aggregates", World Bank, accessed April 4, 2020, http://iresearch.worldbank.org/PovcalNet/povOnDemand.aspx).

[165] Note 138 records the headcount and poverty gap for Mauritania in 2015 and 2018.

[166] Mauritius has a headcount of 0.36% in 2015, and of 0.14% in 2018; it has a poverty gap of 0.05% in 2015, and of 0.02% in 2018; Mauritius' results for 2015 are interpolated, and its most-recent survey year is 2017 ("PovcalNet: Choose economies/aggregates", World Bank, accessed April 4, 2020, http://iresearch.worldbank.org/PovcalNet/povOnDemand.aspx).

[167] The Seychelles has a headcount of 0.91% in 2015, and of 0.84% in 2018; it has a poverty gap of 0.40% in 2015, and of 0.35% in 2018; the Seychelles' most recent survey year is 2013 ("PovcalNet: Choose economies/aggregates", World Bank, accessed April 4, 2020, http://iresearch.worldbank.org/PovcalNet/povOnDemand.aspx). It is submitted that the lack of survey data for the Seychelles beyond 2013 renders these percentages – especially those for 2018 – imprecise.

[168] Notes 158-162, and accompanying text.

[169] Notes 163-167, and accompanying text.

[170] Notes 132-136, and accompanying text.

[171] Notes 137-141, and accompanying text.

LDCs, the headcount and poverty gap for Sub-Saharan Africa[172] are higher in both 2015 and 2018 than those for the LDCs[173] – with the headcount for the Sub-Saharan Africa in both years being in excess of 40%. This statistic is consistent with the hypothesis, stated in the immediately-preceding paragraph, that extreme poverty – measured thus, i.e., by the percentage of population living in households with consumption or income per person below the international poverty line[174] – preponderates over better conditions in Sub-Saharan Africa. As both the headcount below the international poverty line and the poverty gap for Sub-Saharan Africa barely decline between 2015 and 2018, it is submitted that extreme poverty in this region is 'sticky', i.e., very difficult to bring down to any significant and lasting extent. Why does Sub-Saharan Africa perform less well on measures of extreme poverty in both 2015 and 2018 than the LDCs do, when both groups share a majority of their member states? One possible explanation is that levels of severe poverty and/or inequality in some of the Sub-Saharan African countries that are not LDCs – especially significant regional economies such as those of Nigeria and South Africa – are greater than those of the LDCs that are outside Sub-Saharan Africa. Whilst Chapter Four addresses inequality, it is confirmed that the level of extreme poverty in Nigeria is high[175] and that in South Africa is medium[176] – i.e., higher and lower, respectively, than that for both Sub-Saharan Africa as a whole and for the LDCs. On the basis of this partial information, that explanation may be, but is not conclusively, valid.

---

[172] The text to note 157 declares the headcount and poverty gap for Sub-Saharan Africa in both 2015 and 2018.

[173] The text to note 129 specifies the headcount and poverty gap for the LDCs in both 2015 and 2018.

[174] Notes 75 and 76, and accompanying text.

[175] Nigeria has a headcount of 47.01% in 2015, and of 50.85% in 2018; it has a poverty gap of 18.12% in 2015, and of 20.12% in 2018; Nigeria's most recent survey year is 2009 ("PovcalNet: Choose economies/aggregates", World Bank, accessed April 3, 2020, http://iresearch.worldbank.org/PovcalNet/povOnDemand.aspx). It is opined that the lack of survey data for Nigeria beyond 2009 renders these percentages very inexact.

[176] South Africa has a headcount of 18.92% in 2015, and of 19.54% in 2018; it has a poverty gap of 6.21% in 2015, and of 6.42% in 2018; South Africa's most recent survey year is 2014 ("PovcalNet: Choose economies/aggregates", World Bank, accessed April 4, 2020, http://iresearch.worldbank.org/PovcalNet/povOnDemand.aspx). It is suggested that the lack of survey data for South Africa beyond 2014 renders the percentages for its headcount and poverty gap in 2018 approximate.

The aggregated data for the Middle East and North Africa[177] furnish a headcount[178] below the international poverty line[179] of 3.61% in 2015 and of 6.83% in 2018, and a poverty gap[180] of 0.84% in 2015 and of 1.99% in 2018.[181] These data show a low, but increasing, level of extreme poverty in this region – although they may not fully capture the trends in the whole region as PovcalNet omits to provide data on six of that area's nineteen economies.[182] Eleven of the thirteen economies of this region for which PovcalNet supplies data[183] have a headcount of less than 2.5% in 2015 and of less than 3.5% in 2018, and a poverty gap of less than 0.6% in 2015 and of less than 0.4% in 2015.[184] But Syria has a headcount of 14.20% in 2015 and of 43.37% in 2018, and a poverty gap of 2.90% in 2015 and of 12.63% in 2018,[185] and Yemen has a headcount of 30.39% in 2015 and of 51.93% in 2018, and a poverty gap of 8.24% in 2015 and of 17.09% in

---

177 PovcalNet data are available for the following thirteen economies in the Middle East and North Africa: Algeria, Egypt, Iran, Iraq, Israel, Jordan, Lebanon, Morocco, Syria, Tunisia, the United Arab Emirates, West Bank and Gaza, and Yemen ("PovcalNet: Choose economies/aggregates", World Bank, accessed April 4, 2020, http://iresearch.worldbank.org/PovcalNet/povOnDemand.aspx). Hence, PovcalNet data are unavailable for Bahrain, Kuwait, Libya, Oman, Qatar, and Saudi Arabia. Whilst PovcalNet data are available for Cyprus (text to note 74, and notes 85 and 111) this country is judged to be outside the region entitled 'Middle East and North Africa', as, notwithstanding its location in the easternmost part of the Mediterranean Sea, it is a Member State of the European Union.

178 Note 75 defines 'headcount'.

179 Note 76 specifies the current international poverty line.

180 Note 77 defines 'poverty gap'.

181 "PovcalNet: Choose economies/aggregates", World Bank, accessed April 4, 2020, http://iresearch.worldbank.org/PovcalNet/povOnDemand.aspx.
These percentages are given to two decimal places.

182 Note 177 lists the thirteen economies within the Middle East and North Africa for which PovcalNet provides data, and identifies the six countries therein on which PovcalNet omits to supply data.

183 These eleven economies are Algeria, Egypt, Iran, Iraq, Israel, Jordan, Lebanon, Morocco, Tunisia, the United Arab Emirates, and West Bank and Gaza ("PovcalNet: Choose economies/aggregates", World Bank, accessed April 5, 2020, http://iresearch.worldbank.org/PovcalNet/povOnDemand.aspx).

184 "PovcalNet: Choose economies/aggregates", World Bank, accessed April 5, 2020, http://iresearch.worldbank.org/PovcalNet/povOnDemand.aspx.

185 Syria's most recent survey year is 2004 ("PovcalNet: Choose economies/aggregates", World Bank, accessed April 5, 2020, http://iresearch.worldbank.org/PovcalNet/povOnDemand.aspx). It is submitted that the lack of survey data for Syria beyond 2004 renders this state's percentages for headcount and poverty gap in 2015 and 2018 very imprecise.

2018.[186] It is submitted that on-going conflict in both these countries contributes to the raised levels of headcount and poverty gap there – an effect that is particularly marked in the high percentages of headcount and poverty gap for those two states in 2018. These war-driven statistics are reflected in the headcount and poverty gap for the region,[187] which rise considerably between 2015 and 2018 from low levels in the earlier of those two years.

The aggregated data for Central Europe, East Europe, the Caucasus and Central Asia[188] yield a headcount[189] below the international poverty line[190] of 1.61% in 2015 and of 1.19% in 2018, and a poverty gap[191] of 0.45% in 2015 and of 0.35% in 2018.[192] These impressive records include 29 of the 30 regional economies for which PovcalNet provides data,[193] that have a headcount below the international poverty line of less than 6% in 2015 and of less than 5% in 2018, and a poverty gap of less than 2.5% in

---

186 Yemen's most recent survey year is 2014 ("PovcalNet: Choose economies/aggregates", World Bank, accessed April 5, 2020, http://iresearch.worldbank.org/PovcalNet/povOnDemand.aspx). It is opined that the lack of survey data for Yemen beyond 2014 renders the percentages for its headcount and poverty gap in 2018 inexact.

187 The text to note 181 shows the headcount and the poverty gap for the 13 economies in the Middle East and North Africa for which PovcalNet provides data, in both 2015 and 2018. Note 177 lists these 13 economies.

188 PovcalNet data are available for the following 30 countries in Central Europe, East Europe, the Caucasus and Central Asia: Albania, Armenia, Azerbaijan, Belarus, Bosnia and Herzegovina, Bulgaria, Croatia, the Czech Republic, Estonia, Georgia, Hungary, Kazakhstan, Kosovo, Kyrgyzstan, Latvia, Lithuania, Moldova, Montenegro, North Macedonia, Poland, Romania, Russia, Serbia, Slovakia, Slovenia, Tajikistan, Turkey, Turkmenistan, Ukraine, and Uzbekistan ("PovcalNet: Choose economies/aggregates", World Bank, accessed April 5, 2020, http://iresearch.worldbank.org/PovcalNet/povOnDemand.aspx). PovcalNet data are unavailable for Afghanistan (note 125). Whilst PovcalNet data are available for Cyprus (text to note 74, and notes 85, 111 and 177) and Greece (text to note 74, notes 85 and 111, and note 117 and accompanying text), these two states are deemed to be outside the region entitled 'Central Europe, East Europe, the Caucasus and Central Asia'.

189 Note 75 defines 'headcount'.

190 Note 76 specifies the current international poverty line.

191 Note 77 defines 'poverty gap'.

192 "PovcalNet: Choose economies/aggregates", World Bank, accessed April 5, 2020, http://iresearch.worldbank.org/PovcalNet/povOnDemand.aspx.
These percentages are given to two decimal places.

193 Note 188 lists these 30 countries.

2015 and of less 2% than in 2018, the exception being Uzbekistan.[194] On the basis of these figures, there is little extreme poverty in this area of the world.

The aggregated data for South Asia[195] provide a headcount[196] below the international poverty line[197] of 12.30% in 2015 and of 5.32% in 2018, and a poverty gap[198] of 2.16% in 2015 and of 0.79% in 2018.[199] These data include the headcount and poverty gap for India in 2015,[200] but not the headcount and poverty gap for India in 2018 – probably because these latter statistics are not yet available.[201] As each region's aggregate headcount index is the population-weighted mean of the headcount indices across the economies in that area,[202] and as India's population in 2018

---

[194] "PovcalNet: Choose economies/aggregates", World Bank, accessed April 7, 2020, http://iresearch.worldbank.org/PovcalNet/povOnDemand.aspx. Uzbekistan has a headcount of 15.72% in 2015, and of 12.00% in 2018; it has a poverty gap of 4.20% in 2015, and of 3.18% in 2018; Uzbekistan's most recent survey year is 2003 ("PovcalNet: Choose economies/aggregates", World Bank, accessed April 7, 2020, http://iresearch.worldbank.org/PovcalNet/povOnDemand.aspx). It is submitted that the lack of survey data for Uzbekistan beyond 2003 renders these percentages very inexact.

[195] PovcalNet data are available for the following seven states in South Asia: Bangladesh, Bhutan, India (note 69, notes 97 and 100 and accompanying text, and the clause in the text immediately after note 100), the Maldives, Nepal, Pakistan, and Sri Lanka ("PovcalNet: Choose economies/aggregates", World Bank, accessed April 7, 2020, http://iresearch.worldbank.org/PovcalNet/povOnDemand.aspx). PovcalNet data are unavailable for Afghanistan (note 125).

[196] Note 75 defines 'headcount'.

[197] Note 76 specifies the current international poverty line.

[198] Note 77 defines 'poverty gap'.

[199] "PovcalNet: Choose economies/aggregates", World Bank, accessed April 4, 2020, http://iresearch.worldbank.org/PovcalNet/povOnDemand.aspx.
These percentages are given to two decimal places.

[200] India has a headcount of 13.35%, and a poverty gap of 2.36%, in 2015; these data are the weighted sum of the 'India – Urban' and 'India – Rural' headcount above the international poverty line and poverty gap for 2011 ("PovcalNet: Choose economies/aggregates", World Bank, accessed April 7, 2020, http://iresearch.worldbank.org/PovcalNet/povOnDemand.aspx). It is opined that the lack of survey data for India beyond 2010 renders these percentages imprecise.

[201] A two-year wait for the required data is usual (see note 87 and accompanying text, and, for India specifically, the third sentence of note 100).

[202] Note 99 and accompanying text. It is submitted that the region's aggregate poverty gap is likely to be calculated on a similar basis to its aggregate headcount index, i.e., the aggregate poverty gap is the population-weighted mean of the poverty gaps across the economies in the region.

comprises more than three-quarters of the population of South Asia (excluding Afghanistan, for which PovcalNet does not provide data[203]),[204] the figures for the headcount below the international poverty line and the poverty gap in 2018 – which do not include data for India – represent less than one quarter of the population of this region, and are, therefore non-representative. Therefore, it *cannot* be validly concluded from these data and the corresponding statistics for 2015[205] that there has been a substantial fall in headcount and poverty gap in South Asia between 2015 and 2018. Notwithstanding this, both the headcount below the international poverty line and the poverty gap are lower in 2018 than in 2015 for all the non-Indian economies of this region (i.e., Bangladesh,[206] Bhutan,[207] the Maldives,[208] Nepal,[209] Pakistan,[210] and Sri Lanka[211]), which warrants the

---

203 Note 125.

204 Population (South Asia) = Population (Bangladesh) + Population (Bhutan) + Population (India) + Population (the Maldives) + Population (Nepal) + Population (Pakistan) + Population (Sri Lanka); → For the year 2018, Population (South Asia) = 161,360,000 people + 750,000 people + 1,352,620,000 people + 520,000 people + 28,090,000 people + 212,220,000 people + 21,670,000 people = 1,777,230,000 people. Percentage of the population of South Asia that resides in India = [Population (India) / Population (South Asia)] * 100%; → For the year 2018, percentage of the population of South Asia that resides in India = [1,352,620,000 people / 1,777,230,000 people] * 100% = *76.11%*. The ten-digit population data – i.e., those for India and South Asia – are given to six significant figures. The nine-digit population data – i.e., those for Bangladesh and Pakistan – are given to five significant figures. The eight-digit population data – i.e., those for Nepal and Sri Lanka – are given to four significant figures. The six-digit population data – i.e., those for Bhutan and the Maldives – are given to two significant figures. The percentage of the population of South Asia that resides in India is given to two decimal places.

205 Text to note 199.

206 Bangladesh has a headcount of 15.15% in 2015, and of 7.84% in 2018; it has a poverty gap of 2.75% in 2015, and of 1.30% in 2018; Bangladesh's results for 2015 are interpolated, and its most-recent survey year is 2016 ("PovcalNet: Choose economies/aggregates", World Bank, accessed April 7, 2020, http://iresearch.worldbank.org/PovcalNet/povOnDemand.aspx).

207 Note 137 records the headcount and poverty gap for Bhutan in 2015 and 2018.

208 The Maldives has a headcount of 0.07% in 2015, and of 0.00% in 2018; it has a poverty gap of 0.01% in 2015, and of 0.00% in 2018; the Maldives' results for 2015 are interpolated, and its most-recent survey year is 2016 ("PovcalNet: Choose economies/aggregates", World Bank, accessed April 7, 2020, http://iresearch.worldbank.org/PovcalNet/povOnDemand.aspx).

209 Note 140 records the headcount and poverty gap for Nepal in 2015 and 2018.

conclusion that, in the absence of data for India in 2018, the headcount and poverty gap in South Asia appear to have reduced over the ensuing three years from 2015.

The aggregated data for East Asia and the Pacific[212] supply a headcount[213] below the international poverty line[214] of 2.31% in 2015 and of 1.34% in 2018, and a poverty gap[215] of 0.46% in 2015 and of 0.25% in 2018.[216] Whilst these regional figures are both low and decreasing, there is variation from the very small values of headcount and poverty gap in

---

[210] Pakistan has a headcount of 5.33% in 2015, and of 1.61% in 2018; it has a poverty gap of 0.71% in 2015, and of 0.18% in 2018; Pakistan's results for 2015 are interpolated "using estimates at 2013.5 and 2015.5", and its most-recent survey year is stated to be "2015.5" ("PovcalNet: Choose economies/aggregates", World Bank, accessed April 7, 2020, http://iresearch.worldbank.org/PovcalNet/povOnDemand.aspx).

[211] Sri Lanka has a headcount of 1.11% in 2015, and of 0.69% in 2018; it has a poverty gap of 0.14% in 2015, and of 0.08% in 2018; Sri Lanka's results for 2015 are interpolated, and its most-recent survey year is 2016 ("PovcalNet: Choose economies/aggregates", World Bank, accessed April 7, 2020, http://iresearch.worldbank.org/PovcalNet/povOnDemand.aspx).

[212] PovcalNet data are available for the following 19 states of East Asia and the Pacific: China (note 64, and notes 97 and 100 and accompanying text), Fiji, Indonesia (note 70, and notes 97 and 100 and accompanying text), Kiribati, Laos, Malaysia, Micronesia, Mongolia, Myanmar, Papua New Guinea, the Philippines, Samoa, the Solomon Islands, Thailand, Timor-Leste, Tonga, Tuvalu, Vanuatu, and Vietnam ("PovcalNet: Choose economies/aggregates", World Bank, accessed April 8, 2020, http://iresearch.worldbank.org/PovcalNet/povOnDemand.aspx).

[213] Note 75 defines 'headcount'.

[214] Note 76 specifies the current international poverty line.

[215] Note 77 defines 'poverty gap'.

[216] "PovcalNet: Choose economies/aggregates", World Bank, accessed April 8, 2020, http://iresearch.worldbank.org/PovcalNet/povOnDemand.aspx.
These percentages are given to two decimal places.

Malaysia[217] and Thailand[218] to the fairly large numbers for these statistics in the Solomon Islands[219] and Timor-Leste.[220]

The aggregated data for Latin America and the Caribbean[221] furnish a headcount[222] below the international poverty line[223] of 4.09% in 2015 and of 4.39% in 2018, and a poverty gap[224] of 1.51% in 2015 and of 1.71% in 2018.[225] Although these levels of headcount and poverty gap are low, they are increasing. It is submitted that the main contributors to this rise are

---

217 Malaysia has a headcount of 0.01% and a poverty gap of 0.00% in both 2015 and 2018; Malaysia's results for 2015 are interpolated "using estimates at 2013.5 and 2015.33", and its most-recent survey year is stated to be "2015.33" ("PovcalNet: Choose economies/aggregates", World Bank, accessed April 8, 2020, http://iresearch.worldbank.org/PovcalNet/povOnDemand.aspx).

218 Thailand has a headcount of 0.03% in 2015, and of 0.02% in 2018; it has a poverty gap of 0.02% in 2015, and of 0.00% in 2018; Thailand's survey years are 2015 and 2018 ("PovcalNet: Choose economies/aggregates", World Bank, accessed April 8, 2020, http://iresearch.worldbank.org/PovcalNet/povOnDemand.aspx).

219 The Solomon Islands has a headcount of 25.47% in 2015, and of 24.33% in 2018; it has a poverty gap of 6.96% in 2015, and of 6.47% in 2018; the Solomon Islands' most recent survey year is 2013 ("PovcalNet: Choose economies/aggregates", World Bank, accessed April 8, 2020, http://iresearch.worldbank.org/PovcalNet/povOnDemand.aspx). It is submitted that the lack of survey data for the Solomon Islands beyond 2013 renders these percentages – especially those for 2018 – imprecise.

220 Timor-Leste has a headcount of 32.77% in 2015, and of 26.73% in 2018; it has a poverty gap of 7.43% in 2015, and of 5.61% in 2018; Timor-Leste's most recent survey year is 2014 ("PovcalNet: Choose economies/aggregates", World Bank, accessed April 8, 2020, http://iresearch.worldbank.org/PovcalNet/povOnDemand.aspx). It is opined that the lack of survey data for Timor-Leste beyond 2014 renders the percentages for its headcount and poverty gap in 2018 inexact.

221 PovcalNet data are available for the following 25 economies of Latin America and the Caribbean: Argentina – Urban (note 62), Belize, Bolivia, Brazil, Chile, Colombia, Costa Rica, the Dominican Republic, Ecuador, El Salvador, Guatemala, Guyana, Haiti, Honduras, Jamaica, Mexico, Nicaragua, Panama, Paraguay, Peru, Saint Lucia, Suriname, Trinidad and Tobago, Uruguay, and Venezuela ("PovcalNet: Choose economies/aggregates", World Bank, accessed April 8, 2020, http://iresearch.worldbank.org/PovcalNet/povOnDemand.aspx).

222 Note 75 defines 'headcount'.

223 Note 76 specifies the current international poverty line.

224 Note 77 defines 'poverty gap'.

225 "PovcalNet: Choose economies/aggregates", World Bank, accessed April 8, 2020, http://iresearch.worldbank.org/PovcalNet/povOnDemand.aspx.
These percentages are given to two decimal places.

Brazil – whose large population[226] makes the rise in the headcount below the international poverty line from 3.18% in 2015 to 4.44% in 2018, and in the poverty gap from 1.06% in 2015 to 1.65% in 2018[227] a major influence on the change of the region's headcount and poverty gap from 2015 to 2018,[228] and Venezuela – whose headcount below the international poverty line is 9.43% in 2015 and 17.21% in 2018, and whose poverty gap is 6.88% in 2015 and 9.58% in 2018.[229] Whilst Latin America and the Caribbean includes states whose headcount below the international poverty line are very low – in particular Chile,[230] Trinidad and Tobago,[231] and Uruguay,[232] it also contains countries whose headcount and poverty

[226] Brazil's population is 204,470,000 people in 2015, and 209,470,000 people in 2018; Brazil is the most populous country in Latin America and the Caribbean, Mexico being the next – with 121,860,000 people in 2015, and 126,190,000 people in 2018 ("PovcalNet: Choose economies/aggregates", World Bank, accessed April 8, 2020, http://iresearch.worldbank.org/PovcalNet/povOnDemand.aspx). These population data are given to five significant figures.

[227] Brazil's survey years are 2015 and 2018 ("PovcalNet: Choose economies/aggregates", World Bank, accessed April 8, 2020, http://iresearch.worldbank.org/PovcalNet/povOnDemand.aspx).

[228] Notes 99 and 202, and accompanying text.

[229] Venezuela's most recent survey year is 2006 ("PovcalNet: Choose economies/aggregates", World Bank, accessed April 8, 2020, http://iresearch.worldbank.org/PovcalNet/povOnDemand.aspx). It is suggested that the lack of survey data for Venezuela beyond 2006 renders this state's percentages for headcount and poverty gap in 2015 and 2018 very approximate.

[230] Chile has a headcount of 0.30% in 2015, and of 0.28% in 2018; it has a poverty gap of 0.15% in 2015, and of 0.16% in 2018; Chile's survey years are 2015 and 2017 ("PovcalNet: Choose economies/aggregates", World Bank, accessed April 8, 2020, http://iresearch.worldbank.org/PovcalNet/povOnDemand.aspx).

[231] Trinidad and Tobago has a headcount of 0.24% in 2015, and of 0.29% in 2018; it has a poverty gap of 0.12% in 2015, and of 0.13% in 2018; Trinidad and Tobago's most recent survey year is 1992 ("PovcalNet: Choose economies/aggregates", World Bank, accessed April 8, 2020, http://iresearch.worldbank.org/PovcalNet/povOnDemand.aspx). It is submitted that the lack of survey data for Trinidad and Tobago beyond 1992 renders these percentages exceedingly imprecise.

[232] Uruguay has a headcount of 0.13% in 2015, and of 0.06% in 2018; it has a poverty gap of 0.03% in both 2015 and 2018; Uruguay's survey years are 2015 and 2018 ("PovcalNet: Choose economies/aggregates", World Bank, accessed April 8, 2020, http://iresearch.worldbank.org/PovcalNet/povOnDemand.aspx).

gap are quite high – i.e., Belize,[233] Haiti,[234] Honduras,[235] Suriname,[236] and Venezuela.[237]

Thus, modest, mixed progress has been made between 2015 and 2018 towards meeting SDG Target 1.1 – both the headcount below the international poverty line and the poverty gap have reduced globally, and regionally in Central Europe, East Europe, the Caucasus and Central Asia, South Asia, and East Asia and the Pacific, with little change in Sub-Saharan Africa, and increases in the Middle East and North Africa and, to a lesser extent, Latin America and the Caribbean. There is considerable variation in the levels of extreme poverty within regions. The high level of severe poverty in Sub-Saharan Africa presents an especial difficulty in working towards the accomplishment of SDG Target 1.1.

Will SDG Target 1.1 be achieved punctually?

Based on the data presented in the immediately-preceding subsection and on the conclusions drawn from these in that subsection's final paragraph, it

[233] Belize has a headcount of 12.59% in 2015, and of 13.92% in 2018; it has a poverty gap of 5.65% in 2015, and of 6.26% in 2018; Belize's most recent survey year is 1999 ("PovcalNet: Choose economies/aggregates", World Bank, accessed April 8, 2020, http://iresearch.worldbank.org/PovcalNet/povOnDemand.aspx). It is opined that the lack of survey data for Belize beyond 1999 renders these percentages very inexact.

[234] Haiti has a headcount of 24.66% in 2015, and of 25.35% in 2018; it has a poverty gap of 7.99% in 2015, and of 8.34% in 2018; Haiti's most recent survey year is 2012 ("PovcalNet: Choose economies/aggregates", World Bank, accessed April 8, 2020, http://iresearch.worldbank.org/PovcalNet/povOnDemand.aspx). It is suggested that the lack of survey data for Haiti beyond 2012 renders these percentages – particularly those for 2018 – approximate.

[235] Honduras has a headcount of 16.16% in 2015, and of 16.53% in 2018; it has a poverty gap of 5.64% in 2015, and of 6.63% in 2018; Honduras' survey years are 2015 and 2018 ("PovcalNet: Choose economies/aggregates", World Bank, accessed April 8, 2020, http://iresearch.worldbank.org/PovcalNet/povOnDemand.aspx).

[236] Suriname has a headcount of 18.83% in 2015, and of 19.37% in 2018; it has a poverty gap of 14.52% in 2015, and of 14.74% in 2018; Suriname's most recent survey year is 1999 ("PovcalNet: Choose economies/aggregates", World Bank, accessed April 8, 2020, http://iresearch.worldbank.org/PovcalNet/povOnDemand.aspx). It is submitted that the lack of survey data for Suriname beyond 1999 renders these percentages very imprecise.

[237] The text to note 229 states the headcount and poverty gap for Venezuela in 2015 and in 2018.

is submitted that SDG Target 1.1 will not be achieved punctually. There is an extremely high likelihood that it will be missed by 31st December 2030, with Sub-Saharan Africa in particular remaining much adrift with high, persistent levels of extreme poverty. It is opined that the longer-term prognosis for approximating to accomplishment of SDG Target 1.1 is better than this, but will require more investment and knowledge-sharing – especially with regard to the poorest of the LDCs. Furthermore, lower levels of cross-border strife and civil conflict would also facilitate a greater degree of achievement of this target.

The other targets of SDG 1

Progress in the accomplishment of the other targets of SDG 1

A note on SDG Indicators: In July 2017, the General Assembly adopted a set of SDG Indicators, which the UNStC[238] was to refine every year[239] and to review comprehensively in March 2020 at its 51st session and in March

[238] The ECOSOC established the UNStC in February 1946 with five functions (United Nations, Resolution 8(I) of the Economic and Social Council of 16 February 1946 on the Establishment of a Statistical Commission, arts.1 and 2). It modified three of these (i.e., Sub-Paragraphs (a), (d) and (e)) in June 1946 to comprise the following: The UNStC is to assist the ECOSOC: "(a) in promoting the development of national statistics and the improvement of their comparability; (b) in the co-ordination of the statistical work of specialized agencies; (c) in the development of the central statistical services of the Secretariat; (d) in advising the organs of the United Nations on general questions relating to the collection, interpretation and dissemination of statistical information; (e) in promoting the improvement of statistics and statistical methods generally." (Resolution 8(I) of the Economic and Social Council of 16 February 1946 on the Establishment of a Statistical Commission, art.2(b)-(c); United Nations, Resolution 8(II) of the Economic and Social Council adopted 21 June 1946 on the Statistical Commission, art.1(a) and (d)-(e)).

[239] The annual refinements for 2020 that the Inter-Agency and Expert Group on Sustainable Development Indicators proposed to the UNStC for its approval as part of the 2020 Comprehensive Review (note 245 and accompanying text) include the addition of the words 'the' and 'living' to SDG Indicator 1.1.1 (note 39) to read: "Proportion of *the* population *living* below the international poverty line, by sex, age, employment status and geographical location (urban/rural)" (United Nations, Economic and Social Commission: Report of the Inter-Agency and Expert Group on Sustainable Development Goal Indicators, E/CN.3/2020/2, 20 December 2019, 1, and Annex III, 19; emphasis added). The UNStC agreed to, and adopted, these refinements at its 51st session from 3rd-6th March 2020 (note 247).

2025 at its 56th session.[240] Regarding the first of these two comprehensive reviews, the Inter-Agency and Expert Group on Sustainable Development Goal Indicators conducted this process throughout the year 2019, with the aim of submitting its proposed replacement indicators,[241] revisions to existing indicators,[242] proposals for additional indicators,[243] proposed deletions,[244] and annual refinements,[245] to the UNStC's 51st session for the latter's consideration.[246] At this session, the UNStC agreed to, and adopted, these all these proposals, revisions and annual refinements.[247] The SDG Indicators to be used throughout the remainder of this

---

240 United Nations, Resolution 71/313 adopted by the General Assembly on 6 July 2017, art.1; "SDG Indicators: Global indicator framework for the Sustainable Development Goals and targets of the 2030 Agenda for Sustainable Development", United Nations, accessed April 12, 2020, https://unstats.un.org/sdgs/indicators/indicators-list/.

241 Annex II.A to the Report of the Inter-Agency and Expert Group on Sustainable Development Goal Indicators contains these proposed replacement indicators. Note 239 references this Report, pages 14-15 of which comprise Annex II.A.

242 Annex II.B to the Report of the Inter-Agency and Expert Group on Sustainable Development Goal Indicators contains these revisions to existing indicators. Note 239 references this Report, page 16 of which consists of Annex II.B.

243 Annex II.C to the Report of the Inter-Agency and Expert Group on Sustainable Development Goal Indicators contains these proposals for additional indicators. Note 239 references this Report, page 17 of which comprises Annex II.C.

244 Annex II.D to the Report of the Inter-Agency and Expert Group on Sustainable Development Goal Indicators contains these proposed deletions. Note 239 references this Report, page 18 of which consists of Annex II.D.

245 Annex III to the Report of the Inter-Agency and Expert Group on Sustainable Development Goal Indicators contains these annual refinements. Note 239 references this Report, pages 19-21 of which comprise Annex III.

246 United Nations, "IAEG-SDGs: 2020 Comprehensive Review Process", accessed April 12, 2020, https://unstats.un.org/sdgs/iaeg-sdgs/2020-comp-rev/.

247 The Report of the UNStC on its 51st session states: "The Statistical Commission … (d) Agreed to and adopted the proposed major changes and minor refinements put forward in the 2020 comprehensive review, while noting concerns regarding specific indicators and recognized that the work on Sustainable Development Goal indicators is in progress, and asked the [Inter-Agency and Expert] Group [on Sustainable Development Goal Indicators] to continue its annual refinement, research and methodological work to improve the global indicator framework, including addressing important policy issues, such as sustainable tourism and climate change;" (United Nations, Statistical Commission: Report on the fifty-first session (3-6 March 2020), Economic and Social Council Official Records, 2020, Supplement No. 4, E/2020/24-E/CN.3/2020/37 (New York, 2020), 12).

monograph are those immediately following the changes that the 2020 Comprehensive Review made.[248]

SDG Target 1.2: This target is to "reduce at least by half the proportion of men, women and children of all ages living in poverty in all its dimensions according to national definitions", by 2030.[249] The national poverty rate is determined using country-specific poverty lines in domestic currencies – which differ across states in real terms and from the international poverty line; thus, national poverty rates are incomparable between countries.[250] As, due to this country-specificity, there is no aggregation of domestic poverty rates,[251] and as national poverty data beyond 2015 is unavailable for some countries,[252] statistics using such data

---

[248] This up-to-date list of SDG Indicators is found in the document entitled 'Global indicator framework for the Sustainable Development Goals and targets of the 2030 Agenda for Sustainable Development' (note 249), whose references of identification comprise: (i) Resolution 71/313, whose Annex sets out the original list of SDG Indicators in (i.e., A/RES/71/313 (note 240)), (ii) the document whose Annex II contains the annual refinements made to the global indicator framework in March 2018 (i.e., E/CN.3/2018/2), (iii) the document whose Annex II consists of the annual refinements made to the global indicator framework in March 2019 (i.e., E/CN.3/2019/2), and (iv) the main outcome document from the 2020 Comprehensive Review (i.e., E/CN.3/2020/2 (note 239)), whose Annex II (notes 241-244 and accompanying text) comprises changes made to the global indicator framework in March 2020 as part of this audit (note 247), and whose Annex III (note 245 and accompanying text) contains annual refinements made to the global indicator framework in March 2020 (note 247).

[249] Note 15. SDG Target 1.2 has two Indicators, which are as follows: SDG Indicator 1.2.1 – "Proportion of population living below the national poverty line, by sex and age", and SDG Indicator 1.2.2 – "Proportion of men, women and children of all ages living in poverty in all its dimensions according to national definitions" (Resolution 71/313 adopted by the General Assembly on 6 July 2017, Annex, 4; United Nations, Global indicator framework for the Sustainable Development Goals and targets of the 2030 Agenda for Sustainable Development, A/RES/71/313, E/CN.3/2018/2, E/CN.3/2019/2, E/CN.3/2020/2 (New York, 2020), 1). The paragraph in the text that contains the present footnote (i.e., note 249) is wholly devoted to exploration of metadata for SDG Indicator 1.2.1, as metadata for SDG Indicator 1.2.2 are not yet available (United Nations, Department of Economic and Social Affairs – Statistics Division: Metadata for Target 1.2 – Indicator 1.2.2: Last updated: 1st December 2018 (New York, 2018)).

[250] United Nations, Department of Economic and Social Affairs – Statistics Division: Metadata for Target 1.2 – Indicator 1.2.1: World Bank – Last updated: 24 January 2017 (New York, 2017), 4.

[251] Metadata for Target 1.2 – Indicator 1.2.1: World Bank, 4.

[252] Metadata for Target 1.2 – Indicator 1.2.1: World Bank, 5.

via the World Bank's Poverty and Equity DataBank[253] are considered for several countries with large populations,[254] as follows.[255] *Bangladesh*: The

[253] The World Bank's Poverty and Equity DataBank provides two measures of headcount ratio below national poverty lines: (i) "Poverty headcount ratio at national poverty lines (% of population)", and (ii) "Poverty headcount ratio at national poverty lines (% of population), including noncomparable values" ("DataBank: Poverty and Equity", World Bank, accessed April 15, 2020, https://databank.worldbank.org/source/poverty-and-equity). For the twenty countries considered (text to notes 256-268), both measures provide the same reading for the poverty headcount ratio at national poverty lines – except for the value for Thailand in 2018, which is 9.9% using measure (i) (text to note 266) and 9.8% using measure (ii) ("DataBank: Poverty and Equity", World Bank, accessed April 15, 2020, https://databank.worldbank.org/source/poverty-and-equity).

[254] The poverty headcount ratio at national poverty lines is inspected for those of the twenty most populous countries for which the World Bank's Poverty and Equity DataBank provides this ratio from 2015 and/or later. These states – from most populous to least populous – are China, India, the USA, Indonesia, Pakistan, Brazil, Nigeria, Bangladesh, Russia, Mexico, Japan, Ethiopia, the Philippines, Egypt, Vietnam, the Democratic Republic of the Congo, Turkey, Iran, Germany, and Thailand ("Countries in the world by population (2020)", Worldometer, accessed April 15, 2020, https://www.worldometers.info/world-population/population-by-country/).

[255] The UN's guidance notes state: "National poverty estimates are derived from household survey data. Caveats and limitations to survey data applying to the construction of [SDG] indicator 1.1.1 [(note 239), such as the incomplete reporting of required input data being a source of errors in measurement (point (xviii) above (text to note 91)),] apply here as well. To be useful for poverty estimates, surveys must be nationally representative. They must also include enough information to compute a comprehensive estimate of total household consumption or income … and to construct a correctly weighted distribution of consumption or income per person. Consumption is the preferred welfare indicator … . Income is generally more difficult to measure accurately. For example, the poor who work in the informal sector may not receive or report money wages; self-employed workers often experience irregular income flows; many people in rural areas depend on idiosyncratic, agricultural incomes. Moreover, consumption accords better with the idea of the standard of living than income, which can vary over time even if the actual standard of living does not. Thus, whenever possible, consumption-based welfare indicators are used to estimate the poverty measures reported here. But consumption data are not always available. For instance in Latin America and the Caribbean, the vast majority of countries collect primarily income data. In those cases there is little choice but to use income data. … Even if survey data were entirely accurate and comprehensive, the measure of poverty obtained could still fail to capture important aspects of individual welfare. For example, using household consumption measures ignores potential inequalities within households. … The national poverty rate … does not capture income inequality among the poor

poverty headcount ratio at national poverty lines is 24.3% of the Bangladeshi population in 2016.[256] *Brazil, the Democratic Republic of the Congo, Germany, India, Iran, Japan, Nigeria, and the USA*: The Poverty and Equity DataBank provides no information from 2015 onwards on the poverty headcount ratio at national poverty lines for any of these eight states.[257] *China*: The poverty headcount ratio at national poverty lines is 5.7%, 4.5%, 3.1% and 1.7% of the Chinese population, respectively, in 2015, 2016, 2017 and 2018.[258] *Egypt*: The poverty headcount ratio at national poverty lines is 27.8% and 32.5% of the Egyptian population, respectively, in 2015 and 2017.[259] *Ethiopia*: The poverty headcount ratio at national poverty lines is 23.5% of the Ethiopian population in 2015.[260] *Indonesia*: The poverty headcount ratio at national poverty lines is 11.2%, 10.9%, 10.6% and 9.8% of the Indonesian population, respectively, in 2015, 2016, 2017 and 2018.[261] *Mexico*: The poverty headcount ratio at national poverty lines is 43.6% and 41.9% of the Mexican population, respectively, in 2016 and 2018.[262] *Pakistan*: The poverty headcount ratio at national poverty lines is 24.3% of the Pakistani population in 2015.[263] *The Philippines*: The poverty headcount ratio at national poverty lines is 21.6% of the Filipino population in 2015.[264] *Russia*: The poverty headcount ratio at national poverty lines is 13.3%, 13.3%, 13.2% and 12.9% of the Russian population, respectively, in 2015, 2016, 2017 and

---

or the depth of poverty. For instance, it fails to account for the fact that some people may be living just below the poverty line, while others experience far greater shortfalls." (Metadata for Target 1.2 – Indicator 1.2.1: World Bank, 1-3).

256 "DataBank: Poverty and Equity", World Bank, accessed April 15, 2020, https://databank.worldbank.org/source/poverty-and-equity.

257 "DataBank: Poverty and Equity", World Bank, accessed April 15, 2020, https://databank.worldbank.org/source/poverty-and-equity.

258 "DataBank: Poverty and Equity", World Bank, accessed April 15, 2020, https://databank.worldbank.org/source/poverty-and-equity.

259 "DataBank: Poverty and Equity", World Bank, accessed April 15, 2020, https://databank.worldbank.org/source/poverty-and-equity.

260 "DataBank: Poverty and Equity", World Bank, accessed April 15, 2020, https://databank.worldbank.org/source/poverty-and-equity.

261 "DataBank: Poverty and Equity", World Bank, accessed April 15, 2020, https://databank.worldbank.org/source/poverty-and-equity.

262 "DataBank: Poverty and Equity", World Bank, accessed April 15, 2020, https://databank.worldbank.org/source/poverty-and-equity.

263 "DataBank: Poverty and Equity", World Bank, accessed April 15, 2020, https://databank.worldbank.org/source/poverty-and-equity.

264 "DataBank: Poverty and Equity", World Bank, accessed April 15, 2020, https://databank.worldbank.org/source/poverty-and-equity.

2018.[265] *Thailand*: The poverty headcount ratio at national poverty lines is 7.2%, 8.6%, 7.9% and 9.9% of the Thai population, respectively, in 2015, 2016, 2017 and 2018.[266] *Turkey*: The poverty headcount ratio at national poverty lines is 14.3%, 13.5% and 13.9% of the Turkish population, respectively, in 2015, 2016 and 2017.[267] *Vietnam*: The poverty headcount ratio at national poverty lines is 9.8% and 6.7% of the Vietnamese population, respectively, in 2016 and 2018.[268] Thus, there are substantial reductions in the poverty headcount ratio at national poverty lines in China and Vietnam, small decreases in the poverty headcount ratio at national poverty lines in Indonesia, Mexico and Russia, and increases in the poverty headcount ratio at national poverty lines in Egypt and Thailand, with there being no clear pattern for the poverty headcount ratio at national poverty lines in Turkey. These downward trends in China, Indonesia and Vietnam are consistent with the fall between 2015 and 2018 in the headcount below the international poverty line and the poverty gap in the region of East Asia and the Pacific,[269] although the inconstant, upward movement in Thailand is not so compatible.[270] The upward trend in Egypt is accordant with the rise betwixt 2015 and 2018 in the headcount below the international poverty line and the poverty gap in the region of North Africa and the Middle East.[271]

SDG Target 1.3: This target is to "[i]mplement nationally appropriate social protection systems and measures for all, including floors, and by 2030 achieve substantial coverage of the poor and the vulnerable".[272] In

---

[265] "DataBank: Poverty and Equity", World Bank, accessed April 15, 2020, https://databank.worldbank.org/source/poverty-and-equity.

[266] "DataBank: Poverty and Equity", World Bank, accessed April 15, 2020, https://databank.worldbank.org/source/poverty-and-equity. The poverty headcount ratio at national poverty lines for Thailand is 9.8% of the Thai population, if non-comparable values are included in this ratio (note 253).

[267] "DataBank: Poverty and Equity", World Bank, accessed April 15, 2020, https://databank.worldbank.org/source/poverty-and-equity.

[268] "DataBank: Poverty and Equity", World Bank, accessed April 15, 2020, https://databank.worldbank.org/source/poverty-and-equity.

[269] Text to note 216.

[270] Thailand has very low values for the headcount below the international poverty line and the poverty gap in both 2015 and 2018 (note 218).

[271] Text to note 181.

[272] Resolution 70/1 adopted by the General Assembly on 25 September 2015, Transforming our world: the 2030 Agenda for Sustainable Development, 15. SDG Target 1.3 has one Indicator, as follows: SDG Indicator 1.3.1 – "Proportion of population covered by social protection floors/systems, by sex, distinguishing children, unemployed persons, older persons, persons with disabilities, pregnant

line with SDG Indicator 1.3.1,[273] the ILO[274] calculates as a percentage of the respective population the proportion of: (i) children who receive social protection benefits,[275] (ii) women giving birth who gain maternity benefits,[276] (iii) disabled people who obtain disability benefits,[277] (iv) unemployed individuals who collect unemployment benefits,[278] (v) workers who are covered by insurance for injuries at work,[279] (vi) retirees who acquire a pension,[280] and (vii) vulnerable persons who are awarded

women, newborns, work-injury victims and the poor and vulnerable" (Global indicator framework for the Sustainable Development Goals and targets of the 2030 Agenda for Sustainable Development, 1).

[273] Note 272 states SDG Indicator 1.3.1.

[274] In addition to the ILO, the World Bank also provides data that are relevant to SDG Target 1.3 and Indicator 1.3.1. These are from the World Bank's ASPIRE (i.e., Atlas of Social Protection Indicators of Resilience and Equity) database, which measures the effective coverage of social protection, i.e., "the direct and indirect beneficiaries who are actually receiving social protection benefits at the time nationally representative household survey data are collected, as within a target group (total population, for different quintiles, total population in urban and rural areas)" (United Nations, Department of Economic and Social Affairs – Statistics Division: Metadata for Target 1.3 – Indicator 1.3.1: ILO – Last updated: 19th July 2016 (New York, 2018), 1). The ASPIRE database can be accessed at http://datatopics.worldbank.org/aspire/.

[275] This calculation is "ratio of children/households receiving child or family cash benefits to the total number of children/households with children" (United Nations, Department of Economic and Social Affairs – Statistics Division: Metadata for Target 1.3 – Indicator 1.3.1: ILO – Last updated: 8th June 2018 (New York, 2018), 2).

[276] This calculation is "ratio of women receiving cash maternity benefits to women giving birth in the same year" (Metadata for Target 1.3 – Indicator 1.3.1: ILO, 2).

[277] This calculation is "ratio of persons receiving disability cash benefits to persons with severe disabilities[, the latter being] the product of prevalence of disability ratios … and each country's population" (Metadata for Target 1.3 – Indicator 1.3.1: ILO, 2).

[278] This calculation is "ratio of recipients of unemployment cash benefits to the number of unemployed persons" (Metadata for Target 1.3 – Indicator 1.3.1: ILO, 2).

[279] This calculation is "ratio of workers protected by injury insurance to total employment or the labour force" (Metadata for Target 1.3 – Indicator 1.3.1: ILO, 2).

[280] This calculation is "ratio of persons above statutory retirement age receiving an old-age pension to persons above statutory retirement age" (Metadata for Target 1.3 – Indicator 1.3.1: ILO, 2).

social assistance;[281] the aggregate social protection indicator is computed as the percentage of the total population who receive cash benefits or contribute to at least one scheme for social security.[282] *Regional social protection at the initiation of the SDGs. Africa*: 17.8% of the population of Africa are in receipt of at least one cash social protection benefit,[283] with 29.6% of people above statutory pensionable age in that continent collecting old-age pensions,[284] 15.9% of households/children there acquiring family/child cash benefits,[285] 9.5% of vulnerable persons in Africa obtaining non-contributory cash benefits,[286] and 5.6% of unemployed individuals receiving unemployment cash benefits.[287] *The Americas*: 67.6% of the population of the Americas are receiving at least one cash social protection benefit,[288] with 72.9% of individuals with severe disabilities there being given disability cash benefits,[289] 70.8% of people above statutory pensionable age in that region gaining old-age pensions,[290] 68.6% of mothers there with newborn babies obtaining cash maternity benefits,[291] 66.2% of children/households in the Americas acquiring child/family benefits,[292] 38.7% of vulnerable persons in that region

---

[281] This calculation is "ratio of social assistance recipients to the total number of vulnerable persons[, the latter being] calculated by subtracting from total population all people of working age who are contributing to a social insurance scheme or receiving contributory benefits, and all persons above retirement age receiving contributory benefits" (Metadata for Target 1.3 – Indicator 1.3.1: ILO, 2).

[282] Metadata for Target 1.3 – Indicator 1.3.1: ILO, 2.

[283] International Labour Organization, World Social Protection Report 2017-19: Universal social protection to achieve the Sustainable Development Goals (Geneva, 2017), 119 and 123.

[284] World Social Protection Report 2017-19, 119 and 127.

[285] World Social Protection Report 2017-19, 119 and 124.

[286] World Social Protection Report 2017-19, 119 and 129.

[287] World Social Protection Report 2017-19, 126.

[288] World Social Protection Report 2017-19, 119 and 133.

[289] World Social Protection Report 2017-19, 135. Whilst page 119 of the ILO's *World Social Protection Report 2017-19* states that *59.4%* of persons with severe disabilities *in the Americas* receive disability benefits, it is submitted that this percentage is erroneous because it equates in Figure 6.14 of this Report to the percentage of individuals with severe disabilities from *Latin America* who secure these benefits; 96.4% of people with severe disabilities in Northern America are provided with disability benefits (World Social Protection Report 2017-19, 135).

[290] World Social Protection Report 2017-19, 119 and 135.

[291] World Social Protection Report 2017-19, 119 and 134.

[292] World Social Protection Report 2017-19, 119 and 133.

accepting non-contributory cash benefits,[293] and 16.7% of unemployed people there collecting unemployment cash benefits.[294] *Arabia (including Iraq, Jordan, Syria, and West Bank and Gaza)*[295]: Whilst social protection is fragmented in most Arabian countries,[296] 27.4% of individuals above statutory pensionable age receive an old-age pension;[297] limited data permit only a partial assessment of SDG Indicator 1.3.1 to be undertaken for this region.[298] *Asia and the Pacific (comprising South Asia, South-East Asia, East Asia and Oceania)*[299]: 38.9% of the population of Asia and the Pacific are in receipt of at least one cash social protection benefit,[300] with low availability of child/family benefits to children/households in China (2.2%), the Philippines (13.6%) and Thailand (18.9%) but 100% coverage in Australia and Mongolia,[301] 55.2% of persons above statutory pensionable age in Asia and the Pacific collecting old-age pensions,[302] 33.4% of mothers in that region with newborn babies acquiring cash maternity benefits,[303] 22.5% of unemployed people there obtaining unemployment cash benefits,[304] 16.4% of vulnerable persons in Asia and the Pacific securing non-contributory cash benefits,[305] and 9.4% of individuals with severe disabilities there being furnished with disability cash benefits.[306] *Europe and Central Asia*: 84.1% of the population of Europe and Central

---

[293] World Social Protection Report 2017-19, 136.

[294] World Social Protection Report 2017-19, 119 and 134.

[295] World Social Protection Report 2017-19, xxvi and 142.

[296] World Social Protection Report 2017-19, 140.

[297] World Social Protection Report 2017-19, 120 and 143.

[298] World Social Protection Report 2017-19, 120. Note 272 specifies SDG Indicator 1.3.1.

[299] World Social Protection Report 2017-19, 154.

[300] World Social Protection Report 2017-19, 120 and 150.

[301] World Social Protection Report 2017-19, 120 and 150.

[302] World Social Protection Report 2017-19, 120 and 154. The percentage coverage of old-age pensions is 100% in China, Japan, Mongolia and New Zealand, and 99.7% in the Maldives; 77.3%, 74.1%, 31.5% and 23.6% of individuals above statutory pensionable age in East Asia, Oceania, South-East Asia and South Asia, respectively, receive an old-age pension (World Social Protection Report 2017-19, 154).

[303] World Social Protection Report 2017-19, 120 and 151. Mongolia provides cash maternity benefits to all mothers with newborn babies – i.e., 100% coverage (World Social Protection Report 2017-19, 151).

[304] World Social Protection Report 2017-19, 120 and 151.

[305] World Social Protection Report 2017-19, 154.

[306] World Social Protection Report 2017-19, 120 and 152. Australia and Mongolia supply disability cash benefits to all people with severe disabilities – i.e., 100% coverage (World Social Protection Report 2017-19, 152).

Asia are in receipt of at least one social protection benefit,[307] with 95.2% of people above statutory pensionable age in Europe and Central Asia collecting old-age pensions,[308] 87.5% of children/households in that region obtaining child/family cash benefits,[309] 86.7% of individuals with severe disabilities there acquiring disability cash benefits,[310] 81.4% of mothers in Europe and Central Asia with newborn babies accepting cash maternity benefits,[311] 66.7% of vulnerable people securing non-contributory cash

---

307 World Social Protection Report 2017-19, 120 and 159. 100% coverage of social protection is attained in Belgium, Finland, France, Kazakhstan, Slovenia and Sweden, and 99.5% coverage of social protection is achieved in Germany (World Social Protection Report 2017-19, 159).

308 World Social Protection Report 2017-19, 162. Austria, Belarus, Belgium, Bulgaria, Cyprus, the Czech Republic, Denmark, Estonia, Finland, France, Germany, Hungary, Italy, Kyrgyzstan, Latvia, Lithuania, Luxembourg, Malta, the Netherlands, Norway, Poland, Portugal, Romania, Slovakia, Slovenia, Spain, Sweden, Switzerland and the UK supply old-age pensions to all people above statutory pensionable age – i.e., 100% coverage; Bosnia and Herzegovina, and Turkey, give old-age pensions to 29.6% and 20%, respectively, to all individuals above statutory pensionable age (World Social Protection Report 2017-19, 162).

309 World Social Protection Report 2017-19, 120 and 159. Austria, Belgium, Denmark, Estonia, Finland, France, Germany, Hungary, Ireland, Kazakhstan, Latvia, the Netherlands, Norway, Poland, Romania, Russia, Slovakia, Spain, Sweden, Switzerland and the UK provide child/family cash benefits to all children/households living there – i.e., 100%; Armenia, Kyrgyzstan and Tajikistan supply child/family cash benefits to 21.4%, 17.8% and 6.4%, respectively, of children/households residing there coverage (World Social Protection Report 2017-19, 159).

310 World Social Protection Report 2017-19, 120 and 161. Armenia, Azerbaijan, Belgium, Bulgaria, the Czech Republic, Denmark, Estonia, Finland, France, Georgia, Hungary, Iceland, Ireland, Italy, Kazakhstan, Latvia, Lithuania, Luxembourg, the Netherlands, Norway, Poland, Romania, Russia, Slovakia, Slovenia, Sweden, Switzerland and the UK furnish all severely-disabled people with disability cash benefits – i.e., 100% coverage; Cyprus and Turkey provide 26.5% and 5.0%, respectively, of severely-disabled individuals with disability cash benefits (World Social Protection Report 2017-19, 120 and 161).

311 World Social Protection Report 2017-19, 120 and 160. Austria, Belgium, Bulgaria, Croatia, Cyprus, the Czech Republic, Denmark, Estonia, Finland, France, Germany, Greece, Hungary, Iceland, Ireland, Italy, Latvia, Liechtenstein, Lithuania, Luxembourg, Malta, the Netherlands, Norway, Poland, Portugal, Romania, Slovakia, Spain, Sweden, Switzerland, the UK and Ukraine supply cash maternity benefits to all mothers with newborns residing there, – i.e., 100% coverage; Georgia, Kyrgyzstan and Azerbaijan give cash maternity benefits to 24.0%, 23.8% and 14.0%, respectively, of all mothers with newborns living there (World Social Protection Report 2017-19, 160).

benefits,[312] and 42.5% of unemployed persons there receiving unemployment cash benefits.[313] Thus, the provision of social security benefits is most generous in Europe and Central Asia – with 100% coverage for some countries with regard to one or more benefits, and least generous in Africa and in Arabia. Old-age pensions are the best-supported benefit across the regions, and unemployment cash benefit is the least-supported overall. The small percentage of persons with severe disabilities receiving disability cash benefit in Asia and the Pacific is conspicuous in comparison with other regions that report such a statistic; although the data of some populous countries are missing from the relevant graph, for instance those of China and Indonesia, there are low readings for Myanmar (0.4%), Cambodia (0.7%), the Philippines (3.1%), India (5.4%), Vietnam (9.7%), Bangladesh (18.5%), Sri Lanka (20.8%), Timor-Leste (21.3%) and Thailand (35.7%) – with Japan, i.e., a large, advanced economy situated in this region, recording only a medium percentage (55.7%).[314] It is submitted (from experience) that the provision of benefits for people with severe disabilities is an area of high-priority, which one would expect these countries to swiftly address.

SDG Target 1.4: This target is to "ensure that all men and women, in particular the poor and vulnerable, have equal rights to economic resources, as well as access to basic services, ownership and control over land and other forms of property, inheritance, natural resources, appropriate new technology and financial services, including microfinance", by 2030.[315]

---

[312] World Social Protection Report 2017-19, 163. Belgium, Finland, France, Kazakhstan, Slovenia and Sweden furnish all their vulnerable persons with non-contributory cash benefits – i.e., 100% coverage; the Czech Republic, Bulgaria, Cyprus, Armenia, Azerbaijan and Georgia supply 32.0%, 28.8%, 24.1%, 16.2%, 12.6% and 12.0%, respectively, of their vulnerable individuals with non-contributory cash benefits (World Social Protection Report 2017-19, 163).

[313] World Social Protection Report 2017-19, 120 and 161. Austria, Belgium, Finland, Germany and Ireland provide all their jobless workers with unemployment cash benefits – i.e., 100% coverage; Bosnia and Herzegovina, Kyrgyzstan, Azerbaijan, Turkey and Armenia supply 2.0%, 1.7%, 1.6%, 1.4% and 0.0%, respectively, of their jobless workers with unemployment cash benefits (World Social Protection Report 2017-19, 161).

[314] World Social Protection Report 2017-19, 152.

[315] Resolution 70/1 adopted by the General Assembly on 25 September 2015, Transforming our world: the 2030 Agenda for Sustainable Development, 15. SDG Target 1.4 has two Indicators, which are as follows: SDG Indicator 1.4.1 – "Proportion of population living in households with access to basic services", and SDG Indicator 1.4.2 – "Proportion of total adult population with secure tenure rights to land, (*a*) with legally recognized documentation, and (*b*) who perceive

'Basic services' are "public service provision systems that meet human basic needs including drinking water, sanitation and hygiene, energy, mobility, waste collection, health care, education and information technologies".[316] 'Access to basic services' implies that supply is adequate and affordable, with sufficient quality, and includes access to basic: (i) *drinking water* – piped, packaged or delivered water, or water from boreholes, tube wells, protected dug wells or protected springs, is to be within 15 minutes' reach, i.e., collection time including for queueing must be no more than 30 minutes; (ii) *sanitation services* – flush or pour flush to piped sewer systems, septic tanks, pit latrines, ventilated improved pit latrines, pit latrines with slabs or compositing toilets, are to be separately accessible by each household; (iii) *hygiene facilities* – water, soap (i.e., bar soap, liquid soap, powder detergent or soapy water), and a handwashing facility (i.e., a sink with tap water, a bucket with taps, tippy-taps, or a jug or basin designated for handwashing) is to be available on the premises; (iv) *mobility* – access to all-weather roads in rural locations, and to public transport in urban places.[317] Two ways of measuring some of the heads of access to basic services – as SDG Indicator 1.4.1[318] requires – are to check (i), (ii) and (iii) by: (a) examining the joint reports from the UNICEF and the WHO entitled 'Progress on drinking water, sanitation and hygiene',[319] and (b) inspecting the UNDP's MPI for different states using the most recent values of this index – which are those from 2018.[320] (a) *Progress on drinking water, sanitation and hygiene*: Estimates for the percentage of people that use safely-managed drinking water comprise 94% and 96% for

---

their rights to land as secure, by sex and type of tenure" (Global indicator framework for the Sustainable Development Goals and targets of the 2030 Agenda for Sustainable Development, 1).

316 United Nations, Department of Economic and Social Affairs – Statistics Division: Metadata for Target 1.4 – Indicator 1.4.1: United Nations Human Settlements Programme – Last updated: 16th October 2018 (New York, 2018), 2.

317 Metadata for Target 1.4 – Indicator 1.4.1: United Nations Human Settlements Programme, 2.

318 Note 315 states SDG Indicator 1.4.1.

319 The two editions of this report are: (i) World Health Organization and United Nations Children's Fund, Progress on Drinking Water, Sanitation and Hygiene: 2017 Update and SDG Baselines (Geneva, 2017), and (ii) United Nations Children's Fund and World Health Organization, Progress on Household Drinking Water, Sanitation and Hygiene 2000-2017: Special Focus on Inequalities (New York, 2019).

320 "Human Development Reports: The 2019 Global Multidimensional Poverty Index (MPI)", United Nations Development Programme, accessed April 20, 2020, http://hdr.undp.org/en//2018-MPI.

North America and Europe in 2015 and 2017 respectively, 65% and 74% for Latin America and the Caribbean in 2015 and 2017 respectively, 58% and 60% in Central and South Asia in 2015 and 2017 respectively, and 24% and 27% in Sub-Saharan Africa in 2015 and 2017 respectively.[321] Estimates of safely-managed sanitation services comprise 78% and 76% for North America and Europe in 2015 and 2017 respectively, 68% and 72% for Australia and New Zealand in 2015 and 2017 respectively, 55% and 64% for East and South-East Asia in 2015 and 2017 respectively, 34% and 31% for West Asia and North Africa in 2015 and 2017 respectively, 23% and 31% for Latin America and the Caribbean in 2015 and 2017 respectively, and 18% for Sub-Saharan Africa in 2017.[322] Estimates of basic handwashing facilities comprise 76% and 77% in West Asia and North Africa in 2015 and 2017 respectively, 58% in Central and South Asia in 2017, and 15% and 25% in Sub-Saharan Africa in 2015 and 2017 respectively.[323] These percentages show net improvements for access to safely-managed drinking water, safely-managed sanitation services and basic handwashing facilities between 2015 and 2017, with Latin America and the Caribbean advancing 9% and 8% on safely-managed drinking water and basic handwashing facilities respectively in these two years, East and South-East Asia progressing 9% on safely-managed sanitation services in this period, and Sub-Saharan Africa – which has the lowest estimates among those available for the regions for all three basic services (i.e., drinking water, sanitation and hygiene) – progressing 3% on safely-managed drinking water and 10% on basic handwashing facilities. Notwithstanding this, the most prosperous region – North America and Europe – provides less than 80% of its population with safely-managed sanitation services, which shows that the provision of universal access to basic services – as SDG Target 1.4[324] requires – is not yet a reality even there. (b) *The MPI*: The MPI comprises three dimensions of poverty –

---

[321] World Health Organization and United Nations Children's Fund, Progress on Drinking Water, Sanitation and Hygiene: 2017 Update and SDG Baselines (Geneva, 2017), 3; United Nations Children's Fund and World Health Organization, Progress on Household Drinking Water, Sanitation and Hygiene 2000-2017: Special Focus on Inequalities (New York, 2019), 7.

[322] Progress on Drinking Water, Sanitation and Hygiene: 2017 Update and SDG Baselines, 4; Progress on Household Drinking Water, Sanitation and Hygiene 2000-2017: Special Focus on Inequalities, 8.

[323] Progress on Drinking Water, Sanitation and Hygiene: 2017 Update and SDG Baselines, 5; Progress on Household Drinking Water, Sanitation and Hygiene 2000-2017: Special Focus on Inequalities, 9.

[324] The text to note 315 states SDG Target 1.4.

health, education and standard of living, each with equal weight, i.e. ⅓. Health and education each has two indicators – nutrition and child mortality for the former and years of schooling and school attendance for the latter, both with equal weight, i.e., ½ * ⅓ = ⅙; standard of living has six indicators – cooking fuel, sanitation, drinking water, electricity, housing and assets, all with equal weight, i.e., ⅙* ⅓ = 1/18.[325] Each of the ten indicators is given a value of '1' – i.e., the household is deprived *on that measure* – when the condition associated with the measure is met; otherwise, the household is not deprived on that measure, and the value is '0'. The applicable binary value for each indicator is multiplied by the latter's weight, and the weights are summed to give the deprivation score for the household.[326] Table 2.1 provides a hypothetical example of the calculation of this score for a population of two households.

Table 2.1: A hypothetical example of the calculation of a deprivation score for a population comprising Household 1 (four residents) and Household 2 (seven residents)[327]

Indicator	Weight	Value for Household 1	Weight * Value for Household 1	Value for Household 2	Weight * Value for Household 2
At least one member is undernourished	⅙	0	0	0	0
At least one child has died	⅙	1	⅙	1	⅙
No-one has completed six years at school	⅙	0	0	1	⅙
At least one child missing school	⅙	0	0	1	⅙

325 "Human Development Reports: The 2019 Global Multidimensional Poverty Index (MPI)", United Nations Development Programme, accessed April 21, 2020, http://hdr.undp.org/en//2018-MPI.

326 United Nations Development Programme, Human Development Indices and Indicators: 2018 Statistical Update (New York, 2018), 10.

327 Adapted from the tabulated information titled 'Example using hypothetical data', at Human Development Indices and Indicators: 2018 Statistical Update, 11.

No electricity	$\frac{1}{18}$	0	0	1	$\frac{1}{18}$
No access to improved sanitation	$\frac{1}{18}$	0	0	0	0
No access to an improved source of drinking water	$\frac{1}{18}$	0	0	1	$\frac{1}{18}$
House built with inadequate materials	$\frac{1}{18}$	0	0	0	0
Household cooks with charcoal, coal, dung or wood	$\frac{1}{18}$	1	$\frac{1}{18}$	1	$\frac{1}{18}$
Household owns no car or truck, and no more than one of: radio, television, telephone, computer, animal cart, bicycle, motorbike, refrigerator	$\frac{1}{18}$	0	0	1	$\frac{1}{18}$
Household deprivation score (i.e., column total)			$\frac{1}{6} + \frac{1}{18} = \frac{4}{18} =$ **22.22%**[328]		$\frac{1}{6} + \frac{1}{6} + \frac{1}{6} + \frac{1}{18} + \frac{1}{18} + \frac{1}{18} + \frac{1}{18} = \frac{13}{18} =$ **72.22%**[329]

328 This percentage is given to four significant figures.

329 This percentage is given to four significant figures.

If the household deprivation score is at least ⅓, then the household and all its residents are deemed to be multidimensionally poor.[330] The *multidimensional-poverty headcount ratio*, H, is the proportion of multidimensionally-poor individuals in the population, i.e., the number of persons in the population who are multidimensionally poor, q, divided by the total population, n.[331] From Table 2.1, n = 4 residents + 7 residents = 11 residents, and q = 0 residents + 7 residents = 7 residents. Therefore, H = 7 residents / 11 residents = 0.6363.[332] The *intensity of poverty*, A, "reflects the average proportion of the weighted component indicators in which multidimensionally poor people are deprived"; for these individuals, the deprivation sums are added up, and their total is divided by the entire number of multidimensionally-poor persons – i.e., $A = \sum c_i / q$, where c_i is the deprivation score that the ith multidimensionally-poor individual experiences, q is as defined in the immediately-preceding sentence, and $c_i = c_{i1} + c_{i2} + c_{i3} + c_{i4} + c_{i5} + c_{i6} + c_{i7} + c_{i8} + c_{i9} + c_{i10}$ where the subscripts 1, 2, 3, 4, 5, 6, 7, 8, 9 and 10 each represent the weight associated with one of the ten indicators in Table 2.1.[333] From Table 2.1, $\sum c_i$ = 7 residents * $(0 + \frac{1}{6} + \frac{1}{6} + \frac{1}{6} + \frac{1}{18} + 0 + \frac{1}{18} + 0 + \frac{1}{18} + \frac{1}{18})$ = 7 residents * $\frac{13}{18}$ = $\frac{91}{18}$ residents = 5.0556 residents.[334] q = 7 residents. Therefore, A = 5.0556 residents / 7 residents = 0.7222 = 72.22%.[335] The MPI is the product of the multidimensional poverty headcount ratio and the intensity of poverty,[336] i.e., MPI = H * A = 0.6363 * 0.7222 = **0.460**.[337] The greater the extent of multidimensional poverty, the higher is the MPI. For instance, if, for Household 2, the value of the first health indicator – i.e., at least one member of the household is undernourished – is changed from 0 (false) to 1 (true) *ceteris paribus*,[338] then the multidimensional poverty headcount ratio, H, remains unchanged, but the intensity of

---

330 Human Development Indices and Indicators: 2018 Statistical Update, 10.

331 Human Development Indices and Indicators: 2018 Statistical Update, 10.

332 This value of the multidimensional-poverty headcount ratio is given to four significant figures.

333 Human Development Indices and Indicators: 2018 Statistical Update, 10.

334 This value of the sum of the deprivation scores of all multidimensionally-poor people in the population is given to five (rather than four) significant figures, which enables the value for the intensity of poverty to be calculated accurately to four significant figures (note 335 and accompanying text).

335 This value of the intensity of poverty is given to four significant figures.

336 Human Development Indices and Indicators: 2018 Statistical Update, 10.

337 This value of the MPI is given to three significant figures.

338 The Latin phrase '*ceteris paribus*' means "with other conditions remaining the same" (*The New Oxford Dictionary of English*, 299).

poverty increases. Highlighting the results of this change in a bold typeface, $\sum c_i$ = 7 residents * ($1/6 + 1/6 + 1/6 + 1/6 + 1/18 + 0 + 1/18 + 0 + 1/18 + 1/18$) = 7 residents * $\mathbf{16/18}$ = $\mathbf{112/18}$ residents = **6.2222** residents;[339] q remains unaltered; therefore, the intensity of poverty, A = $\sum c_i$ / q = **6.2222** residents / 7 residents = **0.8889** = **88.89%**.[340] MPI = H * A = 0.6363 * **0.8889** = **0.566**.[341] The 2018 MPI dataset, available from the UNDP's website,[342] provides the MPI for 105 developing states and LDCs.[343] The highest readings of the MPI for 2018 (MPI_{2018}) – those values above 0.500 – belong to countries in the northern part of Sub-Saharan Africa, all but one of which are LLDCs and all of which are LDCs, i.e., Burkina Faso (MPI_{2018} = 0.520), Chad (MPI_{2018} = 0.535), Niger (MPI_{2018} = 0.591), Somalia (MPI_{2018} = 0.518), and South Sudan = (MPI_{2018} = 0.581). Assuming all countries in each region to be of equal weight in calculating the MPI for that region,[344] the MPI_{2018} for Sub-Saharan Africa[345] is 0.302,[346] whilst MPI_{2018} for each of South-East Europe,[347] Supra-Saharan

---

339 Note 334.

340 Note 335.

341 Note 337.

342 "Human Development Reports: The 2019 Global Multidimensional Poverty Index (MPI)", United Nations Development Programme, accessed April 23, 2020, http://hdr.undp.org/en//2018-MPI.

343 Note 125 lists all 47 LDCs.

344 This is a simplifying assumption. A more accurate estimate for the MPI in 2018 for each region than that shown in the text would be obtained by weighting the MPI for each country within that region for which data are provided by the share of the total population of the region in 2018 for countries therein for which data are provided.

345 The UNDP's 2018 MPI dataset (note 342 and accompanying text) does not supply data for Botswana, Cabo Verde, Equatorial Guinea, Eritrea, Mauritius, and the Seychelles.

346 MPI (Sub-Saharan Africa) = MPI (Angola + Benin + Burkina Faso + Burundi + Cameroon + Central African Republic + Chad + Comoros + Côte d'Ivoire + the Democratic Republic of the Congo + Djibouti + Eswatini + Ethiopia + Gabon + the Gambia + Ghana + Guinea + Guinea-Bissau + Kenya + Lesotho + Liberia + Madagascar + Malawi + Mali + Mauritania + Mozambique + Namibia + Niger + Nigeria + the Republic of the Congo + Rwanda + São Tomé and Príncipe + Senegal + Sierra Leone + Somalia + South Africa + South Sudan + Sudan + Tanzania + Togo + Uganda + Zambia + Zimbabwe) = (0.283 + 0.346 + 0.520 + 0.404 + 0.244 + 0.465 + 0.535 + 0.181 + 0.236 + 0.378 + 0.170 + 0.083 + 0.490 + 0.067 + 0.286 + 0.132 + 0.337 + 0.373 + 0.179 + 0.146 + 0.331 + 0.453 + 0.244 + 0.457 + 0.261 + 0.412 + 0.183 + 0.591 + 0.294 + 0.185 + 0.266 + 0.092 + 0.293 + 0.422 + 0.518 + 0.032 + 0.581 + 0.280 + 0.275 + 0.250 + 0.279 + 0.262 + 0.149) / Number of countries = 12.965 / 43 = 0.302.

Africa,[348] West Asia,[349] Central Asia,[350] South Asia,[351] South-East Asia,[352] East Asia,[353] and Latin America and the Caribbean,[354] is 0.005,[355] 0.025,[356] 0.051,[357] 0.015,[358] 0.165,[359] 0.106,[360] 0.030,[361] and 0.047,[362] respectively.

---

[347] 'South-East Europe' comprises those countries in that region for which the UNDP's 2018 MPI dataset (note 342 and accompanying text) provides data, which are Albania, Bosnia and Herzegovina, Moldova, Montenegro, North Macedonia, Serbia, and Ukraine.

[348] 'Supra-Saharan Africa' comprises Algeria, Egypt, Libya, Morocco, and Tunisia. The UNDP's 2018 MPI dataset (note 342 and accompanying text) furnishes data for all five of these countries.

[349] 'West Asia' comprises those countries in that region for which the UNDP's 2018 MPI dataset (note 342 and accompanying text) supplies data, which are Armenia, Azerbaijan, Iraq, Jordan, Palestine, Syria, and Yemen.

[350] 'Central Asia' comprises Kazakhstan, Kyrgyzstan, Tajikistan, Turkmenistan, and Uzbekistan. The UNDP's 2018 MPI dataset (note 342 and accompanying text) provides data for all five of these countries.

[351] 'South Asia' comprises those countries in that region for which the UNDP's 2018 MPI dataset (note 342 and accompanying text) furnishes data, which are Afghanistan, Bangladesh, Bhutan, India, the Maldives, Nepal, and Pakistan.

[352] 'South-East Asia' comprises those countries in that region for which the UNDP's 2018 MPI dataset (note 342 and accompanying text) supplies data, which are Cambodia, Indonesia, Laos, Myanmar, the Philippines, Thailand, Timor-Leste, and Vietnam.

[353] 'East Asia' comprises those countries in that region for which the UNDP's 2018 MPI dataset (note 342 and accompanying text) provides data, which are China and Mongolia. This dataset furnishes no data for Oceania, other than for Vanuatu whose MPI for 2018 is 0.174.

[354] 'Latin America and the Caribbean' comprises those countries in that region for which the UNDP's 2018 MPI dataset (note 342 and accompanying text) supplies data, which are Barbados, Belize, Bolivia, Brazil, Colombia, the Dominican Republic, Ecuador, El Salvador, Guatemala, Guyana, Haiti, Honduras, Jamaica, Mexico, Nicaragua, Paraguay, Peru, Saint Lucia, Suriname, and Trinidad and Tobago.

[355] MPI (South-East Europe) = MPI (Albania + Bosnia and Herzegovina + Moldova + Montenegro + North Macedonia + Serbia + Ukraine) = (0.008 + 0.008 + 0.004 + 0.002 + 0.010 + 0.001 + 0.001) / Number of countries = 0.034 / 7 = 0.005.

[356] MPI (Supra-Saharan Africa) = MPI (Algeria + Egypt + Libya + Morocco + Tunisia) = (0.008 + 0.020 + 0.007 + 0.085 + 0.005) / Number of countries = 0.125 / 5 = 0.025.

[357] MPI (West Asia) = MPI (Armenia + Azerbaijan + Iraq + Jordan + Palestine + Syria + Yemen) = (0.001 + 0.019 + 0.059 + 0.005 + 0.004 + 0.029 + 0.241) / Number of countries= 0.358 / 7 = 0.051.

With the exception of South Asia – whose MPI_{2018} is *somewhat* lower than that for Sub-Saharan Africa, the MPI_{2018} of each of the other regions[363] is *much* lower than that for Sub-Saharan Africa. Furthermore, every MPI_{2018} reading for a country that is outside Sub-Saharan Africa is lower than the value of the MPI_{2018} for that region.[364] These data corroborate with the earlier findings that Sub-Saharan Africa has a high level of extreme poverty relative to other regions, and low but improving levels of high-quality drinking water, sanitation and hygiene. There is also scope for improvement in the MPI of South Asia[365] – i.e., the MPI_{2018} readings of Afghanistan, Bangladesh, Bhutan, India, Nepal and Pakistan,[366] whose combined populations account for more than 98% of the residents of this region.[367] SDG Indicator 1.4.2[368] is measured as (0.5 * Part (A)) + (0.5 *

---

358 MPI (Central Asia) = MPI (Kazakhstan + Kyrgyzstan + Tajikistan + Turkmenistan + Uzbekistan) = (0.002 + 0.008 + 0.049 + 0.001 + 0.016) / Number of countries = 0.076 / 5 = 0.015.

359 MPI (South Asia) = MPI (Afghanistan + Bangladesh + Bhutan + India + the Maldives + Nepal + Pakistan) = (0.273 + 0.194 + 0.175 + 0.121 + 0.007 + 0.154 + 0.228) / Number of countries = 1.152 / 7 = 0.165.

360 MPI (South-East Asia) = MPI (Cambodia + Indonesia + Laos + Myanmar + the Philippines + Thailand + Timor-Leste + Vietnam) = (0.158 + 0.029 + 0.211 + 0.176 + 0.038 + 0.003 + 0.211 + 0.020) / Number of countries = 0.846 / 8 = 0.106.

361 MPI (East Asia) = MPI (China + Mongolia) = 0.017 + 0.043 / Number of countries. = 0.060 / 2 = 0.030.

362 MPI (Latin America and the Caribbean) = MPI (Barbados + Belize + Bolivia + Brazil + Colombia + the Dominican Republic + Ecuador + El Salvador + Guatemala + Guyana + Haiti + Honduras + Jamaica + Mexico + Nicaragua + Paraguay + Peru + Saint Lucia + Suriname + Trinidad and Tobago) = (0.009 + 0.017 + 0.094 + 0.016 + 0.021 + 0.016 + 0.018 + 0.033 + 0.134 + 0.014 + 0.231 + 0.090 + 0.018 + 0.025 + 0.074 + 0.019 + 0.052 + 0.007 + 0.041 + 0.002) / Number of countries = 0.931 / 20 = 0.047.

363 No MPI is computed for Oceania, due to a scarcity of data (note 353).

364 This is clear by comparing the value of the MPI at the text to note 346 (i.e., 0.302) with the countries' MPI readings that notes 353, 355, 356, 357, 358, 359, 360, 361 and 362 contain – the highest of which is that of Afghanistan (i.e., 0.273).

365 The MPI for 2018 for South Asia is 0.165 (note 359 and accompanying text).

366 These values are 0.273, 0.194, 0.175, 0.121, 0.154 and 0.228, respectively (note 359).

367 The states that constitute South Asia are Afghanistan, Bangladesh, Bhutan, India, the Maldives, Nepal, Pakistan, and Sri Lanka. Percentage of persons resident in South Asia that are living in Afghanistan, Bangladesh, Bhutan, India, Nepal, or Pakistan = 100% * (Population of Afghanistan + Population of Bangladesh + Population of Bhutan + Population of India + Population of Nepal + Population of Pakistan) / (Population of Afghanistan + Population of Bangladesh + Population of

Part (B)), where Part A = (adults with legally-recognized documentation over land / total adult population) * 100%, and Part B = (adults who perceive their rights as secure[369] / total adult population) * 100%, and is disaggregated by gender and type of tenure.[370] Sources of these data are population censuses, household surveys, and administrative data concerning land tenure from national institutions.[371]

SDG Target 1.5: This target is to "build the resilience of the poor and those in vulnerable situations and reduce their exposure and vulnerability to climate-related extreme events and other economic, social and

---

Bhutan + Population of India + Population of the Maldives + Population of Nepal + Population of Pakistan + Population of Sri Lanka) = 100% * (38,928,346 people + 164,689,383 people + 771,608 people + 1,380,004,385 people + 29,136,808 people + 220,892,340 people) / (38,928,346 people + 164,689,383 people + 771,608 people + 1,380,004,385 people + 540,544 people + 29,136,808 people + 220,892,340 people + 21,413,249 people) = 100% * 1,834,422,870 people / 1,856,376,663 people = 100% * 0.988173847 = 98.8%; percentage given to three significant figures ("Countries of the world by population", Worldometer, accessed April 25, 2020, https://www.worldometers.info/world-population/population-by-country/).

368 Note 315 states SDG Indicator 1.4.2.

369 The UN's guide on metadata for SDG Indicator 1.4.2 states: "For the purposes of constructing the indicator, we define perceptions of tenure to be secure if: (i) The landholder does not report a fear of involuntary loss of the land within the next five years due to, for example, intra-family, community or external threats and (ii) The landholder having the right to bequeath the land (United Nations, Department of Economic and Social Affairs – Statistics Division: Metadata for Target 1.4 – Indicator 1.4.2: United Nations Human Settlements Programme and World Bank – Last updated: 12th February 2018 (New York, 2018), 2). This guide notes: "All forms of tenure should provide people with a degree of tenure security with states protecting legitimate tenure rights, ensuring that people are not arbitrarily evicted and that their legitimate tenure rights are not otherwise extinguished or infringed. Perceptions of tenure matter because they influence the way that the land is used. (Metadata for Target 1.4 – Indicator 1.4.2: United Nations Human Settlements Programme and World Bank, 3).

370 Metadata for Target 1.4 – Indicator 1.4.2: United Nations Human Settlements Programme and World Bank, 5. It is submitted that disaggregation by gender of the recognition of rights over land is essential, as women in developing countries may lose out – see the sentence concerning the 'Bus of Solidarity' in Kyrgyzstan at page 301 of Graeme Baber, *The United Nations System: A Synopsis* (Newcastle-upon-Tyne: Cambridge Scholars Publishing, 2019).

371 Metadata for Target 1.4 – Indicator 1.4.2: United Nations Human Settlements Programme and World Bank, 6.

environmental shocks and disasters", by 2030.[372] The four Indicators for SDG Target 1.5[373] are derived from, and measured together with, the seven global targets of the Sendai Framework for Disaster Risk Reduction 2015-2030,[374] which are as follows.

> (a) Substantially reduce global disaster mortality by 2030, aiming to lower the average per 100,000 global mortality rate in the decade 2020-2030 compared to the period 2005-2015; (b) Substantially reduce the number of affected people globally by 2030, aiming to lower the average global figure per 100,000 in the decade 2020-2030 compared to the period 2005-2015;[375] (c) Reduce direct disaster economic loss in relation to global gross

---

[372] Resolution 70/1 adopted by the General Assembly on 25 September 2015, Transforming our world: the 2030 Agenda for Sustainable Development, 15. SDG Target 1.5 has four Indicators, which are as follows: SDG Indicator 1.5.1 – "Number of deaths, missing persons and directly affected persons attributed to disasters per 100,000 population", SDG Indicator 1.5.2 – "Direct economic loss attributed to disasters in relation to global gross domestic product (GDP)", SDG Indicator 1.5.3 – "Number of countries that adopt and implement national disaster risk reduction strategies in line with the Sendai Framework for Disaster Risk Reduction 2015-2030", and Indicator 1.5.4 – "Proportion of local governments that adopt and implement local disaster risk reduction strategies in line with national disaster risk reduction strategies" (Global indicator framework for the Sustainable Development Goals and targets of the 2030 Agenda for Sustainable Development, 1).

[373] Note 372 contains the four Indicators for SDG Target 1.5.

[374] This Framework was adopted at the Third UN World Conference on Disaster Risk Reduction, which was held in Sendai, Japan, on 18th March 2015 (United Nations, Sendai Framework for Disaster Risk Reduction 2015-2030 (New York, 2015), 5).

[375] SDG Indicator 1.5.1 (note 372) derives from Targets (a) and (b) of the Sendai Framework for Disaster Risk Reduction. SDG Indicator 1.5.1 combines Indicators A-2 (Number of deaths attributed to disasters, per 100,000 population), A-3 (Number of missing persons attributed to disasters, per 100,000 population), and B-1 (Number of directly affected people attributed to disasters, per 100,000 population), from the Sendai Framework for Disaster Risk Reduction (United Nations Office for Disaster Risk Reduction, Technical Guidance for Monitoring and Reporting on Progress in Achieving the Global Targets of the Sendai Framework for Disaster Risk Reduction: Collection of Technical Notes on Data and Methodology: December 2017 (Geneva: 2017), 7 and 20; United Nations, Department of Economic and Social Affairs – Statistics Division: Metadata for Target 1.5 – Indicator 1.5.1: United Nations Office for Disaster Reduction – Last updated: March 2018 (New York, 2018), 2).

domestic product (GDP) by 2030;[376] (d) Substantially reduce disaster damage to critical infrastructure and disruption of basic services, among them health and educational facilities, including through developing their resilience by 2030; (e) Substantially increase the number of countries with national and local disaster risk reduction strategies by 2020;[377] (f) Substantially enhance international cooperation to developing countries through adequate and sustainable support to complement their national actions for implementation of the present Framework by 2030; (g) Substantially increase the availability of and access to multi-hazard early warning systems and disaster risk information and assessments to people by 2030.[378]

SDG Indicator 1.5.1[379] is given by [(A-1 + A-2 + B-1)[380] / Global population] * 100,000.[381] SDG Indicator 1.5.2[382] is calculated as (C-2 + C-

376 SDG Indicator 1.5.2 (note 372) derives from Target (c) of the Sendai Framework for Disaster Risk Reduction. SDG Indicator 1.5.2 combines Indicators C-2 (Direct agricultural loss attributed to disasters), C-3 (Direct economic loss to all other damaged or destroyed productive assets attributed to disasters), C-4 (Direct economic loss in the housing sector attributed to disasters), C-5 (Direct economic loss resulting from damaged or destroyed critical infrastructure attributed to disasters), and C-6 (Direct economic loss to cultural heritage damaged or destroyed attributed to disasters), from the Sendai Framework for Disaster Risk Reduction (Technical Guidance for Monitoring and Reporting on Progress in Achieving the Global Targets of the Sendai Framework for Disaster Risk Reduction, 39; United Nations, Department of Economic and Social Affairs – Statistics Division: Metadata for Target 1.5 – Indicator 1.5.2: United Nations Office for Disaster Reduction – Last updated: March 2018 (New York, 2018), 2).

377 SDG Indicators 1.5.3 and 1.5.4 (note 372) derive from Target (e) of the Sendai Framework for Disaster Risk Reduction. SDG Indicator 1.5.3 is identical to Indicator E-1 (Number of countries that adopt and implement national disaster risk reduction strategies in line with the Sendai Framework for Disaster Risk Reduction 2015-2030) from the Sendai Framework for Disaster Risk Reduction; SDG Indicator 1.5.4 is effectively the same as, although not identical to, Indicator E-2 (Percentage of local governments that adopt and implement local disaster risk reduction strategies in line with national strategies) from the Sendai Framework for Disaster Risk Reduction (Technical Guidance for Monitoring and Reporting on Progress in Achieving the Global Targets of the Sendai Framework for Disaster Risk Reduction, 114).

378 Sendai Framework for Disaster Risk Reduction 2015-2030, 12.

379 Note 372 states SDG Indicator 1.5.1.

380 Note 375 specifies Indicators A-1, A-2 and B-1, which constitute a part of the Sendai Framework for Disaster Risk Reduction 2015-2030.

381 Metadata for Target 1.5 – Indicator 1.5.1: United Nations Office for Disaster Reduction, 2.

382 Note 372 states Indicator 1.5.2.

3 + C-4 + C-5 + C-6)[383] / Global GDP.[384] SDG Indicator 1.5.3[385] is computed as E-1,[386] which, for each country, equals 0.1 * $\sum(KE_i)$, where KE_i is the level of implementation of key element i, i is an integer, and $1 \leq i \leq 10$.[387] Indicator E-1 is also calculated as a global average, which is the

---

383 Note 376 specifies Indicators C-2, C-3, C-4, C-5 and C-6, which constitute a part of the Sendai Framework for Disaster Risk Reduction 2015-2030.

384 Metadata for Target 1.5 – Indicator 1.5.2: United Nations Office for Disaster Reduction, 2.

385 Notes 372 states Indicator 1.5.3.

386 Note 377 specifies Indicator E-1, which constitutes a part of the Sendai Framework for Disaster Risk Reduction 2015-2030.

387 United Nations, Department of Economic and Social Affairs – Statistics Division: Metadata for Target 1.5 – Indicator 1.5.3: United Nations Office for Disaster Reduction – Last updated: 7th July 2017 (New York, 2017), 2; Technical Guidance for Monitoring and Reporting on Progress in Achieving the Global Targets of the Sendai Framework for Disaster Risk Reduction, 117. The ten key elements that implement national disaster risk reduction "strategies are to: i. *Have different timescales, with targets, indicators and time frames* ii. *Have aims at preventing the creation of risk* iii. *Have aims at reducing existing risk* iv. *Have aims at strengthening economic, social, health and environmental resilience* v. … *Based on risk knowledge and assessments to identify risks at the local and national levels of the technical, financial and administrative disaster risk management capacity* vi. … *Mainstream and integrate DRR* [Disaster Risk Reduction] *within and across all sectors with defining roles and responsibilities* vii. … *Guide to allocation of the necessary resources at all levels of administration for the development and the implementation of DRR strategies in all relevant sectors* viii. … *Strengthen disaster preparedness for response and integrate DRR response preparedness and development measures to make nations and communities resilient to disasters* ix. *Promote policy coherence relevant to disaster risk reduction such as sustainable development, poverty eradication, and climate change, notably with the SDGs* [and] *the Paris Agreement* x. *Have mechanisms to follow-up, periodically assess and publicly report on progress* (Technical Guidance for Monitoring and Reporting on Progress in Achieving the Global Targets of the Sendai Framework for Disaster Risk Reduction, 115-116; emphasis original). 1. For each key element i, KE takes a value of 1.00 if there is comprehensive implementation of that element, 0.75 if there is substantial implementation of that element, 0.50 if there is moderate implementation of that element, 0.25 if there is limited implementation of that element, and 0.00 if there is no implementation of that element or if it does not exist (Technical Guidance for Monitoring and Reporting on Progress in Achieving the Global Targets of the Sendai Framework for Disaster Risk Reduction, 117). The Paris Agreement is an international instrument that "enhanc[es] the implementation of the [United Nations Framework] Convention [on Climate Change 1992, and thereby] aims to strengthen the global response to the threat of climate change, in the context of

sum of the values of E-1 for each country divided by the number of countries.[388] SDG Indicator 1.5.4[389] is determined as follows: (i) states are to identify their local governments as "sub-national public administrations with responsibility to develop local disaster risk reduction strategies";[390] (ii) each country is to compute the ratio of the number of local governments with local strategies for disaster risk reduction in accordance with national strategies to the total number of local governments;[391] (iii) the global average is then calculated as the sum of this ratio for all states divided by the number of states.[392] The UNDRR's technical guidance provides an initial survey as to eight of the ten key elements that implement national disaster risk reduction strategies, which are for 32 countries without regional breakdown, as follows.

---

sustainable development and efforts to eradicate poverty" (United Nations, Paris Agreement (Paris, 2015), art.2.1). The Paris Agreement was adopted on 12th December 2015 (Paris Agreement, art.29). It entered into force on 4th November 2016 (United Nations, Secretary-General: Paris Agreement – Depositary Notification C.N.735.2016.TREATIES-XXVII.7.d, 5 October 2016 (New York, 2016)). At the time of writing, 189 Parties of the 197 Parties to the United Nations Framework Convention on Climate Change had ratified the Paris Agreement (United Nations, "Paris Agreement – Status of Ratification", accessed May 4, 2020, https://unfccc.int/process/the-paris-agreement/status-of-ratification).

388 Technical Guidance for Monitoring and Reporting on Progress in Achieving the Global Targets of the Sendai Framework for Disaster Risk Reduction, 117.

389 Notes 372 states Indicator 1.5.4.

390 United Nations, Department of Economic and Social Affairs – Statistics Division: Metadata for Target 1.5 – Indicator 1.5.4: United Nations Office for Disaster Reduction – Last updated: February 2018 (New York, 2018), 2. Countries are to report upon the progress made by the lowest tier of government that is granted the mandate for disaster risk reduction (Metadata for Target 1.5 – Indicator 1.5.4: United Nations Office for Disaster Reduction, 2).

391 Metadata for Target 1.5 – Indicator 1.5.4: United Nations Office for Disaster Reduction, 2.

392 Metadata for Target 1.5 – Indicator 1.5.4: United Nations Office for Disaster Reduction, 2; Technical Guidance for Monitoring and Reporting on Progress in Achieving the Global Targets of the Sendai Framework for Disaster Risk Reduction, 117.

Table 2.2: Elemental assessment of national strategies as to the implementation of disaster risk reduction[393]

Element (i., ii., iii., iv., v., vi., vii., viii., ix, or x., in note 387)	Element present (Number of countries)	Element absent (Number of countries)
Targets (i.)	28	4
Indicators (i.)	22	10
Time frame (i.)	29	3
Prevent the creation of new risk (ii.)	28	4
Reduce existing risk (iii.)	32	0
Strengthen resilience (iv.)	31	1
Based on disaster risk assessment (v.)	29	3
Embedded within/across sectors (vi.)	30	2
Integrate within/across sectors (vi.)	32	0
Define roles and responsibilities (vi.)	30	2
Promote policy coherence (ix.)	32	0
Mechanism for follow-up (x.)	31	1

It is submitted that this information is encouraging: (a) with regard to the attainment of a large number of countries for SDG Indicator 1.5.3 by 31st December 2030,[394] and, consequently, (b) as an element of the achievement of SDG Target 1.5[395] by that date. Notwithstanding this, the national databases for information concerning disaster risk reduction remain in the developmental stage;[396] quick progress is needed to generate

[393] Adapted from the graphical information entitled 'National DRR Strategies', at Technical Guidance for Monitoring and Reporting on Progress in Achieving the Global Targets of the Sendai Framework for Disaster Risk Reduction, 121.

[394] The date 31st December 2030 is introduced pursuant to the use of the phrase 'by 2030' in SDG Target 1.5 (as in SDG Target 1.1 – see text to note 50).

[395] The text to note 372 states SDG Target 1.5.

[396] The UNDRR's programme of work for 2020-2021 states: "All countries should have in place a national disaster loss database system, to enable a comprehensive and credible accounting system for recording and reporting on human, economic and infrastructure losses, and to allow reliable Sendai Framework [for Disaster Risk Reduction 2015-2030] target measurement. UNDRR will support the generation of disaster loss data that is in line with the Sendai Framework requirements in terms of quality and level of disaggregation. Following a review and gap analysis of existing systems, UNDRR will develop a new disaster loss gathering tool using the best available technology that is fully compliant with the

the necessary information to fully support and monitor progress with regard to this Target.

SDG Target 1.a: This target is to "[e]nsure significant mobilization of resources from a variety of sources, including through enhanced development cooperation, in order to provide adequate and predictable means for developing countries, in particular least developed countries, to implement programmes and policies to end poverty in all its dimensions".[397] Whilst metadata for SDG Indicator 1.a.2[398] are not yet available,[399] those for SDG Indicators 1.a.1[400] and 1.b.1[401] "will be finalized shortly".[402] The Development Assistance Committee at the OECD is to provide metadata for SDG Indicator 1.a.1,[403] which will be a specified part[404] of the OECD's database on ODA.[405]

Sendai Framework … . Leveraging a range of existing global and regional partnerships, UNDRR will provide technical assistance and coordinate capacity development in countries to facilitate reporting using the new tool to provide better quality statistical data" (United Nations Office for Disaster Risk Reduction, UNDRR Work Programme 2020-2021 in support of the Sendai Framework for Disaster Risk Reduction (Geneva, 2019), 22).

[397] Resolution 70/1 adopted by the General Assembly on 25 September 2015, Transforming our world: the 2030 Agenda for Sustainable Development, 15. SDG Target 1.a has two Indicators, which are as follows: SDG Indicator 1.a.1 – "Total official development assistance grants from all donors that focus on poverty reduction as a share of the recipient country's gross national income", and SDG Indicator 1.a.2 – "Proportion of total government spending on essential services (education, health and social protection)" (Global indicator framework for the Sustainable Development Goals and targets of the 2030 Agenda for Sustainable Development, 2).

[398] Notes 397 specifies Indicator 1.a.2.

[399] United Nations, Department of Economic and Social Affairs – Statistics Division: Metadata for Target 1.a – Indicator 1.a.2: Last updated: 1st December 2018 (New York, 2018).

[400] Notes 397 states Indicator 1.a.1.

[401] Note 406 specifies Indicator 1.b.1.

[402] United Nations, e-mail of the Statistics Division at the Department of Economic and Social Affairs to Dr. Graeme Baber, 24 April 2020.

[403] United Nations, Department of Economic and Social Affairs – Statistics Division: Reference metadata template for data reported on the Sustainable Development Goals (SDGs) – Target 1.a – Indicator 1.a.3: Last updated: 30th July 2018 (New York, 2018), 4-5. In the 2020 Comprehensive Review of SDG Indicators, Indicator 1.a.1 was deleted, and Indicator 1.a.3 was replaced and re-classified as Indicator 1.a.1 (Report of the Inter-Agency and Expert Group on Sustainable Development Goal Indicators, E/CN.3/2020/2, 20 December 2019,

SDG Target 1.b: This target is to "[c]reate sound policy frameworks at the national, regional and international levels, based on pro-poor and gender-sensitive development strategies, and to support accelerated investment in poverty eradication actions".[406] As the original version of SDG Indicator 1.b.1[407] does not enable effective measurement of SDG Target 1.b, it was replaced in the 2020 Comprehensive Review of SDG Indicators.[408] The UNICEF is the custodian agency for SDG Indicator

---

Annex II.A, 14, and Annex II.D, 18; Statistical Commission: Report on the fifty-first session (3-6 March 2020), E/2020/24-E/CN.3/2020/37, 12).

[404] SDG Indicator 1.a.1 identifies ODA grants that centre on poverty reduction (note 397). Items concerning poverty reduction comprise ODA to basic social services (i.e., basic education, basic health, basic water and sanitation, reproductive health, and population programmes), and developmental food aid (United Nations, Department of Economic and Social Affairs – Statistics Division: Reference metadata template for data reported on the Sustainable Development Goals (SDGs) – Target 1.a – Indicator 1.a.3: Last updated: 30th July 2018 (New York, 2018), 2).

[405] Reference metadata template for data reported on the Sustainable Development Goals (SDGs) – Target 1.a – Indicator 1.a.3, 2-5; "Development finance standards", Organisation for Economic Co-operation and Development, accessed May 1, 2020,
http://www.oecd.org/dac/financing-sustainable-development/development-finance-standards/.

[406] Resolution 70/1 adopted by the General Assembly on 25 September 2015, Transforming our world: the 2030 Agenda for Sustainable Development, 15. SDG Target 1.b has one Indicator, as follows: SDG Indicator 1.b.1 – "Pro-poor public social spending" (Global indicator framework for the Sustainable Development Goals and targets of the 2030 Agenda for Sustainable Development, 2). In the 2020 Comprehensive Review of SDG Indicators, this version of Indicator 1.b.1 replaced the following version of Indicator 1.b.1: "Proportion of government recurrent and capital spending to sectors that disproportionately benefit women, the poor and vulnerable groups" (Report of the Inter-Agency and Expert Group on Sustainable Development Goal Indicators, E/CN.3/2020/2, 20 December 2019, Annex II.A, 14; Statistical Commission: Report on the fifty-first session (3-6 March 2020), E/2020/24-E/CN.3/2020/37, 12). The *replaced* version of SDG Indicator 1.b.1 was the *original* version of it (Resolution 71/313 adopted by the General Assembly on 6 July 2017, Annex, 5).

[407] Note 406 states both the original version of SDG Indicator 1.b.1 and its successor.

[408] Note 406. The proposal that was put to the Inter-Agency and Expert Group on Sustainable Development Goal Indicators stated: "No indicator is currently available to measure effectively target 1.b [text to note 406]. The current indicator 1.b.1 "Proportion of government recurrent and capital spending to sectors that disproportionately benefit women, the poor and vulnerable groups" has no custodian agency and there are no plans to finalise a methodology or collect data.

1.b.1.[409] It will work with the Commitment to Equity Institute at Tulane University[410] and other organizations to compile the data for that SDG Indicator.[411]

Will SDG 1 be achieved punctually?

The immediately-preceding subsection reveals that, whilst suitable data are available to assess progress on some of the targets of SDG 1, appropriate particulars for effective evaluation of others are sparse or yet to be provided – partly in consequence of recent changes to SDG Indicators. Thus, the comment in the current subsection is based upon incomplete information. Given this, the data analysed in the immediately-preceding subsection indicate that poverty is reducing globally but not at a

---

We therefore propose replacing the existing indicator with the new indicator *Pro-poor public social spending*, which is defined as the proportion of government spending towards health and education and direct transfers which benefit directly … the monetary poor. The proposed indicator refines and replaces the previous indicator, by providing clearer definitions of sectors with poverty-reducing effects (health, education and other transfers) and vulnerable groups. Latter covers the monetary poor (as determined by national definition of income or consumption poverty, consistent with SDG [Indicator] 1.2.1 [note 249]. Further developments of the methodology and improvements in data availability may allow [expansion of] this indicator to other vulnerable groups, such as women and children. Government spending on social sectors is a strong measurement of the financial commitment governments make to target their services and transfers on the most vulnerable groups of society, reinforcing pro-poor development strategies. We therefore believe that proposed indicator *Pro-poor public social spending* is [a] suitable measure for the target 1.b." (United Nations Children's Fund/Save the Children, Indicator Proposal Summary Template: Pro-poor public social spending (New York, 2019), 1; emphasis original).

409 Indicator Proposal Summary Template: Pro-poor public social spending, 1. Note 406 specifies Indicator 1.b.1.

410 The Commitment to Equity Institute strives to lower poverty and inequality by means of tax and benefit incidence studies for which it employs a methodology – to which Part 1 of its Handbook entitled 'Commitment to Equity Handbook: Estimating the Impact of Fiscal Policy on Inequality and Poverty' is devoted, the results of which are published in its Data Center and in documents that are accessible from its website ("About CEQ", Commitment to Equity Institute, accessed May 2, 2020, http://commitmentoequity.org/about/; Commitment to Equity Institute, *Commitment to Equity Handbook: Estimating the Impact of Fiscal Policy on Inequality and Poverty*, edited by Nora Lustig (Washington, D.C.: Brookings Institution Press, 2018), iii, v, lix, lxvii and 1).

411 Indicator Proposal Summary Template: Pro-poor public social spending, 2.

rate that would lead to it being substantially lowered by 31st December 2030 – as SDG 1 requires.[412] Furthermore, the evidence examined tends to suggest that: (i) Sub-Saharan Africa is fairly mired in poverty, (ii) West Asia and North Africa have low rates of poverty, but these are not improving and may be deteriorating, and (iii) there remain traces of poverty in the main concentrations of high-income countries, i.e., North America and West Europe. Hence, SDG 1 will not be met punctually – although the *average percentage* of poverty *per person worldwide* is likely to be lower in December 2030 than it was when the SDGs were launched in September 2015.[413]

Conclusion

This Chapter researches whether or not SDG 1 is likely to be accomplished punctually, by methodically exploring the progress made regarding the achievement of MDG 1, MDG Target 1.A, the latter's mapping outcome, i.e., SDG Target 1.1, and SDG 1 – in that order. Whilst MDG Target 1.A was achieved on-time globally – although not in every region, it is opined that neither SDG Target 1.1 nor SDG 1 will be attained punctually. One reason for the lower predicted performance in the timely attainment of SDG Target 1.1 than the recorded result of promptly meeting MDG Target 1.A, is that the latter required extreme poverty to be halved whilst the former aims for it to be eliminated – which is a much stiffer, and arguably unattainable, objective.

---

412 Note 96 of Chapter One, and the text to note 2, state SDG 1. Note 50 explains the introduction of 31st December 2030 as the target date in respect of SDG Target 1.1; this reasoning is also applicable to SDG Targets 1.2 (note 15, and text to note 249) 1.4 (text to note 315), and 1.5 (text to note 372, and note 394), and to the second clause of SDG Target 1.3 (text to note 272). In the document entitled 'Transforming our world: the 2030 Agenda for Sustainable Development', the Heads of State and High Representatives … are committed to ending poverty in all its forms and dimensions, including by eradicating extreme poverty by 2030" (Resolution 70/1 adopted by the General Assembly on 25 September 2015, Transforming our world: the 2030 Agenda for Sustainable Development, paras.1 and 24). It is submitted that, on the basis of these statements, SDG 1 requires the elimination of extreme poverty, and a considerable reduction of all other forms of poverty, by 31st December 2030.

413 The General Assembly adopted Resolution 70/1 on 25th September 2015 (text to note 35 of Chapter One), which comprised the outcome document from the UN's Sustainable Development Summit held at that time (note 61 of Chapter One) entitled 'Transforming our world: the 2030 Agenda for Sustainable Development' (text to note 39 of Chapter One).

The next Chapter investigates progress made on SDG 10 – i.e., "Reduce inequality within and among countries",[414] which is a new Goal that receives no mappings from the MDGs.[415] It assesses the extent to which SDG 10 is likely to be fulfilled by 31st December 2030.

[414] Text to note 36 of Chapter One.

[415] Note 200 of Chapter One, and accompanying text.

CHAPTER THREE

NEW GROUND MICROSTUDY: ADDRESSING GOAL 10 – REDUCE INEQUALITY

Introduction

Inequality is, and has been for a long time, an issue that has troubled societies – for instance, Jesus Christ recognized this concept two millennia ago in his follow-up instruction to the saintly, wealthy young man who wished to gain eternal life, to sell his goods and give the proceeds of their sale to the poor.[1] More recently, inequality has been a matter of concern to some philosophers and legal theorists – such as Drs. John Rawls[2] and

[1] The Gospel according to Saint Matthew reads: "… 'Master, what good deed must I do to possess eternal life?' Jesus said to him, '… [I]f you wish to enter into life, keep the commandments.' … The young man said to him, 'I have kept all these. What more do I need to do?' Jesus said, 'If you wish to be perfect, go and sell what you own and *give the money to the poor*, … then come, follow me.' …"; the Gospel according to Saint Mark states: "… 'Good master, what must I do to inherit eternal life?' Jesus said to him, '… You know the commandments … .' And he said to him, 'Master, I have kept all these from my earliest days.' Jesus … said, 'There is one thing you lack. Go and sell everything that you own and *give the money to the poor*, … then come, follow me.' …"; the Gospel according to Saint Luke reports: "… 'Good master, what have I to do to inherit eternal life?' Jesus said to him, '… You know the commandments … .' He replied, 'I have kept all these from my earliest days till now'. And when Jesus heard this he said, 'There is still one thing you lack. Sell all that you own and *distribute the money to the poor*, … then come, follow me.' …" (*The Jerusalem Bible: Popular Edition* (London: Darton, Longman & Todd Ltd, 1974), Matthew 19: 16-17 and 20-21, Mark 10: 17-21, Luke: 18: 18-22; emphasis added). Jesus' concern was primarily with freeing the young man from his love of possessions, so that he could gain the humble trust in God that is required to enter the latter's kingdom (Tom Wright, *Luke for Everyone* (London: Society for Promoting Christian Knowledge, 2004), 217). It is submitted that Jesus also cared about who received the money from the sale of the petitioner's possessions, i.e., people with great need for it.

[2] John Roemer, "Equality: Its Justification, Nature and Domain", in *The Oxford Handbook of Economic Inequality*, edited by Weimer Salverda, Brian Nolan, and

Ronald Dworkin.[3] There are different notions as to what should be equalized – for example, all goods and services (simple equality), welfare, opportunity for welfare, access to advantage, and capabilities.[4] The broad wording of SDG 10, i.e., "Reduce *inequality within and among* countries",[5] together with the variety of concepts that the targets of SDG 10 contain, such as "social, economic and political inclusion" in Target 10.2,[6] "equal opportunity" and "inequalities of outcome" in Target 10.3,[7]

Timothy Smeeding, 23-39 (Oxford: Oxford University Press, 2009), 25-26. Dr. Rawls (1921-2002) "was an American political philosopher in the liberal tradition. His theory of *justice as fairness* describes a society of free citizens holding equal basic rights and cooperating within an egalitarian economic system. His theory of political liberalism delineates the legitimate use of political power in a democracy, and envisions how civic unity might endure despite the diversity of worldviews that free institutions allow. His writings on the law of peoples set out a liberal foreign policy that aims to create a permanently peaceful and tolerant international order." (Leif Wenar, "John Rawls", in *The Stanford Encyclopedia of Philosophy*, Spring 2017, edited by Edward Zalta, accessed May 10, 2020, https://plato.stanford.edu/archives/spr2017/entries/rawls/; emphasis original). 'Egalitarian' means "of, relating to, or believing in the principle that all people are equal and deserve equal rights and opportunities" (Oxford University Press, *The New Oxford Dictionary of English* (Oxford: Oxford University Press, 1998), 591).

[3] John Roemer, "Equality: Its Justification, Nature and Domain", in *The Oxford Handbook of Economic Inequality*, 23-39, 28-29. Dr. Dworkin (1931-2013) was an American legal theorist with "liberal and egalitarian philosophical views" (Frances Kamm, "In Memoriam: Ronald Dworkin", *Harvard Law Review*, 127(2) (2013): 498-499, 499). Writing and teaching in leading universities in both the UK and the USA, he had trenchant beliefs about the nature of adjudication, which, in essence, allotted no place for judicial discretion in the broad sense of deciding what the law was in a particular case in which no legal rule was specifically applicable to the facts therein, but only for judicial discretion in the narrow sense of determining which rule(s) to apply from the common law in order to achieve the optimal outcome to such proceedings. Note 2 defines 'egalitarian'.

[4] Stefan Gosepath, "Equality", in *The Stanford Encyclopedia of Philosophy*, Spring 2011, edited by Edward Zalta, accessed May 10, 2020, https://plato.stanford.edu/archives/spr2011/entries/equality/.

[5] United Nations, Resolution 70/1 adopted by the General Assembly on 25 September 2015, Transforming our world: the 2030 Agenda for Sustainable Development, 14; emphasis added.

[6] Resolution 70/1 adopted by the General Assembly on 25 September 2015, Transforming our world: the 2030 Agenda for Sustainable Development, 21. The text to note 232 states SDG Target 10.2.

[7] Resolution 70/1 adopted by the General Assembly on 25 September 2015, Transforming our world: the 2030 Agenda for Sustainable Development, 21. The text to note 261 specifies SDG Target 10.3.

and "greater equality [regarding] policies" in Target 10.4,[8] indicates that the *scope* of inequalities that the UN intends to embrace within this Goal is greater than precise definitions of inequality – including those of economic description, for which a variety of methods of measurement are available.[9] Consequently, the next section follows an approach that focuses on every target of SDG 10 separately – to each of which a subsection therein is devoted. Based on that information, the following section addresses the question of whether SDG 10 is likely to be met punctually. The final section concludes.

Targets of SDG 10

SDG Target 10.1 and SDG Indicator 10.1.1

SDG Target 10.1 is to "progressively achieve and sustain income growth of the bottom 40 per cent of the population at a rate higher than the national average" by 2030.[10] Its sole indicator is SDG Indicator 10.1.1, which determines the "[g]rowth rates of household expenditure or income per capita among the bottom 40 per cent of the population and the total population".[11]

The World Bank's Global Database of Shared Prosperity: This database contains information that is relevant to SDG Target 10.1 and Indicator 10.1.1.[12] For each country in the database,[13] the data include: (i)

---

[8] Resolution 70/1 adopted by the General Assembly on 25 September 2015, Transforming our world: the 2030 Agenda for Sustainable Development, 21. The text to note 268 declares SDG Target 10.4.

[9] These methods include the 'variance of the logs' inequality index, percentile ratios, the Gini coefficient, the Generalized Gini (or S-Gini) class of inequality indices, the Pietra ratio, the General Entropy class of inequality indices – including the Theil index, the Mean Logarithmic Deviation, and half the squared coefficient of variation, and the Atkinson family of inequality indices (Stephen Jenkins and Philippe Van Kerm, "The Measurement of Economic Inequality", in *The Oxford Handbook of Economic Inequality*, 40-67, 50-52).

[10] Resolution 70/1 adopted by the General Assembly on 25 September 2015, Transforming our world: the 2030 Agenda for Sustainable Development, 21.

[11] United Nations, Global indicator framework for the Sustainable Development Goals and targets of the 2030 Agenda for Sustainable Development, A/RES/ 71/313, E/CN.3/2018/2, E/CN.3/2019/2, E/CN.3/2020/2 (New York, 2020), 10.

[12] United Nations, Department of Economic and Social Affairs – Statistics Division: Metadata for Target 10.1 – Indicator 10.1.1: World Bank – Last updated: 19th July 2016 (New York, 2016), 4.

the mean per capita income or consumption for the poorer 40% of the welfare distribution and for the total population, in terms of PPP-adjusted USD per day at 2011 prices, (ii) the annualized mean growth rate in per capita real income or real consumption for the lower 40% of the welfare distribution and the total population, (iii) the survey years that define the period for which these growth rates are calculated, and (iv) the type of welfare aggregate that is used to compute the growth rates.[14]

Methodology: The growth rate in the welfare aggregate, i.e., either income or consumption per capita,[15] of the poorer 40% of the population

---

[13] Note 14 lists the countries whose data are included in the Global Database of Shared Prosperity, together with the World Bank's regional grouping to which each is assigned.

[14] Christina Weiser, Methodology for computing the indicator on Shared Prosperity for the Global Database of Shared Prosperity (GDSP) circa 2007-2012: Global Poverty Working Group, October 2015 (Washington, D.C.: World Bank, 2015), 2-3. The welfare aggregate is either income per capita that is estimated from individual income data (i) or grouped income data (I), or consumption per capita that is estimated from individual consumption data (c) or grouped consumption data (C). The countries whose data appear in the Global Database of Shared Prosperity, together with each's type of welfare aggregate, i.e., (i), (I), (c), or (C), are as follows: *Central Europe, East Europe, the Caucasus and Central Asia* – Albania (c), Armenia (c), Belarus (c), Croatia (i), the Czech Republic (i), Estonia (i), Georgia (c), Hungary (i), Kazakhstan (c), Kosovo (c), Kyrgyzstan (c), Latvia (i), Lithuania (i), Moldova (c), Montenegro (i), North Macedonia (i), Poland (i), Romania (i), Russia (c), Serbia (i), Slovakia (i), Slovenia (i), Turkey (c), and Ukraine (c); *East Asia and the Pacific* – China (C), Indonesia (c), Malaysia (i), Mongolia (c), the Philippines (i), Thailand (c), and Vietnam (c); *High-income countries* – Austria (i), Belgium (i), Cyprus (i), Denmark (i), Finland (i), France (i), Germany (I), Greece (i), Iceland (i), Ireland (i), Israel (I), Italy (i), Luxembourg (i), Malta (i), the Netherlands (i), Norway (i), Portugal (i), Spain (i), Sweden (i), Switzerland (i), the UK (i), and the USA (I); *Latin America and the Caribbean* – Argentina – urban areas only (i), Bolivia (i), Brazil (i), Chile (i), Colombia (i), Costa Rica (i), the Dominican Republic (i), Ecuador (i), El Salvador (i), Honduras (i), Panama (i), Paraguay (i), Peru (i), and Uruguay (i); *Middle East and North Africa* – Egypt (c), Iran (c), Tunisia (c), and West Bank and Gaza (c); *South Asia* – Bangladesh (c), Bhutan (c), Pakistan (c), and Sri Lanka (c); *Sub-Saharan Africa* – Benin (c), Botswana (c), Eswatini (c), Ethiopia (c), Ghana (c), Malawi (c), Mauritius (c), Namibia (c), Rwanda (c), Sierra Leone (c), Tanzania (c), Togo (c), Uganda (c), Zambia (c), and Zimbabwe (C/c) (World Bank, Global Database of Shared Prosperity and Median Income/Consumption, circa 2012-2017, as of 17th March 2020, cols 3 and 5, and fns d-e).

[15] Note 14 details the types of welfare aggregate and the particular one of these that each country in the Global Database of Shared Prosperity uses. Consumption is preferred to income as an indicator of welfare (note 255 of Chapter Two). The

notes on the methodology state: "The PovcalNet database of the World Bank Group is used as the primary source for the GDSP [Global Database of Shared Prosperity]. ... The choice of consumption or income to measure G40 for a country is made according to which welfare aggregate is used to estimate extreme poverty in PovcalNet unless there are strong arguments for using a different welfare aggregate. The practice adopted by the World Bank Group for estimating global and regional poverty is, in principle, to use per capita consumption expenditure as the welfare measure wherever available; and to use income as the welfare measure for countries for which consumption is unavailable. However, in some cases data on consumption may be available but are outdated or not shared with the World Bank Group for recent survey years. In these cases, if data on income are available, income is used for estimating G40." (Weiser, Methodology for computing the indicator on Shared Prosperity for the Global Database of Shared Prosperity (GDSP), 3). 'G40' is the annualized average growth rate per capita of real income or real consumption of the lowest 40% of the welfare distribution in a country (Weiser, Methodology for computing the indicator on Shared Prosperity for the Global Database of Shared Prosperity (GDSP), 1). The subsection entitled 'Progress to date in the accomplishment of SDG Target 1.1', in the section titled 'SDG Target 1.1' in Chapter Two, uses the World Bank's PovcalNet database to ascertain regional trends from 2015 to 2018 in extreme poverty. Note 85 of Chapter Two lists every country of those on which PovcalNet provides data (text to note 74 of Chapter Two) concerning which PovcalNet: (i) uses measures of income for both its 2015 database and its 2018 database, (ii) utilizes measures of consumption for both its 2015 database and its 2018 database, and (iii) employs measures of consumption for its 2015 database and measures of income for its 2018 database. Regarding points (i) and (iii) in the context of the current subsection entitled 'SDG Target 10.1 and Indicator 10.1.1', the notes on the methodology specify: "[M]ost middle[-]income countries in Latin America and the Caribbean, as well as Europe and Central Asia, are now using income as a well-accepted measure of poverty and well-being. Therefore, data on income are more readily available than data on consumption and as a result, income is used to estimate G40." (Weiser, Methodology for computing the indicator on Shared Prosperity for the Global Database of Shared Prosperity (GDSP), fn 7, 3). As estimates of annualized mean growth in per capita real income or real consumption are based on income or consumption data gathered in household surveys – as for poverty rates, and as the World Bank's PovcalNet database is the main source of data for the World Bank's Global Database of Shared Prosperity – from which the information pertaining to SDG Target 10.1 and Indicator 10.1.1 are taken (text to note 12), the same issues regarding the quality of the data for poverty rates – and for PovcalNet in particular – apply to the data in the Global Database of Shared Prosperity (Metadata for Target 10.1 – Indicator 10.1.1: World Bank, 2; Weiser, Methodology for computing the indicator on Shared Prosperity for the Global Database of Shared Prosperity (GDSP), 3). The text to note 91 of Chapter Two refers to, among other things, these matters concerning data quality. Moreover, the UN notes: "Analysis of some 20 countries for which both consumption and income of a country is calculated as the annualized mean growth rate in per capita real income or real consumption of the lower 40% of the welfare distribution in that territory from household surveys over a period of minimum three years and maximum seven years.[16] The national average rate of growth in the welfare aggregate[17] is computed as the annualized mean growth rate in per capita real income or real consumption of the total population of a country from household surveys over a period of three to seven years.[18] The rules for selecting the initial survey year, T_0, and the final survey year, T_1, are as follows: (i) choose T_1 for each country to be the year of the most recent household survey available there – but not before 2015,[19] (ii) set T_0 as close as possible to (T_1 – 5 years), within ± 2 years; thus, 3 years $\leq (T_1 - T_0) \leq$ 7 years,[20] (iii) if two surveys are equidistant from (T_1 – 5 years), then, *ceteris paribus*,[21] fix T_0 as the more-recent survey year,[22] and (iv) the comparability of welfare aggregates – income or consumption – for the years selected for T_0 and T_1 is evaluated for every country; if comparability across the two surveys is a significant concern for any state, then criteria (i) to (iii) are re-applied to determine the next-best survey year(s).[23] The welfare aggregates for each country are

---

data were available from the same [household] surveys found income to yield a higher mean than consumption but also higher inequality. When poverty measures based on consumption and income were compared, the two effects roughly cancelled each other out: there was no significant statistical difference." (Metadata for Target 10.1 – Indicator 10.1.1: World Bank, 2).

[16] Metadata for Target 10.1 – Indicator 10.1.1: World Bank, 1; Weiser, Methodology for computing the indicator on Shared Prosperity for the Global Database of Shared Prosperity (GDSP), 2.

[17] Note 15 and accompanying text.

[18] Metadata for Target 10.1 – Indicator 10.1.1: World Bank, 1; Weiser, Methodology for computing the indicator on Shared Prosperity for the Global Database of Shared Prosperity (GDSP), 2.

[19] World Bank, Global Database of Shared Prosperity and Median Income/Consumption, fn c; Weiser, Methodology for computing the indicator on Shared Prosperity for the Global Database of Shared Prosperity (GDSP), 2.

[20] Weiser, Methodology for computing the indicator on Shared Prosperity for the Global Database of Shared Prosperity (GDSP), 2; Metadata for Target 10.1 – Indicator 10.1.1: World Bank, 3.

[21] Note 338 of Chapter Two defines '*ceteris paribus*'.

[22] Weiser, Methodology for computing the indicator on Shared Prosperity for the Global Database of Shared Prosperity (GDSP), 2; Metadata for Target 10.1 – Indicator 10.1.1: World Bank, 3.

[23] Weiser, Methodology for computing the indicator on Shared Prosperity for the Global Database of Shared Prosperity (GDSP), 2; Metadata for Target 10.1 – Indicator 10.1.1: World Bank, 3. The survey years for the countries whose data

calculated in this way: (a) select T_0 and T_1 in accordance with criteria (i) to (iv); (b) estimate the mean per capita real income or real consumption of the lower 40% of the welfare distribution in years T_0 and T_1; (c) compute the annual average growth rate in per capita real income or real consumption of the *lower 40% of the welfare distribution* between T_0 and

---

appears in the current version of the World Bank's Global Database of Shared Prosperity are as follows: *Central Europe, East Europe, the Caucasus and Central Asia* – Albania T_0=2014 T_1=2017, Armenia T_0=2013 T_1=2018, Belarus T_0=2013 T_1=2018, Croatia T_0=2012 T_1=2017, the Czech Republic T_0=2012 T_1=2017, Estonia T_0=2012 T_1=2017, Georgia T_0=2013 T_1=2018, Hungary T_0=2012 T_1=2017, Kazakhstan T_0=2012 T_1=2017, Kosovo T_0=2012 T_1=2017, Kyrgyzstan T_0=2013 T_1=2018, Latvia T_0=2012 T_1=2017, Lithuania T_0=2012 T_1=2017, Moldova T_0=2013 T_1=2018, Montenegro T_0=2012 T_1=2015, North Macedonia T_0=2012 T_1=2017, Poland T_0=2012 T_1=2017, Romania T_0=2012 T_1=2017, Russia T_0=2013 T_1=2018, Serbia T_0=2013 T_1=2017, Slovakia T_0=2011 T_1=2016, Slovenia T_0=2012 T_1=2017, Turkey T_0=2013 T_1=2018, and Ukraine T_0=2013 T_1=2018; *East Asia and the Pacific* – China T_0=2013 T_1=2016, Indonesia T_0=2014 T_1=2018, Malaysia T_0=2012 T_1=2016, Mongolia T_0=2011 T_1=2018, the Philippines T_0=2012 T_1=2015, Thailand T_0=2014 T_1=2018, and Vietnam T_0=2012 T_1=2018; *High-income countries* – Austria T_0=2012 T_1=2017, Belgium T_0=2012 T_1=2017, Cyprus T_0=2012 T_1=2017, Denmark T_0=2012 T_1=2017, Finland T_0=2012 T_1=2017, France T_0=2012 T_1=2017, Germany T_0=2011 T_1=2016, Greece T_0=2012 T_1=2017, Iceland T_0=2010 T_1=2015, Ireland T_0=2011 T_1=2016, Israel T_0=2010 T_1=2016, Italy T_0=2012 T_1=2017, Luxembourg T_0=2012 T_1=2017, Malta T_0=2012 T_1=2017, the Netherlands T_0=2012 T_1=2017, Norway T_0=2012 T_1=2017, Portugal T_0=2012 T_1=2017, Spain T_0=2012 T_1=2017, Sweden T_0=2012 T_1=2017, Switzerland T_0=2012 T_1=2017, the UK T_0=2011 T_1=2016, and the USA T_0=2010 T_1=2016; *Latin America and the Caribbean* – Argentina T_0=2013 T_1=2018, Bolivia T_0=2013 T_1=2018, Brazil T_0=2013 T_1=2018, Chile T_0=2013 T_1=2017, Colombia T_0=2013 T_1=2018, Costa Rica T_0=2013 T_1=2018, the Dominican Republic T_0=2011 T_1=2016, Ecuador T_0=2013 T_1=2018, El Salvador T_0=2013 T_1=2018, Honduras T_0=2013 T_1=2018, Panama T_0=2013 T_1=2018, Paraguay T_0=2013 T_1=2018, Peru T_0=2013 T_1=2018, and Uruguay T_0=2013 T_1=2018; *Middle East and North Africa* – Egypt T_0=2012 T_1=2017, Iran T_0=2014 T_1=2017, Tunisia T_0=2010 T_1=2015, and West Bank and Gaza T_0=2011 T_1=2016; *South Asia* – Bangladesh T_0=2010 T_1=2016, Bhutan T_0=2012 T_1=2017, Pakistan T_0=2010 T_1=2015, and Sri Lanka T_0=2012 T_1=2016; *Sub-Saharan Africa*: Benin T_0=2011 T_1=2015, Botswana T_0=2009 T_1=2015, Eswatini T_0=2009 T_1=2016, Ethiopia T_0=2010 T_1=2015, Ghana T_0=2012 T_1=2016, Malawi T_0=2010 T_1=2016, Mauritius T_0=2012 T_1=2017, Namibia T_0=2009 T_1=2015, Rwanda T_0=2013 T_1=2016, Sierra Leone T_0=2011 T_1=2018, Tanzania T_0=2011 T_1=2018, Togo T_0=2011 T_1=2015, Uganda T_0=2012 T_1=2016, Zambia T_0=2010 T_1=2015, and Zimbabwe T_0=2011 T_1=2017 (World Bank, Global Database of Shared Prosperity and Median Income/Consumption, col 4).

T_1 using the following formula: [(Mean in T_1 / Mean in T_0)$^{1/(T_1 - T_0)}$] – 1; (d) estimate the mean per capita real income or real consumption of the total population in years T_0 and T_1; (e) calculate the annual average growth rate in per capita real income or real consumption of the *total population* between T_0 and T_1 using the formula [(Mean in T_1 / Mean in T_0)$^{1/(T_1 - T_0)}$] – 1.[24]

Calculating regional values for the average annual growth rate in per capita welfare: Recalling that whether welfare aggregates are calculated from consumption or income data collected in household surveys does not significantly affect measures of poverty,[25] it is submitted that the loss of accuracy from aggregating data from countries in the Global Database of Shared Prosperity to form regional figures for the average annual growth rate in per capita welfare is insufficient to invalidate the benefit of using these numbers to assess trends in comparative regional inequality. Thus, such a regional statistic is computed for the poorer 40% of the welfare distribution, R_{40}, and another for the total population, R_T. R_{40} = [(A_{40} * Pn(A)) + (B_{40} * Pn(B)) + … + (N_{40} * Pn(N))] / [Pn(A) + Pn(B) + … Pn(N)], and R_T = [(A_T * Pn(A)) + (B_T * Pn(B)) + … + (N_T * Pn(N))] / [Pn(A) + Pn(B) + … Pn(N)], where A_{40}, B_{40} … N_{40} is the annual average growth rate in per capita real income or real consumption of the lower 40% of the welfare distribution between T_0 and T_1 for country A, B … N, N is the number of countries in the region, A_T, B_T … N_T is the annual average growth rate in per capita real income or real consumption of the total population between T_0 and T_1 for country A, B … N, and Pn(A), Pn(B) … Pn(N) is the population of country A, B … N.[26]

---

[24] Metadata for Target 10.1 – Indicator 10.1.1: World Bank, 3.

[25] The last quote in note 15 is the basis for this clause in the text.

[26] For each region, the data for the population of countries A, B … N are taken from the following website: "Countries in the world by population (2020)", Worldometer, accessed May 15, 2020, https://www.worldometers.info/world-population/population-by-country/, and are as follows: *Central Europe, East Europe, the Caucasus and Central Asia* – Albania 2,877,797 people, Armenia 2,963,243 people, Belarus 9,449,323 people, Croatia 4,105,267 people, the Czech Republic 10,708,981 people, Estonia 1,326,535 people, Georgia 3,989,167 people, Hungary 9,660,351 people, Kazakhstan 18,776,707 people, Kosovo (see point (i), below in this note), Kyrgyzstan 6,524,195 people, Latvia 1,886,198 people, Lithuania 2,722,289 people, Moldova 4,033,963 people, Montenegro 628,066 people, North Macedonia 2,083,374 people, Poland 37,846,611 people, Romania 19,237,691 people, Russia 145,934,462 people, Serbia 8,737,371 people, Slovakia 5,459,642 people, Slovenia 2,078,938 people, Turkey 84,339,067 people, and Ukraine 43,733,762 people; *East Asia and the Pacific* – China 1,439,323,776 people, Indonesia 273,523,615 people, Malaysia 32,365,999 people, Mongolia

Central Europe, East Europe, the Caucasus and Central Asia: R_{40} = [(A_{40} * Pn(A)) + (B_{40} * Pn(B)) + … + (N_{40} * Pn(N))] / [Pn(A) + Pn(B) + … Pn(N)] = [($Albania_{40}$ * Pn(Albania)) + ($Armenia_{40}$ * Pn(Armenia)) + ($Belarus_{40}$ * Pn(Belarus)) + ($Croatia_{40}$ * Pn(Croatia)) + (the Czech $Republic_{40}$ * Pn(the Czech Republic)) + ($Estonia_{40}$ * Pn(Estonia)) + ($Georgia_{40}$ * Pn(Georgia)) + ($Hungary_{40}$ * Pn(Hungary)) + ($Kazakhstan_{40}$ * Pn(Kazakhstan)) + ($Kosovo_{40}$ * Pn(Kosovo)) + ($Kyrgyzstan_{40}$ * Pn(Kyrgyzstan)) + ($Latvia_{40}$ * Pn(Latvia)) + ($Lithuania_{40}$ * Pn(Lithuania))

3,278,290 people, the Philippines 109,581,078 people, Thailand 69,799,978 people, and Vietnam 97,338,579 people; *High-income countries* – Austria 9,006,398 people, Belgium 11,589,623 people, Cyprus 1,207,359 people, Denmark 5,792,202 people, Finland 5,540,720 people, France 65,273,511 people, Germany 83,783,942 people, Greece 10,423,054 people, Iceland 341,243 people, Ireland 4,937,786 people, Israel 8,655,535 people, Italy 60,461,826 people, Luxembourg 625,978 people, Malta 441,543 people, the Netherlands 17,134,872 people, Norway 5,421,241 people, Portugal 10,196,709 people, Spain 46,754,778 people, Sweden 10,099,265 people, Switzerland 8,654,622 people, the UK 67,886,011 people, and the USA 331,002,651 people; *Latin America and the Caribbean* – Argentina – urban areas only (see point (ii), below in this note), Bolivia 11,673,021 people, Brazil 212,559,417 people, Chile 19,116,201 people, Colombia 50,882,891 people, Costa Rica 5,094,118 people, the Dominican Republic 10,847,910 people, Ecuador 17,643,054 people, El Salvador 6,486,205 people, Honduras 9,904,607 people, Panama 4,314,767 people, Paraguay 7,132,538 people, Peru 32,971,854 people, and Uruguay 3,473,730 people; *Middle East and North Africa* – Egypt 102,334,404 people, Iran 83,992,949 people, Tunisia 11,818,619 people, and West Bank and Gaza (see point (iii), below in this note); *South Asia* – Bangladesh 164,689,383 people, Bhutan 771,608 people, Pakistan 220,892,340 people, and Sri Lanka 21,413,249 people; *Sub-Saharan Africa* – Benin 12,123,200 people, Botswana 2,351,627 people, Eswatini 1,160,164 people, Ethiopia 114,963,588 people, Ghana 31,072,940 people, Malawi 19,129,952 people, Mauritius 1,271,768 people, Namibia 2,540,905 people, Rwanda 12,952,218 people, Sierra Leone 7,976,983 people, Tanzania 59,734,218 people, Togo 8,278,724 people, Uganda 45,741,007 people, Zambia 18,383,955 people, and Zimbabwe 14,862,924 people. (i) The population of Kosovo on 15th May 2020 is 1,810,770 people ("Kosovo Population", Countrymeters, accessed May 15, 2020, https://countrymeters.info/en/Kosovo). (ii) The urban population of Argentina in 2020 is 41,919,857 people ("Argentina Population (LIVE)", Worldometer, accessed May 15, 2020, https://www.worldometers.info/world-population/argentina-population/). (iii) The population of the State of Palestine in 2020 is 5,101,414 people ("Countries in the world by population (2020)", Worldometer, accessed May 15, 2020, https://www.worldometers.info/world-population/population-by-country/); the State of Palestine is assumed to comprise the same territory as West Bank and Gaza; therefore, the former's population figure is used for the latter in the list of countries above in this note.

+ (Moldova$_{40}$ * Pn(Moldova)) + (Montenegro$_{40}$ * Pn(Montenegro)) + (North Macedonia$_{40}$ * Pn(North Macedonia)) + (Poland$_{40}$ * Pn(Poland)) + (Romania$_{40}$ * Pn(Romania)) + (Russia$_{40}$ * Pn(Russia)) + (Serbia$_{40}$ * Pn(Serbia)) + (Slovakia$_{40}$ * Pn(Slovakia)) + (Slovenia$_{40}$ * Pn(Slovenia)) + (Turkey$_{40}$ * Pn(Turkey)) + (Ukraine$_{40}$ * Pn(Ukraine))] / [Pn(Albania) + Pn(Armenia) + Pn(Belarus) + Pn(Croatia) + Pn(the Czech Republic) + Pn(Estonia) + Pn(Georgia) + Pn(Hungary) + Pn(Kazakhstan) + Pn(Kosovo) + Pn(Kyrgyzstan) + Pn(Latvia) + Pn(Lithuania) + Pn(Moldova) + Pn(Montenegro) + Pn(North Macedonia) + Pn(Poland) + Pn(Romania) + Pn(Russia) + Pn(Serbia) + Pn(Slovakia) + Pn(Slovenia) + Pn(Turkey) + Pn(Ukraine)] = [(2.46% * 2,877,797 people) + (1.26% * 2,963,243 people) + (0.71% * 9,449,323 people) + (5.47% * 4,105,267 people) + (3.53% * 10,708,981 people) + (7.98% * 1,326,535 people) + (2.65% * 3,989,167 people) + (4.84% * 9,660,351 people) + (-0.02%* 18,776,707 people) + (2.36% * 1,810,770 people) + (3.15% * 6,524,195 people) + (7.91% * 1,886,198 people) + (6.33%* 2,722,289 people) + (1.90% * 4,033,963 people) + (4.72% * 628,066 people) + (7.06% * 2,083,374 people) + (6.01% * 37,846,611 people) + (10.02% * 19,237,691 people) + (-0.44% * 145,934,462 people) + (3.89% * 8,737,371 people) + (-0.58% * 5,459,642 people) + (2.20% * 2,078,938 people) + (2.14% * 84,339,067 people) + (-0.59% * 43,733,762 people)] / [2,877,797 people + 2,963,243 people + 9,449,323 people + 4,105,267 people + 10,708,981 people + 1,326,535 people + 3,989,167 people + 9,660,351 people + 18,776,707 people + 1,810,770 people + 6,524,195 people + 1,886,198 people + 2,722,289 people + 4,033,963 people + 628,066 people + 2,083,374 people + 37,846,611 people + 19,237,691 people + 145,934,462 people + 8,737,371 people + 5,459,642 people + 2,078,938 people + 84,339,067 people + 43,733,762 people] = [7,079,380.62 %people + 3,733,686.18 %people + 6,709,019.33 %people + 22,455,810.49 %people + 37,802,702.93 %people + 10,585,749.30 %people + 10,571,292.55 %people + 46,756,098.84 %people – 375,534.14 %people + 4,273,417.20 %people + 20,551,214.25 %people + 14,919,826.18 %people + 17,232,089.37 %people + 7,664,529.70 %people + 2,964,471.52 %people + 14,708,620.44 %people + 227,458,132.11 %people + 192,761,663.80 %people – 64,211,163.28 %people + 33,988,373.19 %people – 3,166,592.36 %people + 4,573,663.60 %people + 180,485,603.40 %people – 25,802,919.58 %people] / 430,913,770 people = 773,719,135.64 %people / 430,913,770 people = **1.80%**.[27] There are

[27] R_{40} is given to two decimal places. The sixth column of the World Bank's Global Database of Shared Prosperity and Median Income/Consumption provides the data for the annual average growth rate in per capita real income or real

negative values for $Kazakhstan_{40}$,[28] $Russia_{40}$,[29] $Slovakia_{40}$,[30] and $Ukraine_{40}$.[31] These are small in magnitude.[32] Therefore, the large population of Russia[33] does not unite with the value of $Russia_{40}$ to turn R_{40} negative. The biggest positive contributors to R_{40} are Poland, Romania and Turkey. Poland and Romania each combine a medium-sized population[34] with a high value of $Poland_{40}$ and $Romania_{40}$, respectively.[35] Turkey amalgamates a fairly-large population[36] with a middling value of $Turkey_{40}$.[37] R_T = [(A_T * Pn(A)) + (B_T * Pn(B)) + … + (N_T * Pn(N))] / [Pn(A) + Pn(B) + … Pn(N)] = [($Albania_T$ * Pn(Albania)) + ($Armenia_T$ * Pn(Armenia)) + ($Belarus_T$ * Pn(Belarus)) + ($Croatia_T$ * Pn(Croatia)) + (the Czech $Republic_T$ * Pn(the Czech Republic)) + ($Estonia_T$ * Pn(Estonia)) + ($Georgia_T$ * Pn(Georgia)) + ($Hungary_T$ * Pn(Hungary)) + ($Kazakhstan_T$ * Pn(Kazakhstan)) + ($Kosovo_T$ * Pn(Kosovo)) + ($Kyrgyzstan_T$ * Pn(Kyrgyzstan)) + ($Latvia_T$ * Pn(Latvia)) + ($Lithuania_T$ * Pn(Lithuania)) + ($Moldova_T$ * Pn(Moldova)) + ($Montenegro_T$ * Pn(Montenegro)) + (North $Macedonia_T$ * Pn(North Macedonia)) + ($Poland_T$ * Pn(Poland)) + ($Romania_T$ * Pn(Romania)) + ($Russia_T$ * Pn(Russia)) + ($Serbia_T$ * Pn(Serbia)) + ($Slovakia_T$ * Pn(Slovakia)) + ($Slovenia_T$ * Pn(Slovenia)) + ($Turkey_T$ * Pn(Turkey)) + ($Ukraine_T$ * Pn(Ukraine))] / [Pn(Albania) + Pn(Armenia) + Pn(Belarus) + Pn(Croatia) + Pn(the Czech Republic) + Pn(Estonia) + Pn(Georgia) + Pn(Hungary) + Pn(Kazakhstan) + Pn(Kosovo) + Pn(Kyrgyzstan) + Pn(Latvia) + Pn(Lithuania) + Pn(Moldova) + Pn(Montenegro) + Pn(North Macedonia) + Pn(Poland) + Pn(Romania) + Pn(Russia) + Pn(Serbia) + Pn(Slovakia) + Pn(Slovenia) + Pn(Turkey) + Pn(Ukraine)] = [(0.81% * 2,877,797 people) + (2.40% * 2,963,243 people) + (-0.02% * 9,449,323 people) + (4.28% * 4,105,267 people) + (2.82% * 10,708,981 people) + (7.20% * 1,326,535 people) + (1.42% * 3,989,167 people) + (4.60% * 9,660,351 people) + (-0.56%* 18,776,707 people) + (1.89% * 1,810,770 people) + (2.44% * 6,524,195 people) + (8.23% * 1,886,198 people) +

consumption of the lower 40% of the welfare distribution in each country. Note 26 supplies the population figures for each country.

28 $Kazakhstan_{40}$ = -0.02% (text to note 27).

29 $Russia_{40}$ = -0.44% (text to note 27).

30 $Slovakia_{40}$ = -0.58% (text to note 27).

31 $Ukraine_{40}$ = -0.59% (text to note 27).

32 The modulus of each of these negative numbers is less than 0.6% (notes 28-31).

33 Pn(Russia) = 145,934,462 people (note 26).

34 Pn(Poland) = 37,846,611 people; Pn(Romania) = 19,237,691 people (note 26).

35 $Poland_{40}$ = 6.01%; $Romania_{40}$ = 10.02% (text to note 27).

36 Pn(Turkey) = 84,339,067 (note 26).

37 $Turkey_{40}$ = 2.14% (text to note 27).

(7.43%* 2,722,289 people) + (0.32% * 4,033,963 people) + (1.35% * 628,066 people) + (4.31% * 2,083,374 people) + (4.02% * 37,846,611 people) + (9.96% * 19,237,691 people) + (-2.27% * 145,934,462 people) + (1.48% * 8,737,371 people) + (-1.08% * 5,459,642 people) + (1.52% * 2,078,938 people) + (2.67% * 84,339,067 people) + (0.14% * 43,733,762 people)] / [2,877,797 people + 2,963,243 people + 9,449,323 people + 4,105,267 people + 10,708,981 people + 1,326,535 people + 3,989,167 people + 9,660,351 people + 18,776,707 people + 1,810,770 people + 6,524,195 people + 1,886,198 people + 2,722,289 people + 4,033,963 people + 628,066 people + 2,083,374 people + 37,846,611 people + 19,237,691 people + 145,934,462 people + 8,737,371 people + 5,459,642 people + 2,078,938 people + 84,339,067 people + 43,733,762 people] = [2,331,015.57 %people + 7,111,783.20 %people – 188,986.46 %people + 17,570,542.76 %people + 30,199,326.42 %people + 9,551,052.00 %people + 5,664,617.14 %people + 44,437,614.60 %people – 10,514,955.92 %people + 3,422,355.30 %people + 15,919,035.80 %people + 15,523,409.54 %people + 20,226,607.27 %people + 1,290,868.16 %people + 847,889.10 %people + 8,979,341.94 %people + 152,143,376.22 %people + 191,607,402.36 %people – 331,271,228.74 %people + 12,931,309.08 %people – 5,896,413.36 %people + 3,159,985.76 %people + 225,185,308.89 %people + 6,122,726.68 %people] / 430,913,770 people = 426,353,983.31 %people / 430,913,770 people = **0.99%**.[38] There are negative values for Belarus$_T$,[39] Kazakhstan$_T$,[40] Russia$_T$,[41] and Slovakia$_T$.[42] As Russia$_T$ is more than five times as large as Russia$_{40}$,[43] the combination of the former and the considerable Russian population[44] has a more substantial effect on reducing R_T than the merger between that population and Russia$_{40}$ does on lowering R_{40}.[45] The lower level of Poland$_{40}$ than Poland$_T$ contributes to the smaller value of R_T for

---

[38] R_T is given to two decimal places. The eighth column of the World Bank's Global Database of Shared Prosperity and Median Income/Consumption provides the data for the annual average growth rate in per capita real income or real consumption of the total population of each country. Note 26 supplies the population figures for each country.

[39] Belarus$_T$ = -0.02% (text to note 38).

[40] Kazakhstan$_T$ = -0.56% (text to note 38).

[41] Russia$_T$ = -2.27% (text to note 38).

[42] Slovakia$_T$ = -1.08% (text to note 38).

[43] Note 29 states the value of Russia$_{40}$.

[44] Note 33 specifies the population of Russia (i.e., Pn(Russia)).

[45] For Central Europe, East Europe, the Caucuses and Central Asia, R_{40} = 1.80% (text to note 27).

the region than that of R_{40}.[46] As $R_{40} > R_T$, and as both these statistics are positive, the region as a whole has recently improved in its per capita welfare aggregate – with the poorer 40% of its citizens prospering at a greater rate than the population as a whole. This represents a reduction in inequality, *ceteris paribus*,[47] and shows progress by Central Europe, East Europe, the Caucasus and Central Asia towards the accomplishment of SDG Target 10.1.[48]

East Asia and the Pacific: R_{40} = [(A_{40} * Pn(A)) + (B_{40} * Pn(B)) + … + (N_{40} * Pn(N))] / [Pn(A) + Pn(B) + … Pn(N)] = [($China_{40}$ * Pn(China)) + ($Indonesia_{40}$ * Pn(Indonesia)) + ($Malaysia_{40}$ * Pn(Malaysia)) + ($Mongolia_{40}$ * Pn(Mongolia)) + (the $Philippines_{40}$ * Pn(the Philippines)) + ($Thailand_{40}$ * Pn(Thailand)) + ($Vietnam_{40}$ * Pn(Vietnam))] / [Pn(China) + Pn(Indonesia) + Pn(Malaysia) + Pn(Mongolia) + Pn(the Philippines) + Pn(Thailand) + Pn (Vietnam)] = [(8.38% * 1,439,323,776 people) + (5.06% * 273,523,615 people) + (8.30% * 32,365,999 people) + (0.99% * 3,278,290 people) + (5.12% * 109,581,078 people) + (1.45% * 69,799,978 people) + (4.91% * 97,338,579 people)] / [1,439,323,776 people + 273,523,615 people + 32,365,999 people + 3,278,290 people + 109,581,078 people + 69,799,978 people + 97,338,579 people] = [12,061,533,242.88 %people + 1,384,029,491.90 %people + 268,637,791.70 %people + 3,245,507.10 %people + 561,055,119.36 %people + 101,209,968.10 %people + 477,932,422.89 %people] / 2,025,211,315 people = 14,857,643,543.93 %people / 2,025,211,315 people = **7.34%**.[49] R_T = [(A_T * Pn(A)) + (B_T * Pn(B)) + … + (N_T * Pn(N))] / [Pn(A) + Pn(B) + … Pn(N)] = [($China_T$ * Pn(China)) + ($Indonesia_T$ * Pn(Indonesia)) + ($Malaysia_T$ * Pn(Malaysia)) + ($Mongolia_T$ * Pn(Mongolia)) + (the $Philippines_T$ * Pn(the Philippines)) + ($Thailand_T$ * Pn(Thailand)) + ($Vietnam_T$ * Pn(Vietnam))] / [Pn(China) + Pn(Indonesia) + Pn(Malaysia) + Pn(Mongolia) + Pn(the Philippines) + Pn(Thailand) + Pn (Vietnam)] = [(7.12% * 1,439,323,776 people) + (4.93% * 273,523,615 people) + (5.95% * 32,365,999 people) + (0.66% * 3,278,290 people) + (2.56% * 109,581,078 people) + (1.15% * 69,799,978 people) + (5.01% * 97,338,579 people)] / [1,439,323,776 people + 273,523,615 people + 32,365,999 people + 3,278,290 people + 109,581,078 people + 69,799,978 people + 97,338,579 people] = [10,247,985,285.12 %people + 1,348,471,421.95 %people + 192,577,694.05 %people + 2,163,671.40 %people + 280,527,559.68 %people + 80,269,974.70 %people +

[46] Note 35 states the value of $Poland_{40}$. $Poland_T$ = 4.02% (text to note 38).

[47] Note 338 of Chapter Two defines '*ceteris paribus*'.

[48] The text to note 10 states SDG Target 10.1.

[49] Note 27.

487,666,280.79 %people] / 2,025,211,315 people = 12,639,661,887.69 %people / 2,025,211,315 people = **6.24%**.[50] As $R_{40} > R_T$,[51] and as both these figures are positive, the region as a whole has recently improved in its per capita welfare aggregate with the lower 40% of its inhabitants prospering more than the population as a whole. This represents a reduction in inequality, *ceteris paribus*,[52] and shows progress by East Asia and the Pacific towards the attainment of SDG Target 10.1.[53] The large population of China[54] combines with $China_{40}$ and $China_T$,[55] respectively, to provide the main influence on R_{40} and R_T for this region. No state from Oceania is represented among the seven countries whose data are included in the World Bank's Database of Shared Prosperity for East Asia and the Pacific.[56] The values of R_{40} and R_T for this region[57] are both higher than the values of R_{40} and R_T for Central Europe, East Europe, the Caucasus and Central Asia,[58] showing a greater increase in per capita welfare in the former than in the latter over the period.[59]

High-income countries: R_{40} = [(A_{40} * Pn(A)) + (B_{40} * Pn(B)) + … + (N_{40} * Pn(N))] / [Pn(A) + Pn(B) + … Pn(N)] = [($Austria_{40}$ * Pn(Austria)) + ($Belgium_{40}$ * Pn(Belgium)) + ($Cyprus_{40}$ * Pn(Cyprus)) + ($Denmark_{40}$ * Pn(Denmark)) + ($Finland_{40}$ * Pn(Finland)) + ($France_{40}$ * Pn(France)) + ($Germany_{40}$ * Pn(Germany)) + ($Greece_{40}$ * Pn(Greece)) + ($Iceland_{40}$ * Pn(Iceland)) + ($Ireland_{40}$ * Pn(Ireland)) + ($Israel_{40}$ * Pn(Israel)) + ($Italy_{40}$ * Pn(Italy)) + ($Luxembourg_{40}$ * Pn(Luxembourg)) + ($Malta_{40}$ * Pn(Malta)) + (the $Netherlands_{40}$ * Pn(the Netherlands)) + ($Norway_{40}$ * Pn(Norway)) + ($Portugal_{40}$ * Pn(Portugal)) + ($Spain_{40}$ * Pn(Spain)) + ($Sweden_{40}$ * Pn(Sweden)) + ($Switzerland_{40}$ * Pn(Switzerland)) + (the UK_{40} * Pn(the UK)) + (the USA_{40} * Pn(the USA))] / [Pn(Austria) + Pn(Belgium) +

[50] Note 38.

[51] For East Asia and the Pacific, R_{40} = 7.34% (text to note 49).

[52] Note 338 of Chapter Two defines '*ceteris paribus*'.

[53] The text to note 10 specifies SDG Target 10.1.

[54] Pn(China) = 1,439,323,776 people (note 26).

[55] $China_{40}$ = 8.38% (text to note 49). $China_T$ = 7.12% (text to note 50).

[56] World Bank, Global Database of Shared Prosperity and Median Income/Consumption, cols 1 and 3.

[57] For East Asia and the Pacific, R_{40} = 7.34% (text to note 49), and R_T = 6.24% (text to note 50).

[58] For Central Europe, East Europe, the Caucuses and Central Asia, R_{40} = 1.80% (text to note 27), and R_T = 0.99% (text to note 38).

[59] Note 23 states the initial and final survey years, i.e., T_0 and T_1 respectively, for each country whose data appear in the current version of the World Bank's Global Database of Shared Prosperity. The period, P, over which the annual growth of each state's welfare aggregate is being measured, is given by $T_0 \leq P \leq T_1$.

Pn(Cyprus) + Pn(Denmark) + Pn(Finland) + Pn(France) + Pn(Germany) + Pn(Greece) + Pn(Iceland) + Pn(Ireland) + Pn(Israel) + Pn(Italy) + Pn(Luxembourg) + Pn(Malta) + Pn(the Netherlands) + Pn(Norway) + Pn(Portugal) + Pn(Spain) + Pn(Sweden) + Pn(Switzerland) + Pn(the UK) + Pn (the USA)] = [(1.44% * 9,006,398 people) + (0.43% * 11,589,623 people) + (0.29% * 1,207,359 people) + (1.34% * 5,792,202 people) + (0.58% * 5,540,720 people) + (0.61% * 65,273,511 people) + (-0.20% * 83,783,942 people) + (1.80% * 10,423,054 people) + (3.15% * 341,243 people) + (3.43% * 4,937,786 people) + (4.17% * 8,655,535 people) + (0.48% * 60,461,826 people) + (2.96% * 625,978 people) + (3.80% * 441,543 people) + (1.53% * 17,134,872 people) + (0.44% * 5,421,241 people) + (3.32% * 10,196,709 people) + (1.75% * 46,754,778 people) + (1.39% * 10,099,265 people) + (-0.26% * 8,654,622 people) + (1.76% * 67,886,011 people) + (1.31% * 331,002,651 people)] / [9,006,398 people + 11,589,623 people + 1,207,359 people + 5,792,202 people + 5,540,720 people + 65,273,511 people + 83,783,942 people + 10,423,054 people + 341,243 people + 4,937,786 people + 8,655,535 people + 60,461,826 people + 625,978 people + 441,543 people + 17,134,872 people + 5,421,241 people + 10,196,709 people + 46,754,778 people + 10,099,265 people + 8,654,622 people + 67,886,011 people + 331,002,651 people] = [12,969,213.12 %people + 4,983,537.89 %people + 350,134.11 %people + 7,761,550.68 %people + 3,213,617.60 %people + 39,816,841.71 %people – 16,576,788.40 %people + 18,761,497.20 %people + 1,074,915.45 %people + 16,936,605.98 %people + 36,093,580.95 %people + 29,021,676.48 %people + 1,852,894.88 %people + 1,677,863.40 %people + 26,216,354.16 %people + 2,385,346.04 %people + 33,853,073.88 %people + 81,820,861.50 %people + 14,037,978.35 %people – 2,250,201.72 %people + 119,479,379.36 %people + 433,613,472.81 %people] / 765,230,869 people = 866,913,405.43 %people / 765,230,869 people = **1.13%**.[60] R_T = [(A_T * Pn(A)) + (B_T * Pn(B)) + … + (N_T * Pn(N))] / [Pn(A) + Pn(B) + … Pn(N)] = [(Austria$_T$ * Pn(Austria)) + (Belgium$_T$ * Pn(Belgium)) + (Cyprus$_T$ * Pn(Cyprus)) + (Denmark$_T$ * Pn(Denmark)) + (Finland$_T$ * Pn(Finland)) + (France$_T$ * Pn(France)) + (Germany$_T$ * Pn(Germany)) + (Greece$_T$ * Pn(Greece)) + (Iceland$_T$ * Pn(Iceland)) + (Ireland$_T$ * Pn(Ireland)) + (Israel$_T$ * Pn(Israel)) + (Italy$_T$ * Pn(Italy)) + (Luxembourg$_T$ * Pn(Luxembourg)) + (Malta$_T$ * Pn(Malta)) + (the Netherlands$_T$ * Pn(the Netherlands)) + (Norway$_T$ * Pn(Norway)) + (Portugal$_T$ * Pn(Portugal)) + (Spain$_T$ * Pn(Spain)) + (Sweden$_T$ * Pn(Sweden)) + (Switzerland$_T$ * Pn(Switzerland)) + (the UK$_T$ * Pn(the

[60] Note 27.

UK)) + (the USA$_T$ * Pn(the USA))] / [Pn(Austria) + Pn(Belgium) + Pn(Cyprus) + Pn(Denmark) + Pn(Finland) + Pn(France) + Pn(Germany) + Pn(Greece) + Pn(Iceland) + Pn(Ireland) + Pn(Israel) + Pn(Italy) + Pn(Luxembourg) + Pn(Malta) + Pn(the Netherlands) + Pn(Norway) + Pn(Portugal) + Pn(Spain) + Pn(Sweden) + Pn(Switzerland) + Pn(the UK) + Pn (the USA)] = [(1.20% * 9,006,398 people) + (0.42% * 11,589,623 people) + (-0.78% * 1,207,359 people) + (1.68% * 5,792,202 people) + (0.65% * 5,540,720 people) + (0.19% * 65,273,511 people) + (0.80% * 83,783,942 people) + (0.11% * 10,423,054 people) + (3.31% * 341,243 people) + (3.05% * 4,937,786 people) + (2.56% * 8,655,535 people) + (1.04% * 60,461,826 people) + (3.66% * 625,978 people) + (3.74% * 441,543 people) + (1.89% * 17,134,872 people) + (1.02% * 5,421,241 people) + (2.00% * 10,196,709 people) + (1.12% * 46,754,778 people) + (1.98% * 10,099,265 people) + (0.34% * 8,654,622 people) + (2.42% * 67,886,011 people) + (1.66% * 331,002,651 people)] / [9,006,398 people + 11,589,623 people + 1,207,359 people + 5,792,202 people + 5,540,720 people + 65,273,511 people + 83,783,942 people + 10,423,054 people + 341,243 people + 4,937,786 people + 8,655,535 people + 60,461,826 people + 625,978 people + 441,543 people + 17,134,872 people + 5,421,241 people + 10,196,709 people + 46,754,778 people + 10,099,265 people + 8,654,622 people + 67,886,011 people + 331,002,651 people] = [10,807,677.60 %people + 4,867,641.66 %people – 941,740.02 %people + 9,730,899.36 %people + 3,601,468.00 %people + 12,401,967.09 %people + 67,027,153.60 %people + 1,146,535.94 %people + 1,129,514.33 %people + 15,060,247.30 %people + 22,158,169.60 %people + 62,880,299.04 %people + 2,291,079.48 %people + 1,651,370.82 %people + 32,384,908.08 %people + 5,529,665.82 %people + 20,393,418.00 %people + 52,365,351.36 %people + 19,996,544.70 %people + 2,942,571.48 %people + 164,284,146.62 %people + 549,464,400.66 %people] / 765,230,869 people = 1,061,173,290.52 %people / 765,230,869 people = **1.39%**.[61] In the high-income countries as a group, $R_T > R_{40}$,[62] with both these numbers being positive. Thus, over the period between the two household surveys in these states,[63] the latter have

[61] Note 38.

[62] In the high-income countries as a group, R_{40} = 1.13% (text to note 60).

[63] Note 23 specifies the initial and final survey years, i.e., T_0 and T_1 respectively, for each country whose data appear in the present version of the World Bank's Global Database of Shared Prosperity. The period, P, over which the annual growth of each state's welfare aggregate is being measured, is given by $T_0 \leq P \leq T_1$.

collectively improved their income per capita,[64] with the poorer 40 % of their inhabitants prospering less than the population as a whole. This represents an increase in inequality, *ceteris paribus*,[65] and is contrary to the achievement of SDG Target 10.1.[66] This rise in inequality is mainly caused by the greater contribution made to R_T than to R_{40} by the USA,[67] Germany[68], the UK[69] and Italy[70] – in that order.

Latin America and the Caribbean: R_{40} = [(A_{40} * Pn(A)) + (B_{40} * Pn(B)) + … + (N_{40} * Pn(N))] / [Pn(A) + Pn(B) + … Pn(N)] = [(Argentina-urban$_{40}$ * Pn(Argentina-urban))[71] + (Bolivia$_{40}$ * Pn(Bolivia)) + (Brazil$_{40}$ * Pn(Brazil)) + (Chile$_{40}$ * Pn(Chile)) + (Colombia$_{40}$ * Pn(Colombia)) + (Costa Rica$_{40}$ * Pn(Costa Rica)) + (the Dominican Republic$_{40}$ * Pn(the Dominican Republic)) + (Ecuador$_{40}$ * Pn(Ecuador)) + (El Salvador$_{40}$ * Pn (El Salvador))+ (Honduras$_{40}$ * Pn(Honduras)) + (Panama$_{40}$ * Pn(Panama)) + (Paraguay$_{40}$ * Pn(Paraguay)) + (Peru$_{40}$ * Pn(Peru)) + (Uruguay$_{40}$ * Pn(Uruguay))] / [Pn(Argentina-urban) + Pn(Bolivia) + Pn(Brazil) + Pn(Chile) + Pn(Colombia) + Pn(Costa Rica) + Pn (the Dominican Republic) + Pn(Ecuador) + Pn(El Salvador) + Pn(Honduras) + Pn(Panama) + Pn(Paraguay) + Pn(Peru) + Pn(Uruguay)] = [(-1.62% * 41,919,857 people) + (1.78% * 11,673,021 people) + (-0.43% * 212,559,417 people) + (4.92% * 19,116,201 people) + (2.34% * 50,882,891 people) + (1.40% * 5,094,118 people) + (5.19% * 10,847,910 people) + (1.25% * 17,643,054 people) + (3.95% * 6,486,205 people) +

---

64 Each of the 22 states in the group titled 'High-income countries' uses income per capita to measure its welfare aggregate (note 14).

65 Note 338 of Chapter Two defines '*ceteris paribus*'.

66 The text to note 10 states SDG Target 10.1.

67 The USA$_{40}$ = 1.31% (text to note 60). The USA$_T$ = 1.66% (text to note 61). Pn(the USA) = 331,002,651 people (note 26).

68 Germany$_{40}$ = -0.20% (text to note 60). Germany$_T$ = 0.80% (text to note 61). Pn(Germany) = 83,783,942 people (note 26).

69 The UK$_{40}$ = 1.76% (text to note 60). The UK$_T$ = 2.42% (text to note 61). Pn(the UK) = 67,886,011 people (note 26).

70 Italy$_{40}$ = 0.48% (text to note 60). Italy$_T$ = 1.04% (text to note 61). Pn(Italy) = 60,461,826 people (note 26).

71 The data for Argentina in the World Bank's Global Database of Shared Prosperity cover only that country's urban areas (World Bank, Global Database of Shared Prosperity and Median Income/Consumption, col 3 and fn e; note 14). Point (ii) in note 26 specifies the urban population of Argentina in 2020, to which the expression 'Pn(Argentina-urban)' refers. The phrase 'Argentin-urban$_{40}$' represents the welfare aggregate – which is income per capita (note 14 and accompanying text) – of the poorer 40% of the urban population of Argentina (note 15).

(1.30% * 9,904,607 people) + (5.29% * 4,314,767 people) + (1.57% * 7,132,538 people) + (2.45% * 32,971,854 people) + (2.00% * 3,473,730 people)] / [41,919,857 people + 11,673,021 people + 212,559,417 people + 19,116,201 people + 50,882,891 people + 5,094,118 people + 10,847,910 people + 17,643,054 people + 6,486,205 people + 9,904,607 people + 4,314,767 people + 7,132,538 people + 32,971,854 people + 3,473,730 people] = [-67,910,168.34 %people + 20,777,977.38 %people – 91,400,549.31 %people + 94,051,708.92 %people + 119,065,964.94 %people + 7,131,765.20 %people + 56,300,652.90 %people + 22,053,817.50 %people + 25,620,509.75 %people + 12,875,989.10 %people + 22,825,117.43 %people + 11,198,084.66 %people + 80,781,042.30 %people + 6,947,460.00 %people] / 434,020,170 people = 320,319,372.43 %people / 434,020,170 people = **0.74%**.[72] R_T = [(A_T * Pn(A)) + (B_T * Pn(B)) + … + (N_T * Pn(N))] / [Pn(A) + Pn(B) + … Pn(N)] = [(Argentina-urban$_T$ * Pn(Argentina-urban))[73] + (Bolivia$_T$ * Pn(Bolivia)) + (Brazil$_T$ * Pn(Brazil)) + (Chile$_T$ * Pn(Chile)) + (Colombia$_T$ * Pn(Colombia)) + (Costa Rica$_T$ * Pn(Costa Rica)) + (the Dominican Republic$_T$ * Pn(the Dominican Republic)) + (Ecuador$_T$ * Pn(Ecuador)) + (El Salvador$_T$ * Pn(El Salvador))+ (Honduras$_T$ * Pn(Honduras)) + (Panama$_T$ * Pn(Panama)) + (Paraguay$_T$ * Pn(Paraguay)) + (Peru$_T$ * Pn(Peru)) + (Uruguay$_T$ * Pn(Uruguay))] / Pn(Argentina-urban) + Pn(Bolivia) + Pn(Brazil) + Pn(Chile) + Pn(Colombia) + Pn(Costa Rica) + Pn (the Dominican Republic) + Pn(Ecuador) + Pn(El Salvador) + Pn(Honduras) + Pn(Panama) + Pn(Paraguay) + Pn(Peru) + Pn(Uruguay) = [(-1.55% * 41,919,857 people) + (-1.65% * 11,673,021 people) + (0.66% * 212,559,417 people) + (3.83% * 19,116,201 people) + (0.41% * 50,882,891 people) + (0.60% * 5,094,118 people) + (4.25% * 10,847,910 people) + (0.47% * 17,643,054 people) + (1.82% * 6,486,205 people) + (1.72% * 9,904,607 people) + (3.87% * 4,314,767 people) + (0.34% * 7,132,538 people) + (1.49% * 32,971,854 people) + (1.43% * 3,473,730 people)] / [41,919,857 people + 11,673,021 people + 212,559,417 people + 19,116,201 people + 50,882,891 people + 5,094,118 people + 10,847,910 people + 17,643,054 people + 6,486,205 people + 9,904,607 people + 4,314,767 people + 7,132,538 people + 32,971,854 people + 3,473,730 people] = [-64,975,778.35 %people – 19,260,484.65 %people +

[72] Note 27.

[73] The data for Argentina in the World Bank's Global Database of Shared Prosperity cover solely that state's urban territories; the term 'Pn(Argentina-urban)' refers to the urban population of Argentina in 2020 (note 71). The phrase 'Argentina-urban$_T$' represents the welfare aggregate – which is income per capita (note 14 and accompanying text) – of Argentina's urban population (note 15).

140,289,215.22 %people + 73,215,049.83 %people + 20,861,985.31 %people + 3,056,470.80 %people + 46,103,617.50 %people + 8,292,235.38 %people + 11,804,893.10 %people + 17,035,924.04 %people + 16,698,148.29 %people + 2,425,062.92 %people + 49,128,062.46 %people + 4,967,433.90 %people] / 434,020,170 people = 309,641,835.75 %people / 434,020,170 people = **0.71%**.[74] Whilst $R_{40} > R_T$,[75] $0.70\% < R_T$, and $R_{40} < 0.75$, i.e., both R_{40} and R_T are positive at a similar, modest level. These figures represent a small decrease in inequality, *ceteris paribus*,[76] and are consistent with the accomplishment of SDG Target 10.1.[77] Although populous Brazil[78] contributes negatively to R_{40} but positively to R_T, this effect is counterbalanced by the greater beneficial impact of the larger rise in per capita welfare for the poorer 40% of the citizens of Columbia[79] and Peru[80] on R_{40} than the lesser favourable impact of the smaller increase in per capita welfare for the total population of these two countries on R_T.[81]

Middle East and North Africa: R_{40} = [(A_{40} * Pn(A)) + (B_{40} * Pn(B)) + … + (N_{40} * Pn(N))] / [Pn(A) + Pn(B) + … Pn(N)] = [($Egypt_{40}$ * Pn(Egypt)) + ($Iran_{40}$ * Pn(Iran)) + ($Tunisia_{40}$ * Pn(Tunisia)) + (West Bank and $Gaza_{40}$ * Pn(West Bank and Gaza))] / [Pn(Egypt) + Pn(Iran) + Pn(Tunisia) + Pn(West Bank and Gaza)] = [(-2.51% * 102,334,404 people) + (-0.13% * 83,992,949 people) + (5.36% * 11,818,619 people) + (-0.89% * 5,101,414 people)] / [102,334,404 people + 83,992,949 people + 11,818,619 people + 5,101,414 people] = [-256,859,354.04 %people – 10,919,083.37 %people + 63,347,797.84 %people – 4,540,258.46 %people] / 203,247,386 people = -208,970,898.03 %people / 203,247,386 people = **-1.03%**.[82] R_T = [(A_T * Pn(A)) + (B_T * Pn(B)) + … + (N_T * Pn(N))] / [Pn(A) + Pn(B) + … Pn(N)] = [($Egypt_T$ * Pn(Egypt)) + ($Iran_T$ * Pn(Iran)) + ($Tunisia_T$ * Pn(Tunisia)) + (West Bank and $Gaza_T$ * Pn(West

[74] Note 38.

[75] For Latin America and the Caribbean, R_{40} = 0.74% (text to note 72).

[76] Note 338 of Chapter Two defines '*ceteris paribus*'.

[77] The text to note 10 specifies SDG Target 10.1.

[78] $Brazil_{40}$ = -0.43% (text to note 72). $Brazil_T$ = 0.66% (text to note 74). Pn(Brazil) = 212,559,417 people (note 26).

[79] $Colombia_{40}$ = 2.34% (text to note 72). $Colombia_T$ = 0.41% (text to note 74). Pn(Colombia) = 50,882,891 people (note 26).

[80] $Peru_{40}$ = 2.45% (text to note 72). $Peru_T$ = 1.49% (text to note 74). Pn(Peru) = 32,971,854 people (note 26).

[81] Each of the 14 states in Latin America and the Caribbean that provides data to the World Bank's Global Database of Shared Prosperity, utilizes income per capita to measure its welfare aggregate (notes 14 and 15).

[82] Note 27.

Bank and Gaza))] / [Pn(Egypt) + Pn(Iran) + Pn(Tunisia) + Pn(West Bank and Gaza)] = [(-1.14% * 102,334,404 people) + (1.89% * 83,992,949 people) + (3.38% * 11,818,619 people) + (-0.55% * 5,101,414 people)] / [102,334,404 people + 83,992,949 people + 11,818,619 people + 5,101,414 people] = [-116,661,220.56 %people + 158,746,673.61 %people + 39,946,932.22 %people – 2,805,777.70 %people] / 203,247,386 people = 79,226,607.57 %people / 203,247,386 people = **0.39%**.[83] In the Middle East and North Africa – based on a limited sample of four countries – R_T is small and positive, and R_{40} is negative.[84] Consumption per capita[85] has risen slightly over the period,[86] but declined during this time for the poorer 40% of the population. This progression represents an increase in inequality, *ceteris paribus*,[87] and is at variance with the attainment of SDG Target 10.1.[88] The rise in inequality is almost entirely[89] due to the combination of negative growth rates in consumption per capita in, and substantial populations of, Egypt[90] and Iran[91] – especially in relation to R_{40}.

South Asia: R_{40} = [(A_{40} * Pn(A)) + (B_{40} * Pn(B)) + … + (N_{40} * Pn(N))] / [Pn(A) + Pn(B) + … Pn(N)] = [($Bangladesh_{40}$ * Pn(Bangladesh) + ($Bhutan_{40}$ * Pn(Bhutan)) + ($Pakistan_{40}$ * Pn(Pakistan)) + (Sri $Lanka_{40}$ * Pn(Sri Lanka))] / [Pn(Bangladesh) + Pn(Bhutan) + Pn(Pakistan) + Pn(Sri Lanka)] = [(1.35% * 164,689,383 people) + (1.63% * 771,608 people) +

[83] Note 38.

[84] For the Middle East and North Africa, R_{40} = -1.03% (text to note 82).

[85] In Egypt, Iran, Tunisia, and West Bank and Gaza, the growth rate in the welfare aggregate is measured by consumption per capita (note 14 and accompanying text).

[86] Note 23 specifies the initial and final survey years, i.e., T_0 and T_1 respectively, for each country whose data appear in the current version of the World Bank's Global Database of Shared Prosperity. The period, P, over which the annual growth of each state's welfare aggregate is being measured, is given by $T_0 \leq P \leq T_1$.

[87] Note 338 of Chapter Two defines '*ceteris paribus*'.

[88] The text to note 10 states SDG Target 10.1.

[89] The less-negative consumption per capita of the total population in West Bank and Gaza over the period (note 86) than that of the consumption per capita in the poorer 40% of citizens in West Bank and Gaza in this time, makes a small contribution to the rise in inequality. West Bank and $Gaza_{40}$ = -0.89% (text to note 82). West Bank and $Gaza_T$ = -0.55% (text to note 83). Pn(West Bank and Gaza) = 5,101,414 people (note 26 – especially point (iii) in that note).

[90] $Egypt_{40}$ = -2.51% (text to note 82). $Egypt_T$ = -1.14% (text to note 83). Pn(Egypt) = 102,334,404 people (note 26).

[91] $Iran_{40}$ = -0.13% (text to note 82). $Iran_T$ = 1.89% (text to note 83). Pn(Iran) = 83,992,949 people (note 26).

(2.72% * 220,892,340 people) + (4.24% * 21,413,249 people)] / [164,689,383 people + 771,608 people + 220,892,340 people + 21,413,249 people] = [222,330,667.05 %people + 1,257,721.04 %people + 600,827,164.80 %people + 90,792,175.76 %people] / 407,766,580 people = 915,207,728.65 %people / 407,766,580 people = **2.24%**.[92] R_T = [(A_T * Pn(A)) + (B_T * Pn(B)) + … + (N_T * Pn(N))] / [Pn(A) + Pn(B) + … Pn(N)] = [($Bangladesh_T$ * Pn(Bangladesh)) + ($Bhutan_T$ * Pn(Bhutan)) + ($Pakistan_T$ * Pn(Pakistan)) + (Sri $Lanka_T$ * Pn(Sri Lanka))] / [Pn(Bangladesh) + Pn(Bhutan) + Pn(Pakistan) + Pn(Sri Lanka)] = [(1.54% * 164,689,383 people) + (1.67% * 771,608 people) + (4.25% * 220,892,340 people) + (4.72% * 21,413,249 people)] / [164,689,383 people + 771,608 people + 220,892,340 people + 21,413,249 people] = [253,621,649.82 %people + 1,288,585.36 %people + 938,792,445.00 %people + 101,070,535.28 %people] / 407,766,580 people = 1,294,773,215.46 %people / 407,766,580 people = **3.18%**.[93] In South Asia, both R_{40} and R_T are positive[94] – which indicates in increase in consumption per capita[95] over the period.[96] $R_{40} < R_T$. This represents a rise in inequality in the region,[97]

---

[92] Note 27. If $India_{40}$ had been included in the World Bank's Global Database of Shared Prosperity, then R_{40} for South Asia would possibly be materially different to the value shown – as India is by far the most populous country in South Asia (note 204 of Chapter Two).

[93] Note 38. If $India_T$ had been included in the World Bank's Global Database of Shared Prosperity, then R_T for South Asia would possibly be considerably different to the value shown – as India is by far the most populous country in South Asia (note 204 of Chapter Two).

[94] For South Asia, R_{40} = 2.24 (text to note 92).

[95] In Bangladesh, Bhutan, Pakistan, and Sri Lanka, the growth rate in the welfare aggregate is measured by consumption per capita (note 14 and accompanying text).

[96] Note 23 specifies the initial and final survey years, i.e., T_0 and T_1 respectively, for each country whose data appear in the present version of the World Bank's Global Database of Shared Prosperity. The period, P, over which the annual growth of each state's welfare aggregate is being measured, is given by $T_0 \leq P \leq T_1$.

[97] The N_{40} value of all N countries in South Asia for which data are available (i.e., N = 4 countries) is lower than the N_T value (text to note 26), i.e., $Bangladesh_{40}$ (1.35%) < $Bangladesh_T$ (1.54%), $Bhutan_{40}$ (1.63%) < $Bhutan_T$ (1.67%), $Pakistan_{40}$ (2.72%) < $Pakistan_T$ (4.25%), and Sri $Lanka_{40}$ (4.24%) < Sri $Lanka_T$ (4.72%) (text to notes 92 and 93). These percentages, together with the relative population size of Bangladesh, Bhutan, Pakistan and Sri Lanka (note 26) – Pn(Pakistan) > Pn (Bangladesh) > Pn(Sri Lanka) > Pn(Bhutan), show that the data concerning Pakistan contribute the largest input to the rise in inequality in the region – as represented by these four countries.

ceteris paribus,[98] and is in opposition to the achievement of SDG Target 10.1.[99]

Sub-Saharan Africa: R_{40} = [(A_{40} * Pn(A)) + (B_{40} * Pn(B)) + … + (N_{40} * Pn(N))] / [Pn(A) + Pn(B) + … Pn(N)] = [($Benin_{40}$ * Pn(Benin)) + ($Botswana_{40}$ * Pn(Botswana)) + ($Eswatini_{40}$ * Pn(Eswatini))+ ($Ethiopia_{40}$ * Pn(Ethiopia)) + ($Ghana_{40}$ * Pn(Ghana)) + ($Malawi_{40}$ * Pn(Malawi)) + ($Mauritius_{40}$ * Pn(Mauritius)) + ($Namibia_{40}$ * Pn(Namibia)) + ($Rwanda_{40}$ * Pn(Rwanda)) + ($Sierra\ Leone_{40}$ * Pn(Sierra Leone)) + ($Tanzania_{40}$ * Pn(Tanzania)) + ($Togo_{40}$ * Pn(Togo)) + ($Uganda_{40}$ * Pn(Uganda)) + ($Zambia_{40}$ * Pn(Zambia)) + ($Zimbabwe_{40}$ * Pn(Zimbabwe))] / [Pn(Benin) + Pn(Botswana) + Pn(Eswatini) + Pn(Ethiopia) + Pn(Ghana) + Pn(Malawi) + Pn(Mauritius) + Pn (Namibia) + Pn(Rwanda) + Pn(Sierra Leone) + Pn(Tanzania) + Pn(Togo) + Pn(Uganda) + Pn(Zambia) + Pn(Zimbabwe)] = [(-5.20% * 12,123,200 people) + (0.42% * 2,351,627 people) + (4.67% * 1,160,164 people) + (0.35% * 114,963,588 people) + (-0.20% * 31,072,940 people) + (3.05% * 19,129,952 people) + (2.71% * 1,271,768 people) + (5.73% * 2,540,905 people) + (0.31% * 12,952,218 people) + (2.67% * 7,976,983 people) + (-0.15% * 59,734,218 people) + (2.55% * 8,278,724 people) + (-2.20% * 45,741,007 people) + (-0.59% * 18,383,955 people) + (-3.75% * 14,862,924 people)] / [12,123,200 people + 2,351,627 people + 1,160,164 people + 114,963,588 people + 31,072,940 people + 19,129,952 people + 1,271,768 people + 2,540,905 people + 12,952,218 people + 7,976,983 people + 59,734,218 people + 8,278,724 people + 45,741,007 people + 18,383,955 people + 14,862,924 people] = [-63,040,640.00 %people + 987,683.34 %people + 5,417,965.88 %people + 40,237,255.80 %people – 6,214,588.00 %people + 58,346,353.60 %people + 3,446,491.28 %people + 14,559,385.65 %people + 4,015,187.58 %people + 21,298,544.61 %people – 8,960,132.70 %people + 21,110,746.20 %people – 100,630,215.40 %people – 10,846,533.45 %people – 55,735,965.00 %people] / 352,544,173 people = -76,008,460.61 %people / 352,544,173 people = **-0.22%**.[100] R_T = [(A_T * Pn(A)) + (B_T * Pn(B)) + … + (N_T * Pn(N))] / [Pn(A) + Pn(B) + … Pn(N)] = [($Benin_T$ * Pn(Benin)) + ($Botswana_T$ * Pn(Botswana)) + ($Eswatini_T$ * Pn(Eswatini)) + ($Ethiopia_T$ * Pn(Ethiopia)) + ($Ghana_T$ * Pn(Ghana)) + ($Malawi_T$ * Pn(Malawi)) + ($Mauritius_T$ * Pn(Mauritius)) + ($Namibia_T$ * Pn(Namibia)) + ($Rwanda_T$ * Pn(Rwanda)) + ($Sierra\ Leone_T$ * Pn(Sierra Leone)) + ($Tanzania_T$ * Pn(Tanzania)) + ($Togo_T$ * Pn(Togo)) + ($Uganda_T$ * Pn(Uganda)) + ($Zambia_T$ * Pn(Zambia))

[98] Note 338 of Chapter Two defines '*ceteris paribus*'.

[99] The text to note 10 states SDG Target 10.1.

[100] Note 27.

+ (Zimbabwe$_T$ * Pn(Zimbabwe))] / Pn(Benin) + Pn(Botswana) + Pn(Eswatini) + Pn(Ethiopia) + Pn(Ghana) + Pn(Malawi) + Pn(Mauritius) + Pn (Namibia) + Pn(Rwanda) + Pn(Sierra Leone) + Pn(Tanzania) + Pn(Togo) + Pn(Uganda) + Pn(Zambia) + Pn(Zimbabwe) = [(0.06% * 12,123,200 people) + (-3.30% * 2,351,627 people) + (6.14% * 1,160,164 people) + (1.56% * 114,963,588 people) + (1.27% * 31,072,940 people) + (1.57% * 19,129,952 people) + (2.02% * 1,271,768 people) + (6.64% * 2,540,905 people) + (-0.17% * 12,952,218 people) + (2.86% * 7,976,983 people) + (0.92% * 59,734,218 people) + (0.62% * 8,278,724 people) + (-1.01% * 45,741,007 people) + (2.93% * 18,383,955 people) + (-3.50% * 14,862,924 people)] / [12,123,200 people + 2,351,627 people + 1,160,164 people + 114,963,588 people + 31,072,940 people + 19,129,952 people + 1,271,768 people + 2,540,905 people + 12,952,218 people + 7,976,983 people + 59,734,218 people + 8,278,724 people + 45,741,007 people + 18,383,955 people + 14,862,924 people] = [727,392.00 %people – 7,760,369.10 %people + 7,123,406.96 %people + 179,343,197.28 %people + 39,462,633.80 %people + 30,034,024.64 %people + 2,568,971.36 %people + 16,871,609.20 %people – 2,201,877.06 %people + 22,814,171.38 %people + 54,955,480.56 %people + 5,132,808.88 %people – 46,198,417.07 %people + 53,864,988.15 %people – 52,020,234 %people] / 352,544,173 people = 304,717,786.98 %people / 352,544,173 people = **0.87%**.[101] In Sub-Saharan Africa, R_T is positive and R_{40} is negative.[102] These changes in consumption per capita[103] over the period[104] represent an increase in inequality in this region, *ceteris paribus*,[105] and are contrary to the accomplishment of SDG Target 10.1.[106]

Global trend in growth of the welfare aggregate: From the regional figures, R_{40} and R_T, which have been calculated for each area, a global statistic is computed for the poorer 40% of the welfare distribution, G_{40}, and another for the total population G_T. G_{40} = [(R^1_{40} * Pn(R^1)) + (R^2_{40} *

[101] Note 38.

[102] For Sub-Saharan Africa, R_{40} = -0.22 (text to note 100).

[103] In Benin, Botswana, Eswatini, Ethiopia, Ghana, Malawi, Mauritius, Namibia, Rwanda, Sierra Leone, Tanzania, Togo, Uganda, Zambia, and Zimbabwe, the growth rate in the welfare aggregate is measured by consumption per capita (note 14 and accompanying text).

[104] Note 23 states the initial and final survey years, i.e., T_0 and T_1 respectively, for each country whose data appear in the current version of the World Bank's Global Database of Shared Prosperity. The period, P, over which the annual growth of each state's welfare aggregate is being measured, is given by $T_0 \leq P \leq T_1$.

[105] Note 338 of Chapter Two defines '*ceteris paribus*'.

[106] The text to note 10 specifies SDG Target 10.1.

$Pn(R^2)) + \dots + (R^N_{40} * Pn(R^N))] / [Pn(R^1) + Pn(R^2) + \dots Pn(R^N)]$, and $G_T = [(R^1_T * Pn(R^1)) + (R^2_T * Pn(R^2)) + \dots + (R^N_T * Pn(R^N))] / [Pn(R^1) + Pn(R^2) + \dots Pn(R^N)]$, where R^1_{40}, R^2_{40} … R^N_{40} is the annual average growth rate in per capita real income or real consumption of the lower 40% of the welfare distribution between T_0 and T_1 for region R^1, R^2 … R^N, N is the number of regions, R^1_T, R^2_T … R^N_T is the annual average growth rate in per capita real income or real consumption of the total population between T_0 and T_1 for region R^1, R^2 … R^N, and $Pn(R^1)$, $Pn(R^2)$ … $Pn(R^N)$ is the population of region R^1, R^2 … R^N. T_0 and T_1 are as defined previously,[107] taking a value for each region that is a composite of those of its constituent countries[108] weighted according to their population.[109] Thus, $G_{40} = [(R^1_{40} * Pn(R^1)) + (R^2_{40} * Pn(R^2)) + \dots + (R^N_{40} * Pn(R^N))] / [Pn(R^1) + Pn(R^2) + \dots Pn(R^N)]$ = [(R_{40}(Central Asia, East Europe, the Caucuses and Central Asia)[110] * Pn(Central Asia, East Europe, the Caucuses and Central Asia)[111]) + (R_{40}(East Asia and the Pacific)[112] * Pn(East Asia and the Pacific)[113]) + (R_{40}(High-income countries)[114] * Pn(High-income countries)[115]) + (R_{40}(Latin America and the Caribbean)[116] * Pn(Latin America and the Caribbean)[117]) + (R_{40}(Middle East and North Africa)[118] * Pn(Middle East and North Africa)[119]) + (R_{40}(South Asia)[120] + Pn(South Asia)[121]) + (R_{40}(Sub-Saharan Africa)[122] + Pn(Sub-Saharan Africa)[123])] /

---

107 Text to notes 19-23.

108 Note 23 lists the values of T_0 and T_1 for each country whose data are included in the current version of the World Bank's Global Database of Shared Prosperity. In that list, countries are grouped according to the region to which they belong.

109 Note 26 lists states the population in 2020 of each country whose data are included in the World Bank's Global Database of Shared Prosperity. In that list, countries are grouped within the region of which they are part.

110 R_{40}(Central Asia, East Europe, the Caucuses and Central Asia) = 1.80% (text to note 27).

111 Pn(Central Asia, East Europe, the Caucuses and Central Asia) = 430,913,770 people (text to note 27).

112 R_{40}(East Asia and the Pacific) = 7.34% (text to note 49).

113 Pn(East Asia and the Pacific) = 2,025,211,315 people (text to note 49).

114 R_{40}(High-income countries) = 1.13% (text to note 60).

115 Pn(High-income countries) = 765,230,869 people (text to note 60).

116 R_{40}(Latin America and the Caribbean) = 0.74% (text to note 72).

117 Pn(Latin America and the Caribbean) = 434,020,170 people (text to note 72).

118 R_{40}(Middle East and North Africa) = -1.03% (text to note 82).

119 Pn(Middle East and North Africa) = 203,247,386 people (text to note 82).

120 R_{40}(South Asia) = 2.24% (text to note 92).

121 Pn(South Asia) = 407,766,580 people (text to note 92).

122 R_{40}(Sub-Saharan Africa) = -0.22% (text to note 100).

123 Pn(Sub-Saharan Africa) = 352,544,173 people (text to note 100).

[Pn(Central Asia, East Europe, the Caucuses and Central Asia)[124] + Pn(East Asia and the Pacific)[125] + Pn(High-income countries)[126] + Pn(Latin America and the Caribbean)[127] + Pn(Middle East and North Africa)[128] + Pn(South Asia)[129] + Pn(Sub-Saharan Africa)[130]] = [(1.80%[131] * 430,913,770 people[132]) + (7.34%[133] * 2,025,211,315 people[134]) + (1.13%[135] * 765,230,869 people[136]) + (0.74%[137] * 434,020,170 people[138]) + (-1.03%[139] * 203,247,386 people[140]) + (2.24%[141] * 407,766,580 people[142]) + (-0.22%[143] * 352,544,173 people[144])] / [430,913,770 people[145] + 2,025,211,315 people[146] + 765,230,869 people[147] + 434,020,170 people[148] + 203,247,386 people[149] + 407,766,580 people[150] + 352,544,173 people[151]] = [775,644,786.00 %people + 14,865,051,052.10 %people + 864,710,881.97 %people + 321,174,925.80 %people – 209,344,807.58 %people + 913,397,139.20 %people – 77,559,718.06 %people] / 4,618,934,263 people = 17,453,074,259.43 %people / 4,618,934,263

---

[124] Note 111.
[125] Note 113.
[126] Note 115.
[127] Note 117.
[128] Note 119.
[129] Note 121.
[130] Note 123.
[131] Note 110.
[132] Note 111.
[133] Note 112.
[134] Note 113.
[135] Note 114.
[136] Note 115.
[137] Note 116.
[138] Note 117.
[139] Note 118.
[140] Note 119.
[141] Note 120.
[142] Note 121.
[143] Note 122.
[144] Note 123.
[145] Note 111.
[146] Note 113.
[147] Note 115.
[148] Note 117.
[149] Note 119.
[150] Note 121.
[151] Note 123.

people = **3.8%**.[152] The values for R_{40} of six of the seven regions[153] are less than G_{40} (i.e., 3.8%). R_{40}(East Asia and the Pacific)[154] is the only R_{40} statistic that exceeds G_{40}. The large population of East Asia[155] – particularly of China[156] – combines with the high value of R_{40} for this region[157] to raise the value of G_{40}, which would otherwise be considerably lower.[158] Whilst R_{40}(Middle East and North Africa) and R_{40}(Sub-Saharan Africa) are negative,[159] as the population of each of these two regions is smaller than the population of each of the other five regions[160] the effect of these negative values of R_{40} on G_{40} is small.[161] $G_T = [(R^1_T * Pn(R^1)) + (R^2_T$

---

[152] G_{40} is given to one decimal place. The accuracy of G_{40} to two or more decimal places is unreliable, as the values of R^1_{40}, R^2_{40} … R^N_{40} – which are inputs to the calculation of G_{40} – are given two decimal places (note 27).

[153] i.e., N = 7. These values are 1.80% (note 110), 1.13% (note 114), 0.74% (note 116), -1.03% (note 118), 2.24% (note 120) and -0.22% (note 122).

[154] R_{40}(East Asia and the Pacific) = 7.34% (note 112).

[155] Pn(East Asia and the Pacific) = 2,025,211,315 people (note 113).

[156] Pn(China) = 1,439,323,776 people (note 54).

[157] Note 154.

[158] G_{40} excluding R_{40}(East Asia and the Pacific) = [17,453,074,259.43 %people – 14,865,051,052.10 %people] / [4,618,934,263 people – 2,025,211,315 people] = 2,588,023,207.33 %people / 2,593,722,948 people = 1.0%. Thus, the omission of R_{40}(East Asia and the Pacific) from the calculation of G_{40} lowers the latter by 3.8% (text to note 152) – 1.0% = 2.8%.

[159] R_{40}(Middle East and North Africa) = -1.03% (note 118). R_{40}(Sub-Saharan Africa) = -0.22% (note 122).

[160] Pn(Middle East and North Africa) = 203,247,386 people (note 119). Pn(Sub-Saharan Africa) = 352,544,173 people (note 123). Pn(South Asia) = 407,766,580 people (note 121). Pn(Central Asia, East Europe, the Caucuses and Central Asia) = 430,913,770 people (note 111). Pn(Latin America and the Caribbean) = 434,020,170 people (note 117). Pn(High-income countries) = 765,230,869 people (note 115). Pn(East Asia and the Pacific) = 2,025,211,315 people (note 113). Therefore, Pn(Middle East and North Africa) < Pn(Sub-Saharan Africa) < Pn(South Asia) < Pn(Central Asia, East Europe, the Caucuses and Central Asia) < Pn(Latin America and the Caribbean) < Pn(High-income countries) < Pn(East Asia and the Pacific).

[161] G_{40} excluding R_{40}(Middle East and North Africa) and R_{40}(Sub-Saharan Africa) = [17,453,074,259.43 %people + 209,344,807.58 %people + 77,559,718.06 %people] / [4,618,934,263 people – 203,247,386 people – 352,544,173 people] = 17,739,978,785.07 / 4,063,142,704 = 4.4%. Thus, the omission of R_{40}(Middle East and North Africa) and R_{40}(Sub-Saharan Africa) – both of which are negative (note 159) – from the calculation of G_{40} raises the latter by 4.4% – 3.8% (text to note 152) = 0.6%. This reduction in G_{40} is more than four times smaller than the increase in G_{40} that results from the elimination of R_{40}(East Asia and the Pacific) – which is 2.8% (note 158).

$* \text{Pn}(R^2)) + \ldots + (R^N_T * \text{Pn}(R^N))] / [\text{Pn}(R^1) + \text{Pn}(R^2) + \ldots \text{Pn}(R^N)]$ = [(R_T(Central Asia, East Europe, the Caucuses and Central Asia)[162] * Pn(Central Asia, East Europe, the Caucuses and Central Asia)[163]) + (R_T(East Asia and the Pacific)[164] * Pn(East Asia and the Pacific)[165]) + (R_T(High-income countries)[166] * Pn(High-income countries)[167]) + (R_T(Latin America and the Caribbean)[168] * Pn(Latin America and the Caribbean)[169]) + (R_T(Middle East and North Africa)[170] * Pn(Middle East and North Africa)[171]) + (R_T(South Asia)[172] + Pn(South Asia)[173]) + (R_T(Sub-Saharan Africa)[174] + Pn(Sub-Saharan Africa)[175])] / [Pn(Central Asia, East Europe, the Caucuses and Central Asia)[176] + Pn(East Asia and the Pacific)[177] + Pn(High-income countries)[178] + Pn(Latin America and the Caribbean)[179] + Pn(Middle East and North Africa)[180] + Pn(South Asia)[181] + Pn(Sub-Saharan Africa)[182]] = [(0.99%[183] * 430,913,770 people[184]) + (6.24%[185] * 2,025,211,315 people[186]) + (1.39%[187] * 765,230,869 people[188])

---

[162] R_T(Central Asia, East Europe, the Caucuses and Central Asia) = 0.99% (text to note 38).

[163] Pn(Central Asia, East Europe, the Caucuses and Central Asia) = 430,913,770 people (text to note 38; note 111).

[164] R_T(East Asia and the Pacific) = 6.24% (text to note 50).

[165] Pn(East Asia and the Pacific) = 2,025,211,315 people (text to note 50; note 113).

[166] R_T(High-income countries) = 1.39% (text to note 61).

[167] Pn(High-income countries) = 765,230,869 people (text to note 61; note 115).

[168] R_T(Latin America and the Caribbean) = 0.71% (text to note 74).

[169] Pn(Latin America and the Caribbean) = 434,020,170 people (text to note 74; note 117).

[170] R_T(Middle East and North Africa) = 0.39% (text to note 83).

[171] Pn(Middle East and North Africa) = 203,247,386 people (text to note 83; note 119).

[172] R_T(South Asia) = 3.18% (text to note 93).

[173] Pn(South Asia) = 407,766,580 people (text to note 93; note 121).

[174] R_T(Sub-Saharan Africa) = 0.87% (text to note 101).

[175] Pn(Sub-Saharan Africa) = 352,544,173 people (text to note 101; note 123).

[176] Note 163.

[177] Note 165.

[178] Note 167.

[179] Note 169.

[180] Note 171.

[181] Note 173.

[182] Note 175.

[183] Note 162.

[184] Note 163.

[185] Note 164.

+ (0.71%[189] * 434,020,170 people[190]) + (0.39%[191] * 203,247,386 people[192]) + (3.18%[193] * 407,766,580 people[194]) + (0.87%[195] * 352,544,173 people[196])] / [430,913,770 people[197] + 2,025,211,315 people[198] + 765,230,869 people[199] + 434,020,170 people[200] + 203,247,386 people[201] + 407,766,580 people[202] + 352,544,173 people[203]] = [426,604,632.30 %people + 12,637,318,605.60 %people + 1,063,670,907.91 %people + 308,154,320.70 %people + 79,266,480.54 %people + 1,296,697,724.40 %people + 306,713,430.51 %people] / 4,618,934,263 people = 16,118,426,101.96 %people / 4,618,934,263 people = **3.5%**.[204] The values for R_T of six of the seven regions[205] are below G_T (i.e., 3.5%). R_T(East Asia and the Pacific)[206] is the only R_T datum that exceeds G_T. The big population of East Asia[207] – especially of China[208] – unites with the elevated value of R_T for that region[209] to increase the value of G_T, which would elsewise be somewhat lower.[210]

---

186 Note 165.
187 Note 166.
188 Note 167.
189 Note 168.
190 Note 169.
191 Note 170.
192 Note 171.
193 Note 172.
194 Note 173.
195 Note 174.
196 Note 175.
197 Note 163.
198 Note 165.
199 Note 167.
200 Note 169.
201 Note 171.
202 Note 173.
203 Note 175.
204 G_T is given to one decimal place. The accuracy of G_T to two or more decimal places is unreliable, as the values of $R^1{}_T$, $R^2{}_T$ … $R^N{}_T$ – which are inputs to the computation of G_T – are given two decimal places (note 38).
205 These values are 0.99% (note 162), 1.39% (note 166), 0.71% (note 168), 0.39% (note 170), 3.18% (note 172) and 0.87% (note 174).
206 R_T(East Asia and the Pacific) = 6.24% (note 164).
207 Pn(East Asia and the Pacific) = 2,025,211,315 people (note 165).
208 Pn(China) = 1,439,323,776 people (note 54).
209 Note 206.
210 G_T excluding R_T(East Asia and the Pacific) = [16,118,426,101.96 %people – 12,637,318,605.60 %people] / [4,618,934,263 people – 2,025,211,315 people] =

Both G_{40} and G_T are positive,[211] which indicates a rise in the worldwide growth aggregate over the period.[212] $G_{40} > G_T$, which represents a fall in global inequality, *ceteris paribus*,[213] and is consistent with the attainment of SDG Target 10.1.[214] As $3\% < G_T$, and $G_{40} < 4\%$, i.e., both R_{40} and R_T are of similar magnitude. Furthermore, the removal of data concerning East Asia and the Pacific from the global estimates of the change in the welfare aggregate over the period causes the reduction in worldwide inequality to reverse, i.e., G_{40} excluding R_{40}(East Asia and the Pacific)[215] < G_T excluding R_T(East Asia and the Pacific).[216] This immediately-preceding observation shows that the data in the World Bank's Global Database of Shared Prosperity only weakly support progression towards meeting SDG Target 10.1, as removal of the most-populous region from the global figures also eliminates the surplus of G_{40} over G_T.[217]

Comment: Table 3.1 arranges the values for R_{40} and R_T, in order to aid their comparison. $G_{40} = 3.8$.[218] $G_T = 3.5$.[219]

Table 3.1: Calculated values of R_{40} and R_T for each region[220]

Region	R_{40} (%)	R_T (%)
Central Europe, East Europe, the Caucasus and Central Asia	1.80	0.99
East Asia and the Pacific	7.34	6.24
High-income countries	1.13	1.39

3,481,107,496.36 %people / 2,593,722,948 people = 1.3%. Thus, the omission of R_{40}(East Asia and the Pacific) from the calculation of G_{40} lowers the latter by 3.5% (text to note 204) – 1.3% = 2.2%.

211 $G_{40} = 3.8\%$ (text to note 152). $G_T = 3.5\%$ (text to note 204).

212 Note 23 specifies the initial and final survey years, i.e., T_0 and T_1 respectively, for each country whose data appear in the present version of the World Bank's Global Database of Shared Prosperity. The period, P, over which the annual growth of each state's welfare aggregate is being measured, is given by $T_0 \leq P \leq T_1$. In the list of countries in note 23, these are assembled according to the region of which they are part.

213 Note 338 of Chapter Two defines '*ceteris paribus*'.

214 The text to note 10 states SDG Target 10.1.

215 G_{40} excluding R_{40}(East Asia and the Pacific) = 1.0 (note 158).

216 G_T excluding R_T(East Asia and the Pacific) = 1.3 (note 210).

217 Note 211 states G_{40} and G_T, both to one decimal place (notes 152 and 204).

218 Text to note 152.

219 Text to note 204.

220 The text to notes 27, 49, 60, 72, 82, 92 and 100 provide the values of R_{40}. The text to notes 38, 50, 61, 74, 83, 93 and 101 supply the values of R_T.

Latin America and the Caribbean	0.74	0.71
Middle East and North Africa	-1.03	0.39
South Asia	2.24	3.18
Sub-Saharan Africa	-0.22	0.87

In four of the seven listed regions, $R_{40} < R_T$. In the other three regions, $R_{40} > R_T$. These regional statistics indicate a slight *rise* in worldwide inequality. By contrast, the global values show a small *reduction* in worldwide inequality; i.e., $3\% < G_T < G_{40} < 4\%$. Thus, the annualized growth in the welfare aggregate – which Table 3.1 shows to be small in all regions other than East Asia and the Pacific and South Asia, is fairly uncorrelated with level of income or consumption per capita. On the basis of these statistics, it is unlikely that SDG Target 10.1[221] will be achieved by 31st December 2030.[222] The Global Database of Shared Prosperity contains data on 90 countries,[223] whose total population (excluding rural Argentina)[224] is 4,618,934,263 people.[225] The UN comprises 193 Member States,[226] and the world's total population in 2020 is 7,794,798,739 people.[227] Thus, the database comprises 47% of the world[228] by country[229]

---

[221] The text to note 10 specifies SDG Target 10.1.

[222] The date 31st December 2030 is introduced pursuant to the use of the phrase 'by 2030' in SDG Target 10.1 (as in SDG Target 1.1 – see text to note 50 of Chapter Two).

[223] World Bank, Global Database of Shared Prosperity and Median Income/Consumption, col 3.

[224] The data in this database concerning Argentina relate to that country's urban areas only (notes 71 and 99).

[225] Text to notes 152 and 204.

[226] "Member States", United Nations, accessed June 3, 2020, https://www.un.org/en/sections/member-states/. Note 22 of Essay Four in *Essays on International Law* lists these 193 countries (Graeme Baber, *Essays on International Law* (Newcastle-upon-Tyne: Cambridge Scholars Publishing, 2017), 109). A list of these states is also found at the following website – which is homonymous to that cited above in this note: "Member States", United Nations, accessed June 3, 2020, https://www.un.org/en/member-states/. This latter website is the source of the list of Member States in *Essays on International Law* (Baber, *Essays on International Law*, 109).

[227] "World Population by Year", Worldometer, accessed June 3, 2020, https://www.worldometers.info/world-population/world-population-by-year/.

[228] Percentage of the world's countries in the Global Database of Shared Prosperity = (90 countries / 193 countries) * 100% = 47%.

[229] The Member States of the UN do not match precisely with all the countries of the world – although they do match all the recognized independent states of the

and 59% of the global population.[230] If the World Bank were to acquire relevant data to add to its Global Database of Shared Prosperity on the considerable number of jurisdictions that are yet to provide these, then the assessment as to the extent to which SDG Target 10.1 is likely to be met by 31st December 2030[231] would be refined and clarified.

SDG Target 10.2 and SDG Indicator10.2.1

SDG Target 10.2 is to "empower and promote the social, economic and political inclusion of all, irrespective of age, sex, disability, race, ethnicity, origin, religious or economic or other status" by 2030.[232] Its single indicator is SDG Indicator 10.2.1, which measures the "[p]roportion of people living below 50% of median income, by sex, age and persons with disabilities".[233]

The data are collected from household surveys of income or consumption per capita, from which the median – and, thus, 50% of the median – income or consumption per capita is calculated; per capita income or consumption is given by dividing total household income by the size of the household.[234] This median value is measured at 2011 PPP using

---

world. Thus, West Bank and Gaza, and Kosovo – the data of both of which are present in the World Bank's Global Database of Shared Prosperity – are not currently UN Member States (World Bank, Global Database of Shared Prosperity and Median Income/Consumption, col 3; "Member States", United Nations, accessed June 3, 2020, https://www.un.org/en/member-states/). In 2010, the ICJ held that Kosovo's declaration of independence did not contravene any relevant rule of international law, but declined to comment on: (i) Kosovo's status as a state, and (ii) the validity or legal effects of the statements of recognition of Kosovo as an independent state by those countries that had made these (International Court of Justice, *Accordance with International Law of the Unilateral Declaration of Independence in Respect of Kosovo, Advisory Opinion*, Advisory Opinion of 22 July 2010, *I.C.J. Reports 2010*, 403-453, 423-424 and 452-453). In 2012, the UN accorded Palestine – i.e., West Bank and Gaza – "non-member observer State status in the United Nations" (United Nations, Resolution 67/19 adopted by the General Assembly on 29 November 2012, art.2).

230 Percentage of the world's population that the Global Database of Shared Prosperity covers = (4,618,934,263 people / 7,794,798,739 people) * 100% = 59%.

231 Note 222.

232 Resolution 70/1 adopted by the General Assembly on 25 September 2015, Transforming our world: the 2030 Agenda for Sustainable Development, 21.

233 Global indicator framework for the Sustainable Development Goals and targets of the 2030 Agenda for Sustainable Development, 10.

234 United Nations, Department of Economic and Social Affairs – Statistics Division: Metadata for Target 10.2 – Indicator 10.2.1: World Bank – Last updated:

the World Bank's PovcalNet database.[235] As soon as the statistic for 50% of the median is known, the share of the population whose income or consumption per capita is below this threshold, is estimated.[236] The reference year is the year – or the first year in cases where the collection period for the data spans two calendar years – in which the data from the relevant household surveys are gathered.[237]

SDG Indicator 10.2.1 is a country-specific indicator,[238] although aggregation to regional and global values is possible.[239] The data are

---

November 2018 (New York, 2018), 2; Umar Serajuddin, and Espen Prydz, "SDG indicator 10.2.1", Presentation to the 8th meeting of the Inter-Agency and Expert Group on SDG Indicators, Stockholm, 5th-9th November 2018 (Washington, D.C.: World Bank, 2018), 6.

[235] "Data Updates and Errata", World Bank, accessed June 6, 2020, https://datahelpdesk.worldbank.org/knowledgebase/articles/906522-data-updates-and-errata. The subsection entitled 'Progress to date in the accomplishment of SDG Target 1.1', in the section titled 'SDG Target 1.1' in Chapter Two, uses the World Bank's PovcalNet database to ascertain regional trends in extreme poverty from 2015 to 2018.

[236] Metadata for Target 10.2 – Indicator 10.2.1: World Bank, 2; Serajuddin and Prydz, "SDG indicator 10.2.1", Presentation to the 8th meeting of the Inter-Agency and Expert Group on SDG Indicators, 6.

[237] "Data Updates and Errata", World Bank, accessed June 6, 2020, https://datahelpdesk.worldbank.org/knowledgebase/articles/906522-data-updates-and-errata.

[238] Metadata for Target 10.2 – Indicator 10.2.1: World Bank, 3. It is submitted that: (i) SDG Indicator 10.2.1 is country-specific because the level of the median income in each country is dependent upon local factors, i.e., 50% of median income is not a universal standard such as the international poverty line (note 25, and text to notes 23-25 and 33-36, of Chapter Two), and (ii) the proportion of a country's population living below 50% of its median income correlates with income inequality, *ceteris paribus*, because a large range of incomes (i.e., a high level of income inequality) tends to include more data points below the monetary level corresponding to 50% of median income than does a concentration of incomes (i.e., a low level of income inequality). The extent of income inequality determined by the proportion of people living below 50% of median income strongly correlates with the degree of income inequality ascertained by each of the Gini coefficient and 'the share of income of the top 10% of the income distribution divided by the share of income of the bottom 10% of the income distribution' percentile ratio (Serajuddin and Prydz, "SDG indicator 10.2.1", Presentation to the 8th meeting of the Inter-Agency and Expert Group on SDG Indicators, 3).

[239] Serajuddin and Prydz, "SDG indicator 10.2.1", Presentation to the 8th meeting of the Inter-Agency and Expert Group on SDG Indicators, 6. Aggregation could be conducted as for SDG Indicator 1.1.1, with the alignment of each estimate to a reference year – which requires an assumption of distribution-neutral growth

selected from the World Bank's DataBank of World Development Indicators.[240] The data for 2015 – i.e., the year that the SDGs were effected,[241] 2016, 2017 and 2018 – i.e., the most recent year for which data are currently available,[242] are tabulated below in this subsection by continent – Africa (Table 3.2), the Americas (Table 3.3), Asia (Table 3.4) and Europe (Table 3.5). The sole record from Oceania reports that 12.6% of the population of Tonga was living below 50% of median income in 2015.[243]

Table 3.2: The proportion of people living below 50% of median income (%) in African countries for which data are available[244]

Country	2015	2016	2017	2018
Angola				22.8
Benin	20.1			
Botswana	19.7			
Cabo Verde	15.8			
Côte d'Ivoire	15.3			

between the estimate from the pertinent household surveys and the reference year (Metadata for Target 10.2 – Indicator 10.2.1: World Bank, 3). Note 80 of Chapter Two describes the assumption of distribution-neutral growth. Note 39 of Chapter Two states SDG Indicator 1.1.1.

240 "DataBank: World Development Indicators", World Bank, accessed June 7, 2020, https://databank.worldbank.org/source/world-development-indicators.

241 The UN General Assembly adopted the SDGs and their targets in Resolution 70/1, which is dated 25th September 2015 (text to note 35 of Chapter One; note 37 of Chapter One and accompanying text).

242 It takes approximately two years from the reference year for poverty estimates in the World Bank's PovcalNet database to become available (note 87 of Chapter Two and accompanying text). Thus, the World Bank's DataBank of World Development Indicators presently provides for data whose reference year is 2019 to be communicated to the users of this service – but none of these statistics relating to the proportion of people living below 50% of median income are currently available there ("DataBank: World Development Indicators", World Bank, accessed June 7, 2020, https://databank.worldbank.org/source/world-development-indicators).

243 "DataBank: World Development Indicators", World Bank, accessed June 7, 2020, https://databank.worldbank.org/source/world-development-indicators.

244 "DataBank: World Development Indicators", World Bank, accessed June 7, 2020, https://databank.worldbank.org/source/world-development-indicators. The World Bank's DataBank of World Development Indicators gives these percentages to one decimal place.

Djibouti			17.1	
Egypt	4.7		5.2	
Eswatini		19.8		
Ethiopia	12.4			
Gabon			15.7	
The Gambia	10.2			
Ghana		20.6		
Kenya	14.0			
Lesotho			21.0	
Liberia		12.1		
Malawi		9.5		
Mauritius			10.9	
Namibia	24.1			
Rwanda		12.4		
São Tomé and Príncipe			16.9	
Sierra Leone				7.5
Tanzania			9.7	
Togo	18.0			
Tunisia	10.5			
Uganda		13.1		
Zambia	25.3			
Zimbabwe			12.7	

Within Africa, the proportion of people living below 50% of median income is greatest in Zambia, Namibia, Angola and Lesotho, thereby revealing a concentration of income inequality in Southern Africa. Botswana and Eswatini also have high values for this statistic, although, exceptionally in Southern Africa, Malawi, and to a lesser extent, Zimbabwe, do not.

On the basis of records from Egypt and Tunisia only, a fairly small proportion of the people of Supra-Saharan Africa live below 50% of median income. The Gambia, Liberia and, especially, Sierra Leone, have manageable levels of their people living below 50% of median income, which tends to indicate that income inequality is moderate to low in the Westernmost part of Africa. This proportion increases travelling eastward from Sierra Leone through Liberia then Côte d'Ivoire to Ghana – in which it is high, declining slightly in Togo and then rising again in Benin. In the absence of a statistic for populous Nigeria,[245] it is submitted that the proportion of individuals living below 50% of median income in those countries of West Africa bordering the Gulf of Guinea is substantial.

The figures for Central Africa and for East Africa show that a medium to high proportion of people in these areas live below 50% of median income, ranging from 9.7 in Tanzania in 2017 to 17.1 in 2017 in Djibouti. Based on the statistics in Table 3.2, income equality in Africa in general is fairly high.

Table 3.3: The proportion of people living below 50% of median income (%) in American countries for which data are available[246]

Country	2015	2016	2017	2018
Argentina		20.7	19.4	20.3
Bolivia	21.3	21.9	21.5	19.8
Brazil	22.4	23.0	23.1	23.6
Chile	13.6		13.6	
Colombia	21.2	20.7	20.2	20.4
Costa Rica	18.6	19.4	18.7	19.2
The Dominican Republic	17.6	18.6	14.2	14.2
Ecuador	19.0	18.5	19.1	19.3
El Salvador	14.4	16.3	14.5	15.3
Honduras	24.3	25.8	24.7	25.0
Mexico		16.0		15.3
Panama	22.6	22.9	23.5	22.3
Paraguay	20.2	19.1	18.5	18.6
Peru	19.5	20.6	20.1	19.4
Saint Lucia		23.1		
Uruguay	18.2	17.5	17.2	16.9
The USA		18.5		

245 Nigeria is currently the seventh most populous state in the world, and is presently the most populous country in Africa; its population in 2020 is 206,139,589 people ("Countries in the world by population (2020)", Worldometer, accessed June 10, 2020, https://www.worldometers.info/world-population/population-by-country/).

246 "DataBank: World Development Indicators", World Bank, accessed June 7, 2020, https://databank.worldbank.org/source/world-development-indicators. The World Bank's DataBank of World Development Indicators gives these percentages to one decimal place.

The data in Table 3.3 show that the proportion of people in the Americas who live below 50% of median income is high – Chile's figure of 13.6% in both 2015 and 2017 being the lowest figure in this table. On the basis of these statistics, income inequality in the Americas is considerable. Noteworthy are: (i) the smaller proportion of individuals who live below 50% of median income in Chile than in its adjoining countries Argentina, Bolivia and Peru, (ii) the disparity between the somewhat-large proportion of people who live below 50% of median income in El Salvador and the huge percentage of individuals so living in neighbouring Honduras, and (iii) the large fall in the proportion of individuals living below 50% of median income in the Dominican Republic from 2016 and 2017 and the continuance of the 2017 level of this figure in 2018.

Table 3.4: The proportion of people living below 50% of median income (%) in Asian countries for which data are available[247]

Country	2015	2016	2017	2018
Armenia	8.8	11.8	6.9	7.8
Bangladesh		6.1		
Bhutan			13.8	
Georgia	13.4	14.0	14.8	14.6
Iran	14.0	14.4	15.5	
Israel		21.2		
Kazakhstan	3.7	4.5	4.0	
Kyrgyzstan	4.5	3.6	3.8	3.8
Malaysia	16.4			
The Maldives		9.7		
Mongolia		10.2		9.9
Myanmar	9.0		6.7	
Pakistan	4.3			
The Philippines	14.5			
Sri Lanka		9.9		
Tajikistan	11.7			
Thailand	10.0	10.8	11.0	11.3
Turkey	15.6	16.0	15.6	15.6

247 "DataBank: World Development Indicators", World Bank, accessed June 7, 2020, https://databank.worldbank.org/source/world-development-indicators. The World Bank's DataBank of World Development Indicators gives these percentages to one decimal place.

Vietnam		13.4		14.0
West Bank and Gaza		12.8		

Excepting Israel,[248] all countries listed in Table 3.4 show a low or medium proportion of their people living below 50% of median income, which indicates on the basis of limited data[249] that income inequality is fairly small in Asia. This proportion is very low in Kazakhstan, Kyrgyzstan and Pakistan, low in Armenia,[250] Bangladesh, the Maldives, Myanmar and Sri Lanka, and moderate in Bhutan, Georgia,[251] Iran[252] and Tajikistan, which tends to indicate low levels of inequality in Central Asia and South Asia bar pockets therein and to the west of these areas – where these levels are somewhat higher. Indeed, the fragmentary records from West Asia in Table 3.4 show approximately a medium percentage of their people living below 50% of median income: whilst Turkey's proportion is medium-high and Israel's is high,[253] that of neighbouring West Bank and Gaza is moderate – as are those of Georgia[254] and Iran,[255] and that of Armenia[256] is small.

In South-East Asia, the data in Table 3.4 indicate that a middling proportion of people live below 50% of median income. In Mongolia, that proportion is fairly low.

---

248 Text to note 253.

249 In particular, Table 3.4 lacks data on Asia's three most populous countries – China, India and Indonesia, whose combined population is 3,092,851,776 people, i.e., 1,439,323,776 people (China – note 26) + 1,380,004,385 people (India) + 273,523,615 people (Indonesia – note 26) ("Countries in the world by population (2020)", Worldometer, accessed June 10, 2020, https://www.worldometers.info/world-population/population-by-country/).
In 2020, these countries account for [(3,092,851,776 people / 7,794,798,739 people) * 100%] = 40% of the world's population ("World Population (2020 and historical)", Worldometer, accessed June 10, 2020, https://www.worldometers.info/world-population/). This percentage is given to two significant figures.

250 Text to note 256.

251 Text to note 254.

252 Text to note 255.

253 Text to note 248.

254 Text to note 251.

255 Text to note 252.

256 Text to note 250.

Table 3.5: The proportion of people living below 50% of median income (%) in European countries for which data are available[257]

Country	2015	2016	2017	2018
Albania	11.1	12.9	12.0	
Austria	11.3	10.7	10.7	
Belarus	6.2	5.9	5.2	5.2
Belgium	10.5	10.2	10.0	
Bulgaria	16.3	15.7	15.3	
Croatia	13.9	14.1	13.2	
Cyprus	10.1	8.3	8.5	
The Czech Republic	6.5	5.4	4.7	
Denmark	5.9	6.7	6.9	
Estonia	10.6	9.8	9.6	
Finland	6.5	6.5	6.9	
France	10.8	10.4	10.1	
Germany	11.0	11.7		
Greece	17.5	16.2	14.9	
Hungary	12.5	10.2	11.5	
Iceland	6.1			
Ireland	9.8	8.8		
Italy	16.1	15.7	16.0	
Kosovo	5.9	7.0	6.7	
Latvia	11.7	12.5	12.8	
Lithuania	14.7	15.0	13.5	
Luxembourg	12.8	13.1	14.9	
Malta	8.9	10.0	9.4	
Moldova	5.2	4.2	4.5	3.8
Montenegro	20.5			
The Netherlands	7.9	8.5	7.8	
North Macedonia	17.1	18.8	17.7	
Norway	8.0	9.2	8.2	
Poland	12.9	9.9	9.4	
Portugal	13.2	12.5	11.0	
Romania	20.5	18.8	19.2	

[257] "DataBank: World Development Indicators", World Bank, accessed June 7, 2020, https://databank.worldbank.org/source/world-development-indicators. The World Bank's DataBank of World Development Indicators gives these percentages to one decimal place.

Russia	11.6	11.8	11.3	10.8
Serbia	20.4	19.8	18.2	
Slovakia	10.6	9.2		
Slovenia	7.5	7.0	6.4	
Spain	17.4	16.9	16.1	
Sweden	9.6	10.4	10.1	
Switzerland	10.9	11.1	10.9	
The UK	11.3	12.7		
Ukraine	5.0	5.2	5.9	5.0

Regarding East Europe, the proportion of people living below 50% of median income is low in Belarus, Moldova and Ukraine, medium-low in Estonia, moderate in Latvia and Russia, medium-high in Bulgaria and Lithuania and high in Romania, with the net trend in this proportion downwards. In South-East Europe, Montenegro, North Macedonia and Serbia each has a high proportion of its people living below 50% of medium income, Greece, Croatia, Albania and Cyprus each has a medium proportion – moving from medium-high (Greece) through medium to medium-low (Cyprus), and Kosovo and Slovenia each has low proportions of their people living below 50% of medium income.

In Central Europe, Austria, Germany, Hungary, Poland, Slovakia and Switzerland each has a moderate proportion of its people living below 50% of medium income, and the Czech Republic has a low such proportion. Regarding North Europe, the proportion of people living below 50% of medium income is low in Denmark, Finland, Iceland and Norway, and moderate in Sweden. Thus, Central Europe and, especially, North Europe, have small amounts of income inequality.

In West Europe, Spain has a fairly high proportion of its people living below 50% of medium income, with Luxembourg at a slightly lower level but increasing; Belgium, France, Portugal and the UK each has a moderate such proportion, and Ireland and the Netherlands each has a medium-low proportion. The remaining countries, Italy and Malta, are in the centre-south of Europe, each having, respectively, a moderately high and fairly low proportion of its people living below 50% of medium income.

Overall, income equality, as determined by the proportion of people living below 50% of median income, is middling to low in Europe. Thus, the data in Tables 3.2, 3.3, 3.4 and 3.5 tend to support the conclusion that income inequality is, in general, high in the Americas, fairly large in Africa, moderate to low in Europe, and reasonably small in Asia – as far as the limited statistics in Table 3.4[258] on this the largest[259] and most populous continent[260] enable analysis to be undertaken.

SDG Target 10.3 and SDG Indicator10.3.1

SDG Target 10.3 is to "[e]nsure equal opportunity and reduce inequalities of outcome, including by eliminating discriminatory laws, policies and practices and promoting appropriate legislation, policies and action in this regard".[261] Its only indicator is SDG Indicator 10.3.1, which determines the "[p]roportion of population reporting having personally felt discriminated against or harassed in the previous 12 months on the basis of a ground of discrimination prohibited under international human rights law".[262]

---

258 Note 249 identifies the absence of data in Table 3.4 on China, India, and Indonesia.

259 Asia is the largest continent, with an area of 45,036,492 million square kilometers, which exceeds the combined area of North America (24,680,331 square kilometers) and South America (17,815,420 square kilometers) – i.e., the Americas, as well as that of Africa (30,343,578 square kilometers), Antarctica (12,093,000 square kilometers), Europe (9,908,599 square kilometers), and Oceania (8,844,516 square kilometers) (Times Books, *The Times Concise Atlas of the World*, Thirteenth edition (London: Times Books, 2016), 54-57.

260 Asia is the most populous continent, with a population of 4,641,054,775 people, which exceeds that of all the other continents combined, i.e., Africa (1,340,598,147 people), Europe (747,636,026 people), South America (430,759,766 people), North America (368,869,647 people), Oceania (42,677,813 people), and Antarctica (where there are no indigenous inhabitants; approximately 1,100 to 4,400 scientific research personnel in the winter and summer respectively reside there, plus about 1,000 workers in the adjacent waters) ("Continent and Region Populations 2020", World Population Review, accessed June 13, 2020, https://worldpopulationreview.com/continents/; "Antarctica Population 2020", World Population Review, accessed June 13, 2020, https://worldpopulationreview.com/continents/antarctica-population/).
It is submitted that 'North America' in this estimate of population includes the USA – whose population is 331,002,651 people, and Canada – whose population is 37,742,154 people, but not Mexico – whose population is 128,932,753 people ("Total Population by Country 2020", World Population Review, accessed June 21, 2020, https://worldpopulationreview.com/countries/).

261 Resolution 70/1 adopted by the General Assembly on 25 September 2015, Transforming our world: the 2030 Agenda for Sustainable Development, 21.

262 Global indicator framework for the Sustainable Development Goals and targets of the 2030 Agenda for Sustainable Development, 10.

Whilst the first batch of data concerning SDG Indicator 10.3.1 was due for release from National Statistical Offices in the first quarter of 2020, at the time of writing the OHCHR – which is responsible for compiling these data – has not published them.[263] This indicator is subjective, i.e., each recipient of the household survey reports whether or not (s)he experienced discrimination or harassment in the country in which that survey is being presented during the 12 months immediately-preceding the moment of collecting these data.[264] 'Discrimination' means any differential treatment that is directly or indirectly based on any ground of discrimination that international human rights law prohibits,[265] and which is intend to, or has the effect of, annulling or damaging the recognition, exercise or enjoyment, on equal terms, of human rights and fundamental freedoms in any sphere of public life.[266] 'Harassment' is any unwelcome and improper behaviour that might reasonably be perceived or be expected to cause humiliation or offence to another person.[267]

---

263 United Nations, Department of Economic and Social Affairs – Statistics Division: Metadata for Target 10.3 – Indicator 10.3.1: OHCHR – Last updated: 3rd December 2018 (New York, 2018), 5. On enquiry, one of the statisticians at the OHCHR stated that the data regarding SDG Indicator 10.3.1 "will be released for the first time this year through the SDG Global Database and the new OHCHR Dashboard", and are "likely to be released in both platforms in July" (Office of the United Nations High Commissioner for Human Rights, e-mail of Mr. Francisco Guerreiro to Dr. Graeme Baber, 15 June 2020).

264 Office of the United Nations High Commissioner for Human Rights. Guidance Note for Implementation of Survey Module on SDG Indicator 16.b.1 & 10.3.1 (Discrimination) (Geneva, 2020), 4; Metadata for Target 10.3 – Indicator 10.3.1: OHCHR, 1-2.

265 Data collectors may consider the following grounds for discrimination: gender, colour, race, language, political or other opinion, religion, social origin, national origin, property, birth status, age, disability, nationality, health status, marital and family status, gender identity, sexual orientation, place of residence, indigenous status, economic and social situation, pregnancy, and other status – which means that this list is not exhaustive and other grounds may be included (Guidance Note for Implementation of Survey Module on SDG Indicator 16.b.1 & 10.3.1 (Discrimination), 5).

266 Guidance Note for Implementation of Survey Module on SDG Indicator 16.b.1 & 10.3.1 (Discrimination), 5; Metadata for Target 10.3 – Indicator 10.3.1: OHCHR, 1.

267 Guidance Note for Implementation of Survey Module on SDG Indicator 16.b.1 & 10.3.1 (Discrimination), 5.

SDG Target 10.4, and SDG Indicators 10.4.1 and 10.4.2

SDG Target 10.4 is to "[a]dopt policies, especially fiscal, wage and social protection policies, and progressively achieve greater equality".[268] Its two indicators are SDG Indicator 10.4.1 – which measures the "[l]abour share of GDP",[269] and SDG Indicator 10.4.2 – which ascertains the "[r]edistributive impact of fiscal policy".[270]

SDG Indicator 10.4.2 is not yet available on the World Bank's World Development Indicators[271] – it was introduced only recently, i.e., in the 2020 Comprehensive Review of Indicators.[272] The following paragraph summarizes the logic for the introduction of SDG Indicator 10.4.2.

> Fighting poverty and inequality requires a systematic analysis of fiscal policies, accompanied by country-level scrutiny of the impact of the different components of the fiscal system. Developed by the Commitment to Equity Institute (CEQ) at Tulane University,[273] the Redistributive Impact of Fiscal Policy indicator is already being used by both the World Bank and the IMF to guide their own programs and policy advice to countries. The indicator is also included in the Commitment to Reducing Inequality Index developed by Development Finance International[274] and

---

[268] Resolution 70/1 adopted by the General Assembly on 25 September 2015, Transforming our world: the 2030 Agenda for Sustainable Development, 21.

[269] Global indicator framework for the Sustainable Development Goals and targets of the 2030 Agenda for Sustainable Development, 10.

[270] Global indicator framework for the Sustainable Development Goals and targets of the 2030 Agenda for Sustainable Development, 10.

[271] "DataBank: World Development Indicators", World Bank, accessed June 16, 2020, https://databank.worldbank.org/source/world-development-indicators.

[272] United Nations, Economic and Social Commission: Report of the Inter-Agency and Expert Group on Sustainable Development Goal Indicators, E/CN.3/2020/2, 20 December 2019, Annex II.C, 17; United Nations, Statistical Commission: Report on the fifty-first session (3-6 March 2020), Economic and Social Council Official Records, 2020, Supplement No. 4, E/2020/24-E/CN.3/2020/37 (New York, 2020), 12.

[273] Note 410 of Chapter Two describes the role of the Commitment to Equity Institute at Tulane University.

[274], Development Finance International was established in 1992 by Ms. Diane Wilkens ("Development Finance International, Inc.", Devex, accessed June 16, 2020, https://www.devex.com/organizations/development-finance-international-dfi-18748). Development Finance International "is an international business development advisory firm providing a strategy-through-execution approach. We deliver sales and market entry, sustainable supply chains, and measurable social and economic impact in emerging markets ("About DFI", Development Finance International, accessed June 16, 2020, https://www.dfintl.com/our-approach/).

> Oxfam. With its inclusion among the SDG indicators, policy analysts, policy makers and policy advocates throughout the world will be given the opportunity to systematically track progress in fiscal policy's contribution to more equitable societies.[275]

The ILO compiles the data for SDG Indicator 10.4.1[276] from those which National Statistical Offices provide.[277] Labour share of GDP = (Total compensation of employees[278] / GDP) * 100%.[279] Limitations of this calculation include the following: (i) labour share in GDP that is computed purely on the compensation of employees underestimates the percentage of GDP that accrues to total employment – as it omits the labour income of self-employed persons,[280] (ii) the stated figure for GDP may underreport or exclude activities that are hard to measure – such as deals in the informal sector, and (iii) GDP considers the economic, but not the social and environmental, costs of production.[281]

The data for labour income share as a percentage of GDP are taken from both the Department of Statistics at the ILO and the Statistics Division of the Department of Economic and Social Affairs at the UN. Every figure from both those sources has been checked against that from the other source, bar a few items that are included in only one of these two records.[282] The data for 2015 – i.e., the year that the SDGs became

---

[275] Nora Lustig, Chiara Mariotti, and Carolina Sánchez-Páramo, "The redistributive impact of fiscal policy indicator: A new global standard for assessing government effectiveness in tackling inequality within the SDG framework", *World Bank Data Blog*, June 11, 2020, accessed June 16, 2020, https://blogs.worldbank.org/opendata/redistributive-impact-fiscal-policy-indicator-new-global-standard-assessing-government.

[276] The text to note 269 specifies SDG Indicator 10.4.1.

[277] The UN guide on metadata for SDG states: "The recommended primary data sources for this indicator are the national accounts estimates of GDP and compensation of employees." (United Nations, Department of Economic and Social Affairs – Statistics Division: Metadata for Target 10.4 – Indicator 10.4.1: ILO – Last updated: March 2019 (New York, 2019), 3).

[278] Note 280 and accompanying text.

[279] Metadata for Target 10.4 – Indicator 10.4.1: ILO, 2.

[280] In every case in which it is possible, the numerator of the equation (text to note 278) should be expanded to include earnings of self-employed individuals.

[281] Metadata for Target 10.4 – Indicator 10.4.1: ILO, 2.

[282] This data cross-corroboration exercise increases the robustness of these statistics, which are found to match across both sources – save for differences in rounding.

operative,[283] 2016 and 2017 – i.e., the most recent year for which data are presently available, are tabulated below in this subsection.

Table 3.6: Annual modelled estimates of labour income share as a percentage of GDP (%) – supranational series[284]

Region or grouping	2015	2016	2017
World	51.8	51.7	51.4
SIDS[285]	49.4	49.5	49.1

---

[283] The UN General Assembly adopted the SDGs and their targets in Resolution 70/1, which is dated 25th September 2015 (text to note 35 of Chapter One; note 37 of Chapter One and accompanying text).

[284] ILOSTAT explorer: Dataset SDG indicator 10.4.1 – Labour income share as a percent of GDP (%) – Annual", International Labour Organization, accessed June 20, 2020, https://www.ilo.org/shinyapps/bulkexplorer20/?lang=en&segment=&id=SDG_1041_NOC_RT_A; "SDG indicators: United Nations Global SDG Database", United Nations, accessed June 20, 2020, https://unstats.un.org/sdgs/indicators/database/. Table 3.6 shows these percentages to one decimal place.

[285] The SIDS comprise the following 58 states and non-state territories: (i) Member States of the UN – Antigua and Barbuda, the Bahamas, Bahrain, Barbados, Belize, Cabo Verde, Comoros, Cuba, Dominica, the Dominican Republic, Fiji, Grenada, Guinea-Bissau, Guyana, Haiti, Jamaica, Kiribati, the Maldives, the Marshall Islands, Mauritius, Micronesia, Nauru, Palau, Papua New Guinea, Saint Kitts and Nevis, Saint Lucia, Saint Vincent and the Grenadines, Samoa, São Tomé and Príncipe, the Seychelles, Singapore, the Solomon Islands, Suriname, Timor-Leste, Tonga, Trinidad and Tobago, Tuvalu, and Vanuatu; (ii) other areas – American Samoa, Anguilla, Aruba, Bermuda, the British Virgin Islands, the Cayman Islands, the Commonwealth of Northern Marianas, the Cook Islands, Curaçao, French Polynesia, Guadeloupe, Guam, Martinique, Montserrat, New Caledonia, Niue, Puerto Rico, Sint Maarten, the Turks and Caicos Islands, and the United States Virgin Islands ("Small Island Developing States", United Nations Sustainable Development Knowledge Platform, accessed June 20, 2020, https://sustainabledevelopment.un.org/topics/sids/list). Neither source of the annual modelled estimates of labour income share as a percentage of GDP data, i.e., the Department of Statistics at the ILO and the Statistics Division of the Department of Economic and Social Affairs at the UN (note 284), states which of the territories listed in the immediately-preceding sentence contribute to the data for the SIDS that Table 3.6 contains. The annual modelled estimates of labour income share as a percentage of GDP that the ILO compiles include data from the following 32 SIDS: the Bahamas, Bahrain, Barbados, Belize, Cabo Verde, Comoros, Cuba, the Dominican Republic, Fiji, French Polynesia, Guam, Guinea-Bissau, Guyana, Haiti, Jamaica, the Maldives, Mauritius, New Caledonia, Papua New Guinea, Puerto Rico, Saint Lucia, Saint Vincent and the Grenadines, Samoa, São Tomé and

Oceania excluding Australia and New Zealand	42.2	42.6	42.3
Oceania	56.8	55.4	55.6
Australia and New Zealand	57.7	56.1	56.4
Latin America	51.1	51.0	50.5
The Americas	56.6	56.5	56.1
North America	59.3	59.2	58.8
Europe and North America	57.9	57.9	57.6
Europe	56.7	56.9	56.6
Europe and Central Asia	54.8	55.0	54.6
Central Asia	43.1	41.7	41.3
LLDCs[286]	45.4	44.7	44.3

Príncipe, Singapore, the Solomon Islands, Suriname, Timor-Leste, Tonga, Trinidad and Tobago, the United States Virgin Islands, and Vanuatu (ILOSTAT explorer: Dataset SDG indicator 10.4.1 – Labour income share as a percent of GDP (%) – Annual", International Labour Organization, accessed June 20, 2020, https://www.ilo.org/shinyapps/bulkexplorer20/?lang=en&segment=&id=SDG_1041_NOC_RT_A; "SDG indicators: United Nations Global SDG Database", United Nations, accessed June 20, 2020, https://unstats.un.org/sdgs/indicators/database/). Thus, American Samoa, Anguilla, Antigua and Barbuda, Aruba, Bermuda, the British Virgin Islands, the Cayman Islands, the Commonwealth of Northern Marianas, the Cook Islands, Curaçao, Dominica, Grenada, Guadeloupe, Kiribati, the Marshall Islands, Martinique, Micronesia, Montserrat, Nauru, Niue, Palau, Saint Kitts and Nevis, the Seychelles, Sint Maarten, the Turks and Caicos Islands, and Tuvalu are the 26 SIDS for which annual modelled estimates of labour income share as a percentage of GDP are not furnished.

286 The LLDCs comprise the following 32 states: Afghanistan, Armenia, Azerbaijan, Bhutan, Bolivia, Botswana, Burkina Faso, Burundi, Central African Republic, Chad, Eswatini, Ethiopia, Kazakhstan, Kyrgyzstan, Laos, Lesotho, Malawi, Mali, Moldova, Mongolia, Nepal, Niger, North Macedonia, Paraguay, Rwanda, South Sudan, Tajikistan, Turkmenistan, Uganda, Uzbekistan, Zambia, and Zimbabwe ("Office of the High Representative for the Least Developed Countries, Landlocked Developing Countries and Small Island Developing States: List of LLDCs", United Nations, accessed June 21, 2020, https://www.un.org/ohrlls/content/list-lldcs). Neither source of the annual modelled estimates of labour income share as a percentage of GDP data (second sentence of note 285) declares which of the states listed above in this footnote contribute to the data for the LLDCs that Table 3.6 contains. The annual modelled estimates of labour income share as a percentage of GDP that the ILO compiles include data from all 32 LLDCs (ILOSTAT explorer: Dataset SDG indicator 10.4.1 – Labour income share as a percent of GDP (%) – Annual", International Labour Organization, accessed June 20, 2020,

Central and South Asia	46.3	45.9	45.8
South Asia	46.5	46.1	46.1
South-East Asia	40.7	40.5	40.1
East and South-East Asia	50.0	50.0	49.7
East Asia	52.2	52.2	52.0
Arab States[287]	30.9	31.6	32.2
West Asia	34.3	34.9	35.1
North Africa and West Asia	35.8	36.1	36.3
Africa	47.9	47.5	47.4
Sub-Saharan Africa	52.7	52.7	52.5
LDCs[288]	43.8	43.7	43.5

---

https://www.ilo.org/shinyapps/bulkexplorer20/?lang=en&segment=&id=SDG_1041_NOC_RT_A; "SDG indicators: United Nations Global SDG Database", United Nations, accessed June 20, 2020, https://unstats.un.org/sdgs/indicators/database/).

[287] The ILO does not define the term 'Arab States'. It is submitted that these comprise the 22 countries within the League of Arab States, which are Algeria, Bahrain, Comoros, Djibouti, Egypt, Iraq, Jordan, Kuwait, Lebanon, Libya, Mauritania, Morocco, Oman, Palestine – i.e., the Palestine Liberation Organization, Qatar, Saudi Arabia, Somalia, Sudan, Syria, Tunisia, the United Arab Emirates, and Yemen ("Arab League", Encyclopaedia Britannica, accessed June 23, 2020, https://www.britannica.com/topic/Arab-League; "League of Arab States", arab.org, accessed June 23, 2020, https://arab.org/directory/league-of-arab-states/). Neither source of the annual modelled estimates of labour income share as a percentage of GDP data (second sentence of note 285) proclaims which of the countries listed in the immediately-preceding sentence contribute to the data for the Arab States that Table 3.6 contains. The annual modelled estimates of labour income share as a percentage of GDP that the ILO compiles include data from the following 21 'Arab States' – as designated in that sentence: Algeria, Bahrain, Comoros, Djibouti, Egypt, Iraq, Jordan, Kuwait, Lebanon, Libya, Mauritania, Oman, Palestine, Qatar, Saudi Arabia, Somalia, Sudan, Syria, Tunisia, the United Arab Emirates, and Yemen (ILOSTAT explorer: Dataset SDG indicator 10.4.1 – Labour income share as a percent of GDP (%) – Annual", International Labour Organization, accessed June 20, 2020,
https://www.ilo.org/shinyapps/bulkexplorer20/?lang=en&segment=&id=SDG_1041_NOC_RT_A; "SDG indicators: United Nations Global SDG Database", United Nations, accessed June 20, 2020, https://unstats.un.org/sdgs/indicators/database/). Thus, Morocco is the only Arab State from the list above in this footnote for which annual modelled estimates of labour income share as a percentage of GDP are not provided.

[288] Note 125 of Chapter Two lists all 47 LDCs. Neither source of the annual modelled estimates of labour income share as a percentage of GDP data (second sentence of note 285) specifies which of the states listed in note 125 of Chapter Two contribute to the data for the LDCs that Table 3.6 contains. The annual

Neither the ILO nor the UN lists the states and territories that are included in the regional or world totals in Table 3.6.[289] Furthermore, neither[290] provides information as to how these totals are calculated. It is submitted that population is an input variable to the totals. For instance, the population of Australia is 25,499,884 people, and that of New Zealand is 4,822,233 people.[291] Therefore, the population of Oceania excluding Australia and New Zealand = 42,677,813 people[292] – (25,499,884 people + 4,822,233 people) = 42,677,813 people – 30,322,117 people = 12,355,696 people. Let labour income share as a percentage of GDP be represented by L. $L_{(A+B)} = L_A + [(L_B - L_A) * (Pn(B) / (Pn(A) + Pn(B))]$, where A and B are two countries or two regions, L_A, L_B and $L_{(A+B)}$ are the labour income as a share of GDP for A, B, and the combined region of A and B, respectively, Pn(A) is the population of A, Pn(B) is the population of B, and $L_B > L_A$. Thus, $L_{OCEANIA} = L_{(OCEANIA\ EXCLUDING\ AUSTRALIA\ AND\ NEW\ ZEALAND)} + [(L_{(AUSTRALIA\ AND\ NEW\ ZEALAND)} - L_{(OCEANIA\ EXCLUDING\ AUSTRALIA\ AND\ NEW\ ZEALAND)})$ * (Pn(Australia and New Zealand) / (Pn(Oceania excluding Australia and New Zealand) + Pn(Australia and New Zealand))]. For 2015, $L_{OCEANIA}$ = 42.2% + [(57.7% – 42.2%) * (30,322,117 people / (12,355,696 people + 30,322,117 people))] = 42.2% + [15.5% * (30,322,117 people / 42,677,813 people)] = 42.2% + [15.5% *

modelled estimates of labour income share as a percentage of GDP that the ILO compiles include data from the following 45 LDCs: Afghanistan, Angola, Bangladesh, Benin, Bhutan, Burkina Faso, Burundi, Cambodia, Central African Republic, Chad, Comoros, the Democratic Republic of the Congo, Djibouti, Eritrea, Ethiopia, the Gambia, Guinea, Guinea-Bissau, Haiti, Laos, Lesotho, Liberia, Madagascar, Malawi, Mali, Mauritania, Mozambique, Myanmar, Nepal, Niger, Rwanda, São Tomé and Príncipe, Senegal, Sierra Leone, the Solomon Islands, Somalia, South Sudan, Sudan, Tanzania, Timor-Leste, Togo, Uganda, Vanuatu, Yemen, and Zambia (ILOSTAT explorer: Dataset SDG indicator 10.4.1 – Labour income share as a percent of GDP (%) – Annual", International Labour Organization, accessed June 20, 2020, https://www.ilo.org/shinyapps/bulkexplorer20/?lang=en&segment=&id=SDG_1041_NOC_RT_A; "SDG indicators: United Nations Global SDG Database", United Nations, accessed June 20, 2020, https://unstats.un.org/sdgs/indicators/database/). Thus, Kiribati and Tuvalu are the only LDCs for which annual modelled estimates of labour income share as a percentage of GDP are not supplied.

[289] The sources are the Department of Statistics at the ILO and the Statistics Division of the Department of Economic and Social Affairs at the UN (second sentence of note 285).

[290] Note 289.

[291] "Total Population by Country 2020", World Population Review, accessed June 21, 2020, https://worldpopulationreview.com/countries/.

[292] Note 260 states the population of Oceania.

0.710489007] = 42.2% + 11.0% = 53.2%. However, in Table 3.6, the value of $L_{OCEANIA}$ for 2015 is 56.8%, which is considerably nearer to $L_{(AUSTRALIA\ AND\ NEW\ ZEALAND)}$ for 2015 than is the value of $L_{OCEANIA}$ calculated above (i.e., 53.2%). Thus, the ILO may have used one or more variables other than population as an input in its geographical aggregation of the modelled estimates of labour income share as a percentage of GDP. One input variable that it might have employed is land area, which is substantially greater for Australia plus New Zealand than it is for Oceania excluding those two states,[293] thereby bringing $L_{OCEANIA}$ closer to $L_{(AUSTRALIA\ AND\ NEW\ ZEALAND)}$ than the value obtained for $L_{OCEANIA}$ by using population alone as an input variable. A possible alternative or additional explanation for the discrepancy in the value of $L_{OCEANIA}$ for 2015 between that in the calculation above in this paragraph and that in Table 3.6, is that this computation utilizes the total population for Oceania – rather than specifically the population for those territories of Oceania that are included in the ILO's modelled estimates of labour income share as a percentage of GDP (%). The ILO and/or the UN include the following Oceanic states and territories in their annual modelled estimates of labour income share as a percentage of GDP: Australia, Fiji, French Polynesia, Guam, New Caledonia, Papua New Guinea, Samoa, the Solomon Islands, Tonga, and Vanuatu.[294] Thus, Pn (Oceania excluding Australia and New Zealand) = Pn(Fiji) + Pn(French Polynesia) + Pn(Guam) + Pn(New Caledonia) + Pn(Papua New Guinea) + Pn(Samoa) + Pn(the Solomon Islands) + Pn(Tonga) + Pn(Vanuatu) = 896,445 people + 280,908 people + 168,775 people + 285,498 people + 8,947,024 people + 198,414 people + 686,884

---

[293] The land area of Oceania is 8,844,516 square kilometers (note 259). The land area of Australia is 7,692,024 square kilometers, and that of New Zealand is 270,534 square kilometers (*The Times Concise Atlas of the World*, 58 and 67). Therefore, (i) the land area of Australia and New Zealand = 7,692,024 square kilometers + 270,534 square kilometers = 7,962,558 square kilometers, and (ii) the land area of Oceania excluding Australia and New Zealand = 8,844,516 square kilometers – (7,692,024 square kilometers + 270,534 square kilometers) = 8,844,516 square kilometers – 7,962,558 square kilometers = 881,958 square kilometers. The greater part of the last-mentioned land area comprises Papua New Guinea, whose land area is 462,840 square kilometers (*The Times Concise Atlas of the World*, 68).

[294] "ILOSTAT explorer: Dataset SDG indicator 10.4.1 – Labour income share as a percent of GDP (%) – Annual", International Labour Organization, accessed June 20, 2020, https://www.ilo.org/shinyapps/bulkexplorer20/?lang=en&segment=&id=SDG_1041_NOC_RT_A; "SDG indicators: United Nations Global SDG Database", United Nations, accessed June 20, 2020, https://unstats.un.org/sdgs/indicators/database/.

people + 105,695 people + 307,145 people[295] = 11,876,788 people. Next, this value of Pn (Oceania excluding Australia and New Zealand) – i.e., 11,876,788 people, is substituted for the value of Pn (Oceania excluding Australia and New Zealand) used in the calculation of $L_{OCEANIA}$ on the immediately-preceding page – i.e., 12,355,696 people, and the computation is redone. For 2015, $L_{OCEANIA}$ = 42.2% + [(57.7% – 42.2%) * (30,322,117 people / (*11,876,788 people* + 30,322,117 people))] = 42.2% + [15.5% * (30,322,117 people / *42,198,905 people*)] = 42.2% + [15.5% * *0.718552233*] = 42.2% + *11.1%* = *53.3%*.[296] This value of $L_{OCEANIA}$ for 2015 is 0.1% greater than that calculated previously, but is 3.5% less than the value of $L_{OCEANIA}$ for 2015 in Table 3.6. Thus, the precise method that the ILO used to compute its annual modelled estimates of labour income share as a percentage of GDP for each of the regions of the world remains unexplained. Notwithstanding this, the next paragraphs comment on the data in Table 3.6 – using L as shorthand for labour income share as a percentage of GDP.

L_{WORLD} is slightly more than half of GDP in 2015, 2016 and 2017. It declines slowly over this period.

L_{SIDS} is just less than half of GDP in all three of these years. Although Oceania excluding Australia and New Zealand comprises SIDS,[297] L_{SIDS} exceeds $L_{(OCEANIA\ EXCLUDING\ AUSTRALIA\ AND\ NEW\ ZEALAND)}$ in 2015, 2016 and 2017, which reflects the fact that SIDS from regions other than Oceania tend to have higher values for labour income as a percentage of GDP than do Papua New Guinea and the Oceanic Pacific Island states and territories.

$L_{(THE\ AMERICAS)}$ is high, with $L_{(NORTH\ AMERICA)}$ exceeding $L_{(LATIN\ AMERICA)}$ – which is just below L_{WORLD} and narrowly above half of GDP. All three of these variables are declining over the period 2015 to 2017. Table 3.6 shows $L_{(NORTH\ AMERICA)}$ to be the highest value of labour income as a percentage of GDP for any region throughout this time.

L_{EUROPE} is high. It rises by 0.2% from 2015 to 2016, and falls by 0.3% from 2016 to 2017, thereby going against the movement of L_{WORLD} from 2015 to 2016 but following the latter from 2016 to 2017.

$L_{(CENTRAL\ ASIA)}$ is low. It reduces through the period 2015 to 2017 – especially from 2015 to 2016. As all five Central Asian states, i.e., Kazakhstan, Kyrgyzstan, Tajikistan, Turkmenistan and Uzbekistan, are

---

[295] Total Population by Country 2020", World Population Review, accessed June 22, 2020, https://worldpopulationreview.com/countries/.

[296] The italic font is used to emphasize changes in the figures in this calculation of $L_{OCEANIA}$, from those in the computation of $L_{OCEANIA}$ above in this paragraph.

[297] Note 285 lists the 58 states and territories that the UN classifies as SIDS.

LLDCs,[298] it is noteworthy that L_{LLDCS} is also low and falling from 2015 to 2017 – although to a smaller extent than $L_{(\text{CENTRAL ASIA})}$.

Whilst $L_{(\text{SOUTH ASIA})}$ and $L_{(\text{SOUTH-EAST ASIA})}$ are somewhat low and very low, respectively, $L_{(\text{EAST ASIA})}$ is a little above L_{WORLD}. All three of these variables are lower in 2017 than in 2015, with $L_{(\text{EAST ASIA})}$ reducing the least and $L_{(\text{SOUTH-EAST ASIA})}$ falling the most.

$L_{(\text{ARAB STATES})}$, $L_{(\text{WEST ASIA})}$, and $L_{(\text{NORTH AFRICA AND WEST ASIA})}$ are extremely low. All three of these variables are increasing – both from 2015 to 2016 and from 2016 to 2017, which is contrary to the movement of L_{WORLD} and of most of the other regions and groupings in Table 3.6. As the whole of North Africa[299] and much of West Asia[300] comprise Arab States,[301] it is unsurprising that $L_{(\text{ARAB STATES})}$, $L_{(\text{WEST ASIA})}$, and $L_{(\text{NORTH AFRICA AND WEST ASIA})}$ are moving in the same direction. $L_{(\text{ARAB STATES})}$ is rising faster than $L_{(\text{WEST ASIA})}$, which is increasing quicker than $L_{(\text{NORTH AFRICA AND WEST ASIA})}$.

L_{AFRICA} is slightly low, and is slowly declining over the period 2015-2017. Whilst $L_{(\text{SUB-SAHARAN AFRICA})}$ is higher than L_{AFRICA} and a tad above L_{WORLD}, it is considerably greater than L_{LDCS} – which is surprising, as 33 of the 47 LDCs[302] are located in Sub-Saharan Africa.[303]

---

[298] Note 286 lists the 32 states that the UN categorizes as LLDCs.

[299] If it is assumed that 'North Africa' means 'Supra-Saharan Africa', then this area consists of Algeria, Egypt, Libya, Morocco, and Tunisia (note 348 of Chapter Two), all of which are Arab States (note 301).

[300] It is submitted that 'West Asia' contains the following 18 countries: Armenia, Azerbaijan, Bahrain, Georgia, Iran, Iraq, Israel, Jordan, Kuwait, Lebanon, Oman, Palestine (i.e., West Bank and Gaza), Qatar, Saudi Arabia, Syria, Turkey, the United Arab Emirates, and Yemen; whilst the FAO considers West Asia to include Afghanistan and Cyprus – in addition to those countries that the immediately-preceding sentence lists ("Global Forest Resources Assessment 2000 – Chapter 21. West Asia", Food and Agriculture Organization of the United Nations, accessed June 23, 2020, http://www.fao.org/3/y1997e/y1997e0q.htm), it is opined that: (i) Afghanistan is placed more appropriately in the region entitled 'South Asia' (notes 351 and 367 of Chapter Two), and (ii) as Cyprus is a Member State of the European Union, this state should be included in the region titled 'Europe' (note 177 of Chapter Two)). Of these 18 countries that comprise West Asia, 12 are Arab States – i.e., Bahrain, Iraq, Jordan, Kuwait, Lebanon, Oman, Palestine, Qatar, Saudi Arabia, Syria, the United Arab Emirates, and Yemen (note 301).

[301] Note 287 lists the 22 countries that are member states of the League of Arab States – which may be considered to constitute the 'Arab States'.

[302] Note 125 of Chapter Two lists all 47 LDCs. Note 288 specifies the 45 LDCs for which the ILO compiles data concerning SDG Indicator 10.4.1. The text to note 269 states SDG Indicator 10.4.1.

It is submitted that the high values of $L_{(NORTH\ AMERICA)}$, L_{EUROPE}, and $L_{(AUSTRALIA\ AND\ NEW\ ZEALAND)}$, which predominantly comprise advanced economies, tend to indicate that the proportion of resources generated by a national system being received by workers rather than by wealth-owners is greater in developed states than in developing countries. The lowest proportion of labour's income share of GDP is in the Arab States, which may be an indication of traditional allocation of resources in the systems functioning there. Notwithstanding this, differences between the Arab countries and the rest of the world regarding the share of resources apportioned to labour may be reducing, as Table 3.6 shows the Arab States, West Asia and North Africa to be improving in this respect from a meagre supply of resources to workers in the period 2015 to 2017, whilst the other regions are stable or deteriorating from the perspective of the proportion of resources allocated to labour over that time.

Table 3.7: Annual modelled estimates of labour income share as a percentage of GDP (%) – Oceania[304]

Region, area, state or territory	**2015**	**2016**	**2017**
Oceania	*56.8*	*55.4*	*55.6*
Australia and New Zealand	*57.7*	*56.1*	*56.4*
Australia	59.0	57.0	57.2
New Zealand	49.1	50.6	51.2
Oceania excluding Australia and New Zealand	*42.2*	*42.6*	*42.3*
Fiji	45.0	46.4	45.5
French Polynesia	51.4	51.5	51.2
Guam	51.3	51.5	51.2
New Caledonia	51.6	51.8	51.5
Papua New Guinea	30.4	30.8	30.7
Samoa	43.9	42.7	43.7

[303] Note 153 of Chapter Two specifies the 49 states of Sub-Saharan Africa. Note 130 of Chapter Two lists the 33 LDCs that are situated in Sub-Saharan Africa.

[304] ILOSTAT explorer: Dataset SDG indicator 10.4.1 – Labour income share as a percent of GDP (%) – Annual", International Labour Organization, accessed June 20, 2020, https://www.ilo.org/shinyapps/bulkexplorer20/?lang=en&segment=&id=SDG_1041_NOC_RT_A; "SDG indicators: United Nations Global SDG Database", United Nations, accessed June 20, 2020, https://unstats.un.org/sdgs/indicators/database/. Table 3.7 shows these percentages to one decimal place.

The Solomon Islands	49.4	49.2	49.1
Tonga	45.4	45.1	45.7
Vanuatu	69.0	67.8	67.4

$L_{(\text{AUSTRALIA AND NEW ZEALAND})}$ is weighted in favour of Australia rather than New Zealand – the former has a larger population and land area than the latter.[305] Table 3.7 shows $L_{\text{AUSTRALIA}}$ to be high – declining from 2015 to 2016 but increasing slightly from 2016 to 2017, and $L_{(\text{NEW ZEALAND})}$ to be medium – rising over the period 2015 to 2017.

$L_{(\text{PAPUA NEW GUINEA})}$ is exceedingly low in the period 2015 to 2017. This variable causes $L_{(\text{OCEANIA EXCLUDING AUSTRALIA AND NEW ZEALAND})}$ to be low – L_{FIJI}, $L_{(\text{FRENCH POLYNESIA})}$, L_{GUAM}, $L_{(\text{NEW CALEDONIA})}$, L_{SAMOA}, $L_{(\text{THE SOLOMON ISLANDS})}$, L_{TONGA}, and L_{VANUATU} are all higher than $L_{(\text{OCEANIA EXCLUDING AUSTRALIA AND NEW ZEALAND})}$ in 2015, 2016 and 2017.[306] The rise from 2015 to 2016, and fall from 2016 to 2017, in L_{FIJI}, $L_{(\text{FRENCH POLYNESIA})}$, L_{GUAM}, $L_{(\text{NEW CALEDONIA})}$, and $L_{(\text{PAPUA NEW GUINEA})}$ is reflected in $L_{(\text{OCEANIA EXCLUDING AUSTRALIA AND NEW ZEALAND})}$, which increases from 2015 to 2016 and lessens from 2016 to 2017. L_{SAMOA} and L_{TONGA} show the inverse pattern of movement, i.e., a decrease from 2015 to 2016 and a rise from 2016 to 2017. Both $L_{(\text{THE SOLOMON ISLANDS})}$ and L_{VANUATU} are falling over the period 2015 to 2017, the latter from an extremely high level of labour income share as a percentage of GDP.

---

[305] The population of Australia is 25,499,884 people, and that of New Zealand is 4,822,233 people (text to note 291). The land area of Australia is 7,692,024 square kilometers, and that of New Zealand is 270,534 square kilometers (note 293).

[306] The value of $L_{(\text{PAPUA NEW GUINEA})}$ has a large effect on the value of $L_{(\text{OCEANIA EXCLUDING AUSTRALIA AND NEW ZEALAND})}$, as Papua New Guinea is considerably more populous and has a much larger land area than Fiji, French Polynesia, Guam, New Caledonia, Samoa, the Solomon Islands, Tonga and Vanuatu. *Population*: Pn(Papua New Guinea) = *8,947,024 people* (text to note 295). Pn(Fiji) + Pn(French Polynesia) + Pn(Guam) + Pn(New Caledonia) + Pn(Samoa) + Pn(the Solomon Islands) + Pn(Tonga) + Pn(Vanuatu) = 896,445 people + 280,908 people + 168,775 people + 285,498 people + 198,414 people + 686,884 people + 105,695 people + 307,145 people = *2,929,764 people* (text to note 295). *Land area*: The land area of Papua New Guinea is *462,840 square kilometers* (note 293). Let LA represent land area. LA(Fiji) + LA(French Polynesia) + LA(Guam) + LA(New Caledonia) + LA(Samoa) + LA(the Solomon Islands) + LA(Tonga) + LA(Vanuatu) = 18,330 square kilometers + 3,265 square kilometers + 541 square kilometers + 19,058 square kilometers + 2,831 square kilometers + 28,370 square kilometers + 748 square kilometers + 12,190 square kilometers = *85,333 square kilometers* (*The Times Concise Atlas of the World*, 62-63, 67, 69 and 71-72).

Notwithstanding the values of $L_{(PAPUA\ NEW\ GUINEA)}$, those of $L_{OCEANIA}$ are fairly large over the period. It is submitted that $L_{AUSTRALIA}$ is the main contributory influence on $L_{OCEANIA}$, with both decreasing substantially from 2015 to 2016 and increasing slightly from 2016 to 2017 – a contrary movement pattern to that of $L_{(OCEANIA\ EXCLUDING\ AUSTRALIA\ AND\ NEW\ ZEALAND)}$ over the period 2015 to 2017.[307]

Table 3.8: Annual modelled estimates of labour income share as a percentage of GDP (%) – The Americas[308]

Region or state	2015	2016	2017
The Americas	*56.6*	*56.5*	*56.1*
North America	*59.3*	*59.2*	*58.8*
Latin America[309]	*51.1*	*51.0*	*50.5*

---

307 Given the large population and land area of Australia relative to that of Oceania – of which Australia is a part, one would expect $L_{AUSTRALIA}$ to significantly affect $L_{OCEANIA}$. *Population*: Pn(Australia) = 25,499,884 people (text to note 291). Pn(Oceania) = 42,677,813 people (note 260). *Land area*: The land area of Australia is 7,692,024 square kilometers (note 293). The land area of Oceania is 8,844,516 square kilometers (note 259).

308 ILOSTAT explorer: Dataset SDG indicator 10.4.1 – Labour income share as a percent of GDP (%) – Annual", International Labour Organization, accessed June 20, 2020, https://www.ilo.org/shinyapps/bulkexplorer20/?lang=en&segment=&id=SDG_1041_NOC_RT_A; "SDG indicators: United Nations Global SDG Database", United Nations, accessed June 20, 2020, https://unstats.un.org/sdgs/indicators/database/. Table 3.8 shows these percentages to one decimal place.

309 Whilst North America *includes* the countries of Central America *and* the islands in the Caribbean Sea (*The Times Concise Atlas of the World*, 56 and 234-237), most or all of Central America and some of the Caribbean states and territories are also part of Latin America – the precise extent of 'Latin America' depending upon the specific description of this term. For example, (i) the Encyclopaedia Britannica lists the following states and territories as constituting Latin America: Argentina, Belize, Bolivia, Brazil, Chile, Colombia, Costa Rica, Cuba, the Dominican Republic, Ecuador, El Salvador, French Guiana, Guadeloupe, Guatemala, Guyana, Haiti, Honduras, Martinique, Mexico, Nicaragua, Panama, Paraguay, Peru, Puerto Rico, Saint Barthélemy, Sint Maarten, Suriname, Uruguay, and Venezuela ("List of countries in Latin America", Encyclopaedia Britannica, accessed June 24, 2020, https://www.britannica.com/topic/list-of-countries-in-Latin-America-2061416), whilst (ii) WorldAtlas specifies these states and territories are comprising Latin America: Argentina, Bolivia, Brazil, Chile, Colombia, Costa Rica, Cuba, the Dominican Republic, Ecuador, El Salvador, French Guiana, Guadeloupe, Guatemala, Haiti, Honduras, Martinique, Mexico, Nicaragua, Panama, Paraguay, Peru, Puerto

Argentina	59.1	60.1	58.5
The Bahamas	58.4	59.2	58.3
Barbados	57.6	57.6	58.3
Belize	48.9	49.7	50.0
Bolivia	53.5	54.0	54.4
Brazil	61.9	61.6	60.4
Canada	62.4	62.1	61.0
Chile	61.4	62.0	62.1
Colombia	52.7	53.1	53.0
Costa Rica	56.5	55.8	56.0
Cuba	38.6	38.5	38.2
The Dominican Republic	50.4	50.1	50.8
Ecuador	53.2	53.0	52.1
El Salvador	45.3	45.0	45.0
Guatemala	38.3	38.4	38.8
Guyana	55.3	55.0	55.0
Haiti	48.5	48.4	48.4
Honduras	65.5	63.8	65.7
Jamaica	63.7	63.3	63.6
Mexico	34.3	34.4	34.6
Nicaragua	58.9	58.8	58.6
Panama	30.4	30.9	30.3
Paraguay	53.0	51.8	52.3
Peru	46.5	45.6	46.1
Puerto Rico	59.2	59.3	59.6
Saint Lucia	51.0	49.9	50.0
Saint Vincent and the Grenadines	48.5	48.5	48.6
Suriname	47.6	48.0	46.9
Trinidad and Tobago	61.9	64.7	64.1
The United States Virgin Islands	59.1	59.3	59.0
Uruguay	47.0	46.9	46.7

Rico, Saint Barthélemy, Sint Maarten, Uruguay, and Venezuela (Antonia Čirjak, "The Countries That Make Up Latin America", *WorldAtlas*, June 5, 2020, accessed June 24, 2020, https://www.worldatlas.com/articles/the-countries-that-make-up-latin-america.html). List (i) includes all 26 countries on list (ii) plus three further states – Belize, Guyana, and Suriname – that list (ii) omits. Thus, it is difficult to discern exactly which of the states within Table 3.8 the ILO has allotted to 'North America' and which to 'Latin America'. Consequently, the values of $L_{(\text{NORTH AMERICA})}$ and $L_{(\text{LATIN AMERICA})}$ have both been placed within this table – above all the individual countries.

The USA	59.0	59.0	58.6
Venezuela	41.8	42.8	42.6

North America[310]: Table 3.8 shows that the annual modelled estimates of labour income share as a percentage of GDP for the Bahamas, Canada and the USA, i.e., $L_{\text{(THE BAHAMAS)}}$, L_{CANADA}, and $L_{\text{(THE USA)}}$, in the period 2015 to 2017, are high. This concentration of a substantial labour income share of GDP does not extend immediately southwards – L_{MEXICO}, $L_{\text{GUATEMALA}}$, and L_{CUBA} are very low throughout this period. Moving further to the south-east, L_{HONDURAS}, $L_{\text{NICARAGUA}}$, and L_{JAMAICA} are moderately-to-very high during this time, and the annual modelled estimates of labour income share as a percentage of GDP for the other Caribbean states and territories for which data are available are either middling – i.e., L_{HAITI}, $L_{\text{(THE DOMINICAN REPUBLIC)}}$, $L_{\text{(SAINT LUCIA)}}$, and $L_{\text{(SAINT VINCENT AND THE GRENADINES)}}$, or high – i.e. $L_{\text{(PUERTO RICO)}}$, $L_{\text{(THE UNITED STATES VIRGIN ISLANDS)}}$, and L_{BARBADOS}. $L_{\text{(EL SALVADOR)}}$ is somewhat low, thereby forming a continuum between $L_{\text{GUATEMALA}}$ and L_{HONDURAS} – although the labour income share as a percentage of GDP is approximately 20% greater in El Salvador than in Honduras. L_{BELIZE} is a not part of a regional pattern, being of medium value over the period 2015 to 2017 and therefore appreciably higher than the labour income share of its adjoining states, i.e., L_{MEXICO} and $L_{\text{GUATEMALA}}$, over that time – although all three of these values are increasing during that spell. The annual modelled estimate of labour income as a percentage of GDP for Panama – L_{PANAMA} – is the lowest such calculation in the Americas – save the slight possibility of even smaller values from states and territories therein whose data are not included, such as Dominica and French Guiana.

South America: This continent displays middling and high values of labour income share as a percentage of GDP in its centre, east and south – i.e., the high values of L_{CHILE}, $L_{\text{ARGENTINA}}$, and L_{BRAZIL}, and the moderate values of L_{BOLIVIA}, L_{PARAGUAY}, and L_{URUGUAY}. The values of labour income share as a percentage of GDP along South America's north-west and north coasts, i.e., L_{ECUADOR}, L_{COLOMBIA}, L_{GUYANA}, and L_{SURINAME}, are medium over the period 2015 to 2017 – i.e., fairly close to the value of L_{WORLD} during this time; L_{VENZUELA} is the exception in being low. L_{PERU} is somewhat low, and is the smallest value of labour income share as a percentage of its GDP of the states along South America's west coast (i.e., Colombia, Ecuador, Peru, and Chile).

[310] The first sentence of note 309 specifies the geographical extent of North America.

Table 3.9: Annual modelled estimates of labour income share as a percentage of GDP (%) – Europe, Central Asia and South Asia[311]

Region, state or territory	**2015**	**2016**	**2017**
Europe and North America	*57.9*	*57.9*	*57.6*
Europe	*56.7*	*56.9*	*56.6*
Albania	53.6	53.3	53.1
Austria	59.0	61.8	60.9
Belarus	50.0	49.5	49.0
Belgium	64.3	62.7	62.5
Bosnia and Herzegovina	41.6	41.6	41.7
Bulgaria	50.7	51.4	51.4
The Channel Islands	56.8	57.0	56.7
Croatia	59.0	58.3	58.1
Cyprus[312]	49.8	49.2	48.9
The Czech Republic	50.1	50.9	50.4
Denmark	58.7	59.1	58.1
Estonia	57.4	58.5	58.2
Finland	58.4	56.6	56.3
France	62.2	61.8	61.0
Germany	60.6	60.5	60.3
Greece	50.4	50.7	50.3
Hungary	47.9	48.1	47.6
Iceland	61.4	60.6	61.3
Ireland	36.9	36.9	36.6
Italy	58.2	58.2	57.5
Latvia	52.2	53.8	53.4
Lithuania	47.5	47.8	47.6
Luxembourg	54.7	56.0	56.2
Malta	49.5	49.0	48.6
Moldova	60.0	59.2	58.7
Montenegro	45.6	45.7	45.7

[311] ILOSTAT explorer: Dataset SDG indicator 10.4.1 – Labour income share as a percent of GDP (%) – Annual", International Labour Organization, accessed June 20, 2020, https://www.ilo.org/shinyapps/bulkexplorer20/?lang=en&segment=&id=SDG_1041_NOC_RT_A; "SDG indicators: United Nations Global SDG Database", United Nations, accessed June 20, 2020, https://unstats.un.org/sdgs/indicators/database/. Table 3.9 shows these percentages to one decimal place.

[312] Note 300 includes Cyprus in Europe because it is a Member State of the European Union.

The Netherlands	63.7	64.2	63.9
North Macedonia	43.4	43.2	43.7
Norway	52.2	53.8	52.7
Poland	46.6	48.6	48.1
Portugal	54.6	54.7	54.5
Romania	40.5	42.3	44.8
Russia[313]	51.0	52.2	52.0
Serbia	53.1	52.6	52.5
Slovakia	49.8	51.1	51.0
Slovenia	58.4	58.8	58.4
Spain	62.2	61.3	61.2
Sweden	55.6	55.5	55.4
Switzerland	70.2	70.8	70.7
The UK	57.7	57.9	58.0
Ukraine	45.8	42.7	42.8
Europe and Central Asia	*54.8*	*55.0*	*54.6*
Central Asia	*43.1*	*41.7*	*41.3*
Kazakhstan	44.2	41.8	41.0
Kyrgyzstan	38.5	40.0	39.4
Tajikistan	28.9	28.6	28.5
Turkmenistan	46.5	46.5	46.6
Uzbekistan	41.0	41.0	41.4
Central and South Asia	*46.3*	*45.9*	*45.8*
South Asia	*46.5*	*46.1*	*46.1*
Afghanistan[314]	44.8	44.7	44.6
Bangladesh	42.8	42.4	42.2
Bhutan	45.9	45.4	45.2
India	49.2	49.2	49.0
The Maldives	41.6	41.1	41.0
Nepal	39.6	40.8	37.1
Pakistan	42.7	42.7	42.2
Sri Lanka	39.0	38.7	37.1

[313] Russia is bicontinental. Whilst about 75% of Russia's population of 145,934,462 people (notes 26 and 33) lives in Europe, 75% of Russian territory is in Asia ("7 continents", Worldometer, accessed June 27, 2020, https://www.worldometers.info/geography/7-continents/). As SDG Target 10.4 (text to note 268) and SDG Indicator 10.4.1 (text to note 269) concern individuals rather than domains, on the basis of the information provided in the immediately-preceding sentence Russia is included within Europe in Table 3.9.

[314] Note 300 places Afghanistan in South Asia.

Table 3.9 shows the annual modelled estimates of labour income share as a percentage of GDP for Europe, Central Asia and South Asia for 2015, 2016 and 2017. The high value of labour income share as a percentage of GDP for Europe – L_{EUROPE} – during the period 2015 to 2017 is reflected in the medium-high, high, very-high, and (for Switzerland) extremely-high values for labour income share as a percentage of GDP of all the states bar two in North, West, and West-Central Europe in that time – i.e., from north-east anticlockwise to south – L_{LATVIA}, L_{ESTONIA}, L_{FINLAND}, L_{SWEDEN}, L_{DENMARK}, L_{GERMANY}, $L_{\text{LUXEMBOURG}}$, L_{BELGIUM}, $L_{\text{(THE NETHERLANDS)}}$, L_{NORWAY}, L_{ICELAND}, $L_{\text{(THE UK)}}$, $L_{\text{(THE CHANNEL ISLANDS)}}$, L_{PORTUGAL}, L_{SPAIN}, L_{FRANCE}, $L_{\text{SWITZERLAND}}$, L_{AUSTRIA}, L_{ITALY}, L_{SLOVENIA}, and L_{CROATIA}. The two exceptions are Ireland – L_{IRELAND} showing the lowest values of labour income share as a percentage of GDP in Europe during the period 2015 to 2017, and Malta – L_{MALTA} being the on the low side of middling but declining over this time.

By contrast, the values of labour income share as a percentage of GDP over the period 2015 to 2017 for the other countries in Europe for which the ILO compiles data on this series, i.e., L_{RUSSIA}, L_{UKRAINE}, L_{BELARUS}, $L_{\text{LITHUANIA}}$, L_{POLAND}, $L_{\text{(THE CZECH REPUBLIC)}}$, L_{SLOVAKIA}, L_{HUNGARY}, L_{ROMANIA}, L_{BULGARIA}, L_{GREECE}, L_{CYPRUS}, $L_{\text{(NORTH MACEDONIA)}}$, L_{ALBANIA}, $L_{\text{MONTENEGRO}}$, L_{SERBIA}, and $L_{\text{(BOSNIA AND HERZEGOVINA)}}$, are moderate or low, other than the value for Moldova – L_{MOLDOVA} – which is high but decreasing over that time. As these states are located in East, East-Central, and South-East Europe, it is submitted that, within this continent during 2015 to 2017, higher values of labour income share as a percentage of GDP tend to be observed in the more-prosperous North and West, whilst lower such values tend to be found in the less-wealthy East and South-East. This is consistent with the large values of $L_{\text{(NORTH AMERICA)}}$, L_{EUROPE}, and $L_{\text{(AUSTRALIA AND NEW ZEALAND)}}$, which predominantly comprise advanced economies, to which a paragraph above in this subsection refers.[315]

The small values of $L_{\text{(CENTRAL ASIA)}}$ in the period 2015 to 2017 are mirrored in similar readings of its two main economics – Kazakhstan and Uzbekistan, i.e., $L_{\text{KAZAKHSTAN}}$ and $L_{\text{UZBEKISTAN}}$. $L_{\text{TURKMENISTAN}}$ is higher than $L_{\text{(CENTRAL ASIA)}}$, $L_{\text{KAZAKHSTAN}}$, and $L_{\text{UZBEKISTAN}}$, but is nevertheless somewhat low – i.e., about 5% below L_{WORLD}. $L_{\text{KYRGYZSTAN}}$ and $L_{\text{TAJIKISTAN}}$ are less than $L_{\text{(CENTRAL ASIA)}}$, $L_{\text{KAZAKHSTAN}}$, and $L_{\text{UZBEKISTAN}}$ – the first of these only a little but the second much, showing that, on the basis of the data submitted to it, the ILO estimates Tajikistan to have

---

[315] The text to note 303 immediately-precedes the specified paragraph.

exceedingly low annual percentages for labour income as a share of GDP during this time.

The somewhat-low value of labour income share as a percentage of GDP for South Asia – $L_{\text{(SOUTH ASIA)}}$ – over the period 2015 to 2017 is dominated by the most-populous country in this region – India.[316] Labour income share as a percentage of GDP for India – L_{INDIA} – is on the low side of medium for every year in this period, exceeding the corresponding value of $L_{\text{(SOUTH ASIA)}}$. However, $L_{\text{(SOUTH ASIA)}}$ is greater than the annual modelled estimates of labour income share as a percentage of GDP for all the other countries in South Asia during this time – $L_{\text{AFGHANISTAN}}$ and L_{BHUTAN} are fairly low, $L_{\text{BANGLADESH}}$, $L_{\text{(THE MALDIVES)}}$, and L_{PAKISTAN} are low, and L_{NEPAL} and $L_{\text{(SRI LANKA)}}$ are very low. Whilst L_{NEPAL} rises from 2015 to 2016 and L_{INDIA} and L_{PAKISTAN} remain at the same level during those two years, all the other movements in the annual modelled estimates of labour income share as a percentage of GDP for the eight countries of South Asia are in a downwards direction – such that not only is the 2017 value of each of $L_{\text{AFGHANISTAN}}$, $L_{\text{BANGLADESH}}$, L_{BHUTAN}, L_{INDIA}, $L_{\text{(THE MALDIVES)}}$, L_{PAKISTAN}, and $L_{\text{(SRI LANKA)}}$ smaller than its 2016 value, but also the 2017 value is smaller than its 2015 value as well.

Unfortunately, the fact that the 2016 value of labour income share as a percentage of GDP for each of the eight countries of South Asia is lower than its corresponding 2017 value – coupled with the fact that $L_{\text{(SOUTH ASIA)}}$ is 46.1% in both 2016 and 2017, reveals an inconsistency in the ILO's data. This is visible upon careful inspection of the last nine entries in Table 3.9. If $L_{\text{AFGHANISTAN}}$, $L_{\text{BANGLADESH}}$, L_{BHUTAN}, L_{INDIA}, $L_{\text{(THE MALDIVES)}}$, L_{NEPAL}, L_{PAKISTAN}, and $L_{\text{(SRI LANKA)}}$ all decrease between 2016 and 2017, then, by definition, $L_{\text{(SOUTH ASIA)}}$ has to reduce as well. It is opined that the ILO should promptly revisit and, as necessary, rework these statistics.

[316] The population of India is 1,380,004,385 people (note 249). In 2018, India's population comprised more than three-quarters of the population of South Asia excluding Afghanistan (note 204 of Chapter Two and accompanying text).

Table 3.10: Annual modelled estimates of labour income share as a percentage of GDP (%) – South-East Asia and East Asia[317]

Region, state or territory	**2015**	**2016**	**2017**
East and South-East Asia	*50.0*	*50.0*	*49.7*
East Asia	*52.2*	*52.2*	*52.0*
China	51.6	51.5	51.3
The Democratic People's Republic of Korea	30.1	30.1	29.6
Hong Kong	54.0	54.5	54.0
Japan	53.8	54.5	54.2
Macau	31.6	32.6	31.7
Mongolia	40.1	39.8	41.4
The Republic of Korea	54.3	54.3	53.8
Taiwan	53.0	52.9	52.5
South-East Asia	*40.7*	*40.5*	*40.1*
Brunei Darussalam	48.2	48.9	47.9
Cambodia	37.7	37.6	37.6
Indonesia	38.6	38.6	38.1
Laos	50.0	49.9	49.7
Malaysia	42.1	42.2	41.8
Myanmar	44.0	44.3	44.4
The Philippines	27.9	27.0	26.6
Singapore	50.1	50.3	49.2
Thailand	48.0	47.7	48.2
Timor-Leste	46.0	45.7	46.8
Vietnam	40.5	40.3	40.5

Table 3.10 shows the annual modelled estimates of labour income share as a percentage of GDP for South-East Asia and East Asia for 2015, 2016 and 2017. The estimates for East Asia – $L_{(\text{EAST ASIA})}$ – influence more greatly the estimates for the combined region of East and South-East Asia – $L_{(\text{EAST AND SOUTH-EAST ASIA})}$ – than do the estimates for South-East Asia – $L_{(\text{SOUTH-EAST ASIA})}$. One reason that may contribute to explaining this

[317] ILOSTAT explorer: Dataset SDG indicator 10.4.1 – Labour income share as a percent of GDP (%) – Annual", International Labour Organization, accessed June 20, 2020, https://www.ilo.org/shinyapps/bulkexplorer20/?lang=en&segment=&id=SDG_1041_NOC_RT_A; "SDG indicators: United Nations Global SDG Database", United Nations, accessed June 20, 2020, https://unstats.un.org/sdgs/indicators/database/. Table 3.10 shows these percentages to one decimal place.

phenomenon is that the population of East Asia is more than twofold that of South-East Asia.[318] Whilst $L_{\text{(EAST ASIA)}}$ and $L_{\text{(EAST AND SOUTH-EAST ASIA)}}$ fairly-closely reflect the estimates of East Asia's most-populous country China[319] – L_{CHINA}, $L_{\text{(SOUTH-EAST ASIA)}}$ slightly-exceeds the estimates of its most-populous country Indonesia – $L_{\text{INDONESIA}}$, and is considerably greater than those of its second-most populous country the Philippines – $L_{\text{(THE PHILIPPINES)}}$.[320]

East Asia: L_{CHINA}, closely follows L_{WORLD} throughout the period 2015 to 2017 – the former is 0.2%, 0.2% and 0.1% below the latter in 2015, 2016 and 2017, respectively. The annual modelled estimates of labour income share as a percentage of GDP for Hong Kong, Japan, the Republic of Korea and Taiwan – i.e., $L_{\text{(HONG KONG)}}$, L_{JAPAN}, $L_{\text{(THE REPUBLIC OF KOREA)}}$, and L_{TAIWAN}, respectively – are medium-high for the duration of the period. $L_{\text{(THE DEMOCRATIC PEOPLE'S REPUBLIC OF KOREA)}}$ and L_{MACAU} are tremendously low throughout this time; L_{MONGOLIA} is also small over the period – though to a lesser degree than either $L_{\text{(THE DEMOCRATIC PEOPLE'S REPUBLIC OF KOREA)}}$ or L_{MACAU}.

South-East Asia: The annual modelled estimates of labour income share as a percentage of GDP for the Philippines – $L_{\text{(THE PHILIPPINES)}}$ – are extremely low during the period 2015-2017. L_{CAMBODIA} and $L_{\text{INDONESIA}}$ are very small, although markedly greater than $L_{\text{(THE PHILIPPINES)}}$. L_{MALAYSIA} and

---

[318] The population of East Asia is 1,678,089,619 people ("Population of Eastern Asia (2019 and historical)", Worldometer, accessed June 29, 2020, https://www.worldometers.info/world-population/eastern-asia-population/). The population of South-East Asia is 668,619,840 people ("Population of South-Eastern Asia (2019 and historical)", Worldometer, accessed June 29, 2020, https://www.worldometers.info/world-population/south-eastern-asia-population/).

[319] The population of China is 1,439,323,776 people (notes 26 and 249).

[320] In addition to $L_{\text{INDONESIA}}$ and $L_{\text{(THE PHILIPPINES)}}$, the annual modelled estimates of labour income share as a percentage of GDP for South-East Asia's third most-populous country Vietnam – L_{VIETNAM} – are also (albeit slightly) less than $L_{\text{(SOUTH-EAST ASIA)}}$. It is only the estimates of this region's fourth most-populous country Thailand – L_{THAILAND} – that start to provide a counterbalance to those of Indonesia, the Philippines and Vietnam. The population of each of South-East Asia's eleven constituent states, in decreasing order, are as follows: Indonesia – 273,523,615 people (notes 26 and 249), the Philippines – 109,581,078 people (note 26), Vietnam – 97,338,579 people (note 26), Thailand – 69,799,978 people (note 26), Myanmar – 54,409,800 people, Malaysia – 32,365,999 people (note 26), Cambodia – 16,718,965 people, Laos – 7,275,560 people, Singapore – 5,850,342 people, Timor-Leste – 1,318,445 people, and Brunei Darussalam – 437,479 people ("Population of South-Eastern Asia (2019 and historical)", Worldometer, accessed June 29, 2020, https://www.worldometers.info/world-population/south-eastern-asia-population/).

L_{VIETNAM} are low. L_{MYANMAR} and $L_{\text{TIMOR-LESTE}}$ are fairly low. $L_{\text{(BRUNEI DARUSSALAM)}}$, L_{THAILAND}, L_{LAOS}, and $L_{\text{SINGAPORE}}$ are medium-low throughout this time; the first two of these are smaller than the second two.

Table 3.11: Annual modelled estimates of labour income share as a percentage of GDP (%) – Africa and West Asia[321]

Region, state or territory	**2015**	**2016**	**2017**
Africa	*47.9*	*47.5*	*47.4*
Sub-Saharan Africa[322]	*52.7*	*52.7*	*52.5*
Angola	50.6	47.3	47.3
Benin	48.4	47.5	46.6
Botswana	47.0	45.8	46.2
Burkina Faso	49.8	48.9	48.5
Burundi	57.8	57.2	57.0
Cabo Verde	42.2	41.5	42.2
Cameroon	36.2	36.3	36.4
Central African Republic	55.4	55.4	55.3
Chad	54.7	55.8	55.6
Comoros	35.3	35.0	34.8
Côte d'Ivoire	27.8	27.6	27.5
The Democratic Republic of the Congo	39.1	39.6	39.4
Djibouti	40.9	40.8	40.8
Equatorial Guinea	51.9	52.0	51.9
Eritrea	40.1	40.1	39.6

321 ILOSTAT explorer: Dataset SDG indicator 10.4.1 – Labour income share as a percent of GDP (%) – Annual", International Labour Organization, accessed June 20, 2020, https://www.ilo.org/shinyapps/bulkexplorer20/?lang=en&segment=&id=SDG_1041_NOC_RT_A; "SDG indicators: United Nations Global SDG Database", United Nations, accessed June 20, 2020, https://unstats.un.org/sdgs/indicators/database/. Table 3.11 shows these percentages to one decimal place.

322 Whilst neither the ILO nor the UN lists the states and territories that are included within the region entitled 'Sub-Saharan Africa' (text to note 289), the countries placed in that category in Table 3.11 are those for which data on labour income share as a percentage of GDP are provided and which are within the set of 49 states that note 153 of Chapter Two identifies as being situated within Sub-Saharan Africa. This list – in Table 3.11 immediately following the title 'Sub-Saharan Africa' – comprises 48 of those 49 states. The omitted country is the Seychelles, on which no data on labour income share as a percentage of GDP are supplied.

Eswatini	39.9	39.7	39.6
Ethiopia	45.0	44.9	44.1
Gabon	26.4	26.7	27.0
The Gambia	39.5	40.8	39.7
Ghana	49.8	49.7	47.8
Guinea	61.0	57.5	58.1
Guinea-Bissau	39.5	39.4	39.4
Kenya	44.1	41.9	43.9
Lesotho	65.3	65.0	66.7
Liberia	39.1	39.1	38.9
Madagascar	47.7	47.4	47.2
Malawi	35.4	35.4	35.1
Mali	51.2	51.1	50.9
Mauritania	44.1	43.7	43.3
Mauritius	44.7	44.4	45.1
Mozambique	49.5	49.8	49.7
Namibia	47.6	47.2	47.6
Niger	32.4	31.8	30.7
Nigeria	66.2	67.0	66.5
The Republic of the Congo	51.8	53.1	53.2
Rwanda	35.6	35.8	35.7
São Tomé and Príncipe	41.2	41.0	41.0
Senegal	33.6	32.9	32.5
Sierra Leone	49.5	47.4	47.5
Somalia	39.2	39.0	39.6
South Africa	53.0	53.8	54.1
South Sudan	47.6	49.0	48.6
Sudan	34.5	34.2	34.4
Tanzania	43.5	46.8	49.1
Togo	39.4	39.4	39.4
Uganda	38.7	39.9	38.8
Zambia	51.8	51.5	51.4
Zimbabwe	33.8	33.9	33.6
North Africa and West Asia	*35.8*	*36.1*	*36.3*
Algeria	45.5	45.7	46.3
Egypt	36.2	34.6	34.9
Libya	43.2	43.1	41.2
Tunisia	46.2	46.2	45.9

Western Sahara[323]	40.6	40.8	40.5
West Asia	*34.3*	*34.9*	*35.1*
Armenia	47.2	46.6	46.3
Azerbaijan	52.0	51.3	51.2
Bahrain	30.4	30.1	30.0
Georgia	50.5	50.9	49.5
Iran	36.7	34.6	36.2

[323] The region entitled 'North Africa' in Table 3.11 comprises those countries that are within Africa but outside 'Sub-Saharan Africa' as described in note 153 of Chapter Two – i.e., the five states that constitute 'Supra-Saharan Africa' as defined in note 348 of Chapter Two; these are Algeria, Egypt, Libya, Morocco, and Tunisia. However, whilst no data are furnished on labour income share as a percentage of GDP for Morocco, data are provided on Western Sahara – which is included in the list of states of North Africa in Table 3.11. The Government of Morocco claims sovereignty over Western Sahara, whilst the latter's liberation movement – the Polisario Front – would like this territory to be recognized as an independent state (Joseph Huddleston, "Can John Bolton Thaw Western Sahara's Long-Frozen Conflict?", *Foreign Policy*, May 9, 2019, accessed June 30, 2020, https://foreignpolicy.com/2019/05/09/can-john-bolton-thaw-western-saharas-long-frozen-conflict-morocco-western-sahara-polisario-minurso-sahrawi-republic/). The UN has placed Western Sahara – formerly named 'Spanish Sahara' – on its list of Non-Self-Governing Territories since 1963, and its General Assembly annually passes a resolution on Western Sahara ("The United Nations and Decolonization: Non-Self-Governing Territories – Western Sahara", United Nations, accessed June 30, 2020, https://www.un.org/dppa/decolonization/en/nsgt/western-sahara; United Nations, Report of the Committee on Information from Non-Self-Governing Territories, General Assembly Official Records: Eighteenth Session, Supplement No. 14, A/5514 (New York, 1963), Annex III, 34). The latest such document is Resolution 74/97 adopted by the General Assembly on 13 December 2019, which, among other things, "[s]*upports* the process of negotiations ... with a view to achieving a just, lasting and mutually acceptable political solution, which will provide for the self-determination of the people of Western Sahara, and commends the efforts undertaken by the Secretary-General and his Personal Envoy for Western Sahara in this respect" and "[r]*equests* the Special Committee on the Situation with regard to the Implementation of the Declaration on the Granting of Independence to Colonial Countries and Peoples to continue to consider the situation in Western Sahara and to report thereon to the General Assembly at its seventy-fifth session" (United Nations, Resolution 74/97 adopted by the General Assembly on 13 December 2019, arts.2 and 6). Regarding Western Sahara's former denomination as 'Spanish Sahara' – to which this footnote refers, Spain informed the Secretary-General of the UN on 26th February 1976 that from this date onwards it had withdrawn from Western Sahara (United Nations, "The United Nations and Decolonization: Non-Self-Governing Territories", accessed June 30, 2020, https://www.un.org/dppa/decolonization/en/nsgt).

Iraq	27.2	26.9	27.3
Israel	52.0	53.0	53.2
Jordan	36.4	36.5	36.5
Kuwait	29.2	29.1	29.4
Lebanon	47.6	47.5	47.5
Oman	53.4	53.3	54.9
Qatar	18.5	18.6	18.6
Saudi Arabia	29.2	30.6	31.5
State of Palestine/Occupied Palestinian Territory	37.0	37.7	38.2
Syria	39.5	39.3	39.4
Turkey[324]	36.6	37.0	36.2
The United Arab Emirates	34.3	36.2	36.8
Yemen	43.4	43.3	42.6

---

324 Turkey is bicontinental. Turkey's population of 84,339,067 people (notes 26 and 36) resides preponderantly in Asia, with the remainder living in Europe; in 2019, the address-based population of Turkey comprised 83,154,997 people, of whom 413,903 people lived in the Thracian region of Edirne, 361,836 people resided in the Thracian region of Kirklareli, 1,055,412 people habitated the Thracian region of Tekirdağ, 15,519,267 people lived in the mainly-Thracian and partly-Anatolian region of Istanbul, and 542,157 people resided in the predominantly-Anatolian and partly-Thracian region of Çanakkale ("Main Statistics", Turkish Statistical Institute, accessed June 30, 2020, http://www.turkstat.gov.tr/UstMenu.do?metod=temelist; *The Times Concise Atlas of the World*, 211 and 213). As all Thracian Turkey – i.e., European Turkey – is constituted by the regions of Edirne, Kirklareli, Tekirdağ, Istanbul, and Çanakkale, and as the regions of Istanbul and Çanakkale include some residents of Anatolian Turkey – i.e., Asian Turkey – the European population of Turkey in 2019 was *less than* Pn(Edirne) + Pn(Kirklareli) + Pn(Tekirdağ) + Pn (Istanbul) + Pn(Çanakkale) = 413,903 people + 361,836 people + 1,055,412 people + 15,519,267 people + 542,157 people = 17,892,575 people. Therefore, in 2019 the percentage of residents of Turkey that lived in Europe was *less than* [(17,892,575 people / 83,154,997 people) * 100%] = 21.52%. This statistic is given to two decimal places. Thus, in 2019, the majority of the residents of Turkey lived in Asia. Furthermore, the land area of Anatolian Turkey exceeds that of Thracian Turkey, i.e., most of Turkey is in Asia ("Turkey", Encyclopaedia Britannica, accessed June 30, 2020, https://www.britannica.com/place/Turkey; Joseph Kiprop, "Is Turkey in Europe or Asia?", *WorldAtlas*, April 25, 2015, accessed June 30, 2020, https://www.worldatlas.com/articles/is-turkey-in-europe-or-asia.html; Tunga Kiyak, "Turkey", Encyclopedia of the Nations, accessed June 30, 2020, https://www.nationsencyclopedia.com/economies/Asia-and-the-Pacific/Turkey.html). Given these conclusions concerning the distribution of Turkey's population and land area between Asia and Europe, Turkey is included within West Asia rather than in Europe.

Sub-Saharan Africa: Further to the above comment that $L_{\text{(SUB-SAHARAN AFRICA)}}$ is considerably higher than L_{LDCS} – even though 33 of the 47 LDCs are located in Sub-Saharan Africa,[325] Table 3.11 shows $L_{\text{(SUB-SAHARAN AFRICA)}}$ to be greater than the annual modelled estimates of labour income share as a percentage of GDP over the period 2015 to 2017 for most of the 48 states of that region for which data are provided. This observation may result from the fact that Africa's most-populous state – Nigeria[326] – has a labour income share as a percentage of GDP that is tremendously high – if, as discussed earlier in this subsection,[327] the regional and world totals of labour income share as a percentage of GDP are weighted by population of the constituent countries. Whilst L_{NIGERIA} is the highest value of labour incomes share as a percentage of GDP in Africa in 2015 and 2016, and the second-largest value in 2017 – being surpassed in that year by L_{LESOTHO}, to the east L_{CHAD} and $L_{\text{(CENTRAL AFRICAN REPUBLIC)}}$ are somewhat high. With the exception of Guinea – L_{GUINEA} is high (especially in 2015), the states to the west and north of Nigeria have exceedingly-low-to-medium values of labour income as a share of GDP – i.e., in increasing order, $L_{\text{(CÔTE D'IVOIRE)}}$, L_{NIGER}, L_{SENEGAL}, L_{LIBERIA}, L_{TOGO}, $L_{\text{(GUINEA BISSAU)}}$, $L_{\text{(THE GAMBIA)}}$, $L_{\text{(CABO VERDE)}}$, $L_{\text{MAURITANIA}}$, L_{BENIN}, $L_{\text{(SIERRA LEONE)}}$, L_{GHANA}, $L_{\text{(BURKINA FASO)}}$, and L_{MALI}. To the south of Nigeria, the middling level of $L_{\text{(EQUATORIAL GUINEA)}}$, is conspicuous among the low, very-low and extremely-low values of $L_{\text{(SÃO TOMÉ AND PRÍNCIPE)}}$, L_{CAMEROON}, and L_{GABON}, respectively – although bordering the latter two states to the east is the medium reading of the Republic of the Congo – i.e., $L_{\text{(REPUBLIC OF THE CONGO)}}$. The annual modelled estimates of labour income share as a percentage of GDP in the period 2015 to 2017 are low for the Democratic Republic of the Congo – i.e., $L_{\text{(DEMOCRATIC REPUBLIC OF THE CONGO)}}$, and very-low-to-moderate for all the states of South and East Africa, i.e., in rising order, L_{ZIMBABWE}, L_{SUDAN}, L_{COMOROS}, L_{MALAWI}, L_{RWANDA}, L_{UGANDA}, L_{SOMALIA}, L_{ESWATINI}, L_{ERITREA}, L_{DJIBOUTI}, L_{KENYA}, L_{ETHIOPIA}, $L_{\text{MAURITIUS}}$, L_{BOTSWANA}, L_{TANZANIA}, $L_{\text{MADAGASCAR}}$, L_{NAMIBIA}, L_{ANGOLA}, $L_{\text{(SOUTH SUDAN)}}$, $L_{\text{MOZAMBIQUE}}$, and L_{ZAMBIA}, bar South Africa, Burundi, and Lesotho – $L_{\text{(SOUTH AFRICA)}}$, L_{BURUNDI}, and L_{LESOTHO} are slightly high, fairly high, and very high, respectively during the period 2015 to 2017. Three notable features are

---

[325] The text to note 303 includes this comment.

[326] The population of Africa is 1,340,598,147 people (note 260). The population of Nigeria is 206,139,589 people ("Population of Nigeria (2020 and historical)", Worldometer, accessed July 1, 2020, https://www.worldometers.info/world-population/nigeria-population/).

[327] This discussion uses the value of L_{OCEANIA} for 2015 as an example, and is contained in the paragraph that immediately follows Table 3.6.

that: (i) L_{TOGO} remains unchanged from 2015 through 2016 to 2017, although this level of labour income share as a percentage of GDP is low, (ii) L_{ANGOLA} falls by 3.3% from 2015 to 2016, and in 2017 remains unchanged from its level in 2016, and (iii) L_{TANZANIA} rises by 3.3% from 2015 to 2016, and increases by 2.3% from 2016 to 2017. There is a downward movement pattern through the period 2015 to 2017 in the annual modelled estimates of labour income share as a percentage of GDP in the following adjacent states in West Africa: Côte d'Ivoire, Burkina Faso, Benin, Niger, Mali, and Mauritania. There is a pattern of increase from 2015 to 2016 and decrease from 2016 to 2017 in the annual modelled estimates of labour income share as a percentage of GDP in the following adjoining countries in Central-East Africa: South Sudan, the Democratic Republic of the Congo, Rwanda, and Uganda.

North Africa: L_{ALGERIA} and L_{TUNISIA} are somewhat low. L_{LIBYA} and $L_{\text{(WESTERN SAHARA)}}$ are small. L_{EGYPT} is very low. Thus, no country in North Africa whose data the ILO compiles has an annual modelled estimate of labour income above L_{WORLD}.

West Asia: The annual modelled estimates of labour income as a percentage of GDP for Qatar – L_{QATAR} – over the period 2015 to 2017 comprises the lowest values of those for all the states and territories for which data are submitted. In 2017, Qatar had the highest PPP GDP per capita of all states.[328] As, in that year, the ILO estimates that only 18.6% of that GDP was paid to workers,[329] the majority of income there went to owners of capital. Thus, Qatar does not follow the observed tendency for the proportion of resources created by a national system being received by labour rather than by wealth-owners, to be greater in advanced states than in developing countries.[330] Other than Oman – L_{OMAN} is slightly high, all the states of the Persian Gulf have low to tremendously low annual modelled estimates of labour income share as a percentage of GDP, i.e., in decreasing order, L_{YEMEN}, $L_{\text{(THE UNITED ARAB EMIRATES)}}$, $L_{\text{(SAUDI ARABIA)}}$, L_{BAHRAIN}, and L_{KUWAIT}. The exceedingly-low value of L_{KUWAIT} is surpassed by the even-smaller value of Kuwait's neighbour Iraq, i.e., L_{IRAQ}. Of the states and territories to the west of Iraq, only Israel and Lebanon have middling values of annual modelled estimates of labour income share as a

328 "GDP per capita", Worldometer, accessed July 2, 2020, https://www.worldometers.info/gdp/gdp-per-capita/.

329 Table 3.11 contains this datum.

330 The first sentence of the paragraph immediately-preceding Table 3.7 includes this comment. The remainder of that paragraph is also relevant to the analysis of data for North Africa and West Asia in the current paragraph entitled 'West Asia' and the one immediately-above it titled 'North Africa'.

percentage of GDP – with L_{ISRAEL} being greater than L_{WORLD}, which is larger than $L_{LEBANON}$, L_{JORDAN}, $L_{PALESTINE}$, and L_{SYRIA}. L_{TURKEY}, and L_{IRAN} are very low. A three-country row along the 35° North Parallel – which comprises Syria, Iraq, and Iran,[331] has decreasing values of labour income share as a percentage of GDP from 2015 to 2016 and increasing readings of this variable from 2016 to 2017. The annual modelled estimates of labour income share as a percentage of GDP in the years 2015 to 2017 are moderate in adjoining states Georgia, Armenia and Azerbaijan, with $L_{AZERBAIJAN}$ exceeding $L_{GEORGIA}$, which is higher than $L_{ARMENIA}$. Taken as a whole in sub-regions of West Asia, these estimates are lower in the Persian Gulf than they are in the Levant, which are smaller than those in the Caucasus. Notably, Azerbaijan is the only country in the Caucasus in which Muslims are in a majority[332] – and no Caucasian countries are Arab States.[333]

SDG Target 10.5 and SDG Indicator 10.5.1

SDG Target 10.5 is to "[i]mprove the regulation and monitoring of global financial markets and institutions and strengthen the implementation of such regulations".[334] Its indicator is SDG Indicator 10.5.1, which states "Financial Soundness Indicators".[335] These financial indicators are as follows: (i) the ratio of Regulatory Tier 1 capital (as determined in the Basel Framework)[336] to total assets on the balance sheet, (ii) the ratio of

---

331 *The Times Concise Atlas of the World*, 130-131.

332 "Armenian people", Encyclopaedia Britannica, accessed July 2, 2020, https://www.britannica.com/topic/Armenian-people; "Azerbaijan", Encyclopaedia Britannica, accessed July 2, 2020, https://www.britannica.com/place/Azerbaijan; "Georgia", accessed July 2, 2020, https://www.britannica.com/place/Georgia; "Russia", accessed July 2, 2020, https://www.britannica.com/place/Russia.

333 Note 287 lists the 22 countries within the League of Arab States – which include no Caucasian countries. For a comment on labour's income per share of GDP in the Arab States, see the paragraph to which note 330 refers – and also the paragraph that precedes it next-but-one.

334 Resolution 70/1 adopted by the General Assembly on 25 September 2015, Transforming our world: the 2030 Agenda for Sustainable Development, 21.

335 Global indicator framework for the Sustainable Development Goals and targets of the 2030 Agenda for Sustainable Development, 10.

336 For a comprehensive summary of the Basel Framework, see pages 245-330 of Graeme Baber, *International Financial Law: Quo Vadis?* (New York: Nova Science Publishers, Inc.), 2017). The calculation of Regulatory Tier 1 capital is based upon the Basel I Accords, the Basel II Accords, or the Basel III Accords, depending upon the supervisory practices of the relevant country (United Nations,

Regulatory Tier 1 capital to risk-weighted assets (both as determined in the Basel Framework),[337] (iii) the ratio of non-performing loans[338] less specific loan-loss provisions[339] to total regulatory capital (as determined in the Basel Framework),[340] (iv) the ratio of non-performing loans[341] to the total value of the loan portfolio,[342] (v) return on total assets,[343] (vi) the ratio of liquid assets[344] to short-term liabilities,[345] (vii) the ratio of net open

---

Department of Economic and Social Affairs – Statistics Division: Metadata for Target 10.5 – Indicator 10.5.1: IMF – Last updated: 3rd December 2018 (New York, 2018), 2).

337 Note 336.

338 A loan is 'non-performing' "when payment of principal or interest is past due by 90 days or more, or evidence exists that a full or partial amount of a loan is not going to be recovered"; data for this Financial Soundness Indicator omit accrued interest on non-performing loans (Metadata for Target 10.5 – Indicator 10.5.1: IMF, 3).

339 Specific loan-loss provisions allocate charges against the value of particular loans (Metadata for Target 10.5 – Indicator 10.5.1: IMF, 3).

340 For a thorough synopsis of the Basel Framework, see Baber, *International Financial Law: Quo Vadis?*, 245-330. The calculation of total regulatory capital is based upon the Basel I Accords, the Basel II Accords, or the Basel III Accords, depending upon the supervisory practices of the country in question loans (Metadata for Target 10.5 – Indicator 10.5.1: IMF, 3).

341 Note 338.

342 The total value of the loan portfolio includes that of non-performing loans without deducting specific loan-loss provisions (Metadata for Target 10.5 – Indicator 10.5.1: IMF, 1). Note 339 describes 'specific loan-loss provisions'.

343 This Financial Soundness Indicator divides annualized net income before extraordinary items and taxes by the average value of total assets – financial and non-financial – over the same period (Metadata for Target 10.5 – Indicator 10.5.1: IMF, 1 and 3).

344 Countries *must* use the *core* measure of liquid assets as the numerator for this Financial Soundness Indicator, which comprises financial assets – including currency and deposits – that are obtainable within three months, and *may* calculate values for an additional indicator that utilizes the *broad* measure of liquid assets as the numerator – which adds to the core measure of liquid assets those securities that are traded in liquid markets and which can be transformed into cash with only a minimum alteration in their value (Metadata for Target 10.5 – Indicator 10.5.1: IMF, 1-3).

345 'Short-term liabilities' comprise "short-term elements of debt liabilities plus net (short-term) market value of financial derivatives position" – which "is calculated as financial derivatives liability position minus financial derivatives asset position"; 'short-term' means three months, which refers to the instrument's remaining maturity – or its original maturity when its remaining maturity is unavailable (Metadata for Target 10.5 – Indicator 10.5.1: IMF, 3).

position in foreign exchange[346] to total regulatory capital (as determined in the Basel Framework[347]).[348]

The national central banks or supervisory agencies collect the data for the construction of the Financial Soundness Indicators, which include balance sheet, profit and loss account, and supervisory series – such as Regulatory Tier 1 capital, Regulatory Tier 2 capital, and risk-weighted assets.[349] The Financial Soundness Indicators that the IMF disseminates are compiled on the basis of the IMF's *FSI Compilation Guide*,[350] which furnishes guidance on definitions, concepts, sources and techniques for the assembling of data that are comparable across countries in order to aid national and global scrutiny of financial systems.[351]

As the Financial Soundness Indicators are not aggregated across countries to produce regional totals,[352] and since the data on those indicators are extensive, a subset of these data for the twenty most-populous states of the world is analysed – as for SDG Target 1.2 and SDG Indicator 1.2.2.[353] In the remainder of this subsection, each of the seven Financial Soundness Indicators listed above[354] is allocated a table in which the value of the indicator is given for the financial institutions of each of these twenty countries over the period 2015[355] to 2018.[356]

---

346 The 'net open position in foreign exchange' is "the foreign-currency and foreign-currency linked element of balance sheet assets and off-balance sheet exposures minus the foreign-currency and foreign-currency linked element of balance sheet liabilities and off-balance sheet exposures"; financial instruments that are 'foreign-currency linked' are "accounts denominated in national currency [whose] payments are linked to exchange rates, [and] thus [they are] subject to foreign exchange risk" (Metadata for Target 10.5 – Indicator 10.5.1: IMF, 3).

347 Note 340.

348 Metadata for Target 10.5 – Indicator 10.5.1: IMF, 1-2.

349 Metadata for Target 10.5 – Indicator 10.5.1: IMF, 5.

350 The *FSI Compilation Guide* is available from the IMF's website – in English, French, Mandarin, Russian, and Spanish – at https://data.imf.org/?sk=51B096FA-2CD2-40C2-8D09-0699CC1764DA&sId=1390288795525.

351 Metadata for Target 10.5 – Indicator 10.5.1: IMF, 4.

352 Metadata for Target 10.5 – Indicator 10.5.1: IMF, 4.

353 Note 254 of Chapter Two and accompanying text. Note 254 of Chapter Two lists these twenty countries from the most populous of them (China) to the least populous of them (Thailand). The text to note 249 of Chapter Two states ADG Target 1.2. Note 249 of Chapter 2 specifies SDG Indicators 1.2.1 and 1.2.2.

354 Text to note 348.

355 2015 is selected as the start of the period for data presentation, as this is the year in which the SDGs became effective (note 283).

356 2018 is the most recent year for which data compiled on the Financial Soundness Indicators are currently available – except for Nigeria, for which data

Table 3.12: The ratio of Regulatory Tier 1 capital to total assets on the balance sheet (%) for the financial institutions of the world's twenty most-populous countries[357]

State: in decreasing population order	2015	2016	2017	2018
China	8.44	8.14	8.56	9.07
India	7.21	7.16	7.39	7.53
The USA	11.71	11.59	11.65	11.69
Indonesia	13.61	14.41	15.22	15.12
Pakistan	8.42	7.82	7.12	7.14
Brazil	8.46	9.27	10.05	10.06
Nigeria[358]	12.38	11.37	5.68	8.11
Bangladesh	5.55	5.63	5.18	4.74
Russia	8.92	10.36	10.51	9.97
Mexico	10.45	9.94	10.40	10.70
Japan	-	-	-	-
Ethiopia	-	-	-	-
The Philippines	9.99	9.74	10.02	10.67
Egypt	-	-	-	-
Vietnam	8.26	7.77	7.36	7.68
The Democratic Republic of the Congo	-	-	-	-
Turkey	11.00	10.73	10.72	10.79
Iran	-	-	-	-
Germany	5.94	5.98	6.33	6.47
Thailand	10.03	10.46	10.73	10.78

Table 3.12 shows that the financial institutions of Bangladesh and Germany have the lowest levels of Regulatory Tier 1 capitalization of the

assembled on these indicators is accessible for 2019 (notes 358, 361, 365, 367, 370, 375 and 377).

357 "SDG indicators: United Nations Global SDG Database", United Nations, accessed July 5, 2020, https://unstats.un.org/sdgs/indicators/database/. The values in Table 3.12 for the ratio of Regulatory Tier 1 capital to total assets on the balance sheet are given to two decimal places. Data on the ratio of Regulatory Tier 1 capital to total assets on the balance sheet are not provided for Japan, Ethiopia, Egypt, the Democratic Republic of the Congo, and Iran.

358 The ratio of Regulatory Tier 1 capital to total assets on the balance sheet for Nigeria for 2019 is 7.29%; this datum is given to two decimal places. ("SDG indicators: United Nations Global SDG Database", United Nations, accessed July 5, 2020, https://unstats.un.org/sdgs/indicators/database/).

fifteen states for which it provides data. Whilst Germany's capitalization rises over the period 2015 to 2018, that of Bangladesh falls to 4.74%. Whilst this pattern is also observed in Table 3.13 for the ratio of Regulatory Tier 1 capital to risk-weighted assets for the financial institutions of Bangladesh through the period, these percentages are higher than those for Bangladesh in Table 3.12. However, that country's capitalization of risk-weighted assets is the lowest of the fifteen states whose data Table 3.13 contains.

Both Table 3.12 and Table 3.13 show that Indonesia's financial institutions have the highest level of Regulatory Tier 1 capitalization every year from 2015 to 2018 of those of the fifteen countries whose data these tables contain. Nigeria's financial institutions show an erratic pattern of Regulatory Tier 1 capitalization – reducing from 2015 to 2016, markedly falling from 2016 to 2017, rising from 2017 to 2018 and then decreasing slightly from 2018 to 2019.[359] The risk-weighted asset composition of the financial institutions of Russia is concerning, as this is the only state listed in Tables 3.12 and 3.13 whose ratio of Regulatory Tier 1 capital to total assets on the balance sheet in each of the years 2015, 2016, 2017 and 2018 exceeds its ratio of Regulatory Tier 1 capital to risk-weighted assets for the same year.

Table 3.13: The ratio of Regulatory Tier 1 capital to risk-weighted assets (%) for the financial institutions of the world's twenty most-populous countries[360]

State: in decreasing population order	2015	2016	2017	2018
China	11.31	11.25	11.35	11.58
India	10.08	10.70	11.02	11.91
The USA	13.09	13.17	13.53	13.78
Indonesia	18.76	22.22	22.65	21.20
Pakistan	14.39	13.08	12.88	13.24
Brazil	12.69	13.70	14.46	14.56
Nigeria[361]	18.15	16.29	8.43	13.54

[359] Tables 3.12 and 3.13 contain the data regarding Nigeria for 2015 to 2018, and notes 358 and 361 for 2019, to which this sentence in the text refers.

[360] "SDG indicators: United Nations Global SDG Database, United Nations, accessed July 5, 2020, https://unstats.un.org/sdgs/indicators/database/. The values in Table 3.13 for the ratio of Regulatory Tier 1 capital to risk-weighted assets are given to two decimal places. Data concerning the ratio of Regulatory Tier 1 capital to risk-weighted assets are not supplied for Japan, Ethiopia, Egypt, the Democratic Republic of the Congo, and Iran.

Bangladesh	7.98	8.14	7.45	6.77
Russia	8.46	9.17	8.50	8.88
Mexico	13.28	13.22	14.17	14.22
Japan	-	-	-	-
Ethiopia	-	-	-	-
The Philippines	12.84	12.60	12.71	13.30
Egypt	-	-	-	-
Vietnam	10.14	9.37	8.77	9.43
The Democratic Republic of the Congo	-	-	-	-
Turkey	13.18	13.14	14.06	13.99
Iran	-	-	-	-
Germany	15.72	16.28	16.93	16.62
Thailand	13.91	14.47	15.07	15.04

In Table 3.14, the financial institutions of China, Brazil, and Mexico return negative values for the ratio of non-performing loans less specific loan-loss provisions to total regulatory capital over the period 2015 to 2018.[362] It is submitted that this may be because the total value of financial institutions' specific loan-loss provisions for each of these states exceeds the total value of those organizations' non-performing loans.

Table 3.14 shows that the financial institutions of Russia, India, and Bangladesh have the third-or-fourth-highest,[363] second-largest and highest, respectively, ratio of non-performing loans less specific loan-loss provisions to total regulatory capital of such organizations of the fifteen countries whose data this table contains, for each of the years 2015, 2016, 2017 and 2018. These observations for Bangladesh corroborate the low Regulatory Tier 1 capitalization ratios which Table 3.12 and Table 3.13 specify for that country's financial institutions during this time.

---

361 The ratio of Regulatory Tier 1 capital to risk-weighted assets for Nigeria for 2019 is 12.76%; this statistic is given to two decimal places. ("SDG indicators: United Nations Global SDG Database", United Nations, accessed July 5, 2020, https://unstats.un.org/sdgs/indicators/database/).

362 In 2019, the financial institutions of Nigeria yield a negative value for the ratio of non-performing loans less specific loan-loss provisions to total regulatory capital (note 365).

363 Table 3.14 shows that the financial institutions of Nigeria have a higher ratio of non-performing loans less specific loan-loss provisions to total regulatory capital than those of Russia in 2016 and 2017, but not in 2015 and 2018.

Table 3.14: The ratio of non-performing loans less specific loan-loss provisions to total regulatory capital (%) for the financial institutions of the world's twenty most-populous countries[364]

State: in decreasing population order	2015	2016	2017	2018
China	-7.87	-7.81	-8.25	-9.18
India	24.01	38.71	41.62	26.92
The USA	7.23	6.62	5.67	4.73
Indonesia	5.89	5.66	4.98	4.38
Pakistan	7.65	7.30	5.79	7.83
Brazil	-12.95	-13.06	-12.99	-13.76
Nigeria[365]	5.53	36.23	23.89	0.05
Bangladesh	44.19	44.08	49.66	53.36
Russia	20.29	17.33	17.25	16.71
Mexico	-5.00	-6.18	-5.96	-5.59
Japan	-	-	-	-
Ethiopia	-	-	-	-
The Philippines	3.12	3.02	3.09	3.50
Egypt	-	-	-	-
Vietnam	11.02	11.42	10.65	8.76
The Democratic Republic of the Congo	-	-	-	-
Turkey	3.94	3.78	3.16	5.93
Iran	-	-	-	-
Germany	17.36	14.68	11.89	9.13
Thailand	7.98	8.43	9.08	9.11

Furthermore, the ratio of non-performing loans less specific loan provisions to total regulatory capital for Bangladesh's financial institutions falls slightly from 2015 to 2016, and rises over the period 2016 to 2018.

---

364 "SDG indicators: United Nations Global SDG Database", United Nations, accessed July 5, 2020, https://unstats.un.org/sdgs/indicators/database/. The values in Table 3.14 for the ratio of non-performing loans less specific loan-loss provisions to total regulatory capital are given to two decimal places. Data on the ratio of non-performing loans less specific loan-loss provisions to total regulatory capital are not furnished for Japan, Ethiopia, Egypt, the Democratic Republic of the Congo, and Iran.

365 The ratio of non-performing loans less specific loan-loss provisions to total regulatory capital for Nigeria for 2019 is -11.10%; this figure is given to two decimal places. ("SDG indicators: United Nations Global SDG Database", United Nations, accessed July 5, 2020, https://unstats.un.org/sdgs/indicators/database/).

This information confirms the findings in Tables 3.12 and 3.13 that the Regulatory Tier 1 capitalization of these Bangladeshi organizations increases a small amount from 2015 to 2016, and decreases from 2016 to 2018.

Table 3.15: The ratio of non-performing loans to the total value of the loan portfolio (%) for the financial institutions of the world's twenty most-populous countries[366]

State: in decreasing population order	2015	2016	2017	2018
China	1.67	1.74	1.74	1.83
India	5.88	9.19	9.98	9.46
The USA	1.47	1.32	1.13	0.91
Indonesia	2.43	2.90	2.56	2.29
Pakistan	11.36	10.06	8.43	7.97
Brazil	3.31	3.92	3.59	3.05
Nigeria[367]	4.86	12.82	14.81	11.67
Bangladesh	8.40	8.86	8.90	9.89
Russia	8.35	9.44	10.00	10.12
Mexico	2.52	2.09	2.09	2.05
Japan	-	-	-	-
Ethiopia	-	-	-	-
The Philippines	1.89	1.72	1.58	1.67
Egypt	-	-	-	-
Vietnam	2.34	2.28	1.82	1.80
The Democratic Republic of the Congo	-	-	-	-
Turkey	2.99	3.11	2.84	3.69
Iran	-	-	-	-
Germany	1.97	1.71	1.50	1.24
Thailand	2.68	2.99	3.07	3.08

366 "SDG indicators: United Nations Global SDG Database, United Nations, accessed July 5, 2020, https://unstats.un.org/sdgs/indicators/database/. The values in Table 3.15 for the ratio of non-performing loans to the total value of the loan portfolio are given to two decimal places. Data regarding the ratio of non-performing loans to the total value of the loan portfolio are not provided for Japan, Ethiopia, Egypt, the Democratic Republic of the Congo, and Iran.

367 The ratio of non-performing loans to the total value of the loan portfolio for Nigeria for 2019 is 6.03%; this percentage is given to two decimal places. ("SDG indicators: United Nations Global SDG Database", United Nations, accessed July 5, 2020, https://unstats.un.org/sdgs/indicators/database/).

Whilst Table 3.15 shows the financial institutions of Bangladesh – as well as those of India and Russia – to have high ratios of non-performing loans to the total value of the loan portfolio over the period 2015 to 2018, thereby corroborating the data in Table 3.14 that show these organizations to have the largest ratios of non-performing loans less specific loan-loss provisions to total regulatory capital among such entities of the fifteen states whose data that table contains during this period,[368] Table 3.15 also indicates that the financial institutions of Nigeria and Pakistan manifest large ratios of non-performing loans to the total value of the loan portfolio during this time. It is submitted that this is a worrying trend in these countries, as the high percentage of non-performing loans may render it difficult for their banks to repay the funds of depositors on demand – causing possible crises of cashflow at those institutions.

Table 3.16: Return on total assets (%) for the financial institutions of the world's twenty most-populous countries[369]

State: in decreasing population order	2015	2016	2017	2018
China	1.10	0.98	0.92	0.90
India	0.45	0.37	0.33	-0.01
The USA	0.36	0.37	0.34	0.39
Indonesia	2.25	2.12	2.41	2.51
Pakistan	1.52	1.27	0.93	0.81
Brazil	1.49	1.12	1.47	1.58
Nigeria[370]	2.50	1.27	2.42	2.03
Bangladesh	0.93	1.28	1.37	0.86
Russia	0.23	1.20	1.01	1.59
Mexico	1.63	1.69	2.05	2.20
Japan	-	-	-	-
Ethiopia	-	-	-	-

[368] This statement concerning the corroboration of data in Table 3.14 is subject to an exception concerning Russia and Nigeria in 2016 and 2017 that note 363 specifies.

[369] "SDG indicators: United Nations Global SDG Database", United Nations, accessed July 5, 2020, https://unstats.un.org/sdgs/indicators/database/. The values in Table 3.16 for return on total assets are given to two decimal places. Data concerning return on total assets are not supplied for Japan, Ethiopia, Egypt, the Democratic Republic of the Congo, and Iran.

[370] Return on total assets for Nigeria for 2019 is 2.53%; this number is given to two decimal places. ("SDG indicators: United Nations Global SDG Database", United Nations, accessed July 5, 2020, https://unstats.un.org/sdgs/indicators/database/).

The Philippines	1.38	1.35	1.34	1.32
Egypt	-	-	-	-
Vietnam	0.47	0.53	0.62	0.90
The Democratic Republic of the Congo	-	-	-	-
Turkey	1.48	1.89	2.04	1.78
Iran	-	-	-	-
Germany	0.40	0.37	0.37	0.32
Thailand	1.37	1.39	1.24	1.31

Table 3.16 shows that the return on total assets is highest for the financial institutions of Nigeria, Indonesia, Mexico and Turkey over the period 2015 to 2018, among such organizations for the fifteen states whose data this table contains. Profit margins are lowest for the financial institutions of India, the USA, and Germany, during this time.[371] Whilst it is submitted that German and American banks may be able to function efficiently on profit margins as low as 0.3% to 0.4% – due to these countries advanced economies and sophisticated financial systems, this is unlikely to be true of Indian banks – as India is a large, developing country with a progressing financial sector. This concern for the regular returns on assets of Indian banks is illustrated by the marginal loss of -0.01% return on assets that Table 3.16 shows for that country's financial institutions in 2018.

Table 3.17 shows the ratio of liquid assets to short-term liabilities to be highest for financial institutions in Brazil, Russia and Germany over the period 2015 to 2018, relative to that of such organizations in the other twelve states whose data this table contains. In these countries, domestic banks are likely to be able to repay their depositors on demand.

Table 3.17 also shows that the ratio of liquid assets to short-term liabilities in each of the years 2015, 2016, 2017 and 2018 is lowest for financial institutions in India, Indonesia, Nigeria[372] and Thailand, in comparison with such organizations in the other countries for which that table furnishes data. It is submitted that, of the states whose data Table 3.17 contains, these four countries are more likely to suffer a run on their

[371] In 2015, the financial institutions of Russia have the smallest return on total assets among such organizations of the fifteen countries whose data Table 3.16 contains. The table shows the return on total assets of these Russian financial institutions to be considerably higher in 2016, 2017 and 2018 than in 2015.

[372] This ratio for the financial institutions of Nigeria is also low in 2019 (note 375) – although this value of the ratio is higher than those of these organizations in the four immediately-preceding years.

banks – as those banks would tend to be the first to be unable to repay their depositors on demand, *ceteris paribus*.[373]

Table 3.17: The ratio of liquid assets to short-term liabilities (%) for the financial institutions of the world's twenty most-populous countries[374]

State: in decreasing population order	2015	2016	2017	2018
China	48.01	47.55	50.03	55.31
India	24.56	32.27	24.73	22.34
The USA	91.20	98.20	97.74	89.26
Indonesia	35.05	32.62	31.66	31.97
Pakistan	88.02	94.99	92.12	86.45
Brazil	190.04	236.30	237.55	241.92
Nigeria[375]	27.13	24.46	27.18	34.15
Bangladesh	47.83	45.95	34.00	44.48
Russia	139.25	144.96	167.38	166.44
Mexico	45.51	42.43	42.19	42.27
Japan	-	-	-	-
Ethiopia	-	-	-	-
The Philippines	60.64	54.64	51.83	50.74
Egypt	-	-	-	-
Vietnam				
The Democratic Republic of the Congo	-	-	-	-
Turkey	69.57	66.92	66.24	64.01
Iran	-	-	-	-
Germany	146.50	146.62	151.25	151.70
Thailand	33.12	30.73	32.55	30.67

373 Note 338 of Chapter Two defines '*ceteris paribus*'.

374 "SDG indicators: United Nations Global SDG Database", United Nations, accessed July 5, 2020, https://unstats.un.org/sdgs/indicators/database/. The values in Table 3.17 for the ratio of liquid assets to short-term liabilities are given to two decimal places. Data on the ratio of liquid assets to short-term liabilities are not furnished for Japan, Ethiopia, Egypt, the Democratic Republic of the Congo, and Iran.

375 The ratio of liquid assets to short-term liabilities for Nigeria for 2019 is 35.32%; this datum is given to two decimal places. ("SDG indicators: United Nations Global SDG Database", United Nations, accessed July 5, 2020, https://unstats.un.org/sdgs/indicators/database/).

The lowest percentage in Table 3.17 is the ratio of liquid assets to short-term liabilities of Indian financial institutions in 2018. This ratio of 22.34% corroborates the slightly-negative return on assets that Table 3.16 shows for those organizations in the same year. India's low values for the ratio of liquid assets to short-term liabilities also support the comment made in the final sentence of the paragraph succeeding Table 3.15, following the detection in the first sentence of that paragraph that this table showed the financial institutions of India – among other states – to exhibit a high ratio of non-performing loans to the total value of their loan portfolio over the period 2015 to 2018; essentially, Indian domestic banks may have difficulties in returning large amounts of cash to their depositors on demand.

Table 3.18: The ratio of net open position in foreign exchange to total regulatory capital (%) for the financial institutions of the world's twenty most-populous countries[376]

State: in decreasing population order	2015	2016	2017	2018
China	3.67	3.54	2.54	2.44
India	8.24	7.05	8.34	8.59
The USA	-	-	-	-
Indonesia	0.91	1.78	1.59	1.68
Pakistan	-0.73	-0.62	-0.25	-0.02
Brazil	0.50	0.89	0.66	0.71
Nigeria[377]	0.00	16.96	21.60	9.26
Bangladesh	5.34	4.93	4.49	7.43
Russia	0.97	1.00	2.21	2.96
Mexico	-0.43	0.78	1.06	1.22
Japan	-	-	-	-
Ethiopia	-	-	-	-

[376] "SDG indicators: United Nations Global SDG Database", United Nations, accessed July 5, 2020, https://unstats.un.org/sdgs/indicators/database/. The values in Table 3.18 for the ratio of net open position in foreign exchange to total regulatory capital are given to two decimal places. Data regarding the ratio of net open position in foreign exchange to total regulatory capital are not provided for the USA, Japan, Ethiopia, Egypt, Vietnam, the Democratic Republic of the Congo, Iran, and Thailand.

[377] The ratio of net open position in foreign exchange to total regulatory capital for Nigeria for 2019 is 4.71%; this statistic is given to two decimal places. ("SDG indicators: United Nations Global SDG Database", United Nations, accessed July 5, 2020, https://unstats.un.org/sdgs/indicators/database/).

The Philippines	2.43	2.00	7.93	4.72
Egypt	-	-	-	-
Vietnam	-	-	-	-
The Democratic Republic of the Congo	-	-	-	-
Turkey	-0.40	0.21	0.71	1.52
Iran	-	-	-	-
Germany	4.62	4.00	3.67	3.19
Thailand	-	-	-	-

Table 3.18 shows the ratio of the net open position in foreign exchange to total regulatory capital to be highest for the financial institutions of India, Nigeria,[378] and Bangladesh for each of 2015, 2016, 2017 and 2018 – except for Nigeria in 2015 and Bangladesh in 2017. Thus, the banks of these countries carry the greatest risk of insolvency caused by swings in foreign exchange rates, in comparison with those of the other nine countries for which this table provides data. This risk is of particular concern in respect of Nigerian financial institutions, whose levels of this ratio in 2016 and 2017 are extremely high and whose fluctuations in the ratio through the period 2015 to 2019 are considerable.

The above review of Financial Soundness Indicators for the twenty most-populous countries of the world reveals that financial institutions of Bangladesh tend to have capitalization difficulties, those of India tend to have problems with cashflow, and those of Nigeria tend to be unstable by virtue of some fluctuating ratios through the years for which data are supplied. Furthermore, the IMF has currently not presented the Financial Soundness Indicators that it is compiling on five of these states[379] – plus three further countries for the ratio on net open position in foreign exchange to total regulatory capital.[380] The publication and analysis of these data from a time substantially prior to 2030 is necessary for the identification and implementation of requisite improvements in the management of financial institutions, in order to satisfy requirements for the fulfilment of SDG Target 10.5 by the end of that year.[381]

---

[378] Note 377 specifies the ratio of net open position in foreign exchange to total regulatory capital for financial institutions in Nigeria in 2019 to be fairly high – but less raised than these organizations' value for this ratio in 2016, 2017 and 2018.

[379] Notes 357, 360, 364, 366, 369, 374 and 376 each specify these five states. The list of countries in note 376 also identifies the three countries to which the text to note 380 refers.

[380] Note 376 lists these three states, together with the five countries to which the text to note 379 refers.

[381] The text to note 334 states SDG Target 10.5.

SDG Target 10.6 and SDG Indicator 10.6.1

SDG Target 10.6 is to "[e]nsure enhanced representation and voice for developing countries in decision-making in global international economic and financial institutions in order to deliver more effective, credible, accountable and legitimate institutions".[382] Its solitary indicator is SDG Indicator 10.6.1, which determines the "[p]roportion of members and voting rights of developing countries in international organizations".[383]

SDG Indicator 10.6.1 is computed independently for the following international institutions: the UN General Assembly, the UNSC, the ECOSOC, the IMF, the IBRD, the IFC, the AfDB, the AsDB, the IADB, the WTO, and the FSB.[384] Aggregation of data across all these institutions is done in conformity with the UN's M49 statistical standard, which includes the allocation of states and territories to 'developed regions'[385] and 'developing regions'[386] – whilst a continuing review attempts to reach

---

382 Resolution 70/1 adopted by the General Assembly on 25 September 2015, Transforming our world: the 2030 Agenda for Sustainable Development, 21.

383 Global indicator framework for the Sustainable Development Goals and targets of the 2030 Agenda for Sustainable Development, 11.

384 United Nations, Department of Economic and Social Affairs – Statistics Division: Metadata for Target 10.6 – Indicator 10.6.1: Financing for Development Office at the Department of Economic and Social Affairs – Last updated: 19th July 2016 (New York, 2016), 1.

385 The 'developed regions' comprise the following states and territories: the Åland Islands, Albania, Andorra, Australia, Austria, Belarus, Belgium, Bermuda, Bosnia and Herzegovina, Bulgaria, Canada, Christmas Island, the Cocos (Keeling) Islands, Croatia, Cyprus, the Czech Republic, Denmark, Estonia, the Faroe Islands, Finland, France, Germany, Gibraltar, Greece, Greenland, Guernsey, Heard Island and McDonald Islands, the Holy See, Hungary, Iceland, Ireland, the Isle of Man, Israel, Italy, Japan, Jersey, Latvia, Liechtenstein, Lithuania, Luxembourg, Malta, Moldova, Monaco, Montenegro, the Netherlands, New Zealand, Norfolk Island, North Macedonia, Norway, Poland, Portugal, Romania, Russia, Saint Pierre and Miquelon, San Marino, Sark, Serbia, Slovakia, Slovenia, Spain, Svalbard and Jan Mayen Islands, Sweden, Switzerland, the UK, Ukraine, and the USA ("Methodology: Standard country or area codes for statistical use (M49) – Developed Regions", United Nations, accessed July 9, 2020, https://unstats.un.org/unsd/methodology/m49/#developed).

386 The 'developing regions' consist of the following states and territories: Afghanistan, Algeria, American Samoa, Angola, Anguilla, Antigua and Barbuda, Argentina, Armenia, Aruba, Azerbaijan, the Bahamas, Bahrain, Bangladesh, Barbados, Belize, Benin, Bhutan, Bolivia, Bonaire and Sint Eustatius and Saba, Botswana, Bouvet Island, Brazil, British Indian Ocean Territory, the British Virgin Islands, Brunei Darussalam, Burkina Faso, Burundi, Cabo Verde, Cambodia,

agreement on the definition of these terms for the purposes of monitoring progress towards the accomplishment of the SDGs.[387]

The two parts of SDG Indicator 10.6.1[388] – i.e., (i) the proportion of *members* of a developing state or territory in an international organization, and (ii) the proportion of *voting rights* of a such a country therein – are calculated as follows: (i) proportion of members = number of members that are developing countries / total number of members, and (ii) proportion of voting rights = number of voting rights allotted to members that are developing countries / total number of voting rights.[389] These computations use data concerning the published membership and voting

---

Cameroon, the Cayman Islands, Central African Republic, Chad, Chile, China, Colombia, Comoros, the Cook Islands, Costa Rica, Côte d'Ivoire, Cuba, Curaçao, the Democratic People's Republic of Korea, the Democratic Republic of the Congo, Djibouti, Dominica, the Dominican Republic, Ecuador, Egypt, El Salvador, Equatorial Guinea, Eritrea, Eswatini, Ethiopia, the Falkland Islands, Fiji, French Guiana, French Polynesia, French Southern Territories, Gabon, the Gambia, Georgia, Ghana, Grenada, Guadeloupe, Guam, Guatemala, Guinea, Guinea-Bissau, Guyana, Haiti, Honduras, Hong Kong, India, Indonesia, Iran, Iraq, Jamaica, Jordan, Kazakhstan, Kenya, Kiribati, Kuwait, Kyrgyzstan, Laos, Lebanon, Lesotho, Liberia, Libya, Macau, Madagascar, Malawi, Malaysia, the Maldives, Mali, the Marshall Islands, Martinique, Mauritania, Mauritius, Mayotte, Mexico, Micronesia, Mongolia, Montserrat, Morocco, Mozambique, Myanmar, Namibia, Nauru, Nepal, New Caledonia, Nicaragua, Niger, Nigeria, Niue, the Northern Mariana Islands, Oman, Pakistan, Palau, Panama, Papua New Guinea, Paraguay, Peru, the Philippines, the Pitcairn Islands, Puerto Rico, Qatar, the Republic of the Congo, the Republic of Korea, Réunion, Rwanda, Saint Barthélemy, Saint Helena, Saint Kitts and Nevis, Saint Lucia, Saint Martin (French Part), Saint Vincent and the Grenadines, Samoa, São Tomé and Príncipe, Saudi Arabia, Senegal, the Seychelles, Sierra Leone, Singapore, Sint Maarten (Dutch Part), the Solomon Islands, Somalia, South Africa, South Georgia and the South Sandwich Islands, South Sudan, Sri Lanka, the State of Palestine, Sudan, Suriname, Syria, Tajikistan, Tanzania, Thailand, Timor-Leste, Togo, Tokelau, Tonga, Trinidad and Tobago, Tunisia, Turkey, Turkmenistan, the Turks and Caicos Islands, Tuvalu, Uganda, the United Arab Emirates, the United States Minor Outlying Islands, the United States Virgin Islands, Uruguay, Uzbekistan, Vanuatu, Venezuela, Vietnam, the Wallis and Futuna Islands, Western Sahara, Yemen, Zambia, and Zimbabwe ("Methodology: Standard country or area codes for statistical use (M49) – Developing Regions", United Nations, accessed July 9, 2020, https://unstats.un.org/unsd/methodology/m49/#developing).

[387] Metadata for Target 10.6 – Indicator 10.6.1: Financing for Development Office at the Department of Economic and Social Affairs, 1.

[388] The text to note 383 states SDG Indicator 10.6.1.

[389] Metadata for Target 10.6 – Indicator 10.6.1: Financing for Development Office at the Department of Economic and Social Affairs, 2.

rights of each of the above international institutions[390] from its annual report.[391] The Financing for Development Office at the UN Department of Economic and Social Affairs compiles those statistics, and calculates the proportions from them.[392]

The data that the UN Global SDG Database[393] furnishes on SDG Indicator 10.6.1[394] include statistics for each country and specified aggregates.[395] The proportions are summed from those country-specific entries in the database for one of the eleven international institutions – the IMF.[396] The data for the year that the SDGs were operationalized – i.e., 2015 – are used,[397] together with those for the most recent year for which the UN Global SDG Database provides statistics regarding SDG Indicator 10.6.1 – which is 2019. The proportions that the database contains are given as percentages; therefore, the following equations are appropriate.

$\sum\%(Dd)_M = \%(DdC_1)_M + \%(DdC_2)_M + \%(DdC_3)_M + \ldots \%(DdC_N)_M$, where $\%(DdC_1)_M + \%(DdC_2)_M + \%(DdC_3)_M + \ldots \%(DdC_N)_M$ are the percentages of members of developed countries in the relevant international organization for countries 1, 2, 3 … N, respectively, and N is the number of developed countries whose data are in the UN Global SDG Database for SDG Indicator 10.6.1. $\sum\%(Dg)_M = \%(DgC_1)_M + \%(DgC_2)_M + \%(DgC_3)_M + \ldots \%(DgC_N)_M$, where $\%(DgC_1)_M + \%(DgC_2)_M + \%(DgC_3)_M + \ldots \%(DgC_N)_M$ are the percentages of members of developing countries in the relevant international organization for countries 1, 2, 3 … N,

[390] The text to note 384 lists the eleven international organizations for which Financing for Development Office at the UN Department of Economic and Social Affairs compiles data regarding SDG Indicator 10.6.1 (text to note 392). The text to note 383 specifies SDG Indicator 10.6.1.

[391] Metadata for Target 10.6 – Indicator 10.6.1: Financing for Development Office at the Department of Economic and Social Affairs, 2.

[392] Metadata for Target 10.6 – Indicator 10.6.1: Financing for Development Office at the Department of Economic and Social Affairs, 5.

[393] SDG indicators: United Nations Global SDG Database", United Nations, accessed July 9, 2020, https://unstats.un.org/sdgs/indicators/database/.

[394] The text to note 383 states SDG Indicator 10.6.1.

[395] The UN Global SDG Database aggregates its data for SDG Indicator 10.6.1 into the following categories: (i) LDCs, and (ii) developing regions.

[396] The IMF connects voting power to size of the quota that its members provide – almost in direct proportion but with a slightly-diminishing marginal allocation of votes as the amount of the quota increases (Baber, *Essays on International Law*, 245).

[397] The UN General Assembly adopted the SDGs and their targets in Resolution 70/1, which is dated 25th September 2015 (text to note 35 of Chapter One; note 37 of Chapter One and accompanying text).

respectively, and N is the number of developing countries whose data are in the UN Global SDG Database for SDG Indicator 10.6.1. If $\sum\%(Dd)_M + \sum\%(Dg)_M \neq 100\%$, then the percentage of developed countries within the relevant international organization *based on the records currently in the database* is given by $[\sum\%(Dd)_M / (\sum\%(Dd)_M + \sum\%(Dg)_M)] * 100\%$, and the percentage of developing countries within the relevant international organization *based on the records currently in the database* is given by $[\sum\%(Dg)_M / (\sum\%(Dd)_M + \sum\%(Dg)_M)] * 100\%$. These latter two percentages must sum to 100%. The above series of equations are repeated to attain the proportion of *voting rights* of developing countries within the relevant international organization, but with the subscript 'M' – which means 'members' – replaced by the subscript 'VR', which stands for 'voting rights'. Each country is classified as 'developed' or 'developing' in accordance with its allocation to one or other of these two categories under the M49 statistical standard.[398]

1. The percentage of members: For the IMF in 2015, $\sum\%(Dd)_M = \%(DdC_1)_M + \%(DdC_2)_M + \%(DdC_3)_M + \ldots + \%(DdC_N)_M$ = %(Albania)$_M$ + %(Australia)$_M$ + %(Austria)$_M$ + %(Belarus)$_M$ + %(Belgium)$_M$ + %(Bosnia and Herzegovina)$_M$ + %(Bulgaria)$_M$ + %(Canada)$_M$ + %(Croatia)$_M$ + %(Cyprus)$_M$ + %(the Czech Republic)$_M$ + %(Denmark)$_M$ + %(Estonia)$_M$ + %(Finland)$_M$ + %(France)$_M$ + %(Germany)$_M$ + %(Greece)$_M$ + %(Hungary)$_M$ + %(Iceland)$_M$ + %(Ireland)$_M$ + %(Israel)$_M$ + %(Italy)$_M$ + %(Japan)$_M$ + %(Kosovo[399])$_M$ + %(Latvia)$_M$ + %(Lithuania)$_M$ + %(Luxembourg)$_M$ + %(Malta)$_M$ + %(Moldova)$_M$ + %(Montenegro)$_M$ + %(the Netherlands)$_M$ + %(New Zealand)$_M$ + %(North Macedonia)$_M$ + %(Norway)$_M$ + %(Poland)$_M$ + %(Portugal)$_M$ + %(Romania)$_M$ + %(Russia)$_M$ + %(San Marino)$_M$ + %(Serbia)$_M$ + %(Slovakia)$_M$ + %(Slovenia)$_M$ + %(Spain)$_M$ + %(Sweden)$_M$ + %(Switzerland)$_M$ + %(the

---

[398] Note 385 specifies the states and territories that the UN's M49 statistical standard lists as those comprising the 'developed regions'. Note 386 identifies the states and territories that the UN's M49 statistical standard lists as those constituting the 'developing regions'.

[399] The UN's M40 statistical standard omits to classify Kosovo as a country ("Methodology: Standard country or area codes for statistical use (M49) – Countries or areas / geographical regions", accessed July 12, 2020, https://unstats.un.org/unsd/methodology/m49/). Consequently, Kosovo is absent from both its list of states and territories that constitute 'developed regions' (note 385) and its list of states and territories that comprise 'developing regions' (note 386). As the M40 statistical standard allocates Serbia to its list of developed regions (note 385), Kosovo is considered to be a developed country for the purposes of SDG Target 10.6 and SDG Indicator 10.6.1. The text to note 382 declares SDG Target 10.6. The text to note 383 specifies SDG Indicator 10.6.1.

UK)$_M$ + %(Ukraine)$_M$ + %(the USA)$_M$ = 0.53191% + 0.53191% = 48 * 0.53191% = *25.53168%*. For the IMF in 2015, $\sum$%(Dg)$_M$ = %(DgC$_1$)$_M$ + %(DgC$_2$)$_M$ + %(DgC$_3$)$_M$ + … + %(DgC$_N$)$_M$ = %(Afghanistan)$_M$ + %(Algeria)$_M$ + %(Angola)$_M$ + %(Antigua and Barbuda)$_M$ + %(Argentina)$_M$ + %(Armenia)$_M$ + %(Azerbaijan)$_M$ + %(the Bahamas)$_M$ + %(Bahrain)$_M$ + %(Bangladesh)$_M$ + %(Barbados)$_M$ + %(Belize)$_M$ + %(Benin)$_M$ + %(Bhutan)$_M$ + %(Bolivia)$_M$ + %(Botswana)$_M$ + %(Brazil)$_M$ + %(Brunei Darussalam)$_M$ + %(Burkina Faso)$_M$ + %(Burundi)$_M$ + %(Cabo Verde)$_M$ + %(Cambodia)$_M$ + %(Cameroon)$_M$ + %(Central African Republic)$_M$ + %(Chad)$_M$ + %(Chile)$_M$ + %(China)$_M$ + %(Colombia)$_M$ + %(Comoros)$_M$ + %(Costa Rica)$_M$ + %(Côte d'Ivoire)$_M$ + %(the Democratic Republic of the Congo)$_M$ + %(Djibouti)$_M$ + %(Dominica)$_M$ + %(the Dominican Republic)$_M$ + %(Ecuador)$_M$ + %(Egypt)$_M$ + %(El Salvador)$_M$ + %(Equatorial Guinea)$_M$ + %(Eritrea)$_M$ + %(Eswatini)$_M$ + %(Ethiopia)$_M$ + %(Fiji)$_M$ + %(Gabon)$_M$ + %(the Gambia)$_M$ + %(Georgia)$_M$ + %(Ghana)$_M$ + %(Grenada)$_M$ + %(Guatemala)$_M$ + %(Guinea)$_M$ + %(Guinea-Bissau)$_M$ + %(Guyana)$_M$ + %(Haiti)$_M$ + %(Honduras)$_M$ + %(India)$_M$ + %(Indonesia)$_M$ + %(Iran)$_M$ + %(Iraq)$_M$ + %(Jamaica)$_M$ + %(Jordan)$_M$ + %(Kazakhstan)$_M$ + %(Kenya)$_M$ + %(Kiribati)$_M$ + %(Kuwait)$_M$ + %(Kyrgyzstan)$_M$ + %(Laos)$_M$ + %(Lebanon)$_M$ + %(Lesotho)$_M$ + %(Liberia)$_M$ + %(Libya)$_M$ + %(Madagascar)$_M$ + %(Malawi)$_M$ + %(Malaysia)$_M$ + %(the Maldives)$_M$ + %(Mali)$_M$ + %(the Marshall Islands)$_M$ + %(Mauritania)$_M$ + %(Mauritius)$_M$ + %(Mexico)$_M$ + %(Micronesia)$_M$ + %(Mongolia)$_M$ + %(Morocco)$_M$ + %(Mozambique)$_M$ + %(Myanmar)$_M$ + %(Namibia)$_M$ + %(Nepal)$_M$ + %(Nicaragua)$_M$ + %(Niger)$_M$ + %(Nigeria)$_M$ + %(Oman)$_M$ + %(Pakistan)$_M$ + %(Palau)$_M$ + %(Panama)$_M$ + %(Papua New Guinea)$_M$ + %(Paraguay)$_M$ + %(Peru)$_M$ + %(the Philippines)$_M$ + %(Qatar)$_M$ + %(the Republic of the Congo)$_M$ + %(the Republic of Korea)$_M$ + %(Rwanda)$_M$ + %(Saint Kitts and Nevis)$_M$ + %(Saint Lucia)$_M$ + %(Saint Vincent and the Grenadines)$_M$ + %(Samoa)$_M$ + %(São Tomé and Príncipe)$_M$ + %(Saudi Arabia)$_M$ + %(Senegal)$_M$ + %(the Seychelles)$_M$ + %(Sierra Leone)$_M$ + %(Singapore)$_M$ + %(Solomon Islands)$_M$ + %(Somalia)$_M$ + %(South Africa)$_M$ + %(South

Sudan)$_M$ + %(Sri Lanka)$_M$ + %(Sudan)$_M$ + %(Suriname)$_M$ + %(Syria)$_M$ + %(Tajikistan)$_M$ + %(Tanzania)$_M$ + %(Thailand)$_M$ + %(Timor-Leste)$_M$ + %(Togo)$_M$ + %(Tonga)$_M$ + %(Trinidad and Tobago)$_M$ + %(Tunisia)$_M$ + %(Turkey)$_M$ + %(Turkmenistan)$_M$ + %(Tuvalu)$_M$ + %(Uganda)$_M$ + %(United Arab Emirates)$_M$ + %(Uruguay)$_M$ + %(Uzbekistan)$_M$ + %(Vanuatu)$_M$ + %(Venezuela)$_M$ + %(Vietnam)$_M$ + %(Yemen)$_M$ + %(Zambia)$_M$ + %(Zimbabwe)$_M$ = 0.53191% +0.53191% + 0.53191% = 140 * 0.53191% = *74.46740%*. ∑%(Dd)$_M$ + ∑%(Dg)$_M$ = 25.53168% + 74.46740% = 99.99908% ≠ 100%. The percentage of developed countries that were members of the IMF in 2015 = [∑%(Dd)$_M$ / (∑%(Dd)$_M$ + ∑%(Dg)$_M$)] * 100% = [25.53168% / 99.99908%] * 100% = ***25.53191%***.[400] The percentage of developing countries that were members of the IMF in 2015 = [∑%(Dg)$_M$ / (∑%(Dd)$_M$ + ∑%(Dg)$_M$)] * 100% = [74.46740% /

[400] This percentage is given to five decimal places.

99.99908%] * 100% = ***74.46809%***.[401] *Check:* The percentage of developing countries that were members of the IMF in 2015 = 100% – the percentage of developed countries that were members of the IMF in 2015 = 100% – 25.53191% = 74.46809%. Crucially, this percentage of 74.49809% is identical to that which the UN Global SDG Database specifies for the proportion of developing regions that are members of the IMF in 2015.[402] As this exact number is independently arrived at for the same specific aggregated total by both the UN statisticians and the author, it is submitted that this particular item of information is a robust datum.

For the IMF in 2019, $\sum$%(Dd)$_M$ = %(DdC$_1$)$_M$ + %(DdC$_2$)$_M$ + %(DdC$_3$)$_M$ + … + %(DdC$_N$)$_M$ = %(Albania)$_M$ + %(Australia)$_M$ + %(Austria)$_M$ + %(Belarus)$_M$ + %(Belgium)$_M$ + %(Bosnia and Herzegovina)$_M$ + %(Bulgaria)$_M$ + %(Canada)$_M$ + %(Croatia)$_M$ + %(Cyprus)$_M$ + %(the Czech Republic)$_M$ + %(Denmark)$_M$ + %(Estonia)$_M$ + %(Finland)$_M$ + %(France)$_M$ + %(Germany)$_M$ + %(Greece)$_M$ + %(Hungary)$_M$ + %(Iceland)$_M$ + %(Ireland)$_M$ + %(Israel)$_M$ + %(Italy)$_M$ + %(Japan)$_M$ + %(Kosovo[403])$_M$ + %(Latvia)$_M$ + %(Lithuania)$_M$ + %(Luxembourg)$_M$ + %(Malta)$_M$ + %(Moldova)$_M$ + %(Montenegro)$_M$ + %(the Netherlands)$_M$ + %(New Zealand)$_M$ + %(North Macedonia)$_M$ + %(Norway)$_M$ + %(Poland)$_M$ + %(Portugal)$_M$ + %(Romania)$_M$ + %(Russia)$_M$ + %(San Marino)$_M$ + %(Serbia)$_M$ + %(Slovakia)$_M$ + %(Slovenia)$_M$ + %(Spain)$_M$ + %(Sweden)$_M$ + %(Switzerland)$_M$ + %(the UK)$_M$ + %(Ukraine)$_M$ + %(the USA)$_M$ = 0.529% + 0.529% = 48 * 0.529% = *25.392%*. For the IMF in 2019, $\sum$%(Dg)$_M$ = %(DgC$_1$)$_M$ + %(DgC$_2$)$_M$ + %(DgC$_3$)$_M$ + … + %(DgC$_N$)$_M$ = %(Afghanistan)$_M$ + %(Algeria)$_M$ + %(Angola)$_M$ + %(Antigua and Barbuda)$_M$ + %(Argentina)$_M$ + %(Armenia)$_M$ + %(Azerbaijan)$_M$ + %(the Bahamas)$_M$ +%(Bahrain)$_M$ + %(Bangladesh)$_M$ +

[401] This statistic is given to five decimal places.

[402] SDG indicators: United Nations Global SDG Database", United Nations, accessed July 9, 2020, https://unstats.un.org/sdgs/indicators/database/. Row 5792 of the spreadsheet concerning SDG Indicator 10.6.1 that was downloaded from this webpage on 9th July 2020, contains this datum.

[403] Note 399 classifies Kosovo as a developed country for the purposes of SDG Target 10.6 and SDG Indicator 10.6.1.

%(Barbados)$_{M}$ + %(Belize)$_{M}$ + %(Benin)$_{M}$ + %(Bhutan)$_{M}$ + %(Bolivia)$_{M}$ + %(Botswana)$_{M}$ + %(Brazil)$_{M}$ + %(Brunei Darussalam)$_{M}$ + %(Burkina Faso)$_{M}$ + %(Burundi)$_{M}$ + %(Cabo Verde)$_{M}$ + %(Cambodia)$_{M}$ + %(Cameroon)$_{M}$ + %(Central African Republic)$_{M}$ + %(Chad)$_{M}$ + %(Chile)$_{M}$ + %(China)$_{M}$ + %(Colombia)$_{M}$ + %(Comoros)$_{M}$ + %(Costa Rica)$_{M}$ + %(Côte d'Ivoire)$_{M}$ + %(the Democratic Republic of the Congo)$_{M}$ + %(Djibouti)$_{M}$ + %(Dominica)$_{M}$ + %(the Dominican Republic)$_{M}$ + %(Ecuador)$_{M}$ + %(Egypt)$_{M}$ + %(El Salvador)$_{M}$ + %(Equatorial Guinea)$_{M}$ + %(Eritrea)$_{M}$ + %(Eswatini)$_{M}$ + %(Ethiopia)$_{M}$ + %(Fiji)$_{M}$ + %(Gabon)$_{M}$ + %(the Gambia)$_{M}$ + %(Georgia)$_{M}$ + %(Ghana)$_{M}$ + %(Grenada)$_{M}$ + %(Guatemala)$_{M}$ + %(Guinea)$_{M}$ + %(Guinea-Bissau)$_{M}$ + %(Guyana)$_{M}$ + %(Haiti)$_{M}$ + %(Honduras)$_{M}$ + %(India)$_{M}$ + %(Indonesia)$_{M}$ + %(Iran)$_{M}$ + %(Iraq)$_{M}$ + %(Jamaica)$_{M}$ + %(Jordan)$_{M}$ + %(Kazakhstan)$_{M}$ + %(Kenya)$_{M}$ + %(Kiribati)$_{M}$ + %(Kuwait)$_{M}$ + %(Kyrgyzstan)$_{M}$ + %(Laos)$_{M}$ + %(Lebanon)$_{M}$ + %(Lesotho)$_{M}$ + %(Liberia)$_{M}$ + %(Libya)$_{M}$ + %(Madagascar)$_{M}$ + %(Malawi)$_{M}$ + %(Malaysia)$_{M}$ + %(the Maldives)$_{M}$ + %(Mali)$_{M}$ + %(the Marshall Islands)$_{M}$ + %(Mauritania)$_{M}$ + %(Mauritius)$_{M}$ + %(Mexico)$_{M}$ + %(Micronesia)$_{M}$ + %(Mongolia)$_{M}$ + %(Morocco)$_{M}$ + %(Mozambique)$_{M}$ + %(Myanmar)$_{M}$ + %(Namibia)$_{M}$ + %(Nauru[404])$_{M}$ + %(Nepal)$_{M}$ + %(Nicaragua)$_{M}$ + %(Niger)$_{M}$ + %(Nigeria)$_{M}$ + %(Oman)$_{M}$ + %(Pakistan)$_{M}$ + %(Palau)$_{M}$ + %(Panama)$_{M}$ + %(Papua New Guinea)$_{M}$ + %(Paraguay)$_{M}$ + %(Peru)$_{M}$ + %(the Philippines)$_{M}$ + %(Qatar)$_{M}$ + %(the Republic of the Congo)$_{M}$ + %(the Republic of Korea)$_{M}$ + %(Rwanda)$_{M}$ + %(Saint Kitts and Nevis)$_{M}$ + %(Saint Lucia)$_{M}$ + %(Saint Vincent and the Grenadines)$_{M}$ + %(Samoa)$_{M}$ + %(São Tomé and Príncipe)$_{M}$ + %(Saudi Arabia)$_{M}$ + %(Senegal)$_{M}$ + %(the Seychelles)$_{M}$ + %(Sierra Leone)$_{M}$ + %(Singapore)$_{M}$ + %(Solomon Islands)$_{M}$ + %(Somalia)$_{M}$ + %(South Africa)$_{M}$ + %(South Sudan)$_{M}$ + %(Sri Lanka)$_{M}$ + %(Sudan)$_{M}$ +

---

[404] Nauru is the 189th country to become a member of the IMF, and is the only state that joined the IMF between 1st January 2015 and 31st December 2019, i.e., over the period to which the data in the current and immediately-preceding paragraphs in the text relate; Nauru's effective date of membership of the IMF is 12th April 2016 ("List of Members", International Monetary Fund, last updated April 15, 2020, accessed July 14, 2020, https://www.imf.org/external/np/sec/memdir/memdate.htm). The UN Global SDG Database provides data on membership of the IMF for 188 countries in 2015, and for 189 countries in 2019 ("SDG indicators: United Nations Global SDG Database", United Nations, accessed July 9, 2020, https://unstats.un.org/sdgs/indicators/database/), which respectively matches the number of members of the IMF during those particular years ("List of Members", International Monetary Fund, last updated April 15, 2020, accessed July 14, 2020, https://www.imf.org/external/np/sec/memdir/memdate.htm).

%(Suriname)$_M$ + %(Syria)$_M$ + %(Tajikistan)$_M$ + %(Tanzania)$_M$ + %(Thailand)$_M$ + %(Timor-Leste)$_M$ + %(Togo)$_M$ + %(Tonga)$_M$ + %(Trinidad and Tobago)$_M$ + %(Tunisia)$_M$ + %(Turkey)$_M$ + %(Turkmenistan)$_M$ + %(Tuvalu)$_M$ + %(Uganda)$_M$ + %(United Arab Emirates)$_M$ + %(Uruguay)$_M$ + %(Uzbekistan)$_M$ + %(Vanuatu)$_M$ + %(Venezuela)$_M$ + %(Vietnam)$_M$ + %(Yemen)$_M$ + %(Zambia)$_M$ + %(Zimbabwe)$_M$ = 0.529% + 0.529% + 0.529% + 0.529% + 0.529% + 0.529% + 0.529% + 0.529% + 0.529% + 0.529% + 0.529% +0.529% + 0.529% = 141 * 0.529% = *74.589%*. ∑%(Dd)$_M$ + ∑%(Dg)$_M$ = 25.392% + 74.589% = 99.981% ≠ 100%. The percentage of developed countries that were members of the IMF in 2019 = [∑%(Dd)$_M$ / (∑%(Dd)$_M$ + ∑%(Dg)$_M$)] * 100% = [25.392% / 99.981%] * 100% = ***25.39683%***.[405] The percentage of developing countries that were members of the IMF in 2019 = [∑%(Dg)$_M$ / (∑%(Dd)$_M$ + ∑%(Dg)$_M$)] * 100% = [74.589% / 99.981%] * 100% = ***74.60317%***.[406] *Check:* The percentage of developing countries that were members of the IMF in 2019 = 100% – the percentage of developed countries that were members of the IMF in 2019 = 100% – 25.39683% = 74.60317%. Critically, this percentage of 74.60317% is identical to that which the UN Global SDG Database specifies for the proportion of developing regions that are members of the

405 This statistic is given to five decimal places.

406 This datum is given to five decimal places.

IMF in 2019.[407] As this precise number is independently reached for the same specific aggregated total by both the UN statisticians and the author, it is submitted that this particular item of information is a robust datum. Furthermore, since the UN Global SDG Database and the author agree exactly on the magnitude of both the totals for developing regions that the latter has calculated from the country-specific data in this database on the proportion of developing countries in international organizations – one of which relates to 2015 and the other to 2019, it is assumed that this aggregate as provided in the UN Global SDG Database is accurate for all eleven international organizations[408] which the database includes for these two years and for those between them – i.e., 2015, 2016, 2017, 2018 and 2019. Accordingly, Table 3.19 shows the percentage of members of these institutions that are developing countries for each of these five years.

Table 3.19: The proportion of members of international institutions, by organization, that are developing countries (%) – for each of the years 2015, 2016, 2017, 2018 and 2019[409]

Organization	2015	2016	2017	2018	2019
AfDB	77.5	77.5	77.5	77.5	-
AsDB	68.65672	67.16418	67.16418	-	-
ECOSOC	64.81481	64.81481	64.81481	66.66667	68.51852
FSB	50	50	50	50	50
IADB	60.41667	60.41667	60.41667	-	-
IBRD	74.47	74.47	74.60317	74.60317	74.60317

[407] SDG indicators: United Nations Global SDG Database", United Nations, accessed July 9, 2020, https://unstats.un.org/sdgs/indicators/database/. Row 5830 of the spreadsheet regarding SDG Indicator 10.6.1 that was downloaded from this webpage on 9th July 2020, includes this figure.

[408] The text to note 384 lists these eleven international institutions for which the UN Global SDG Database publishes data concerning SDG Indicator 10.6.1. The text to note 383 states SDG Indicator 10.6.1. The text to note 416 alphabetizes these eleven organizations.

[409] "SDG indicators: United Nations Global SDG Database", United Nations, accessed July 9, 2020, https://unstats.un.org/sdgs/indicators/database/. Rows 5784-5833 inclusive of the spreadsheet concerning SDG Indicator 10.6.1 that was downloaded from this webpage on 9th July 2020, contain the data in Table 3.19. As Table 3.19 shows, this spreadsheet omits aggregated data: (a) for 2018 and 2019 on the proportion of members of (i) the AsDB, and (ii) the IADB, that are developing countries, and (b) for 2019 on the proportion of members of the AfDB that are developing countries.

IFC	74.45652	74.45652	74.45652	74.45652	74.45652
IMF	74.46809	74.46809	74.60317	74.60317	74.60317
UN General Assembly	74.09326	74.09326	74.09326	74.09326	74.09326
UNSC	53.33333	46.66667	46.66667	53.33333	53.33333
WTO	71.25	71.6	71.95122	71.95122	71.95122

Of the 193 Member States of the UN,[410] the following 50 are developed countries according to the UN's M49 statistical standard:[411] Albania, Andorra, Australia, Austria, Belarus, Belgium, Bosnia and Herzegovina, Bulgaria, Canada, Croatia, Cyprus, the Czech Republic, Denmark, Estonia, Finland, France, Germany, Greece, Hungary, Iceland, Ireland, Israel, Italy, Japan, Latvia, Liechtenstein, Lithuania, Luxembourg, Malta, Moldova, Monaco, Montenegro, the Netherlands, New Zealand, North Macedonia, Norway, Poland, Portugal, Romania, Russia, San Marino, Serbia, Slovakia, Slovenia, Spain, Sweden, Switzerland, the UK, Ukraine, and the USA.[412] Thus, the number of developing countries that are UN Member States – under the M49 statistical standard – is equal to the total number of UN Member States, i.e., 193 countries, less the number of developed countries that are UN Member States, i.e., 50 countries, which is 143 countries. The percentage of developing countries that are UN Member States = [the number of developing countries that are UN Member States / the total number of UN Member States] * 100% = [143 countries / 193 countries] * 100% = *74.09326%*.[413] This percentage is identical to that which the UN Global SDG Database provides for the proportion of members of the UN General Assembly that are developing countries for 2015, 2016, 2017, 2018 and 2019 – as Table 3.19 shows. Since the Member States of the UN are identical to the Member States of the UN General Assembly,[414] and as the membership of the UN remained constant throughout the period 2015 to 2019,[415] the percentage calculated

410 Text to note 226.

411 Note 385 lists the states and territories that the UN's M49 statistical standard classifies as 'developed regions'.

412 Note 226; Baber, *Essays on International Law*, 109.

413 This percentage is given to five decimal places.

414 "Member States", United Nations, accessed July 15, 2020, https://www.un.org/en/member-states/; "Member States", United Nations, accessed July 15, 2020, https://www.un.org/en/sections/member-states/.

415 South Sudan was admitted on 14th July 2011 as the 193rd Member State of the UN ("Member States", United Nations, accessed July 15, 2020, https://www.un.org/en/sections/member-states/).

above in this paragraph, i.e., 74.09326%, should equal the proportion of members of the UN General Assembly that are developing countries during this time. Table 3.19 confirms this equality, which corroborates the assumption of accuracy of the UN Global SDG Database's aggregate for the proportion of members that are developing countries regarding the AfDB, the AsDB, the ECOSOC, the FSB, the IADB, the IBRD, the IFC, the IMF, the UN General Assembly, the UNSC and the WTO, for each of the years 2015, 2016, 2017, 2018 and 2019[416] – which Table 3.19 shows, and that assumption's underlying claims of robust data in respect of the values of the aggregate for the IMF in 2015[417] and 2019.[418]

If this statistic of 74.09326% – 74% to two significant figures – is considered to be the benchmark for equality of membership in international organizations between developing countries and developed states – i.e., if for there to equality between these two groups in respect of such membership 74% of the members are to be the former and 26% the latter, then, pursuant to the data in Table 3.19: (i) membership of the AfDB over the period 2015 to 2018 rather favours developing states, (ii) membership of the AsDB from 2015 to 2017 moderately favours developed countries, (iii) membership of the ECOSOC during the period 2015 to 2019 somewhat favours developed states – though less so in 2018 than in 2015, 2016 and 2017 and less so in 2019 than in 2018, (iv) membership of the WTO throughout the period 2015 to 2019 mildly favours developed countries – though less so in 2016 than in 2015 and less so in 2017, 2018 and 2019 than in 2016, (v) membership of the IADB between 2015 and 2017 substantially favours developed states, (vi) membership of the FSB and of the UNSC from 2015 to 2019 hugely favours developed states, (vii) membership of the UN General Assembly over the period 2015 to 2019 is equal between developing and developed countries, and (viii) membership of the IBRD, the IFC and the IMF during the period 2015 to 2019 is approximately equal between developing and developed states, although very-slightly favouring developing states – with the latter's membership of the IBRD and the IMF being a little higher in 2017, 2018 and 2019 than in 2015 and 2016. It is submitted that, *on the basis of these data and this benchmark*, developing countries need

[416] The text to note 408 comprises this assumption.

[417] The sentence immediately following the text to note 402 contains this statement for the percentage of developing countries that were members of the IMF in 2015.

[418] The sentence immediately succeeding the text to note 407 consists of this statement for the percentage of developing countries that were members of the IMF in 2019.

enhanced representation – as SDG Target 10.6[419] requires – on the FSB and the UNSC and, to a lesser extent, the IADB, but *not* on the AfDB, the IBRD, the IFC, the IMF and the UN General Assembly.

2. The percentage of voting rights: For the IMF in 2015, $\sum\%(Dd)_{VR}$ = $\%(DdC_1)_{VR}$ + $\%(DdC_2)_{VR}$ + $\%(DdC_3)_{VR}$ + … $\%(DdC_N)_{VR}$ = %(Albania)$_{VR}$ + %(Australia)$_{VR}$ + %(Austria)$_{VR}$ + %(Belarus)$_{VR}$ + %(Belgium)$_{VR}$ + %(Bosnia and Herzegovina)$_{VR}$ + %(Bulgaria)$_{VR}$ + %(Canada)$_{VR}$ + %(Croatia)$_{VR}$ + %(Cyprus)$_{VR}$ + %(the Czech Republic)$_{VR}$ + %(Denmark)$_{VR}$ + %(Estonia)$_{VR}$ + %(Finland)$_{VR}$ + %(France)$_{VR}$ + %(Germany)$_{VR}$ + %(Greece)$_{VR}$ + %(Hungary)$_{VR}$ + %(Iceland)$_{VR}$ + %(Ireland)$_{VR}$ + %(Israel)$_{VR}$ + %(Italy)$_{VR}$ + %(Japan)$_{VR}$ + %(Kosovo[420])$_{VR}$ + %(Latvia)$_{VR}$ + %(Lithuania)$_{VR}$ + %(Luxembourg)$_{VR}$ + %(Malta)$_{VR}$ + %(Moldova)$_{VR}$ + %(Montenegro)$_{VR}$ + %(the Netherlands)$_{VR}$ + %(New Zealand)$_{VR}$ + %(North Macedonia)$_{VR}$ + %(Norway)$_{VR}$ + %(Poland)$_{VR}$ + %(Portugal)$_{VR}$ + %(Romania)$_{VR}$ + %(Russia)$_{VR}$ + %(San Marino)$_{VR}$ + %(Serbia)$_{VR}$ + %(Slovakia)$_{VR}$ + %(Slovenia)$_{VR}$ + %(Spain)$_{VR}$ + %(Sweden)$_{VR}$ + %(Switzerland)$_{VR}$ + %(the UK)$_{VR}$ + %(Ukraine)$_{VR}$ + %(the USA)$_{VR}$ = 0.05308%[421] + 1.31327% + 0.86794% + 1.85633% + 0.09637% + 0.28327% + 0.18258% + 2.55617% + 0.17413% + 0.09204% + 0.42689% + 0.77966% + 0.06653% + 0.53067% + 4.28962% + 5.80793% + 0.46640% + 0.44125% + 0.07594% + 0.52821% + 0.45026% + 3.15647% + 6.22966% + 0.05269% + 0.08566% + 0.10224% + 0.19539% + 0.06975% + 0.07816% + 0.04019% + 2.07739% + 0.38420% + 0.77661% + 0.69913% + 0.43780% + 0.43800% + 2.38803% + 0.03817% + 0.21483% + 0.19888% + 0.13838% + 1.62550% + 0.97966% + 1.40139% + 0.57360% + 0.05661% + 4.28962% + 16.74073% = *64.80728%*. For the IMF in 2015, $\sum\%(Dg)_{VR}$ = $\%(DgC_1)_{VR}$ + $\%(DgC_2)_{VR}$ + $\%(DgC_3)_{VR}$ + … $\%(DgC_N)_{VR}$ = %(Afghanistan)$_{VR}$ + %(Algeria)$_{VR}$ + %(Angola)$_{VR}$ + %(Antigua and Barbuda)$_{VR}$ + %(Argentina)$_{VR}$ + %(Armenia)$_{VR}$ + %(Azerbaijan)$_{VR}$ + %(the Bahamas)$_{VR}$ + %(Bahrain)$_{VR}$ + %(Bangladesh)$_{VR}$ + %(Barbados)$_{VR}$ + %(Belize)$_{VR}$ + %(Benin)$_{VR}$ + %(Bhutan)$_{VR}$ + %(Bolivia)$_{VR}$ + %(Botswana)$_{VR}$ + %(Brazil)$_{VR}$ + %(Brunei

---

[419] The text to note 382 states SDG Target 10.6.

[420] Note 399 categorizes Kosovo as a developed country for the purposes of SDG Target 10.6 and SDG Indicator 10.6.1. The text to note 382 specifies SDG Target 10.6. The text to note 383 states SDG Indicator 10.6.1.

[421] Whilst these numbers correspond to the percentage of voting rights in the IMF in 2015 of each of the countries listed in this calculation, the ordering of these figures in this computation is that in which the UN Global SDG Database displays those countries and their data – rather than the alphabetical list of the countries as shown above in this equation.

Darussalam)$_{VR}$ + %(Burkina Faso)$_{VR}$ + %(Burundi)$_{VR}$ + %(Cabo Verde)$_{VR}$ + %(Cambodia)$_{VR}$ + %(Cameroon)$_{VR}$ + %(Central African Republic)$_{VR}$ + %(Chad)$_{VR}$ + %(Chile)$_{VR}$ + %(China)$_{VR}$ + %(Colombia)$_{VR}$ + %(Comoros)$_{VR}$ + %(Costa Rica)$_{VR}$ + %(Côte d'Ivoire)$_{VR}$ + %(the Democratic Republic of the Congo)$_{VR}$ + %(Djibouti)$_{VR}$ + %(Dominica)$_{VR}$ + %(the Dominican Republic)$_{VR}$ + %(Ecuador)$_{VR}$ + %(Egypt)$_{VR}$ + %(El Salvador)$_{VR}$ + %(Equatorial Guinea)$_{VR}$ + %(Eritrea)$_{VR}$ + %(Eswatini)$_{VR}$ + %(Ethiopia)$_{VR}$ + %(Fiji)$_{VR}$ + %(Gabon)$_{VR}$ + %(the Gambia)$_{VR}$ + %(Georgia)$_{VR}$ + %(Ghana)$_{VR}$ + %(Grenada)$_{VR}$ + %(Guatemala)$_{VR}$ + %(Guinea)$_{VR}$ + %(Guinea-Bissau)$_{VR}$ + %(Guyana)$_{VR}$ + %(Haiti)$_{VR}$ + %(Honduras)$_{VR}$ + %(India)$_{VR}$ + %(Indonesia)$_{VR}$ + %(Iran)$_{VR}$ + %(Iraq)$_{VR}$ + %(Jamaica)$_{VR}$ + %(Jordan)$_{VR}$ + %(Kazakhstan)$_{VR}$ + %(Kenya)$_{VR}$ + %(Kiribati)$_{VR}$ + %(Kuwait)$_{VR}$ + %(Kyrgyzstan)$_{VR}$ + %(Laos)$_{VR}$ + %(Lebanon)$_{VR}$ + %(Lesotho)$_{VR}$ + %(Liberia)$_{VR}$ + %(Libya)$_{VR}$ + %(Madagascar)$_{VR}$ + %(Malawi)$_{VR}$ + %(Malaysia)$_{VR}$ + %(the Maldives)$_{VR}$ + %(Mali)$_{VR}$ + %(the Marshall Islands)$_{VR}$ + %(Mauritania)$_{VR}$ + %(Mauritius)$_{VR}$ + %(Mexico)$_{VR}$ + %(Micronesia)$_{VR}$ + %(Mongolia)$_{VR}$ + %(Morocco)$_{VR}$ + %(Mozambique)$_{VR}$ + %(Myanmar)$_{VR}$ + %(Namibia)$_{VR}$ + %(Nepal)$_{VR}$ + %(Nicaragua)$_{VR}$ + %(Niger)$_{VR}$ + %(Nigeria)$_{VR}$ + %(Oman)$_{VR}$ + %(Pakistan)$_{VR}$ + %(Palau)$_{VR}$ + %(Panama)$_{VR}$ + %(Papua New Guinea)$_{VR}$ + %(Paraguay)$_{VR}$ + %(Peru)$_{VR}$ + %(the Philippines)$_{VR}$ + %(Qatar)$_{VR}$ + %(the Republic of the Congo)$_{VR}$ + %(the Republic of Korea)$_{VR}$ + %(Rwanda)$_{VR}$ + %(Saint Kitts and Nevis)$_{VR}$ + %(Saint Lucia)$_{VR}$ + %(Saint Vincent and the Grenadines)$_{VR}$ + %(Samoa)$_{VR}$ + %(São Tomé and Príncipe)$_{VR}$ + %(Saudi Arabia)$_{VR}$ + %(Senegal)$_{VR}$ + %(the Seychelles)$_{VR}$ + %(Sierra Leone)$_{VR}$ + %(Singapore)$_{VR}$ + %(Solomon Islands)$_{VR}$ + %(Somalia)$_{VR}$ + %(South Africa)$_{VR}$ + %(South Sudan)$_{VR}$ + %(Sri Lanka)$_{VR}$ + %(Sudan)$_{VR}$ + %(Suriname)$_{VR}$ + %(Syria)$_{VR}$ + %(Tajikistan)$_{VR}$ + %(Tanzania)$_{VR}$ + %(Thailand)$_{VR}$ + %(Timor-Leste)$_{VR}$ + %(Togo)$_{VR}$ + %(Tonga)$_{VR}$ + %(Trinidad and Tobago)$_{VR}$ + %(Tunisia)$_{VR}$ + %(Turkey)$_{VR}$ + %(Turkmenistan)$_{VR}$ + %(Tuvalu)$_{VR}$ + %(Uganda)$_{VR}$ + %(United Arab Emirates)$_{VR}$ + %(Uruguay)$_{VR}$ + %(Uzbekistan)$_{VR}$ + %(Vanuatu)$_{VR}$ + %(Venezuela)$_{VR}$ + %(Vietnam)$_{VR}$ + %(Yemen)$_{VR}$ + %(Zambia)$_{VR}$ + %(Zimbabwe)$_{VR}$ = 0.09351%[422] + 0.52706% + 0.14286% + 0.03464% + 0.09311% + 0.86921% + 0.08097% + 0.08284% + 0.24086% + 0.06578% + 0.05606% + 0.03178% + 0.09732% + 0.06411%

---

[422] Whilst these figures correspond to the percentage of voting rights in the IMF in 2015 of each of the countries listed in this calculation, the ordering of these numbers in this computation is that in which the UN Global SDG Database displays those states and their data – rather than the alphabetical list of the countries as shown above in this equation.

+ 1.71560% + 0.03674% + 0.03341% + 0.11466% + 0.13180% + 0.05983% + 0.06399% + 0.10295% + 0.03372% + 0.05138% + 0.19329% + 0.05570% + 0.36892% + 3.80854% + 0.33635% + 0.03281% + 0.06284% + 0.24074% + 0.09438% + 0.05384% + 0.03253% + 0.11612% + 0.16726% + 0.09724% + 0.05003% + 0.08232% + 0.03559% + 0.05717% + 0.03559% + 0.09050% + 0.08891% + 0.04162% + 0.17567% + 0.03150% + 0.03392% + 0.11267% + 0.07177% + 0.06534% + 0.06177% + 0.08066% + 2.33887% + 0.85421% + 0.62327% + 0.50076% + 0.15830% + 0.13779% + 0.19900% + 0.09692% + 0.13695% + 1.36485% + 0.57721% + 0.06451% + 0.05027% + 0.13497% + 0.04313% + 0.08054% + 0.47509% + 0.07776% + 0.05681% + 0.73305% + 0.03325% + 0.06629% + 0.05483% + 0.06959% + 1.46772% + 0.04955% + 0.26264% + 0.07435% + 0.12331% + 0.08343% + 0.05757% + 0.03602% + 0.08085% + 0.05538% + 0.72484% + 0.03130% + 0.03067% + 0.03051% + 0.43938% + 0.11124% + 0.08149% + 0.06891% + 0.28256% + 0.43367% + 0.03491% + 0.03356% + 0.14933% + 0.06106% + 0.03281% + 0.03535% + 0.03257% + 0.03221% + 2.80067% + 0.09347% + 0.03360% + 0.07042% + 0.58788% + 0.21206% + 0.04681% + 0.77058% + 0.16949% + 0.07808% + 0.09661% + 0.06582% + 0.04939% + 0.14576% + 0.06380% + 0.60078% + 0.05840% + 0.03202% + 0.16242% + 0.32782% + 0.14294% + 0.60685% + 0.05911% + 0.02999% + 0.10089% + 0.40368% + 0.10819% + 0.05316% + 0.15088% + 0.13862% + 1.08424% + 0.03388% + 0.12588% + 0.22332% = *35.19270%*. $\sum\%(Dd)_{VR}$ + $\sum\%(Dg)_{VR}$ = 64.80728% + 35.19270% = 99.99998% ≠ 100%. The percentage of voting rights in the IMF in 2015 of developed countries = [$\sum\%(Dd)_{VR}$ / ($\sum\%(Dd)_{VR}$ + $\sum\%(Dg)_{VR}$)] * 100% = [64.80728% / 99.99998%] * 100% = ***64.80729%***.[423] The percentage of voting rights in the IMF in 2015 held by developing countries = [$\sum\%(Dg)_{VR}$ / ($\sum\%(Dd)_{VR}$ + $\sum\%(Dg)_{VR}$)] * 100% = [35.19270% / 99.99998%] * 100% = ***35.19271%***.[424] *Check:* The percentage of voting rights in the IMF in 2015 held by developing countries = 100% – the percentage of voting rights in the IMF in 2015 held by developed countries = 100% – 64.80729% = 35.19271%. This percentage of 35.19271% is 0.00003% lower than that which the UN Global SDG Database specifies for the proportion of voting rights in the IMF in 2015 that are held by developing countries – which is 35.19274% of the total voting rights in the IMF.[425] It is submitted that 0.00003% is a negligible difference between

[423] This statistic is given to five decimal places.

[424] This datum is given to five decimal places.

[425] SDG indicators: United Nations Global SDG Database", United Nations, accessed July 9, 2020, https://unstats.un.org/sdgs/indicators/database/. Row 15344

the UN statisticians' calculation of this aggregated total and the author's computation of it, which may be explained (at least in part) by differences in the rounding of numerals. The statistic – which is unequivocally 35.1927% to four decimal places – is sufficiently certain to be considered a robust datum, although to a lesser degree than the two pairs of identical values resulting from the UN statisticians' and the author's calculations of the percentage of developing countries that were members of the IMF in 2015[426] and in 2019.[427]

For the IMF in 2019, $\sum\%(Dd)_{VR}$ = $\%(DdC_1)_{VR}$ + $\%(DdC_2)_{VR}$ + $\%(DdC_3)_{VR}$ + … $\%(DdC_N)_{VR}$ = %(Albania)$_{VR}$ + %(Australia)$_{VR}$ + %(Austria)$_{VR}$ + %(Belarus)$_{VR}$ + %(Belgium)$_{VR}$ + %(Bosnia and Herzegovina)$_{VR}$ + %(Bulgaria)$_{VR}$ + %(Canada)$_{VR}$ + %(Croatia)$_{VR}$ + %(Cyprus)$_{VR}$ + %(the Czech Republic)$_{VR}$ + %(Denmark)$_{VR}$ + %(Estonia)$_{VR}$ + %(Finland)$_{VR}$ + %(France)$_{VR}$ + %(Germany)$_{VR}$ + %(Greece)$_{VR}$ + %(Hungary)$_{VR}$ + %(Iceland)$_{VR}$ + %(Ireland)$_{VR}$ + %(Israel)$_{VR}$ + %(Italy)$_{VR}$ + %(Japan)$_{VR}$ + %(Kosovo[428])$_{VR}$ + %(Latvia)$_{VR}$ + %(Lithuania)$_{VR}$ + %(Luxembourg)$_{VR}$ + %(Malta)$_{VR}$ + %(Moldova)$_{VR}$ + %(Montenegro)$_{VR}$ + %(the Netherlands)$_{VR}$ + %(New Zealand)$_{VR}$ + %(North Macedonia)$_{VR}$ + %(Norway)$_{VR}$ + %(Poland)$_{VR}$ + %(Portugal)$_{VR}$ + %(Romania)$_{VR}$ + %(Russia)$_{VR}$ + %(San Marino)$_{VR}$ + %(Serbia)$_{VR}$ + %(Slovakia)$_{VR}$ + %(Slovenia)$_{VR}$ + %(Spain)$_{VR}$ + %(Sweden)$_{VR}$ + %(Switzerland)$_{VR}$ + %(the UK)$_{VR}$ + %(Ukraine)$_{VR}$ + %(the USA)$_{VR}$ = 0.05679%[429] + 1.33499% + 0.81036% + 1.30286% + 0.08180% + 0.20720% + 0.16452% + 2.21946% + 0.17165% + 0.08947% + 0.46230% + 0.71249% + 0.07751% + 0.50807% + 4.03375% + 5.32114% + 0.51171% + 0.41457% + 0.09305% + 0.71457% + 0.41077% + 3.02339% + 6.15288% + 0.04552% + 0.09513% + 0.11685% + 0.29174% +

of the spreadsheet regarding SDG Indicator 10.6.1 that was downloaded from this webpage on 9th July 2020, contains this statistic.

426 The text to note 402 and the sentence immediately following that statement concern the matching value and robustness, respectively, of the percentage of developing countries that were members of the IMF in 2015.

427 The text to note 407 and the sentence immediately succeeding that statement concern the matching value and robustness, respectively, of the percentage of developing countries that were members of the IMF in 2019.

428 Note 399 classifies Kosovo as a developed country for the purposes of SDG Target 10.6 and SDG Indicator 10.6.1.

429 Whilst these numbers correspond to the percentage of voting rights in the IMF in 2019 of each of the countries listed in this calculation, the ordering of these figures in this computation is that in which the UN Global SDG Database displays those countries and their data – rather than the alphabetical list of the countries as shown above in this equation.

0.06255% + 0.06338% + 0.04113% + 1.76498% + 0.27789% + 0.77513% + 0.84283% + 0.43843% + 0.38902% + 2.59296% + 0.03888% + 0.15921% + 0.22800% + 0.14564% + 1.92373% + 0.90931% + 1.17578% + 0.42884% + 0.05698% + 4.03375% + 16.51934% = *62.29230%*. For the IMF in 2019, $\sum\%(Dg)_{VR} = \%(DgC_1)_{VR} + \%(DgC_2)_{VR} + \%(DgC_3)_{VR} + \ldots \%(DgC_N)_{VR}$ = %(Afghanistan)$_{VR}$ + %(Algeria)$_{VR}$ + %(Angola)$_{VR}$ + %(Antigua and Barbuda)$_{VR}$ + %(Argentina)$_{VR}$ + %(Armenia)$_{VR}$ + %(Azerbaijan)$_{VR}$ + %(the Bahamas)$_{VR}$ + %(Bahrain)$_{VR}$ + %(Bangladesh)$_{VR}$ + %(Barbados)$_{VR}$ + %(Belize)$_{VR}$ + %(Benin)$_{VR}$ + %(Bhutan)$_{VR}$ + %(Bolivia)$_{VR}$ + %(Botswana)$_{VR}$ + %(Brazil)$_{VR}$ + %(Brunei Darussalam)$_{VR}$ + %(Burkina Faso)$_{VR}$ + %(Burundi)$_{VR}$ + %(Cabo Verde)$_{VR}$ + %(Cambodia)$_{VR}$ + %(Cameroon)$_{VR}$ + %(Central African Republic)$_{VR}$ + %(Chad)$_{VR}$ + %(Chile)$_{VR}$ + %(China)$_{VR}$ + %(Colombia)$_{VR}$ + %(Comoros)$_{VR}$ + %(Costa Rica)$_{VR}$ + %(Côte d'Ivoire)$_{VR}$ + %(the Democratic Republic of the Congo)$_{VR}$ + %(Djibouti)$_{VR}$ + %(Dominica)$_{VR}$ + %(the Dominican Republic)$_{VR}$ + %(Ecuador)$_{VR}$ + %(Egypt)$_{VR}$ + %(El Salvador)$_{VR}$ + %(Equatorial Guinea)$_{VR}$ + %(Eritrea)$_{VR}$ + %(Eswatini)$_{VR}$ + %(Ethiopia)$_{VR}$ + %(Fiji)$_{VR}$ + %(Gabon)$_{VR}$ + %(the Gambia)$_{VR}$ + %(Georgia)$_{VR}$ + %(Ghana)$_{VR}$ + %(Grenada)$_{VR}$ + %(Guatemala)$_{VR}$ + %(Guinea)$_{VR}$ + %(Guinea-Bissau)$_{VR}$ + %(Guyana)$_{VR}$ + %(Haiti)$_{VR}$ + %(Honduras)$_{VR}$ + %(India)$_{VR}$ + %(Indonesia)$_{VR}$ + %(Iran)$_{VR}$ + %(Iraq)$_{VR}$ + %(Jamaica)$_{VR}$ + %(Jordan)$_{VR}$ + %(Kazakhstan)$_{VR}$ + %(Kenya)$_{VR}$ + %(Kiribati)$_{VR}$ + %(Kuwait)$_{VR}$ + %(Kyrgyzstan)$_{VR}$ + %(Laos)$_{VR}$ + %(Lebanon)$_{VR}$ + %(Lesotho)$_{VR}$ + %(Liberia)$_{VR}$ + %(Libya)$_{VR}$ + %(Madagascar)$_{VR}$ + %(Malawi)$_{VR}$ + %(Malaysia)$_{VR}$ + %(the Maldives)$_{VR}$ + %(Mali)$_{VR}$ + %(the Marshall Islands)$_{VR}$ + %(Mauritania)$_{VR}$ + %(Mauritius)$_{VR}$ + %(Mexico)$_{VR}$ + %(Micronesia)$_{VR}$ + %(Mongolia)$_{VR}$ + %(Morocco)$_{VR}$ + %(Mozambique)$_{VR}$ + %(Myanmar)$_{VR}$ + %(Namibia)$_{VR}$ + %(Nauru[430])$_{VR}$ + %(Nepal)$_{VR}$ + %(Nicaragua)$_{VR}$ + %(Niger)$_{VR}$ + %(Nigeria)$_{VR}$ + %(Oman)$_{VR}$ + %(Pakistan)$_{VR}$ + %(Palau)$_{VR}$ + %(Panama)$_{VR}$ + %(Papua New Guinea)$_{VR}$ + %(Paraguay)$_{VR}$ + %(Peru)$_{VR}$ + %(the Philippines)$_{VR}$ + %(Qatar)$_{VR}$ + %(the Republic of the Congo)$_{VR}$ + %(the Republic of Korea)$_{VR}$ + %(Rwanda)$_{VR}$ + %(Saint Kitts and Nevis)$_{VR}$ + %(Saint Lucia)$_{VR}$ + %(Saint Vincent and the Grenadines)$_{VR}$ + %(Samoa)$_{VR}$ + %(São Tomé and Príncipe)$_{VR}$ + %(Saudi Arabia)$_{VR}$ + %(Senegal)$_{VR}$ + %(the Seychelles)$_{VR}$ + %(Sierra Leone)$_{VR}$ + %(Singapore)$_{VR}$ + %(Solomon Islands)$_{VR}$ + %(Somalia)$_{VR}$ + %(South Africa)$_{VR}$ + %(South Sudan)$_{VR}$ + %(Sri Lanka)$_{VR}$ + %(Sudan)$_{VR}$ +

[430] Note 404 provides information concerning Nauru's accession to membership of the IMF.

%(Suriname)$_{VR}$ + %(Syria)$_{VR}$ + %(Tajikistan)$_{VR}$ + %(Tanzania)$_{VR}$ + %(Thailand)$_{VR}$ + %(Timor-Leste)$_{VR}$ + %(Togo)$_{VR}$ + %(Tonga)$_{VR}$ + %(Trinidad and Tobago)$_{VR}$ + %(Tunisia)$_{VR}$ + %(Turkey)$_{VR}$ + %(Turkmenistan)$_{VR}$ + %(Tuvalu)$_{VR}$ + %(Uganda)$_{VR}$ + %(United Arab Emirates)$_{VR}$ + %(Uruguay)$_{VR}$ + %(Uzbekistan)$_{VR}$ + %(Vanuatu)$_{VR}$ + %(Venezuela)$_{VR}$ + %(Vietnam)$_{VR}$ + %(Yemen)$_{VR}$ + %(Zambia)$_{VR}$ + %(Zimbabwe)$_{VR}$ = 0.09344%[431] + 0.41852% + 0.17616% + 0.03308% + 0.10694% + 0.66240% + 0.06535% + 0.10759% + 0.24103% + 0.05470% + 0.04788% + 0.03316% + 0.07681% + 0.06829% + 2.22306% + 0.03441% + 0.03324% + 0.08897% + 0.13179% + 0.05971% + 0.06388% + 0.08395% + 0.03382% + 0.05124% + 0.14411% + 0.05696% + 0.37569% + 6.08580% + 0.43533% + 0.03265% + 0.06130% + 0.24091% + 0.10250% + 0.05371% + 0.03139% + 0.12396% + 0.16774% + 0.08617% + 0.06040% + 0.08885% + 0.03227% + 0.04866% + 0.03543% + 0.07203% + 0.07091% + 0.04147% + 0.17574% + 0.03133% + 0.03237% + 0.11427% + 0.07167% + 0.06523% + 0.06165% + 0.07874% + 2.63483% + 0.95271% + 0.73786% + 0.35969% + 0.15834% + 0.10519% + 0.25927% + 0.09728% + 0.13696% + 1.73442% + 0.41328% + 0.06440% + 0.05013% + 0.15498% + 0.04298% + 0.08045% + 0.34169% + 0.07767% + 0.05669% + 0.75111% + 0.03332% + 0.06618% + 0.05470% + 0.05736% + 1.79999% + 0.04347% + 0.20682% + 0.07425% + 0.13728% + 0.06708% + 0.02966% + 0.06028% + 0.03384% + 0.08077% + 0.05526% + 0.51680% + 0.03012% + 0.02980% + 0.02972% + 0.43265% + 0.10398% + 0.08140% + 0.06912% + 0.29426% + 0.43501% + 0.03475% + 0.03419% + 0.17517% + 0.06094% + 0.03159% + 0.03336% + 0.03143% + 0.03205% + 2.01455% + 0.09340% + 0.03366% + 0.07032% + 0.80240% + 0.25822% + 0.03789% + 0.63536% + 0.16954% + 0.07799% + 0.06283% + 0.05472% + 0.04471% + 0.08744% + 0.06368% + 0.66729% + 0.05828% + 0.03185% + 0.12245% + 0.48832% + 0.13743% + 0.95473% + 0.07652% + 0.02961% + 0.10084% + 0.43386% + 0.10815% + 0.05303% + 0.11437% + 0.13863% + 0.76878% + 0.03233% + 0.12587% + 0.22347% = *37.70771%*. ∑%(Dd)$_{VR}$ + ∑%(Dg)$_{VR}$ = 62.29230% + 37.70771% = 100.00001% ≠ 100%. The percentage of voting rights in the IMF in 2015 held by developed countries = [∑%(Dd)$_{VR}$ / (∑%(Dd)$_{VR}$ + ∑%(Dg)$_{VR}$)] *

[431] Whilst these figures correspond to the percentage of voting rights in the IMF in 2019 of each of the countries listed in this calculation, the ordering of these numbers in this computation is that in which the UN Global SDG Database displays those states and their data – rather than the alphabetical list of the countries as shown above in this equation.

100% = [62.29230% / 100.00001%] * 100% = ***62.29229%***.[432] The percentage of voting rights in the IMF in 2019 held by developing countries = [$\sum$%$(Dg)_{VR}$ / ($\sum$%$(Dd)_{VR}$ + $\sum$%$(Dg)_{VR}$)] * 100% = [37.70771% / 100.00001%] * 100% = ***37.70771%***.[433] *Check:* The percentage of voting rights in the IMF in 2019 held by developing countries = 100% – the percentage of voting rights in the IMF in 2019 held by developed countries = 100% – 62.29229% = 37.70771%. This percentage of 37.70771% is 0.00001% higher than that which the UN Global SDG Database specifies for the proportion of voting rights in the IMF in 2019 that are held by developing countries – which is 37.70770% of the total voting rights in the IMF.[434] It is submitted that 0.00001% is a negligible difference between the UN statisticians' calculation of this aggregated total and the author's computation of it, which may be explained by differences in the rounding of numerals. This statistic – which is incontrovertibly 37.7077% to four decimal places – is sufficiently certain to be deemed a robust datum. Moreover, since the UN Global SDG Database and the author agree exactly to four decimal places – notwithstanding the above-mentioned[435] differences to five decimal places – on the size of both the totals for developing regions that the latter has computed from the country-specific data in this database on the proportion of voting rights held by developing countries in international organizations – one of which relates to 2015 and the other to 2019, it is assumed that this aggregate as supplied in the UN Global SDG Database is accurate for all eleven international institutions[436] which the database includes for these two and their intervening years – i.e., 2015, 2016, 2017, 2018 and 2019. Accordingly, Table 3.20 shows the percentage of voting rights in these organizations that developing countries hold, for each of these five years.

---

[432] This percentage is given to five decimal places.

[433] This datum is given to five decimal places.

[434] SDG indicators: United Nations Global SDG Database", United Nations, accessed July 9, 2020, https://unstats.un.org/sdgs/indicators/database/. Row 15344 of the spreadsheet concerning SDG Indicator 10.6.1 that was downloaded from this webpage on 9th July 2020, includes this percentage – although it is specified there to four, rather than to five, decimal places (note 439).

[435] Text to notes 425 and 434.

[436] The text to note 384 lists these eleven international institutions for which the UN Global SDG Database publishes data regarding SDG Indicator 10.6.1. The text to note 383 specifies SDG Indicator 10.6.1. The text to note 416 alphabetizes these eleven organizations.

Table 3.20: The proportion of voting rights held by developing countries in international institutions, by organization, (%) – for each of the years 2015, 2016, 2017, 2018 and 2019[437]

Organization	2015	2016	2017	2018	2019
AfDB	62.82	62.66458	62.66458	62.66458	-
AsDB	58.065	45.323	45.323	45.323	-
ECOSOC	64.81481	64.81481	64.81481	66.66667	68.51852
FSB	43.85965	43.85965	43.85965	43.85965	43.85965
IADB	50.069	50.072	50.072	50.072	-
IBRD	38.11	37.86	38.81087	39.7005	39.18491
IFC	32.15193	32.15193	32.11692	32.11692	31.87957
IMF	35.1927[438]	37.2	37.67887	37.6914	37.7077[439]
UN General Assembly	74.09326	74.09326	74.09326	74.09326	74.09326
UNSC	53.33333	46.66667	46.66667	53.33333	53.33333
WTO	71.25	71.6	71.95122	71.95122	71.95122

Table 3.20 shows the percentage of voting rights that developing countries hold in each of the ECOSOC, the UN General Assembly, the UNSC and the WTO to be identical to the percentage of members of this international organization that are developing countries in every year from 2015 to 2019 – as displayed in Table 3.19. In each of the other institutions which Tables 3.19 and 3.20 list – i.e., the AfDB, the AsDB, the FSB, the IADB, the IBRD, the IFC and the IMF, and in all five years, the percentage of voting rights that are held by developing countries in this

[437] "SDG indicators: United Nations Global SDG Database", United Nations, accessed July 9, 2020, https://unstats.un.org/sdgs/indicators/database/. Rows 15334-15385 inclusive of the spreadsheet concerning SDG Indicator 10.6.1 that was downloaded from this webpage on 9th July 2020, contain the data in Table 3.20. As Table 3.20 shows, this spreadsheet omits aggregated data for 2019 on the proportion of voting rights that are held by developing countries in (i) the AfDB, (ii) the AsDB, and (iii) the IADB.

[438] Table 3.20 specifies this datum to four decimal places – as the UN statisticians and the author agree on it to that degree of precision, but not to five decimal places (text to note 425).

[439] Table 3.20 states this percentage to four decimal places – as the UN statisticians and the author agree on it to that extent of precision, but not to five decimal places (text to note 434). The datum is specified to four decimal places in the spreadsheet to which notes 434 and 437 refer – i.e., it appears there as '37.7077' rather than as '37.70770' (note 434).

organization is lower than the percentage of members of it that are those states. Thus, on average, a member of one of these seven organizations that is an advanced economy is able to exercise more votes than a member of this same institution that is a developing state.

Before concluding that developing countries are therefore under-represented in international institutions on matters that require a vote, it is noted that developed states provide much of the funding for these organizations. Why should countries be prepared to provide this money without incremental benefits for doing so? One way of benefiting is to receive a greater share of the vote on matters requiring voting in the relevant international organization than those states who do not pay towards the relevant institution's upkeep or who give a smaller amount.

Furthermore, six of the seven international institutions that Tables 3.19 and 3.20 show to have an underrepresentation of developing-country votes relative to members, are organizations that provide funding to developing states – the exception being the FSB.[440] Consequently, it may be argued that the FSB should promptly modify its voting structure in order to increase the number of votes allocated to its members that are developing countries from 43.85965%[441] to 50% – the latter being the percentage of its members that are developing states.[442] It is opined that the AfDB, the AsDB, the IADB, the IBRD, the IFC and the IMF should each review – or continue to review – its voting structure, in order to ensure that the balance between the proportion of its members that are developing countries and the percentage of its votes that those states hold is compatible with SDG Target 10.6[443] and SDG Indicator 10.6.1.[444]

---

440 The 'Mandate of the FSB' section on the FSB's website states: "The FSB promotes international financial stability; it does so by coordinating national financial authorities and international standard-setting bodies as they work toward developing strong regulatory, supervisory and other financial sector policies. It fosters a level playing field by encouraging coherent implementation of these policies across sectors and jurisdictions. The FSB, working through its members, seeks to strengthen financial systems and increase the stability of international financial markets. The policies developed in the pursuit of this agenda are implemented by jurisdictions and national authorities. ..." ("About the FSB", Financial Stability Board, accessed July 20, 2020, https://www.fsb.org/about/).

441 Table 3.20.

442 Table 3.19.

443 The text to note 382 states SDG Target 10.6.

444 The text to note 383 specifies SDG Target 10.6.1.

SDG Target 10.7, and SDG Indicators 10.7.1, 10.7.2, 10.7.3 and 10.7.4

SDG Target 10.7 is to "[f]acilitate orderly, safe, regular and responsible migration and mobility of people, including through the implementation of planned and well-managed migration policies".[445] Its four indicators are SDG Indicator 10.7.1 – which measures the "[r]ecruitment cost borne by employee as a proportion of monthly income earned in country of destination",[446] SDG Indicator 10.7.2 – which ascertains the "[n]umber of countries with migration policies that facilitate orderly, safe, regular and responsible migration and mobility of people",[447] SDG Indicator 10.7.3 – which determines the "[n]umber of migrants killed while attempting to cross maritime, land and air borders",[448] and SDG Indicator 10.7.4 – which calculates the "[p]roportion of the population who are refugees, by country of origin".[449]

SDG Indicators 10.7.3 and 10.7.4

SDG Indicators 10.7.3 and 10.7.4 were introduced only lately – in the 2020 Comprehensive Review of Indicators.[450] The UNHCR is the custodian agency and the data compiler for SDG Indicator 10.7.4,[451] but has not yet made these statistics available.[452]

---

445 Resolution 70/1 adopted by the General Assembly on 25 September 2015, Transforming our world: the 2030 Agenda for Sustainable Development, 21.

446 Global indicator framework for the Sustainable Development Goals and targets of the 2030 Agenda for Sustainable Development, 11.

447 Global indicator framework for the Sustainable Development Goals and targets of the 2030 Agenda for Sustainable Development, 11.

448 Global indicator framework for the Sustainable Development Goals and targets of the 2030 Agenda for Sustainable Development, 11.

449 Global indicator framework for the Sustainable Development Goals and targets of the 2030 Agenda for Sustainable Development, 11.

450 Report of the Inter-Agency and Expert Group on Sustainable Development Goal Indicators, E/CN.3/2020/2, 20 December 2019, Annex II.C, 17; Statistical Commission: Report on the fifty-first session (3-6 March 2020), E/2020/24-E/CN.3/2020/37, 12.

451 Documentation relating to SDG Indicator 10.7.4 specifies that the UNHCR is to fulfil these roles; as those records were published when that Office was attempting to present this indicator for acceptance as SDG Indicator 16.3.3, they refer to 'SDG Indicator 16.3.3' rather than to 'SDG Indicator 10.7.4' (Office of the United Nations High Commissioner for Refugees. Indicator Proposal Summary Template: Proportion of population who are refugees by country of origin (New York, 2019),

The IOM compiles the data for SDG Indicator 10.7.3, which are provided by various sources – including local authorities, NGOs and surveys with migrants who survive.[453] These data are contained in the IOM's Missing Migration Project database,[454] which is updated twice each week.[455] The latest-recorded incident in the database was on Wednesday 22nd July 2020.[456] The data therein comprise a subset of all migration-related deaths over the period to which they relate,[457] which commences

---

1; United Nations, Department of Economic and Social Affairs – Statistics Division: Reference metadata template for data reported on the Sustainable Development Goals (SDGs) – Target 16.3 – Indicator 16.3.3: Last updated: 3rd December 2018 (New York, 2018), 5). The UNHCR remarks: "… [I]n the original indicator framework, designed to measure progress towards meeting the SDGs, there was not a single indicator mentioning refugees or displacement. This is of critical importance. … With more than 230 existing indicators, there was little appetite for more. It was therefore essential to have a tier 1 indicator which would not add to the reporting burden on countries, i.e. that was based upon data which we already collected through UNHCR with good availability and a clear and international agreed methodology. This led to the following proposal: *The number of refugees by country of origin as a proportion of the national population of that country of origin*. … We also needed to make the case regarding which SDG target was not yet being adequately measured. [I]t was decided to promote the indicator under target 16.3 concerning the rule of law. …" (Petra Nahmias, and Natalia Baal, "Including forced displacement in the SDGs: a new refugee indicator", *UNHCR Blogs*, December 2, 2019, accessed July 21, 2020, https://www.unhcr.org/blogs/including-forced-displacement-in-the-sdgs-a-new-refugee-indicator/; emphasis original).

452 Regarding SDG Indicator 10.7.4, the recently-published *Report on UNHCR's global strategy priorities* merely states: "SDG indicator 10.7.4 on refugees per country of origin was included in the indicator framework for the 2030 Agenda." (Office of the United Nations High Commissioner for Refugees, Report on UNHCR's global strategic priorities, EC/71/SC/CRP.13/Rev.1, 6 July 2020 (Geneva, 2020), 16).

453 United Nations, Department of Economic and Social Affairs – Statistics Division: Metadata for Target 10.7 – Indicator 10.7.3: IOM – Last updated: 5th July 2020 (New York, 2020), 8.

454 Metadata for Target 10.7 – Indicator 10.7.3: IOM, 1.

455 Metadata for Target 10.7 – Indicator 10.7.3: IOM, 8.

456 "Download Missing Migrants Project data," International Organization for Migration, accessed July 24, 2020, https://missingmigrants.iom.int/downloads.

457 The webpage on the IOM's website that explains the methodological framework of the Missing Migrants Project states the following: "Missing Migrants Project counts *migrants* who have died at the external borders of states, or in the process of migration towards an international destination, regardless of their legal status. The Project records only those migrants who die during their journey to a country

on Monday 6th January 2014.[458] Table 3.21 contains data from the Missing Migration Project database from 1st January 2015 – as 2015 was the year during which the SDGs became effective,[459] until the latest datum that is currently available.[460]

The Missing Migrants Project categorizes locations for migration purposes according to the geographical sub-regions that the UN's M49 statistical standard specifies.[461] It also classifies them according to the following regions: North America (comprising Canada, Greenland, and the USA excluding the land next to the border with Mexico), the USA-Mexico

---

different from their country of residence. Missing Migrants Project data include the deaths of migrants who die in transportation accidents, shipwrecks, violent attacks, or due to medical complications during their journeys. It also includes the number of corpses found at border crossings that are categorized as the bodies of migrants, on the basis of belongings and/or the characteristics of the death. For instance, a death of an unidentified person might be included if the decedent is found without any identifying documentation in an area known to be on a migration route. Deaths during migration may also be identified based on the cause of death, especially if [it] is related to trafficking, smuggling, or means of travel such as on top of a train, in the back of a cargo truck, as a stowaway on a plane, in unseaworthy boats, or crossing a border fence. While the location and cause of death can provide strong evidence that an unidentified decedent should be included in Missing Migrants Project data, this should always be evaluated in conjunction with migration history and trends. … The count excludes deaths that occur in immigration detention facilities or after deportation to a migrant's homeland, as well as deaths more loosely connected with migrants' irregular status, such as those resulting from labour exploitation. Migrants who die or go missing after they are established in a new home are also not included in the data, so deaths in refugee camps or housing are excluded. The deaths of internally displaced persons who die within their country of origin are also excluded." ("Methodology", International Organization for Migration, accessed July 24, 2020, accessed July 24, 2020, https://missingmigrants.iom.int/methodology; emphasis original).

458 "Download Missing Migrants Project data," International Organization for Migration, accessed July 24, 2020, https://missingmigrants.iom.int/downloads.

459 The UN General Assembly adopted the SDGs and their targets in Resolution 70/1, which is dated 25th September 2015 (text to note 35 of Chapter One; note 37 of Chapter One and accompanying text).

460 Text to note 456.

461 "Regional classifications", International Organization for Migration, accessed July 25, 2020, https://missingmigrants.iom.int/regional-classifications. These geographical sub-regions are listed on the following webpage: https://unstats.un.org/unsd/methodology/m49/. Note 385 states those of the M49 statistical standard's sub-regions that this standard classifies as 'developed regions'. The standard categorizes the remaining sub-regions as 'developing regions', which are listed in note 386.

Border, Central America (comprising Belize, Costa Rica, El Salvador, Guatemala, Honduras, Nicaragua, Panama, and Mexico excluding the territory adjacent to the border with the USA), the Caribbean, South America, Europe (including Siberia, but excluding Thracian Turkey[462]), the Mediterranean Sea, North Africa (comprising Algeria, Egypt, Libya, Morocco including Western Sahara[463], Sudan, and Tunisia), the Horn of Africa (comprising Djibouti, Eritrea, Ethiopia, and Somalia), Sub-Saharan Africa (comprising the remaining states of Africa – i.e., Angola, Benin, Botswana, Burkina Faso, Burundi, Cabo Verde, Cameroon, Central African Republic, Chad, Comoros, Côte d'Ivoire, the Democratic Republic of the Congo, Equatorial Guinea, Eswatini, Gabon, the Gambia, Ghana, Guinea, Guinea-Bissau, Kenya, Lesotho, Liberia, Madagascar, Malawi, Mali, Mauritania, Mauritius, Mozambique, Namibia, Niger, Nigeria, the Republic of the Congo, Rwanda, São Tomé and Príncipe, Senegal, the Seychelles, Sierra Leone, South Africa, South Sudan, Tanzania, Togo, Uganda, Zambia, and Zimbabwe), the Middle East (excluding Iran, but including Armenia, Azerbaijan, Georgia, and Turkey), South Asia (including Iran), Central Asia, East Asia, South-East Asia, and Oceania.[464] Table 3.21 uses these regional designations.

---

462 Thracian Turkey is that part of Turkey that is in Europe. Note 324 provides information concerning the population of Thracian Turkey.

463 Note 323 supplies information regarding the status of Western Sahara.

464 "Regional classifications", International Organization for Migration, accessed July 25, 2020, https://missingmigrants.iom.int/regional-classifications. The 'Regional classifications' webpage declares: "These regions … differ from the UN geoscheme in several ways. Firstly, several regions have modified names – most notably, states in the UN-designated region of 'Western Asia' are categorized here under 'Middle East'. Secondly, some regions are combined because they have similar patterns of migration; for example, Europe is defined as one region instead of four. Additionally, the US-Mexico border is counted as a distinct region, as it has a particular migration context relating to instances of migrant deaths and disappearances. The Mediterranean is also included as a geographic region on this list for the same reason. The regional break-down for Africa also deviates from the UN geoscheme, again in the interest of grouping areas with strongly related migration trends. For instance, the Horn of Africa is counted as its own region, as migration in Ethiopia, Somalia, Djibouti, and Eritrea have migration flows distinct from the UN-designated regions of Northern and Eastern Africa. Similarly, North Africa includes all deaths in the Sahara Desert, as well as those between north-western Africa and the Canary Islands. Eastern African countries not in the Horn, as well as those in the Western, Middle and Southern African regions are combined into 'Sub-Saharan Africa' as comparatively few deaths are recorded in this area." ("Regional classifications", International Organization for Migration, accessed July 25, 2020, https://missingmigrants.iom.int/regional-classifications).

Table 3.21: The number of migrants recorded as dead or missing (italic numerals) in 2015, 2016, 2017, 2018 and 2019, and from 1st January 2020 until 22nd July 2020[465]

Region	2015	2016	2017	2018	2019	2020	Total
North America	0 *0*	0 *0*	1 *0*	0 *0*	1 *0*	2 *0*	**4 *0***
USA-Mexico Border	336 *3*	398 *3*	408 *9*	437 *3*	509 *9*	139 *7*	**2,227 *34***
Central America	110 *0*	179 *0*	90 *3*	74 *3*	113 *1*	22 *0*	**588** *7*
Caribbean	33 *35*	22 *93*	44 *126*	14 *27*	65 *95*	7 *52*	**185 *428***
South America	2 *0*	27 *6*	0 *0*	27 *3*	32 *5*	11 *0*	**99 *14***
Europe	137 *0*	63 *0*	84 *14*	108 *7*	134 *14*	39 *2*	**565 *37***
Mediterranean Sea	2,175 *1,892*	1,484 *3,506*	936 *2,203*	722 *1,577*	447 *1,438*	169 *234*	**5,933 *10,850***
North Africa	762 *62*	1,354 *151*	1,013 *0*	716 *27*	676 *106*	92 *81*	**4,613 *427***
Horn of Africa	102 *33*	178 *56*	161 *12*	286 *18*	91 *33*	0 *0*	**818 *152***
Sub-Saharan Africa	54 *20*	90 *2*	480 *74*	578 *15*	962 *11*	106 *10*	**2,270 *132***
Middle East	14 *0*	100 *0*	98 *0*	140 *5*	174 *0*	70 *5*	**596 *10***
South Asia	22 *0*	14 *0*	211 *0*	27 *0*	129 *0*	33 *0*	**436 *0***
Central Asia	0 *0*	0 *0*	0 *0*	52 *0*	0 *0*	0 *0*	**52 *0***
East Asia	0 *15*	1 *2*	1 *0*	3 *0*	5 *0*	0 *0*	**10** *17*
South-East Asia	297 *492*	149 *38*	197 *102*	87 *18*	237 *5*	111 *54*	**1,078 *709***
Oceania	0 *0*	0 *0*	0 *0*	0 *0*	0 *0*	0 *0*	**0 *0***
Total	**4,044** *2,552*	**4,059** *3,857*	**3,724** *2,543*	**3,271** *1,703*	**3,575** *1,717*	**801** *445*	**19,474** *12,817*

465 "Download Missing Migrants Project data," International Organization for Migration, accessed July 24, 2020, https://missingmigrants.iom.int/downloads. It is submitted that, as the numbers in Table 3.21 are totals of data which the author has calculated from 7,171 rows of chronologically-ordered records that the IOM holds on its 'Missing Migrants' spreadsheet, these figures may not be 100% accurate. The author takes responsibility for any errors made in the process of summing and tabulating these migration statistics.

Table 3.21 shows that, unlike the comment on the IOM's website,[466] hundreds of deaths are recorded in Sub-Saharan Africa in 2017, 2018 and, especially, 2019 – in which more horrific figures are reported for only the Mediterranean Sea. More than 5,000 deaths and 10,000 missing migrants are recorded for the latter region in the period that Table 3.21 covers, which is approximately 50% of all reported deaths and disappearances of migrants worldwide during this time.[467] High numbers of deaths of migrants are also reported for North Africa and, to a lesser extent, the Horn of Africa over the period – although the no deaths or disappearances are recorded for the Horn of Africa in 2020. These observations, together with the frequency of the recorded migrant deaths and disappearances in the Mediterranean Sea and North Africa – which tend to show that the migration patterns in these two areas increased from 2015 to 2016 and then reduced from 2016 until the current time, reveal a correlation between the intensity of migration over the Mediterranean Sea and the intensity of migration across North Africa.

If linear extrapolation is used to estimate figures for migrant deaths and disappearances throughout 2020, then these projections show low totals for these deaths and disappearances for this year compared to the corresponding figures in Table 3.21 for the preceding years. Table 3.22 displays these estimates – the linear extrapolation multiplication factor is 1.794117647.[468] It is opined that the advent of the COVID-19 pandemic[469] – including the fear of migrants of contracting COVID-19 in transit or at the destination of migration, contributes to the reduced totals for 2020.

---

[466] The last sentence of note 464 states that "comparatively few deaths are recorded in" 'Sub-Saharan Africa' as defined by the IOM's Missing Migrations Project (text to note 464).

[467] Number of deaths and disappearances of refugees in the Mediterranean Sea from 1st January 2015 to 22nd July 2020 = 5,933 + 10,850 = 16,783. Total number of deaths and disappearances of refugees from 1st January 2015 to 22nd July 2020 = 19,474 + 12,817 = 32,291. → Percentage of all recorded deaths and disappearances of refugees that are reported for the Mediterranean Sea = [16,783 / 32,291] * 100% = 52%.

[468] The Missing Migrant Project database contains records up to and including 22nd July 2020 (text to note 456). Number of days from 1st January 2020 to 22nd July 2020 inclusive = 31 + 29 + 31 + 30 + 31 + 30 + 22) days = 204 days. Number of days in 2020 = 366 days. Linear extrapolation multiplication factor = 366 days / 204 days = 1.794117647.

[469] The WHO declared the outbreak and spread of COVID-19 as a pandemic on 11th March 2020 (note 53 of Chapter Two).

Table 3.22: Estimates made by using linear extrapolation of the number of migrants that will be recorded as dead or missing in 2020

Region	**Recorded number of dead migrants**[470]	***Extrapolated number of dead migrants***[471]	**Recorded number of missing migrants**[472]	***Extrapolated number of missing migrants***[473]
North America	2	*4*[474]	0	*0*[475]
USA-Mexico Border	139	*249*[476]	7	*13*[477]
Central America	22	*39*[478]	0	*0*[479]
Caribbean	7	*13*[480]	52	*93*[481]
South America	11	*20*[482]	0	*0*[483]
Europe	39	*70*[484]	2	*4*[485]
Mediterranean Sea	169	*303*[486]	234	*420*[487]
North Africa	92	*165*[488]	81	*145*[489]
Horn of Africa	0	*0*[490]	0	*0*[491]

---

[470] The first figure in each row of the seventh column of Table 3.21 gives this number for the corresponding region.
[471] Extrapolated number of dead migrants = Recorded number of dead migrants * Linear extrapolation multiplication factor. The linear extrapolation multiplication factor is 1.794117647 (note 468).
[472] The second figure in each row of the seventh column of Table 3.21 gives this number for the corresponding region.
[473] Extrapolated number of missing migrants = Recorded number of missing migrants * Linear extrapolation multiplication factor. The linear extrapolation multiplication factor is 1.794117647 (note 468).
[474] 2 * 1.794117647 = 3.588235294.
[475] 0 * 1.794117647 = 0.
[476] 139 * 1.794117647 = 249.382352933.
[477] 7 * 1.794117647 = 12.558823529.
[478] 22 * 1.794117647 = 39.470588234.
[479] 0 * 1.794117647 = 0.
[480] 7 * 1.794117647 = 12.558823529.
[481] 52 * 1.794117647 = 93.294117644.
[482] 11 * 1.794117647 = 19.735294117.
[483] 0 * 1.794117647 = 0.
[484] 39 * 1.794117647 = 69.970588233.
[485] 2 * 1.794117647 = 3.588235294.
[486] 169 * 1.794117647 = 303.205882343
[487] 234 * 1.794117647 = 419.823529398.
[488] 92 * 1.794117647 = 165.058823524.
[489] 81 * 1.794117647 = 145.323529407.

Sub-Saharan Africa	106	*190*[492]	10	*18*[493]
Middle East	70	*126*[494]	5	*9*[495]
South Asia	33	*59*[496]	0	*0*[497]
Central Asia	0	*0*[498]	0	*0*[499]
East Asia	0	*0*[500]	0	*0*[501]
South-East Asia	111	*199*[502]	54	*97*[503]
Oceania	0	*0*[504]	0	*0*[505]
Total	**801**	***1437***[506]	**445**	***799***[507]

Table 3.21 and 3.22 show that, other than in the Mediterranean Sea in 2015, the number of missing migrants in this region and in the Caribbean exceeds that of those reported to be found dead. It is submitted that most of these missing people were drowned in the sea. Table 3.23 shows the hundred most major incidents from the IOM's Missing Migrants database that happened over the period 1st January 2015 to 22nd July 2020, with these events primarily ranked according to the total number of migrants dead or missing, secondarily prioritized according to the proportion of that

490 0 * 1.794117647 = 0.
491 0 * 1.794117647 = 0.
492 106 * 1.794117647 = 190.176470582.
493 10 * 1.794117647 = 17.941176470.
494 70 * 1.794117647 = 125.588235290.
495 5 * 1.794117647 = 8.970588235.
496 33 * 1.794117647 = 59.205882351.
497 0 * 1.794117647 = 0.
498 0 * 1.794117647 = 0.
499 0 * 1.794117647 = 0.
500 0 * 1.794117647 = 0.
501 0 * 1.794117647 = 0.
502 111 * 1.794117647 = 199.147058817.
503 54 * 1.794117647 = 96.882352938.
504 0 * 1.794117647 = 0.
505 0 * 1.794117647 = 0.
506 Check: 801 * 1.794117647 = 1437.088235247.
507 Check: 445 * 1.794117647 = 798.382352915. The difference between the output from this check and the total in Table 3.22 corresponding to the current footnote is a rounding error, i.e., 799 – 798.382352915 = 0.617647085 = (0 – 0) + (13 – 12.558823529) + (0 – 0) + (93 – 93.294117644) + (0 – 0) + (4 – 3.588235294) + (420 – 419.823529398) + (145 – 145.323529407) + (0 – 0) + (18 – 17.941176470) + (9 – 8.970588235) + (0 – 0) +(0 – 0) + (0 – 0) + (97 – 96.882352938) + (0 – 0).

total recorded as dead rather than missing, and tertiarily ordered with the more or most recent incident first.

Table 3.23: The hundred most major incidents from the IOM's Missing Migrants database that took place between 1st January 2015 and 22nd July 2020[508]

Region	Total number of migrants dead or missing	Date of the incident	Cause of death	Approximate location of the incident
Mediterranean Sea	1,022	18th April 2015	Drowning	North of western Libya
Mediterranean Sea	550	26th May 2016	Drowning	North of western Libya
Mediterranean Sea	459	9th April 2016	Drowning	North of western Egypt
Mediterranean Sea	400	13th April 2015	Drowning	North of the Libyan coast
Mediterranean Sea	339	3rd June 2016	Drowning	Off the coast of Crete
Mediterranean Sea	307	9th February 2015	Drowning	North of western Libya
Mediterranean Sea	288	21st September 2016	Drowning	North-East of Alexandria, Egypt
Mediterranean Sea	255	25th May 2016	Drowning	North of western Libya
Mediterranean Sea	245	29th May 2016	Drowning	North of western Libya
South-East Asia	243	31st March 2015	Mixed	Andaman Sea
Mediterranean Sea	222	6th August 2015	Drowning	North of western Libya

508 "Download Missing Migrants Project data," International Organization for Migration, accessed July 24, 2020, https://missingmigrants.iom.int/downloads.

Mediterranean Sea	202	27th August 2015	Drowning	North of the Libyan coast
Mediterranean Sea	176	14th January 2017	Drowning	North of western Libya
Mediterranean Sea	156	19th May 2017	Drowning	North of western Libya
Mediterranean Sea	150	25th July 2019	Drowning	North of western Libya
Mediterranean Sea	135	14th November 2016	Drowning	Between Libya and Italy
Mediterranean Sea	130[509]	1st September 2018	Drowning	North of western Libya
Mediterranean Sea	130[510]	23rd March, 2017	Drowning	North of western Libya
South-East Asia	130[511]	31st March 2015	Drowning	Bay of Bengal near Rakhine state, Myanmar
Mediterranean Sea	128	2nd November 2016	Drowning	Between Libya and Italy
Mediterranean Sea	126	15th June 2017	Drowning	North of the Libyan coast
USA-Mexico Border	123	31st December 2015	Mixed	Texas
Mediterranean Sea	120[512]	31st July 2016	Drowning	North of western Libya

[509] 2 of these 130 migrants are recorded as dead, and the others as missing.
[510] All 130 migrants are recorded as missing rather than dead.
[511] All 130 migrants are recorded as missing rather than dead.
[512] All 120 migrants are recorded as dead rather than missing.

Mediterranean Sea	120[513]	30th August 2017	Drowning	Off the coast of Tunisia near the border with Libya
Mediterranean Sea	118	19th February 2017	Drowning	North of western Libya
Mediterranean Sea	117	18th January 2019	Drowning	North of western Libya
Mediterranean Sea	114	1st July 2018	Drowning	North of western Libya
Mediterranean Sea	112	2nd June 2018	Drowning	East of Sfax, Tunisia
Mediterranean Sea	111	1st November 2016	Drowning	North of the Libyan coast
Mediterranean Sea	110	17th June 2017	Drowning	North of western Libya
South-East Asia	106	25th May 2015	Unknown	Along the Malaysian border with Thailand
Mediterranean Sea	104	29th June 2018	Drowning	North of western Libya
Mediterranean Sea	103	16th November 2016	Drowning	Between Libya and Italy
Mediterranean Sea	102	7th May 2017	Drowning	North of western Libya
Mediterranean Sea	101	19th June 2018	Drowning	North of western Libya
Mediterranean Sea	100[514]	15th July 2015	Drowning	North of western Libya

[513] All 120 migrants are recorded as missing rather than dead.
[514] All 100 migrants are recorded as dead rather than missing.

Mediterranean Sea	100[515]	1st February 2018	Drowning	North of western Libya
Mediterranean Sea	100[516]	19th August 2019	Drowning	North of the Libyan coast
Mediterranean Sea	100[517]	9th January 2018	Drowning	North of western Libya
Mediterranean Sea	99	15th November 2016	Drowning	Between Libya and Italy
Mediterranean Sea	97[518]	26th October 2016	Drowning	North of western Libya
Mediterranean Sea	97[519]	20th September 2016	Drowning	North of western Libya
Mediterranean Sea	97[520]	13th April 2017	Drowning	North of western Libya
Mediterranean Sea	95	5th October 2015	Drowning	North of western Libya
Mediterranean Sea	94	21st November 2019	Drowning	North of the Libyan coast
Mediterranean Sea	91	9th February 2019	Drowning	North of western Libya
Mediterranean Sea	90	30th March 2016	Drowning	North of western Libya

[515] 14 of these 100 migrants are recorded as dead, and the others as missing.
[516] All 100 migrants are recorded as missing rather than dead.
[517] All 100 migrants are recorded as missing rather than dead.
[518] All 97 migrants are recorded as dead rather than missing.
[519] 7 of these 97 migrants are recorded as dead, and the others as missing.
[520] All 97 migrants are recorded as missing rather than dead.

Mediterranean Sea	87	13th December 2016	Drowning	North of western Libya
USA-Mexico Border	84[521]	20th December 2019	Mixed	Texas
Mediterranean Sea	84[522]	29th April 2016	Drowning	North of western Libya
Mediterranean Sea	84[523]	28th March 2016	Drowning	North of the Libyan coast
Mediterranean Sea	83	3rd July 2019	Drowning, hypothermia	Off the coast of Tunisia near the border with Libya
Mediterranean Sea	82[524]	26th May 2017	Drowning	Between North Africa and Italy
Mediterranean Sea	82[525]	7th May 2017	Drowning	Between Libya and Italy
Mediterranean Sea	76[526]	3rd November 2017	Drowning	Between Libya and Italy
Mediterranean Sea	76[527]	12th June 2018	Drowning	North of the Libyan Coast
Mediterranean Sea	74	20th February 2017	Drowning	North of western Libya
Mediterranean Sea	73[528]	9th June 2020	Drowning	East of Sfax, Tunisia

[521] All 84 migrants are recorded as dead rather than missing.
[522] All 84 migrants are recorded as missing rather than dead.
[523] All 84 migrants are recorded as missing rather than dead.
[524] All 82 migrants are recorded as missing rather than dead.
[525] All 82 migrants are recorded as missing rather than dead.
[526] 23 of these 76 migrants are recorded as dead, and the others as missing.
[527] All 76 migrants are recorded as missing rather than dead.
[528] 68 of these 73 migrants are recorded as dead, and the others as missing.

Mediterranean Sea	73[529]	26th November 2019	Drowning	Alboran Sea
Europe	71	27th August, 2015	Suffocation	On motorway near Vienna, Austria
South-East Asia	70[530]	15th April 2020	Dehydration, starvation, violence	Andaman Sea
Horn of Africa	70[531]	29th January 2019	Drowning	East of northern Djibouti
Mediterranean Sea	70[532]	30th January 2016	Drowning	Between Tunisia and Sicily
Mediterranean Sea	70[533]	29th November 2019	Drowning	In Malta's territorial waters
Mediterranean Sea	70[534]	19th June 2018	Drowning	North of western Libya
Caribbean	68[535]	24th January 2017	Drowning	Near the Turks and Caicos Islands
Mediterranean Sea	68[536]	21st March 2017	Drowning	North of western Libya
Mediterranean Sea	68[537]	3rd October 2017	Drowning	North of western Libya
Mediterranean Sea	65	20th November 2019	Drowning	North of western Libya

529 All 73 migrants are recorded as missing rather than dead.
530 All 70 migrants are recorded as dead rather than missing.
531 52 of these 70 migrants are recorded as dead, and the others as missing.
532 6 of these 70 migrants are recorded as dead, and the others as missing.
533 All 70 migrants are recorded as missing rather than dead.
534 All 70 migrants are recorded as missing rather than dead.
535 17 of these 68 migrants are recorded as dead, and the others as missing.
536 2 of these 68 migrants are recorded as dead, and the others as missing.
537 All 68 migrants are recorded as missing rather than dead.

Sub-Saharan Africa	64[538]	24th March 2020	Asphyxiation	Inside lorry in Tete province, Mozambique
Mediterranean Sea	64[539]	6th January 2018	Unknown	North of the Libyan coast
South-East Asia	63	28th September 2017	Drowning	Off the coast of Bangladesh near the border with Myanmar
Horn of Africa	62	6th June 2018	Drowning	Gulf of Aden
Mediterranean Sea	61[540]	23rd December 2016	Drowning	North of western Libya
Mediterranean Sea	61[541]	3rd September 2018	Drowning	Alboran Sea
South-East Asia	61[542]	3rd September 2015	Drowning	Off the west coast of Malaysia
South-East Asia	60[543]	2nd November 2016	Drowning	Near Indonesia
South-East Asia	60[544]	11th February 2020	Drowning	Bay of Bengal near border of Bangladesh and Myanmar
Mediterranean Sea	60[545]	2nd July 2019	Drowning	North of western Libya

[538] All 64 migrants are recorded as dead rather than missing.
[539] 8 of these 64 migrants are recorded as dead, and the others as missing.
[540] 5 of these 61 migrants are recorded as dead, and the others as missing.
[541] All 61 migrants are recorded as missing rather than dead.
[542] All 61 migrants are recorded as missing rather than dead.
[543] 54 of these 60 migrants are recorded as dead, and the others as missing.
[544] 15 of these 60 migrants are recorded as dead, and the others as missing.
[545] All 60 migrants are recorded as missing rather than dead.

Mediterranean Sea	60[546]	30th June 2017	Drowning	Between Libya and Italy
Mediterranean Sea	60[547]	11th August 2015	Drowning	Between Tunisia and Sicily
South-East Asia	60[548]	1st June 2015	Mixed	Bay of Bengal and Andaman Sea
Middle East	59[549]	28th June 2020	Drowning	Van Lake, Turkey
Mediterranean Sea	59[550]	10th May 2019	Drowning	East of Sfax, Tunisia
Mediterranean Sea	58	22nd December 2016	Unknown	Between Tunisia and Sicily
Mediterranean Sea	57[551]	27th May 2017	Drowning	Between Libya and Italy
South-East Asia	57[552]	29th January 2015	Drowning	Bay of Bengal
Mediterranean Sea	57[553]	19th October 2019	Drowning	North of western Libya
North Africa	57[554]	13th May 2016	Drowning	Between Western Sahara and the Canary Islands, Spain

[546] All 60 migrants are recorded as missing rather than dead.
[547] All 60 migrants are recorded as missing rather than dead.
[548] All 60 migrants are recorded as missing rather than dead.
[549] All 59 migrants are recorded as dead rather than missing.
[550] 4 of these 59 migrants are recorded as dead, and the others as missing.
[551] 33 of these 57 migrants are recorded as dead, and the others as missing.
[552] 8 of these 57 migrants are recorded as dead, and the others as missing.
[553] All 57 migrants are recorded as missing rather than dead.
[554] All 57 migrants are recorded as missing rather than dead.

Mediterranean Sea	56[555]	16th December 2019	Drowning	North of western Algeria
North Africa	56[556]	7th February 2016	Sickness, lack of access to medicines	Between Western Sahara and the Canary Islands, Spain
Mediterranean Sea	54	27th October 2018	Drowning	Alboran Sea
Mediterranean Sea	53[557]	28th September 2019	Drowning	Off the north-west coast of Morocco
Mediterranean Sea	53[558]	17th January 2019	Drowning	Alboran Sea
Central Asia	52[559]	18th January 2018	Bus fire	Aktobe province, Kazakhstan
Mediterranean Sea	52[560]	26th August 2015	Suffocation	North of the Libyan coast
Mediterranean Sea	52[561]	29th August 2018	Drowning	Alboran Sea near border of Algeria and Morocco
Sub-Saharan Africa	52[562]	25th June 2017	Exposure to sunny, dry and hot conditions	The Sahara Desert within Niger

555 All 56 migrants are recorded as missing rather than dead.
556 All 56 migrants are recorded as missing rather than dead.
557 18 of these 53 migrants are recorded as dead, and the others as missing.
558 All 53 migrants are recorded as missing rather than dead.
559 All 52 migrants are recorded as dead rather than missing.
560 All 52 migrants are recorded as dead rather than missing.
561 13 of these 52 migrants are recorded as dead, and the others as missing.
562 1 of these 52 migrants is recorded as dead, and the others are reported as missing.

Mediterranean Sea	52[563]	10th June 2017	Drowning	North of the Libyan coast
Mediterranean Sea	51	19th March 2016	Drowning	North of western Libya

Most of the incidents that Table 3.23 shows are cases of drowning. Many of these events occur in the Mediterranean Sea north of western Libya. It is submitted that the ongoing civil war in Libya has enabled people-traffickers to establish bases in ports in western Libya, and that many migrants from Sub-Saharan Africa have crossed the Sahara Desert and attempted to reach Italy by boat – using the paid services of those peddlers. But, as Table 3.23 reveals, the cost to many has been greater than the money handed to the dealers.

Table 3.21 shows that the number of migrants recorded as dead or missing over the period from 1st January 2015 to 22nd July 2020 is low or very low in South America, Central Asia, East Asia, and North America (i.e., Canada, Greenland, and the USA excluding the land adjacent to the last-mentioned state's border with Mexico[564]) – in decreasing order. No migrants are reported as dead or missing in Oceania during this time.

Tables 3.21 and 3.23 indicate that, whilst some regions – in particular Central Asia – excepting the bus fire in Kazakhstan[565], East Asia, Canada and Greenland, and Oceania, appear to be fulfilling SDG Target 10.7[566] in respect of the transit of migrants, other regions, especially North Africa and Sub-Saharan Africa – both on their own accounts and with regard to the contribution that each makes to the loss of migrants in the Mediterranean Sea, do not currently meet this Target. It is opined that Libya is a particularly weak link in the process of orderly, safe, regular and responsible migration, and that the international community should take reasonable steps to ensure that the ports of western Libya operate responsibly concerning the transportation of migrants over the Mediterranean Sea to European destinations – notwithstanding the continuance of that country's civil war.

563 All 52 migrants are recorded as missing rather than dead.

564 Text to note 464.

565 Note 559 and accompanying entry in Table 3.23. This incident wholly constitutes the only non-zero datum for Central Asia in Table 3.21.

566 The text to note 445 states SDG Target 10.7.

SDG Indicator 10.7.2

In 2015, the IOM developed a Migration Governance Framework, which includes the following six dimensions of migration governance:[567] migrants' rights,[568] whole-of-government approach to the management of migration,[569] partnerships,[570] well-being of migrants,[571] mobility dimensions of crises,[572] and safe, orderly and dignified migration.[573] In accordance

[567] "Migration Governance Indicators", International Organization for Migration, accessed August 5, 2020, https://gmdac.iom.int/migration-governance-indicators.
[568] The IOM states: "Indicators in this domain assess the extent to which migrants have the same status as citizens in terms of access to basic social services such as health[care], education, and social security. It also describes the rights of migrants to family reunification, to work and to residency and citizenship. The ratification of the main international conventions is also included within this domain." ("Migration Governance Indicators", International Organization for Migration, accessed August 5, 2020, https://gmdac.iom.int/migration-governance-indicators).
[569] The IOM declares: "Indicators in this domain assess countries' institutional, legal, and regulatory frameworks related to migration policies. Domain 2 also reviews the existence of national migration strategies that are in-line with development, as well as institutional transparency and coherence in relation to migration management. This domain also investigates the extent to which governments collect and use migration data." ("Migration Governance Indicators", International Organization for Migration, accessed August 5, 2020, https://gmdac.iom.int/migration-governance-indicators).
[570] The IOM proclaims: "This domain focuses on countries' efforts to cooperate on migration-related issues with other states and with relevant non-governmental actors, including civil society organizations and the private sector. Cooperation can lead to improvements in governance by aligning and raising standards, increasing dialogue and providing structures to overcome challenges." ("Migration Governance Indicators", International Organization for Migration, accessed August 5, 2020, https://gmdac.iom.int/migration-governance-indicators).
[571] The IOM asseverates: "This domain includes indicators on countries' policies for managing the socioeconomic well-being of migrants, through aspects such as the recognition of migrants' educational and professional qualifications, provisions regulating student migration and the existence of bilateral labour agreements between countries. Indicators equally focus on policies and strategies related to diaspora engagement and migrant remittances." ("Migration Governance Indicators", International Organization for Migration, accessed August 5, 2020, https://gmdac.iom.int/migration-governance-indicators).
[572] The IOM avers: "This domain studies the type and level of preparedness of countries when they are faced with mobility dimensions of crises, linked to either disasters, the environment and/or conflict. The questions are used to identify the processes in place for nationals and non-nationals both during and after disasters, including whether humanitarian assistance is equally available to migrants as it is

with the IOM's Migration Governance Framework, the methodology for SDG Indicator 10.7.2[574] comprises six policy domains, each of which has a corresponding proxy measure.[575] Table 3.24 shows these domains and their proxy measures.

Table 3.24: The policy domains and proxy measures for SDG Indicator 10.7.2[576]

Policy domain	**Proxy measure**
1. Migrant rights	The extent to which migrants have the same access as nationals to services
2. Whole-of-government/Evidence based policies	Dedicated institutions, legal frameworks and policies or strategies to regulate migration
3. Co-operation and partnerships	Government measures to nurture co-operation and encourage the inclusion and participation of stakeholders in migration policy
4. Socioeconomic well-being of migrants	Government measures to maximize the positive-development impact of migration and the socioeconomic well-being of migrants
5. Mobility dimensions of crises	Government measures to provide comprehensive responses to persons who are forcibly displaced
6. Safe, orderly and regular migration	Government measures to address the regularity of migration

---

to citizens." ("Migration Governance Indicators", International Organization for Migration, accessed August 5, 2020, https://gmdac.iom.int/migration-governance-indicators).

573 The IOM writes: "This domain analyses countries' approach to migration management in terms of border control and enforcement policies, admission criteria for migrants, preparedness and resilience in the case of significant and unexpected migration flows, as well as the fight against trafficking in human beings and smuggling of migrants. It also assesses efforts and incentives to help integrate returning citizens." ("Migration Governance Indicators", International Organization for Migration, accessed August 5, 2020, https://gmdac.iom.int/migration-governance-indicators).

574 The text to note 447 states SDG Indicator 10.7.2.

575 United Nations, Department of Economic and Social Affairs – Statistics Division: Metadata for Target 10.7 – Indicator 10.7.2: Department of Economic and Social Affairs and IOM – Last updated: September 2019 (New York, 2019), 2.

576 Adapted from Table 1 at Metadata for Target 10.7 – Indicator 10.7.2: Department of Economic and Social Affairs and IOM, 2.

For each of these domains and its corresponding proxy measure, a question was constructed – informed by five sub-categories to encapsulate essential aspects of the range of national migration policies, whilst permitting the indicator to detect pertinent variations across countries and through time.[577] The question for Policy Domain 1 (i.e., migrant rights) asks: *Does the government provide non-nationals with equal access to the following services, welfare benefits and rights?*[578] The five sub-classes for Domain 1 comprise these 'following services', which are: (i) essential and/or emergency healthcare, (ii) public education, (iii) equal pay for equal work, (iv) social security, and (v) access to justice.[579] Tables 3.25, 3.26, 3.27, 3.28 and 3.29 each contains the questions and sub-categories for Policy Domains 2 (i.e., whole of government/evidence-based policies), 3 (i.e., co-operation and partnerships), 4 (i.e., socioeconomic well-being of migrants), 5 (i.e., mobility dimensions of crises), and 6 (i.e., safe, orderly and regular migration), respectively.

Table 3.25: Question and sub-classes for Policy Domain 2 (SDG Indicator 10.7.2)[580]

Does the government have any of the following institutions, policies or strategies to govern immigration or emigration?
(i) a dedicated government agency to implement national migration policy
(ii) a national policy or strategy for regular migration pathways
(iii) a national policy or strategy to promote the inclusion or integration of immigrants
(iv) formal mechanisms to ensure that the migration policy is responsive to gender
(v) a mechanism to ensure that migration policy is informed by data

[577] Metadata for Target 10.7 – Indicator 10.7.2: Department of Economic and Social Affairs and IOM, 2.
[578] Metadata for Target 10.7 – Indicator 10.7.2: Department of Economic and Social Affairs and IOM, 2.
[579] Metadata for Target 10.7 – Indicator 10.7.2: Department of Economic and Social Affairs and IOM, 2.
[580] Adapted from Table 2 at Metadata for Target 10.7 – Indicator 10.7.2: Department of Economic and Social Affairs and IOM, 2.

Table 3.26: Question and sub-classes for Policy Domain 3 (SDG Indicator 10.7.2)[581]

Does the government take any of the following measures to foster co-operation amongst countries and encourage the inclusion and participation of stakeholders in migration policy?
(i) an inter-ministerial co-ordination mechanism on migration
(ii) bilateral agreements on migration
(iii) regional agreements that promote mobility
(iv) agreements for co-operation with other countries on the return and readmission of migrants
(v) formal mechanisms to engage civil society and the private sector in the formulation and implementation of migration policy

Table 3.27: Question and sub-classes for Policy Domain 4 (SDG Indicator 10.7.2)[582]

Does the government take any of the following measures to maximize the positive-development impact of migration and the socioeconomic well-being of migrants?
(i) align, through periodic assessments, policies on the migration of labour with actual and projected needs of the labour market
(ii) facilitate the portability of social security benefits
(iii) facilitate the recognition of qualifications and skills acquired abroad
(iv) facilitate or promote the flow of migrant remittances
(v) promote fair and ethical recruitment of migrant workers

581 Adapted from Table 2 at Metadata for Target 10.7 – Indicator 10.7.2: Department of Economic and Social Affairs and IOM, 3.

582 Adapted from Table 2 at Metadata for Target 10.7 – Indicator 10.7.2: Department of Economic and Social Affairs and IOM, 3.

Table 3.28: Question and sub-classes for Policy Domain 5 (SDG Indicator 10.7.2)[583]

Does the government take any of the following measures to respond to refugees and other persons who are forcibly displaced across international borders?
(i) a system for receiving, processing and identifying individuals who are forced to flee across international borders
(ii) contingency planning for displaced populations in terms of their basic needs – such as food, sanitation, education and medical care
(iii) specific measures to provide assistance to citizens who reside abroad in countries in crisis or post-crisis situations
(iv) a national disaster risk reduction strategy with specific provisions to address the impact of disasters regarding the displacement of people
(v) the granting of permissions for temporary stay or temporary protection for persons who are forcibly displaced across international borders and for individuals who are unable to return to their home state

Table 3.29: Question and sub-classes for Policy Domain 6 (SDG Indicator 10.7.2)[584]

Does the government address regular or irregular migration through any of the following measures?
(i) a system to monitor migrants who have lived in a country beyond the time at which their visa permits them to do so
(ii) pre-arrival authorization controls
(iii) provisions for unaccompanied minors or separated children
(iv) information and awareness-raising campaigns on migration
(v) formal strategies to address trafficking in persons and smuggling of migrants

Thus, SDG Indicator 10.7.2[585] comprises thirty sub-categories, under six policy domains and questions; all of these sub-classes, except for those under Domain 1,[586] have dichotomous 'Yes/No' answers that are coded '1'

---

[583] Adapted from Table 2 at Metadata for Target 10.7 – Indicator 10.7.2: Department of Economic and Social Affairs and IOM, 3.
[584] Adapted from Table 2 at Metadata for Target 10.7 – Indicator 10.7.2: Department of Economic and Social Affairs and IOM, 3.
[585] The text to note 447 specifies SDG Indicator 10.7.2.
[586] The text to note 579 lists the five sub-categories for Domain 1.

for 'Yes' and '0' for 'No'.[587] For the sub-categories under Domain 1, the possible answers are 'Yes, regardless of immigration status' – which is coded '1', 'Yes, only for those individuals with legal immigration status' – which is coded '0.5', and 'No' – which is coded '0'.[588] For each policy domain, the unweighted average of the coded values across its sub-classes, D_i, is calculated as $D_i = [\sum_j s_{ji} / n] * 100\%$, where D_i is the coded value for domain i, $\sum_j s_{ji}$ is the sum of the coded values across sub-classes – indexed by j – under domain i, and n is the total number of sub-classes in a domain – which is 5.[589] For each domain, i, $0\% \leq D_i \leq 100\%$.[590] The overall SDG Indicator 10.7.2 for each country is reached by calculating the unweighted average of the coded values of the thirty sub-categories under the six domains, with values ranging from 0% to 100%.[591]

The country-level averages, both by domain and for the overall SDG Indicator 10.7.2, are grouped as follows: values of less than 40% are coded as 'Requires further progress – 1', values of 40% to less than 80% are coded as 'Partially meets – 2', values of 80% to less than 100% are coded as 'Meets – 3', and values of 100% are coded as 'Fully meets – 4'.[592] To ensure that SDG Indicator 10.7.2 is comparable across countries and over time, missing values are coded '0'.[593] The providers of the data underpinning SDG Indicator 10.7.2 are the governments of: (i) the Member States of the UN, (ii) its two Permanent Observers,[594] and two

---

587 Metadata for Target 10.7 – Indicator 10.7.2: Department of Economic and Social Affairs and IOM, 5.

588 Metadata for Target 10.7 – Indicator 10.7.2: Department of Economic and Social Affairs and IOM, 5.

589 Metadata for Target 10.7 – Indicator 10.7.2: Department of Economic and Social Affairs and IOM, 5.

590 Metadata for Target 10.7 – Indicator 10.7.2: Department of Economic and Social Affairs and IOM, 5.

591 Metadata for Target 10.7 – Indicator 10.7.2: Department of Economic and Social Affairs and IOM, 5.

592 Metadata for Target 10.7 – Indicator 10.7.2: Department of Economic and Social Affairs and IOM, 5; "SDG indicators: United Nations Global SDG Database", United Nations, accessed August 5, 2020, https://unstats.un.org/sdgs/indicators/database/.

593 Metadata for Target 10.7 – Indicator 10.7.2: Department of Economic and Social Affairs and IOM, 5.

594 The UN's two Permanent Observers are the Holy See and the State of Palestine ("Non-member States", United Nations, accessed August 6, 2020, https://www.un.org/en/sections/member-states/non-member-states/index.html).

non-Member States.[595] The data compilers for SDG Indicator 10.7.2 are the IOM, the Department of Economic and Social Affairs at the UN, and the OECD.[596] The UN Global SDG Database currently supplies these data for 2019 only.[597]

Whilst the UN Global SDG Database provides these grouped data for many states[598] and territories,[599] Table 3.30 contains those countries from

---

[595] Metadata for Target 10.7 – Indicator 10.7.2: Department of Economic and Social Affairs and IOM, 8. The UN's guide on SDG Indicator 10.7.2 (i.e., the document referred to as 'Metadata for Target 10.7 – Indicator 10.7.2') does not impart the identity of the two non-Member States of the UN that provide data for the calculation of SDG Indicator 10.7.2.

[596] Metadata for Target 10.7 – Indicator 10.7.2: Department of Economic and Social Affairs and IOM, 8. The UN's guide on SDG Indicator 10.7.2 states: "The source of data is the UN Inquiry among governments on Population and Development, which has been used to survey global population policies since 1963, including policies on international migration. … The Twelfth Inquiry is divided into three thematic modules: Module I on population aging and urbanization; Module II on fertility, family planning and reproductive health; and Module III on international migration. Module III of the Twelfth Inquiry has been updated to include core questions for all the six migration policy domains … ." (Metadata for Target 10.7 – Indicator 10.7.2: Department of Economic and Social Affairs and IOM, 6). Table 3.24 lists the six policy domains for SDG Indicator 10.7.2.

[597] "SDG indicators: United Nations Global SDG Database", United Nations, accessed August 5, 2020, https://unstats.un.org/sdgs/indicators/database/.

[598] The UN Global SDG Database contains grouped data for 2019 for the following states: Albania, Angola, Argentina, Armenia, Australia, Azerbaijan, Bahrain, Bangladesh, Belarus, Belgium, Botswana, Brazil, Burkina Faso, Cambodia, Cameroon, Canada, Central African Republic, Chad, Chile, China, Colombia, Côte d'Ivoire, the Czech Republic, Denmark, Djibouti, El Salvador, Equatorial Guinea, Estonia, Ethiopia, Fiji, Finland, France, Gabon, the Gambia, Germany, Georgia, Ghana, Greece, Grenada, Guatemala, Guinea, Guinea-Bissau, Honduras, Iraq, Ireland, Italy, Jamaica, Japan, Jordan, Kazakhstan, Kenya, Kuwait, Kyrgyzstan, Latvia, Liberia, Libya, Lithuania, Luxembourg, Malawi, Malta, the Marshall Islands, Mauritania, Mauritius, Mexico, Micronesia, Moldova, Mongolia, Montenegro, Mozambique, Nepal, New Zealand, Niger, Nigeria, Norway, Palau, Panama, Papua New Guinea, Paraguay, Peru, the Philippines, Portugal, Puerto Rico, Qatar, the Republic of the Congo, Romania, Russia, Samoa, São Tomé and Príncipe, Senegal, Serbia, Sierra Leone, Slovenia, the Solomon Islands, Somalia, South Sudan, Spain, Sweden, Switzerland, Tajikistan, Tanzania, Thailand, Togo, Tunisia, Turkey, Uganda, the UK, Ukraine, Uruguay, Vietnam, Yemen, and Zambia ("SDG indicators: United Nations Global SDG Database", United Nations, accessed August 5, 2020, https://unstats.un.org/sdgs/indicators/database/).

Table 3.30: Country-level averages for the world's twenty most-populous states for 2019 for each policy domain and for the overall SDG Indicator 10.7.2 (i.e., All domains), where 1 = requires further progress towards meeting the objective of facilitating orderly, safe, regular and responsible migration and mobility of people, 2 = partially meets this objective, 3 = meets this objective, and 4 = fully meets this objective[600]

State: in decreasing population order	Number of policy domain (1 to 6)[601]						All domains
	1	2	3	4	5	6	
China	2	2	3	4	1[602]	3	2[603]
India	-	-	-	-	-	-	-
The USA	-	-	-	-	-	-	-
Indonesia	-	-	-	-	-	-	-
Pakistan	-	-	-	-	-	-	-
Brazil	4	2	3	3	3	3	3

599 The UN Global SDG Database contains grouped data for 2019 for the following non-state territories: the Åland Islands, American Samoa, Anguilla, Aruba, Bermuda, Bonaire and Sint Eustatius and Saba, British Indian Ocean Territory, the British Virgin Islands, the Cayman Islands, the Channel Islands (with additional separate records for Guernsey and for Jersey), Christmas Island, the Cocos (Keeling) Islands, Curaçao, the Falkland Islands, the Faroe Islands, French Guinea, French Polynesia, French Southern Territories, Gibraltar, Greenland, Guadeloupe, Guam, Heard Island and McDonald Islands, Hong Kong, the Isle of Man, Macau, Martinique, Mayotte, Montserrat, New Caledonia, Norfolk Island, the Northern Mariana Islands, the Pitcairn Islands, Réunion, Saint Barthélemy, Saint Helena, Saint Martin (French Part), Saint Pierre and Miquelon, Sint Maarten (Dutch Part), South Georgia and the South Sandwich Islands, Svalbard and Jan Mayen Islands, Tokelau, the Turks and Caicos Islands, the United States Minor Outlying Islands, the United States Virgin Islands, the Wallis and Futuna Islands, and Western Sahara; the entries for all these territories in the downloaded spreadsheet are accompanied by the datum 'N' in place of the coded values of '1', '2', '3', or '4' that represent the country-level averages of the values for the sub-categories for each policy domain (text to note 592) ("SDG indicators: United Nations Global SDG Database", United Nations, accessed August 5, 2020, https://unstats.un.org/sdgs/indicators/database/). The text to notes 578 and 579, and Tables 3.25-3.29, specify the five sub-categories for each of the six policy domains.

600 "SDG indicators: United Nations Global SDG Database", United Nations, accessed August 5, 2020, https://unstats.un.org/sdgs/indicators/database/.

601 Table 3.24 lists the six policy domains for SDG Indicator 10.7.2.

602 China's item non-response for Domain 5 of SDG Indicator 10.7.2 is ≥ 10%.

603 China's item non-response for the overall SDG Indicator 10.7.2 is ≥ 10%.

Nigeria	2	4	4	4	4	2	3
Bangladesh	2	4	4	3	4	3	3
Russia	2	4	4	2[604]	3[605]	3	2[606]
Mexico	1	2	1	1	1	1	1
Japan	3	3	3	2[607]	2[608]	3	2[609]
Ethiopia	2	4	4	3	4	4	3
The Philippines	3	4	4	4	4	4	3
Egypt	-	-	-	-	-	-	-
Vietnam	2	2	4	4	2	3	2
The Democratic Republic of the Congo	-	-	-	-	-	-	-
Turkey	2[610]	3[611]	2[612]	1[613]	2[614]	4	2[615]
Iran	-	-	-	-	-	-	-
Germany	3	3	4	3[616]	1[617]	4	2[618]
Thailand	3	4	4	4	4	4	3

the twenty most-populous states in the world[619] for which this database contains this information.

Table 3.30 shows that data are currently absent from the UN Global SDG Database for the country-level averages for 2019 for India, the USA, Indonesia, Pakistan, Egypt, the Democratic Republic of the Congo, and Iran. Of the thirteen states whose data Table 3.30 contains, the Philippines and Thailand have the best results – fully meeting the objective of facilitating orderly, safe, regular and responsible migration and mobility of

---

604 Russia's item non-response for Domain 4 of SDG Indicator 10.7.2 is ≥ 10%.
605 Russia's item non-response for Domain 5 of SDG Indicator 10.7.2 is ≥ 10%.
606 Russia's item non-response for the overall SDG Indicator 10.7.2 is ≥ 10%.
607 Japan's item non-response for Domain 4 of SDG Indicator 10.7.2 is ≥ 10%.
608 Japan's item non-response for Domain 5 of SDG Indicator 10.7.2 is ≥ 10%.
609 Japan's item non-response for the overall SDG Indicator 10.7.2 is ≥ 10%.
610 Turkey's item non-response for Domain 1 of SDG Indicator 10.7.2 is ≥ 10%.
611 Turkey's item non-response for Domain 2 of SDG Indicator 10.7.2 is ≥ 10%.
612 Turkey's item non-response for Domain 3 of SDG Indicator 10.7.2 is ≥ 10%.
613 Turkey's item non-response for Domain 4 of SDG Indicator 10.7.2 is ≥ 10%.
614 Turkey's item non-response for Domain 5 of SDG Indicator 10.7.2 is ≥ 10%.
615 Turkey's item non-response for the overall SDG Indicator 10.7.2 is ≥ 10%.
616 Germany's item non-response for Domain 4 of SDG Indicator 10.7.2 is ≥ 10%.
617 Germany's item non-response for Domain 5 of SDG Indicator 10.7.2 is ≥ 10%.
618 Germany's item non-response for the overall SDG Indicator 10.7.2 is ≥ 10%.
619 Note 254 of Chapter Two lists these twenty countries from the most populous of them (China) to the least populous of them (Thailand).

people regarding Policy Domains 2, 3, 4, 5 and 6, and fulfilling this objective concerning Policy Domain 1 and the overall SDG Indicator 10.7.2. Nigeria, Bangladesh and Ethiopia also display very good outcomes – each fully meeting the objective on three (Bangladesh) or four (Nigeria and Ethiopia) of the six Policy Domains, and satisfying it as regards the overall SDG Indicator 10.7.2. Whilst Brazil, Russia, Japan, Vietnam and Germany exhibit reasonable results for meeting the objective in respect of the Policy Domains, all these countries bar Brazil fall short of fulfilling the objective concerning the overall SDG Indicator 10.7.2. The results for China are varying, those for Turkey are weak, and the outcomes for Mexico are abysmal – with the last-mentioned country requiring further progress towards meeting the objective of facilitating orderly, safe, regular and responsible migration and mobility of people concerning five of the six Policy Domains and the overall SDG Indicator 10.7.2.

Table 3.21 shows that hundreds of migrants die each year attempting to cross the USA-Mexico Border. Whilst, some of these tragedies are recorded as major events – especially towards the end of the year,[620] the preponderance of them are reported as occurrences that each involve the death of a single migrant.[621] Given these circumstances and Mexico's low-grade migration management – as indicated by the that state's entry in Table 3.30, it may be constructive to consider the country-level averages for Colombia, Panama, Costa Rica, Nicaragua, Honduras, El Salvador, and Guatemala – through which – save El Salvador – migrants from South America wishing to reach the USA must travel if they journey by road and/or rail.

Table 3.31 shows that data are presently missing from the UN Global SDG Database for the country-level averages for 2019 for Costa Rica and Nicaragua. Colombia, El Salvador and Guatemala fully meet the objective of facilitating orderly, safe, regular and responsible migration and mobility of people on three (Colombia) or four (El Salvador and Guatemala) of the six Policy Domains, and satisfy it in respect of the overall SDG Indicator 10.7.2. Whilst Colombia and El Salvador complete an excellent record by fulfilling the objective concerning those two (El Salvador) or three (Colombia)

[620] Table 3.23 contains an entry pertaining to 123 dead or missing migrants for the USA-Mexico Border dated 31st December 2015, and an entry referring to 84 dead migrants dated 20th December 2019. In the IOM's Missing Migration Project database, the 123 migrants are all recorded as dead rather than missing ("Download Missing Migrants Project data," International Organization for Migration, accessed July 24, 2020, https://missingmigrants.iom.int/downloads).

[621] Download Missing Migrants Project data," International Organization for Migration, accessed July 24, 2020, https://missingmigrants.iom.int/downloads.

Table 3.31: Country-level averages for the states through which migrants travel by road and/or rail to reach the USA for 2019 for each policy domain and for the overall SDG Indicator 10.7.2 (i.e., All domains), where 1 = requires further progress towards meeting the objective of facilitating orderly, safe, regular and responsible migration and mobility of people, 2 = partially meets this objective, 3 = meets this objective, and 4 = fully meets this objective[622]

State: in order of migrant travel	Number of policy domain (1 to 6)[623]						All domains
	1	2	3	4	5	6	
Colombia	4	3	3	4	3	4	3
Panama	3	3	3	1	1[624]	3	2
Costa Rica	-	-	-	-	-	-	-
Nicaragua	-	-	-	-	-	-	-
Honduras	2	2[625]	1[626]	1[627]	1[628]	4	2[629]
El Salvador	3	4	3	4	4	4	3
Guatemala	4	1	4	2	4	4	3
Mexico (Table 3.30)	1	2	1	1	1	1	1

Policy Domains for which these countries do not fully meet that aim, Guatemala's otherwise-superb statistics are diminished by requiring further progress to meet the objective with respect to Policy Domain 2 and by partially satisfying that goal as regards Policy Domain 4. Panama requires further progress to fulfil the objective of facilitating orderly, safe, regular and responsible migration and mobility of people on Policy Domains 4 and 5, and only partially meets it in respect of the overall SDG Indicator 10.7.2. Honduras displays the weakest outcomes bar Mexico of the states which Table 3.31 contains, with its only recommendable datum therein being it fully meeting the objective regarding Policy Domain 6. Of particular concern is the poor performance of Mexico and Honduras with respect to Policy Domain 3, as that Domain's requirements for bilateral

---

622 "SDG indicators: United Nations Global SDG Database", United Nations, accessed August 5, 2020, https://unstats.un.org/sdgs/indicators/database/.
623 Table 3.24 lists the six policy domains for SDG Indicator 10.7.2.
624 Panama's item non-response for Domain 5 of SDG Indicator 10.7.2 is ≥ 10%.
625 Honduras' item non-response for Domain 2 of SDG Indicator 10.7.2 is ≥ 10%.
626 Honduras' item non-response for Domain 3 of SDG Indicator 10.7.2 is ≥ 10%.
627 Honduras' item non-response for Domain 4 of SDG Indicator 10.7.2 is ≥ 10%.
628 Honduras' item non-response for Domain 5 of SDG Indicator 10.7.2 is ≥ 10%.
629 Honduras' item non-response for the overall SDG Indicator 10.7.2 is ≥ 10%.

agreements on migration[630] and agreements for co-operation with other countries on the return and readmission of migrants[631] are essential in effectively managing the movement of migrants from South America through Central America and Mexico to the USA.

Table 3.32 provides the aggregated data from the UN Global SDG Database concerning SDG Indicator 10.7.2.[632] Whilst these totals are compiled from the statistics of a limited number of states,[633] and whilst the UN's guide on SDG Indicator 10.7.2[634] does not impart the information as to which non-state territories,[635] if any,[636] and which states, are included in the various aggregates, these comprise information on the extent to which countries are either meeting or fully meeting the objective of facilitating orderly, safe, regular and responsible migration and mobility of people for each Policy Domain of SDG Indicator 10.7.2 and for 'All domains', i.e., for the overall SDG Indicator 10.7.2.[637]

---

[630] This requirement is sub-category (ii) in Table 3.26.

[631] This requirement is sub-class (iv) in Table 3.26.

[632] The text to note 447 states SDG Indicator 10.7.2.

[633] Note 598 lists the states for which the UN Global SDG Database contains grouped data for 2019.

[634] Note 595 specifies the UN's guide on SDG Indicator 10.7.2.

[635] Note 599 lists the non-state territories for which the UN Global SDG Database contains grouped data for 2019, and points out that their data entries do not contain the stipulated coded values for the country-level averages.

[636] The absence of suitably-coded values for the country-level averages of the non-state territories (note 635) may preclude the inclusion of these places in the data aggregates for SDG Indicator 10.7.2.

[637] The UN's guide on SDG Indicator 10.7.2 states: "The regional and global aggregates are calculated and reported as the proportion of countries in that region (or globally) that "Require further progress", "Partially meet" and "Meet or fully meet" target 10.7 as conceptualized and measured by indicator 10.7.2, among those that responded to the Inquiry module on international migration. The regional and global aggregates can be presented for both the overall indicator and by domain." (Metadata for Target 10.7 – Indicator 10.7.2: Department of Economic and Social Affairs and IOM, 6). Table 3.32 reports the "Percentage of countries that "Meet or fully meet" the criteria for SDG target 10.7 as conceptualised and measured by indicator 10.7.2, among those that responded to the Inquiry module on international migration" within each region ("SDG indicators: United Nations Global SDG Database", United Nations, accessed August 5, 2020, https://unstats.un.org/sdgs/indicators/database/). These figures form a binary test as to the compliance of countries with the objective of facilitating orderly, safe, regular and responsible migration and mobility of people, rather than the ternary test that UN's guide on SDG Indicator 10.7.2 specifies in

Table 3.32: The proportion of countries with migration policies to facilitate orderly, safe, regular and responsible migration and mobility of people, by policy domain (%)[638]

Region or grouping	Number of policy domain (1 to 6)[639]						All domains
	1	2	3	4	5	6	
World[640]	55.0	67.6	79.3	58.6 [641]	62.2	77.5	54.1
Africa[642]	45.7	48.6	77.1	42.9	71.4	68.6	45.7
South America[643]	100.0	85.7	85.7	85.7	71.4	100.0	100.0
Oceania[644]	55.6	55.6	77.8	66.7	44.4	66.7	33.3

the first quoted sentence above in this footnote. Note 596 describes the constituent modules of the UN Inquiry among governments on Population and Development.

638 "SDG indicators: United Nations Global SDG Database", United Nations, accessed August 5, 2020, https://unstats.un.org/sdgs/indicators/database/. The percentages in Table 3.32 are given to one decimal place. The entries in the column headed 'Region or Grouping' in Table 3.32 are placed in the same order in this table as they are located in the spreadsheet downloaded from the webpage to which this footnote refers on 5th August 2020.

639 Table 3.24 lists the six policy domains for SDG Indicator 10.7.2.

640 The 'World' aggregates are calculated from data provided by 111 countries. The UN comprises 193 Member States (text to note 226), and has 2 Permanent Observers – the Holy See and the State of Palestine (note 594). Thus, the World contains 195 states.

641 The item non-response of ≥ 20% of the constituent countries of the 'World' aggregate for Domain 4 of SDG Indicator 10.7.2 is ≥ 10%.

642 The 'Africa' aggregates are calculated from data provided by 35 countries. Africa contains 54 of the UN's Member States (note 153 of Chapter Two).

643 The 'South America' aggregates are calculated from data provided by 7 countries. South America comprises French Guiana – which is an Overseas Department of France – and the following 12 states: Argentina, Bolivia, Brazil, Chile, Colombia, Ecuador, Guyana, Paraguay, Peru, Suriname, Uruguay, and Venezuela (*The Times Concise Atlas of the World*, 62 and 270-271).

644 The 'Oceania' aggregates are calculated from data provided by 9 countries. Oceania contains the following 14 states: Australia, Fiji, Kiribati, the Marshall Islands, Micronesia, Nauru, New Zealand, Palau, Papua New Guinea, Samoa, the Solomon Islands, Tonga, Tuvalu, and Vanuatu (*The Times Concise Atlas of the World*, 84-85 and 103). Oceania includes the following non-state territories: American Samoa, the Ashmore and Carter Islands, Baker Island, the Cook Islands, Coral Sea Islands Territory, French Polynesia, Guam, Howland Island, Jarvis Island, Johnston Atoll, Kingman Reef, Lord Howe Island, Macquarie Island, New Caledonia, Niue, Norfolk Island, the Northern Mariana Islands, Palmyra Atoll, the

West Africa[645]	69.2	69.2	92.3	61.5[646]	84.6	76.9[647]	69.2
Central America[648]	60.0	40.0	60.0	20.0	40.0[649]	80.0	40.0
East Africa[650]	36.4	63.6	90.9	54.5	90.9	81.8	54.5
North Africa[651]	0.0[652]	50.0	50.0[653]	0.0[654]	0.0[655]	50.0[656]	0.0[657]

Pitcairn Islands, Tokelau, Wake Island, the Wallis and Futuna Islands, and the outlying islands of New Zealand – of which the Auckland Islands and the Chatham Islands, for instance, are part (*The Times Concise Atlas of the World*, 84-85).

[645] The 'West Africa' aggregates are calculated from data provided by 13 countries. West Africa comprises the following 16 states: Benin, Burkina Faso, Cabo Verde, Côte d'Ivoire, the Gambia, Ghana, Guinea, Guinea-Bissau, Liberia, Mali, Mauritania, Niger, Nigeria, Senegal, Sierra Leone, and Togo (United Nations, Department of Field Support – Cartographic Section: West Africa – Map No. 4533, October 2014).

[646] The item non-response of ≥ 20% of the constituent countries of the 'West Africa' aggregate for Domain 4 of SDG Indicator 10.7.2 is ≥ 10%.

[647] The item non-response of ≥ 20% of the constituent countries of the 'West Africa' aggregate for Domain 6 of SDG Indicator 10.7.2 is ≥ 10%.

[648] The 'Central America' aggregates are calculated from data provided by 5 countries. Central America comprises the following 7 states: Belize, Costa Rica, El Salvador, Guatemala, Honduras, Nicaragua, and Panama (*The Times Concise Atlas of the World*, 262-263). As the UN Global SDG Database includes grouped data for 2019 for El Salvador, Guatemala, Honduras, Mexico and Panama, but not for Belize, Costa Rica and Nicaragua (note 598 and Table 3.31), it is submitted that the five countries that the data compilers for SDG Indicator 10.7.2 (text to note 596) have included in the 'Central America' region are El Salvador, Guatemala, Honduras, Mexico and Panama. This postulate is corroborated by the inclusion in the UN Global SDG Database of grouped data for 2019 of one only country in North America (note 664) – which is Canada rather than the USA (note 598).

[649] The item non-response of ≥ 20% of the constituent countries of the 'Central America' aggregate for Domain 5 of SDG Indicator 10.7.2 is ≥ 10%.

[650] The 'East Africa' aggregates are calculated from data provided by 11 countries. It is opined that East Africa comprises the following 17 states: Burundi, Comoros, Djibouti, Eritrea, Ethiopia, Kenya, Madagascar, Malawi, Mauritius, Mozambique, Rwanda, the Seychelles, Somalia, South Sudan, Sudan, Tanzania, and Uganda.

[651] The 'North Africa' aggregates are calculated from data provided by 2 countries. North Africa contains 5 states (note 323).

[652] The item non-response of ≥ 20% of the constituent countries of the 'North Africa' aggregate for Domain 1 of SDG Indicator 10.7.2 is ≥ 10%.

[653] The item non-response of ≥ 20% of the constituent countries of the 'North Africa' aggregate for Domain 3 of SDG Indicator 10.7.2 is ≥ 10%.

Central Africa[658]	37.5	0.0	37.5	12.5	50.0	50.0	12.5
Southern Africa[659]	0.0[660]	0.0	100.0	0.0[661]	0.0[662]	0.0	0.0[663]
North America[664]	100.0	100.0	100.0	100.0	100.0	100.0	100.0

[654] The item non-response of ≥ 20% of the constituent countries of the 'North Africa' aggregate for Domain 4 of SDG Indicator 10.7.2 is ≥ 10%.
[655] The item non-response of ≥ 20% of the constituent countries of the 'North Africa' aggregate for Domain 5 of SDG Indicator 10.7.2 is ≥ 10%.
[656] The item non-response of ≥ 20% of the constituent countries of the 'North Africa' aggregate for Domain 6 of SDG Indicator 10.7.2 is ≥ 10%.
[657] The item non-response of ≥ 20% of the constituent countries of the 'North Africa' aggregate for the overall SDG Indicator 10.7.2 is ≥ 10%.
[658] The 'Central Africa' aggregates are calculated from data provided by 8 countries. It is submitted that Central Africa comprises the following 10 states: Angola, Cameroon, Central African Republic, Chad, the Democratic Republic of the Congo, Equatorial Guinea, Gabon, the Republic of the Congo, São Tomé and Príncipe, and Zambia.
[659] The 'Southern Africa' aggregates are calculated from data provided by 1 country. This region is entitled 'Southern Africa' rather than 'South Africa', in order to avoid confusion with the country of the latter name. It is opined that Southern Africa consists of the following 6 states: Botswana, Eswatini, Lesotho, Namibia, South Africa, and Zimbabwe.
[660] The item non-response of ≥ 20% of the constituent countries of the 'Southern Africa' aggregate for Domain 1 of SDG Indicator 10.7.2 is ≥ 10%.
[661] The item non-response of ≥ 20% of the constituent countries of the 'Southern Africa' aggregate for Domain 4 of SDG Indicator 10.7.2 is ≥ 10%.
[662] The item non-response of ≥ 20% of the constituent countries of the 'Southern Africa' aggregate for Domain 5 of SDG Indicator 10.7.2 is ≥ 10%.
[663] The item non-response of ≥ 20% of the constituent countries of the 'Southern Africa' aggregate for the overall SDG Indicator 10.7.2 is ≥ 10%.
[664] The 'North America' aggregates are calculated from data provided by 1 country. This country is Canada rather than the USA (note 598) or Mexico (note 648). *Check*: the grouped values of Canada for Policy Domains 1, 2, 3, 4, 5 and 6 of SDG Indicator 10.7.2 and the overall SDG Indicator 10.7.2, respectively, are 3, 4, 4, 4, 4, 4 and 3 ("SDG indicators: United Nations Global SDG Database", (United Nations, accessed August 5, 2020, https://unstats.un.org/sdgs/indicators/database/). Thus, Canada is meeting (i.e., grouped value 3 (text to note 592)) or fully meeting (i.e., grouped value 4 (text to note 592)) the objective of facilitating orderly, safe, regular and responsible migration and mobility of people for each Policy Domain of SDG Indicator 10.7.2 and for the overall SDG Indicator 10.7.2 (text to note 637). If Canada were to be the solitary country to be included in the 'North America' aggregates, then these

Caribbean[665]	50.0	100.0	100.0	100.0	100.0	100.0	100.0
East Asia[666]	33.3 [667]	66.7 [668]	66.7 [669]	33.3 [670]	0.0[671]	66.7 [672]	0.0[673]
South Asia[674]	50.0	50.0	50.0	100.0	100.0	100.0	50.0
South-East Asia[675]	75.0	75.0	100.0	100.0	75.0	75.0	75.0
South Europe[676]	40.0	80.0	90.0	60.0 [677]	60.0	70.0	60.0[678]

outcomes would translate to a value of 100% for all Policy Domains and for the overall SDG Indicator 10.7.2. These are the readings that Table 3.32 provides for North America. It is submitted that the region entitled North America as described here – i.e., omitting Central America and the Caribbean – comprises the non-state territory of Greenland and the following 3 states: Canada, Mexico, and the USA. The continent titled 'North America' also includes the countries of Central America and the islands in the Caribbean Sea (note 309).

665 The 'Caribbean' aggregates are calculated from data provided by 2 countries. The Caribbean contains the following 13 states: Antigua and Barbuda, the Bahamas, Barbados, Cuba, Dominica, the Dominican Republic, Grenada, Haiti, Jamaica, Saint Kitts and Nevis, Saint Lucia, Saint Vincent and the Grenadines, and Trinidad and Tobago (*The Times Concise Atlas of the World*, 237 and 266-267).

666 The 'East Asia' aggregates are calculated from data provided by 3 countries. East Asia contains the following 5 states: China (including Hong Kong, Macau, and Taiwan), the Democratic People's Republic of Korea, Japan, Mongolia, and the Republic of Korea (*The Times Concise Atlas of the World*, 100-101 and 110-111).

667 The item non-response of ≥ 20% of the constituent countries of the 'East Asia' aggregate for Domain 1 of SDG Indicator 10.7.2 is ≥ 10%.

668 The item non-response of ≥ 20% of the constituent countries of the 'East Asia' aggregate for Domain 2 of SDG Indicator 10.7.2 is ≥ 10%.

669 The item non-response of ≥ 20% of the constituent countries of the 'East Asia' aggregate for Domain 3 of SDG Indicator 10.7.2 is ≥ 10%.

670 The item non-response of ≥ 20% of the constituent countries of the 'East Asia' aggregate for Domain 4 of SDG Indicator 10.7.2 is ≥ 10%.

671 The item non-response of ≥ 20% of the constituent countries of the 'East Asia' aggregate for Domain 5 of SDG Indicator 10.7.2 is ≥ 10%.

672 The item non-response of ≥ 20% of the constituent countries of the 'East Asia' aggregate for Domain 6 of SDG Indicator 10.7.2 is ≥ 10%.

673 The item non-response of ≥ 20% of the constituent countries of the 'East Asia' aggregate for the overall SDG Indicator 10.7.2 is ≥ 10%.

674 The 'South Asia' aggregates are calculated from data provided by 2 countries. South Asia comprises 8 states (note 367 of Chapter Two).

675 The 'South-East Asia' aggregates are calculated from data provided by 4 countries. South-East Asia comprises 11 states (note 320).

Australia and New Zealand[679]	50.0[680]	100.0	100.0	100.0	50.0[681]	100.0	50.0[682]
Melanesia[683]	100.0	33.3	100.0	33.3	33.3	66.7	33.3
Micronesia[684]	33.3	33.3[685]	33.3	66.7	33.3	66.7[686]	33.3
Polynesia[687]	0.0	100.0	100.0	100.0	100,0	0.0	0.0

[676] The 'South Europe' aggregates are calculated from data provided by 10 countries. 'South Europe' consists of the following 15 states: Albania, Andorra, Bosnia and Herzegovina, Croatia, Greece, the Holy See, Italy, Malta, Montenegro, North Macedonia, Portugal, San Marino, Serbia, Slovenia, and Spain ("How many Countries in Europe?", Worldometer, accessed August 14, 2020, https://www.worldometers.info/geography/how-many-countries-in-europe/).
[677] The item non-response of ≥ 20% of the constituent countries of the 'South Europe' aggregate for Domain 4 of SDG Indicator 10.7.2 is ≥ 10%.
[678] The item non-response of ≥ 20% of the constituent countries of the 'South Europe' aggregate for the overall SDG Indicator 10.7.2 is ≥ 10%.
[679] The 'Australia and New Zealand' aggregates are calculated from data provided by 2 countries.
[680] The item non-response of ≥ 20% of the constituent countries of the 'Australia and New Zealand' aggregate for Domain 1 of SDG Indicator 10.7.2 is ≥ 10%.
[681] The item non-response of ≥ 20% of the constituent countries of the 'Australia and New Zealand' aggregate for Domain 5 of SDG Indicator 10.7.2 is ≥ 10%.
[682] The item non-response of ≥ 20% of the constituent countries of the 'Australia and New Zealand' aggregate for the overall SDG Indicator 10.7.2 is ≥ 10%.
[683] The 'Melanesia' aggregates are calculated from data provided by 3 countries. The following 4 states are in Melanesia: Fiji, Papua New Guinea, the Solomon Islands, and Vanuatu ("Countries & Regions: Melanesia", University of Central Florida, accessed August 14, 2020, https://guides.ucf.edu/countries/melanesia; "Reference map of Melanesia", Nations Online Project, accessed August 14, 2020, https://www.nationsonline.org/oneworld/map/melanesia_map.htm).
[684] The 'Micronesia' aggregates are calculated from data provided by 3 countries. The following 5 states are in Micronesia: Kiribati, the Marshall Islands, Micronesia (Federated States of), Nauru, and Palau ("Countries & Regions: Micronesia", University of Central Florida, accessed August 14, 2020, https://guides.ucf.edu/countries/micronesia).
[685] The item non-response of ≥ 20% of the constituent countries of the 'Micronesia' aggregate for Domain 2 of SDG Indicator 10.7.2 is ≥ 10%.
[686] The item non-response of ≥ 20% of the constituent countries of the 'Micronesia' aggregate for Domain 6 of SDG Indicator 10.7.2 is ≥ 10%.
[687] The 'Polynesia' aggregates are calculated from data provided by 1 country. The following 3 states are in Polynesia: Samoa, Tonga, and Tuvalu ("Countries & Regions: Polynesia", University of Central Florida, accessed August 14, 2020, https://guides.ucf.edu/countries/polynesia).

Central and South Asia[688]	60.0	80.0	80.0	100.0	80.0	100.0	80.0
Asia[689]	50.0	77.3	77.3	68.2[690]	54.5[691]	77.3	50.0[692]
Central Asia[693]	66.7	100.0	100.0	100.0	66.7[694]	100.0	100.0
West Asia[695]	40.0[696]	80.0[697]	70.0	50.0[698]	50.0[699]	70.0	40.0[700]

688 The 'Central and South Asia' aggregates are calculated from data provided by 5 countries. Central and South Asia comprises 13 states, i.e., the 5 countries of Central Asia (note 693) plus the 8 states of South Asia (note 674).

689 The 'Asia' aggregates are calculated from data provided by 22 countries. Asia comprises 48 states, i.e., the 5 states of East Asia (note 666) plus the 8 countries of South Asia (note 674) plus the 11 states of South-East Asia (note 675) plus the 5 countries of Central Asia (note 693) plus the 19 states of West Asia (note 695).

690 The item non-response of ≥ 20% of the constituent countries of the 'Asia' aggregate for Domain 4 of SDG Indicator 10.7.2 is ≥ 10%.

691 The item non-response of ≥ 20% of the constituent countries of the 'Asia' aggregate for Domain 5 of SDG Indicator 10.7.2 is ≥ 10%.

692 The item non-response of ≥ 20% of the constituent countries of the 'Asia' aggregate for the overall SDG Indicator 10.7.2 is ≥ 10%.

693 The 'Central Asia' aggregates are calculated from data provided by 3 countries. Central Asia comprises 5 states (note 350 of Chapter Two).

694 The item non-response of ≥ 20% of the constituent countries of the 'Central Asia' aggregate for Domain 5 of SDG Indicator 10.7.2 is ≥ 10%.

695 The 'West Asia' aggregates are calculated from data provided by 10 countries. West Asia comprises 19 states, i.e., the 18 countries that the first sentence of note 300 lists, plus Cyprus, which – unlike the opinion expressed in point (ii) in note 300 – is not considered to be part of Europe by virtue of its omission from the listings for South Europe (note 676) and East Europe (note 704).

696 The item non-response of ≥ 20% of the constituent countries of the 'West Asia' aggregate for Domain 1 of SDG Indicator 10.7.2 is ≥ 10%.

697 The item non-response of ≥ 20% of the constituent countries of the 'West Asia' aggregate for Domain 2 of SDG Indicator 10.7.2 is ≥ 10%.

698 The item non-response of ≥ 20% of the constituent countries of the 'West Asia' aggregate for Domain 4 of SDG Indicator 10.7.2 is ≥ 10%.

699 The item non-response of ≥ 20% of the constituent countries of the 'West Asia' aggregate for Domain 5 of SDG Indicator 10.7.2 is ≥ 10%.

700 The item non-response of ≥ 20% of the constituent countries of the 'West Asia' aggregate for the overall SDG Indicator 10.7.2 is ≥ 10%.

Europe[701]	56.7	83.3	83.3	63.3 [702]	60.0	83.3	60.0 [703]
East Europe[704]	33.3	83.3	66.7	50.0 [705]	50.0 [706]	83.3	33.3 [707]
North Europe[708]	66.7	77.8	88.9	66.7 [709]	66.7 [710]	88.9	66.7
West Europe[711]	100.0	100.0	80.0	80.0 [712]	60.0	100.0	80.0
LDCs[713]	50.0	50.0	78.6	53.6	75.0	78.6	57.1

---

[701] The 'Europe' aggregates are calculated from data provided by 30 countries. There are 44 states in Europe (How many Countries in Europe?", Worldometer, accessed August 14, 2020, https://www.worldometers.info/geography/how-many-countries-in-europe/; *The Times Concise Atlas of the World*, 146-147).

[702] The item non-response of ≥ 20% of the constituent countries of the 'Europe' aggregate for Domain 4 of SDG Indicator 10.7.2 is ≥ 10%.

[703] The item non-response of ≥ 20% of the constituent countries of the 'Europe' aggregate for the overall SDG Indicator 10.7.2 is ≥ 10%.

[704] The 'East Europe' aggregates are calculated from data provided by 6 countries. 'East Europe' comprises the following 10 states: Belarus, Bulgaria, the Czech Republic, Hungary, Moldova, Poland, Romania, Russia, Slovakia, and Ukraine ("How many Countries in Europe?", Worldometer, accessed August 14, 2020, https://www.worldometers.info/geography/how-many-countries-in-europe/).

[705] The item non-response of ≥ 20% of the constituent countries of the 'East Europe' aggregate for Domain 4 of SDG Indicator 10.7.2 is ≥ 10%.

[706] The item non-response of ≥ 20% of the constituent countries of the 'East Europe' aggregate for Domain 5 of SDG Indicator 10.7.2 is ≥ 10%.

[707] The item non-response of ≥ 20% of the constituent countries of the 'East Europe' aggregate for the overall SDG Indicator 10.7.2 is ≥ 10%.

[708] The 'North Europe' aggregates are calculated from data provided by 9 countries. 'North Europe' consists of the following 10 states: Denmark, Estonia, Finland, Iceland, Ireland, Latvia, Lithuania, Norway, Sweden, and the UK ("How many Countries in Europe?", Worldometer, accessed August 14, 2020, https://www.worldometers.info/geography/how-many-countries-in-europe/).

[709] The item non-response of ≥ 20% of the constituent countries of the 'North Europe' aggregate for Domain 4 of SDG Indicator 10.7.2 is ≥ 10%.

[710] The item non-response of ≥ 20% of the constituent countries of the 'North Europe' aggregate for Domain 5 of SDG Indicator 10.7.2 is ≥ 10%.

[711] The 'West Europe' aggregates are calculated from data provided by 5 countries. West Europe comprises the following 9 states: Austria, Belgium, France, Germany, Liechtenstein, Luxembourg, Monaco, the Netherlands, and Switzerland ("How many Countries in Europe?", Worldometer, accessed August 14, 2020, https://www.worldometers.info/geography/how-many-countries-in-europe/).

[712] The item non-response of ≥ 20% of the constituent countries of the 'West Europe' aggregate for Domain 4 of SDG Indicator 10.7.2 is ≥ 10%.

Sub-Saharan Africa[714]	48.5	48.5	78.8	45.5 [715]	75.8	69.7	48.5
Latin America and the Caribbean [716]	78.6	71.4	78.6	64.3	64.3	92.9	78.6
LLDCs[717]	60.0	60.0	75.0	50.0	60.0	70.0	55.0
Europe and North America[718]	58.1	83.9	83.9	64.5 [719]	61.3	83.9	61.3 [720]
Developed regions[721]	58.8	85.3	85.3	64.7 [722]	58.8 [723]	85.3	58.8 [724]

---

713 The 'LDCs' aggregates are calculated from data provided by 28 countries. 47 states are LDCs (note 125 of Chapter Two).

714 The 'Sub-Saharan Africa' aggregates are calculated from data provided by 33 countries. It is opined that 49 of the 54 UN Member States that are situated in Africa, are located in Sub-Saharan Africa (note 153 of Chapter Two).

715 The item non-response of ≥ 20% of the constituent countries of the 'Sub-Saharan Africa' aggregate for Domain 4 of SDG Indicator 10.7.2 is ≥ 10%.

716 The 'Latin America and the Caribbean' aggregates are calculated from data provided by 14 countries. It is submitted that Latin America and the Caribbean comprises 30 states, i.e., the 20 states but not the 6 non-state territories on the shorter list constituting 'Latin America' in note 309 – i.e., list (ii), plus the 13 states of the Caribbean (note 665), less those 3 states of the Caribbean (i.e., Cuba, the Dominican Republic, and Haiti) that are in Latin America (i.e., that are on list (ii) in note 309).

717 The 'LLDCs' aggregates are calculated from data provided by 20 countries. 32 states are LLDCs (note 286).

718 The 'Europe and North America' aggregates are calculated from data provided by 31 countries. Europe and North America comprises 47 states, i.e., the 44 countries of Europe (note 701) plus the 3 states of North America (note 664).

719 The item non-response of ≥ 20% of the constituent countries of the 'Europe and North America' aggregate for Domain 4 of SDG Indicator 10.7.2 is ≥ 10%.

720 The item non-response of ≥ 20% of the constituent countries of the 'Europe and North America' aggregate for the overall SDG Indicator 10.7.2 is ≥ 10%.

721 The 'Developed regions' aggregates are calculated from data provided by 34 countries. The 'Developed regions' include the following 51 states: Albania, Andorra, Australia, Austria, Belarus, Belgium, Bosnia and Herzegovina, Bulgaria, Canada, Croatia, Cyprus, the Czech Republic, Denmark, Estonia, Finland, France, Germany, Greece, the Holy See, Hungary, Iceland, Ireland, Israel, Italy, Japan, Latvia, Liechtenstein, Lithuania, Luxembourg, Malta, Moldova, Monaco, Montenegro, the Netherlands, New Zealand, North Macedonia, Norway, Poland, Portugal,

Developing regions[725]	53.2	59.7	76.6	55.8	63.6	74.0	51.9
Oceania excluding Australia and New Zealand[726]	57.1	42.9	71.4	57.1	42.9	57.1	28.6

Romania, Russia, San Marino, Serbia, Slovakia, Slovenia, Spain, Sweden, Switzerland, the UK, Ukraine, and the USA (note 385).

[722] The item non-response of ≥ 20% of the constituent countries of the 'Developed regions' aggregate for Domain 4 of SDG Indicator 10.7.2 is ≥ 10%.

[723] The item non-response of ≥ 20% of the constituent countries of the 'Developed regions' aggregate for Domain 5 of SDG Indicator 10.7.2 is ≥ 10%.

[724] The item non-response of ≥ 20% of the constituent countries of the 'Developed regions' aggregate for the overall SDG Indicator 10.7.2 is ≥ 10%.

[725] The 'Developing regions' aggregates are calculated from data provided by 77 countries. The 'Developing regions' include the following 144 states: Afghanistan, Algeria, Angola, Antigua and Barbuda, Argentina, Armenia, Azerbaijan, the Bahamas, Bahrain, Bangladesh, Barbados, Belize, Benin, Bhutan, Bolivia, Botswana, Brazil, Brunei Darussalam, Burkina Faso, Burundi, Cabo Verde, Cambodia, Cameroon, Central African Republic, Chad, Chile, China, Colombia, Comoros, Costa Rica, Côte d'Ivoire, Cuba, the Democratic People's Republic of Korea, the Democratic Republic of the Congo, Djibouti, Dominica, the Dominican Republic, Ecuador, Egypt, El Salvador, Equatorial Guinea, Eritrea, Eswatini, Ethiopia, Fiji, Gabon, the Gambia, Georgia, Ghana, Grenada, Guatemala, Guinea, Guinea-Bissau, Guyana, Haiti, Honduras, India, Indonesia, Iran, Iraq, Jamaica, Jordan, Kazakhstan, Kenya, Kiribati, Kuwait, Kyrgyzstan, Laos, Lebanon, Lesotho, Liberia, Libya, Madagascar, Malawi, Malaysia, the Maldives, Mali, the Marshall Islands, Mauritania, Mauritius, Mexico, Micronesia, Mongolia, Morocco, Mozambique, Myanmar, Namibia, Nauru, Nepal, Nicaragua, Niger, Nigeria, Oman, Pakistan, Palau, Panama, Papua New Guinea, Paraguay, Peru, the Philippines, Qatar, the Republic of the Congo, the Republic of Korea, Rwanda, Saint Kitts and Nevis, Saint Lucia, Saint Vincent and the Grenadines, Samoa, São Tomé and Príncipe, Saudi Arabia, Senegal, the Seychelles, Sierra Leone, Singapore, the Solomon Islands, Somalia, South Africa, South Sudan, Sri Lanka, the State of Palestine, Sudan, Suriname, Syria, Tajikistan, Tanzania, Thailand, Timor-Leste, Togo, Tonga, Trinidad and Tobago, Tunisia, Turkey, Turkmenistan, Tuvalu, Uganda, the United Arab Emirates, Uruguay, Uzbekistan, Vanuatu, Venezuela, Vietnam, Yemen, Zambia, and Zimbabwe (note 386).

[726] The 'Oceania excluding Australia and New Zealand' aggregates are calculated from data provided by 7 countries. Oceania excluding Australia and New Zealand comprises 12 states, i.e., the 14 states of Oceania (note 644) less 2 countries (i.e., Australia and New Zealand).

SIDS[727]	50.0	50.0	75.0	58.3	50.0	75.0	41.7
North Africa and West Asia[728]	33.3 [729]	75.0 [730]	66.7 [731]	41.7 [732]	41.7 [733]	66.7 [734]	33.3 [735]
East and South-East Asia[736]	57.1	71.4	85.7	71.4 [737]	42.9 [738]	71.4	42.9 [739]

It is submitted that the information in Table 3.32 is difficult to analyze both because: (i) there are several classifications of region and grouping therein, and (ii) data are absent regarding many countries. Therefore, representativeness – and presentation – of the percentages that Table 3.32 contains are addressed, as follows.

---

727 The 'SIDS' aggregates are calculated from data provided by 12 countries. 38 states are SIDS (list (i) in the first sentence of note 285).

728 The 'North Africa and West Asia' aggregates are calculated from data provided by 12 countries. North Africa and West Asia consists of 24 states, i.e., the 5 countries of North Africa (note 651) plus the 19 states of West Asia (note 695).

729 The item non-response of ≥ 20% of the constituent countries of the 'North Africa and West Asia' aggregate for Domain 1 of SDG Indicator 10.7.2 is ≥ 10%.

730 The item non-response of ≥ 20% of the constituent countries of the 'North Africa and West Asia' aggregate for Domain 2 of SDG Indicator 10.7.2 is ≥ 10%.

731 The item non-response of ≥ 20% of the constituent countries of the 'North Africa and West Asia' aggregate for Domain 3 of SDG Indicator 10.7.2 is ≥ 10%.

732 The item non-response of ≥ 20% of the constituent countries of the 'North Africa and West Asia' aggregate for Domain 4 of SDG Indicator 10.7.2 is ≥ 10%.

733 The item non-response of ≥ 20% of the constituent countries of the 'North Africa and West Asia' aggregate for Domain 5 of SDG Indicator 10.7.2 is ≥ 10%.

734 The item non-response of ≥ 20% of the constituent countries of the 'North Africa and West Asia' aggregate for Domain 6 of SDG Indicator 10.7.2 is ≥ 10%.

735 The item non-response of ≥ 20% of the constituent countries of the 'North Africa and West Asia' aggregate for the overall SDG Indicator 10.7.2 is ≥ 10%.

736 The 'East and South-East Asia' aggregates are calculated from data provided by 7 countries. East and South-East Asia comprises 16 states, i.e., the 5 countries of East Asia (note 666) plus the 11 states of South-East Asia (note 675).

737 The item non-response of ≥ 20% of the constituent countries of the 'East and South-East Asia' aggregate for Domain 4 of SDG Indicator 10.7.2 is ≥ 10%.

738 The item non-response of ≥ 20% of the constituent countries of the 'East and South-East Asia' aggregate for Domain 5 of SDG Indicator 10.7.2 is ≥ 10%.

739 The item non-response of ≥ 20% of the constituent countries of the 'East and South-East Asia' aggregate for the overall SDG Indicator 10.7.2 is ≥ 10%.

Representativeness: Any aggregate to which only one country provides data is not necessarily representative of the region or grouping associated with that total. Thus, no comment is made on the sole-country aggregates relating to Southern Africa,[740] North America,[741] and Polynesia.[742] The greater the percentage of countries within a region or grouping on which data are provided, the more representative is its aggregate of the countries of that region or grouping, *ceteris paribus*.[743] Table 3.33 provides these percentages for the non-sole-country aggregates in Table 3.32, classifying the representativeness of those of > 60% as high, 40%-60% as medium, and < 40% as low. No comment is made on those aggregates with low representativeness. Remarks in respect of aggregates with medium representativeness should be interpreted cautiously.

Table 3.33: The representativeness of the number of countries providing data for the region or grouping as a whole – > 60% = high, 40%-60% = medium, < 40% = low

Region or grouping	No. of states providing data (x)	No. of states in region or grouping (y)	Percentage of states providing data [(x/y) * 100%] (%)[744]	Represent-iveness (high, medium, or low)
Australia and New Zealand	2[745]	2	100	high
North Europe	9[746]	10[747]	90	high
West Africa	13[748]	16[749]	81	high
Central	8[750]	10[751]	80	high

[740] Note 659.
[741] Note 664.
[742] Note 687.
[743] Note 338 of Chapter Two defines '*ceteris paribus*'.
[744] The numbers in this column are given to the nearest percentage point.
[745] Note 679.
[746] Note 708.
[747] Note 708.
[748] Note 645.
[749] Note 645.
[750] Note 658.

Africa				
Melanesia	3[752]	4[753]	75	high
Central America	5[754]	7[755]	71[756]	high[757]
Europe	30[758]	44[759]	68	high
Developed regions	34[760]	51[761]	67	high
Sub-Saharan Africa	33[762]	49[763]	67	high
South Europe	10[764]	15[765]	67	high
Europe and	31[766]	47[767]	66[768]	high[769]

751 Note 658.
752 Note 683.
753 Note 683.
754 Note 648.
755 Notes 648 and 756.
756 The UN Global SDG Database includes grouped data for 2019 for El Salvador, Guatemala, Honduras, Mexico and Panama, but not for Belize, Costa Rica and Nicaragua (note 648). Mexico is not one of the 7 states of Central America (note 648). Notwithstanding this, Mexico may be one of the 5 countries that the data compilers for SDG Indicator 10.7.2 have included in the 'Central America' region (note 648). Thus, for accurate categorization of these data, 'Central America' may need to be enlarged to include Mexico – which would alter the number of states in this region from 7 to 8. This change reduces the percentage of states providing data for the region's aggregates from 71% to [(5/8) * 100%] = 63%.
757 The level of representativeness, i.e., high, is unaffected by the decrease in the percentage of states providing data from 71% to 63% that note 756 suggests.
758 Note 701.
759 Note 701.
760 Note 721.
761 Note 721.
762 Note 714.
763 Note 714.
764 Note 676.
765 Note 676.
766 Note 718.
767 Notes 718 and 768.
768 The 31 countries from which data are provided to calculate the 'Europe and North America' aggregates (note 718) comprise the 30 countries for which data are supplied to compute the 'Europe' aggregates (note 701) and the 1 country for which data are furnished to determine the 'North America' aggregates (note 664). This latter country is Canada (note 664). The data for Mexico are omitted from the

North America				
Africa	35[770]	54[771]	65	high
East Africa	11[772]	17[773]	65	high
Oceania	14[774]	9[775]	64	high
LLDCs	20[776]	32[777]	63	high
LDCs	28[778]	47[779]	60	medium
East Europe	6[780]	10[781]	60	medium
Central Asia	3[782]	5[783]	60	medium
East Asia	3[784]	5[785]	60	medium
Micronesia	3[786]	5[787]	60	medium

'North America' aggregates (note 664), and may have been included in the 'Central America' aggregates instead (note 648). Whilst note 664 opines that the region entitled North America (i.e., that omitting Central America and the Caribbean) consists of the non-state territory of Greenland and the states of Canada, Mexico and the USA, the omission of the data for Mexico from the 'North America' aggregate necessitates the removal of Mexico from the region entitled 'North America' – which therefore includes only 2 states, i.e., Canada and the USA. This change necessitates the number of states in the region titled 'Europe and North America' to be reduced by one, i.e., from 47 states to 46 states. Consequently, the percentage of states providing data for the 'Europe and North America' aggregates rises from 66% to [(31/46) * 100%] = 67%.

[769] The level of representativeness, i.e., high, is unaltered by the increase in the percentage of states providing data from 66% to 67% that note 768 specifies.

[770] Note 642.

[771] Note 642.

[772] Note 650.

[773] Note 650.

[774] Note 644.

[775] Note 644.

[776] Note 717.

[777] Note 717.

[778] Note 713.

[779] Note 713.

[780] Note 704.

[781] Note 704.

[782] Note 693.

[783] Note 693.

[784] Note 666.

[785] Note 666.

[786] Note 684.

[787] Note 684.

Oceania excluding Australia and New Zealand	7[788]	12[789]	58	medium
South America	7[790]	12[791]	58	medium
World	111[792]	195[793]	57	medium
West Europe	5[794]	9[795]	56	medium
Developing regions	77[796]	144[797]	53	medium
West Asia	10[798]	19[799]	53	medium
North Africa and West Asia	12[800]	24[801]	50	medium
Latin America and the Caribbean	14[802]	30[803]	47	medium
Asia	22[804]	48[805]	46	medium
East and	7[806]	16[807]	44	medium

788 Note 726.
789 Note 726.
790 Note 643.
791 Note 643.
792 Note 640.
793 Note 640.
794 Note 711.
795 Note 711.
796 Note 725.
797 Note 725.
798 Note 695.
799 Note 695.
800 Note 728.
801 Note 728.
802 Note 716.
803 Note 716.
804 Note 689.
805 Note 689.
806 Note 736.
807 Note 736.

South-East Asia				
North Africa	2[808]	5[809]	40	medium
Central and South Asia	5[810]	13[811]	38	low
South-East Asia	4[812]	11[813]	36	low
SIDS	12[814]	38[815]	32	low
South Asia	2[816]	8[817]	25	low
Caribbean	2[818]	13[819]	15	low

Presentation: The data in Table 3.32 is separated into clusters that are presented in subsidiary tables, each of which contains countries' records that together provide high or medium representativeness of the region or grouping according to their classification as such in Table 3.33. Comments are made on the data in these tables. The first of these – Table 3.34 – shows the aggregates for the world and the groupings that qualify as per the criterion of representativeness.

Table 3.34 shows that 50% or more of states worldwide, developed and developing countries, LLDCs and LDCs have migration policies in place to facilitate orderly, safe, regular and responsible migration and mobility of people – for each policy domain and for the overall SDG Indicator 10.7.2.[820] This bodes well for the punctual accomplishment of SDG Target 10.7.[821]

[808] Note 651.
[809] Note 651.
[810] Note 688.
[811] Note 688.
[812] Note 675.
[813] Note 675.
[814] Note 727.
[815] Note 727.
[816] Note 674.
[817] Note 674.
[818] Note 665.
[819] Note 665.
[820] The text to note 447 specifies SDG Indicator 10.7.2.
[821] The text to note 445 states SDG Target 10.7.

Table 3.34: The proportion of countries globally and in various groupings with migration policies to facilitate orderly, safe, regular and responsible migration and mobility of people, by policy domain (%)[822]

Grouping	Representativeness (Table 3.33)	Number of policy domain (1 to 6)[823]						All domains
		1	2	3	4	5	6	
World	medium	55	68	79	59	62	78	54
Developed regions	high	59	85	85	65	59	85	59
Developing regions	medium	53	60	77	56	64	74	52
LLDCs	high	60	60	75	50	60	70	55
LDCs	medium	50	50	79	54	75	79	57

Table 3.35: The proportion of countries in Oceania with migration policies to facilitate orderly, safe, regular and responsible migration and mobility of people, by policy domain (%)[824]

Region	Representativeness (Table 3.33)	Number of policy domain (1 to 6)[825]						All domains
		1	2	3	4	5	6	
Oceania	high	56	56	78	67	44	67	33
Australia and New Zealand	high	50	100	100	100	50	100	50
Oceania excluding Australia and New Zealand	medium	57	43	71	57	43	57	29
Melanesia	high	100	33	100	33	33	67	33
Micronesia	medium	33	33	33	67	33	67	33

822 The numbers in Table 3.34 are given to the nearest percentage point. Note 637 and its accompanying text detail what the aggregates in this table are measuring – in the eighth line of note 637, please read 'Table 3.34' for 'Table 3.32'.

823 Table 3.24 lists the six policy domains for SDG Indicator 10.7.2.

824 The numbers in Table 3.35 are given to the nearest percentage point. Note 637 and its accompanying text detail what the aggregates in this table are measuring – in the eighth line of note 637, please read 'Table 3.35' for 'Table 3.32'.

825 Table 3.24 lists the six policy domains for SDG Indicator 10.7.2.

Table 3.35 shows that, whilst the region entitled 'Australia and New Zealand' to a considerable extent effects migration policies to facilitate orderly, safe, regular and responsible migration and mobility of people – and whilst the majority of the states in Oceania as a whole do so for five of the six policy domains, few countries in Oceania – and even less when Australia and New Zealand are omitted – have such policies in place regarding the overall SDG Indicator 10.7.2.[826]

Only one of the three Melanesian countries providing data,[827] and just one of the three Micronesian states furnishing statistics,[828] operate migration policies to facilitate orderly, safe, regular and responsible migration and mobility of people in respect of the overall SDG Indicator 10.7.2. In Micronesia, for no policy domain do all three countries supplying data employ these policies.

Whilst good national migration policies concerning Policy Domain 6 are prevalent in Oceania, such policies for Policy Domain 5 are in the minority there. Whilst substantial progress towards the timely achievement of SDG Target 10.7[829] over the area of national migration policies has been made in Oceania, this region should continue to improve those policies – especially regarding Policy Domain 5.

Table 3.36: The proportion of countries in Europe with migration policies to facilitate orderly, safe, regular and responsible migration and mobility of people, by policy domain (%)[830]

Region	Representativeness (Table 3.33)	Number of policy domain (1 to 6)[831]						All domains
		1	2	3	4	5	6	
Europe	high	57	83	83	63	60	83	60
East Europe	medium	33	83	67	50	50	83	33
North Europe	high	67	78	89	67	67	89	67
South Europe	high	40	80	90	60	60	70	60

826 The text to note 447 specifies SDG Indicator 10.7.2.

827 Note 683.

828 Note 684.

829 The text to note 445 states SDG Target 10.7.

830 The numbers in Table 3.36 are given to the nearest percentage point. Note 637 and its accompanying text detail what the aggregates in this table are measuring – in the eighth line of note 637, please read 'Table 3.36' for 'Table 3.32'.

831 Table 3.24 lists the six policy domains for SDG Indicator 10.7.2.

West Europe	medium	100	100	80	80	60	100	80
Europe and North America	high	58	84	84	65	61	84	61

Table 3.36 shows that more than 50% of countries in Europe – and in Europe and North America – have migration policies in place to facilitate orderly, safe, regular and responsible mobility of people, for each policy domain and for the overall SDG Indicator 10.7.2.[832] Two-thirds or more of states in North Europe, and at least 60% of countries in West Europe, operate such migration policies for each policy domain and for the overall SDG Indicator 10.7.2.

60% or more of states in South Europe have working migration policies to facilitate orderly, safe, regular and responsible mobility of people for each policy domain bar Policy Domain 1, and for the overall SDG Indicator 10.7.2. 50% or more of countries in East Europe employ such policies for each policy domain save Policy Domain 1, but only 33% of these states use these policies for the overall SDG Indicator 10.7.2. Thus, countries in South Europe and those in East Europe should improve their migration policies in respect of Policy Domain 1. States in East Europe should ameliorate those policies regarding the overall SDG Indicator 10.7.2. Notwithstanding these issues, it is submitted that Europe is progressing well regarding its migration policies towards the punctual attainment of SDG Target 10.7.[833]

Table 3.37: The proportion of countries in Latin America with migration policies to facilitate orderly, safe, regular and responsible migration and mobility of people, by policy domain (%)[834]

Region	Representativeness (Table 3.33)	Number of policy domain (1 to 6)[835]						All domains
		1	2	3	4	5	6	
Latin America	medium	79	71	79	64	64	93	79

[832] The text to note 447 specifies SDG Indicator 10.7.2.

[833] The text to note 445 states SDG Target 10.7.

[834] The numbers in Table 3.37 are given to the nearest percentage point. Note 637 and its accompanying text detail what the aggregates in this table are measuring – in the eighth line of note 637, please read 'Table 3.37' for 'Table 3.32'.

[835] Table 3.24 lists the six policy domains for SDG Indicator 10.7.2.

and the Caribbean								
Central America	high	60	40	60	20	40	80	40
South America	medium	100	86	86	86	71	100	100

Table 3.37 shows that more than 70% of countries in South America, and more than 60% of states in Latin America and the Caribbean, have migration policies in place to facilitate orderly, safe, regular and responsible migration and mobility of people – for each policy domain and for the overall SDG Indicator 10.7.2.[836] South America is progressing particularly well with regard to the alignment of its constituent countries' migration policies with SDG Target 10.7[837] – 100% of the seven constituent countries that provided data for the calculation of the 'South America' aggregate[838] operate such migration policies for the overall SDG Indicator 10.7.2 and for Policy Domains 1 and 6.

Less than 50% of the states in Central America employ functional migration policies to facilitate orderly, safe, regular and responsible migration and mobility of people in respect of Policy Domains 2, 4 and 5 and the overall SDG Indicator 10.7.2. It is opined that these are areas over which countries in Central America should improve their migration policies with a view to timely accomplishment of SDG Target 10.7.

Table 3.38: The proportion of countries in Asia with migration policies to facilitate orderly, safe, regular and responsible migration and mobility of people, by policy domain (%)[839]

Region	**Representativeness (Table 3.33)**	**Number of policy domain (1 to 6)[840]**						**All domains**
		1	**2**	**3**	**4**	**5**	**6**	
Asia	medium	50	77	77	68	55	77	50
East and South-	medium	57	71	86	71	43	71	43

[836] The text to note 447 specifies SDG Indicator 10.7.2.

[837] The text to note 445 states SDG Target 10.7.

[838] Note 643.

[839] The numbers in Table 3.38 are given to the nearest percentage point. Note 637 and its accompanying text detail what the aggregates in this table are measuring – in the eighth line of note 637, please read 'Table 3.38' for 'Table 3.32'.

[840] Table 3.24 lists the six policy domains for SDG Indicator 10.7.2.

East Asia								
East Asia	medium	33	67	67	33	0	67	0
Central Asia	medium	67	100	100	100	67	100	100
West Asia	medium	40	80	70	50	50	70	40
North Africa and West Asia	medium	33	75	67	42	42	67	33

Table 3.38 shows that 50% or more of countries in Asia have migration policies in place to facilitate orderly, safe, regular and responsible migration and mobility of people – for each policy domain and for the overall SDG Indicator 10.7.2.[841] All three states in Central Asia that furnished data for the computation of the 'Central Asia' and 'Central and South Asia' aggregates[842] apply such migration policies for the overall SDG Indicator 10.7.2 and for Policy Domains 2, 3, 4 and 6, and two of these countries do so for Policy Domains 1 and 5 – showing that Central Asia is progressing effectively in respect of the alignment of its constituent countries' migration policies with SDG Target 10.7.[843]

Fewer than 50% of countries in East and South-East Asia, East Asia, West Asia, and North Africa and West Asia, have migration policies in place to facilitate orderly, safe, regular and responsible migration and mobility of people for at least one of the six Policy Domains and for the overall SDG Indicator 10.7.2. The totals in Table 3.38 for East Asia are of particular concern, as none of the three countries in this region that supplied data for the calculation of the 'East Asia' and 'East and South-East Asia' aggregates[844] operate such migration policies for the overall SDG Indicator 10.7.2 and for Policy Domain 5. It is opined that states in East Asia should ameliorate their migration policies over these areas, in order to improve their chances of a punctual achievement of SDG Target 10.7.

---

[841] The text to note 447 specifies SDG Indicator 10.7.2.

[842] Notes 693 and 688, respectively. Due to the low-representativeness of the data submitted by 38% of countries in respect of the 'Central and South Asia' aggregates (Table 3.33), these totals are omitted from Table 3.38.

[843] The text to note 445 states SDG Target 10.7.

[844] Notes 666 and 736, respectively.

Table 3.39: The proportion of countries in Africa with migration policies to facilitate orderly, safe, regular and responsible migration and mobility of people, by policy domain (%)[845]

Region	Representativeness (Table 3.33)	Number of policy domain (1 to 6)[846]						All domains
		1	2	3	4	5	6	
Africa	high	46	49	77	43	71	69	46
North Africa	medium	0	50	50	0	0	50	0
Sub-Saharan Africa	high	49	49	79	46	76	70	49
Central Africa	high	38	0	38	13	50	50	13
East Africa	high	36	64	91	55	91	82	55
West Africa	high	69	69	92	62	85	77	69

Table 3.39 shows that 43% to 77% of countries in Africa have migration policies in place to facilitate orderly, safe, regular and responsible migration and mobility of people for the six policy domains, with 46% of these states operating such policies for the overall SDG Indicator 10.7.2.[847] The percentage of countries in Sub-Saharan Africa with these policies is slightly greater than for Africa for each policy domain[848] and for the overall SDG Indicator 10.7.2, but follows a similar pattern among the policy domains. As Africa = Sub-Saharan Africa + North Africa,[849] the aggregates for North Africa have modestly worsened the Sub-Saharan totals on combining with these to form the aggregates for Africa. This is because, in this merger, the two countries with poor

[845] The numbers in Table 3.39 are given to the nearest percentage point. Note 637 and its accompanying text detail what the aggregates in this table are measuring – in the eighth line of note 637, please read 'Table 3.39' for 'Table 3.32'.
[846] Table 3.24 lists the six policy domains for SDG Indicator 10.7.2.
[847] The text to note 447 specifies SDG Indicator 10.7.2.
[848] Whilst Table 3.39 shows that 49% of countries in Africa and 49% of states in Sub-Saharan Africa have migration policies in place to facilitate orderly, safe, regular and responsible migration and mobility of people for Policy Domain 2, Table 3.32 shows the former percentage to be 48.6% to one decimal place and the latter percentage to be 48.5% to one decimal place.
[849] Note 323.

migration policies that constitute the aggregates for North Africa[850] are added to the 33 states that form the totals for Sub-Saharan Africa.[851] Table 3.39 shows that neither of these states in North Africa has working migration policies to facilitate orderly, safe, regular and responsible migration and mobility of people for the overall SDG Indicator 10.7.2 and for Policy Domains 1, 4 and 5, and only one of those two countries operates such migration policies in respect of Policy Domains 2, 3 and 6. These countries are Libya and Tunisia.[852] Table 3.40 shows the coded country-level averages for those two states for each policy domain and for the overall SDG Indicator 10.7.2.

Table 3.40: Country-level averages for Libya and Tunisia for 2019 for each policy domain and for the overall SDG Indicator 10.7.2 (i.e., All domains), where 1 = requires further progress towards meeting the objective of facilitating orderly, safe, regular and responsible migration and mobility of people, 2 = partially meets this objective, 3 = meets this objective, and 4 = fully meets this objective[853]

State: in order of migrant travel	Number of policy domain (1 to 6)[854]						All domains
	1	2	3	4	5	6	
Libya	2[855]	1	1	2[856]	1	4	2
Tunisia	1[857]	3	3[858]	1[859]	1[860]	1[861]	1[862]

Further to the comments made concerning the loss of migrants in the Mediterranean Sea,[863] scrutiny of the migration policy of Tunisia and,

850 Note 651 and accompanying row in Table 3.32.
851 Note 714.
852 An inspection of the list of states in note 598 in the light of the information in the first sentence of note 323 reveals that Libya and Tunisia are the two countries in North Africa that contribute data to the 'North Africa' aggregates.
853 "SDG indicators: United Nations Global SDG Database", United Nations, accessed August 5, 2020, https://unstats.un.org/sdgs/indicators/database/.
854 Table 3.24 lists the six policy domains for SDG Indicator 10.7.2.
855 Libya's item non-response for Domain 1 of SDG Indicator 10.7.2 is ≥ 10%.
856 Libya's item non-response for Domain 4 of SDG Indicator 10.7.2 is ≥ 10%.
857 Tunisia's item non-response for Domain 1 of SDG Indicator 10.7.2 is ≥ 10%.
858 Tunisia's item non-response for Domain 3 of SDG Indicator 10.7.2 is ≥ 10%.
859 Tunisia's item non-response for Domain 4 of SDG Indicator 10.7.2 is ≥ 10%.
860 Tunisia's item non-response for Domain 5 of SDG Indicator 10.7.2 is ≥ 10%.
861 Tunisia's item non-response for Domain 6 of SDG Indicator 10.7.2 is ≥ 10%.
862 Tunisia's item non-response for the overall SDG Indicator 10.7.2 is ≥ 10%.

especially, Libya – given the use of the latter country's western ports to convey migrants from Africa to Europe – may provide insights into ways of improving this situation. The information available to help to do this includes: (i) the grouped country-level averages for Libya and Tunisia in Table 3.40, (ii) the question and five sub-categories for each policy domain,[864] the answers to which yield those averages by means of (iii) the methodology for determining values of SDG Indicator 10.7.2,[865] most of which is revisited forthwith.

All the sub-categories, save those under Policy Domain 1, have 'Yes/No' answers that are coded '1' for 'Yes' and '0' for No.[866] The sub-classes under Policy Domain 1 have these possible coded answers *and* 'Yes, only for those individuals with legal immigration status' – which is coded '0.5'.[867] For each policy domain, the unweighted average of the coded values across its sub-categories, D_i, is calculated as $D_i = [\sum_j s_{ji} / n] * 100\%$, where D_i is the coded value for domain i, $\sum_j s_{ji}$ is the sum of the coded values across sub-categories – indexed by j – under domain i, and n is the total number of sub-categories in a domain – which is 5.[868] For each domain, i, $0\% \leq D_i \leq 100\%$.[869] The overall SDG Indicator 10.7.2 for each country is reached by computing the unweighted average of the coded values of the thirty sub-categories under the six domains, with values ranging from 0% to 100%.[870] Once these country-level averages have been computed – for each policy domain and for the overall SDG Indicator 10.7.2, they are grouped as follows: values of less than 40% are coded as 'Requires further progress – 1', values of 40% to less than 80% are coded as 'Partially meets – 2', values of 80% to less than 100% are coded as 'Meets – 3', and values of 100% are coded as 'Fully meets – 4'.[871] Tables 3.30, 3.31 and 3.40 contain grouped country-level averages for each policy domain and for the overall SDG Indicator 10.7.2, which have been calculated thus.

---

[863] The antepenultimate and final paragraphs of the subsection entitled 'SDG Indicators 10.7.3 and 10.7.4', above in the current section (i.e., that titled 'SDG Target 10.7, and SDG Indicators 10.7.1, 10.7.2, 10.7.3 and 10.7.4') contain these reflections.

[864] The text to notes 578 and 579, and Tables 3.25-3.29, state the question and five sub-categories for each of the six policy domains.

[865] The text to note 447 specifies SDG Indicator 10.7.2.

[866] Text to note 587.

[867] Text to note 588.

[868] Text to note 589.

[869] Text to note 590.

[870] Text to note 591.

[871] Text to note 592.

In Table 3.40, Libya's country-level average for Policy Domain 1 has a coded value of 2, and Tunisia's has a coded value of 1. This means that 40% to 79% of Libya's answers to the question for Policy Domain 1 are in the affirmative, whilst less than 40% of Tunisia's are so. Thus, given the possible coded answers to the sub-categories under Policy Domain 1,[872] Libya's coded answers to the question applied to each of that policy domain's five sub-categories sum to 2, 2.5, 3 or 3.5 out of 5, and Tunisia's coded answers regarding Policy Domain 1 total to 0, 0.5, 1 or 1.5. Therefore, the Libyan Government provides non-nationals with the same access as its citizens to some of: (i) essential and/or emergency healthcare, (ii) public education, (iii) equal pay for equal work, (iv) social security, and (v) access to justice,[873] whilst the Tunisian Government supplies non-nationals with the same access as its nationals to none or few of these benefits.

Table 3.40 shows that Libya's country-level average for each of Policy Domains 2 and 3 has a coded value of 1, whilst Tunisia's has a coded value of 3. Given the possible coded answers to the sub-classes under Policy Domains 2, 3, 4, 5 and 6,[874] Libya's coded answers to the question for Policy Domain 2 applied to each of that policy domain's five sub-categories, and also to the question in Policy Domain 3 applied to each of the latter's five sub-classes, sum to 0 or 1 out of 5. Therefore, subject to the possibility of one exception from among the following, Libya does not have any of: (i) a dedicated government agency to implement its national migration policy, (ii) a national policy or strategy for regular migration pathways, (iii) a national policy or strategy to promote the inclusion or integration of immigrants, (iv) formal mechanisms to ensure that the migration policy is responsive to gender, or (v) a mechanism to ensure that migration policy is informed by data.[875] Nor does Libyan Government, conditional upon the possibility of one exception from among the following, take any of these measures to nurture co-operation between countries and encourage the inclusion and participation of stakeholders in its migration policy: (i) an inter-ministerial co-ordination mechanism on migration, (ii) bilateral agreements on migration, (iii) regional agreements that promote mobility, (iv) agreements for co-operation with other countries on the return and readmission of migrants, or (v) formal mechanisms to engage civil society and the private sector in the

[872] Text to note 867.
[873] Text to note 579.
[874] Text to note 866.
[875] Table 3.25.

formulation and implementation of migration policy.[876] It is submitted that absence of these institutions, policies, strategies, mechanisms and agreements is a contributory factor to the migration melee that has been recorded at and around the coast of western Libya in recent years.

In Table 3.40, Libya's country-level average for Policy Domain 4 has a coded value of 2, whilst Tunisia's has a coded value of 1. Given the possible coded answers to the sub-categories under Policy Domains 2 to 6,[877] Libya's coded answers to the question for Policy Domain 4 applied to each of that policy domain's five sub-categories total to 2 or 3 out of 5, and Tunisia's coded answers regarding Policy Domain 4 sum to 0 or 1. Thus, subject to the possibility of one exception among the following measures, the Tunisian Government does not: (i) align, using periodic assessments, policies on the migration of labour with actual and projected needs of the labour market, (ii) facilitate the portability of social security benefits, (iii) facilitate the recognition of qualifications and skills acquired abroad, (iv) facilitate or promote the flow of migrant remittances, or (v) promote fair and ethical recruitment of migrant workers.[878] The Libyan Government takes two or three of these five measures. It is opined that, if Tunisia improves its migration policy regarding these five actions under Policy Domain 4, it may be able to ease the migration bottleneck in western Libya and the adjacent part of the Mediterranean Sea – in particular, the recognition of migrant qualifications and skills might enable some of the migrants in western Libya to move to Tunisia to seek skilled or semi-skilled work, which would ease the pressure on the Libyan ports, the Mediterranean Sea and destinations in Europe.

Table 3.40 shows that both Libya's and Tunisia's country-level average for Policy Domain 5 have a coded value of 1. Given the possible coded answers to the sub-categories under Policy Domains 2 to 6,[879] both Libya's and Tunisia's coded answers to the question for Policy Domain 5 applied to each of that policy domain's five sub-classes total to 0 or 1 out of 5. Thus, conditional to the possibility of one exception for either or both governments among the following measures, neither the Libyan Government nor the Tunisian Government responds to persons forcibly displaced across international borders by taking any of the following measures: (i) a system for receiving, processing and identifying individuals who are forced to flee across international borders, (ii) contingency planning for displaced populations in terms of their basic

[876] Table 3.26.

[877] Text to note 866.

[878] Table 3.27.

[879] Text to note 866.

needs, (iii) specific measures to provide assistance to citizens who reside abroad in countries in crisis or post-crisis situations, (iv) a national disaster risk reduction strategy with specific provisions to address the impact of disasters regarding the displacement of people, or (v) the granting of permissions for temporary stay or temporary protection for persons who are forcibly displaced across international borders and for individuals who are unable to return to their home country.[880] As Africa is a hot continent that is prone to tribal conflict, refugees are likely to number among the migrants within North Africa. Therefore, it is important that Libya and Tunisia reform their migration policies regarding Policy Domain 5, in order to better provide for the needs of people who are forcibly moved across international borders.

In Table 3.40, Libya's country-level average for Policy Domain 6 has a coded value of 4, whilst Tunisia's has a coded value of 1. Given the possible coded answers to the sub-classes under Policy Domains 2 to 6,[881] Libya's coded answers to the question for Policy Domain 6 applied to each of that policy domain's five sub-categories total to 5 out of 5 – i.e., Libya has answered all five sub-classes for Policy Domain 6 pursuant to that policy domain's question in the affirmative, and Tunisia's coded answers concerning Policy Domain 6 sum to 0 or 1. Thus, unlike the Tunisian Government – which implements no more than one of the following measures, the Libyan government addresses migration through all these: (i) a system to monitor migrants who have lived in a country beyond the time at which their visa permits them to do so, (ii) pre-arrival authorization controls, (iii) provisions for unaccompanied minors or separated children, (iv) information and awareness-raising campaigns on migration, and (v) formal strategies to combat trafficking in persons and smuggling of migrants.[882]

Thus, the Libyan Government operates a system of migration management – which is evidenced by the measures that it takes to address migration under Policy Domain 6.[883] However, this system is neither comprehensive nor effectively integrated with that of Libya's neighbouring states – as evidenced by the lack of institutions, policies, strategies, mechanisms and agreements recommended under Policy Domains 2 and 3.[884] These inferences are reflected in Libya's country-level average for

[880] Table 3.28.
[881] Text to note 866.
[882] Table 3.29.
[883] Text to note 882.
[884] Text to notes 875 and 876.

the overall SDG Indicator 10.7.2 – calculated as specified above,[885] whose coded value Table 3.40 shows to be 2. Explaining this statement in terms of the methodology,[886] that coded country-level average of 2 means that 40% to 79% of Libya's answers to the questions associated with those the six policy domains applied to the corresponding sub-classes are in the affirmative,[887] which, given the coding system for these answers[888] including that used exclusively for those under Policy Domain 1,[889] means that Libya's coded answers total to 12, 12.5, 13, 13.5, 14, 14.5, 15, 15.5, 16, 16.5, 17, 17.5, 18, 18.5, 19, 19.5, 20, 20.5, 21, 21.5, 22, 22.5, 23 or 23.5 out of 30. It is submitted that, given the prevalence of coded country-level averages of 1 in Libya's data – Table 3.40 shows that Libya has this value for Policy Domains 2, 3 and 5, the total of Libya's coded answers for the overall SDG Indicator 10.7.2 is likely to be in the lower part of the range of 12 to 23.5. The highest possible total for Libya's coded answers for the overall SDG Indicator 10.7.2 is equal to 3.5 (Libya's coded country-level average for Policy Domain 1 is 2) plus 1 (Libya's coded country-level average for Policy Domain 2 is 1) plus 1 (Libya's coded country-level average for Policy Domain 3 is 1) plus 3 (Libya's coded country-level average for Policy Domain 4 is 2) plus 1 (Libya's coded country-level average for Policy Domain 5 is 1) plus 5 (Libya's coded country-level average for Policy Domain 6 is 4), which sums to 14.5 out of 30. Thus, Libya's coded answers for the overall SDG Indicator 10.7.2 total to 12, 12.5, 13, 13.5, 14 or 14.5 out of 30, from which it may be inferred that whilst the Libyan Government has put a substantial number of the required measures to fully meet the objective of facilitating orderly, safe, regular and responsible migration in place, many of the issues raised in the policy domains' subcategories remain to be addressed.

In Table 3.40, Tunisia's coded country-level average for the overall SDG Indicator 10.7.2 is 1. Thus, less than 40% of Tunisia's answers to the questions linked to the six policy domains applied to the corresponding sub-categories are in the affirmative,[890] which, given the coding system for those answers[891] including that solely for those under Policy Domain 1,[892]

---

[885] Text to note 870.

[886] The text to notes 866-871 specify the preponderant part of the methodology for ascertaining values of SDG Indicator 10.7.2.

[887] Text to notes 870 and 871.

[888] Text to note 866.

[889] Text to note 867.

[890] Text to notes 870 and 871.

[891] Text to note 866.

[892] Text to note 867.

means that Tunisia's coded answers sum to 0, 0.5, 1, 1.5, 2, 2.5, 3, 3.5, 4, 4.5, 5, 5.5, 6, 6.5, 7, 7.5, 8, 8.5, 9, 9.5, 10, 10.5, 11 or 11.5 out of 30. The lowest possible total for Tunisia's coded answers for the overall SDG Indicator 10.7.2 is equal to 0 (Libya's coded country-level average for Policy Domain 1 is 1) plus 4 (Libya's coded country-level average for Policy Domain 2 is 3) plus 4 (Libya's coded country-level average for Policy Domain 3 is 3) plus 0 (Libya's coded country-level average for Policy Domain 4 is 1) plus 0 (Libya's coded country-level average for Policy Domain 5 is 1) plus 0 (Libya's coded country-level average for Policy Domain 6 is 1), which sums to 8 out of 30. Consequently, Tunisia's coded answers for the overall SDG Indicator 10.7.2 total to 8, 8.5, 9, 9.5, 10, 10.5, 11 or 11.5 out of 30, from which it may be concluded that, whilst the Tunisian Government has taken some of the measures that are necessary to fully satisfy the objective of facilitating orderly, safe, regular and responsible migration, most of the actions required for this purpose are still to be performed. To this end, Tunisia may need financial assistance. The following promised contribution would be a start.

> Italy offered Tunisia €11 million [i.e., 11,000,000 EUR] yesterday to enlist its support in stemming a new wave of Mediterranean migration, after 728 migrants arrived on the Italian island of Lampedusa in small boats at the weekend. The offer came as two Italian ministers and two EU commissioners [i.e., European Commissioners] visited Tunis for talks on the migration crisis. Luigi Di Maio, the Five Star foreign minister, and Luciana Lamorgese, the politically unaffiliated interior minister, were accompanied by Ylva Johansson, the European commissioner for home affairs, and Oliver Varhelyi, who is responsible for strengthening relations with the EU's [European Union's] neighbours. The group met President Saied of Tunisia and Hichem Mechichi, the prime minister-designate, to press for stronger measures to reduce the number of migrants leaving Tunisia.[893]

Returning to Table 3.39, Sub-Saharan Africa comprises Central Africa, East Africa, West Africa and Southern Africa – the last of which is omitted from that table because only one country in that region provides data to compute the 'Southern Africa' aggregates,[894] and these statistics are not necessarily representative of Southern Africa.[895] 62% to 92% of

---

893 Philip Willan, "Rome offers Tunis €11m to stop flow of migrants", *The Times*, August 18, 2020, No. 73241, 31.

894 Text to note 659. The one state in Southern Africa to supply data to calculate the 'Southern Africa' for 2019 is Botswana (note 598).

895 Text to note 740.

states in West Africa have migration policies in place to facilitate orderly, safe, regular and responsible migration and mobility of people for the six policy domains, with 69% of these countries employing such policies for the overall SDG Indicator 10.7.2.[896] Each of these seven percentages exceeds the corresponding percentage for Sub-Saharan Africa.

Table 3.39 shows that 36% to 91% of states in East Africa operate policies which facilitate orderly, safe, regular and responsible migration and mobility of people for the six policy domains – the lowest percentage concerns Policy Domain 1 and the highest applies to Policy Domains 3 and 5, with 55% of these states using these policies for the overall SDG Indicator 10.7.2. Other than for Policy Domain 1, the proportion of countries in East Africa with migration policies in place to facilitate orderly, safe, regular and responsible migration and mobility of people for each policy domain and for the overall SDG Indicator 10.7.2 exceeds the corresponding percentage for Sub-Saharan Africa.

In Table 3.39, 50% of countries in Central Africa employ policies that facilitate orderly, safe, regular and responsible migration and mobility of people for Policy Domains 5 and 6, 38% of these states operate such policies for Policy Domains 1 and 3, 13% do so for Policy Domain 4 and the overall SDG Indicator 10.7.2, and none do so for Policy Domain 2. Each of these percentages subceeds the corresponding percentage for Sub-Saharan Africa. In view of the tendency of migrants to move from west to east and, especially, south to north, across the Sahara Desert, it is noteworthy that Cameroon, Central African Republic and Chad are among the eight states in Central Africa that provide data for the calculation of the 'Central Africa' aggregates.[897] Table 3.41 shows the coded country-level averages for these three states for each policy domain and for the overall SDG Indicator 10.7.2.

Whilst none of these states – except for Chad in respect of Policy Domain 2 and Cameroon concerning Policy Domains 3 and 5 – meet (or fully meet) the objective of facilitating orderly, safe, regular and responsible migration and mobility of people regarding each policy domain and the overall SDG Indicator 10.7.2,[898] Central African Republic falls further short of this standard than do Cameroon or Chad. Given the possible coded answers for the relevant question applied to the five sub-categories for each of

---

[896] The text to note 447 specifies SDG Indicator 10.7.2.

[897] Notes 598 and 658.

[898] The text to note 447 states SDG Indicator 10.7.2.

Table 3.41: Country-level averages for Cameroon, Central African Republic and Chad for 2019 for each policy domain and for the overall SDG Indicator 10.7.2 (i.e., All domains), where 1 = requires further progress towards meeting the objective of facilitating orderly, safe, regular and responsible migration and mobility of people, 2 = partially meets this objective, 3 = meets this objective, and 4 = fully meets this objective[899]

State: in order of migrant travel	Number of policy domain (1 to 6)[900]						All domains
	1	2	3	4	5	6	
Cameroon	1	1	3	2	3	2	2
Central African Republic	1	1	1	1	2	2	1
Chad	3	2	1	1	2	2	2

Policy Domains 2 to 6[901] and those for the question and sub-classes for Policy Domain 1,[902] the lowest possible total for Central African Republic is equal to 0 (Central African Republic's coded country-level average for Policy Domain 1 is 1) plus 0 (Central African Republic's coded country-level average for Policy Domain 2 is 1) plus 0 (Central African Republic's coded country-level average for Policy Domain 3 is 1) plus 0 (Central African Republic's coded country-level average for Policy Domain 4 is 1) plus 2 (Central African Republic's coded country-level average for Policy Domain 5 is 2) plus 2 (Central African Republic's coded country-level average for Policy Domain 6 is 2), which sums to 4 out of 30,[903] and the highest possible total for Central African Republic is equal to 1.5 (Central African Republic's coded country-level average for Policy Domain 1 is 1) plus 1 (Central African Republic's coded country-level average for Policy Domain 2 is 1) plus 1 (Central African Republic's coded country-level average for Policy Domain 3 is 1) plus 1 (Central African Republic's coded country-level average for Policy Domain 4 is 1) plus 3 (Central African Republic's coded country-level average for Policy Domain 5 is 2)

[899] "SDG indicators: United Nations Global SDG Database", United Nations, accessed August 5, 2020, https://unstats.un.org/sdgs/indicators/database/.

[900] Table 3.24 lists the six policy domains for SDG Indicator 10.7.2.

[901] Text to note 866.

[902] Text to note 867.

[903] The text to note 870 states this calculation generically, which, in the current instance of it, yields a country-level average of less than 40% (i.e., (4/30) * 100% = 13% to the nearest percentage point) – which is coded as 'Requires further progress – 1' (text to note 871).

plus 3 (Central African Republic's coded country-level average for Policy Domain 6 is 2), which sums to 10.5 out of 30.[904] Thus, Central African Republic's coded answers for the overall SDG Indicator 10.7.2 total to 4, 4.5, 5, 5.5, 6, 6.5, 7, 7.5, 8, 8.5, 9, 9.5, 10 or 10.5 out of 30, all values of which translate to a coded country-level average of 1,[905] and from which it may be inferred that this State's Government has yet to put in place the majority of the measures that are required to meet the objective of facilitating orderly, safe, regular and responsible migration.

SDG Indicator 10.7.1

A crucial role of migration policies is to lower the financial costs of recruitment that migrant workers incur, which deplete their incomes – including that which their families send to them – and remittances.[906] SDG Indicator 10.7.1[907] measures the total amount that an international migrant worker and/or this employee's family paid to find, qualify for, and obtain a firm job offer from a foreign employer and to arrive at the place of employment for the worker's first job abroad, relative to the actual income which this employee received for the last month in that job – including bonuses and overtime pay – adjusted for deductions made for taxes and social security contributions and for the employer to recover any recruitment costs that it paid at the outset.[908] The calculation of SDG Indicator 10.7.1 is given by RCI = f (C_k / E_k), where RCI – the Recruitment

[904] The text to note 870 states this calculation generically, which, in the present instance of it, yields a country-level average of less than 40% (i.e., (10.5/30) * 100% = 35%) – which is coded as 'Requires further progress – 1' (text to note 871).

[905] As the minimum (note 903) and the maximum (note 904) values of these aggregate coded answers for the overall SDG Indicator 10.7.2 for Central African Republic both yield a country-level average of less than 40% – which is coded as 'Requires further progress – 1' (text to note 871), all the other (i.e., the intervening) values of these aggregate coded answers also yield a country-level average of less than 40% – coded as 'Requires further progress – 1'. Consequently, the coded country-level average for Central African Republic is 1, which corroborates the value that Table 3.41 shows for this statistic.

[906] United Nations, Department of Economic and Social Affairs – Statistics Division: Metadata for Target 10.7 – Indicator 10.7.1: ILO and World Bank – Last updated: November 2018 (New York, 2018), 1.

[907] Note 446 states SDG Indicator 10.7.1.

[908] Metadata for Target 10.7 – Indicator 10.7.2: Department of Economic and Social Affairs and IOM, 2.

Costs Indicator[909] – is the proportion of recruitment costs in monthly employment earnings, f is a function – which may be, for instance, the mean, the median or the fourth quintile, C_k represents the recruitment costs that migrant worker k pays, and E_k represents the monthly earnings of the same migrant worker k.[910]

In order to minimize the operational challenges and costs of collecting the input data for SDG Indicator 10.7.1, household-based surveys – such as a survey of the labour force, a household income and expenditure survey, or a multi-purpose survey that includes questions on migration and employment, are the main instruments for collecting data, as these rely on existing programmes that countries conduct regularly.[911] The custodian agencies – and data compliers – for SDG Indicator 10.7.1, which are the ILO and the World Bank,[912] are to make a stand-alone module that includes a set of questions available to the data providers for this SDG Indicator – which are the National Statistical Offices[913] – for integration in household survey instruments that are already in place.[914]

Whilst data pertaining to SDG Indicator 10.7.1 was scheduled for collection from the first quarter of 2019 – and for release from the third quarter of that year,[915] it is currently unavailable from the UN Global SDG Database.[916] However, from 2015 to 2017, KNOMAD[917] – in partnership

---

909 World Bank, Migration and Remittances: Recent Developments and Outlook – Migration and Development Brief 29, April 2018 (Washington, D.C., 2018), 14.

910 Metadata for Target 10.7 – Indicator 10.7.2: Department of Economic and Social Affairs and IOM, 3.

911 Metadata for Target 10.7 – Indicator 10.7.2: Department of Economic and Social Affairs and IOM, 4.

912 Metadata for Target 10.7 – Indicator 10.7.2: Department of Economic and Social Affairs and IOM, 1 and 6.

913 Metadata for Target 10.7 – Indicator 10.7.2: Department of Economic and Social Affairs and IOM, 6.

914 Metadata for Target 10.7 – Indicator 10.7.2: Department of Economic and Social Affairs and IOM, 5.

915 Metadata for Target 10.7 – Indicator 10.7.2: Department of Economic and Social Affairs and IOM, 6.

916 United Nations Global SDG Database", United Nations, accessed August 20, 2020, https://unstats.un.org/sdgs/indicators/database/.

917 Based at the World Bank's headquarters in Washington, D.C., KNOMAD is a non-exclusive multidisciplinary knowledge partnership that advises policymakers in countries from which migrants depart, through which they travel, and in which they settle ("Overview", Global Knowledge Partnership on Migration and Development, accessed August 21, 2020, https://www.knomad.org/about-us).

with the ILO – interviewed more than 5,500 migrant workers[918] from 19 bilateral migration corridors[919] in order to systematically record the costs that these individuals incurred seeking jobs abroad and their conditions of work in the countries of destination.[920] These survey data showed the Recruitment Cost Indicator[921] to be especially high for low-income migrant workers and for those whom brokers recruited, and revealed that migrants who used the services of these intermediaries tended to incur additional expenses.[922] Migrants incurring higher recruitment costs

---

[918] The KNOMAD-ILO Migration Cost Surveys 2015 interviewed 3,149 migrants; the KNOMAD-ILO Migration Cost Surveys 2016 interviewed 2,454 migrants ("KNOMAD-ILO Migration and Recruitment Costs Surveys", Global Knowledge Partnership on Migration and Development, accessed August 21, 2020, https://www.knomad.org/data/recruitment-costs). Note 920 specifies accessibility of these two datasets.

[919] Taken together, the seven KNOMAD-ILO Migration Costs Surveys 2015 cover the following ten bilateral migration corridors: El Salvador to Mexico, Ethiopia to Saudi Arabia, Guatemala to Mexico, Honduras to Mexico, India to Qatar, Nepal to Qatar, Pakistan to Saudi Arabia, Pakistan to the United Arab Emirates, the Philippines to Qatar, and Vietnam to Malaysia; as a group, the five KNOMAD-ILO Migration Costs Surveys 2016 include the following nine bilateral migration corridors: India to Saudi Arabia, Kyrgyzstan to Russia, Nepal to Malaysia, Nepal to Qatar, Nepal to Saudi Arabia, the Philippines to Saudi Arabia, Tajikistan to Russia, Uzbekistan to Russia, and West African states to Italy ("KNOMAD-ILO Migration and Recruitment Costs Surveys", Global Knowledge Partnership on Migration and Development, accessed August 21, 2020, https://www.knomad.org/data/recruitment-costs). Note 920 details accessibility of these two datasets.

[920] World Bank, Migration and Remittances: Recent Developments and Outlook, 14. The KNOMAD-ILO Migration Cost Surveys 2015 and the KNOMAD-ILO Migration Cost Surveys 2016 are currently available for download from the World Bank's Microdata Library to registered users of this databank who are logged in to it ("KNOMAD-ILO Migration Costs Surveys 2015", World Bank, accessed August 21, 2020, https://microdata.worldbank.org/index.php/catalog/2938/get-microdata; "KNOMAD-ILO Migration Costs Surveys 2016", World Bank, accessed August 21, 2020, https://microdata.worldbank.org/index.php/catalog/2944/get-microdata).

[921] The text to note 910 defines the Recruitment Cost Indicator as used to calculate values of SDG Indicator 10.7.1. The World Bank's report titled 'Migration and Remittances: Recent Developments and Outlook' – which note 909 references – defines the Recruitment Cost Indicator as "the worker-paid recruitment costs of securing an overseas job, expressed as a multiple of monthly foreign earnings" (World Bank, Migration and Remittances: Recent Developments and Outlook, 14).

[922] World Bank, Migration and Remittances: Recent Developments and Outlook, 14.

received less income than that contractually-promised, were more likely to be paid irregularly, and were less likely to be compensated when injured at work, *ceteris paribus*.[923]

Comment

The data in Tables 3.21, 3.23, 3.31, 3.40 and 3.41 impart the information that all is not well concerning Africa-to-Europe and South/Central-to-North America migration. Whilst the worst incidents regarding migration over the period 1st January 2015 to 22nd July 2020 took place towards the beginning of this period[924] in the Mediterranean Sea[925] – especially off the coast of north-west Libya,[926] such tragedies have not completely subsided – even in the throes of the COVID-19 pandemic[927] – as the following excerpt indicates.

> Forty-five people … have drowned in the Mediterranean in the worst tragedy this year, the UN said yesterday. The victims were among 82 people on an overcrowded boat that capsized on Monday after its engine exploded in Libyan waters off the port of Zuwara [which is on the coast of

---

923 World Bank, Migration and Remittances: Recent Developments and Outlook, 14. Note 338 of Chapter Two defines '*ceteris paribus*'. The World Bank's Migration and Development Brief states: "While these results are tentative, they suggest a plausible pattern of exploitation whereby vulnerable migrants experience both higher costs and more adverse working conditions. Efforts to reduce recruitment costs would require better monitoring of recruitment agents (or subagents) and allowing direct recruitment by certified, *bona fide* overseas employers." (World Bank, Migration and Remittances: Recent Developments and Outlook, 14-15; emphasis added). '*Bona fide*' means "genuine, real", and is the ablative singular of the Latin phrase '*bona fides*' – "literally 'with good faith'" (*The New Oxford Dictionary of English*, 202).

924 Table 3.23 shows that the twelve most major incidents in the period 1st January 2015 to 22nd July 2020 in terms of the total number of migrants dead or missing took place between 9th February 2015 and 21st September 2016.

925 Table 3.23 shows that all the nine most major incidents – and seventeen of the eighteen most major incidents – in the period 1st January 2015 to 22nd July 2020 in terms of the total number of migrants dead or missing, occurred in the Mediterranean Sea.

926 Table 3.23 records six of the nine most major incidents – and twelve of the eighteen most major incidents – in terms of the total number of migrants dead or missing, as happening north of western Libya.

927 The WHO declared the outbreak and spread of COVID-19 to be a pandemic on 11th March 2020 (text to note 53 of Chapter Two).

> north-west Libya].[928] Another 37 people were rescued by fishermen and returned to Libya … . The migrants were mainly from Senegal, Mali … , Chad and Ghana.[929]

The migration-related problems in North Africa and the Mediterranean Sea cannot remain unaddressed until the target date for the SDGs to be realized approaches, [930] as these difficulties are too serious. The UN should swiftly act to help Libya, Tunisia and other relevant countries to fully meet the objective of having migration policies in place that facilitate orderly, safe, regular and responsible migration and mobility of people – which, if accomplished, may reduce to low levels the fatal mishaps that have tended to strike migrants in the Mediterranean Sea.

SDG Target 10.a and SDG Indicator 10.a.1

SDG Target 10.a is to "[i]mplement the principle of special and differential treatment[931] for developing countries, in particular least developed countries, in accordance with World Trade Organization agreements".[932] Its one indicator is SDG Indicator 10.a.1, which determines the "[p]roportion of tariff lines applied to imports from least developed countries and developing countries with zero-tariff".[933]

Duty-free treatment (i.e., zero tariffs) is not always synonymous with preferential treatment regarding tariffs[934] for a country benefiting from

---

[928] The IOM's 'Missing Migrants' spreadsheet (note 465) contains several entries that refer to fatal incidents involving migrants which occurred off the Libyan coast near Zuwara.

[929] Philip Willan, "45 killed as boat capsizes", *The Times*, August 21, 2020, No. 73244, 9.

[930] This target date is 31st December 2030, pursuant to the use of the phrase "by 2030' in some of the SDG Targets, such as SDG Target 1.1 (note 99 of Chapter One, text to note 6 of Chapter Two, and note 50 of Chapter Two and accompanying text) and SDG Target 10.1 (text to note 10, and note 222 and accompanying text).

[931] For further information concerning special and differential treatment for developing countries, see Baber, *Essays on International Law*, 177-181.

[932] Resolution 70/1 adopted by the General Assembly on 25 September 2015, Transforming our world: the 2030 Agenda for Sustainable Development, 21.

[933] Global indicator framework for the Sustainable Development Goals and targets of the 2030 Agenda for Sustainable Development, 11.

[934] Tariffs are "customs duties on merchandise imports, levied either on an *ad valorem* basis (percentage of value) or on a specific basis (e.g. [USD]7 per 100 kg" (Metadata for Target 10.a – Indicator 10.a.1: International Trade Centre, UNCTAD and WTO – Last updated: 19th July 2016 (New York, 2016), 1; emphasis added).

special and differential treatment within the WTO Agreements, because some MFN tariffs[935] are already at, or near to, zero, particularly for fuels and minerals.[936] SDG Indicator 10.a.1 measures the percentage of the total number of tariff lines[937] that are applied to products imported from developing countries and LDCs which correspond to a tariff rate of 0% in Chapters 1 (i.e., 01) to 97 of the Harmonized Commodity Description and Coding System.[938]

The computation of SDG Indicator 10.a.1 permits observation of the extent to which special and differential treatment has been accorded to various developing countries and LDCs in terms of import tariffs.[939] Furthermore, the evolution of this SDG Indicator will present information

---

[935] For the Most-Favoured-Nation (MFN) Rule, which is contained in Article 1:1 of the General Agreement on Tariffs and Trade, see Graeme Baber, *Preferential Trade Agreements and International Law*, (Abingdon and New York: Routledge, 2019), 3.

[936] Metadata for Target 10.a – Indicator 10.a.1: International Trade Centre, UNCTAD and WTO, 2.

[937] Note 938 describes National Tariff Line codes, which determines the concept of a National Tariff Line – i.e., a tariff line.

[938] Metadata for Target 10.a – Indicator 10.a.1: International Trade Centre, UNCTAD and WTO, 1. For information concerning the Harmonized Commodity Description and Coding System, see Baber, *Preferential Trade Agreements and International Law*, 120, fn 105 (of Chapter 2 therein), and Baber, *Preferential Trade Agreements and International Law*, 173, fn 24 (of Chapter 4 therein). National Tariff Line codes are the classification codes that individual countries apply to merchandise goods based on the 6-digit Harmonization Commodity Description and Coding System but with additional digits; for example, the 6-digit Harmonization Commodity Description and Coding System Code 0101.20 refers to Asses, mules and hinnies, live, whereas the USA's National Tariff Line code 010120.10 refers to live purebred breeding asses, 010120.20 to live asses other than purebred breeding asses, and 010120.30 to mules and hinnies imported for immediate butchery (Metadata for Target 10.a – Indicator 10.a.1: International Trade Centre, UNCTAD and WTO, 1). A National Tariff Line – i.e., a tariff line – is the product code that is used at the national level, beyond the six digits of the 6-digit Harmonization Commodity Description and Coding System, which differs between countries ("Trade Knowledgebase: Tariff Line", United Nations. accessed August 23, 2020, https://unstats.un.org/unsd/tradekb/Knowledgebase/50291/Tariff-Line). In the above example, 10 is the tariff line for code 010120.10, 20 is the tariff line for code 010120.20, and 30 is the tariff line for code 010120.30; all three of these tariff lines are specific to the USA.

[939] Metadata for Target 10.a – Indicator 10.a.1: International Trade Centre, UNCTAD and WTO, 1.

on the extent to which tariffs are being phased out on goods from these states.[940]

SDG Indicator 10.a.1[941] is calculated as the mean share of national tariff lines that are free from tariffs, disaggregated by sector (e.g., agricultural products, textiles), geographical regions, and country income level (e.g., LDCs, developing, developed).[942] SDG Indicator 10.a.1 is computed mainly from import tariff data, which are retrieved from various sources (for instance, national statistical offices and ministries of trade) and stored in the databases of the data compilers – the International Trade Centre,[943] the UNCTAD and the WTO, which jointly report on this SDG Indicator.[944] Table 3.42 shows the worldwide aggregates[945] for SDG Indicator 10.a.1.

Table 3.42 shows that approximately 52% of national tariff lines worldwide are applied to tariff-free imports, with this percentage decreasing from 2015 to 2016, rising considerably from 2016 to 2017, and increasing further from 2017 to 2018. These patterns are consistent with special and differential treatment being accorded to developing countries in 2017 and 2018 with regard to the import of their goods to advanced economies.

---

940 Metadata for Target 10.a – Indicator 10.a.1: International Trade Centre, UNCTAD and WTO, 1.

941 The text to note 933 states SDG Indicator 10.a.1.

942 Metadata for Target 10.a – Indicator 10.a.1: International Trade Centre, UNCTAD and WTO, 2. Missing values at country, regional and global levels are computed using those for the most recent year available; regional aggregates comprise the share of duty-free tariff lines in the total number of tariff lines by country or groups of countries (Metadata for Target 10.a – Indicator 10.a.1: International Trade Centre, UNCTAD and WTO, 2).

943 Founded in 1964, the International Trade Centre is a joint agency of the UN and the WTO whose mission is "to foster inclusive and sustainable economic development, and contribute to achieving the United Nations Global Goals for Sustainable Development [i.e., the SDGs,] work[ing] towards creating 'trade impact for good'"; its objectives are to: (i) fortify the integration of developing countries' business sector into the worldwide economy, (ii) ameliorate the performance of institutions that support trade and investment for the good of SMEs, and (iii) improve the global competitiveness of SMEs ("About ITC", International Trade Centre, accessed August 23, 2020, https://www.intracen.org/itc/about/).

944 Metadata for Target 10.a – Indicator 10.a.1: International Trade Centre, UNCTAD and WTO, 3-4.

945 173 countries contributed data to the global aggregates (Metadata for Target 10.a – Indicator 10.a.1: International Trade Centre, UNCTAD and WTO, 3). The world contains 195 states (note 640).

Table 3.42: The proportion of tariff lines applied to imports with a tariff rate of 0% – global aggregate for each of the years 2015, 2016, 2017 and 2018, disaggregated by product sector (%)[946]

Product sector	2015	2016	2017	2018
Total or no breakdown	50.50223	48.43139	53.45238	54.36070
Agricultural products	47.76753	49.03004	51.54110	52.17857
Arms	45.76861	44.31352	52.72472	53.36493
Clothing	36.54185	32.65001	41.73089	42.99142
Industrial products	52.31954	50.46325	55.02445	55.95402
Oil	79.97481	80.13029	86.90344	87.97753
Textiles	45.42298	41.75575	49.16732	49.90859

This general pattern over the period 2015 to 2018 is also observed for the global totals disaggregated by product sector. The proportion of national tariff lines applied to zero-tariff imports in all six sectors (i.e., agricultural products, arms, clothing, industrial products, oil and textiles) – save agricultural products and oil from 2015 to 2016 – decreases between those latter two years, rises substantially from 2016 to 2017, and increases further from 2017 to 2018. The proportion of national tariff lines applied to imports with a tariff rate of 0% from 2015 to 2018 is highest for the oil sector, and lowest for the clothing sector.

Table 3.43 shows that more than 60% of national tariff lines in Africa are applied to tariff-free imports, with this percentage decreasing from 2015 to 2016, rising from 2016 to 2017, and increasing at a slower rate from 2016 to 2017 to surpass 65%. This general pattern through the period 2015 to 2018 is also present for the regional totals for Africa disaggregated by product sector. The proportion of national tariff lines applied to zero-tariff imports from 2015 to 2018 is highest for the oil sector and lowest for the clothing sector. These patterns are similar to those that Table 3.42 records for the global aggregates, although all the regional totals for Africa exceed the corresponding worldwide statistics.

946 "SDG indicators: United Nations Global SDG Database", United Nations, accessed August 22, 2020, https://unstats.un.org/sdgs/indicators/database/. The UN Global SDG Database gives these percentages to five decimal places.

Table 3.43: The proportion of tariff lines applied to imports with a tariff rate of 0% – regional aggregate for Africa for each of the years 2015, 2016, 2017 and 2018, disaggregated by product sector (%)[947]

Product sector	2015	2016	2017	2018
Total or no breakdown	63.75304	61.50059	64.34646	65.42178
Agricultural products	62.68416	62.62551	66.15803	66.71846
Arms	63.88060	62.18750	66.56442	69.93865
Clothing	46.89051	43.14200	47.92114	49.50942
Industrial products	66.00631	63.81146	66.18743	67.32673
Oil	86.70886	86.36364	88.46154	88.46154[948]
Textiles	66.67666	63.67639	66.38211	67.05932

Table 3.44: The proportion of tariff lines applied to imports with a tariff rate of 0% – regional aggregate for the Americas for each of the years 2015, 2016, 2017 and 2018, disaggregated by product sector (%)[949]

Product sector	2015	2016	2017	2018
Total or no breakdown	52.79688	52.20041	53.12069	54.11657
Agricultural products	49.05665	49.18529	50.88866	52.26076
Arms	36.70316	39.61708	41.50694	42.87634

[947] "SDG indicators: United Nations Global SDG Database", United Nations, accessed August 22, 2020, https://unstats.un.org/sdgs/indicators/database/. The UN Global SDG Database gives these percentages to five decimal places. 49 countries contributed data to the regional aggregates for Africa (Metadata for Target 10.a – Indicator 10.a.1: International Trade Centre, UNCTAD and WTO, 3). Africa contains 54 of the UN's Member States (note 153 of Chapter Two).

[948] It is submitted that, as this value is identical to that for the same product sector in the immediately-preceding year, the relevant datum for the later year (i.e., 2018) is missing (note 942).

[949] "SDG indicators: United Nations Global SDG Database", United Nations, accessed August 22, 2020, https://unstats.un.org/sdgs/indicators/database/. The UN Global SDG Database gives these percentages to five decimal places.

Clothing	42.04433	40.12752	43.81571	44.80819
Industrial products	54.25413	53.67529	54.28790	55.22577
Oil	83.87097	83.84615	94.26752	94.19355
Textiles	50.03723	50.01017	50.78232	51.74759

Table 3.44 shows that approximately 53% of national tariff lines in the Americas are applied to tariff-free imports, with a slight fall in this percentage from 2015 to 2016, and small rises in it from 2016 to 2017 and from 2017 to 2018. The figures for the product sectors tend to follow the trend in the general aggregate (i.e., Total or no breakdown), though the rises in the agricultural products sector's – and especially the arms sector's – percentages exceed those of that general aggregate – starting from a lower level than the latter, and the percentage for the oil sector increases more than 10% between 2016 and 2017 – barely falling back in 2018. The proportion of national tariff lines applied to zero-tariff imports from 2015 to 2018 is highest for the oil sector and lowest for the arms sector – followed fairly closely by the clothing sector.

Table 3.45: The proportion of tariff lines applied to imports with a tariff rate of 0% – regional aggregate for Asia for each of the years 2015, 2016, 2017 and 2018, disaggregated by product sector (%)[950]

Product sector	**2015**	**2016**	**2017**	**2018**
Total or no breakdown	43.64701	43.14685	46.37685	47.44432
Agricultural products	44.34527	43.93127	47.87742	48.63956
Arms	38.82476	42.12874	43.22479	43.13725
Clothing	27.36909	26.87984	32.24084	33.48180
Industrial products	46.09203	45.57620	48.55166	49.63933
Oil	78.57143	76.83824	84.30769	84.82972
Textiles	34.52148	35.33863	38.16512	39.21543

950 "SDG indicators: United Nations Global SDG Database", United Nations, accessed August 22, 2020, https://unstats.un.org/sdgs/indicators/database/. The UN Global SDG Database gives these percentages to five decimal places.

Table 3.45 shows that approximately 45% of national tariff lines in Asia are applied to tariff-free imports, with this percentage decreasing slightly from 2015 to 2016, increasing from 2016 to 2017, and rising further from 2017 to 2018. This general pattern over the period 2015 to 2018 is observed for the following sectors: agricultural products, clothing, industrial products and oil. The proportion of national tariff lines applied to zero-tariff imports in the arms and textiles sectors in Asia rises throughout this time, bar a miniscule fall in that percentage for the arms sector from 2017 to 2018. The proportion of national tariff lines applied to imports with a tariff rate of 0% from 2015 to 2018 is highest for the oil sector and lowest for the clothing sector. These patterns are fairly similar to those that Table 3.42 records for the global aggregates, although all the regional totals for Asia subceed the corresponding worldwide statistics.

Table 3.46: The proportion of tariff lines applied to imports with a tariff rate of 0% – regional aggregate for Europe for each of the years 2015, 2016, 2017 and 2018, disaggregated by product sector (%)[951]

Product sector	2015	2016	2017	2018
Total or no breakdown	53.65794	62.20099	57.94656	58.67450
Agricultural products	47.19956	63.31193	51.85248	52.10136
Arms	50.30356	52.10084	59.64683	60.32166
Clothing	43.02994	43.17673	50.90385	52.13797
Industrial products	55.06198	63.65540	59.11033	59.89207
Oil	74.10072	84.09091	86.63366	89.34010
Textiles	53.59091	64.78199	58.34902	58.66805

Table 3.46 shows that approximately 58% of national tariff lines in Europe are applied to zero-tariff imports, with this percentage rising considerably from 2015 to 2016, falling from 2016 to 2017, and increasing slightly from 2017 to 2018. Except for the arms and clothing sectors – in which the rise from 2015 to 2016 is smaller, the proportion of national tariff lines applied to imports with a tariff rate of 0% increases markedly in

[951] "SDG indicators: United Nations Global SDG Database", United Nations, accessed August 22, 2020, https://unstats.un.org/sdgs/indicators/database/. The UN Global SDG Database gives these percentages to five decimal places.

2016 in each product sector. In the arms and clothing sectors, there is a substantial rise in this proportion between 2016 and 2017, whilst that percentage decreases from 2016 to 2017 in the industrial products, textiles and, especially, the agricultural products sectors – with the oil sector's proportion of national tariff lines applied to tariff-free imports rising somewhat between those two years.

In all six product sectors that Table 3.46 lists, the proportion of national tariff lines applied to imports with a tariff rate of 0% increases slightly (agricultural products, arms, industrial products and textiles), somewhat (clothing), or moderately (oil), from 2017 to 2018, which reflects the rise in the general aggregate (i.e., Total or no breakdown) during this time. The proportion of national tariff lines applied to zero-tariff imports from 2015 to 2018 is highest for the oil sector and lowest for the clothing sector.

Table 3.47: The proportion of tariff lines applied to imports with a tariff rate of 0% – regional aggregate for Oceania for each of the years 2015, 2016, 2017 and 2018, disaggregated by product sector (%)[952]

Product sector	2015	2016	2017	2018
Total or no breakdown	48.25494	45.39953	49.65282	50.48682
Agricultural products	44.39377	41.59469	48.12225	49.14660
Arms	47.27273	46.40884	46.79803	43.00000
Clothing	32.70522	35.31974	37.36660	38.72769
Industrial products	50.04676	46.80174	50.92383	51.67698
Oil	67.64706	63.88889	71.42857	78.78788
Textiles	41.02526	42.59635	45.92030	47.07107

Table 3.47 shows that approximately 48% of national tariff lines in Oceania are applied to tariff-free imports, with this percentage decreasing moderately from 2015 to 2016, increasing substantially from 2016 to 2017, and rising a little further from 2017 to 2018. Agricultural products,

952 "SDG indicators: United Nations Global SDG Database", United Nations, accessed August 22, 2020, https://unstats.un.org/sdgs/indicators/database/. The UN Global SDG Database gives these percentages to five decimal places.

industrial products and oil sectors follow a similar trajectory to the general aggregate (i.e., Total or no breakdown).

The arms sector is exceptional among the product sectors for Oceania in its proportion of national tariff lines that are applied to tariff-free imports decreasing between 2017 and 2018. Unlike the other product sectors, clothing and textiles each shows a rise in its proportion of tariff lines applied to zero-tariff imports in each year on the previous year over the period 2015 to 2018. The proportion of national tariff lines applied to imports with a tariff rate of 0% from 2015 to 2018 is highest for the oil sector and lowest for the clothing sector – although these percentages for the oil sector are smaller than those for all the other regions for each corresponding year.[953]

Whilst recalling the view that the annual movement in the global general aggregate (i.e., Total or no breakdown) in Table 3.42 is compatible with the application of special and differential treatment,[954] it should be noted that Tables 3.43, 3.44, 3.45 and 3.47 show that the general aggregate for Africa, the Americas, Asia and Oceania, respectively, each follows a similar year-by-year movement to the worldwide general aggregate. In analysing these figures in depth, a possible specific explanation for this almost-ubiquitous[955] regional pattern should be sought – which may or may not be related to the implementation of special and differential treatment. It is not yet possible to estimate with reasonable precision – on the basis of the global and high-level regional data for 2015 to 2018 concerning its sole indicator, i.e., SDG Indicator 10.a.1,[956] the extent to which SDG Target 10.a[957] is likely to be achieved promptly.

---

[953] For example, Tables 3.43 to 3.47 show that the proportion of tariff lines in the oil sector in 2017 applied to imports with a tariff rate of 0% in Africa, the Americas, Asia, Europe and Oceania, respectively, is 88.46154%, 94.26752%, 84.30769%, 86.63366% and 71.42857%.

[954] The sentence immediately-preceding Table 3.42 states: "These patterns are consistent with special and differential treatment being accorded to developing countries in 2017 and 2018 with regard to the import of their goods to advanced economies.".

[955] Table 3.46 shows that the movement in the general aggregate (i.e., Total or no breakdown) for Europe differs from those of the world, Africa, America, Asia and Oceania in that the proportion of national tariff lines in Europe applied to imports with a tariff rate of 0% rises substantially from 2015 to 2016 and falls from 2016 to 2017.

[956] The text to note 933 specifies SDG Indicator 10.a.1.

[957] The text to note 932 states SDG Target 10.a.

SDG Target 10.b and SDG Indicator 10.b.1

SDG Target 10.b is to "[e]ncourage official development assistance and financial flows, including foreign direct investment, to States where the need is greatest, in particular least developed countries, African countries, small island developing States and landlocked developing countries, in accordance with their national plans and programmes".[958] Its unique indicator is SDG Indicator 10.b.1, which ascertains the "[t]otal resource flows for development, by recipient and donor countries and type of flow (e.g. official development assistance, foreign direct investment and other flows)".[959]

Total resource flows to developing countries quantify the overall funds that donor states supply to developing countries.[960] These total flows comprise official flows and private flows, the first of which comprises ODA and other official flows, and the second of which consists of flows on market terms and charitable grants.[961] The OECD, which is the data compiler for SDG Indicator 10.b.1,[962] defines the term 'ODA flows' – starting with data for 2018 – thus.

> Official development assistance flows are defined as those flows to countries and territories on the DAC [i.e., the OECD Development Assistance Committee[963]] List of ODA Recipients[964] and to multilateral

---

[958] Resolution 70/1 adopted by the General Assembly on 25 September 2015, Transforming our world: the 2030 Agenda for Sustainable Development, 21.

[959] Global indicator framework for the Sustainable Development Goals and targets of the 2030 Agenda for Sustainable Development, 11.

[960] United Nations, Department of Economic and Social Affairs – Statistics Division: Metadata for Target 10.b – Indicator 10.b.1: OECD – Last updated: 19th July 2016 (New York, 2016), 1.

[961] Metadata for Target 10.b – Indicator 10.b.1: OECD, 1.

[962] Metadata for Target 10.b – Indicator 10.b.1: OECD, 3.

[963] The overarching aim of the OECD Development Assistance Committee from 2018 to 2022 "is to promote development co-operation and other relevant policies so as to contribute to implementation of the 2030 Agenda for Sustainable Development, including sustained, inclusive and sustainable economic growth, poverty eradication, improvement of living standards in developing countries, and to a future in which no country will depend on aid" ("The Development Assistance Committee's Mandate", Organisation for Economic Co-operation and Development, accessed August 27, 2020, http://www.oecd.org/dac/thedevelopmentassistancecommitteesmandate.htm).

[964] The following three versions of the DAC List of ODA Recipients are relevant: (i) *DAC List of ODA Recipients: Effective for reporting on 2014, 2015, 2016 and 2017 flows*, which concerns the data points in Tables 3.48 to 3.51 for 2015, 2016

and 2017, (ii) *DAC List of ODA Recipients: Effective for reporting on aid in 2018 and 2019*, which bears on the data points in Tables 3.48 to 3.51 for 2018, and (iii) *DAC List of ODA Recipients: Effective for reporting on 2020 flows*, which is currently in force. The headings in the DAC List of ODA Recipients are as follows: (a) *LDCs*, which in all three of these versions of the DAC List of ODA Recipients comprises the 47 states that are presently LDCs (note 125 of Chapter Two) – with Equatorial Guinea also present on list (i) but absent from lists (ii) and (iii), (b) *Other Low Income Countries*, which consists of the Democratic People's Republic of Korea, Kenya, Tajikistan, and Zimbabwe on list (i), and the Democratic People's Republic of Korea and Zimbabwe on lists (ii) and (iii), (c) *Lower Middle Income Countries and Territories*, which comprises Armenia, Bolivia, Cabo Verde, Cameroon, Côte d'Ivoire, Egypt, El Salvador, Eswatini, Georgia, Ghana, Guatemala, Guyana, Honduras, India, Indonesia, Kosovo, Kyrgyzstan, Micronesia, Moldova, Mongolia, Morocco, Nicaragua, Nigeria, Pakistan, Papua New Guinea, Paraguay, the Philippines, the Republic of the Congo, Samoa, Sri Lanka, Syria, Tokelau, Ukraine, Uzbekistan, Vietnam, and West Bank and Gaza Strip on list (i), and Armenia, Bolivia, Cabo Verde, Cameroon, Côte d'Ivoire, Egypt, El Salvador, Eswatini, Georgia, Ghana, Guatemala, Honduras, India, Indonesia, Jordan, Kenya, Kosovo, Kyrgyzstan, Micronesia, Moldova, Mongolia, Morocco, Nicaragua, Nigeria, Pakistan, Papua New Guinea, the Philippines, the Republic of the Congo, Sri Lanka, Syria, Tajikistan, Tokelau, Tunisia, Ukraine, Uzbekistan, Vietnam, and West Bank and Gaza Strip on lists (ii) and (iii), and (d) *Upper Middle Income Countries and Territories*, which consists of Albania, Algeria, Antigua and Barbuda, Argentina, Azerbaijan, Belarus, Belize, Bosnia and Herzegovina, Botswana, Brazil, Chile, China, Colombia, the Cook Islands, Costa Rica, Cuba, Dominica, the Dominican Republic, Ecuador, Fiji, Gabon, Grenada, Iran, Iraq, Jamaica, Jordan, Kazakhstan, Lebanon, Libya, Malaysia, the Maldives, the Marshall Islands, Mauritius, Mexico, Montenegro, Montserrat, Namibia, Nauru, Niue, North Macedonia, Palau, Panama, Peru, Saint Helena, Saint Lucia, Saint Vincent and the Grenadines, Serbia, the Seychelles, South Africa, Suriname, Thailand, Tonga, Tunisia, Turkey, Turkmenistan, Uruguay, Venezuela, and the Wallis and Futuna Islands on list (i), Albania, Algeria, Antigua and Barbuda, Argentina, Azerbaijan, Belarus, Belize, Bosnia and Herzegovina, Botswana, Brazil, China, Colombia, the Cook Islands, Costa Rica, Cuba, Dominica, the Dominican Republic, Ecuador, Equatorial Guinea, Fiji, Gabon, Grenada, Guyana, Iran, Iraq, Jamaica, Kazakhstan, Lebanon, Libya, Malaysia, the Maldives, the Marshall Islands, Mauritius, Mexico, Montenegro, Montserrat, Namibia, Nauru, Niue, North Macedonia, Palau, Panama, Paraguay, Peru, Saint Helena, Saint Lucia, Saint Vincent and the Grenadines, Samoa, Serbia, South Africa, Suriname, Thailand, Tonga, Turkey, Turkmenistan, Venezuela, and the Wallis and Futuna Islands on list (ii), and all the states and territories on list (ii) except for the Cook Islands on list (iii) (Organisation for Economic Co-operation and Development, DAC List of ODA Recipients: Effective for reporting on 2014, 2015, 2016 and 2017 flows (Paris, 2017); Organisation for Economic Co-operation and Development, DAC List of ODA

> development institutions which are: i. provided by official agencies, including state and local governments, or by their executive agencies, and ii. each transaction of which: a. is administered with the promotion of the economic development and welfare of developing countries as its main objective; and b. is concessional in character. In DAC statistics, this implies a grant element of at least … – **45 per cent** in the case of bilateral loans to the official sector of LDCs and other LICs [Low Income Countries] (calculated at a rate of discount of 9 per cent). – **15 per cent** in the case of bilateral loans to the official sector of LMICs [Low Middle Income Countries and Territories] (calculated at a rate of discount of 7 per cent). – **10 per cent** in the case of bilateral loans to the official sector of UMICs [Upper Middle Income Countries and Territories] (calculated at a rate of discount of 6 per cent) – **10 per cent** in the case of loans to multilateral institutions … (calculated at a rate of discount of 5 per cent for global institutions and multilateral development banks, and 6 per cent for other organisations, including sub-regional organisations) … . Loans whose terms are not consistent with the IMF Debt Limits Policy and/or the World Bank's Non-Concessional Borrowing Policy are not reportable as ODA. … [965]

The OECD publishes data on SDG Indicator 10.b.1[966] annually in December for capital flows the previous year[967] – making 2018 the latest year for which these statistics are currently available. The data providers are statistical reporters in governments, which disclose them "on an annual

---

Recipients: Effective for reporting on aid in 2018 and 2019 (Paris, 2019); DAC List of ODA Recipients: Effective for reporting on 2020 flows (Paris, 2019)).

965 "Official development assistance – definition and coverage", Organisation for Economic Co-operation and Development, accessed August 27, 2020, https://www.oecd.org/dac/financing-sustainable-development/development-finance-standards/officialdevelopmentassistancedefinitionandcoverage.htm; emphasis original. The OECD's definition of the term 'ODA flows' for data up to and including those of 2017 is as follows: "those flows to countries and territories on the DAC List of ODA Recipients and to multilateral institutions which are: i. provided by official agencies, including state and local governments, or by their executive agencies; and ii. each transaction of which: a. is administered with the promotion of the economic development and welfare of developing countries as its main objective; and b. is concessional in character and conveys a grant element of at least 25 per cent (calculated at a rate of discount of 10 per cent)" ("Official development assistance – definition and coverage", Organisation for Economic Co-operation and Development, accessed August 27, 2020, https://www.oecd.org/dac/financing-sustainable-development/development-finance-standards/officialdevelopmentassistancedefinitionandcoverage.htm).

966 The text to note 959 specifies SDG Indicator 10.b.1.

967 Metadata for Target 10.b – Indicator 10.b.1: OECD, 3.

calendar year basis".[968] These data are available "[o]n a donor basis for" members of the OECD Development Assistance Committee,[969] and "[o]n a recipient basis for countries that are eligible for ODA".[970]

The data comprise the sum of official and private capital flows from donors to developing countries.[971] Regional statistics are founded on the sum of total resource flows to these states and territories.[972] Table 3.48 contains these aggregates for each of the years 2015[973] to 2018,[974] for Asia and its sub-regions.

Table 3.48 shows that total resource flows for development in Asia rise from 2015 to 2016, fall slightly from 2016 to 2017, and decrease substantially from 2017 to 2018. Whilst the sub-regions tend to follow this trend, notable differences include: (i) the decline in total resource flows to and from countries of Central Asia throughout the period 2015 to 2018 – the flows turning negative in 2017 – which is also reflected in the statistics for Caucasus and Central Asia, (ii) the relatively small magnitude of the capital flows into the states of East Asia excluding China and Japan – with the datum for 2016 being more than twice the magnitude of that for each of the other three years, and (iii) the constancy of the total resource flows for West Asia and, especially, South-East Asia.

---

968 Metadata for Target 10.b – Indicator 10.b.1: OECD, 3.

969 The OECD Development Assistance Committee currently comprises the following thirty members: Australia, Austria, Belgium, Canada, the Czech Republic, Denmark, the European Union, Finland, France, Germany, Greece, Hungary, Iceland, Ireland, Italy, Japan, Luxembourg, the Netherlands, New Zealand, Norway, Poland, Portugal, the Republic of Korea, Slovakia, Slovenia, Spain, Sweden, Switzerland, the UK, and the USA ("Development Assistance Committee (DAC)", Organisation for Economic Co-operation and Development, accessed September 7, 2020, http://www.oecd.org/dac/development-assistance-committee/).

970 Metadata for Target 10.b – Indicator 10.b.1: OECD, 3. Note 964 lists those states and territories that are eligible for ODA.

971 Metadata for Target 10.b – Indicator 10.b.1: OECD, 2.

972 Metadata for Target 10.b – Indicator 10.b.1: OECD, 3.

973 The first year selected for data to be included in Tables 3.48 to 3.51 is 2015, because this is the time during which the SDGs entered into effect – the UN General Assembly adopted the SDGs and their targets in Resolution 70/1, which is dated 25th September 2015 (text to note 35 of Chapter One; note 37 of Chapter One and accompanying text).

974 At the present time, the UN Global SDG Database does not include data beyond 2018 concerning SDG Indicator 10.b.1 ("SDG indicators: United Nations Global SDG Database", United Nations, accessed August 22, 2020, https://unstats.un.org/sdgs/indicators/database/).

Table 3.48: Total resource flows for development, by recipient and donor countries for each of the years 2015, 2016, 2017 and 2018 (millions of current USD) – Asia[975]

Region or sub-region	2015	2016	2017	2018
Asia	120,193.696	155,511.571	148,770.721	114,842.022
Caucasus and Central Asia	13,025.878	7,750.176	2,681.684	-3,079.986
Central Asia	9,162.822	4,309.965	-895.653	-5,114.816
East Asia	18,884.250	43,272.197	39,722.800	27,073.750
East Asia excluding China and Japan	820.794	1,803.244	732.376	751.241
South Asia	25,670.838	34,006.080	38,727.355	26,052.880
South Asia excluding India	13,396.558	14,578.476	15,388.661	11,114.698
South-East Asia	31,420.312	32,643.823	31,660.497	29,066.298
West Asia	35,055.475	41,279.506	39,555.723	37,763.911

Table 3.49 shows low levels of total resource flows for development for developed regions, and huge such flows for developing regions – particularly in 2017. Total resource flows for development into LDCs are substantial and rising throughout the period 2015 to 2018. Total resource flows for development into LLDCs are fairly large and falling throughout this time. Whilst total resource flows for development into SIDS increase from 2015 to 2016 and rise substantially from 2016 to 2017, these flows plummet from 2017 to 2018.

975 "SDG indicators: United Nations Global SDG Database", United Nations, accessed August 22, 2020, https://unstats.un.org/sdgs/indicators/database/. Table 3.48 gives these percentages to three decimal places.

Table 3.49: Total resource flows for development, by recipient and donor countries for each of the years 2015, 2016, 2017 and 2018 (millions of current USD) – developed regions, developing regions, LDCs, LLDCs and SIDS[976]

Grouping	2015	2016	2017	2018
Developed regions[977]	2,899.256	3,813.435	8,176.181	6,102.058
Developing regions	313,875.824	316,744.056	420,301.244	271,249.257
LDCs	48,595.493	52,023.981	55,538.675	58,393.738
LLDCs	38,256.794	34,627.018	31,639.083	24,932.883
SIDS	5,981.003	7,637.743	10,789.891	2,818.790

Whilst the growing total resource flows for development over the period 2015 to 2018 for LDCs, and from 2015 to 2017 for SIDS, are consistent with the accomplishment of SDG Target 10.b,[978] the dwindling resource flows for development from 2015 to 2018 for LLDCs are contrary to the achievement of this SDG Target. The collapse of the flows into SIDS from 2017 to 2018 is worrying – an explanation for this sudden diminution should be sought.

Table 3.50 shows that the total resource flows for development to the countries of Africa are sizeable, falling sharply from 2015 to 2016, rising from 2016 to 2017, and decreasing from 2017 to 2018. The total flows for development to the countries of North Africa are of appreciable magnitude, but are declining throughout the period 2015 to 2018. The total flows for development for Sub-Saharan Africa follow a similar pattern to those of Africa, reducing dramatically from 2015 to 2016, increasing from 2016 to 2017, and reducing from 2017 to 2018.

---

[976] "SDG indicators: United Nations Global SDG Database", United Nations, accessed August 22, 2020, https://unstats.un.org/sdgs/indicators/database/. Table 3.49 gives these percentages to three decimal places.

[977] The spreadsheet downloaded from the webpage to which this footnote refers on 22nd August 2020 states that the developed regions comprise "Europe, Cyprus, Israel, Northern America, Japan, Australia & New Zealand" ("SDG indicators: United Nations Global SDG Database", United Nations, accessed August 22, 2020, https://unstats.un.org/sdgs/indicators/database/).

[978] The text to note 958 states SDG Target 10.b.

Table 3.50: Total resource flows for development, by recipient and donor countries for each of the years 2015, 2016, 2017 and 2018 (millions of current USD) – Africa[979]

Region or sub-region	2015	2016	2017	2018
Africa	89,919.434	58,261.395	75,670.336	61,333.465
North Africa	18,614.554	17,271.261	13,287.974	11,846.322
Sub-Saharan Africa	71,304.880	40,990.134	62,382.362	49,487.143
Central Africa	5,459.268	11,003.877	6,363.560	4,219.421
East Africa	22,326.051	22,892.653	29,815.549	25,587.761
Southern Africa[980]	6,860.226	5,370.031	5,468.946	3,943.940
West Africa	36,659.335	1,723.573	20,734.307	15,736.020

Within Sub-Saharan Africa, states of East Africa and of West Africa together attract the majority of the resource inflows for development. Whilst the total resource flows for development for East Africa are fairly steady, those for West Africa are turbulent – reducing from approximately 36.7 billion USD in 2015 to 1.7 billion USD in 2016, recovering to 20.7 billion USD in 2017, and falling to 15.5 billion USD in 2018. The major fall in the resource flows for development for West Africa from 2015 to 2016 and the substantial rise in these movements of funds from 2016 to 2017, are reflected in large movements of total resource flows for development for Sub-Saharan Africa and for Africa over the period 2015 to 2017.

The total resource flows for development for Central Africa and Southern Africa are quite small in magnitude, with the former peaking in 2016 then declining and the latter being fairly steady but tending to reduce over the period 2015 to 2018. Overall, the trend for foreign investment in Africa during this time is running against the attainment of SDG Target 10.b.[981] Table 3.51 shows the total resource flows for development for

[979] "SDG indicators: United Nations Global SDG Database", United Nations, accessed August 22, 2020, https://unstats.un.org/sdgs/indicators/database/. Table 3.50 gives these percentages to three decimal places.

[980] This area is entitled 'Southern Africa' rather than 'South Africa', in order to avoid confusion with the state of the latter name.

[981] The text to note 958 states SDG Target 10.b.

developing regions other than Asia and Africa, i.e., South America, Central America, the Caribbean and Oceania.

Table 3.51: Total resource flows for development, by recipient and donor countries for each of the years 2015, 2016, 2017 and 2018 (millions of current USD) – South America, Central America, the Caribbean and Oceania[982]

Region or sub-region	2015	2016	2017	2018
Latin America and the Caribbean	97,376.600	44,639.935	57,393.735	59,314.408
South America	70,298.933	29,748.947	21,717.305	31,819.678
Central America	23,014.644	9,936.038	32,375.788	24,864.470
The Caribbean	4,063.022	4,954.950	3,300.642	2,630.259
Oceania	1,911.183	2,238.756	2,716.441	609.300
Melanesia	-1,792.589	889.370	951.961	1,172.076
Micronesia[983]	3,308.884	995.163	1,377.672	-961.282
Polynesia	394.888	354.222	386.807	398.506

The total resource flows for development for Latin America and the Caribbean fall sharply from 2015 to 2016, rise from 2016 to 2017, and increase slightly further from 2017 to 2018. The total resource flows for development for South America and for Central America also decrease greatly from 2015 to 2016, although the smaller total resource flows for

[982] "SDG indicators: United Nations Global SDG Database", United Nations, accessed August 22, 2020, https://unstats.un.org/sdgs/indicators/database/. Table 3.51 gives these percentages to three decimal places.

[983] This title refers to Micronesia the sub-region of Oceania, which contains five states – Kiribati, the Marshall Islands, Micronesia (Federated States of), Nauru, and Palau (note 684), rather than to the country entitled 'Micronesia' (i.e., the Federated States of Micronesia) – upon which the UN Global SDG Database also provides data concerning SDG Indicator 10.b.1 ("SDG indicators: United Nations Global SDG Database", United Nations, accessed August 22, 2020, https://unstats.un.org/sdgs/indicators/database/). The text to note 959 specifies SDG Indicator 10.b.1.

development for the Caribbean rise during this time. The total capital movement into states of Central America increases more than threefold from 2016 to 2017 – exceeding that into countries of South America in the latter year. The total resource flows for development for South America grow from 2017 to 2018, whilst those for Central America decline through this time, thereby enabling the total capital movement into countries of South America during 2018 to exceed that into states of Central America in that year – as it did in 2015 and in 2016. The total resource flows for development for the Caribbean lessen over the period 2016 to 2018.

The total resource flows for development for Oceania over the period 2015 to 2018 subceed those of the Caribbean during that period. These flows rise from 2015 to 2016 and from 2016 to 2017, and plunge from 2017 to 2018. The total resource flows for development for Melanesia and, especially, Micronesia, are erratic over the period 2015 to 2018, with the former trending upwards during this time and the latter downwards. The total resource flows for Polynesia are modest, and are fairly constant during the period 2015 to 2018.

It is submitted that, taken as a whole, the data in Tables 3.48, 3.49, 3.50 and 3.51 are not encouraging for the timely accomplishment of SDG Target 10.b.[984] The primary exception to this view is the LDCs as a group, to which total resource flows for development have steadily risen over the period 2015 to 2018.[985] This problem might be redressed by requesting African countries, LLDCs and SIDS,[986] in accordance with SDG Target 10.b, to publish in depth their national plans and programmes – so that official and private donors from developed countries are able to carefully examine the ongoing and proposed projects into which their funds may be invested most appropriately.

SDG Target 10.c and SDG Indicator 10.c.1

SDG Target 10.c is to "reduce to less than 3 per cent the transaction costs of migrant remittances and eliminate remittance corridors with costs higher than 5 per cent" by 2030.[987] Its lone indicator is SDG Indicator

[984] The text to note 958 states SDG Target 10.b.

[985] See the fourth row of Table 3.49 and the commentary thereon.

[986] LDCs are omitted from this list, because, as the text to note 985 points out, on the basis of the data in Table 3.49 these states as a group are progressing towards attainment of SDG Target 10.b.

[987] Resolution 70/1 adopted by the General Assembly on 25 September 2015, Transforming our world: the 2030 Agenda for Sustainable Development, 21.

10.c.1, which measures "[r]emittance costs as a proportion of the amount remitted".[988]

SDG Target 10.c comprises two components, which require two separate computations: (i) the worldwide average of remittance costs is to be lowered to under 3% of the amount of those remittances – which is calculated as the mean of the total cost for all services that are included in the World Bank's Remittance Prices Worldwide database,[989] and (ii) senders of remittances are to be able to transmit money to their receivers at a cost of 5% or less of the amount sent – which is computed as the mean cost of the three cheapest available services in each country corridor that fulfil a set of minimum requirements – as defined in the World Bank's SmarRT methodology.[990]

---

[988] Global indicator framework for the Sustainable Development Goals and targets of the 2030 Agenda for Sustainable Development, 11.

[989] The World Bank's Remittance Prices Worldwide database contains data on the cost of sending and receiving international transfers of small sums of money (i.e., remittances) from one country to another; the database covers 367 country corridors, which include 48 remittance-sending countries and 105 remittance-receiving countries ("Remittance Prices Worldwide: About Us", World Bank, accessed August 30, 2020, https://remittanceprices.worldbank.org/en/about-remittance-prices-worldwide).

[990] United Nations, Department of Economic and Social Affairs – Statistics Division: Metadata for Target 10.c – Indicator 10.c.1: World Bank – Last updated: 2nd February 2018 (New York, 2018), 2-3. The section entitled 'Methodology for calculation' in the document entitled 'Getting SmaRT about remittance price monitoring' states: "SmaRT is calculated using a simple average of the three cheapest services for sending the equivalent of USD 200 in each [country] corridor and is expressed as a percentage of the total amount sent. In order to ensure both availability and accessibility, the three cheapest services must meet the following criteria to be included in the calculation of SmarRT: 1. *Transaction is available to recipient within five days after money is sent.* – This information is already available in RPW [i.e., the World Bank's Remittance Prices Worldwide database] for all services … . 2. *Transaction can be originated in all relevant areas of the sending country.* – This information, categorized as high, medium or low, is only available starting in Q[uarter]1 [of] 2016. The categories are assigned based on a qualitative analysis, supported by the available quantitative data, based on whether a service is accessible to a large extent to remittance senders in the [country] corridors where it is available. [Only readings of 'high' are eligible for SmaRT (Table 1 on page 7 of 'Getting SmaRT about remittance price monitoring')] 3. *Transaction can be delivered to the recipient nationwide, or at least in all relevant areas of the receiving country.* – This information is already available in RPW for all services … and can be high, medium or low. Only services with a [network] coverage area deemed as "high" will be included in SmaRT. 4. *If the service*

Remittance service providers supply data for SDG Indicator 10.c.1[991] by means of "a mystery shopping exercise" conducted every three months,[992] in which the average cost is computed as the mean of total costs that each remittance service provider working in a country corridor quotes – with the sample of remittance service providers comprising at least 80% of the market share of remittances in each country corridor.[993] Data pertaining to a sample of country corridors is collected for each sending and receiving state; it is assumed that the costs of other country corridors to/from each country are within a similar pecuniary range.[994] Regional aggregates are calculated by computing simple averages of individual services concerning remittances to the recipient countries in the region for which there are data; it is assumed that missing statistics are within the same monetary range as data that have been collected.[995] The custodian agency and data complier for SDG Indicator 10.c.1 is the World Bank.[996]

Table 3.52 comprises all the data for 2015, 2017 and 2018 concerning SDG Indicator 10.c.1 that are currently available on the UN Global SDG Database.[997] The first year selected is 2015, because this is period during

---

requires access to a transactional account [i.e., a deposit or e-money account held with a regulated service provider] *or other technologies, such as the Internet or mobile phones, access to these technologies should be nearly universal for senders and receivers in that* [country] *corridor.* – … [No] available data show whether migrant workers have access to transactional accounts, the internet and/or mobile phones, which may be necessary to access certain remittance services. In order to estimate the accessibility of a service, a set of indicators on transaction account, internet, and mobile phone penetration have been constructed and used to estimate the likelihood of a migrant worker being able to access a service that requires one or more of these. …" (World Bank, Getting SmaRT about remittance price monitoring: Methodology for the Smart Remitter Target (SmaRT): a new approach to measuring the progress towards the global objectives of reducing the cost of international remittances, Payment Systems Development Group, June 2016 (Washington, D.C., 2016), 5-6; emphasis added).

[991] The text to note 988 specifies SDG Indicator 10.c.1.

[992] Metadata for Target 10.c – Indicator 10.c.1: World Bank, 4.

[993] Metadata for Target 10.c – Indicator 10.c.1: World Bank, 2.

[994] Metadata for Target 10.c – Indicator 10.c.1: World Bank, 3.

[995] Metadata for Target 10.c – Indicator 10.c.1: World Bank, 3.

[996] Metadata for Target 10.c – Indicator 10.c.1: World Bank, 1 and 5.

[997] At the time of writing, the UN Global SDG Database does not contain data beyond 2018 regarding SDG Indicator 10.c.1 ("SDG indicators: United Nations Global SDG Database", United Nations, accessed August 22, 2020, https://unstats.un.org/sdgs/indicators/database/).

which the SDGs came into force.[998] This database presently lacks data for 2016 regarding SDG Indicator 10.c.1.[999]

Table 3.52: Remittance costs as a proportion of the amount remitted for each of the years 2015, 2017 and 2018[1000]

Country or global/regional aggregate	2015	2017	2018
World	7.5	7.2	6.9
Central and South Asia	5.4	5.3	5.4
East and South-East Asia	7.4	7.6	6.9
Europe and North America	6.6	6.8	6.7
Latin America and the Caribbean	6.3	5.7	5.9
North Africa and West Asia	7.5	7.0	6.8
Oceania excluding Australia and New Zealand	10.1	10.9	9.6
Sub-Saharan Africa	9.8	9.2	9.0
Afghanistan	-	9.9	9.2
Albania	7.9	8.4	8.4
Algeria	11.9	8.3	10.9
Angola	16.6	18.7	19.4
Armenia	1.5	4.0	5.7

[998] The UN General Assembly adopted the SDGs and their targets in Resolution 70/1, which is dated 25th September 2015 (text to note 35 of Chapter One; note 37 of Chapter One and accompanying text).
[999] "SDG indicators: United Nations Global SDG Database", United Nations, accessed August 22, 2020, https://unstats.un.org/sdgs/indicators/database/.
[1000] "SDG indicators: United Nations Global SDG Database", United Nations, accessed August 22, 2020, https://unstats.un.org/sdgs/indicators/database/. The UN Global SDG Database gives these percentages to one decimal place.

Azerbaijan	1.1	1.0	1.3
Bangladesh	4.2	4.4	4.9
Belarus	-	18.3	1.6
Benin	1.4	1.3	12.3
Bolivia	7.1	4.1	5.9
Bosnia and Herzegovina	7.3	6.5	6.9
Botswana	19.7	19.1	18.2
Brazil	7.0	6.3	7.1
Bulgaria	9.2	8.2	8.6
Cabo Verde	-	15.1	9.4
Cambodia	-	4.4	14.5
Cameroon	10.7	10.2	4.2
China	10.2	10.0	8.0
Colombia	6.2	5.4	5.0
Comoros	-	4.8	4.8
Costa Rica	6.0	5.5	6.6
Côte d'Ivoire	4.1	6.3	5.5
Croatia	-	11.0	6.2
Cuba	6.0	8.7	10.8
The Dominican Republic	6.4	6.8	6.7
Ecuador	4.3	4.0	4.1
Egypt	5.7	5.3	5.0
El Salvador	4.2	3.9	4.0
Eritrea	9.1	11.5	8.0
Estonia	5.8	6.4	4.3
Eswatini	13.8	15.9	17.9
Ethiopia	7.9	6.5	6.3
Fiji	9.6	8.9	8.6
Gambia	10.0	9.7	12.7
Georgia	1.2	1.3	1.3
Ghana	9.4	7.2	7.0
Guatemala	4.7	5.0	5.2
Guyana	8.7	8.5	6.5
Haiti	9.4	8.1	7.2
Honduras	4.2	4.2	4.1
Hungary	6.1	8.1	8.5
India	6.5	6.0	5.7
Indonesia	6.9	7.1	6.8

Jamaica	8.5	8.9	8.2
Jordan	5.8	5.7	5.4
Kazakhstan	1.4	1.3	1.5
Kenya	8.8	7.9	8.4
Kyrgyzstan	1.2	4.0	5.5
Latvia	4.8	5.1	4.0
Lebanon	13.1	11.7	11.0
Lesotho	13.8	15.9	15.1
Liberia	5.0	5.5	4.9
Lithuania	8.2	7.1	6.7
Laos	-	16.3	15.7
Madagascar	-	7.9	8.2
Malawi	9.1	17.0	15.8
Malaysia	5.7	8.1	7.4
Mali	5.1	5.1	5.1
Mexico	5.6	4.9	4.1
Moldova	5.7	5.7	5.8
Morocco	7.0	6.8	6.0
Mozambique	18.2	14.7	11.5
Myanmar	-	12.1	14.4
Namibia	-	27.6	26.9
Nepal	3.6	4.7	5.0
Nicaragua	4.1	4.2	5.1
Nigeria	7.7	8.5	7.6
North Macedonia	-	10.4	10.2
Pakistan	5.4	4.8	5.5
Panama	4.7	4.9	4.6
Paraguay	7.1	5.4	7.0
Peru	6.0	4.6	4.9
The Philippines	6.2	5.5	5.1
Poland	6.6	5.7	5.0
The Republic of the Congo	-	5.7	8.2
Romania	6.1	5.1	4.8
Rwanda	13.8	11.5	12.9
Samoa	8.5	10.5	9.0
Senegal	5.6	5.1	5.2
Serbia	9.2	9.2	8.3
Sierra Leone	5.2	8.3	10.4

Somalia	6.5	8.4	7.3
South Africa	9.0	8.1	8.1
South Sudan	-	9.7	9.5
Sri Lanka	5.6	5.3	4.5
The State of Palestine	-	7.3	6.3
Sudan	-	4.9	7.1
Suriname	6.5	5.6	8.6
Syria	-	4.6	6.4
Tajikistan	1.5	4.6	4.3
Tanzania	9.6	10.6	11.1
Thailand	7.6	9.2	8.3
Togo	8.6	7.0	8.0
Tonga	8.3	9.5	9.4
Tunisia	6.1	8.5	8.6
Turkey	7.0	6.8	7.1
Uganda	12.8	10.6	9.0
Ukraine	4.7	6.8	6.4
Uzbekistan	1.7	1.7	1.4
Vanuatu	15.7	16.7	12.1
Vietnam	7.9	7.6	7.2
Yemen	3.7	5.4	5.6
Zambia	15.7	15.2	14.7
Zimbabwe	11.9	11.2	10.6

Table 3.52 shows that remittance costs as a proportion of the amount remitted are, on the basis of all countries included therein – as shown in the global aggregate, i.e., 'World', falling over the period 2015 to 2018, which is in line with the timely attainment of SDG Target 10.c.[1001] However, the 2018 value of this total – 6.9% – is more than twice this SDG Target's ceiling for the transaction costs of migrant remittances – which is 3%. Thus, further reductions need to be made to at least some of the remittance costs listed in Table 3.52.

The highest regional values in Table 3.52 are those of Oceania excluding Australia and New Zealand, and of Sub-Saharan Africa, both of which are gently reducing. The data for Sub-Saharan Africa are raised by a cluster of high remittance costs as a proportion of the amount remitted in Southern, South-Central and South-East Africa, i.e., those of Angola

[1001] The text to note 987 states SDG Target 10.c.

(16.6% → 18.7% → 19.4%), Botswana (19.7% → 19.1% → 18.2%), Eswatini (13.8% → 15.9% → 17.9%), Lesotho (13.8% → 15.9% → 15.1%), Malawi (9.1% → 17.0% → 15.8%), Mozambique (18.2% → 14.7% → 11.5%), Namibia (27.6% → 26.9%), Zambia (15.7% → 15.2% → 14.7%) and Zimbabwe (11.9% → 11.2% → 10.6%), with South Africa's remittance costs (9.0% → 8.1% → 8.1%) being lower than those of the aforementioned states but higher than the SDG Target's ceiling of 3%.

The remittance costs as a proportion of the amount remitted are declining for the world's two most populous countries – China[1002] (10.2% → 10.0% → 8.0%) and India[1003] (6.5% → 6.0% → 5.7%). In addition to China and India, other populous states have remittance costs as a proportion of the amount remitted that are moving in the right direction for possible timely achievement of SDG Target 10.c; these include Colombia (6.2% → 5.4% → 5.0%), Egypt (5.7% → 5.3% → 5.0%), Ethiopia (7.9% → 6.5% → 6.3%), Mexico (5.6% → 4.9% → 4.1%), the Philippines (6.2 → 5.5% → 5.1%), Uganda (12.8% → 10.6% → 9.0%) and Vietnam (7.9% → 7.6% → 7.2%). However, not all such countries are progressing thus regarding their remittance costs, for instance, the smaller number with rising percentages (Bangladesh (4.2% → 4.4% → 4.9%), Myanmar (12.1% → 14.4%), Sudan (4.9% → 7.1%) and Tanzania (9.6% → 10.6% → 11.1%)), and the greater number with equivocal numbers (Algeria (11.9% → 8.3% → 10.9%), Brazil (7.0% → 6.3% → 7.1%), Indonesia (6.9% → 7.1% → 6.8%), Kenya (8.8% → 7.9% → 8.4%), Nigeria (7.7% → 8.5% → 7.6%), Pakistan (5.4% → 4.8% → 5.5%), South Africa (9.0% → 8.1% → 8.1%), Thailand (7.6% → 9.2% → 8.3%), Turkey (7.0% → 6.8% → 7.1%) and Ukraine (4.7% → 6.8% → 6.4%)).

As some of the states in the Caucasus or Central Asia – namely Azerbaijan (1.1% → 1.0% → 1.3%), Georgia (1.2% → 1.3% → 1.3%), Kazakhstan (1.4% → 1.3% → 1.5%) and Uzbekistan (1.7% → 1.7% → 1.4%) – display low percentages of remittance costs as a proportion of the amount remitted over the period 2015 to 2018, it is submitted that the aim of SDG Target 10.c[1004] to lower the transaction costs of migrant remittances to less than 3% is a realistic goal for other countries. However,

---

1002 The population of China is 1,439,323,776 people (note 26).

1003 The population of India is 1,380,004,385 people (note 249). As the population of the world is 7,794,798,739 people (text to note 227; note 249), China and India together contain [(1,439,323,776 people + 1,380,004,385 people) / 7,794,798,739 people) * 100%] [(2,819,328,161 people / 7,794,798,739 people) * 100%] = 36% of the world's population. This percentage is given to two significant figures.

1004 The text to note 987 specifies SDG Target 10.c.

the fact that remittance costs as a proportion of the amount remitted have risen to exceed this ceiling of 3% during 2015 to 2018 in other states located in the Caucasus or Central Asia – namely Armenia (1.5% → 4.0% → 5.7%), Kyrgyzstan (1.2% → 4.0% → 5.5%) and Tajikistan (1.5% → 4.6% → 4.3%) – is a caution to countries that are succeeding in lowering their remittance costs that, even if they succeed in reducing these expenses to below the target of 3% of migrant remittances, their governments will need to continue to monitor the relevant remittance service providers carefully in order to ensure that these remittance costs do not suddenly and/or substantially rise.

Will SDG 10 be achieved punctually?

SDG 10[1005] comprises diverse targets and indicators, the data for which show signs of progression towards accomplishment of at least some of those SDG Targets. However, this chapter's foregoing analyses reveal the presence of inequalities and ongoing difficulties that are incompatible with the punctual achievement of this SDG – unless the wording 'reduce inequality' in SDG 10 is interpreted to mean that a very slight net improvement in overall equality across all the targets of SDG 10 has been demonstrated by 31st December 2030.[1006]

Notwithstanding the improbability of achieving SDG 10 punctually – its non-accomplishment being the likely outcome to an assessment by the aforementioned date[1007] of this attainment by means of the application of any reasonable measure(s) for conducting the evaluation, it is probable that progress will have been made by that time towards reaching most or all of the targets of SDG 10. Thus, the considerable resources employed by the UN System, national governments and others towards realizing SDG 10 are likely to prove to have been used constructively in the substantial effort to improve equality locally, nationally, regionally and globally.

Conclusion

This Chapter investigates whether or not SDG 10 is likely to be achieved punctually, by systematically appraising data supporting its targets and indicators that cover the period from the year in which the SDGs became

---

1005 The text to note 5 states SDG 10.

1006 The target date for the SDGs to be realized is 31st December 2030 (note 930 and accompanying text).

1007 This date is 31st December 2030 (note 1006).

effective – i.e., 2015,[1008] until the present – i.e., the latest statistics available at the time of writing. On the basis of this analysis, it was inferred that SDG 10 is unlikely to be promptly accomplished, but that valuable work towards attainment of this SDG will have been made by its target date. Furthermore, the research in this Chapter shows that such work is currently in progress, for instance, with regard to issues concerning national policies for international migration – though more needs to be done.

The next Chapter extends the 'micro' analysis in Chapter Two of the likelihood of prompt attainment of SDG 1, which follows from MDG 1[1009] – with MDG Target 1.A continuing from SDG Target 1.1,[1010] to the other SDGs that Table 1.4 classifies as proceeding from the MDGs, i.e., SDGs 2, 3, 4, 5, 6, 14, 15 and 17. This is a 'macro' analysis, which uses the content of published reports as its basis.

[1008] The UN General Assembly adopted the SDGs and their targets in Resolution 70/1, which is dated 25th September 2015 (text to note 35 of Chapter One; note 37 of Chapter One and accompanying text).

[1009] Text to notes 95 and 96 of Chapter One. These footnotes respectively state MDG 1 and SDG 1.

[1010] Text to notes 98 and 99 of Chapter One. These footnotes respectively specify MDG Target 1.A and SDG Target 1.1.

CHAPTER FOUR

CONTINUATION MACROSTUDY: PROGRESS TOWARDS FULFILLING THE SUSTAINABLE DEVELOPMENT GOALS THAT RELATE TO THE MILLENNIUM DEVELOPMENT GOALS

Introduction

Chapter Two – the 'Continuation Microstudy' – investigates whether or not SDG 1[1] is likely to be achieved punctually, by methodically looking at the progress made towards the accomplishment of MDG 1,[2] MDG Target 1.A,[3] SDG Target 1.1[4] – to which MDG Target 1.A maps,[5] and SDG 1[6] – in that sequence. In the present Chapter – the 'Continuation Macrostudy', this procedure is extended from SDG 1 to the other SDGs that Table 1.4 classifies as proceeding from the MDGs, i.e., SDGs 2, 3, 4, 5, 6, 14, 15 and 17, using the content of published reports as the basis for analysis. The size of this task is demonstrated by replicating as Table 4.1 that part of Table 1.2 which shows those mappings from MDGs or MDG Targets that are received by the above list of SDGs and their targets.

---

[1] SDG 1 is to "[e]nd poverty in all its forms everywhere" (note 96 of Chapter One; text to note 2 of Chapter Two).

[2] MDG 1 is to "[e]radicate extreme poverty and hunger" (note 95 of Chapter One; text to note 4 of Chapter Two).

[3] MDG Target 1.A is to "[h]alve, between 1990 and 2015, the proportion of people whose income is less than one dollar a day" (note 98 of Chapter One; text to note 7 of Chapter Two). The pinpoint phrase 'less than one dollar a day' may be replaced by the generic expression 'below the international poverty line' (text to note 37 of Chapter Two, and the sentence that immediately follows that text).

[4] SDG Target 1.1 is to "eradicate extreme poverty for all people everywhere …" (note 99 of Chapter One; text to notes 6 and 39 of Chapter Two).

[5] Text to notes 98 and 99 of Chapter One.

[6] MDG 1 maps to SDG 1 and to SDG 2 (text to notes 95-97 of Chapter One).

Table 4.1: The number of mappings to each SDG considered in Chapter Four and to its targets

SDG Number	***Number of mappings from MDGs to the relevant SDG***	**Total number of targets of the relevant SDG**	***Number of these SDG Targets to which MDG Targets are mapped***	***Total number of mappings to the targets of the relevant SDG***
2	*1*	8	*1*	*1*
3	*3*	13	*4*	*7*
4	*1*	10	*2*	*2*
5	*2*	9	*1*	*1*
6	*1*	8	*4*	*4*
14	*1*	10	*4*	*5*
15	*1*	12	*5*	*5*
17	*1*	19	*8*	*10*

Next, these mappings are displayed by transferring them from Chapter One – but grouped according to SDG, rather than by MDG as in that earlier Chapter. The titles and subtitles of the current Chapter are labelled accordingly, following the sequence that Chapter Two uses for SDG 1[7] – but commenting on each MDG and the MDG Targets of that MDG that map to the relevant SDG together in the initial subsection of the section devoted to this SDG, rather than in separate subsections as in Chapter Two.[8]

SDG 2: SDG 2 receives a mapping from MDG 1.[9] SDG Target 2.1 receives a mapping from MDG Target 1.C.[10]

SDG 3: SDG 3 receives a mapping from each of MDG 4,[11] MDG 5[12] and MDG 6.[13] SDG Target 3.1 receives a mapping from MDG Target

[7] The first sentence of the current section (i.e., that entitled 'Introduction') describes this order.

[8] The section entitled 'MDG 1' in Chapter Two comprises subsections titled 'General comments concerning the accomplishment of MDG 1', 'The international poverty line and inferences from it', 'Progress in the accomplishment of MDG Target 1.A', and 'From MDG Target 1.A to SDG 1.1', whilst the first two subsections of the section entitled 'SDG 2' in the current Chapter are titled 'MDG 1 and MDG Target 1.C' and 'From MDG Target 1.C to SDG Target 2.1'.

[9] Text to notes 95 and 97 of Chapter One.

[10] Text to notes 102 and 103 of Chapter One.

[11] Text to notes 112 and 113 of Chapter One.

[12] Text to notes 116 and 117 of Chapter One.

[13] Text to notes 123 and 124 of Chapter One.

5.A.[14] SDG Target 3.2 receives a mapping from MDG Target 4.A.[15] SDG Target 3.3 receives a mapping from each of MDG Target 6.A,[16] MDG Target 6.B[17] and MDG Target 6.C.[18] SDG Target 3.8 receives a mapping from each of MDG Target 6.B[19] and MDG Target 8.E.[20]

SDG 4: SDG 4 receives a mapping from MDG 2.[21] SDG Target 4.1 receives a mapping from MDG Target 2.A.[22] SDG Target 4.5 receives a mapping from MDG Target 3.A.[23]

SDG 5: SDG 5 receives a mapping from each of MDG 3[24] and MDG 5.[25] SDG Target 5.6 receives a mapping from MDG Target 5.B.[26]

SDG 6: SDG 6 receives a mapping from MDG 7.[27] SDG Target 6.1 and SDG Target 6.2 each receives a mapping from MDG Target 7.C.[28] SDG Target 6.4 receives a mapping from MDG Target 7.A.[29] SDG Target 6.6 receives a mapping from MDG Target 7.B.[30]

SDG 14: SDG 14 receives a mapping from MDG 7.[31] SDG Target 14.2 receives a mapping from each of MDG Target 7.A[32] and MDG Target 7.B.[33] SDG Target 14.4 receives a mapping from MDG Target 7.A.[34] SDG Target 14.5 and SDG Target 14.c each receives a mapping from MDG Target 7.B.[35]

SDG 15: SDG 15 receives a mapping from MDG 7.[36] SDG Target 15.2, SDG Target 15.3 and SDG Target 15.9 each receives a mapping

[14] Text to notes 119 and 120 of Chapter One.
[15] Text to notes 114 and 115 of Chapter One.
[16] Text to notes 125 and 126 of Chapter One.
[17] Text to notes 127 and 128 of Chapter One.
[18] Text to notes 130 and 131 to Chapter One.
[19] Text to notes 127 and 129 of Chapter One.
[20] Text to notes 170 and 171 of Chapter One.
[21] Text to notes 104 and 105 of Chapter One.
[22] Text to notes 106 and 107 of Chapter One.
[23] Text to notes 110 and 111 of Chapter One.
[24] Text to notes 108 and 109 of Chapter One.
[25] Text to notes 116 and 118 of Chapter One.
[26] Text to notes 121 and 122 of Chapter One.
[27] Text to notes 132 and 133 of Chapter One.
[28] Text to notes 152, 153 and 154 of Chapter One.
[29] Text to notes 137 and 138 of Chapter One.
[30] Text to notes 145 and 146 of Chapter One.
[31] Text to notes 132 and 135 of Chapter One.
[32] Text to notes 137 and 140 of Chapter One.
[33] Text to notes 145 and 147 of Chapter One.
[34] Text to notes 137 and 141 of Chapter One.
[35] Text to notes 145, 148 and 149 of Chapter One.
[36] Text to notes 132 and 136 of Chapter One.

from MDG Target 7.A.[37] SDG Target 15.4 and SDG Target 15.5 each receives a mapping from MDG Target 7.B.[38]

SDG 17: SDG 17 receives a mapping from MDG 8.[39] SDG Target 17.4 receives a mapping from MDG Target 8.D.[40] SDG Target 17.5 and SDG Target 17.12 each receives a mapping from MDG Target 8.B.[41] SDG Target 17.6 and SDG Target 17.7 each receives a mapping from MDG Target 8.F.[42] SDG Target 17.8 receives a mapping from each of MDG Target 8.B[43] and MDG Target 8.F.[44] SDG Target 17.10 receives a mapping from MDG Target 8.A.[45] SDG Target 17.18 receives a mapping from each of MDG Target 8.B[46] and MDG Target 8.C.[47]

SDG 2: End Hunger and Promote Sustainable Agriculture

MDG 1 and MDG Target 1.C

MDG 1 is to "[e]radicate extreme poverty and hunger".[48] It comprises three targets, as follows: (i) MDG Target 1.A – to "[h]alve, between 1990 and 2015, the proportion of people whose income is below the international poverty line",[49] (ii) MDG Target 1.B – to "[a]chieve full and productive employment and decent work for all, including women and young people",[50] and (iii) MDG Target 1.C – to "[h]alve, between 1990 and 2015, the proportion of people who suffer from hunger".[51] Whilst the number of people worldwide living in extreme poverty was halved from its 1990 level in 2010[52] – rendering MDG Target 1.A successfully fulfilled at the global level,[53] most but not all developing regions satisfied this

[37] Text to notes 137, 142, 143 and 144 of Chapter One.
[38] Text to notes 145, 150 and 151 of Chapter One.
[39] Text to notes 157 and 158 of Chapter One.
[40] Text to notes 168 and 169 of Chapter One.
[41] Text to notes 161, 162 and 164 of Chapter One.
[42] Text to notes 172, 173 and 174 of Chapter One.
[43] Text to notes 161 and 163 of Chapter One.
[44] Text to notes 172 and 175 of Chapter One.
[45] Text to notes 159 and 160 of Chapter One.
[46] Text to notes 161 and 165 of Chapter One.
[47] Text to notes 166 and 167 of Chapter One.
[48] Note 2.
[49] Note 3.
[50] Note 100 of Chapter One; text to note 20 of Chapter Two.
[51] Note 102 of Chapter One.
[52] Note 12 of Chapter Two.
[53] Text to notes 10, 12 and 41 of Chapter Two.

MDG Target.[54] Although MDG Target 1.B was not met,[55] it is submitted that the disappointment of this outcome is mitigated by this MDG Target being an unrealistic goal.[56] MDG Target 1.C was almost realized.[57] Thus, the outcome in 2015 to MDG 1 is successful – given comparable conditions over the areas of its targets in 1990,[58] notwithstanding the fact that the application of a literal interpretation to the *prima facie* requirements of MDG 1[59] would have made this MDG impossible to meet.[60]

---

[54] Notes 43 and 44 of Chapter Two, and accompanying text.

[55] Note 21 of Chapter Two, and accompanying text. The worldwide employment-to-population ratio, i.e., the percentage of the working-age population that is employed, fell from 62% in 1991 to 60% in 2015 (United Nations, The Millennium Development Goals Report 2015 (New York, 2015), 17; "We can end poverty: Millennium Development Goals and Beyond 2015 – Goal 1: Eradicate extreme poverty & hunger", United Nations, accessed September 3, 2020, https://www.un.org/millenniumgoals/poverty.shtml).

[56] The sentence immediately-following the text to note 22 of Chapter Two opines that full employment is very difficult to attain, even in ideal conditions.

[57] Notes 11 and 13 of Chapter Two; text to note 13 of Chapter Two; text to notes 61 and 62.

[58] The final sentence of the subsection entitled 'General comments concerning the accomplishment of MDG 1', in the section titled 'MDG 1' in Chapter Two, reaches this conclusion.

[59] '*Prima facie*' is a Latin phrase from *primus* (i.e., first) and *facies* (i.e., face) that means "based on the first impression; accepted as correct until proved otherwise" (Oxford University Press, *The New Oxford Dictionary of English* (Oxford: Oxford University Press, 1998), 1471). Dr. McFarlane defines this expression as "[o]n the face of things; at first sight" (Gavin McFarlane, *The Layman's Dictionary of English Law* (London: Waterlow Publishers Limited), 1984). A literal interpretation of the requirements of MDG 1 examines the words that comprise the statement constituting this Goal, and thereby determines these requirements based on the ordinary meaning of those words; in this approach to interpreting the requirements of MDG 1, the targets of MDG 1 are no more than an aid to interpretation of the meaning of the statement constituting MDG 1, in places within that statement in which this is in doubt.

[60] MDG 1 is to "*[e]radicate* extreme poverty and hunger" (text to note 48; emphasis added). 'Eradicate' means "destroy completely; put an end to" (*The New Oxford Dictionary of English*, 623). It is opined that the UN and other interested parties did not put an end to extreme poverty and hunger by 2015, and, *in this literal sense*, they were unsuccessful in promptly realizing MDG 1. Note 52 of Chapter Two and its accompanying text consider the problem of eradicating extreme poverty – which SDG Target 1.1 requires. Note 4 states SDG Target 1.1.

The percentage of the population in the developing regions who were undernourished fell from 23.3% in 1990-1992 to 12.9% in 2014-2016.[61] Whilst this percentage fall is by almost half,[62] and, therefore, nearly fulfils MDG Target 1.C,[63] there are regional differences, with the Caucasus and Central Asia, East Asia, Latin America, and South-East Asia meeting this MDG Target, and the Caribbean, Oceania, South Asia, Sub-Saharan Africa, and West Asia failing to attain it.[64] The proportion of children under five years of age who are severely or moderately underweight declined by 50% or more from 1990 to 2015 in the Caucuses and Central Asia, East Asia, Latin America and the Caribbean, North Africa, and West Asia, dropped by less than half in South Asia, South-East Asia, and Sub-Saharan Africa, and rose slightly in Oceania.[65]

From MDG Target 1.C to SDG Target 2.1

SDG Target 2.1 is to "end hunger and ensure access by all people, in particular the poor and people in vulnerable situations, including infants, to safe, nutritious, and sufficient food all year round" by 2030.[66] This SDG Target provides a considerable part of the wording of SDG 2, which is to "*[e]nd hunger, achieve food security*[67] and improved nutrition and promote sustainable agriculture".[68]

The progression from MDG Target 1.C to SDG Target 2.1 is from halving the percentage of people who suffer from hunger to ending

---

[61] The Millennium Development Goals Report 2015, 20. It is submitted that the 2014-2016 statistic of 12.9% is partly or wholly based on estimates (note 13 of Chapter Two).

[62] The Millennium Development Goals Report 2015, 20.

[63] The Millennium Development Goals Report 2015, 20. The text to note 51 specifies MDG Target 1.C.

[64] The Millennium Development Goals Report 2015, 21.

[65] The Millennium Development Goals Report 2015, 22.

[66] Note 103 of Chapter One.

[67] The CFS published the following definition of 'food security' in 2011: 'Food Security' exists "when all people, at all times, have physical, social, and economic access to sufficient, safe, and nutritious food to meet their dietary needs and food preferences for a healthy and active life" (Committee on World Food Security, Thirty-seventh session, Rome, 17-22 October 2011, Item V: Policy Roundtable – Gender, Food Security and Nutrition, CFS:2011/5, September 2011 (Rome, 2011), 2). It is submitted that, on the basis of this definition, SDG Target 2.1 could be summarily worded 'To end hunger and achieve food security by 2030'. The text to note 66 states SDG Target 2.1.

[68] Note 97 of Chapter One; emphasis added.

hunger. As for extreme poverty,[69] whilst headway on meeting MDG Target 1.C demonstrated that it was possible to *halve* the proportion of people suffering from hunger,[70] it is submitted that it is impossible to *end*[71] hunger because shortages of food in exceptional circumstances – such as widespread flooding in an area whose population is mainly reliant on the growth of crops for subsistence – may precipitate hunger. However, if there is a satisfactory system for providing food security[72] in place – which is also a subject of SDG Target 2.1 and SDG 2,[73] then it should be possible to end *starvation* – at least in the absence of war or civil war, even though short-lived occurrences of hunger are nevertheless possible.[74] Thus, as for the discussion concerning extreme poverty in Chapter Two,[75] the comments in the next two subsections consider the *extent to which* SDG Target 2.1 might be accomplished by 31st December 2030.[76]

Progress to date in the accomplishment of SDG Target 2.1

The average level of global moderate food insecurity[77] has *increased* from 14.1% in 2014 to 16.3% in 2019, and of worldwide severe food insecurity[78] has *risen* from 8.3% in 2014 to 9.7% in 2019.[79] Both moderate

---

69 Text to notes 51 and 52 of Chapter Two.

70 Text to notes 61-63.

71 'End' means "come or bring to a final point; finish" (*The New Oxford Dictionary of English*, 608).

72 Note 67 defines 'food security'.

73 Note 67 and accompanying text. The text to note 66 specifies SDG Target 2.1. The text to note 68 states SDG 2.

74 It is submitted that the issue of food logistics, i.e., the difficulty, time and expense of supplying stored food to people in need of nourishment, especially if they are located in remote places and/or isolated due to being surrounded by difficult terrain such as flooded fields, is a contributory factor to making it impossible to end hunger, i.e., bring hunger to its final point (note 71).

75 The sentence immediately-following the text to note 54 of Chapter Two makes the corresponding point for SDG Target 1.1.

76 The target date for the SDGs to be achieved is 31st December 2030 (note 930 of Chapter Three and accompanying text).

77 Individuals who "experience[e] moderate food insecurity are typically unable to eat a healthy, balanced diet on a regular basis because of income or other resource constraints" (United Nations, The Sustainable Development Goals Report 2020 (New York, 2020), 26). Note 67 defines 'food security'.

78 Persons who "fac[e] severe insecurity … tend to run out of food and, at worst, go a day, or days, without eating" (The Sustainable Development Goals Report 2020, 26). Note 67 defines 'food security'.

79 The Sustainable Development Goals Report 2020, 26.

and severe food insecurity have increased over the period 2014 to 2019 in Central and South Asia, East and South-East Asia, Latin America, and Sub-Saharan Africa.[80] Furthermore, although the global occurrence of undernourishment has remained slightly under 9% since 2014, the total number of people suffering hunger has slowly risen for several years in succession – nearly 690 million individuals were undernourished in 2019 – up by almost 60 million persons from 2014.[81]

The COVID-19 pandemic[82] is a threat to food systems, because it indirectly diminishes purchasing power and the capacity to supply and distribute food.[83] It is opined that this pandemic will adversely affect the worldwide and regional percentages for food insecurity for both 2020 and 2021, which will render punctual attainment of SDG Target 2.1 even more unlikely than it appears to be – based on the data that the immediately-preceding paragraph contains.

Will SDG Target 2.1 be achieved punctually?

It is submitted that SDG Target 2.1[84] will not be achieved by 31st December 2030.[85] The statistics in the foregoing subsection show that the majority of regions are moving away from the attainment of this SDG Target. Notwithstanding this, if an effective and safe vaccine for COVID-19 is soon widely accepted, distributed and administered, then barring the realization of any other international catastrophe that affects food systems, the relevant authorities within the UN System and these regions should be able to effectively address issues of food security, thereby moving countries located therein in the correct direction towards accomplishment of SDG Target 2.1 by 31st December 2030.

Progress to date in accomplishment of SDG 2 as a whole

Bar SDG Target 2.1,[86] the targets of SDG 2[87] are condensed as follows.

---

[80] The Sustainable Development Goals Report 2020, 26.

[81] The Sustainable Development Goals Report 2020, 26.

[82] The WHO designated the outbreak and spread of COVID-19 as a pandemic on 11th March 2020 (note 53 of Chapter Two).

[83] The Sustainable Development Goals Report 2020, 26.

[84] The text to note 66 specifies SDG Target 2.1.

[85] The target date for the SDGs to be met is 31st December 2030 (note 930 of Chapter Three and accompanying text).

[86] The text to note 66 states SDG Target 2.1.

[87] The text to note 68 specifies SDG 2.

> 2.2 By 2030, end all forms of malnutrition … and address the nutritional needs of adolescent girls, pregnant and lactating women and older persons[.] 2.3 By 2030, double the agricultural productivity and incomes of small-scale producers … [.] 2.4 By 2030, ensure sustainable food production and implement resilient agricultural practices that increase productivity and production, that help [to] maintain ecosystems, that strengthen capacity for adaptation to … disasters and that progressively improve land and soil quality[.] 2.5 By 2020, maintain the genetic diversity of seeds, cultivated plants and farmed and domesticated animals and their related wild species … and promote access to and fair and equitable sharing of benefits arising from the utilization of genetic resources and associated traditional knowledge, as international agreed[.] 2.a Increase investment … in rural infrastructure, agricultural research and extension services, technology development and plant and livestock gene banks … [.] 2.b Correct and prevent trade restrictions and distortions in world agricultural markets … in accordance with the mandate of the Doha Development Round[.] 2.c Adopt measures to ensure the proper functioning of food commodity markets and their derivatives and facilitate timely access to market information, … in order to help [to] limit extreme food price volatility[.][88]

Regarding SDG Target 2.2: (i) the percentage of children of less than five years of age globally who endure chronic malnutrition – or stunting – fell from 23.1% in 2015 to 21.3% in 2019, (ii) 6.9% of children under five years of age worldwide were afflicted with acute malnutrition – or wasting – in 2019, and (iii) 5.6% of children under five years of age globally were overweight.[89] With respect to SDG Targets 2.3, 2.4 and 2.a: (i) the agriculture orientation index – i.e., the ratio of the governments' contributions to agriculture to the agriculture sector's contribution to GDP fell from 0.42 in 2001 to 0.31 in 2015, and further to 0.28 in 2018, and (ii) the share of aid to agriculture in developing countries declined from almost 25% of the sector-allocable aid of all donors in the mid-1980s to 5% in 2018.[90] As regards SDG Target 2.c: (i) there were abrupt rises in food prices in Sub-Saharan Africa, caused by production shocks,

---

[88] United Nations, Resolution 70/1 adopted by the General Assembly on 25 September 2015, Transforming our world: the 2030 Agenda for Sustainable Development, 15-16.

[89] United Nations, Economic and Social Council: High-level political forum on sustainable development, convened under the auspices of the Economic and Social Council – Progress towards the Sustainable Development Goals: Report of the Secretary-General, E/2020/xxx (New York, 2020), 5.

[90] Progress towards the Sustainable Development Goals: Report of the Secretary-General, E/2020/xxx, 5; The Sustainable Development Goals Report 2020, 27.

macroeconomic problems, and – in some parts of this region – prolonged conflicts and extreme weather conditions,[91] (ii) the depreciation of local currencies contributed to high food prices in Latin America, and (iii) an increase in demand for food and interruptions to supply chains, both precipitated by the COVID-19 pandemic,[92] formed the basis for rises in food prices in several countries during March and April 2020.[93]

The above catalogue of data suggests there has been little progress by 2020, if any, towards the accomplishment of SDG 2. Furthermore, it is submitted the targets of SDG 2[94] are specific and diverse, requiring detailed attention backed by suitably-targeted financial resources.

Will SDG 2 be achieved punctually?

On the basis of the limited information that the immediately-preceding subsection provides, it is probable that SDG 2 will not be achieved by 31st December 2030.[95] It is opined that the European Union is among the leading regions in progress towards accomplishment of this SDG, as the bloc is constructively engaging with issues presented by that Goal's targets – as summarized in the following statement.

> [T]he EU [i.e., European Union] has made progress in making agricultural production more sustainable over the past few years. However, there is still room for improvement in terms of the environmental impacts of agriculture, where the picture is mixed.[96]

It is submitted that other regions need to do similarly to the European Union, in order to make possible substantial progress towards punctual accomplishment of SDG 2.

---

[91] Progress towards the Sustainable Development Goals: Report of the Secretary-General, E/2020/xxx, 5; The Sustainable Development Goals Report 2020, 27.

[92] The Sustainable Development Goals Report 2020, 27.

[93] The Sustainable Development Goals Report 2020, 27.

[94] The text to note 88 quotes the essence of SDG Targets 2.2 to 2.c. The text to note 66 states SDG Target 2.1.

[95] The target date for the SDGs to be fulfilled is 31st December 2030 (note 930 of Chapter Three and accompanying text).

[96] Eurostat, Sustainable development in the European Union: Monitoring report on progress towards the SDGs in an EU context: 2020 edition (Luxembourg: Publications Office of the European Union, 2020), 55.

SDG 3: Ensure Healthy Lives and Promote Well-Being

MDG 5 and MDG Target 5.A

MDG 5 is to "[i]mprove maternal health".[97] It comprises the following targets: (i) MDG Target 5.A – to "[r]educe by three quarters, between 1990 and 2015, the maternal mortality ratio",[98] and (ii) MDG Target 5.B – to "[a]chieve, by 2015, universal access to reproductive health".[99]

MDG Target 5.A was not met – the global maternal mortality ratio fell from 380 maternal deaths per 100,000 live births in 1990 to 210 maternal deaths per 100,000 live births in 2013,[100] Furthermore, MDG Target 5.B was not reached – an average of 52% of pregnant women in the developing regions received the WHO's recommended quantity of at least four antenatal care visits during pregnancy.[101] Thus, whilst progress was made towards achieving MDG 5, this was not enough to fulfil that Goal.

Regarding MDG Target 5.A, none of the regions achieved a 75% reduction in the maternal mortality ratio between 1990 and 2013.[102] The bar chart declares a fall in this ratio over that period of 65%, 64%, 57%, 57%, 51%, 49%, 44%, 43%, 40% and 36% for East Asia, South Asia, North Africa, South-East Asia, Oceania, Sub-Saharan Africa, the Caucasus and Central Asia, West Asia, Latin America, and the Caribbean, respectively.[103]

From MDG Target 5.A to SDG Target 3.1

SDG Target 3.1 is to "reduce the global maternal mortality ratio to less than 70 per 100,000 live births" by 2030.[104] This absolute target contrasts with the proportional target that constitutes MDG Target 5.A.[105] As the

---

[97] Note 116 of Chapter One.

[98] Note 119 of Chapter One.

[99] Note 121 of Chapter One.

[100] The Millennium Development Goals Report 2015, 38. MDG Target 5.A for the global maternal mortality ratio was, in absolute terms, to reduce this value from 380 maternal deaths per 100,000 live births in 1990 to [380 * (1 – ¾) = 380 * ¼ =] 95 maternal deaths per 100,000 live births in 2015.

[101] The Millennium Development Goals Report 2015, 41.

[102] The Millennium Development Goals Report 2015, 38.

[103] The Millennium Development Goals Report 2015, 38. In these statistics, Latin America (40%) is treated as a separate region to the Caribbean (36%).

[104] Note 120 of Chapter One.

[105] The text to note 98 specifies MDG Target 5.A.

worldwide maternal mortality ratio in 2013 was 210 maternal deaths per 100,000 live births,[106] SDG Target 3.1 translates to a percentage target of [((210 – 70) maternal deaths per 100,000 live births / 210 maternal deaths per 100,000 live births) * 100%] = 67%.[107] That is to say, on the basis of the above datum[108] SDG Target 3.1 is equivalent to the following proportional target: 'Reduce by *two thirds*, between 2013 and 2030, the maternal mortality ratio'. A two-third reduction in the maternal mortality ratio over seventeen years (i.e., 2013 to 2030) is equivalent to an annual reduction of [(1 – $(\frac{1}{3})^{\frac{1}{17}}$) * 100%] = 6.258036949%.[109] A three-quarters reduction in the maternal mortality ratio over twenty-five years (i.e., 1990 to 2015, in accordance with MDG Target 5.A) is equivalent to annual reduction of [(1 – $(\frac{1}{4})^{\frac{1}{25}}$) * 100%] = 5.394235327%.[110] Thus, in proportional terms, SDG

[106] Text to note 100.

[107] This percentage is given to two significant figures.

[108] Text to note 106.

[109] This percentage is given to nine decimal places. Thus, if the initial maternal mortality in 2013 takes a value of 1, then the maternal mortality in each subsequent year should be reduced multiplying that annual figure by [1 – 0.06258036949 = 0.93741963051], in order yield to a maternal mortality of ⅓ in 2030. In essence, $(0.93741963051)^{17}$ = ⅓, and [210 * $(0.93741963051)^{17}$] = 70. This compounding method can be used to estimate whether the world is on track to meet SDG Target 3.1 in any given year. For example, 2025 is the twelfth year beyond 2013. Therefore, for the global maternal mortality ratio to be on target to reach 70 maternal deaths per 100,000 live births in 2030, the maternal mortality ratio in 2025 should be equal to or less than [210 * $(0.93741963051)^{12}$] maternal deaths per 100,000 live births = 96.7003 maternal deaths per 100,000 live births. This number is given to six significant figures and four decimal places. *Check*: 2030 is five years beyond 2025; therefore, [96.7003 * $(0.93741963051)^{5}$] maternal deaths per 100,000 live births ≡ 70 maternal deaths per 100,000 live births → [96.7003 * 0.72388506965] maternal deaths per 100,000 live births ≡ 70 maternal deaths per 100,000 live births → 69.9999 maternal deaths per 100,000 live births ≡ 70 maternal deaths per 100,000 live births, which is true to five significant figures and three decimal places.

[110] This percentage is given to nine decimal places. Therefore, if the initial maternal mortality in 1990 takes a value of 1, then the maternal mortality in each subsequent year should be reduced multiplying that annual figure by [1 – 0.05394235327 = 0.94605764673], in order yield to a maternal mortality of ¼ in 2015. Fundamentally, $(0.94605764673)^{25}$ = ¼, and, using the datum for the global maternal mortality ratio in 1990 of 380 maternal deaths to 100,000 live births (text to note 100), [380 * $(0.94605764673)^{25}$] = 95. *Check:* MDG Target 5.A is to reduce the maternal mortality ratio between 1990 and 2015 by three quarters (text to note 98), which, for the global mortality ratio, means aiming to lower this value

Target 3.1 is a more demanding objective in respect of lowering the worldwide maternal mortality ratio than MDG Target 5.A – which, as stated above,[111] was not met.

Progress to date in the accomplishment of SDG Target 3.1

An estimated 295,000 maternal deaths happened in 2017, resulting in a global maternal mortality ratio of 211 maternal deaths per 100,000 live births – with the majority of these occurring in low-income and lower-middle-income countries.[112] The majority of these were in Sub-Saharan Africa,[113] with a further 20% of the worldwide total in South Asia.[114]

The global maternity mortality ratio remains almost unchanged from 2013 to 2017.[115] Hence, no progress has been made towards realizing SDG Target 3.1.

Will SDG Target 3.1 be achieved punctually?

A greater annual percentage reduction in the worldwide maternal mortality ratio is required to meet SDG Target 3.1[116] by 2030 than was needed to realize MDG Target 5.A[117] by 2015.[118] Furthermore, MDG Target 5.A was

---

from 380 maternal deaths per 100,000 live births in 1990 to 95 maternal deaths per 100,000 live births in 2015 (note 100).

111 Text to note 100.

112 Progress towards the Sustainable Development Goals: Report of the Secretary-General, E/2020/xxx, 5.

113 Sub-Saharan Africa accounted for 66% of the worldwide maternal deaths in 2017 (Progress towards the Sustainable Development Goals: Report of the Secretary-General, E/2020/xxx, 5).

114 Sub-Saharan Africa and South Asia together accounted for 86% of the worldwide maternal deaths in 2017 (The Sustainable Development Goals Report 2020, 28). Percentage of global maternal deaths occurring in South Asia = Percentage of global maternal deaths occurring in Sub-Saharan Africa and South Asia – Percentage of global maternal deaths occurring in Sub-Saharan Africa = 86% (first sentence of current footnote) – 66% (note 113) = 20%.

115 The worldwide maternal mortality ratio was 210 maternal deaths per 100,000 live births in 2013 (text to note 100) and 211 maternal deaths per 100,000 live births in 2017 (text to note 112), which is a tiny increase over four years. Notwithstanding this, the UN recently reported a 4% reduction in the global maternal mortality ratio from 2015 to 2017 (Progress towards the Sustainable Development Goals: Report of the Secretary-General, E/2020/xxx, 5).

116 The text to note 104 states SDG Target 3.1.

117 The text to note 98 specifies MDG Target 5.A.

not achieved.[119] Additionally, the COVID-19 pandemic[120] may overturn earlier progress in reducing maternal and infant deaths, by undermining health systems, disrupting routine healthcare, and restricting access to nourishing diets and vital nutrition services.[121] In the light of these three statements, it is improbable that SDG Target 3.1 will be attained punctually,[122] i.e., by 31st December 2030.[123]

---

118 MDG Target 5.A necessitated an annual reduction in the global maternal mortality rate of 5.39% (text to note 110). On the basis of a starting-point of 210 maternal deaths per 100,000 live births in 2013 (text to note 100), SDG Target 3.1 requires an annual reduction in the worldwide maternal mortality rate of 6.26% (text to note 109). The UN states that the annual reduction in the global maternal mortality rate needed to meet SDG Target 3.1 is 6.4% (The Sustainable Development Goals Report 2020, 28). It is submitted that this 6.4% annual reduction may be based upon a starting point of 211 maternal deaths per 100,000 live births in 2017 (text to note 112), rather than a starting point of 210 maternal deaths per 100,000 live births in 2013 (text to note 100) – which requires a 6.26% annual reduction in order to fulfil SDG Target 3.1 (text to note 109). *Check:* Required annual reduction corresponding to that of [211 – 70 = 141] maternal deaths per 100,000 live births over [2030 – 2017 = 13] years = [(1 – $(70/211)^{1/13}$) * 100%] = 8.137203875%. This percentage is given to nine decimal places. If the initial maternal mortality in 2017 takes a value of 1, then the maternal mortality in each subsequent year should be reduced multiplying that annual figure by [1 – 0.08137203875 = 0.91862796125], in order yield to a maternal mortality of [70/211 = 0.3317535545] in 2030. In essence, $(0.91862796125)^{13}$ = 0.331754 to six significant figures, and [211 * $(0.91862796125)^{13}$] = 70. *Thus, based on the UN-reported datum of 211 maternal deaths per 100,000 deaths per 100,000 live births in 2017* (note 112 and accompanying text; The Sustainable Development Goals Report 2020, 28), *SDG Target 3.1 requires an annual reduction in the worldwide maternal mortality rate of 8.14% from 2017, in order to be met in 2030.*

119 Text to note 100.

120 The WHO classified the outbreak and spread of COVID-19 as a pandemic on 11th March 2020 (note 53 of Chapter Two).

121 The Sustainable Development Goals Report 2020, 28.

122 The Secretary-General of the UN opined: "With the current rate of progress, the world will fall short of the SDG Target [as to the global maternal mortality ratio, i.e., SDG Target 3.1]" (Progress towards the Sustainable Development Goals: Report of the Secretary-General, E/2020/xxx, 5).

123 The target date for the SDGs to be accomplished is 31st December 2030 (note 930 of Chapter Three and accompanying text).

MDG 4 and MDG Target 4.A

MDG 4 is to "[r]educe child mortality".[124] Its sole target – MDG Target 4.A – is to "[r]educe by two thirds, between 1990 and 2015, the under-five [child] mortality rate".[125]

Preliminary estimates claim that the worldwide under-five mortality ratio fell from 90 infants per 1,000 live births in 1990 to 43 infants per 1,000 live births in 2015.[126] As the datum for 1990 translates to a required absolute value of [90 * (1 – ⅔) = 90 * ⅓] = 30 infants per 1,000 live births for MDG Target 4.A to be accomplished punctually, on this basis MDG Target 4.A was not met.

The bar chart which graphs these forecasts proclaims that the under-five mortality ratio per 1,000 infants decreased in all regions between 1990 and 2015, with reductions of 31%, 52%, 55%, 60%, 62%, 65%, 67%, 69% and 78% in Oceania, Sub-Saharan Africa, the Caucasus and Central Asia, South Asia, South-East Asia, West Asia, North Africa, Latin America and the Caribbean, and East Asia, respectively.[127] Thus, going by these percentages, North Africa, Latin America and the Caribbean, and East Asia, all achieved MDG Target 4.A,[128] but Oceania, Sub-Saharan Africa, the Caucasus and Central Asia, South Asia, South-East Asia, and West Asia did not attain it.

The annual rate of reduction of under-five mortality is: (i) higher over the period 2005 to 2013 than through any of the quinquennia 1990 to 1995, 1995 to 2000 and 2000 to 2005, in Oceania, South Asia, and Sub-Saharan Africa, (ii) lower than during any of those lustra in Latin America and the Caribbean, North Africa, and South-East Asia, and (iii) second to the annual rate of reduction from 2000 to 2005 in the Caucasus and Central Asia, and East Asia, and to that from 1995 to 2000 in West Asia.[129] Whilst the subtitle for these data in *The Millennium Development Goals Report 2015* "Child mortality rates are falling faster than ever"[130] is overenthusiastic, the information presented above in the current subsection[131] is supportive of a claim that MDG 4[132] has been met, which a

[124] Note 112 of Chapter One.
[125] Note 114 of Chapter One.
[126] The Millennium Development Goals Report 2015, 33.
[127] The Millennium Development Goals Report 2015, 32.
[128] The text to note 125 specifies MDG Target 4.A.
[129] The Millennium Development Goals Report 2015, 35.
[130] The Millennium Development Goals Report 2015, 35.
[131] Text to notes 126, 127 and 128.
[132] The text to note 124 states MDG 4.

literal interpretation[133] of that Goal's *prima facie*[134] requirements would reinforce[135] – notwithstanding the fact that MDG Target 4.A has not been fulfilled.

From MDG Target 4.A to SDG Target 3.2

SDG Target 3.2 is to "end preventable deaths of newborns and children under 5 years of age, with all countries aiming to reduce neonatal mortality to at least as low as 12 per 1,000 live births and under-5 mortality to at least as low as 25 per 1,000 live births", by 2030.[136] This absolute SDG Target follows-on from proportional MDG Target 4.A.[137] It also expands from the latter to include a requirement concerning preventable deaths of neonates and infants, and another regarding mortality of babies.

Progress to date in the accomplishment of SDG Target 3.2

The worldwide under-five mortality ratio decreased from 76 infants per 1,000 live births in 2000 to 42 infants per 1,000 live births in 2015, and thence to 39 infants per 1,000 live births in 2018.[138] By 2018, 121 countries had fulfilled SDG Target 3.2[139] as to under-five mortality.[140]

The global neonatal mortality ratio reduced from 31 babies per 1,000 live births in 2000 to 18 babies per 1,000 live births in 2018.[141] Both the

---

[133] Note 59 explains the concept of a 'literal interpretation', as applied to MDG 1.

[134] Note 59 defines the phrase '*prima facie*'.

[135] MDG 4 is to "*[r]educe child* mortality" (text to note 124; emphasis added). 'Reduce' – in this sense of the word – means "make smaller in amount, degree or size" (*The New Oxford Dictionary of English*, 1556). 'Child' – in this sense of the word – means 'a young human being below the age of full physical development' (*The New Oxford Dictionary of English*, 317). The data in the current subsection (i.e., that entitled 'MDG 4 and MDG Target 4.A') suggest that the mortality of individuals under five years – which is below the age of full physical development – has been made smaller in degree, i.e., reduced. Thus, a literal interpretation of the requirements of MDG 4 would reinforce a claim that, on the basis of these statistics, this Goal has been realized.

[136] Note 115 of Chapter One.

[137] The text to note 125 specifies MDG Target 4.A.

[138] Progress towards the Sustainable Development Goals: Report of the Secretary-General, E/2020/xxx, 6; The Sustainable Development Goals Report 2020, 28.

[139] The text to note 136 states SDG Target 3.2.

[140] The Sustainable Development Goals Report 2020, 28.

[141] The Sustainable Development Goals Report 2020, 28.

worldwide under-five mortality ratio and the global neonatal mortality ratio declined in every region between 2000 and 2018.[142]

Will SDG Target 3.2 be achieved punctually?

The data in the immediately-preceding subsection suggest that both the global under-five mortality ratio and the worldwide neonatal mortality ratio are moving in the correct direction for there to be a possibility of attaining one or both of the corresponding goals in SDG Target 3.2[143] by 31st December 2030.[144] However, the COVID-19 pandemic[145] may reverse earlier headway in lowering maternal and infant deaths.[146] Furthermore, the UN should define 'preventable deaths', so that it is possible to assess the level of these with a view to the objective in SDG Target 3.2 of ending them by 31st December 2030.[147] On the basis of these statements, it is submitted that, whilst one or even two of the three heads of SDG Target 3.2 may be achieved punctually, this target as a whole will not be achieved by 31st December 2030.

MDG 6 and MDG Targets 6.A, 6.B and 6.C

MDG 6 is to "[c]ombat HIV/AIDS, malaria and other diseases".[148] This MDG comprises the following three targets: (i) MDG Target 6.A – to "[h]ave halted by 2015 and begun to reverse the spread of HIV/AIDS",[149] (ii) MDG Target 6.B – to "[a]chieve, by 2010, universal access to

---

142 The Sustainable Development Goals Report 2020, 28.

143 The text to note 136 states SDG Target 3.2. These 'corresponding goals' are: (i) for the global under-five mortality ratio, 25 infants per 1,000 live births, and (ii) for the worldwide neonatal mortality ratio, 12 babies per 1,000 live births (text to note 136).

144 The target date for the SDGs to be realized is 31st December 2030 (note 930 of Chapter Three and accompanying text).

145 The WHO categorized the outbreak and spread of COVID-19 as a pandemic on 11th March 2020 (note 53 of Chapter Two).

146 Text to note 121.

147 At present, there is no SDG Indicator which corresponds to that part of SDG Target 3.2 which aims to "end preventable deaths of newborns and children under 5 years of age" (United Nations, Global indicator framework for the Sustainable Development Goals and targets of the 2030 Agenda for Sustainable Development, A/RES/71/313, E/CN.3/2018/2, E/CN.3/2019/2, E/CN.3/2020/2 (New York, 2020), 3).

148 Note 123 of Chapter One.

149 Note 125 of Chapter One.

treatment for HIV/AIDS for all those who need it",[150] and (iii) MDG Target 6.C – to "[h]ave halted by 2015 and begun to reverse the incidence of malaria and other major diseases".[151]

Regarding MDG Target 6.A, an estimated 35 million individuals were living with HIV in 2013 – a figure which is rising as more of these people live longer due to greater use of antiretroviral therapy, and as the number of new HIV infections continues to be high.[152] Thus, by 2013, the spread of HIV/AIDS had not been halted – and, therefore, the target at this point had not been achieved. Notwithstanding this, the estimated number of people newly-infected with HIV in 2013 is smaller than this figure in 2000 for the five geographical areas most affected by this disease in the earlier year – from highest to lowest: Southern Africa,[153] East Africa, West Africa, South Asia, and Central Africa.[154] New HIV infections worldwide declined by approximately 40% between 2000 and 2013.[155]

With respect to MDG Target 6.B, globally 13.6 million people living with HIV were receiving antiretroviral therapy – an enormous rise from 375,000 individuals taking this treatment in 2003.[156] Notwithstanding this, an estimated 64% of the individuals subject to HIV in developing regions were not being given antiretroviral therapy in 2013,[157] which supports a conclusion that MDG Target 6.B was not met.

As regards MDG Target 6.C: (i) the worldwide incidence of malaria decreased by an estimated 37% from 2000 to 2015, and the global mortality rate from that disease fell by 58% over this period,[158] (ii) the tuberculosis incidence rate declined in all regions since 2000 – at a mean

---

[150] Note 127 of Chapter One.

[151] Note 130 of Chapter One.

[152] The Millennium Development Goals Report 2015, 45.

[153] In *The Millennium Development Goals Report 2015*, 'Southern Africa' comprises Angola, Botswana, Eswatini, Lesotho, Malawi, Mozambique, Namibia, South Africa, Zambia, and Zimbabwe (The Millennium Development Goals Report 2015, 71). This sub-region of Africa is entitled 'Southern Africa' rather than 'South Africa', in order to avoid confusion with the state of the latter name.

[154] The Millennium Development Goals Report 2015, 44.

[155] The Millennium Development Goals Report 2015, 45.

[156] The Millennium Development Goals Report 2015, 46.

[157] *The Millennium Development Goals Report 2015* states: "only an estimated 36 per cent of the 31.5 million people living with HIV in developing regions were receiving ART [i.e., antiretroviral therapy] in 2013" (The Millennium Development Goals Report 2015, 47). As 36% of the individuals subject to HIV in developing regions were receiving antiretroviral therapy in 2013, 100% – 36% = 64% of these people were not being given this treatment in that year.

[158] The Millennium Development Goals Report 2015, 47.

annual rate of approximately 1.5% between that year and 2013, and the global mortality rate from tuberculosis diminished by 45% during this time,[159] and (iii) an outbreak of Ebola commenced in December 2013 in rural Guinea – close to its border with Liberia and Sierra Leone, precipitating more than 27,000 suspected, probable and confirmed cases and 11,000 deaths by late May 2015.[160] On the basis of this information, it is opined that MDG Target 6.C has been met for malaria and for tuberculosis – which is one of the "other major diseases";[161] however, the recurrent[162] rise in the incidence of Ebola – another major disease – in Sub-Saharan Africa from 2013 to 2015 precludes submission of an inference that this MDG Target has been fulfilled.

As MDG Targets 6.A, 6.B and 6.C have not been met, it can be reasonably argued that MDG 6 has not been achieved. However, a literal interpretation[163] as to the *prima facie*[164] requirements of MDG 6 would support a claim that this Goal has been fulfilled.[165]

From MDG Targets 6.A, 6.B and 6.C to SDG Target 3.3

SDG Target 3.3 is to "end the epidemics of AIDS, tuberculosis, malaria and neglected tropical diseases and combat hepatitis, water-borne diseases and other communicable diseases", by 2030.[166] This SDG Target proceeds

---

[159] The Millennium Development Goals Report 2015, 49.

[160] The Millennium Development Goals Report 2015, 51.

[161] Text to note 151.

[162] Sporadic outbreaks of this viral disease across equatorial Africa between 1976 and 2012 have infected about 2,400 individuals and caused approximately 1,600 deaths (The Millennium Development Goals Report 2015, 51).

[163] Note 59 explains the concept of a 'literal interpretation', as applied to MDG 1.

[164] Note 59 defines the phrase '*prima facie*'.

[165] MDG 6 is to "*[c]ombat* HIV/AIDS, malaria and other diseases" (text to note 148; emphasis added). 'Combat' means "take action to reduce, destroy, or prevent (something bad or undesirable)" (*The New Oxford Dictionary of English*, 364). The information in the current subsection (i.e., that entitled 'MDG 6 and MDG Targets 6.A., 6.B and 6.C') suggests that action has been taken since 2000 to reduce the incidence of HIV/AIDS, malaria and tuberculosis – all of which are undesirable. As this conclusion that HIV/AIDS, malaria and tuberculosis have been combatted – as MDG 6 requires – is unambiguous, it is unnecessary to refer to the targets of MDG 6 as an aid to interpretation of the meaning of the statement constituting MDG 6 (note 59). Thus, a literal interpretation of the requirements of MDG 6 would support a claim that, on the basis of these data, this Goal has been met.

[166] Note 126 of Chapter One.

from all three targets of MDG 6[167]: (i) MDG Target 6.A[168] requires the spread of AIDS to be halted and reversed, whilst SDG Target 3.3 necessitates that the widespread occurrence of AIDS be brought to a final point;[169] (ii) MDG Target 6.B[170] requires all people who suffer from HIV/AIDS to have access to treatment for it, whilst SDG Target 3.3 entails this access in order to reduce – and thence bring to its final point – the widespread occurrence of AIDS,[171] and (iii) MDG Target 6.C[172] requires the spread of malaria and other major diseases to be halted and reversed, whilst SDG Target 3.3 necessitates that the widespread occurrence of malaria, tuberculosis and tropical diseases to which proper attention has not been paid, be brought to a final point, and that action be taken to reduce, destroy or prevent other communicable diseases.[173]

Progress to date in the accomplishment of SDG Target 3.3

HIV/AIDS: The worldwide incidence of HIV among adults aged 15 to 49 years decreased by 18% from 2010 to 2018.[174] In 2018, there were an estimated 1.7 million people were newly-infected with HIV, which is an incidence rate of 0.24 per 1,000 uninfected individuals – nearly unchanged from 0.26 per 1,000 uninfected persons in 2015.[175]

Malaria: The global incidence of malaria reduced from 81 cases per 1,000 population in 2000 to 57 cases per 1,000 population in 2014, and

---

[167] The text to note 148 states MDG 6.

[168] The text to note 149 specifies MDG Target 6.A.

[169] A literal interpretation as to the *prima facie* requirements of SDG Target 3.3 calls for a definition of the words 'end', 'epidemic', 'neglect' and 'combat'. 'End' means "come or bring to a final point; finish" (note 71). An 'epidemic' is "a widespread occurrence of an infectious disease in a community at a particular time" (note 53 of Chapter Two). 'Neglect' – in this sense of the word – means "not pay proper attention to; disregard" (*The New Oxford Dictionary of English*, 1240). 'Combat' means "take action to reduce, destroy, or prevent (something bad or undesirable)" (note 165). Note 59 explains the concept of a 'literal interpretation', as applied to MDG 1, and defines the phrase '*prima facie*'.

[170] The text to note 150 states MDG Target 6.B.

[171] Note 169.

[172] The text to note 151 specifies MDG Target 6.C.

[173] Note 169.

[174] The Sustainable Development Goals Report 2020, 30.

[175] Progress towards the Sustainable Development Goals: Report of the Secretary-General, E/2020/xxx, 6.

remained at a similar level to that of 2014 through to 2018.[176] The spread of COVID-19 within countries in which malaria is endemic may potentially disrupt services that are aimed at preventing the latter disease.[177]

Tuberculosis: The worldwide incidence of tuberculosis fell from 141 cases per 100,000 population in 2015 to 132 cases per 100,000 population in 2018.[178] The mortality rate from this disease declined by 8.3% between 2015 and 2018.[179] In 2018, there were 484,000 new cases of tuberculosis that was resistant to rifampicin.[180]

Hepatitis: The use of a vaccine for hepatitis B in infants has substantially lowered the incidence of new, persistent infections of this disease.[181] The proportion of children of less than five years of age who became chronically-infected with hepatitis B declined from 4.7% before the introduction of the vaccine to 0.9% in 2018.[182]

Neglected tropical diseases: In 2018, 1.76 billion individuals were reported to require treatment and care for neglected tropical diseases – which is lower than the corresponding numbers of people who were announced to need this in 2010 (2.19 billion people) and 2015 (1.80 billion people).[183] At least one neglected tropical disease was eradicated in each of forty countries.[184]

---

[176] Progress towards the Sustainable Development Goals: Report of the Secretary-General, E/2020/xxx, 6; The Sustainable Development Goals Report 2020, 30.

[177] The Sustainable Development Goals Report 2020, 30.

[178] Progress towards the Sustainable Development Goals: Report of the Secretary-General, E/2020/xxx, 6; The Sustainable Development Goals Report 2020, 30.

[179] Progress towards the Sustainable Development Goals: Report of the Secretary-General, E/2020/xxx, 6.

[180] The Sustainable Development Goals Report 2020, 30. 'Rifampicin', alternatively called 'rifampin', is "a semisynthetic antibiotic $C_{43}H_{58}N_4O_{12}$ used especially in the treatment of tuberculosis and to treat asymptomatic carriers of meningococci" ("rifampin", Merriam-Webster, accessed September 7, 2020, https://www.merriam-webster.com/dictionary/rifampin). This definition includes the molecular formula of rifampicin – $C_{43}H_{58}N_4O_{12}$. The formula summarizes the information that each molecule of rifampicin comprises 43 atoms of carbon (C), 58 atoms of hydrogen (H), four atoms of nitrogen (N), and twelve atoms of oxygen (O).

[181] Progress towards the Sustainable Development Goals: Report of the Secretary-General, E/2020/xxx, 6.

[182] Progress towards the Sustainable Development Goals: Report of the Secretary-General, E/2020/xxx, 6.

[183] Progress towards the Sustainable Development Goals: Report of the Secretary-General, E/2020/xxx, 6; The Sustainable Development Goals Report 2020, 30.

[184] Progress towards the Sustainable Development Goals: Report of the Secretary-General, E/2020/xxx, 6; The Sustainable Development Goals Report 2020, 30.

Conclusion: Whilst the UN concluded that the progress regarding the global incidence of HIV/AIDS, malaria and tuberculosis was at an insufficient pace to meet SDG Target 3.3[185] as applied to each of these three diseases,[186] it is submitted that – on the basis of the information provided above in this subsection[187] – this target as applied to hepatitis B has already been realized. Notwithstanding this, it is opined that the requirement to 'combat' hepatitis within SDG Target 3.3 is less onerous than any of the four requirements within that SDG Target to 'eradicate the epidemics of' AIDS, tuberculosis, malaria, and neglected tropical diseases.[188]

Will SDG Target 3.3 be achieved punctually?

Further to the data that the foregoing subsection contains, it is probable that SDG Target 3.3[189] will not be met punctually, i.e., by 31st December 2030.[190] Moreover, disruptions concerning COVID-19 to health, prevention and supply services may deteriorate the prognosis for the timely achievement of SDG Target 3.3.[191]

From MDG Targets 6.B and 8.E to SDG Target 3.8

MDG Target 8.E is to "provide access to affordable essential drugs in developing countries", "[i]n cooperation with pharmaceutical companies".[192] Notwithstanding a paucity of data on sustainable access to such drugs, the few surveys undertaken in low-income and lower-middle-income countries between 2007 and 2014 indicate that generic medicines were available in

---

185 The text to note 166 states SDG Target 3.3.

186 Progress towards the Sustainable Development Goals: Report of the Secretary-General, E/2020/xxx, 6; The Sustainable Development Goals Report 2020, 30.

187 Text to notes 181 and 182.

188 This opinion is supported by comparing the definitions of the word 'combat' with that of 'end' in note 169.

189 The text to note 166 specifies SDG Target 3.3.

190 The target date for the SDGs to be attained is 31st December 2030 (note 930 of Chapter Three and accompanying text).

191 *The Sustainable Development Goals Report 2020* asseverates: "In spite of gains on many fronts, COVID-19-related service disruptions could cause hundreds of thousands of additional deaths from AIDS, malaria, tuberculosis and neglected tropical diseases." (The Sustainable Development Goals Report 2020, 30).

192 Note 170 of Chapter One.

58% of public health facilities there – on average, but in 67% of facilities in the private sector – on average.[193]

SDG Target 3.8 is to "[a]chieve universal health coverage,[194] including financial risk protection, access to quality essential health-care services and access to safe, effective, quality and affordable essential medicines and vaccines for all".[195] This SDG Target follows on from MDG Target 8.E, but is comprehensive – requiring access to the aforementioned medicines and vaccines for everyone. By contrast, MDG Target 8.E only requires a provision of access to drugs in developing countries. Furthermore, MDG Target 8.E uses only two descriptors for these drugs – 'affordable' and 'essential', compared with five descriptors for medicines and vaccines in SDG Target 3.8 – which must not only be 'affordable' and 'essential' but also 'safe', 'effective' and 'quality'.

SDG Target 3.8 broadens MDG Target 6.B[196] from access for everyone who needs it to treatment for HIV/AIDS to access for everyone to coverage for their health-related needs. It is submitted that SDG Target 3.8 wishes to cater for non-emergency and non-critical healthcare needs – provided these are not superfluous demands from the public – which is more extensive than the specific – and necessary – treatment for HIV/AIDS.

Progress to date in the accomplishment of SDG Target 3.8

The number of individuals who were covered by essential health services in 2017 was estimated to be between 2.5 billion people and 3.7 billion people.[197] Between 12% and 27% of the population in low-income countries had coverage for their health needs in 2017.[198] If present trends continue, between 39% and 63% of the world's population[199] will be covered by essential health services in 2030.[200]

---

193 The Millennium Development Goals Report 2015, 49.

194 *The Sustainable Development Goals Report 2020* explains: "Universal health coverage means that all people have access to the health services they need, when and where they need them, without financial hardship. It includes the full range of essential health services, from health promotion to prevention, treatment, rehabilitation and palliative care." (The Sustainable Development Goals Report 2020, 31).

195 Note 129 of Chapter One.

196 The text to note 150 states MDG Target 6.B.

197 The Sustainable Development Goals Report 2020, 31.

198 The Sustainable Development Goals Report 2020, 31.

199 The population of the world is 7,794,798,739 people (text to note 227 of Chapter Three; note 249 of Chapter Three).

200 The Sustainable Development Goals Report 2020, 31.

Will SDG Target 3.8 be achieved punctually?

The figures in the immediately-preceding subsection suggest that universal health coverage[201] – which is the aim that SDG Target 3.8[202] contains – will not be realized punctually, i.e., by 31st December 2030.[203] Furthermore, some essential health services have been suspended in order to release resources to: (i) treat patients who suffer from COVID-19 and, (ii) lower the risk of transmission of this virus.[204]

Progress to date in accomplishment of SDG 3 as a whole

SDG 3 is to "[e]nsure healthy lives and promote well-being for all at all ages".[205] Save SDG Targets 3.1,[206] 3.2,[207] 3.3[208] and 3.8,[209] the targets of SDG 3 are abridged as follows.

> 3.4 By 2030, reduce by one third premature mortality from non-communicable diseases … and promote mental health and well-being[.] 3.5 Strengthen the prevention and treatment of substance abuse … [.] 3.6 By 2020, halve the number of global deaths and injuries from road traffic accidents[.] 3.7 By 2030, ensure universal access to sexual and reproductive health-care services … and the integration of reproductive health into national strategies and programmes[.] … 3.9 By 2030, substantially reduce the number of deaths and illnesses from hazardous chemicals and air, water and soil pollution and contamination[.] 3.a Strengthen the implementation of the World Health Organization Framework Convention on Tobacco Control[210] … [.] 3.b Support the research and development of vaccines and

---

[201] Note 194 explains the UN's understanding of the meaning of the term 'universal health coverage'.

[202] The text to note 195 specifies SDG Target 3.8.

[203] The target date for the SDGs to be achieved is 31st December 2030 (note 930 of Chapter Three and accompanying text).

[204] The Sustainable Development Goals Report 2020, 31.

[205] Note 113 of Chapter One.

[206] The text to note 104 states SDG Target 3.1.

[207] The text to note 136 specifies SDG Target 3.2.

[208] The text to note 166 states SDG Target 3.3.

[209] The text to note 195 specifies SDG Target 3.8.

[210] The WHO Framework Convention on Tobacco Control was adopted by the World Health Assembly on 21st May 2003, and came into force on 27th February 2005 ("About the WHO Framework Convention on Tobacco Control", World Health Organization, accessed September 8, 2020, https://www.who.int/fctc/about/en/). It aims to address the some of the causes of the tobacco epidemic, including complex determinants with cross-border effects,

> medicines for the communicable and non-communicable diseases that primarily affect developing countries, provide access to affordable essential medicines and vaccines … and … provide access to medicines for all[.] 3.c Substantially increase health financing and the recruitment, development, training and retention of the health workforce in developing countries … [.] 3.d Strengthen the capacity of all countries … for early warning, risk reduction and management of national and global health risks[.][211]

Regarding SDG Target 3.4, the probability of dying from cardiovascular disease, cancer, chronic respiratory disease or diabetes between the ages of 30 years and 70 years fell from 19% in 2010 to 18% in 2016.[212] With respect to SDG Targets 3.5 and 3.a, an estimated 8.1 million people died from a tobacco-related illness in 2017, and 38.6% of men and 8.5% of women worldwide smoked or chewed tobacco in 2018.[213] As regards SDG Target 3.9, air pollution in houses and immediate surroundings gave rise to 7 million deaths in 2016, and insufficient water, hygiene and sanitation resulted in 870,000 deaths in that year.[214]

Regarding SDG Target 3.b, global vaccination coverage among infants rose from 72% in 2000 to 85% in 2015, and to 86% in 2018 – although an estimated 19.4 million babies did not receive the critical vaccines during the first year of their lives.[215] In respect of SDG Target 3.c: (i) the proportion of the world's population spending more than 10% of their budgets to pay for health services rose continuously from 9.4% in 2000 to 12.7% in 2015,[216] (ii) 41% of medical doctors and 88% of nurses worldwide are women – based on data from 2013 to 2018,[217] and (iii) more than 40% of all countries employ fewer than ten medical doctors per

such as the liberalization of trade, tobacco advertising, and illegal trade in products made from tobacco (World Health Organization, The WHO Framework on Tobacco Control: an overview, January 2015 (Geneva, 2015), 1).

211 Resolution 70/1 adopted by the General Assembly on 25 September 2015, Transforming our world: the 2030 Agenda for Sustainable Development, 16-17.

212 Progress towards the Sustainable Development Goals: Report of the Secretary-General, E/2020/xxx, 7; The Sustainable Development Goals Report 2020, 29.

213 Progress towards the Sustainable Development Goals: Report of the Secretary-General, E/2020/xxx, 7.

214 Progress towards the Sustainable Development Goals: Report of the Secretary-General, E/2020/xxx, 7.

215 Progress towards the Sustainable Development Goals: Report of the Secretary-General, E/2020/xxx, 7.

216 Progress towards the Sustainable Development Goals: Report of the Secretary-General, E/2020/xxx, 7; The Sustainable Development Goals Report 2020, 31.

217 The Sustainable Development Goals Report 2020, 31.

10,000 people, and over 55% of countries have less than forty nurses and midwives per 10,000 people.[218] As regards SDG Target 3.d, 166 countries reported in 2019 on their readiness to detect, report on, and respond to, health emergencies by means of implementing the International Health Regulations;[219] steady progress was made from 2018 to 2019 in all the Regulations' core capacities – other than human resources in which the same level was retained.[220]

Will SDG 3 be achieved punctually?

The data in the foregoing subsection, together with those relating to SDG Targets 3.1,[221] 3.2,[222] 3.3[223] and 3.8,[224] tend to support the view that, although progress has been, and is being, made towards achievement of the targets of SDG 3, this headway is insufficient to make it probable that SDG 3[225] will be fulfilled punctually, i.e., by 31st December 2030.[226] Furthermore,

---

[218] The Sustainable Development Goals Report 2020, 31.

[219] The International Health Regulations have the following purpose and ambit: "to prevent, protect against, control and provide a public health response to the international spread of disease in ways that are commensurate with and restricted to public health risks, and which avoid unnecessary interference with international traffic and trade" (World Health Organization. International Health Regulations 2005, Second edition (Geneva, 2008), art.2).

[220] Progress towards the Sustainable Development Goals: Report of the Secretary-General, E/2020/xxx, 8; The Sustainable Development Goals Report 2020, 31.

[221] The subsection entitled 'Progress to date in the accomplishment of SDG Target 3.1', above in the current section (i.e., that titled 'SDG 3: Ensure Healthy Lives and Promote Well-Being'), contains data concerning SDG Target 3.1. The text to note 104 states SDG Target 3.1.

[222] The subsection entitled 'Progress to date in the accomplishment of SDG Target 3.2', above in the present section (i.e., that titled 'SDG 3: Ensure Healthy Lives and Promote Well-Being'), contains data on SDG Target 3.2. The text to note 136 specifies SDG Target 3.2.

[223] The subsection entitled 'Progress to date in the accomplishment of SDG Target 3.3', above in the current section (i.e., that titled 'SDG 3: Ensure Healthy Lives and Promote Well-Being'), contains data regarding SDG Target 3.3. The text to note 166 states SDG Target 3.3.

[224] The subsection entitled 'Progress to date in the accomplishment of SDG Target 3.8', above in the present section (i.e., that titled 'SDG 3: Ensure Healthy Lives and Promote Well-Being'), contains data concerning SDG Target 3.8. The text to note 195 specifies SDG Target 3.8.

[225] The text to note 205 states SDG 3.

[226] The target date for the SDGs to be met is 31st December 2030 (note 930 of Chapter Three and accompanying text).

the UN considers that, whilst advances continued in many areas of health until the close of 2019, the rate of progress has slowed down and will be insufficient to attain most of the targets of SDG 3.[227]

SDG 4: Ensure Quality Education and Promote Learning

MDG 2 and MDG Target 2.A

MDG 2 is to "[a]chieve universal primary education".[228] Its single target is MDG Target 2.A, which is to "[e]nsure that, by 2015, children everywhere, boys and girls alike, will be able to complete a full course of primary schooling.[229]

The adjusted net enrolment rate in primary education[230] in the developing regions rose from 80% in 1990 to 83% in 2000 and thence to 90% in 2007, with a projection of 91% for 2015.[231] Corresponding percentages for the developed regions in 1990, 2000 and 2015 are 96%, 97% and 96%, respectively.[232] Sub-Saharan Africa is the region with the lowest adjusted net enrolment rate in primary education, which increased from 52% in 1990 to 60% in 2000 and thence to 78% in 2012, with an estimate of 80% for 2015.[233]

The number of out-of-school children worldwide fell from 99.8 million in 2000 to 57.8 million in 2012, with most of these – 97.5 million in 2000 and 55.2 million in 2012 – being from the developing regions.[234] Approximately half of these absentees – 43.7 million in 2000 and 32.7 million in 2012 – were in Sub-Saharan Africa.[235]

Survey data from 72 countries that represented 86% of the population of low-income and middle-income countries suggests that the completion rate in primary education, as reported by youths of fourteen to sixteen

---

[227] Progress towards the Sustainable Development Goals: Report of the Secretary-General, E/2020/xxx, 5; The Sustainable Development Goals Report 2020, 28.
[228] Note 104 of Chapter One.
[229] Note 106 of Chapter One.
[230] The 'adjusted net enrolment rate in primary education' is "the number of pupils of the official age for primary education enrolled either in primary or secondary school, expressed as a percentage of the total population in that age group" (The Millennium Development Goals Report 2015, 24).
[231] The Millennium Development Goals Report 2015, 24-25.
[232] The Millennium Development Goals Report 2015, 24.
[233] The Millennium Development Goals Report 2015, 24-25.
[234] The Millennium Development Goals Report 2015, 25.
[235] The Millennium Development Goals Report 2015, 25.

years of age, increased from: (i) 43% in 1992 to 47% in 1999 and thence to 57% in 2008, for low-income countries, (ii) 65% in 1992 to 73% in 1999 and thence to 81% in 2008, for lower-middle-income countries, and (iii) 89% in 1992 to 95% in 1999 and thence to 96% in 2008, for upper-middle-income countries.[236] Survey data from 2007 to 2013 from 73 developing countries indicates that 34.4% of adolescents in the poorest quintile relinquished their primary-school education, whilst 6.5% of youths in the wealthiest quintile gave up this schooling.[237]

On the basis of these statistics, neither MDG 2[238] nor MDG Target 2.A[239] was met. Notwithstanding this, and in view of the fact that a threshold of 97% enrolment is often used to decide whether or not universal enrolment in primary school has been attained,[240] it is submitted that both MDG 2 and MDG Target 2.1 have proved to be essential in succeeding to focus attention in developing states on the need for their children of appropriate age to be in primary school – as attendance rates in these countries rise to approach those of such youngsters in advanced economies.

From MDG Target 2.A to SDG Target 4.1

SDG Target 4.1 is to "ensure that all girls and boys complete free, equitable and quality primary and secondary education leading to relevant and effective learning outcomes", by 2030.[241] This SDG Target follows on from MDG Target 2.A,[242] and enhances the latter in the following respects: (i) it emphases the 'universal' aspect of the education goal that is explicit in MDG 2[243] but not in MDG Target 2.A by referring to 'all girls and boys' – rather than to 'children everywhere, boys and girls alike', (ii) it adds secondary education, (iii) it qualifies 'primary and secondary education' with the descriptors 'free', 'equitable' and 'quality', which are all absent from MDG Target 2.A, and (iv) it requires the education to 'lead to relevant and effective learning outcomes', which is not demanded by

[236] The Millennium Development Goals Report 2015, 26.
[237] The Millennium Development Goals Report 2015, 26.
[238] The text to note 228 states MDG 2.
[239] The text to note 229 specifies MDG Target 2.A.
[240] The Millennium Development Goals Report 2015, 25.
[241] Note 107 of Chapter One.
[242] The text to note 229 states MDG Target 2.A.
[243] The text to note 228 specifies MDG 2.

MDG Target 2.A – obliging 'a full course of primary schooling' but no evaluation as to its result.[244]

Progress to date in the accomplishment of SDG Target 4.1

The global primary school completion rate rose from 70% in 2000 to 84% in 2018 and thence to 85% in 2019, and is forecast to reach 89% by 2030.[245] Data from 2014 to 2018 suggest that the richest quintile had a primary school completion rate of 78.5%, 96.5%, 98.0% and 99.5% in low-income, lower-middle-income, upper-middle-income and high-income countries, respectively, and that the poorest quintile had a primary school completion rate of 34.3%, 68.4%, 89.8% and 94.5% in those groupings, respectively.[246] Wealth-related disparities were also found in completion rates for lower secondary and upper secondary schools.[247] Parity between children or youths from the richest and poorest quintiles of the population was achieved in 25%, 21% and 1% of countries for primary, lower secondary and upper secondary education, respectively.[248]

Will SDG Target 4.1 be achieved punctually?

The statistics in the immediately-preceding subsection indicate that not all children complete primary education. As the Secretary-General of the UN predicts,[249] the rate of increase in the proportion of youngsters fulfilling their attendance requirements at primary school is such that the worldwide completion rate is likely to fall short of the universal completion which SDG Target 4.1 specifies is to be attained by 2030.[250] Therefore, it is probable that SDG Target 4.1 will not be met punctually.

---

244 Further to point (iv), it is submitted that learning outcomes are absent from MDG Target 2.A because this target does not mention secondary education – which leads either to employment or tertiary education and, therefore, includes public assessments in the later stage(s) of its curriculum.

245 Progress towards the Sustainable Development Goals: Report of the Secretary-General, E/2020/xxx, 8; The Sustainable Development Goals Report 2020, 32.

246 The Sustainable Development Goals Report 2020, 32.

247 The Sustainable Development Goals Report 2020, 32.

248 Progress towards the Sustainable Development Goals: Report of the Secretary-General, E/2020/xxx, 8.

249 Text to note 245.

250 The text to note 241 states SDG Target 4.1.

From MDG Target 3.A to SDG Target 4.5

MDG Target 3.A is to "Eliminate gender disparity in primary and secondary education, preferably by 2005, and in all levels of education no later than 2015".[251] This translates to a gender parity index – the ratio of the gross enrolment ratio for girls to that of boys for each level of education – of between 0.97 and 1.03,[252] which – on the basis of projected figures for 2015[253] – is achieved: (i) in the Caucasus and Central Asia, East Asia, Latin America and the Caribbean, South Asia, and South-East Asia for primary education, (ii) in the Caucasus and Central Asia, East Asia, North Africa, South Asia, and South-East Asia for secondary education, and (iii) in West Asia for tertiary education.[254]

SDG Target 4.5 is to "eliminate gender disparities in education and ensure equal access to all levels of education and vocational training for the vulnerable, including persons with disabilities, indigenous peoples and children in vulnerable situations", by 2030.[255] This SDG Target is a progression from MDG Target 3.A, as both require gender parity in education whilst the former adds an objective to ensure equal access to education and vocational training for people in vulnerable circumstances as that enjoyed by the majority of the population.

Progress to date in accomplishment of SDG Target 4.5

Approximately 5.5 million more girls than boys of primary school age were out of school in 2018.[256] The disadvantage that girls face in comparison with boys is more pronounced in Sub-Saharan Africa, were 128 girls for every 100 boys were out of school in 2018.[257]

Disrupted education that the closure of schools – to halt the spread of COVID-19 – has caused, is adversely affecting both learning outcomes and social and behavioural development of youths and children.[258] Even though many schools are offering remote learning to pupils through virtual classrooms to lessen the impact of these closures, children and adolescents

[251] Note 110 of Chapter One.
[252] The Millennium Development Goals Report 2015, 28.
[253] The Millennium Development Goals Report 2015, 28.
[254] The Millennium Development Goals Report 2015, 29.
[255] Note 111 of Chapter One.
[256] The Sustainable Development Goals Report 2020, 32.
[257] The Sustainable Development Goals Report 2020, 32.
[258] Progress towards the Sustainable Development Goals: Report of the Secretary-General, E/2020/xxx, 8; The Sustainable Development Goals Report 2020, 32.

in vulnerable and disadvantaged communities – such as those living in extreme poverty, fragile countries, refugee camps and remote areas – may have neither a computer, nor significant computer-related skills, nor access to the Internet at home.[259] In 2019, about 87% of households in Europe – in general a more prosperous continent than Africa – had access to the Internet at home, compared with 18% of families in Africa.[260] 78% of families in Europe owned a computer in 2019, whilst 11% of households in Africa possessed one.[261]

The limited information in the current subsection suggests that both the 'gender parity' goal and the 'equal access for the vulnerable' objective of SDG Target 4.5[262] are progressing slowly or not at all. The impact of COVID-19 is a factor in the poor performance-to-date regarding this SDG Target, which was unforeseeable when this target was introduced.

Will SDG Target 4.5 be achieved punctually?

Further to the foregoing subsection, it is unlikely that SDG Target 4.5 will be met punctually, i.e., by 31st December 2030.[263] It is submitted that the UN, the WHO and other relevant parties will need to bring COVID-19 under strict control globally – in order that schools and colleges are able to remain open, for there to be a chance of approaching punctual realization of this SDG Target.

Progress to date in accomplishment of SDG 4 as a whole

SDG4 is to "[e]nsure inclusive and equitable quality education and promote lifelong learning opportunities for all".[264] Except for SDG Targets 4.1[265] and 4.5,[266] the targets of SDG 4 are compressed as follows.

> 4.2 By 2030, ensure that all girls and boys have access to quality early childhood development, care and pre-primary education … [.] 4.3 By

---

[259] Progress towards the Sustainable Development Goals: Report of the Secretary-General, E/2020/xxx, 8; The Sustainable Development Goals Report 2020, 33.
[260] The Sustainable Development Goals Report 2020, 33.
[261] The Sustainable Development Goals Report 2020, 33.
[262] The text to note 255 specifies SDG Target 4.5.
[263] The target date for the SDGs to be fulfilled is 31st December 2030 (note 930 of Chapter Three and accompanying text).
[264] Note 105 of Chapter One.
[265] The text to note 241 states SDG Target 4.1.
[266] The text to note 255 specifies SDG Target 4.5.

> 2030, ensure equal access for all women and men to affordable and quality technical, vocational and tertiary education, including university[.] 4.4 By 2030, substantially increase the number of youth and adults who have relevant skills … for employment, decent jobs and entrepreneurship[.] … 4.6 By 2030, ensure that all youth and a substantial proportion of adults, both men and women, achieve literacy and numeracy[.] 4.7 By 2030, ensure that all learners acquire the knowledge and skills needed to promote sustainable development … [.] 4.a Build and upgrade education facilities that are child, disability and gender sensitive and provide safe, non-violent, inclusive and effective learning environments for all[.] 4.b By 2020, substantially expand globally the number of scholarships available to developing countries … for enrolment in higher education … in developed countries and other developing countries[.] 4.c By 2030, substantially increase the supply of qualified teachers … [.][267]

Regarding SDG Target 4.2: (i) in 74 countries whose data are comparable for the period 2011 to 2019, about seven in ten infants of three or four years of age were on track in at least three of the following four developmental domains: learning, literacy-numeracy, physical development and social-emotional development, and (ii) participation worldwide in organized learning one year prior to the official entry age to primary school increased steadily from 62% in 2010 to 67% in 2017, with a large variation between countries ranging from 9% to almost 100%.[268] With respect to SDG Target 4.6: (i) in 2018, approximately 773 million adults globally – two-thirds of whom are women – could neither read nor write, (ii) almost half of the world's illiterate population live in South Asia, and a quarter of these people reside in Sub-Saharan Africa, and (iii) in 2018, the worldwide adult literacy rate was 86% and the global youth literacy rate was 92%.[269]

As regards SDG Target 4.a: (i) in 2019, fewer than one-half of primary and lower secondary schools in Sub-Saharan Africa had access to basic handwashing facilities, electricity, computers, and the Internet,[270] (ii) data from 2016 to 2018 suggest that, globally, only 65% of primary schools, 71% of lower secondary schools, and 76% of upper secondary schools

---

[267] Resolution 70/1 adopted by the General Assembly on 25 September 2015, Transforming our world: the 2030 Agenda for Sustainable Development, 17.

[268] Progress towards the Sustainable Development Goals: Report of the Secretary-General, E/2020/xxx, 8.

[269] Progress towards the Sustainable Development Goals: Report of the Secretary-General, E/2020/xxx, 8-9.

[270] Progress towards the Sustainable Development Goals: Report of the Secretary-General, E/2020/xxx, 9.

have basic handwashing facilities,[271] and (iii) these data indicate that 85%, 89%, 74% and 61% of upper secondary schools throughout the world have access to drinking water, electricity, computers, and the Internet, respectively.[272] In respect of SDG Target 4.b, ODA for scholarships rose from USD 1.3 billion in 2017 to USD 1.6 billion in 2018.[273] Regarding SDG Target 4.c, data from 129 countries suggest that, from 2015, 85% of primary school teachers worldwide are recorded as having received the minimum pedagogical training under national standards – with Sub-Saharan Africa and South Asia at 64% and 72%, respectively.[274]

Will SDG 4 be achieved punctually?

Whilst the information in the immediately-preceding subsection concerning progress in respect of SDG Targets 4.2[275] and, especially, 4.b,[276] is encouraging, it is submitted that the statistics in that subsection – together with the data concerning headway as to SDG Targets 4.1[277] and 4.5,[278] suggest that advancement is needed regarding the targets of SDG 4[279] taken as a whole, in order for fulfilment of SDG 4 to be within reach. *The Sustainable Development Goals Report 2020* states: "Despite progress, the world is not on track to meet 2030 education targets."[280] It is submitted that this view is correct – especially in the light of the adverse effect of

271 The Sustainable Development Goals Report 2020, 33.
272 The Sustainable Development Goals Report 2020, 33.
273 Progress towards the Sustainable Development Goals: Report of the Secretary-General, E/2020/xxx, 9.
274 Progress towards the Sustainable Development Goals: Report of the Secretary-General, E/2020/xxx, 9; The Sustainable Development Goals Report 2020, 33.
275 Text to note 268. The text to note 267 condenses SDG Target 4.2.
276 Text to note 273. The text to note 267 abridges SDG Target 4.b.
277 The subsection entitled 'Progress to date in the accomplishment of SDG Target 4.1', above in the current section (i.e., that titled 'SDG 4: Ensure Quality Education and Promote Learning'), contains data on SDG Target 4.1. The text to note 241 states SDG Target 4.1.
278 The subsection entitled 'Progress to date in the accomplishment of SDG Target 4.5', above in the present section (i.e., that titled 'SDG 4: Ensure Quality Education and Promote Learning'), contains data concerning SDG Target 4.5. The text to note 255 specifies SDG Target 4.5.
279 The text to note 264 states SDG 4.
280 The Sustainable Development Goals Report 2020, 32.

COVID-19 on education, schools and colleges. It is unlikely that SDG 4 will be met by 31st December 2030.[281]

SDG 5: Achieve Gender Equality and Empower Women

MDG 5 and MDG Target 5.B

MDG 5 is to "[i]mprove maternal health".[282] It is commented above that neither of the two targets of MDG 5 – i.e., MDG Targets 5.A[283] and 5.B – were met and, that the progress made was insufficient to fulfil this Goal.[284] MDG Target 5.B is to "[a]chieve, by 2015, universal access to reproductive health".[285]

From MDG Target 5.B to SDG Target 5.6

SDG Target 5.6 is to "[e]nsure universal access to sexual and reproductive health and reproductive rights as agreed in accordance with the Programme of Action of the International Conference on Population and Development[286] and the Beijing Platform for Action[287] and the outcome

---

[281] The target date for the SDGs to be accomplished is 31st December 2030 (note 930 of Chapter Three and accompanying text).

[282] Text to note 97.

[283] Text to note 98.

[284] Text to notes 100 and 101, and the sentence that follows the text to note 101.

[285] Text to note 99.

[286] The Programme of Action of the International Conference on Population and Development was adopted at the International Conference on Population and Development, which was held in Cairo from 5th September 1994 to 13th September 1994 (United Nations, Report of the International Conference on Population and Development, Cairo, 5-13 September 1994 (New York, 1995), 1). Paragraph 7.6 of the Programme of Action states: "All countries should strive to make accessible through the primary health-care system, reproductive health to all individuals of appropriate ages as soon as possible and no later than the year 2015. …" (Report of the International Conference on Population and Development, 41).

[287] The Beijing Platform for Action was adopted at the Fourth World Conference on Women, which took place in Beijing from 4th September 1995 to 15th September 1995 (United Nations, Beijing Declaration and Platform for Action, The Fourth World Conference on Women, 4-15 September 1994 (Beijing, 1995), 1). Paragraph 106(a) of the Beijing Platform for Action requires governments to: "[s]upport and implement the commitments made in the Programme of Action of the International Conference on Population and Development" (Beijing Declaration and Platform for Action, 38). Paragraph 106(i) of the Beijing Platform

documents of their review conferences".[288] This SDG Target matches MDG Target 5.B[289] in aiming for universal access to reproductive health. Furthermore, SDG Target 5.6 extends the scope of MDG Target 5.B by: (i) seeking universal access to sexual health – in so far as 'sexual and reproductive health' is a broader concept than 'reproductive health', and (ii) pursuing universal access to reproductive rights. It is submitted that SDG Target 5.6 mentions the Programme of Action of the International Conference on Population and Development and the Beijing Plan of Action in order to: (i) offer guidance on what the universal access to reproductive health, sexual health, and reproductive rights should include, and (ii) provide consistency with previous work of the UN System and its partnering organizations over the area of reproductive health.

Progress to date in the accomplishment of SDG Target 5.6

Data from 75 countries suggested that, in 2019, states had enacted: (i) 73% of the laws and regulations that are necessary to guarantee full and equal access to sexual and reproductive health and rights, (ii) 87% of the laws and regulations which are needed for HIV counselling and testing services, (iii) 91% of the laws and regulations that are required for HIV treatment and care services, (iv) 96% of the laws and regulations which are necessary for HIV confidentiality, and (v) 79% of the laws and regulations that provide for full, free and informed consent of any individual before (s)he receives contraceptive services.[290] A global aggregation of data from 2007 to 2018 from 57 countries indicated that 55%, 75%, 91% and 75% of women of 15 to 49 years of age make their own decisions regarding sexual and reproductive health and rights, whether or not to have sexual intercourse, on the use of contraception, and concerning their own healthcare, respectively.[291]

---

for Action calls for governments to: "[s]trengthen and reorient health services, particularly primary health care, in order to ensure universal access to quality health services for women and girls" (Beijing Declaration and Platform for Action, 39).

288 Note 122 of Chapter One.

289 The text to note 285 specifies MDG Target 5.B.

290 The Sustainable Development Goals Report 2020, 35.

291 The Sustainable Development Goals Report 2020, 35.

Will SDG Target 5.6 be achieved punctually?

On the basis of the finite quantity of statistics that the foregoing subsection contains, there is a reasonable likelihood that most or even all countries will provide their female citizens with full and equal access to sexual and reproductive health and to reproductive rights – in accordance with SDG Target 5.6[292] – by 31st December 2030.[293] Thus, it is realistic to anticipate that this SDG Target will be attained punctually.

MDG 3

MDG 3 is to "[p]romote gender equality and empower women".[294] It has one target – MDG Target 3.A,[295] which concerns the elimination of gender disparity in education and is considered in relation to SDG Target 4.5.[296]

Dimensions of MDG 3 other than gender parity in education include the following. *Women's access to paid employment:* The global proportion of women in wage employment outside the agricultural sector rose from 35% in 1990 to 38% in 2000, and thence to a projected 41% in 2015.[297] *Women's political representation:* From data on 174 countries that are available for the period 1995 to 2005, the worldwide average proportion of women in national parliaments increased from 11% in 1995 to 14% in 2000, and thence to an estimated 22% in 2015.[298]

Whilst considerable progress has been made towards women's and girls' equality with men and boys, respectively, in education, employment and political representation since 1995, imbalances between males and females persist in areas that the MDGs did not address, such as violence against women and girls,[299] the unequal division of unpaid care and domestic work,[300] and women's differing participation to men in public[301]

---

[292] The text to note 288 states SDG Target 5.6.

[293] The target date for the SDGs to be realized is 31st December 2030 (note 930 of Chapter Three and accompanying text).

[294] Note 108 of Chapter One.

[295] The text to note 251 specifies MDG Target 3.A.

[296] The subsection entitled 'From MDG Target 3.A to SDG Target 4.5', in the section above titled 'SDG 4: Ensure Quality Education and Promote Learning', provides: (i) information concerning gender parity in education and the extent to which MDG Target 3.A has been met, and (ii) comment regarding the relationship between MDG Target 3.A and SDG Target 4.5.

[297] The Millennium Development Goals Report 2015, 30.

[298] The Millennium Development Goals Report 2015, 31.

[299] SDG Target 5.2 addresses this matter (text to note 313).

[300] SDG Target 5.4 attends to this issue (text to note 314).

and private decision-making.[302] On the basis of this view, the statistics in the immediately-preceding paragraph, the information given on gender parity in education and the extent to which MDG Target 3.A has been attained,[303] and a literal interpretation[304] of the *prima facie*[305] requirements of MDG 3,[306] MDG 3 has largely been accomplished.

From MDG 3 to SDG 5

SDG 5 is to "[a]chieve gender equality and empower all women and girls".[307] This SDG progresses from MDG 3,[308] as follows: (i) the standard, and the level of difficulty in meeting the first part of the Goal, are both raised by changing the verb from '*promote*[309] gender equality' in MDG 3 to '*achieve* gender equality' in SDG 5, and (ii) the scope of the second part of the Goal is widened by changing the object of the verb 'empower'[310] from 'women' in MDG 3 to "*all* women *and girls*" in SDG 5 – which, if read as 'all women and *all* girls" rather than "all women and

---

301 SDG Target 5.5 focuses on women's participation in public decision-making (text to note 315).

302 The Millennium Development Goals Report 2015, 31.

303 Point (i) in note 296 specifies the location in the text of this information.

304 Note 59 explains the concept of a 'literal interpretation', as applied to MDG 1.

305 Note 59 defines the phrase '*prima facie*'.

306 MDG 3 is to "*[p]romote* gender equality and *empower* women" (text to note 294; emphasis added). 'Promote' – in this sense of the word – means "further the progress of (something, especially a cause, venture or aim); support or actively encourage" (*The New Oxford Dictionary of English*, 1484). 'Empower' – in this sense of the word – means "make (someone) stronger and more confident, especially in controlling their life and claiming their rights" (*The New Oxford Dictionary of English*, 605). It is submitted that the UN and other stakeholders furthered the progress of gender equality – for instance, by encouraging a rise in the percentage of women in national parliaments (text to note 298) and helped women to claim their rights – for example, by backing an increase in the percentage of women in paid employment (i.e., the right to work – which is enshrined in Article 23(1) of the UDHR, i.e., "Everyone has the right to work, to free choice of employment, to just and favourable conditions of work and to protection against unemployment." (United Nations, Universal Declaration of Human Rights (Paris, 1948), art.23(1)). *In this literal sense*, these entities successfully achieved MDG 3.

307 Note 109 of Chapter One.

308 The text to note 294 states MDG 3.

309 Note 306 defines 'promote'.

310 Note 306 defines 'empower'.

some girls", is a *much* more demanding requirement than the second element of MDG 3.[311]

Areas of gender inequality and empowerment of women that MDG 3 did not, in practice, see to[312] include: (i) violence against women and girls, which SDG Target 5.2 addresses: "Eliminate all forms of violence against all women and girls in the public and private spheres, including trafficking and sexual and other types of exploitation",[313] (ii) the uneven division between men and women of unsalaried care and domestic work, which SDG Target 5.4 attends to: "Recognize and value unpaid care and domestic work through the provision of public services, infrastructure and social protection policies and the promotion of shared responsibility within the household and the family as nationally appropriate",[314] and (iii) the lesser extent of women's participation in decision-making than that of men, the public aspect of which SDG Target 5.5 confronts: "Ensure women's full and effective participation and equal opportunities for leadership at all levels of decision-making in political, economic and public life".[315]

Progress in the accomplishment of SDG 5 as a whole

Bar SDG Targets 5.2,[316] 5.4,[317] 5.5[318] and 5.6,[319] the targets of SDG 5[320] are abbreviated as follows:

> 5.1 End all forms of discrimination against all women and girls everywhere[.] … 5.3 Eliminate all harmful practices [against women and girls.] … 5.a Undertake reforms to give women equal rights to economic

[311] To empower all women and some girls is a more demanding requirement than to empower women – i.e., the second part of MDG 3, but a less demanding requirement than to empower all women and all girls.
[312] The text to note 299 states that the MDGs did not address these areas of imbalance between the sexes.
[313] Resolution 70/1 adopted by the General Assembly on 25 September 2015, Transforming our world: the 2030 Agenda for Sustainable Development, 18.
[314] Resolution 70/1 adopted by the General Assembly on 25 September 2015, Transforming our world: the 2030 Agenda for Sustainable Development, 18.
[315] Resolution 70/1 adopted by the General Assembly on 25 September 2015, Transforming our world: the 2030 Agenda for Sustainable Development, 18.
[316] The text to note 313 specifies SDG Target 5.2.
[317] The text to note 314 states SDG Target 5.4.
[318] The text to note 315 specifies SDG Target 5.5.
[319] The text to note 288 states SDG Target 5.6.
[320] The text to note 307 specifies SDG 5.

> resources, as well as access to ownership and control over … property, financial services, inheritance and national resources, in accordance with national laws[.] 5.b Enhance the use of enabling technology … to promote the empowerment of women[.] 5.c Adopt and strengthen sound policies and enforceable legislation for the promotion of gender equality and the empowerment of all women and girls at all levels[.][321]

Regarding SDG Target 5.2, surveys carried out between 2005 and 2017 in 106 countries disclosed that 18% of ever-partnered girls and women between 15 and 49 years of age had experienced physical and sexual violence by a current or former close partner in the year immediately prior to the conduct of the relevant survey.[322] In respect of SDG Target 5.3: (i) the latest-available data from 91 countries from women of 20 to 24 years of age collected during the period 2013 to 2019 showed that 20.2% of these people were married or in partnership before the age of 18 years, compared with 23.8% from an analogous population of women ten years' earlier,[323] and (ii) at least 200 million girls and women have suffered female genital mutilation, based on recent data from 31 countries in which this malpractice is concentrated.[324]

As regards SDG Target 5.4, the latest-available data from 2001 to 2018 from 89 countries and areas revealed that, on an average day, women spent approximately three times as many hours on unpaid care and domestic work as men – with a small decline in the time spent by the former on these tasks compared with that spent by the latter.[325] With respect to SDG Target 5.5: (i) on 1st January 2020, women's representation in the either unicameral, or the lower chamber of bicameral, national parliaments was 24.9%, compared with 22.3% in 2015,[326] (ii) data from 133 countries and areas suggest that women hold 36.3% of elected seats in local deliberative entities,[327] and (iii) in 2019, women constituted 39% of the world's working population but only 28% of its managerial positions – up from 25% in 2000.[328] Regarding SDG Target 5.b, data from 2016 to 2018 from

---

[321] Resolution 70/1 adopted by the General Assembly on 25 September 2015, Transforming our world: the 2030 Agenda for Sustainable Development, 18.

[322] The Sustainable Development Goals Report 2020, 34.

[323] The Sustainable Development Goals Report 2020, 34.

[324] Progress towards the Sustainable Development Goals: Report of the Secretary-General, E/2020/xxx, 9; The Sustainable Development Goals Report 2020, 34.

[325] The Sustainable Development Goals Report 2020, 35.

[326] Progress towards the Sustainable Development Goals: Report of the Secretary-General, E/2020/xxx, 9; The Sustainable Development Goals Report 2020, 35.

[327] The Sustainable Development Goals Report 2020, 35.

[328] The Sustainable Development Goals Report 2020, 35.

66 countries recorded women's ownership of mobile telephones as being 6.8% less than that of men, on average.[329]

Will SDG 5 be achieved punctually?

There are areas over which females are strongly underrepresented relative to males – for instance three times as many men sit in national parliaments as do women, with this ratio changing in favour of the latter but not at a sufficient rate to reach parity of representation there by 31st December 2030.[330] Therefore, notwithstanding the favourable opinion given in respect of the possibility of timely attainment of SDG Target 5.6,[331] it is improbable that SDG 5 – the first part of which requires gender equality to be achieved[332] – will be punctually accomplished.

SDG 6: Ensure Availability of Water and Sanitation

MDG 7 and MDG Targets 7.A, 7.B and 7.C

MDG 7 is to "[e]nsure environmental sustainability".[333] It comprises four targets – MDG Targets 7.A, 7.B, 7.C and 7.D – the first three of which map to targets of SDG 6,[334] which is to "[e]nsure availability and sustainable management of water and sanitation for all".[335]

MDG Target 7.A is to "[i]ntegrate the principles of sustainable development into country policies and programmes and reverse the loss of environmental resources".[336] *Sustainable forest management:* The net loss

---

[329] Progress towards the Sustainable Development Goals: Report of the Secretary-General, E/2020/xxx, 10; The Sustainable Development Goals Report 2020, 34.

[330] Text to note 326. The target date for the SDGs to be attained is 31st December 2030 (note 930 of Chapter Three and accompanying text).

[331] This view is presented in the subsection titled 'Will SDG Target 5.6 be achieved punctually?', above in the present section (i.e., that titled 'SDG 5: Achieve Gender Equality and Empower Women'). The text to note 288 states SDG Target 5.6.

[332] SDG 5 is to "[a]chieve gender equality and empower all women and girls" (text to note 307).

[333] Note 132 of Chapter One.

[334] MDG 7 maps to SDG 6, MDG Target 7.A maps to SDG Target 6.4, MDG Target 7.B maps to SDG Target 6.6, and MDG Target 7.C maps to SDG Targets 6.1 and 6.2 (text to notes 27-30; text to notes 132, 133, 137, 138, 145, 146, 152, 153 and 154 of Chapter One).

[335] Note 133 of Chapter One.

[336] Note 137 of Chapter One.

in global forest area reduced from 8.3 billion hectares annually in the 1990s to an estimated 5.2 million hectares annually in the 2000s.[337] The total stock of carbon held in forest biomass decreased by an estimated 0.5 gigatonnes each year from 2005 to 2010 – mainly due to a diminution in forest area worldwide.[338] *Emissions of carbon dioxide:* Whilst emissions of carbon dioxide in the developed regions fell from 14.9 billion tonnes in 1990 to 13.9 billion tonnes in 2000 and are estimated to be 13.1 billion tonnes in 2012, such discharges rose in the developing regions from 6.7 billion tonnes in 1990 to 9.9 billion tonnes and are estimated to be 19.8 billion tonnes in 2012.[339] As a consequence of the acceleration in the rate of emissions of carbon dioxide, the increase in global emissions has also speeded up – rising by 10% from 1990, when they were 21.6 billion tonnes, i.e., 14.9 billion tonnes plus 6.7 billion tonnes, to 2000, when they were 23.8 billion tonnes, i.e., 13.9 billion tonnes plus 9.9 billion tonnes, and increasing by 38% from 2000 to 2012.[340] *The ozone layer:* The Montreal Protocol on Substances that Deplete the Ozone Layer was adopted on 16th September 1987,[341] and has been ratified by all 193 Member States of the UN,[342] plus the Cook Islands, the European Union, the Holy See, Niue, and the State of Palestine.[343] By 2015, 197 parties[344]

---

337 The Millennium Development Goals Report 2015, 52.

338 The Millennium Development Goals Report 2015, 52.

339 The Millennium Development Goals Report 2015, 53.

340 The Millennium Development Goals Report 2015, 53. The estimated figures in *The Millennium Development Goals Report 2015* for global emissions of carbon dioxide in 2012 do not match exactly. This may due to rounding errors. The 'World' amount is 33.0 billion tonnes, whilst the total of the numbers for the developed regions (13.1 billion tonnes) and the developing regions (19.8 billion tones) is 32.9 billion tonnes. The percentage increase in worldwide emissions from 2000 to 2012 is 38.7% to three significant figures, i.e., [((33.0 billion tonnes – 23.8 billion tonnes) / 23.8 billion tonnes) * 100%], when the estimate for 2012 is 33.0 billion tonnes of carbon dioxide; it is 38.2% to three significant figures, i.e., [((32.9 billion tonnes – 23.8 billion tonnes) / 23.8 billion tonnes) * 100%], when the estimate for 2012 is 32.9 billion tonnes carbon dioxide (The Millennium Development Goals Report 2015, 53).

341 "The Montreal Protocol on Substances that Deplete the Ozone Layer – Article 20: Authentic Texts", United Nations Environment Programme, accessed September 11, 2020, https://ozone.unep.org/treaties/montreal-protocol/articles/article-20-authentic-texts.

342 Note 226 of Chapter Three and accompanying text.

343 "Chapter XXVII Environment: 2. a Montreal Protocol on Substances that Deplete the Ozone Layer", United Nations Treaty Collection, accessed September 11, 2020,

had phase out 98% of all significant ozone-depleting substances that were present in 1990.[345] *Marine fish stocks:* The percentage of global marine fish stocks within safe biological limits decreased from 90% in 1974 to 71% in 2011, resulting in worldwide fish stocks being below the level at which they are able to supply maximum sustainable yields.[346] The total marine catch across the world fell from a peak of 88 million tonnes in 1996 to about 82 million tonnes in 2013.[347] *Water stress and water scarcity:* At present, agriculture uses 69% of the fresh water withdrawn globally – mostly for irrigation, industries 19% of such water, and municipalities 12%.[348] Whilst agriculture, industries and municipalities together withdraw 9% of renewable freshwater resources worldwide in 2011 – which is below the 25% threshold that defines the start of physical water stress,[349] 41 countries experienced water stress or water scarcity,[350] which is up from 36 countries in 1998.[351] *Has MDG Target 7.A been achieved?:* On the basis of these statistics, it is submitted that the first part of MDG Target 7.A, i.e., 'integrate the principles of sustainable development into country policies and programmes', has not been met, and that the second part of MDG Target 7.A, i.e., 'reverse the loss of environmental resources', has been partially fulfilled – in particular by

---

https://treaties.un.org/pages/ViewDetails.aspx?src=TREATY&mtdsg_no=XXVII-2-a&chapter=27&lang=en.

344 The State of Palestine was the 198th party to ratify the Montreal Protocol on Substances that Deplete the Ozone Layer, and did so on 18th March 2019 ("Chapter XXVII Environment: 2. a Montreal Protocol on Substances that Deplete the Ozone Layer", United Nations Treaty Collection, accessed September 11, 2020, https://treaties.un.org/pages/ViewDetails.aspx?src=TREATY&mtdsg_no=XXVII-2-a&chapter=27&lang=en).

345 The Millennium Development Goals Report 2015, 54.

346 The Millennium Development Goals Report 2015, 54. Nevertheless, successes have been reported in rebuilding overfished stocks, especially in Europe, Oceania and North America (The Millennium Development Goals Report 2015, 55).

347 The Millennium Development Goals Report 2015, 55.

348 The Millennium Development Goals Report 2015, 55.

349 Water stress and water scarcity can be *physical* – insufficient water of adequate quality, *economic* – lack of satisfactory infrastructure, or *institutional* – shortage of institutions for a dependable, safe and equitable supply of water (The Millennium Development Goals Report 2015, 55).

350 Ten of these countries – located in Arabia, Central Asia or North Africa – withdrew more than 100% of renewable freshwater resources, thereby depleting their renewable groundwater resources (The Millennium Development Goals Report 2015, 55).

351 The Millennium Development Goals Report 2015, 55.

countries' action under the Montreal Protocol on Substances that Deplete the Ozone Layer to discontinue the use of ozone-depleting substances.[352]

MDG Target 7.B is to "[r]educe biodiversity loss, achieving, by 2010, a significant reduction in the rate of loss".[353] *Terrestrial and marine protected areas:*[354] In 2014, 15.2% of the world's terrestrial and inland water areas – up from 8.7% in 1990 and 11.8% in 2000 – and 8.4% of its coastal marine areas – the sea from 0 to 200 nautical miles from the shore – were protected, whilst 0.25% of thalassic areas beyond 200 nautical miles were safeguarded.[355] *Risk of extinction:* 26% of 5,500 species of mammals, 13% of 10,400 species of birds, 41% of 6,000 species of amphibians, 33% of 845 species of reef-building corals, and 63% of 340 species of cycads, are endangered – with the extinction risk of reef-building corals rising the quickest of these classes (mammals, birds and amphibians)[356] or orders (stony corals – some of whose families are reef-building corals,[357] and cycadales[358]).[359] *Has MDG Target 7.B been achieved?:* It is opined that, on the basis of the limited information that this paragraph furnishes, MDG Target 7.B has not been accomplished.

MDG Target 7.C is to "[h]alve, by 2015, the proportion of people without sustainable access to safe drinking water and basic sanitation".[360] *Safe drinking water:* Between 1990 and 2015, the proportion of the worldwide population using an improved source of drinking water rose from 76% to a projected 91% – surpassing the objective in the first part of MDG Target 7.C, i.e., to halve the proportion of people without sustainable access to safe drinking water – which was attained in 2010.[361] *Basic sanitation:* Between 1990 and 2015, the proportion of the global population employing an improved sanitation facility increased from 54%

---

352 Text to notes 343 and 345.

353 Note 145 of Chapter One.

354 These zones "help to prevent loss of biodiversity, maintain food security and water supplies, strengthen climate resilience and improve human health and well-being" (The Millennium Development Goals Report 2015, 56).

355 The Millennium Development Goals Report 2015, 56.

356 "Animal Classification", A-Z Animals, accessed September 12, 2020, https://a-z-animals.com/reference/animal-classification/.

357 "Scleractinia", Wikipedia, accessed September 12, 2020, https://en.wikipedia.org/wiki/Scleractinia.

358 "Cycad", Wikipedia, accessed September 12, 2020, https://en.wikipedia.org/wiki/Cycad; "Cycadales", Wikipedia, accessed September 12, 2020, https://en.wikipedia.org/wiki/Cycadales.

359 The Millennium Development Goals Report 2015, 57.

360 Note 152 of Chapter One.

361 The Millennium Development Goals Report 2015, 58.

to a projected 68% – underreaching the aim in the second part of MDG Target 7.C, i.e., to halve the proportion of people without access to basic sanitation.[362] Notwithstanding this, the Caucasus and Central Asia, East Asia, North Africa, and West Asia achieved this goal; the developed regions, Latin America and the Caribbean, and South-East Asia missed it by a slim margin.[363] *Has MDG Target 7.C been achieved?:* The aim in the first part of MDG Target 7.C was met in 2010.[364] The objective in the second part of MDG Target 7.C was not attained,[365] but four developing regions – three of these in Asia – accomplished it.[366]

MDG Target 7.D is "to have achieved a significant improvement in the lives of at least 100 million slum dwellers", by 2020.[367] Between 2000 and 2014, more than 320 million individuals gained access to improved water, improved sanitation, durable housing or more spacious conditions for housing.[368] Thus, MDG Target 7.D was met.[369]

As MDG Target 7.B was not fulfilled,[370] MDG Target 7.A was attained only in small part,[371] MDG Target 7.C was moderately realized,[372] and MDG Target 7.D was satisfied,[373] MDG 7[374] was not met. The application of a literal interpretation[375] to the *prima facie*[376] requirements of MDG 7 supports the view that this Goal was not achieved.[377]

---

362 The Millennium Development Goals Report 2015, 59.
363 The Millennium Development Goals Report 2015, 59.
364 Text to note 361.
365 Text to note 362.
366 Text to note 363.
367 Note 155 of Chapter One.
368 The Millennium Development Goals Report 2015, 60.
369 The Millennium Development Goals Report 2015, 60. Whilst the proportion of the urban population in the developing regions living in slums decreased from 39% in 2000 to 30% in 2014, the number of urban residents living in slums is estimated to be 880 million residents – which is up from 792 million urban residents in 2000 and 689 million urban residents in 1990 (The Millennium Development Goals Report 2015, 60).
370 The sentence immediately-following the text to note 359 opines that MDG Target 7.B has not been achieved.
371 Text to note 352.
372 Text to notes 364, 365 and 366.
373 Text to note 369.
374 The text to note 333 states MDG 7.
375 Note 59 explains the concept of a 'literal interpretation', as applied to MDG 1.
376 Note 59 defines the phrase '*prima facie*'.
377 MDG 7 is to "*[e]nsure* environmental sustainability" (text to note 333; emphasis added). 'Ensure' – in this sense of the word – means "make certain that (something) will occur or be the case" (*The New Oxford Dictionary of English*,

From MDG Target 7.C to SDG Targets 6.1 and 6.2

SDG Target 6.1 is to "achieve universal and equitable access to safe and affordable drinking water for all" by 2030.[378] SDG Target 6.2 is to "achieve access to adequate and equitable sanitation and hygiene for all and end open defecation, paying special attention to the needs of women and girls and those in vulnerable situations", by 2030.[379]

The first part of MDG Target 7.C,[380] i.e., to 'halve the proportion of people without sustainable access to safe drinking water', extends and expands into SDG Target 6.1. The 'extension' is the progression from halving the proportion of people without access to safe drinking water, to achieving universal access to safe drinking water. The 'expansion' is the replacement of the descriptor 'sustainable' in MDG Target 7.C with the descriptors 'universal', 'equitable', 'affordable' and 'for all' in SDG Target 6.2 – although 'universal' and 'for all' convey the same meaning, making the inclusion therein of the word 'for all' tautologous.[381]

The second part of MDG Target 7.C, i.e., to 'halve the proportion of people without sustainable access to basic sanitation' extends and expands into SDG Target 6.2. The 'extension' is the advancement from halving the proportion of people without access to sanitation, to attaining access to

---

614). Thus, MDG 7 aims to make certain that environmental sustainability will occur. It is submitted that, although progress regarding the targets of MDG 7 includes making certain that sustainment of some aspects of the environment – for instance the ozone layer (text to note 345) – will occur, it has not satisfactorily made certain that sustainment of other dimensions of the environment – such as the availability of fresh water (text to note 351) – will happen. Therefore, it is submitted that, although the UN and other interested parties *addressed* environmental sustainability, they have not *ensured* it. 'Address' – in this sense of the word – means "think about and begin to deal with (an issue or problem)" (*The New Oxford Dictionary of English*, 20).

378 Note 153 of Chapter One.

379 Note 154 of Chapter One.

380 The text to note 360 specifies MDG Target 7.C.

381 'Universal' – in this sense of the word – means "of, affecting, or done by all people or things in the world or in a particular group; applicable to all cases" (*The New Oxford Dictionary of English*, 2024). Is it submitted that 'access to safe and affordable drinking water that is applicable to all people' (i.e., universal), is the same as 'access to safe and affordable drinking water for all' – unless one is pedantic, e.g., a hypothetical SDG Target might provide for access to safe and affordable drinking water for children and old people – which is a restricted group rather than 'all' – but provide universal access to that water, so that, for instance, a mother could bring the water for her children even though she would not be encouraged to drink it herself.

sanitation for all. The 'expansion' is threefold: (i) the replacement of the descriptors 'sustainable' and 'basic' in MDG Target 7.C with the descriptors 'adequate', 'equitable' and 'for all' in SDG Target 6.2, (ii) the substitution of the word 'sanitation' in MDG Target 7.C with the phrase 'sanitation and hygiene' in SDG Target 6.2, and (iii) the addition of the requirement in SDG Target 6.2 to 'end open defecation' – which is one manifestation of poor sanitation and, therefore, already covered by the requirement in SDG Target 6.2 for 'adequate sanitation', making the introduction of this clause one of emphasis.

Progress to date in the accomplishment of SDG Target 6.1

The proportion of the worldwide population that used safely-managed drinking water services rose from 61% in 2000 to 71% in 2017.[382] The percentage of the global population with access to basic drinking water increased from 81% in 2000 to 90% in 2017.[383]

Will SDG Target 6.1 be achieved punctually?

The sizeable rises between 2000 and 2017 in the proportion of the worldwide population with access to basic drinking water and to safely-managed drinking water that the foregoing subsection shows, indicate that considerable progress has been made towards the realization of SDG Target 6.1.[384] However, the remaining headway that is necessary to accomplish universal access to safely-managed drinking water – as SDG Target 6.1 requires – is unlikely to be completed by 31st December 2030.[385] Therefore, it is doubtful whether SDG Target 6.1 will be met punctually.

Progress to date in the accomplishment of SDG Target 6.2

Sanitation: The proportion of the global population with access to safely-managed sanitation grew from 28% in 2000 to 45% in 2017.[386] The

---

[382] The Sustainable Development Goals Report 2020, 36.
[383] The Sustainable Development Goals Report 2020, 36.
[384] The text to note 378 states SDG Target 6.1.
[385] The target date for the SDGs to be achieved is 31st December 2030 (note 930 of Chapter Three and accompanying text).
[386] The Sustainable Development Goals Report 2020, 36.

percentage of the worldwide population that used basic sanitation services rose from 56% in 2000 to 74% in 2017.[387]

Hygiene: In 2017, 60% of the global population, 51% of people in the SIDS, 34% of individuals in the LLDCs, and 28% of people in the LDCs, had access to a handwashing facility with soap and water at home.[388] In that year, only 25% of the population of Sub-Saharan Africa had access to such a facility at home – compared with 77% of people in North Africa and West Asia, and with 58% of individuals in Central and South Asia.[389] In 2016, only 53% of schools worldwide possessed handwashing equipment with soap and water.[390]

Will SDG Target 6.2 be achieved punctually?

Whilst the first paragraph of the immediately-preceding subsection shows the rate of progress from 2000 to 2017 in providing access to basic sanitation and to safely-managed sanitation to be considerable, it is opined that the remaining headway which needs to be made in order to achieve access to adequate, equitable sanitation for everyone – as SDG Target 6.2[391] requires – is beyond that which can be accomplished by 31st December 2030.[392] Furthermore, the second paragraph of the foregoing subsection reveals that the majority of people in Sub-Saharan Africa, the LDCs and the LLDCs do not have access to handwashing facilities with soap and water in their homes, which renders the attainment of access to adequate, equitable hygiene for all – as called for by SDG Target 6.2 – beyond that which can be realized by 31st December 2030. Consequently, it is unlikely that SDG Target 6.2 will be achieved punctually.

From MDG Target 7.A to SDG Target 6.4

SDG Target 6.4 is to "substantially increase water-use efficiency across all sectors and ensure sustainable withdrawals and supply of freshwater to address water scarcity and substantially reduce the number of people

---

387 The Sustainable Development Goals Report 2020, 36.

388 The Sustainable Development Goals Report 2020, 36.

389 The Sustainable Development Goals Report 2020, 36.

390 The Sustainable Development Goals Report 2020, 36.

391 The text to note 379 specifies SDG Target 6.2.

392 The target date for the SDGs to be met is 31st December 2030 (note 930 of Chapter Three and accompanying text).

suffering from water scarcity", by 2030.[393] This SDG Target is a development on MDG Target 7.A,[394] as applied specifically to water.

The connection between MDG Target 7.A and SDG Target 6.4 is via a constructed portion of MDG Target 7.A – which is dubbed 'MDG Target 7.A(W)[395] and reads: 'integrate the principles and policies of sustainable development into country policies and programmes *for the management of water supply and water usage*, and reverse the loss of *water* resources'. MDG Target 7.A(W) was not met.[396]

Thus, both parts of MDG Target 7.A are narrowed to fashion MDG Target 7.A(W). The first part of MDG Target 7.A(W), i.e., 'integrate the principles and policies of sustainable development into country policies and programmes for the management of water supply and water usage' is progressed into the main part of SDG Target 6.4, i.e., 'substantially increase water-use efficiency across all sectors and ensure sustainable withdrawals and supply of freshwater to address water scarcity' – the latter being more functional and specific than the former. The second part of MDG Target 7.A(W), i.e., 'reverse the loss of water resources' is reoriented to become the final part SDG Target 6.4, i.e., 'substantially reduce the number of people suffering from water scarcity' – the latter focusing on the result of water scarcity and the former on the cause of it.

Progress to date in the accomplishment of SDG Target 6.4

Water stress and water scarcity: In 2017, the world's population withdrew 17.0% of its available fresh water.[397] Higher levels than this were recorded in North Africa (102.9%), Central Asia (87.9%), South Asia (70.7%), West Asia (53.8%) and East Asia (45.8%).[398]

Lack of fresh water in the poorest countries: In 2018, slightly more than 2.1% of land worldwide was covered by fresh water – with developed countries having 3.5% freshwater coverage and developing countries 1.4% freshwater coverage.[399] In that year, the freshwater coverage of the LDCs

---

[393] Note 138 of Chapter One.

[394] The text to note 336 states MDG Target 7.A.

[395] 'W' stands for 'water'.

[396] 41 countries suffered water stress or water scarcity in 2011, which is an increase on 36 countries in 1998 (text to note 351).

[397] The Sustainable Development Goals Report 2020, 37.

[398] The Sustainable Development Goals Report 2020, 37.

[399] Progress towards the Sustainable Development Goals: Report of the Secretary-General, E/2020/xxx, 11; The Sustainable Development Goals Report 2020, 37.

and the SIDS was 1.2% and 1%, respectively – these low levels raising the vulnerability of these places to water scarcity and to climate change.[400]

Will SDG Target 6.4 be achieved punctually?

The statistics in the first paragraph of the immediately-preceding subsection show that, in 2017, there was a low level of water stress globally,[401] whilst there were very high levels of water stress in North Africa and Central Asia.[402] In 2011, countries in these regions were experiencing severe water stress.[403] It is submitted that the persistence of this problem in these regions precludes the punctual achievement of SDG Target 6.4,[404] the last part of which requires a substantial reduction by 2030 in the number of people who suffer from water scarcity.

From MDG Target 7.B to SDG Target 6.6

SDG Target 6.6 is to "protect and restore water-related ecosystems, including mountains, forests, wetlands, rivers, aquifers and lakes", by 2020.[405] If water-related ecosystems are protected and restored – as SDG Target 6.6 requires, then biodiversity in these habitats is likely to be maintained.

As MDG Target 7.B[406] requires a significant reduction in the rate of loss of biodiversity to be achieved by 2010, and as this MDG Target was not punctually met,[407] then attempting to safeguard and restore ecosystems is a way of realizing the general objective that MDG Target 7.B contains, i.e., to reduce biodiversity loss. SDG Target 6.6 advocates the protection

---

400 Progress towards the Sustainable Development Goals: Report of the Secretary-General, E/2020/xxx, 11; The Sustainable Development Goals Report 2020, 37. The Secretary-General of the UN declares: "The adverse effects of climate change can further decrease freshwater body extent and hence, worsen our ecosystems and livelihoods." (Progress towards the Sustainable Development Goals: Report of the Secretary-General, E/2020/xxx, 11).

401 Text to note 397.

402 Text to note 398.

403 In 2011, ten countries in Arabia, Central Asia or North Africa withdrew more than 100% of their renewable freshwater resources (note 350).

404 The text to note 393 specifies SDG Target 6.4.

405 Note 146 of Chapter One.

406 The text to note 353 states MDG Target 7.B.

407 The sentence immediately-following the text to note 359 opines that MDG Target 7.B has not been fulfilled.

and restoration of ecosystems in the context of water, and is, therefore, a goal that forms part of this realization.

Progress to date in the accomplishment of SDG Target 6.6

The following eleven countries had a greater than 20% positive change in the extent of their water-related ecosystems over time – from a baseline-year period of 2001-2005 until 2016, pursuant to SDG Indicator 6.6.1[408] and its sub-indicators:[409] Botswana (245%), Algeria (78%), Eswatini (55%), Eritrea (51%), the Dominican Republic (49%), Niger (48%), Namibia (36%), Sudan (33%), Pakistan (31%), Morocco (25%), and Portugal (22%).[410] The following four states had a greater than 20% negative change in the extent of their water-related ecosystems over the same time – i.e., from a baseline-year period of 2001-2005 until 2016, in accordance with SDG Indicator 6.6.1 and its sub-indicators: Ukraine (-77%), Uzbekistan (-44%), Afghanistan (-24%), and Argentina (-22%).[411] All 163 other countries on which these data are provided, record a change in the extent of their water-related ecosystems over time – from a baseline-year period of 2001-2005 until 2016, of between 20% and -20%.[412]

Will SDG Target 6.6 be achieved punctually?

The data in the foregoing subsection suggest that the extent of countries' water-related ecosystems tends to be fairly stable, but with a slight

[408] SDG Indicator 6.6.1 measures the "[c]hange in the extent of water-related ecosystems over time" (Global indicator framework for the Sustainable Development Goals and targets of the 2030 Agenda for Sustainable Development, 7).

[409] The sub-indicators of SDG Indicator 6.6.1 are: (i) the spatial extent of water-related ecosystems, (ii) water quality of lakes and artificial water bodies, (iii) the quantity of water in rivers and estuaries, (iv) water quality imported from SDG Indicator 6.3.2, and (v) the quantity of groundwater within aquifers ("Indicator 6.6.1 – Water-related ecosystems", United Nations Water, accessed September 13, 2020, https://sdg6data.org/indicator/6.6.1). SDG Indicator 6.3.2 measures the "[p]roportion of bodies of water with good ambient water quality" (Global indicator framework for the Sustainable Development Goals and targets of the 2030 Agenda for Sustainable Development, 7).

[410] "Indicator 6.6.1 – Water-related ecosystems", United Nations Water, accessed September 13, 2020, https://sdg6data.org/indicator/6.6.1.

[411] "Indicator 6.6.1 – Water-related ecosystems", United Nations Water, accessed September 13, 2020, https://sdg6data.org/indicator/6.6.1.

[412] "Indicator 6.6.1 – Water-related ecosystems", United Nations Water, accessed September 13, 2020, https://sdg6data.org/indicator/6.6.1.

propensity to increase over time. It is submitted these statistics are compatible with the requirement of SDG Target 6.6[413] to 'protect water-related ecosystems'. There is insufficient information to determine whether these data are consistent with the requirement of SDG Target 6.6 to 'restore water-related ecosystems', as information on neither the dimensions nor the biodiversity of these ecosystems at any time prior to 2001 is provided therein. It is opined that it is possible for SDG Target 6.6 to be met punctually, i.e., by 31st December 2030,[414] but that considerable reconstruction work on those ecosystems which have been eroded would need to be undertaken during the 2020s, in order to satisfy the 'restore' requirement of this SDG Target by this date.[415]

Progress to date in accomplishment of SDG 6 as a whole

Save SDG Targets 6.1,[416] 6.2,[417] 6.4[418] and 6.6,[419] the targets of SDG 6[420] are condensed as follows.

> 6.3 By 2030, improve water quality by reducing pollution, eliminating dumping and minimizing release of hazardous chemicals and materials, halving the proportion of untreated wastewater and substantially increasing recycling and safe reuse globally[.] … 6.5 By 2030, implement integrated water resources management at all levels, including through transboundary cooperation as appropriate[.] … 6.a By 2030, expand international cooperation and capacity-building support to developing countries in water- and sanitation-related activities and programmes … [.] 6.b Support and strengthen the participation of local communities in improving water and sanitation management[.][421]

Regarding SDG Target 6.3, preliminary estimates from 79 mainly high-income and high-middle-income countries in 2019 indicate that, in

---

413 The text to note 405 states SDG Target 6.6.

414 The target date for the SDGs to be fulfilled is 31st December 2030 (note 930 of Chapter Three and accompanying text).

415 Whilst SDG Target 6.6 is scheduled to be accomplished by 2020 (text to note 405), it is submitted that the extent of its realization should be assessed alongside that of other SDG Targets.

416 The text to note 378 states SDG Target 6.1.

417 The text to note 379 specifies SDG Target 6.2.

418 The text to note 393 states SDG Target 6.4.

419 The text to note 405 specifies SDG Target 6.6.

420 The text to note 335 states SDG 6.

421 Resolution 70/1 adopted by the General Assembly on 25 September 2015, Transforming our world: the 2030 Agenda for Sustainable Development, 18-19.

approximately one quarter of these states, less than half of all household wastewater flows are treated safely.[422] In respect of SDG Target 6.5: (i) 60% of the 172 countries that reported in 2018 disclosed very low, low or medium-low levels of implementation of integrated water resources management,[423] and (ii) data from 67 out of 153 countries that share transboundary waters suggest that, whilst the mean share of national transboundary basins that were covered by a functional arrangement was 59% over the period 2017 to 2018, only 17 countries stated that these arrangements applied to all their transboundary basins.[424] As regards SDG Target 6.a: (i) Commitments of ODA[425] to the water sector fell by 9% from 2017 to 2018, down from a 38% rise in these commitments from 2016 to 2017,[426] (ii) data from 20 developing countries and territories revealed a gap of 61% between identified financial needs to meet national drinking-water, sanitation and hygiene targets and available funding,[427] (iii) disbursements of ODA[428] to the water sector rose by 6% from 2017 to 2018, reaching USD 9.4 billion in the latter year[429] – notwithstanding the

---

[422] Progress towards the Sustainable Development Goals: Report of the Secretary-General, E/2020/xxx, 10.

[423] Progress towards the Sustainable Development Goals: Report of the Secretary-General, E/2020/xxx, 11; The Sustainable Development Goals Report 2020, 37.

[424] Progress towards the Sustainable Development Goals: Report of the Secretary-General, E/2020/xxx, 11; The Sustainable Development Goals Report 2020, 36.

[425] Commitments of ODA "measure donors' intentions and permit monitoring of the targeting of resources to specific purposes and recipient countries. They fluctuate as aid policies change, and reflect how donors' political commitments translate into action. They thus give an indication about future flows [of ODA to countries and territories on the DAC List of ODA Recipients (note 964 of Chapter Three and accompanying text) and to multilateral development institutions (text to note 965 of Chapter Three)]." ("Frequently Asked Questions", Organisation for Economic Co-operation and Development, accessed September 14, 2020, https://www.oecd.org/dac/stats/faq.htm).

[426] The Sustainable Development Goals Report 2020, 37.

[427] Progress towards the Sustainable Development Goals: Report of the Secretary-General, E/2020/xxx, 11; The Sustainable Development Goals Report 2020, 37.

[428] Disbursements of ODA "show actual payments in each year. They show the realisation of donors' intentions and the implementation of their policies. They are required to examine the contribution of donors' actions in development achievements. They better describe aid flows [than do commitments of ODA (note 425)] from a recipient's point of view." ("Frequently Asked Questions", Organisation for Economic Co-operation and Development, accessed September 14, 2020, https://www.oecd.org/dac/stats/faq.htm).

[429] Progress towards the Sustainable Development Goals: Report of the Secretary-General, E/2020/xxx, 11; The Sustainable Development Goals Report 2020, 37.

overall reduction of 1.9% in disbursements of ODA across all sectors,[430] and (iv) disbursements of ODA to the water and sanitation sectors combined increased by 9% from 2017 to 2018 – including an increase of USD 346 million to Sub-Saharan Africa for drinking-water systems, water-sector policy and administrative management.[431]

Will SDG 6 be achieved punctually?

Despite the view given above that the undertaking of substantial reconstruction work on water-related ecosystems during the 2020s would be necessary to satisfy the 'restore' requirement in SDG Target 6.6[432] – thereby raising the likelihood of this SDG Target being met punctually,[433] i.e., by 31st December 2020,[434] the data in the immediately-preceding session together with those concerning SDG Targets 6.1,[435] 6.2[436] and 6.4[437], form the basis for submitting that SDG 6[438] will probably not be realized by that date. Besides, *The Sustainable Development Goals Report 2020* avers that the targets of SDG 6 will not be attained by 2030, unless present rates of progress rise appreciably.[439] The application of a literal interpretation[440] to the *prima facie*[441] requirements of SDG 6 endorses the conclusion that this Goal is unlikely to be achieved punctually.[442]

---

430 The Sustainable Development Goals Report 2020, 37.

431 The Sustainable Development Goals Report 2020, 37.

432 The text to note 405 specifies SDG Target 6.6.

433 This opinion is given in the subsection titled 'Will SDG Target 6.6 be achieved punctually?', above in the current section (i.e., that titled 'SDG 6: Ensure Availability of Water and Sanitation').

434 The target date for the SDGs to be accomplished is 31st December 2030 (note 930 of Chapter Three and accompanying text).

435 The text to notes 382 and 383 contains these statistics. The text to note 378 states SDG Target 6.1.

436 The text to notes 386-390 comprises these data. The text to note 379 specifies SDG Target 6.2.

437 The text to notes 397-400 consists of these statistics. The information that note 403 contains contextualizes the data that the text to note 398 presents. The text to note 393 states SDG Target 6.4.

438 The text to note 335 states SDG 6.

439 The Sustainable Development Goals Report 2020, 36.

440 Note 59 explains the concept of a 'literal interpretation', as applied to MDG 1.

441 Note 59 defines the phrase '*prima facie*'.

442 SDG 6 is to "*[e]nsure* availability and sustainable management of water and sanitation for all" (text to note 335; emphasis added). 'Ensure' – in this sense of the word – means "make certain that (something) will occur or be the case" (note

SDG 14: Conserve the Oceans, Seas and Their Resources

MDG 7 and MDG Targets 7.A and 7.B

MDG 7 is to "[e]nsure environmental sustainability".[443] It consists of four targets – MDG Targets 7.A, 7.B, 7.C and 7.D – the first two of which map to targets of SDG 14,[444] which is to "[c]onserve and sustainably use the oceans, seas and marine resources for sustainable development".[445] MDG 7 and MDG Targets 7.A and 7.B are considered in the subsection entitled 'MDG 7 and MDG Targets 7.A, 7.B and 7.C', in the section above titled 'SDG 6: Ensure Availability of Water and Sanitation'.

From MDG Targets 7.A and 7.B to SDG Target 14.2

SDG Target 14.2 is to "sustainably manage and protect marine and coastal ecosystems to avoid significant adverse impacts, including by strengthening their resilience, and take action for their restoration in order to achieve healthy and productive oceans", by 2020.[446] This SDG Target builds on an aspect of MDG Target 7.A,[447] i.e., the integration of the principles of sustainable development into national policies and programmes concerning marine and coastal ecosystems and the reversing of the loss of resources within those ecosystems, and on a dimension of

---

377). The information that the current section (i.e., that entitled 'SDG 6: Ensure Availability of Water and Sanitation') provides, tends to support the views that: (i) it will not be the case that water and sanitation beyond the most basic facilities will be available to everyone by 31st December 2030, and (ii) nor will it be the situation that everybody will benefit from the sustainable management of water and sanitation by this date. Therefore, it is submitted that, although the UN and other stakeholders will have *addressed* the availability and the sustainable management of water and sanitation with a view to their universality by 31st December 2030, they will not by then have *ensured* that these facilities are available to everyone or sustainably-managed for the benefit of all. The final sentence of note 377 defines 'address'.

443 Text to note 333.

444 MDG 7 maps to SDG 14, MDG Target 7.A maps to SDG Targets 14.2 and 14.4, and MDG Target 7.B maps to SDG Targets 14.2, 14.5 and 14.c (text to notes 31-35; text to notes 132, 135, 137, 140, 141, 145, 147, 148 and 149 of Chapter One).

445 Note 135 of Chapter One.

446 Note 140 of Chapter One.

447 The text to note 336 specifies MDG Target 7.A.

MDG Target 7.B,[448] i.e., the reduction in the rate of loss of biodiversity of marine and coastal ecosystems. Over the area of these habitats, SDG Target 14.2 moves beyond MDG Targets 7.A and 7.B, as the latter two targets aim to reverse the loss of environmental resources and biodiversity, respectively, whereas the former progresses to take action for the restoration of coastal and marine ecosystems in order to attain healthy and productive oceans.

Progress to date in the accomplishment of SDG Target 14.2

In December 2019, more than 17% of waters globally between the shore and 200 nautical miles out to sea perpendicular to the coast comprised protected areas – with this coverage more than doubling since 2010.[449] The worldwide mean percentage of each marine key biodiversity area constituted by protected areas rose from 30.5% in 2010 to 44.8% in 2015, and thence to 46.0% in 2019.[450] Whilst the mean percentage of each thalassic key biodiversity area covered by protected areas rose both from 2010 to 2015 and from 2015 to 2019 in all[451] eight regions,[452] the LDCs and the SIDS, these latter two groupings lagged behind the global mean percentage of 46% in 2019 at 25.4% and 23.7%, respectively, for that year.[453]

Will SDG Target 14.2 be achieved punctually?

On the basis of the aggregated data that the foregoing subsection provides, it is submitted that SDG Target 14.2[454] will not be achieved punctually,

---

448 The text to note 353 states MDG Target 7.B.

449 Progress towards the Sustainable Development Goals: Report of the Secretary-General, E/2020/xxx, 18; The Sustainable Development Goals Report 2020, 52.

450 The Sustainable Development Goals Report 2020, 52.

451 There is one exception to the statement in this 'Whilst' clause – the mean percentage of each marine key biodiversity area covered by protected areas in Central and South Asia was the same in 2019 as it had been in 2015 (The Sustainable Development Goals Report 2020, 52).

452 These regions are – from greatest coverage in 2019 of their marine key biodiversity areas covered by protected areas to least – Europe and North America, Australia and New Zealand, Latin America and the Caribbean, Sub-Saharan Africa, Central and South Asia, East and South-East Asia, North Africa and West Asia, and Oceania excluding Australia and New Zealand (The Sustainable Development Goals Report 2020, 52).

453 The Sustainable Development Goals Report 2020, 52.

454 The text to note 446 specifies SDG Target 14.2.

i.e., by 31st December 2030.[455] Whilst progress concerning the safeguarding of marine key biodiversity areas is in the correct direction regarding SDG Target 14.2,[456] such headway needs to accelerate in order to support a finding that the first part of this SDG Target, i.e., to sustainably manage and protect marine and coastal ecosystems, has been accomplished by that date.

From MDG Target 7.A to SDG Target 14.4

SDG Target 14.4 is to "effectively regulate harvesting and end overfishing, illegal, unreported and unregulated fishing and destructive fishing practices and implement science-based management plans, in order to restore fish stocks in the shortest time feasible, at least to levels that can produce maximum sustainable yield as determined by their biological characteristics", by 2020.[457] Marine fish stocks are a component of the environment resources with which MDG Target 7.A[458] is concerned.[459] SDG Target 14.4 advances preservation of this element of that MDG Target in specific terms – with the aim of restoring these stocks as quickly as is reasonably possible.

Progress to date in the accomplishment of SDG Target 14.4

As at 14th February 2020, the number of parties to the Agreement on Port State Measures[460] rose to 66 – up from 58 parties in 2019.[461] In 2020,

---

[455] The target date for the SDGs to be realized is 31st December 2030 (note 930 of Chapter Three and accompanying text). Whilst SDG Target 14.2 is scheduled to be met by 2020 (text to note 446), it is opined that the extent of its attainment should be assessed alongside that of other SDG Targets.

[456] Text to notes 450 and 453.

[457] Note 141 of Chapter One.

[458] The text to note 336 states MDG Target 7.A.

[459] The text to notes 346 and 347 report on the decline in global thalassic fish stocks from 1974 to 2011, and the fall in the worldwide marine catch of fish from 1996 to 2013, respectively.

[460] The Agreement on Port State Measures to Prevent, Deter and Eliminate Illegal, Unreported and Unregulated Fishing was approved by the FAO Conference at its Thirty-Sixth Session in November 2009, and came into force on 5th June 2016 ("Agreement on Port State Measures (PSMA): Parties to the PSMA", Food and Agriculture Organization of the United Nations, accessed September 14, 2020, http://www.fao.org/port-state-measures/background/parties-psma/en/).

The Agreement is the first binding international instrument to specifically focus on illegal, unreported and unregulated fishing ("Agreement on Port State Measures

almost 75% of countries reported scoring highly in their degree of implementation of international instruments that combat illegal, unreported and unregulated fishing, compared with 70% in 2018.[462]

The proportion of marine fish stocks worldwide that are within biologically-sustainable levels fell from 90.0% in 1974 to 71% in 2011, to 66.7% in 2015, and thence to 65.8% in 2017 – thus showing a reduction in the rate of decline in recent years.[463] In both 2015 and 2017, the thalassic areas with the lowest percentage of fish stocks within biologically-sustainable levels were the Mediterranean Sea and the Black Sea (37.5% in 2017), the South-East Pacific Ocean (45.5% in 2017), and the South-West Atlantic Ocean (46.7% in 2017).[464]

Will SDG Target 14.4 be achieved punctually?

Countries that have ratified the Agreement on Port State Measures to Prevent, Deter and Eliminate Illegal, Unreported and Unregulated Fishing, are introducing legislation to combat illegal, unreported and unregulated fishing.[465] Simultaneously with the introduction of these national rules, the rate of decrease of the global percentage of marine fish stocks that are

---

(PSMA)", Food and Agriculture Organization of the United Nations, accessed September 14, 2020, http://www.fao.org/port-state-measures/en/).
The Agreement's objective "is to prevent, deter and eliminate IUU [illegal, unreported and unregulated] fishing through the implementation of effective port State measures, and thereby to ensure the long-term conservation and sustainable use of living marine resources and marine ecosystems" (Food and Agriculture Organization of the United Nations, Agreement on Port State Measures to Prevent, Deter and Eliminate Illegal, Unreported and Unregulated Fishing (Rome, 2009), art.2).

461 Progress towards the Sustainable Development Goals: Report of the Secretary-General, E/2020/xxx, 18-19; The Sustainable Development Goals Report 2020, 53.

462 Progress towards the Sustainable Development Goals: Report of the Secretary-General, E/2020/xxx, 19; The Sustainable Development Goals Report 2020, 53.

463 The Sustainable Development Goals Report 2020, 53; text to note 346. The Secretary-General of the UN states that the proportion of marine fish stocks within biologically-sustainable levels was "at 65.8% in 2017, down from 90% in 1974 and *0.8 percentage point lower than 2015 levels*" (Progress towards the Sustainable Development Goals: Report of the Secretary-General, E/2020/xxx, 18; emphasis added), and is thus at variance with the corresponding datum for 2015 in *The Sustainable Development Goals Report 2020*. It is submitted that the 0.1% difference in this statistic between these two sources may be due to a rounding error regarding this datum.

464 The Sustainable Development Goals Report 2020, 53.

465 Text to notes 461 and 462.

within biologically-sustainable levels is falling.[466] It is submitted that national implementation of this Agreement may lead to the end of this type of fishing, as SDG Target 14.4[467] requires, by 31st December 2030,[468] if the majority of states ratify the Agreement within the next few years.

In addition to ending illegal, unreported and unregulated fishing, SDG Target 14.4 also aims to: (i) effectively regulate harvesting, (ii) end overfishing, (iii) end destructive fishing practices, and (iv) implement science-based management plans.[469] It is opined that not all these goals will be fully realized by 31st December 2030, and, therefore, that SDG Target 14.4 will not be achieved punctually in every aspect of its coverage.

From MDG Target 7.B to SDG Targets 14.5 and 14.c

SDG Target 14.5 is to "conserve at least 10 per cent of coastal and marine areas, consistent with national and international law and based on the best available scientific information", by 2020.[470] SDG Target 14.c is to "[e]nhance the conservation and sustainable use of oceans and their resources by implementing international law as reflected in the United Nations Convention on the Law of the Sea, which provides the legal framework for the conservation and sustainable use of oceans and their resources …".[471]

SDG Target 14.5 attempts to reduce biodiversity loss – which MDG Target 7.B[472] requires, by advocating protection of 10% or more of coastal and thalassic areas. SDG Target 14.c also endeavours to lessen biodiversity loss – which MDG Target 7.B prescribes, by calling for countries to put into effect the relevant international law for the preservation and sustainable use of oceans and their resources.

---

466 Text to note 463.

467 The text to note 457 specifies SDG Target 14.4.

468 The target date for the SDGs to be attained is 31st December 2030 (note 930 of Chapter Three and accompanying text). Whilst SDG Target 14.4 is scheduled to be achieved by 2020 (text to note 457), it is submitted that the extent of its fulfilment should be assessed alongside that of other SDG Targets.

469 Text to note 457.

470 Note 148 of Chapter One.

471 Note 149 of Chapter One.

472 The text to note 353 states MDG Target 7.B.

Progress to date in the accomplishment of SDG Target 14.5

In December 2019, more than 17% of waters worldwide up to 200 nautical miles from the shore perpendicular to the coast were covered by protected areas.[473] This percentage has risen substantially over the years, and has more than doubled since 2010.[474] Much of this overlay with protected areas is concentrated in Oceania, and in Latin America and the Caribbean.[475]

Will SDG Target 14.5 be achieved punctually?

Provided that conservation of those parts of coastal and marine areas up to 200 nautical miles from the shore that are within protected areas is in accordance with international and national law and founded on the best-available scientific information – in accordance with SDG Target 14.5,[476] then at least 10% of these coastal waters are 'conserved' within the meaning of SDG Target 14.5, which – in respect of these seas – has been met by 2020, as required. If 'marine areas' in SDG Target 14.5 includes some or all of the high seas, then this SDG Target's required conservation extends to 10% or more of these waters, too.

Progress to date in the accomplishment of SDG Target 14.c

At the time of writing, there are 168 States Parties to the United Nations Convention on the Law of the Sea.[477] The States Parties are able to discuss issues of mutual concern at their meetings convened under Article 319(2)(e) of the Convention,[478] which, over the area of sustainable development, include a rise in the level of the sea, coastal flooding and impeded drainage, storm surges and the movement of tidal waters into

---

[473] Text to note 449.

[474] The Sustainable Development Goals Report 2020, 52; text to note 449.

[475] Progress towards the Sustainable Development Goals: Report of the Secretary-General, E/2020/xxx, 18.

[476] The text to note 470 specifies SDG Target 14.5.

[477] "States Parties", International Tribunal for the Law of the Sea, accessed September 14, 2020, https://www.itlos.org/the-tribunal/states-parties/.

[478] The Secretary-General of the UN shall "convene necessary meetings of States Parties in accordance with this Convention" (United Nations, United Nations Convention on the Law of the Sea (Montego Bay, 1982), art.319(2)(e)).

estuaries and rivers, and the salinization of soils, surface water and groundwater.[479]

Will SDG Target 14.c be achieved punctually?

As most of the states of the world have ratified the United Nations Convention on the Law of the Sea,[480] it is submitted that there is acceptance by the majority of countries that this instrument is a part of international law. National implementation of the provisions of the Convention tends to follow from this ratification and that acceptance. Thus, it is opined that SDG Target 14.c will be accomplished punctually, i.e., by 31st December 2020.[481]

Progress to date in accomplishment of SDG 14 as a whole

Except for SDG Targets 14.2,[482] 14.4,[483] 14.5[484] and 14.c,[485] targets of SDG 14[486] are abridged as follows.

> 14.1 By 2025, prevent and significantly reduce marine pollution of all kinds … [.] … 14.3 Minimize and address the impacts of ocean acidification … [.] … 14.6 By 2020, prohibit certain forms of fisheries subsidies which contribute to overcapacity and overfishing, eliminate subsidies that contribute to illegal, unreported and unregulated fishing and refrain from introducing new such subsidies … [.] 14.7 By 2030, increase the economic benefits to small island developing States and least developed countries from the sustainable use of marine resources … [.] 14.a Increase scientific knowledge, develop research capacity and transfer marine technology … in order to improve ocean health and to enhance the contribution of marine biodiversity to the development of developing countries … 14.b Provide access for small-scale artisanal fishers to marine resources and markets[.] …[487]

---

[479] United Nations, Oceans and the law of the sea: Report of the Secretary-General, A/75/50, 16 March 2020 (New York, 2020), 7.

[480] Text to note 477. The world contains 195 states (note 640 of Chapter Three).

[481] The target date for the SDGs to be achieved is 31st December 2030 (note 930 of Chapter Three and accompanying text).

[482] The text to note 446 states SDG Target 14.2.

[483] The text to note 457 specifies SDG Target 14.4.

[484] The text to note 470 states SDG Target 14.5.

[485] The text to note 471 specifies SDG Target 14.c.

[486] The text to note 445 states SDG 14.

[487] Resolution 70/1 adopted by the General Assembly on 25 September 2015, Transforming our world: the 2030 Agenda for Sustainable Development, 23-24.

Regarding SDG Target 14.3: (i) the ocean absorbs about 23% of annual emissions of carbon dioxide that human activity generates,[488] (ii) the carbon dioxide thus absorbed has caused seawater to become more acidic – there has been a 26% fall in pH levels since before industrialization,[489] and (iii) there has been a rise in pH variability of between 10% and 30% over the last five years, and an increase in the acidity of the ocean over the period 2015 to 2019.[490] In respect of SDG Target 14.7: (i) whilst the contribution of sustainable fisheries to worldwide GDP has been stable at approximately 0.1% per year, this input to GDP has been significantly higher in Oceanic SIDS and in LDCs – where fishing activities are essential for local communities and indigenous people,[491] and (ii) the share of sustainable fisheries in the GDP of Oceanic SIDS and of LDCs for the period 2011 to 2017 averaged 1.55% and 1.11%, respectively.[492] As regards SDG Target 14.b: (i) whilst small-scale fishers contribute more than 50% of the total output of fisheries in developing countries, they continue to be marginalized, and (ii) the COVID-19 pandemic[493] is adversely affecting the income of these food producers, as global demand for seafood declines and restrictions on transportation prevent their access to the market.[494]

---

[488] Progress towards the Sustainable Development Goals: Report of the Secretary-General, E/2020/xxx, 18; The Sustainable Development Goals Report 2020, 52.
[489] The Sustainable Development Goals Report 2020, 52.
[490] Progress towards the Sustainable Development Goals: Report of the Secretary-General, E/2020/xxx, 18; The Sustainable Development Goals Report 2020, 52.
[491] Progress towards the Sustainable Development Goals: Report of the Secretary-General, E/2020/xxx, 19; The Sustainable Development Goals Report 2020, 53.
[492] The Sustainable Development Goals Report 2020, 53. The Secretary-General of the UN states: "The contribution of sustainable marine capture fisheries remains stable at global level, with regional variation and the largest contribution to the GDP in the Pacific SIDS and LDCs, averaging 1.55% and *1.15%*, respectively, in 2011-2017 (Progress towards the Sustainable Development Goals: Report of the Secretary-General, E/2020/xxx, 19; emphasis added). It is submitted that the 0.04% difference between the percentage for the share of sustainable fisheries in the GDP of LDCs as recorded in *The Sustainable Development Goals Report 2020*, i.e., 1.11%, and this value as noted in the Report of the Secretary-General, i.e., 1.15%, is due to an erratum in one of these two documents.
[493] The WHO designated the outbreak and spread of COVID-19 as a pandemic on 11th March 2020 (note 53 of Chapter Two).
[494] The Sustainable Development Goals Report 2020, 53.

Will SDG 14 be achieved punctually?

SDG Targets 14.2,[495] 14.3,[496] 14.4[497] and 14.b[498] are unlikely to be fulfilled punctually, i.e., by 31st December 2030.[499] SDG Target 14.5[500] as applied to coastal and marine areas within 200 nautical miles of the shore, has been achieved subject to one proviso.[501] SDG Targets 14.7[502] and 14.c[503] are likely to be attained punctually. It is submitted that SDG 14[504] will not be realized by 31st December 2030, because not all its targets will have been accomplished by that date.

SDG 15: Protect Ecosystems and Halt Biodiversity Loss

MDG 7 and MDG Targets 7.A and 7.B

MDG 7 is to "[e]nsure environmental sustainability".[505] It comprises four targets – MDG Targets 7.A, 7.B, 7.C and 7.D – the first two of which map to targets of SDG 15,[506] which is to "[p]rotect, restore and promote sustainable use of territorial ecosystems, sustainably manage forests, combat desertification, and halt and reverse land degradation and halt biodiversity loss".[507] MDG 7 and MDG Targets 7.A and 7.B are appraised in the subsection entitled 'MDG 7 and MDG Targets 7.A, 7.B and 7.C', in the section above titled 'SDG 6: Ensure Availability of Water and Sanitation'.

---

[495] Text to note 455. The text to note 446 specifies SDG Target 14.2.
[496] Text to notes 488-490. The text to note 487 abridges SDG Target 14.3.
[497] Text to note 469, and the sentence that immediately follows that text. The text to note 457 specifies SDG Target 14.4.
[498] Text to note 494. The text to note 487 states SDG Target 14.b.
[499] The target date for the SDGs to be met is 31st December 2030 (note 930 of Chapter Three and accompanying text).
[500] The text to note 470 specifies SDG Target 14.5.
[501] Text to note 476.
[502] Text to notes 491 and 492. The text to note 487 abridges SDG Target 14.7.
[503] Text to notes 480 and 481. The text to note 471 states SDG Target 14.c.
[504] The text to note 445 specifies SDG 14.
[505] Text to note 333.
[506] MDG 7 maps to SDG 15, MDG Target 7.A maps to SDG Targets 15.2, 15.3 and 15.9, and MDG Target 7.B maps to SDG Targets 15.4 and 15.5 (text to notes 36-38; text to notes 132, 136, 137, 142, 143, 144, 145, 150 and 151 of Chapter One).
[507] Note 136 of Chapter One.

From MDG Target 7.A to SDG Targets 15.2, 15.3 and 15.9

SDG Target 15.2 is to "promote the implementation of sustainable management of all types of forests, halt deforestation, restore degraded forests and substantially increase afforestation and reforestation globally", by 2020.[508] MDG Target 7.A[509] connects to SDG Target 15.2 by means of a constructed element of the former – which is dubbed 'MDG Target 7.A(F)'[510] and reads: 'integrate the principles and policies of sustainable development into country policies and programmes *for the management of forests*, and reverse *deforestation*'.[511] MDG Target 7.A(F) was not achieved.[512] The first part of MDG Target 7.A(F), i.e., 'integrate the principles and policies of sustainable development into country policies and programmes', is condensed into the first clause of SDG Target 15.2, i.e., 'promote the implementation of sustainable management of all types of forests". The second section of MDG Target 7.A(F), i.e., 'reverse deforestation', is expanded into the remainder of SDG Target 15.2, i.e., 'halt deforestation, restore degraded forests and substantially increase afforestation and reforestation globally'.

SDG Target 15.3 is to "combat desertification, restore degraded land and soil, including land affected by desertification, drought and floods, and strive to achieve a land degradation-neutral world", by 2030.[513] SDG Target 15.3 is an instance of a specific development from the second goal of MDG Target 7.A,[514] i.e., 'reverse the loss of environmental resources' – the particular environmental resource is land. The interim target narrowed from this objective of MDG Target 7.A is dubbed 'MDG Target 7.A(L)'[515] and reads: 'Reverse the *degradation of land*'.[516] MDG Target 7.A(L) is

---

[508] Note 142 of Chapter One.

[509] The text to note 336 states MDG Target 7.A.

[510] 'F' stands for 'forests'.

[511] The creation of MDG Target 7.A(F) in the progression from MDG Target 7.A to SDG Target 15.2, is analogous to the generation of MDG Target 7.A(W) in the advance from MDG Target 7.A to SDG Target 6.4 (text to note 395). The text to note 393 specifies SDG Target 6.4.

[512] Whilst the annual loss in worldwide forest area was lower in the 2000s than in the 1990s (text to note 337), deforestation was not reversed – as the second part of MDG Target 7.A(F) requires.

[513] Note 143 of Chapter One.

[514] The text to note 336 states MDG Target 7.A.

[515] 'L' stands for 'land'.

[516] Whilst the fashioning of MDG Target 7.A(F) from MDG Target 7.A (text to note 511), and of MDG Target 7.A(W) from MDG Target 7.A (text to note 395), each requires a narrowing of both parts of MDG Target 7.A, the forming of MDG

broadened into the first two parts of SDG Target 15.3, i.e., 'combat desertification, restore degraded land and soil', and progressed by the addition of the third section of that SDG Target, i.e., 'strive to achieve a land degradation-neutral world'.

SDG Target 15.9 is to "integrate ecosystem and biodiversity values into national and local planning, development processes, poverty reduction strategies and accounts", by 2020.[517] This SDG Target preserves the first part of MDG Target 7.A,[518] i.e., 'integrate the principles of sustainable development into country policies and programmes', which becomes 'integrate ecosystem and biodiversity values into national and local planning' in SDG Target 15.9 – whilst adding a degree of specificity, i.e., the principles of sustainable development' in MDG Target 7.A becomes 'ecosystem and biodiversity values' in SDG Target 15.9. This SDG Target widens the scope of the integration to include 'development processes, poverty reduction strategies and accounts'.

Progress to date in the accomplishment of SDG Target 15.2

From 2015 to 2020, the rate of deforestation worldwide was estimated to be 10 million hectares per annum, which is lower than the yearly loss of 12 million hectares of forest over the period 2010 to 2015.[519] The global proportion of forest area decreased from 31.9% of total land area in 2000 to 31.2% of total land area in 2020, representing a net loss of nearly 100 million hectares of the world's forests – which was mainly due to the conversion of this land into a form suitable for agricultural use.[520]

In 2020, management plans were in place for more than half of the 4.06 billion hectares of forest worldwide.[521] Data from 2017 and from 2020 showed that the percentage of forests in protected areas and subject

---

Target 7.A(L) involves a straightening of only the second segment of MDG Target 7.A.

[517] Note 144 of Chapter One. It is submitted that SDG Target 15.9 is based upon Aichi Biodiversity Target 2 of the Strategic Plan for Biodiversity 2011-2020, to which it is similar. The last sentence of note 541 states Aichi Biodiversity Target 2.

[518] The text to note 336 specifies MDG Target 7.A.

[519] The Sustainable Development Goals Report 2020, 55.

[520] Progress towards the Sustainable Development Goals: Report of the Secretary-General, E/2020/xxx, 19; The Sustainable Development Goals Report 2020, 55.

[521] The Sustainable Development Goals Report 2020, 55.

to long-term management plans, and the certified area of forest,[522] rose or continued to be stable, both globally and in most of the world's regions.[523]

From 2000 to 2020, forest area enlarged in Asia, Europe, and North America.[524] It materially diminished in Latin America, South-East Asia, and Sub-Saharan Africa over this vicennium.[525]

Will SDG Target 15.2 be achieved punctually?

On the basis of the limited information that the foregoing subsection provides, the stage of realization of the goals within SDG Target 15.2[526] are as follows: (i) 'promote the implementation of sustainable management of all types of forests' – more than half of the world's forests are covered by management plans,[527] and the percentage of forests subject to these plans is stable or increasing,[528] (ii) 'halt deforestation' – the rate of

---

522 The FAO describes 'forest certification' as follows: "Forest certification is a voluntary process whereby an independent third party (the "certifier") assesses the quality of forest management and production against a set of requirements ("standards") predetermined by a public or private certification organization. Forest certification, and associated labelling, is a way of informing consumers about the sustainability of the forests from which wood and other forest products were produced. There are two types of certification 1. certification of forest management, which assesses whether forests are being managed according to a specified set of standards; and 2. certification of the chain of custody … , which verifies that certified material is identified or kept separate from non-certified or non-controlled material through the production process, from the forest to the final consumer. To label an end-product as certified, both forest management certification and chain-of custody certification are required. Most forest management certification standards address a wide range of economic, social, environmental and technical aspects of forest management, including the well-being of workers and of families living in and around the forest area subject to certification." ("Sustainable Forest Management (SFM) Toolbox: Forest Certification – Basic Knowledge", Food and Agriculture Organization of the United Nations, accessed September 16, 2020, http://www.fao.org/sustainable-forest-management/toolbox/modules/forest-certification/basic-knowledge/en/).

523 Progress towards the Sustainable Development Goals: Report of the Secretary-General, E/2020/xxx, 19; The Sustainable Development Goals Report 2020, 55.

524 Progress towards the Sustainable Development Goals: Report of the Secretary-General, E/2020/xxx, 19.

525 Progress towards the Sustainable Development Goals: Report of the Secretary-General, E/2020/xxx, 19.

526 The text to note 508 states SDG Target 15.2.

527 Text to note 521.

528 Text to note 523.

deforestation has fallen for the period 2015 to 2020, relative to that for 2010 to 2015,[529] and forest area substantially lessened in Latin America, South-East Asia and Sub-Saharan Africa from 2000 to 2020,[530] (iii) 'restore degraded forests' – no data are furnished, and (iv) 'substantially increase afforestation and reforestation globally' – forest area rose in Asia, Europe, and North America from 2000 to 2020.[531] It is submitted that, if countries can be persuaded to stop deforestation in order to release more land for agricultural use, it is possible for SDG Target 15.2 to be achieved punctually, i.e., by 31st December 2030.[532]

Progress to date in the accomplishment of SDG Target 15.3

One fifth of the world's land area is degraded.[533] From 2000 to 2015, worldwide trends in land cover suggested a net loss in natural and semi-natural categories of land – determinants of which include deforestation, unsustainable agricultural practices, urbanization, and issues of land tenure.[534] By early 2020, 123 countries had pledged to set non-mandatory targets to attain land-degradation neutrality, and the governments of 60 of these had officially endorsed those objectives.[535]

Will SDG Target 15.3 be achieved punctually?

Whilst land degradation was increasing from 2000 to 2015,[536] the undertaking of so many countries to attempt to halt this practice[537] is in accord with the third aim of SDG Target 15.3,[538] which is to 'strive to achieve a land degradation-neutral world'. Thus, it is opined that there is a

---

[529] Text to note 519.
[530] Text to note 525.
[531] Text to note 524.
[532] The target date for the SDGs to be fulfilled is 31st December 2030 (note 930 of Chapter Three and accompanying text). Whilst SDG Target 15.2 is scheduled to be realized by 2020 (text to note 508), it is submitted that the extent of its accomplishment should be evaluated alongside that of other SDG Targets.
[533] The Sustainable Development Goals Report 2020, 54.
[534] The Sustainable Development Goals Report 2020, 54.
[535] Progress towards the Sustainable Development Goals: Report of the Secretary-General, E/2020/xxx, 19; The Sustainable Development Goals Report 2020, 54.
[536] Text to note 534.
[537] Text to note 535.
[538] The text to note 513 specifies SDG Target 15.3.

fairly-high probability of this SDG Target being met punctually, i.e., by 31st December 2030.[539]

Progress to date in the accomplishment of SDG Target 15.9

In January 2020: (i) 129 parties to the Convention on Biological Diversity,[540] including the European Union, had each submitted its sixth report under the Convention, and (ii) 113 parties to the Convention had assessed progress towards national biodiversity targets that were established in line with Aichi Biodiversity Target 2 of the Strategic Plan for Biodiversity 2011-2020.[541] Approximately 32% of these 113 parties are on track to meet or exceed these national biodiversity targets, as stated in their reports under the Convention on Biological Diversity.[542]

---

[539] The target date for the SDGs to be accomplished is 31st December 2030 (note 930 of Chapter Three and accompanying text).

[540] The Convention on Biological Diversity was adopted at the United Nations Conference on Environment and Development in 1992, and has three objectives: (i) the conservation of biodiversity, (ii) sustainable use of the elements of biodiversity, and (iii) sharing the benefits from the use of genetic resources in a way that is equitable and fair (Secretariat of the Convention on Biological Diversity, Sustaining life on Earth: How the Convention on Biological Diversity promotes nature and human well-being, April 2000 (Montreal, 2000). 8).

[541] Progress towards the Sustainable Development Goals: Report of the Secretary-General, E/2020/xxx, 20; The Sustainable Development Goals Report 2020, 55. The Strategic Plan for Biodiversity 2011-2020 is "[a] ten-year framework for action by all countries and stakeholders to save biodiversity and enhance its benefits for people" (Secretariat of the Convention on Biological Diversity, Strategic Plan for Biodiversity 2011-2020 and the Aichi Targets (Montreal, 2010), 1). The twenty Aichi Biodiversity Targets were adopted as part of the Strategic Plan for Biodiversity 2011-2020 (Secretariat of the Convention on Biological Diversity, Living in harmony with nature: Strategic Plan for Biodiversity 2011-2020 (Montreal, 2010), 1). Aichi Biodiversity Target 2 is as follows: "By 2020, at the latest, biodiversity values have been integrated into national and local development and poverty reduction strategies and planning processes and are being incorporated into national accounting, as appropriate, and reporting systems." (Strategic Plan for Biodiversity 2011-2020 and the Aichi Targets, 2).

[542] Progress towards the Sustainable Development Goals: Report of the Secretary-General, E/2020/xxx, 20; The Sustainable Development Goals Report 2020, 55.

Will SDG Target 15.9 be achieved punctually?

Given the resemblance of SDG Target 15.9[543] to Aichi Biodiversity Target 2 of the Strategic Plan for Biodiversity 2011-2020,[544] the fact that countries' national biodiversity targets were established in accordance with Aichi Biodiversity Target 2[545] means that they may be considered to be set up in conformity to SDG Target 15.9 as well. Thus, the fact that about 32% of reporting countries are on course to fulfil or exceed their national biodiversity targets[546] may be interpreted that these states are on schedule to accomplish SDG Target 15.9. Given that this SDG Target is to be attained 'by 2020',[547] it is probable that these countries and some others, too, will have met or exceeded their national biodiversity targets by 31st December 2030.[548] Therefore, it is submitted that there is a considerable likelihood that SDG Target 15.9 will be achieved punctually.

From MDG Target 7.B to SDG Targets 15.4 and 15.5

SDG Target 15.4 is to "ensure the conservation of mountain ecosystems, including their biodiversity, in order to enhance their capacity to provide benefits that are essential for sustainable development", by 2030.[549] MDG Target 7.B[550] links to SDG Target 15.4 via a constructed portion of the former – which is dubbed 'MDG Target 7.B(ME)'[551] and reads: 'reduce biodiversity loss in *mountain ecosystems*, achieving, by 2010, a significant reduction in the rate of loss'.[552] SDG Target 15.4 presents a positive way

---

[543] The text to note 517 states SDG Target 15.9.

[544] The final sentence of note 541 specifies Aichi Biodiversity Target 2 of the Strategic Plan for Biodiversity 2011-2020.

[545] Text to note 541.

[546] Text to note 542.

[547] Text to note 517. Whilst SDG Target 15.2 is scheduled to be achieved by 2020, it is opined that the extent of its fulfilment should be evaluated alongside that of other SDG Targets (note 548).

[548] The target date for the SDGs to be realized is 31st December 2030 (note 930 of Chapter Three and accompanying text).

[549] Note 150 of Chapter One.

[550] The text to note 353 states MDG Target 7.B.

[551] 'ME' stands for 'mountain ecosystems'.

[552] The introduction of MDG Target 7.B(ME) in the progression from MDG Target 7.B to SDG Target 15.4 is akin to the insertion of: (i) MDG Target 7.A(W) in the development from MDG Target 7.A to SDG Target SDG Target 6.4 (text to note 395), (ii) MDG Target 7.A(F) in the progression from MDG Target 7.A to SDG Target 15.2 (text to note 511), and (iii) MDG Target 7.A(L) in the advance from

of addressing the requirement to 'reduce biodiversity loss in mountain ecosystems' in MDG Target 7.B(ME)', which is to 'ensure the conservation of mountain ecosystems'. As 'ensure' means "make certain that (something) will occur or be the case",[553] SDG Target 15.4 takes a firm approach in requiring the conservation of mountain ecosystems to occur by 2030, which is likely to be beneficial for their biodiversity.

SDG Target 15.5 is to "[t]ake urgent and significant action to reduce the degradation of natural habitats, halt the loss of biodiversity and, by 2020, protect and prevent the extinction of threatened species".[554] This SDG Target progresses MDG Target 7.B, which aims for 'a significant reduction in the rate of loss' of biodiversity, by requiring 'urgent and significant action to … halt the loss of biodiversity'. Furthermore, SDG Target 15.5 broadens the scope of MDG Target 7.B by: (i) adding a requirement to 'take urgent and significant action to reduce the degradation of natural habitats', and (ii) by setting a deadline of 2020 for a new objective, which is to 'protect and prevent the extinction of threatened species'.

Progress to date in the accomplishment of SDG Target 15.4

In 2020, on average, globally 41% of each mountain Key Biodiversity Area was within protected areas.[555] This is a rise of about 12-13% since 2000.[556]

Will SDG Target 15.4 be achieved punctually?

On the basis of the limited information in the immediately-preceding subsection, the rate of increase in the percentage of Key Biodiversity Areas that are within protected areas is insufficient for 100% of the former to be within the latter by 31st December 2030.[557] Assuming that the goal

---

MDG Target 7.A to SDG Target 15.3 (text to note 516, and the sentence that immediately follows that text).

553 Note 377.

554 Note 151 of Chapter One.

555 Progress towards the Sustainable Development Goals: Report of the Secretary-General, E/2020/xxx, 19.

556 Progress towards the Sustainable Development Goals: Report of the Secretary-General, E/2020/xxx, 19.

557 The target date for the SDGs to be attained is 31st December 2030 (note 930 of Chapter Three and accompanying text).

within SDG Target 15.4,[558] i.e., to 'ensure the conservation of mountain ecosystems, including their biodiversity', is synonymous with a requirement to 'place 100% of the terrain in all mountain Key Biodiversity Areas worldwide within protected areas', it is improbable that SDG Target 15.4 will be met punctually, i.e., by 31st December 2030.

Progress to date in the accomplishment of SDG Target 15.5

Worldwide species extinction risk has risen by approximately 10% over the last thirty years, with the overall Red List Index[559] value for all the taxa combined decreasing from 0.82% in 1990 to 0.75 in 2015, and thence to 0.73 in 2020.[560] This means that more than 31,000 species are threatened with extinction, which is mainly due to habitat loss from deforestation, the spread of invasive foreign species, and unsustainable agriculture, harvest and trade.[561]

Will SDG Target 15.5 be achieved punctually?

The information in the foregoing subsection suggests that insufficient action has been taken – as SDG Target 15.5[562] requires – 'to reduce the degradation of natural habitats'. Furthermore, this SDG Target wishes to

---

558 The text to note 549 specifies SDG Target 15.4.

559 The Red List Index "shows trends in overall extinction risk for species, and is used by governments to track their progress towards targets for reducing biodiversity loss" ("Red List Index", International Union for Conservation of Nature and Natural Resources, accessed September 17, 2020, https://www.iucnredlist.org/assessment/red-list-index).

560 Progress towards the Sustainable Development Goals: Report of the Secretary-General, E/2020/xxx, 19-20; The Sustainable Development Goals Report 2020, 55; "Red List Index", International Union for Conservation of Nature and Natural Resources, accessed September 17. 2020, https://www.iucnredlist.org/assessment/red-list-index. A Red List Index "value of 1.0 equates to all species qualifying as Least Concern (i.e., not expected to become Extinct in the near future). A[Red List Index] value of 0 equates to all species having gone Extinct. A constant [Red List Index] value over time indicates that the overall extinction risk for the group is unchanged. If the rate of biodiversity loss were reducing, [then] the [Red List Index] would show an upward trend" ("Red List Index", International Union for Conservation of Nature and Natural Resources, accessed September 17. 2020, https://www.iucnredlist.org/assessment/red-list-index).

561 The Sustainable Development Goals Report 2020, 55.

562 The text to note 554 states SDG Target 15.5.

'protect and prevent the extinction of threatened species', which has not been accomplished, as sought, 'by 2020'. It is submitted that SDG Target 15.5 is unlikely to be met punctually, i.e., by 31st December 2030.[563]

Progress to date in accomplishment of SDG 15 as a whole

Bar SDG Targets 15.2,[564] 15.3,[565] 15.4,[566] 15.5[567] and 15.9,[568] targets of SDG 15[569] are compressed as follows.

> 15.1 By 2020, ensure the conservation, restoration and sustainable use of terrestrial and inland freshwater systems and their services … in line with obligations under international agreements[.] … 15.6 Promote fair and equitable sharing of the benefits arising from the utilization of genetic resources and promote appropriate access to such resources, as internationally agreed[.] 15.7 Take urgent action to end poaching and trafficking of protected species of flora and fauna and address both demand and supply of illegal wildlife products[.] 15.8 By 2020, introduce measures to prevent the introduction and significantly reduce the impact of invasive alien species … and control or eradicate the priority species[.] … 15.a Mobilize and significantly increase financial resources … to conserve and sustainably use biodiversity and ecosystems[.] 15.b Mobilize significant resources … to finance sustainable forest management and provide adequate incentives to developing countries to advance such management … [.] 15.c Enhance global support for efforts to combat poaching and trafficking of protected species … [.][570]

Regarding SDG Target 15.1, in 2020, on average, 44% of each terrestrial Key Biodiversity Area and 41% of each freshwater Key Biodiversity Area, worldwide, were within protected areas – which are increases of approximately 12-13% since 2000.[571] In respect of SDG Target 5.6: (i) As of 1st February 2020, the European Union and 122 countries had ratified

---

563 The target date for the SDGs to be achieved is 31st December 2030 (note 930 of Chapter Three and accompanying text).
564 The text to note 508 specifies SDG Target 15.2.
565 The text to note 513 states SDG Target 15.3.
566 The text to note 549 specifies SDG Target 15.4.
567 The text to note 554 states SDG Target 15.5.
568 The text to note 517 specifies SDG Target 15.9.
569 The text to note 507 states SDG 15.
570 Resolution 70/1 adopted by the General Assembly on 25 September 2015, Transforming our world: the 2030 Agenda for Sustainable Development, 24-25.
571 Progress towards the Sustainable Development Goals: Report of the Secretary-General, E/2020/xxx, 19; The Sustainable Development Goals Report 2020, 55.

the Nagoya Protocol on Access to Genetic Resources and the Fair and Equitable Sharing of Benefits Arising from the Utilization to the Convention on Biological Diversity[572] – a rise of 53 from 2019, and the European Union and 63 states had shared information about their frameworks on access and benefit-sharing,[573] and (ii) at the time of writing of the Report of the Secretary-General to the UN,[574] there were 146 Contracting Parties to the International Treaty on Plant Genetic Resources for Food and Agriculture, and 56 countries have supplied information about their measures on access and benefit-sharing concerning the genetic materials of crops, training for food and agriculture, and breeding.[575] As

---

[572] The Nagoya Protocol on Access to Genetic Resources and the Fair and Equitable Sharing of Benefits Arising from their Utilization to the Convention on Biological Diversity "is a supplementary agreement to the Convention on Biological Diversity [note 540]. It provides a transparent legal framework for the effective implementation of one of the three objectives of the CBD [Convention on Biological Diversity]: the fair and equitable sharing of benefits arising out of the utilization of genetic resources. The Nagoya Protocol on ABS [access and benefit-sharing] was adopted on 29 October 2010 in Nagoya, Japan and entered into force on 12 October 2014, 90 days after the deposit of the fiftieth instrument of ratification. Its objective is the fair and equitable sharing of benefits arising from the utilization of genetic resources, thereby contributing to the conservation and sustainable use of biodiversity." ("About the Nagoya Protocol", Secretariat of the Convention on Biological Diversity, accessed September 18, 2020, https://www.cbd.int/abs/about/default.shtml/).

[573] Progress towards the Sustainable Development Goals: Report of the Secretary-General, E/2020/xxx, 20.

[574] This report was released to the public on 19th May 2020, and "draws on the latest available data on the indicators contained in the global SDG indicator framework as of April 2020" ("UN Secretary-General Releases 2020 SDG Progress Report", International Institute for Sustainable Development, accessed September 18, 2020, https://sdg.iisd.org/news/un-secretary-general-releases-2020-sdg-progress-report/).

[575] Progress towards the Sustainable Development Goals: Report of the Secretary-General, E/2020/xxx, 20; "International Treaty on Plant Genetic Resources for Food and Agriculture", Food and Agriculture Organization of the United Nations, accessed September 18, 2020, http://www.fao.org/plant-treaty/overview/en/. The International Treaty on Plant Genetic Resources for Food and Agriculture was adopted on 3rd November 2001 by the Thirty-First Session of the Conference of the FAO; it aims to: (i) "recogniz[e] the enormous contribution of farmers to the diversity of crops that feed the world", (ii) establish[] a global system to provide farmers, plant breeders and scientists with access to plant genetic materials", and (iii) "ensur[e] that recipients share benefits they derive from the use of these genetic materials with the countries where they have been originated" ("International Treaty on Plant Genetic Resources for Food and Agriculture", Food and

regards SDG Targets 15.7 and 15.c: (i) the number of whole-pangolin equivalents globally that were seized for trafficking rose from 13.9 in 2014 to 35.8 in 2015, and thence to 75.9 in 2016 and 101.0 in 2017, and from there to an estimated 141.9 in 2018 – more than tenfold the amount for 2014,[576] and (ii) between 2014 and 2018, the equivalent of 370,000 pangolins were seized across the world, indicating that millions of these mammals were trafficked and killed – notwithstanding the international ban on legal, commercial trade in all eight species of pangolin that entered into force on 2nd January 2017.[577]

Will SDG 15 be achieved punctually?

Subject to one condition, SDG Target 15.2[578] may be attained punctually,[579] i.e., by 31st December 2030,[580] as may SDG Targets 15.3[581] and 15.9.[582] SDG Targets 15.4[583] and 15.5[584] are unlikely to be accomplished by that date. From the information that the foregoing subsection provides, it is submitted that: (i) SDG Targets 15.1[585] and 15.7[586] will probably not be fulfilled by 31st December 2020, (ii) SDG Target 15.6[587] may be realized by that date, and (iii) although the trafficking of pangolins appears to be rife,[588] there remains time to enhance worldwide support for attempts to tackle trafficking and poaching

---

Agriculture Organization of the United Nations, accessed September 18, 2020, http://www.fao.org/plant-treaty/overview/en/).

576 Agenda for Sustainable Development, 54.

577 Agenda for Sustainable Development, 54; Russell Scott and Emma Howard, "Even after a global ban, pangolins are still legally traded", *Unearthed (Greenpeace UK)*, July 23, 2020, accessed September 18, 2020, https://unearthed.greenpeace.org/2020/07/23/pangolin-ban-legal-trade-cites-china-us/.

578 The text to note 508 states SDG Target 15.2.

579 Text to note 532.

580 The target date for the SDGs to be met is 31st December 2030 (note 930 of Chapter Three and accompanying text).

581 Text to note 539. The text to note 513 specifies SDG Target 15.3.

582 Text to note 548, and the sentence that immediately follows that text. The text to note 517 states SDG Target 15.9.

583 Text to note 558. The text to note 549 states SDG Target 15.4,

584 Text to note 563. The text to note 554 specifies SDG Target 15.5.

585 Text to note 571. The text to note 570 compresses SDG Target 15.1.

586 Text to notes 576 and 577. The text to note 570 states SDG Target 15.7.

587 Text to notes 573 and 575. The text to note 570 specifies SDG Target 15.6.

588 Text to notes 576 and 577.

of protected species – and so SDG Target 15.c[589] may be achieved punctually. Taking all this together, it may be concluded that, whilst it is unlikely that every target of SDG 15[590] – and indeed every aim within the title of SDG 15 – will be met by 31st December 2030, one or more of these objectives are likely to be so satisfied by that date.

SDG 17: Revitalize the Global Partnership

MDG 8 and MDG Targets 8.A, 8.B, 8.C, 8.D and 8.F

MDG 8 is to "[d]evelop a global partnership for development".[591] It comprises six targets – MDG Targets 8.A, 8.B, 8.C, 8.D, 8.E and 8.F – five of which map to targets of SDG 17,[592] which is to "[s]trengthen the means of implementation and revitalize the Global Partnership for Sustainable Development".[593] MDG Target 8.E – which is the only target of MDG 8 not to map to a target of SDG 17 – is as follows: "In cooperation with pharmaceutical companies, provide access to affordable essential drugs in developing countries".[594] Generic medicines were available in 58% – on average – of public health facilities in low-income and lower-middle-income countries that were covered by the few surveys undertaken between 2007 and 2014, but in 67% – on average – of facilities in the private sector.[595]

---

[589] The text to note 570 compresses SDG Target 15.c.

[590] The text to note 507 states SDG 15.

[591] Note 157 of Chapter One. It is submitted that this MDG is not written in the Queen's English. More suitable alternatives might be to '*establish* a global partnership for development', '*fashion* a global partnership for development', '*institute* a global partnership for development' or '*put in place* a global partnership for development'.

[592] MDG 8 maps to SDG 17, MDG Target 8.A maps to SDG Target 17.10, MDG Target 8.B maps to SDG Targets 17.5, 17.8, 17.12 and 17.18, MDG Target 8.C maps to SDG Target 17.18, MDG Target 8.D maps to SDG Target 17.4, and MDG Target 8.F maps to SDG Targets 17.6, 17.7 and 17.8 (text to notes 39-47; text to notes 157-169 and 172-175 of Chapter One).

[593] Note 158 of Chapter One,

[594] Note 170 of Chapter One, and text to note 192. MDG Target 8.E maps to SDG Target 3.8 (text to notes 170 and 171 of Chapter One). The text to note 195 specifies SDG Target 3.8.

[595] Text to note 193.

MDG Target 8.A is to "[d]evelop further an open, rule-based, predictable, non-discriminatory trading and financial system".[596] The proportion of imports to developed states that they admitted duty-free, from developing countries and LDCs was, respectively, 54% and 78% in 1996, 65% and 70% in 2000, 75% and 81% in 2004, and 79% and 84% in 2014 – a slight fall from the respective values in 2013.[597] The share of exports from LDCs that were accorded preferential treatment – beyond that of Most-Favoured-Nation status – rose from 53% in 2011 to about 60% in 2014.[598] Regarding each of agricultural products, clothing and textiles, the average tariffs that developed states imposed on imports from: (i) developing countries, and (ii) LDCs, fell between 1996 and 2005.[599] Whilst the average tariffs that developed countries placed on imports of both clothing and textiles from developing states decreased from 2005 to 2014, those imposed on imports of clothing from LDCs rose slightly from 2005 to 2010 and declined very slightly from 2010 to 2014 – and those placed on imports of textiles from LDCs remained at the 2005 level in 2010 and 2014.[600] Conversely, the mean tariffs that developed states imposed on agricultural products from LDCs fell from 2005 to 2014, whilst those placed on such products from developing countries lessened from 2005 to 2010 and increased a little from 2010 to 2014.[601] Whilst on average, LDCs benefit from a wider margin of trade preference beyond Most-Favoured-Nation status on imports from developing countries than do other developing nations, this margin varies considerably across exporting regions.[602] ODA from developed countries rose by 66% in real terms between 2000 and 2014 to USD 135.2 billion.[603] It is submitted that these data are consistent with the development of an open, rule-based, predictable, non-discriminatory trading and financial system, but that it cannot be concluded therefrom that MDG Target 8.A[604] has been achieved.

---

596 Note 159 of Chapter One.
597 The Millennium Development Goals Report 2015, 64.
598 The Millennium Development Goals Report 2015, 64.
599 The Millennium Development Goals Report 2015, 64.
600 The Millennium Development Goals Report 2015, 64.
601 The Millennium Development Goals Report 2015, 64.
602 The Millennium Development Goals Report 2015, 65.
603 "We can end poverty: Millennium Development Goals and Beyond 2015 – Goal 8: Develop a global partnership for development", United Nations, accessed September 19, 2020, https://www.un.org/millenniumgoals/global.shtml.
604 The text to note 596 states MDG Target 8.A.

MDG Target 8.B is to "[a]ddress the special needs of the least developed countries".[605] In 2014, bilateral aid to LDCs dropped by 16% in real terms, reaching USD 25 billion at constant 2013 prices – although much of this reduction is attributable to debt relief for Myanmar in 2013.[606] Preliminary data for 2014 suggest that bilateral ODA to Sub-Saharan Africa – where 33 of the 47 LDCs are situated[607] – fell by 5% in real terms from the immediately-preceding year, attaining USD 25 billion at constant 2013 prices – although this decrease was only 2% if debt relief is factored out.[608] Notwithstanding these falls in bilateral aid and ODA to LDCs from 2013 to 2014, it is submitted that the provision of such bilateral aid, ODA and debt relief, together with the progressive – although irregular – reduction and elimination of tariffs on imports to developed countries from LDCs that data in the foregoing paragraph concerning MDG Target 8.A[609] present,[610] shows that the UN and other interested parties have 'addressed the special needs of LDCs' as MDG Target 8.B requires,[611] and, therefore, that this MDG Target has been met.

MDG Target 8.C is to "[a]ddress the special needs of landlocked developing countries and small island developing States ...".[612] In 2016, the OECD stated the following regarding aid to LDCs, LLDCs and SIDS.

> ODA from the nineteen EU [European Union] countries that are DAC [Development Assistance Committee[613]] members[614] was USD 73.5 billion in 2015, representing an increase of 12.7% in real terms ... . The United

---

605 Note 161 of Chapter One.

606 The Millennium Development Goals Report 2015, 63.

607 Note 130 of Chapter Two and accompanying text.

608 The Millennium Development Goals Report 2015, 63.

609 The text to note 596 specifies MDG Target 8.A.

610 Text to notes 597-602.

611 The text to note 605 states MDG Target 8.B.

612 Note 166 of Chapter One.

613 Note 963 of Chapter Three states the overall aim of the OECD Development Assistance Committee.

614 Note 969 of Chapter Three lists the thirty members of the OECD, which, as of 7th September 2020, included nineteen Member States of the European Union (Austria, Belgium, the Czech Republic, Denmark, Finland, France, Germany, Greece, Hungary, Ireland, Italy, Luxembourg, the Netherlands, Poland, Portugal, Slovakia, Slovenia, Spain, and Sweden) and the European Union itself. This list of nineteen countries is not identical to the 'nineteen EU countries' to which the text refers, as the UK was a Member State of the European Union at the date of the OECD Report that the text quotes – 13th April 2016, but was not a Member State of the European Union at the date of the list in note 969 of Chapter Three – 7th September 2020.

> States [of America] continued to be the largest donor by volume with net ODA flows amounting to USD 31.1 billion in 2015, a fall of 7.0% in real terms compared to 2014. … CPA [Country Programmable Aid[615]] to least developed countries (LDCs) and other low-income countries (Other LICs) increased by 3% in real terms to USD 39.8 billion in 2015 compared to 2014. … The [2016 Development Assistance Committee] Survey [on Forward Spending Plans] results suggest a large increase in 2016 of global CPA of USD 5.2 billion (constant 2015 prices), stemming from both bilateral and multilateral providers. This increase will benefit countries across all income groups, but primarily LDCs and fragile states, where an increase of 6% in real terms is noted due to larger disbursements by multilateral agencies. … On a geographical basis, the largest increases in 2016 can be expected for populous countries in Asia … and for countries in sub-Saharan Africa, such as Ethiopia [which is an LLDC (note 286 of Chapter Three)], Nigeria, and Uganda [which is an LLDC]. Slight decreases are, however, to be expected for countries in the Americas [which include several SIDS (note 285 of Chapter Three)] and in Oceania [where there are also a number of SIDS]. … Global CPA is projected to remain stable up to 2019 with a continued upward trajectory for the LDCs … . The Survey projects declining levels of CPA for some individual LDCs between 2016 and 2019, such as Guinea and Niger [which is an LLDC] … . Aid is also expected to rise, although at a slower pace than for LDCs, to other countries most in need, such as other low-income countries, fragile and conflict-affected states and economies, landlocked developing countries and small island developing states.[616]

It is opined that, on the basis of the information in the above passage,[617] the donor countries of aid to developing states and territories have not tended to address the special needs of LLDCs and SIDS, with the latter in particular being of low priority relative to LDCs as a grouping for the receipt of foreign aid. Therefore, it is submitted that MDG Target 8.C[618] has not been fulfilled.

---

[615] Country Programmable Aid "is the portion of aid that providers can programme for individual countries or regions, and over which partner countries could have a significant say. [It] is a closer proxy of aid that goes to partner countries than the concept of official development assistance (ODA)" ("Country programmable aid (CPA)", Organisation for Economic Co-operation and Development, accessed September 20, 2020, http://www.oecd.org/dac/financing-sustainable-development/development-finance-standards/cpa.htm).

[616] Organisation for Economic Co-operation and Development, Development aid in 2015 continues to grow despite costs for in-donor refugees, 13 April 2016 (Paris, 2016), 2, 4 and 5).

[617] Text to note 616.

[618] The text to note 612 specifies MDG Target 8.C.

MDG Target 8.D is to "[d]eal comprehensively with the debt problems of developing countries through national and international measures in order to make debt sustainable in the long term".[619] In 2013, the external debt service of those developing countries that observe the World Bank's Debtor Reporting System was 3.1% of their export revenue, which is down from 12.0% in 2000, 7.7% in 2004 and in 2005, and 3.6% in 2008, but has slowly risen from 2.9% in 2011 and 3.0% in 2012.[620] The reduction in the burden of developing countries' external debt service has resulted from improved management of debt, expansion of trade, considerable debt relief for very poor countries, and favourable conditions for borrowing funds on international capital markets.[621] It is submitted that, whilst these data show the debt problems of developing countries to be less severe in 2013 than in 2000, it is not certain that these difficulties have been comprehensively addressed such that debt is sustainable in the long term – as MDG Target 8.D requires.[622] Thus, it is opined that MDG Target 8.D may not have been accomplished.

MDG Target 8.F is to "make available the benefits of new technologies, especially information and communications", "[i]n cooperation with the private sector".[623] The proportion of the world's population covered by a 2G mobile-cellular network rose from 58% in 2001 to 95% in 2015.[624] The number of mobile-cellular subscriptions has increased from 738 million in 2000 to more than 7 billion in 2015.[625] The number of users of the Internet has grown from slightly more than 6% of the global population in 2000 to 43% of that population in 2015.[626] Preliminary data for 2015 suggest that a little more than one third of the population in developing regions then used the Internet, whilst 82%, less than 21%, and less than 10% of the population in developed regions, Sub-Saharan Africa and LDCs, respectively, did so.[627] Whilst the worldwide mobile-cellular penetration rate was 97% in 2015, this rate in LDCs reached 64% in that year.[628] On the basis of these data it is submitted that, whilst the proportion of the population of LDCs using mobile telephones and the Internet is

---

[619] Note 168 of Chapter One.
[620] The Millennium Development Goals Report 2015, 66.
[621] The Millennium Development Goals Report 2015, 66.
[622] The text to note 619 specifies MDG Target 8.D.
[623] Note 172 of Chapter One.
[624] The Millennium Development Goals Report 2015, 67.
[625] The Millennium Development Goals Report 2015, 67.
[626] The Millennium Development Goals Report 2015, 67.
[627] The Millennium Development Goals Report 2015, 68.
[628] The Millennium Development Goals Report 2015, 68.

lower than that of the world, global usage of these technologies has risen so much between 2000 and 2015 that it should be concluded that: (i) new technologies have been made available to the public over this period – in accordance with MDG Target 8.F,[629] and (ii) therefore, this MDG Target has been achieved.

Thus, MDG Targets 8.B[630] and 8.F[631] have been accomplished, but MDG Target 8.C[632] has not been realized and MDG Targets 8.A,[633] 8.D[634] and 8.E[635] may or may not have been attained. It is submitted that, as at least one-third of the targets of MDG 8 have been met, this MDG should be considered to have been partly fulfilled but not to have been achieved in full.

From MDG Target 8.D to SDG Target 17.4

SDG Target 17.4 is to "[a]ssist developing countries in attaining long-term debt sustainability through coordinated policies aimed at fostering debt financing, debt relief and debt restructuring, as appropriate, and address the external debt of highly indebted poor countries to reduce debt distress".[636] This SDG Target follows on from MDG Target 8.D[637] in also aiming to achieve long-term debt sustainability in developing countries, but is more specific than the latter in its approach to attaining this goal. Whilst MDG Target 8.D wished to 'deal comprehensively with the debt problems of developing countries through national and international measures', without stating what measures or types of measures might be suitable, SDG Target 17.4 recommends 'coordinated policies aimed at fostering debt financing, debt relief and debt restructuring'.

In addition, SDG Target 17.4 adds a new objective that MDG Target 8.D did not explicitly require – namely 'address the external debt of highly indebted poor countries to reduce debt distress'. It is submitted that this aim was within the ambit of MDG Target 8.D. Nevertheless, by including

---

629 The text to note 623 states MDG Target 8.F.

630 Text to note 611. The text to note 605 states MDG Target 8.B.

631 Point (ii) of the final sentence of the immediately-preceding paragraph. The text to note 623 specifies MDG Target 8.F.

632 Text to note 618. The text to note 612 states MDG Target 8.C.

633 Text to note 604. The text to note 596 specifies MDG Target 8.A.

634 Text to note 622, and the sentence that immediately follows that text. The text to note 619 specifies MDG Target 8.D.

635 Text to note 595. The text to note 594 states MDG Target 8.E.

636 Note 169 of Chapter One.

637 The text to note 619 specifies MDG Target 8.D.

this goal expressly, SDG Target 17.4 creates an expectation of developed countries that they should go further in their assistance for 'highly indebted poor countries' in order to alleviate the latter's debt distress, than they are expected to do for other developing states in pursuit of long-term debt sustainability.

Progress to date in the accomplishment of SDG Target 17.4

SDG Indicator 17.4.1 measures "[d]ebt service as a proportion of exports of goods and services.[638] Table 4.2 shows total debt service as a percentage of exports of goods, services and primary income, for a sample of twenty developing countries with large populations – for 2015, i.e., the year in which the SDGs became effective,[639] and for 2017, which is the latest year for which data on this SDG Indicator are currently available.

Table 4.2: Total debt service as a proportion of exports of goods, services and primary income (%) for twenty developing countries with large populations[640]

Country	2015 value	2017 value	% change on 2015 value
Bangladesh	4.73	5.52	+16.70[641]
Brazil	38.10	36.19	-5.01[642]
China	4.89	7.62	+55.83[643]
Colombia	28.05	41.63	+48.41[644]
Egypt	9.98	15.12	+51.50[645]
India	11.21	10.07	-10.17[646]

[638] Global indicator framework for the Sustainable Development Goals and targets of the 2030 Agenda for Sustainable Development, 20.
[639] The UN General Assembly adopted the SDGs and their targets in Resolution 70/1, which is dated 25th September 2015 (text to note 35 of Chapter One; note 37 of Chapter One and accompanying text).
[640] "Debt service of exports of goods and services", Our World in Data, accessed September 21, 2020, https://ourworldindata.org/grapher/debt-service-of-exports-of-goods-services?tab=table&time=2015. These percentages are given to two decimal places.
[641] [(5.52% – 4.73%) / 4.73%] * 100% = 16.70%.
[642] [(36.19% – 38.10%) / 38.10%] * 100% = -5.01%.
[643] [(7.62% – 4.89%) / 4.89%] * 100% = 55.83%.
[644] [(41.63% – 28.05%) / 28.05%] * 100% = 48.41%.
[645] [(15.12% – 9.98%) / 9.98%] * 100% = 51.50%.

Indonesia	31.99	33.96	+6.16[647]
Kenya	8.21	14.78	+80.02[648]
Mexico	13.16	14.01	+6.46[649]
Myanmar	8.08	5.22	-35.40[650]
Nigeria	2.85	6.83	+139.65[651]
Pakistan	13.97	22.80	+63.21[652]
The Philippines	12.93	11.31	-12.53[653]
South Africa	7.77	12.19	+56.89[654]
Sudan	10.65	4.22	-60.38[655]
Tanzania	3.95	8.38	+112.15[656]
Thailand	6.87	4.71	-31.44[657]
Turkey	27.44	40.22	+46.57[658]
Uganda	2.00	3.76	+88.00[659]
Vietnam	3.82	5.94	+55.50[660]

Table 4.2 shows that the total debt service as a proportion of exports of goods, services and primary income has risen from 2015 to 2017 in thirteen of the twenty populous developing countries whose data this table contains. Of these countries, Brazil, Colombia, Indonesia and Turkey each has total debt service in 2015 of more than 20% of its exports of goods services and primary income, and would, it is submitted, be considered to be 'highly indebted' – as worded in SDG Target 17.4.[661] The total debt service as a proportion of exports has increased from 2015 to 2017 in three

646 [(10.07% – 11.21%) / 11.21%] * 100% = -10.17%.
647 [(33.96% – 31.99%) / 31.99%] * 100% = 6.16%.
648 [(14.78% – 8.21%) / 8.21%] * 100% = 80.02%.
649 [(14.01% – 13.16%) / 13.16%] * 100% = 6.46%.
650 [(5.22% – 8.08%) / 8.08%] * 100% = -35.40%.
651 [(6.83% – 2.85%) / 2.85%] * 100% = 139.65%.
652 [(22.80% – 13.97%) / 13.97%] * 100% = 63.21%.
653 [(11.31% – 12.93%) / 12.93%] * 100% = -12.53%.
654 [(12.19% – 7.77%) / 7.77%] * 100% = 56.89%.
655 [(4.22% – 10.65%) / 10.65% * 100% = -60.38%.
656 [(8.38% – 3.95%) / 3.95%] * 100% = 112.15%.
657 [(4.71% – 6.87%) / 6.87%] * 100% = -31.44%.
658 [(40.22% – 27.44%) / 27.44%] * 100% = 46.57%.
659 [(3.76% – 2.00%) / 2.00%] * 100% = 88.00%.
660 [(5.94% – 3.82%) / 3.82%] * 100% = 55.50%.
661 The text to note 636 states SDG Target 17.4. These four countries might not be regarded as 'poor' in SDG Target 17.4, as none of them are LDCs. Note 125 of Chapter Two lists the 47 states that the UN currently classifies as LDCs.

of these four states, i.e., Colombia, Indonesia and Turkey – with the latter two countries each exceeding total debt service of 40% of its exports of goods, services and primary income in 2017.

Will SDG Target 17.4 be achieved punctually?

The data in Table 4.2 tend to support the view that little is being done to help developing countries to attain long-term debt sustainability, and that the issue of raised external debt is not being adequately addressed. Thus, on the basis of this information, it is unlikely that SDG Target 17.4[662] will be achieved punctually, i.e., by 31st December 2030.[663]

From MDG Target 8.B to SDG Targets 17.5 and 17.12

SDG Target 17.5 is to "[a]dopt and implement investment promotion regimes for least developed countries".[664] SDG Target 17.12 is to "[r]ealize timely implementation of duty-free and quota-free market access on a lasting basis for all least developed countries, consistent with World Trade Organization decisions, including by ensuring that preferential rules of origin applicable to imports from least developed countries are transparent and simple, and contribute to facilitating market access".[665]

SDG Target 17.5 and SDG Target 17.12 are each an instance of MDG Target 8.B,[666] which requires the 'special needs of the LDCs' to be addressed. SDG Target 17.5 requires states to 'adopt and implement investment promotion regimes for LDCs', and SDG Target 17.12 calls for countries to 'realize timely implementation of duty-free and quota-free market access on a lasting basis for all LDCs'.

Progress to date in the accomplishment of SDG Target 17.5

SDG Indicator 17.5.1 determines the "[n]umber of countries that adopt and implement investment promotion regimes for developing countries,

---

[662] The text to note 636 specifies SDG Target 17.4.
[663] The target date for the SDGs to be fulfilled is 31st December 2030 (note 930 of Chapter Three and accompanying text).
[664] Note 162 of Chapter One.
[665] Note 164 of Chapter One.
[666] The text to note 605 states MDG Target 8.B.

including the least developed countries".[667] The UN Global SDG Database presently lacks data concerning SDG Indicator 17.5.1.[668]

FDI inflows to African LDCs was up 27% on the low of 2017 to USD 12 billion in 2018, which remained more than 40% below the annual average of 2012 to 2016.[669] Led by Bangladesh – which was up 68% on its FDI level of 2017 to USD 3.6 billion in 2018, Asian and Oceanic LDCs reached a new high in FDI inflows of USD 12 billion in 2018.[670]

Following a temporary recovery in 2017, FDI inflows to the LLDCs decreased again in 2018 – by 2% to USD 23 billion, which is 1.7% of worldwide FDI inflows for that year.[671] FDI inflows to LLDCs remained directed at a few economies – Azerbaijan, Ethiopia, Kazakhstan, Mongolia, and Turkmenistan accounted for 56% of total FDI inflows to this grouping.[672]

FDI inflows to the SIDS fell for a second successive year to USD 3.7 billion in 2018, with an 11% reduction in these funds to the Caribbean SIDS.[673] FDI inflows to the Asian and Oceanic SIDS stayed constant at USD 1 billion.[674] Those to the African SIDS declined by 22% to USD 0.6 billion.[675]

In 2018, 55 economies instituted at least 112 policy measures affecting foreign investment, 66% of which sought to liberalize, advance and facilitate new investment, and 34% of which introduced new regulations

---

[667] Global indicator framework for the Sustainable Development Goals and targets of the 2030 Agenda for Sustainable Development, 20.

[668] "SDG indicators: United Nations Global SDG Database", United Nations, accessed September 22, 2020, https://unstats.un.org/sdgs/indicators/database/.

[669] United Nations Conference on Trade and Development, World Investment Report 2019: Special Economic Zones – Key Messages and Overview (Geneva: United Nations, 2019), 13.

[670] World Investment Report 2019: Special Economic Zones – Key Messages and Overview, 13.

[671] World Investment Report 2019: Special Economic Zones – Key Messages and Overview, 13.

[672] World Investment Report 2019: Special Economic Zones – Key Messages and Overview, 14.

[673] World Investment Report 2019: Special Economic Zones – Key Messages and Overview, 14.

[674] World Investment Report 2019: Special Economic Zones – Key Messages and Overview, 14.

[675] World Investment Report 2019: Special Economic Zones – Key Messages and Overview, 14.

or restrictions for FDI – the highest percentage since 2003.[676] In 2018, forty new international investment agreements were signed, which comprised thirty bilateral investment treaties and ten treaties with investment provisions.[677]

Will SDG Target 17.5 be achieved punctually?

On the basis of the information in the immediately-preceding subsection, it is submitted that there is some appetite for investment in Asian LDCs and in some mainly large LLDCs, but little for investment in SIDS. It is opined that this is fairly unsupportive of SDG Target 17.5,[678] and that this SDG Target is unlikely to be met punctually, i.e., by 31st December 2030.[679]

Progress to date in the accomplishment of SDG Target 17.12

SDG Indicator 17.12.1 ascertains the "[w]eighted average tariffs faced by developing countries, least developed countries and small island developing States".[680] SDG Target 17.12[681] is concerned with 'duty-free and quota-free market access on a lasting basis for *all least developed countries*'. Therefore, the weighted average tariff rate for all products exported from those LDCs for which data are available is shown in Table 4.3 – for 2015, i.e., the year in which the SDGs came into force,[682] and for 2018, i.e., the latest year for which these statistics are available.

---

[676] World Investment Report 2019: Special Economic Zones – Key Messages and Overview, 15.

[677] World Investment Report 2019: Special Economic Zones – Key Messages and Overview, 17.

[678] The text to note 664 specifies SDG Target 17.5.

[679] The target date for the SDGs to be accomplished is 31st December 2030 (note 930 of Chapter Three and accompanying text).

[680] Global indicator framework for the Sustainable Development Goals and targets of the 2030 Agenda for Sustainable Development, 21.

[681] The text to note 665 states SDG Target 17.12.

[682] The UN General Assembly adopted the SDGs and their targets in Resolution 70/1, which is dated 25th September 2015 (text to note 35 of Chapter One; note 37 of Chapter One and accompanying text).

Table 4.3: Weighted average tariff rate applied by developed countries (preferential status) for all products exported from the 46 LDCs for which data are available (%)[683]

LDC	2015 value	2018 value	% change on 2015 value
LDCs	*1.15977*	*1.12650*	*-2.86867[684]*
Afghanistan	0.29994	0.28324	-5.56778[685]
Angola	0.00414	0.02082	+402.89855[686]
Bangladesh	4.16870	4.08093	-2.10545[687]
Benin	0.09608	0.09226	-3.97585[688]
Bhutan	0.30245	0.29978	-0.88279[689]
Burkina Faso	0.16082	0.05825	-63.77938[690]
Burundi	0.01950	0.03198	+64.00000[691]
Cambodia	5.38777	5.20200	-3.44799[692]
Central African Republic	0.02837	0.02223	-21.64258[693]
Chad	0.63184	0.13445	-78.72088[694]
Comoros	0.07549	0.07480	-0.91403[695]
The Democratic Republic of the Congo	0.00865	0.01060	+22.54335[696]
Djibouti	0.26079	0.24336	-6.68354[697]

683 "SDG indicators: United Nations Global SDG Database", United Nations, accessed September 22, 2020, https://unstats.un.org/sdgs/indicators/database/. These percentages are given to five decimal places. The spreadsheet concerning SDG Indicator 17.12.1 that was downloaded from this webpage on 22nd September 2020 does not include data on South Sudan.

684 [(1.12650% – 1.15977%) / 1.15977%] * 100% = -2.86867%.

685 [(0.28324% – 0.29994%) / 0.29994%] * 100% = -5.56778%.

686 [(0.02082% – 0.00414%) / 0.00414%] * 100% = 402.89855%.

687 [(4.08093% – 4.16870%) / 4.16870%] * 100% = -2.10545%.

688 [(0.09226% – 0.09608%) / 0.09608%] * 100% = -3.97585%.

689 [(0.29978% – 0.30245%) / 0.30245%] * 100% = -0.88279%.

690 [(0.05825% – 0.16082%) / 0.16082%] * 100% = -63.77938%.

691 [(0.03198% – 0.01950%) / 0.01950%] * 100% = 64.00000%.

692 [(5.20200% – 5.38777%) / 5.38777%] * 100% = -3.44799%.

693 [(0.02223% – 0.02837%) / 0.02837%] * 100% = -21.64258%.

694 [(0.13445% – 0.63184%) / 0.63184%] * 100% = -78.72088%.

695 [(0.07480% – 0.07549%) / 0.07549%] * 100% = -0.91403%.

696 [(0.01060% – 0.00865%) / 0.00865%] * 100% = 22.54335%.

Eritrea	0.29904	0.28643	-4.21683[698]
Ethiopia	0.02360	0.02470	+4.66102[699]
The Gambia	0.33346	0.34694	+4.04246[700]
Guinea	0.02043	0.02628	+28.63436[701]
Guinea-Bissau	0.23987	0.26475	+10.37228[702]
Haiti	0.29225	0.24691	-15.51411[703]
Kiribati	0.02855	0.23296	+715.97198[704]
Laos	4.48702	4.51322	+0.58391[705]
Lesotho	0.25616	0.22947	-10.41927[706]
Liberia	0.00412	0.00422	+2.42718[707]
Madagascar	0.35929	0.32042	-10.81856[708]
Malawi	6.24696	6.24096	-0.09605[709]
Mali	0.17131	0.07698	-55.06392[710]
Mauritania	0.10709	0.15815	+47.67952[711]
Mozambique	0.03754	0.03886	+3.51625[712]
Myanmar	5.22181	4.80438	-7.99397[713]
Nepal	2.64777	2.61017	-1.42006[714]
Niger	0.06097	0.05130	-15.86026[715]
Rwanda	0.01884	0.02876	+52.65393[716]

697 [(0.24336% – 0.26079%) / 0.26079%] * 100% = -6.68354%.
698 [(0.28643% – 0.29904%) / 0.29904%] * 100% = -4.21683%.
699 [(0.02470% – 0.02360%) / 0.02360%] * 100% = 4.66102%.
700 [(0.34694% – 0.33346%) / 0.33346%] * 100% = 4.04246%.
701 [(0.02628% – 0.02043%) / 0.02043%] * 100% = 28.63436%.
702 [(0.26475% – 0.23987%) / 0.23987%] * 100% = 10.37228%.
703 [(0.24691% – 0.29225%) / 0.29225%] * 100% = -15.51411%.
704 [(0.23296% – 0.02855%) / 0.02855%] * 100% = 715.97198%.
705 [(4.51322% – 4.48702%) / 4.48702%] * 100% = 0.58391%.
706 [(0.22947% – 0.25616%) / 0.25616%] * 100% = -10.41927%.
707 [(0.00422% – 0.00412%) / 0.00412%] * 100% = 2.42718%.
708 [(0.32042% – 0.35929%) / 0.35929%] * 100% = -10.81856%.
709 [(6.24096% – 6.24696%) / 6.24696%] * 100% = -0.09605%.
710 [(0.07698% – 0.17131%) / 0.17131%] * 100% = -55.06392%.
711 [(0.15815% – 0.10709%) / 0.10709%] * 100% = 47.67952%.
712 [(0.03886% – 0.03754%) / 0.03754%] * 100% = 3.51625%.
713 [(4.80438% – 5.22181%) / 5.22181%] * 100% = -7.99397%.
714 [(2.61017% – 2.64777%) / 2.64777%] * 100% = -1.42006%.
715 [(0.05130% – 0.06097%) / 0.06097%] * 100% = -15.86026%.
716 [(0.02876% – 0.01884%) / 0.01884%] * 100% = 52.65393%.

São Tomé and Príncipe	0.21846	0.29843	+36.60624[717]
Senegal	0.22011	0.24043	+9.23175[718]
Sierra Leone	0.02762	0.02570	-6.95148[719]
The Solomon Islands	0.08191	0.11565	+41.19155[720]
Somalia	0.10802	0.13055	+20.85725[721]
Sudan	0.48589	0.48136	-0.93231[722]
Tanzania	0.17238	0.15976	-7.32103[723]
Timor-Leste	0.00147	0.00202	+37.41497[724]
Togo	0.07491	0.10319	+37.75197[725]
Tuvalu	0.28154	0.17800	-36.77630[726]
Uganda	0.35317	0.30604	-13.34484[727]
Vanuatu	0.09328	0.11591	+24.26029[728]
Yemen	0.01889	0.05277	+179.35416[729]
Zambia	0.05965	0.06267	+5.06287[730]

The weighted average tariff rates applied by developed countries for all products exported from LDCs are remarkably low, being between 1.1% and 1.2% on average, and declining by just under 3% between 2015 and 2017. The highest values are for the LDCs in South and South-East Asia – Cambodia (5.4% in 2015 and 5.2% in 2017), Myanmar (5.2% in 2015 and 4.8% in 2017), Laos (4.5% in both 2015 and 2017), Bangladesh (4.2% in 2015 and 4.1% in 2017), and Nepal (2.6% in both 2015 and 2017), except for Malawi (6.2% in both 2015 and 2017). All the other LDCs in Table 4.3 have weighted average tariff rates applied by developed countries for their exports that are below 1%, in both 2015 and 2017. For 22 of the 46 LDCs

717 [(0.29843% – 0.21846%) / 0.21846%] * 100% = 36.60624%.
718 [(0.24093% – 0.22011%) / 0.22011%] * 100% = 9.23175%.
719 [(0.02570% – 0.02762%) / 0.02762%] * 100% = -6.95148%.
720 [(0.11565% – 0.08191%) / 0.08191%] * 100% = 41.19155%.
721 [(0.13055% – 0.10802%) / 0.10802%] * 100% = 20.85725%.
722 [(0.48136% – 0.48589%) / 0.48589%] * 100% = -0.93231%.
723 [(0.15976% – 0.17238%) / 0.17238%] * 100% = -7.32103%.
724 [(0.00202% – 0.00147%) / 0.00147%] * 100% = 37.41497%.
725 [(0.10319% – 0.07491%) / 0.07491%] * 100% = 37.75197%.
726 [(0.17800% – 0.28154%) / 0.28154%] * 100% = -36.77630%.
727 [(0.30604% – 0.35317%) / 0.35317%] * 100% = -13.34484%.
728 [(0.11591% – 0.09328%) / 0.09328%] * 100% = 24.26029%.
729 [(0.05277% – 0.01889%) / 0.01889%] * 100% = 179.35416%.
730 [(0.06267% – 0.05965%) / 0.05965%] * 100% = 5.06287%.

in Table 4.3, the weighted average tariff rate applied by developed countries to the exports of the former has risen. For the other 24 LDCs in Table 4.3, this weighted average tariff rate has fallen.

Will SDG Target 17.12 be achieved punctually?

The data in Table 4.3 show that tariff rates that developed countries apply to exports from LDCs tend to be low, and that these are, on average, a little smaller in 2017 than in 2015. Thus, countries are on their way to 'realizing timely implementation of duty-free market access on a lasting basis for all LDCs', in accordance with SDG Target 17.12.[731] However, neither these data – nor any statistics that are associated with SDG Indicator 17.12.1[732] – provide information as to whether states, in line with SDG Target 17.12, are either 'realizing timely implementation of quota-free market access on a lasting basis for all LDCs' or 'ensuring that preferential rules of origin applicable to imports from LDCs are transparent and simple, and contribute to facilitating market access'. It is submitted that, whilst it is feasible for LDCs to attain quota-free access by 31st December 2030,[733] it is less likely that preferential rules of origin which apply to imports from LDCs will be universally transparent and simple by then – as this area of the law of international trade is complex. In the light of these observations and comments, it is opined that SDG Target 17.12 will not be punctually achieved in full – although it may be in part.

From MDG Target 8.F to SDG Targets 17.6 and 17.7

SDG Target 17.6 is to "[e]nhance North-South, South-South and triangular regional and international cooperation on and access to science, technology and innovation and enhance knowledge sharing on mutually agreed terms, including through improved coordination among existing mechanisms, in particular at United Nations level, and through a global technology facilitation mechanism".[734] This SDG Target is a progression of MDG Target 8.F[735] regarding information, communication and

---

[731] The text to note 665 specifies SDG Target 17.12.

[732] The text to note 680 states SDG Indicator 17.12.1.

[733] The target date for the SDGs to be realized is 31st December 2030 (note 930 of Chapter Three and accompanying text).

[734] Note 173 of Chapter One. North' represents developed countries, and 'South' less-developed economies (note 173 of Chapter One).

[735] The text to note 623 specifies MDG Target 8.F.

technology. In particular, MDG Target 8.F disseminates new technologies, whilst SDG Target 17.6 introduces a worldwide technology facilitation mechanism.

SDG Target 17.7 is to "[p]romote the development, transfer, dissemination and diffusion of environmentally sound technologies to developing countries on favourable terms, including on concessional and preferential terms, as mutually agreed".[736] This SDG Target is a very-specific application of MDG Target 8.F, as the latter makes the benefits of new technologies generally-available, whilst the former concentrates on advancing environmentally sound technologies and offering these to developing states on agreed favourable terms.

Progress to date in the accomplishment of SDG Target 17.6

SDG Indicator 17.6.1 determines the "[f]ixed Internet broadband subscriptions per 100 inhabitants, by speed".[737] Whilst this Indicator does not 'enhance North-South, South-South and triangular cooperation and international cooperation on and access to science, to technology and innovation' – as SDG Target 17.6[738] requires, it reveals the ability of countries to access information on science, technology and innovation. Thus, the following information on Internet access and broadband descriptions is given in relation to SDG Target 17.6.

At the end of 2019, 53.6% of people worldwide were estimated to be using the Internet.[739] In 2018, only 20% of the Oceanic population – excluding that of Australia and New Zealand – and 26% in Sub-Saharan Africa were using the Internet, whilst 84% of people in Europe, the USA, Canada and Greenland,[740] and 87% of Australians and New Zealanders, were using the Internet.[741]

---

[736] Note 174 of Chapter One.

[737] Global indicator framework for the Sustainable Development Goals and targets of the 2030 Agenda for Sustainable Development, 20.

[738] The text to note 734 states SDG Target 17.6.

[739] Progress towards the Sustainable Development Goals: Report of the Secretary-General, E/2020/xxx, 22; The Sustainable Development Goals Report 2020, 59.

[740] *The Sustainable Development Goals Report 2020* refers to 'Europe and Northern America' (The Sustainable Development Goals Report 2020, 59). 'Northern America' comprises the USA, Canada and Greenland (The Sustainable Development Goals Report 2020, 63). Reference to 'Northern America' is avoided in the text, in order to avoid confusion with 'North America', which, in addition to the USA, Canada and Greenland, includes the countries of Central America and the islands in the Caribbean Sea (note 309 of Chapter Three).

[741] The Sustainable Development Goals Report 2020, 59.

Globally, fixed-broadband subscriptions have almost doubled from 7.6 per 100 inhabitants in 2010 to 14.9 per 100 inhabitants in 2019.[742] In 2019, developed states had 33.6 fixed-broadband subscriptions per 100 inhabitants, whilst developing countries had 11.2 fixed-broadband subscriptions per 100 inhabitants.[743] LDCs had few fixed broadband connections, due to the lack and high cost of infrastructure.[744]

Will SDG Target 17.6 be achieved punctually?

It is submitted that both the 'enhance' aims within SDG Target 17.6[745] – especially the second – are achievable punctually, i.e., by 31st December 2020.[746] The data in the foregoing subsection are supportive of this result, although there is room for improvement both in the number of people using the Internet and in the number of fixed-broadband subscriptions – especially in the poorest countries and regions.

Progress to date in the accomplishment of SDG Target 17.7

SDG Indicator 17.7.1 measures the "[t]otal amount of funding for developing countries to promote the development, transfer, dissemination and diffusion of environmentally sound technologies".[747] Unfortunately, there are no data available concerning either this SDG Indicator or SDG Target 17.7[748] at the time of writing.[749]

---

[742] The Sustainable Development Goals Report 2020, 59.
[743] The Sustainable Development Goals Report 2020, 59.
[744] The Sustainable Development Goals Report 2020, 59.
[745] The text to note 734 specifies SDG Target 17.6.
[746] The target date for the SDGs to be attained is 31st December 2030 (note 930 of Chapter Three and accompanying text).
[747] Global indicator framework for the Sustainable Development Goals and targets of the 2030 Agenda for Sustainable Development, 20.
[748] The text to note 736 states SDG Target 17.7.
[749] The UN Global SDG Database currently presents no data on SDG Target 17.7 ("SDG indicators: United Nations Global SDG Database", United Nations, accessed September 24, 2020, https://unstats.un.org/sdgs/indicators/database/). SDG Tracker states: "We are currently not aware of data for this indicator [i.e., SDG Indicator 17.7.1]. You can notify us of available data for this indicator via our feedback form." ("Sustainable Development Goal 17: Revitalize the global partnership for sustainable development", SDG Tracker, accessed September 24, 2020, https://sdg-tracker.org/global-partnerships). In addition, neither the Report of the Secretary General of the UN nor *The Sustainable Development Goals Report 2020* contains information concerning SDG Target 17.7 (Progress towards the

Will SDG Target 17.7 be achieved punctually?

Notwithstanding the absence of data on SDG Target 17.7,[750] the application of a literal interpretation[751] to the *prima facie*[752] requirements of this SDG Target tends to support a reasonable probability of its punctual achievement.[753] This tentative prediction of a successful result is

---

Sustainable Development Goals: Report of the Secretary-General, E/2020/xxx, 21-23; The Sustainable Development Goals Report 2020, 58-59).

750 Note 749 and accompanying text. The text to note 736 specifies SDG Target 17.7.

751 Note 59 explains the concept of a 'literal interpretation', as applied to MDG 1.

752 Note 59 defines the phrase '*prima facie*'.

753 SDG Target 17.7 is to "*[p]romote* the *development*, *transfer*, *dissemination and diffusion* of *environmentally sound technologies* to developing countries *on favourable terms* ... as *mutually agreed*" (text to note 736; emphasis added). 'Promote' – in this sense of the word – means "further the progress of (something, especially a cause, venture or aim); support or actively encourage" (note 306). On the basis of this definition, it is submitted that 'promote' is a gentle requirement, compared with, say, 'significantly achieve' or 'firmly deliver'. 'Environmentally sound technologies' is a broad term, which should include any technical advance that does not cause harm to either the Earth or its atmosphere. This term has four descriptors – 'development', 'transfer', 'dissemination' and 'diffusion', which are connected by the conjunction 'and' – meaning that all these descriptors need to be satisfied for the SDG Target to be fulfilled. This is the hardest part of the test. However, the first two descriptors are sequential, and the third and fourth descriptors follow the second descriptor and have similar meanings: to 'disseminate' is to 'spread or disperse (something, especially information) widely' (*The New Oxford Dictionary of English*, 534), and to 'diffuse' – in this sense of the word – is to "spread or cause to spread over a wide area or between a large number of people" (*The New Oxford Dictionary of English*, 514). 'On favourable terms' in this context means that the package of 'development, transfer, dissemination and diffusion of environmentally sound technologies' must be of overall benefit to the developing countries to which these technologies are transferred, disseminated and dispersed. Finally, the promotion of the development, transfer, dissemination and diffusion of environmentally sound technologies to developing countries on favourable terms must be 'as mutually agreed', i.e., as agreed between the country – be it an advanced country or a developing country – that develops and transfers these technologies and the developing country to which the technologies are transferred – and in which these are to be disseminated and diffused. Thus, it is submitted that, for accomplishment of SDG Target 17.7 to be declared with regard to these two countries, there must be an agreement between them as to the promotion by the former of the development, transfer, dissemination and diffusion of environmentally sound technologies to the latter on favourable terms. It is opined that this is achievable punctually, i.e., by 31st December 2030.

subject to a reassessment, pending the forthcoming receipt of relevant information.

From MDG Targets 8.B and 8.F to SDG Target 17.8

SDG Target 17.8 is to "[f]ully operationalize the technology bank and science, technology and innovation capacity-building mechanism for least developed countries by 2017 and enhance the use of enabling technology, in particular information and communications technology".[754] This SDG Target comprises two objectives: (i) to 'fully operationalize the technology bank and science, technology and innovation capacity-building mechanism for LDCs by 2017', and (ii) to 'enhance the use of enabling technology'.

The first objective of SDG Target 17.8 is an instance MDG Target 8.B,[755] i.e., the former 'addresses a special need of the LDCs', namely, the operationalization of the technology bank and science, technology innovation capacity-building mechanism for these countries.

Both objectives of SDG Target 17.8 are applications of MDG Target 8.F.[756] Objective (i) of SDG Target 17.8 'makes available the benefits of new technologies' in accordance with that MDG Target, by requiring operationalization of a technology-related capacity-building mechanism for LDCs. Objective (ii) of SDG Target 17.8 also 'makes available the benefits of new technologies' in line with MDG Target 8.F, by requiring enhancement of the use of – i.e., an increase in the take-up of – enabling technology.[757]

Progress to date in the accomplishment of SDG Target 17.8

SDG Indicator 17.8.1 ascertains the "[p]roportion of individuals using the Internet".[758] As detailed above,[759] just over half of people globally were estimated to be using the Internet in 2019 – with data for 2018 showing Australia and New Zealand, and Europe, the USA, Canada and

[754] Note 163 of Chapter One.
[755] The text to note 605 states MDG Target 8.B.
[756] The text to note 623 specifies MDG Target 8.F.
[757] 'Enhance' means 'intensify, increase, or further improve the quality, value, or extent of' (*The New Oxford Dictionary of English*, 612).
[758] Global indicator framework for the Sustainable Development Goals and targets of the 2030 Agenda for Sustainable Development, 20.
[759] Text to notes 739 and 741.

Greenland,[760] to have a much greater proportion of people than this using the Internet, and Sub-Saharan Africa and Oceania to have a considerably smaller proportion of people there using the Internet. Furthermore, the technology bank and science, technology and innovation capacity-building mechanism for LDCs was established in September 2017 and inaugurated on 4th June 2018,[761] which means that the first objective of SDG Target 17.8[762] has been achieved.

Will SDG Target 17.8 be achieved punctually?

Whilst the first objective of SDG Target 17.8[763] has been accomplished,[764] the second objective, i.e., to 'enhance the use of enabling technology, in particular information and communications technology', is also likely to be satisfied punctually, i.e., by 31st December 2030.[765] It is opined that the latter objective means 'an increase in the take up of enabling technology, in particular information and communications technology'.[766] SDG Indicator 17.8.1[767] determines the percentage of people who use the Internet, which lags in some developing regions in comparison with developed countries.[768] Notwithstanding this, it is opined that the number of users of the Internet is increasing worldwide – which would support the claim that the second objective of SDG Target 17.8 – and, therefore, this SDG Target as a whole (as its first objective has been fulfilled), is likely to be realized by 31st December 2030.

---

760 Whilst *The Sustainable Development Goals Report 2020* refers to 'Europe and Northern America' rather than to 'Europe, the USA, Canada and Greenland', reference in the text to 'Northern America' is avoided in order to avoid confusion with 'North America' (note 740).
761 "Technology Bank Inaugurated in Turkey, Work Under Way in 16 LDCs: 7 June 2018", International Institute for Sustainable Development, accessed September 25, 2020, http://sdg.iisd.org/news/technology-bank-inaugurated-in-turkey-work-under-way-in-16-ldcs/.
762 The text to note 754 states SDG Target 17.8. Point (i) in the sentence immediately-following that text comprises the first objective of SDG Target 17.8.
763 The text to note 754 specifies SDG Target 17.8.
764 Text to note 762.
765 The target date for the SDGs to be met is 31st December 2030 (note 930 of Chapter Three and accompanying text).
766 Text to note 757.
767 The text to note 758 states SDG Indicator 17.8.1.
768 Text to note 759.

From MDG Target 8.A to SDG Target 17.10

SDG Target 17.10 is to "[p]romote a universal, rules-based, open, non-discriminatory and equitable multilateral trading system under the World Trade Organization, including through the conclusion of negotiations under its Doha Development Agenda".[769] This SDG Target is an application of MDG Target 8.A[770] that is limited to trade, and which progresses from this MDG Target to be universal and equitable. SDG Target 17.10 adds to MDG Target 8.A a condition for the former's fulfilment – that negotiations under the WTO's Doha Development Agenda have been concluded.

Progress to date in the accomplishment of SDG Target 17.10

With regard to the Doha Development Agenda, the WTO states the following.

> The next step will be agreement on "modalities" – the way or method of doing something. In the Doha Development Agenda negotiations[,] these are blueprints for the final deal, e[.]g[.], how to cut tariffs, and reduce agricultural subsidies and support, along with flexibilities to deal with various sensitivities. Once the modalities have been settled, countries will apply the formulas to tariffs on thousands of products and to a range of support programmes. Added to that will be pledges on how open their markets will be for services. The result will be the "schedules of commitments", which will take up tens of thousands of pages of the final deal. And also in the final deal will be new or revised agreements, the WTO's rule book.[771]

Based on this description of the tasks still to be done regarding the WTO's Doha Development Agenda, it is submitted that there are still many hours of work ahead for governments to bring their negotiations on this matter to a successful conclusion.

---

[769] Note 160 of Chapter One.

[770] The text to note 596 specifies MDG Target 8.A.

[771] "The Doha Round texts – introduction", World Trade Organization, accessed September 25, 2020, https://www.wto.org/english/tratop_e/dda_e/texts_intro_e.htm.

Will SDG Target 17.10 be achieved punctually?

Notwithstanding the outstanding work to be done on the Doha Development Agenda, the WTO currently has no Director-General, with the sixth Director-General Mr. Roberto Azevêdo having stepped down from this position on 31st August 2020 – one year in advance of the expiry of his second term,[772] Moreover, the Appellate Body of the WTO[773] is presently dysfunctional.[774] Further to these circumstances, and to the excerpt[775] and comment in the immediately-preceding subsection, it is opined that SDG Target 17.10[776] will not be attained punctually, i.e., by 31st December 2030.[777]

From MDG Targets 8.B and 8.C to SDG Target 17.18

SDG Target 17.18 is to "enhance capacity-building support to developing countries, including for least developed countries and small island developing States, to increase significantly the availability of high-quality, timely and reliable data disaggregated by income, gender, age, race, ethnicity, migratory status, disability, geographical location and other characteristics relevant in national contexts", by 2020.[778] MDG Target

---

[772] "Roberto Azevêdo, WTO Director-General, 2013 to 2020", accessed September 25, 2020, https://www.wto.org/english/thewto_e/dg_e/ra_e.htm.

[773] The Appellate Body of the WTO "was established in 1995 under Article 17 of the Understanding on Rules and Procedures Governing the Settlement of Disputes (DSU). It is a standing body of seven persons that hears appeals from reports issued by panels in disputes brough by WTO Members. The Appellate Body can uphold, modify or reverse the legal findings and conclusions of a panel, and Appellate Body Reports, once adopted by the Dispute Settlement Body (DSB) must be accepted by the parties to the dispute." ("Appellate Body", World Trade Organization, accessed September 25, 2020, https://www.wto.org/english/tratop_e/dispu_e/appellate_body_e.htm).

[774] A Division of three Members of the Appellate Body of the WTO is needed to hear each appeal from a Panel, but there is currently only one Member (and Chairperson) of the Appellate Body – Dr. Hong Zhao – whose term expires on 30th November 2020 ("Appellate Body Members", World Trade Organization, accessed September 25, 2020, https://www.wto.org/english/tratop_e/dispu_e/ab_members_descrp_e.htm).

[775] Text to note 771.

[776] The text to note 769 specifies SDG Target 17.10.

[777] The target date for the SDGs to be fulfilled is 31st December 2030 (note 930 of Chapter Three and accompanying text).

[778] Note 165 of Chapter One.

8.B[779] requires the special needs of the LDCs to be addressed. MDG Target 8.C[780] calls for the special needs of SIDS and LLDCs to be addressed. SDG Target 17.18 is an instance of both MDG Target 8.B and MDG Target 8.C, as this SDG Target requires 'the enhancement of capacity-building support to developing countries, *including for LDCs and SIDS*, to increase the availability of high-quality, timely and reliable data disaggregated by characteristics relevant in national contexts, by 2020'.

Progress to date in the accomplishment of SDG Target 17.18

For the period 2014 to 2018, 147 countries have birth registration data that are 90% or more complete, and 153 countries have death registration data which are 75% or more complete.[781] In 2019, 132 countries reported that they had national statistical legislation which observed the UN Fundamental Principles of Official Statistics[782] – a progression from 111 countries in 2018.[783]

---

[779] The text to note 605 states MDG Target 8.B.

[780] The text to note 612 specifies MDG Target 8.C.

[781] Progress towards the Sustainable Development Goals: Report of the Secretary-General, E/2020/xxx, 23.

[782] The General Assembly of the United Nations endorsed the Fundamental Principles of Official Statistics in Resolution 68/261 of 29 January 2014 ("Fundamental Principles of National Official Statistics", United Nations, accessed September 25. 2020, https://unstats.un.org/unsd/dnss/gp/fundprinciples.aspx). There are ten Fundamental Principles of Official Statistics, which are condensed as follows: "Principle 1: … [O]fficial statistics that meet the test of practical utility are to be compiled and made available on an impartial basis by official statistical agencies to honour citizens' entitlement to public information. Principle 2: … [T]he statistical agencies need to decide according to strictly professional considerations, including scientific principles and professional ethics, on the methods and procedures for the collection, processing, storage and presentation of statistical data. Principle 3: … [T]he statistical agencies are to present information according to scientific standards on the sources, methods and procedures of the statistics. Principle 4: … The statistical agencies are entitled to comment on erroneous interpretation and misuse of statistics. Principle 5: … Data for statistical purposes may be drawn from all types of sources … . Statistical agencies are to choose the source with regard to quality, timeliness, costs and the burden on respondents. Principle 6: … Individual data collected by statistical agencies for statistical compilation … are to be strictly confidential and used exclusively for statistical purposes. Principle 7: … The laws, regulations and measures under which the statistical systems operate are to be made public. Principle 8: … Coordination among statistical agencies within countries is essential to achieve consistency and efficiency in the statistical system. Principle 9: The use by

In 2019, 141 countries reported that they were implementing a national statistical plan, which is up from 129 countries in 2018.[784] Only 25% of national statistical plans were fully-funded in Sub-Saharan Africa – i.e., those of 9 out of 36 countries that were implementing these plans; this is the region with the lowest proportion of fully-funded plans.[785]

Will SDG Target 17.18 be achieved punctually?

The key factors as to the standard to be applied for SDG Target 17.18[786] are: (i) the definition of 'enhance' – which is 'intensify, increase, or further improve the quality, value or extent of'[787] – and (ii) to increase significantly the availability of high-quality, timely and reliable data disaggregated by characteristics relevant in national contexts'. It is submitted that, on the basis of this definition, only a small rise in capacity-building support to developing countries – including LDCs and SIDS – is required, as long as data with the above three descriptors is increased significantly – which is the harder part of SDG Target 17.18 to satisfy (i.e., the enhancement of the capacity-building support is the easier part of this SDG Target to fulfil). The UN Fundamental Principles of Statistics includes requirements for quality (Principles 2, 3, 4, 5, 9 and 10), timeliness (Principles 5 and 8) and reliability (Principles 2, 3, 8 and 9).[788] Therefore, the substantial rise in countries from 2018 to 2019 that report national statistics legislation which complies with the UN Fundamental Principles of Official Statistics[789] is a promising sign for the achievement of the harder part of SDG Target 17.18. Regarding the easier part of this SDG Target to accomplish, there should be a rise in the

---

statistical agencies in each country of international concepts, classifications and methods promotes the consistency and efficiency of statistical systems at all official levels. Principle 10: … Bilateral and multilateral cooperation in statistics contributes to the improvement of systems of official statistics in all countries." (United Nations, Resolution 68/261 adopted by the General Assembly on 29 January 2014).

783 Progress towards the Sustainable Development Goals: Report of the Secretary-General, E/2020/xxx, 23.

784 Progress towards the Sustainable Development Goals: Report of the Secretary-General, E/2020/xxx, 23; The Sustainable Development Goals Report 2020, 59.

785 Progress towards the Sustainable Development Goals: Report of the Secretary-General, E/2020/xxx, 23; The Sustainable Development Goals Report 2020, 59.

786 The text to note 778 states SDG Target 17.18.

787 Note 757.

788 Note 782 condenses the UN Fundamental Principles of Statistics.

789 Text to note 783.

number of national statistical plans that are fully-funded.[790] The fairly-ubiquitous availability of comprehensive birth and death registration data[791] illustrates that data of the type that SDG Target 17.18 describes – i.e., high-quality, timely and reliable, may be available over important areas such as records of national births and deaths. On the basis of these observations, it is opined that there is a considerable likelihood that SDG Target 17.18 will be realized punctually, i.e., by 31st December 2020.[792]

Progress to date in accomplishment of SDG 17 as a whole

Except for SDG Targets 17.4,[793] 17.5,[794] 17.6,[795] 17.7,[796] 17.8,[797] 17.10,[798] 17.12[799] and 17.18,[800] targets of SDG 17[801] are abbreviated as follows.

> 17.1 Strengthen domestic resource mobilization … to improve domestic capacity for … revenue collection[.] 17.2 Developed countries to implement fully their official development assistance commitments … [.] 17.3 Mobilize additional financial resources for developing countries from multiple sources[.] … 17.9 Enhance international support for implementing effective and targeted capacity-building in developing countries to support national plans to implement all the Sustainable Development Goals … [.] … 17.11 Significantly increase the exports of developing countries, in particular with a view to doubling the least developed countries' share of global exports by 2020[.] … 17.13 Enhance global macroeconomic stability, including through policy coordination and policy coherence[.] 17.14 Enhance policy coherence for sustainable development[.] 17.15 Respect each country's policy space and leadership to establish and implement policies for poverty eradication and sustainable development[.] 17.16 Enhance the Global Partnership for Sustainable Development … to

---

790 Text to note 785.

791 Text to note 781.

792 The target date for the SDGs to be accomplished is 31st December 2030 (note 930 of Chapter Three and accompanying text). Whilst SDG Target 17.18 is scheduled to be achieved by 2020 (text to note 778), it is submitted that the extent of its attainment should be assessed alongside that of other SDG Targets.

793 The text to note 636 specifies SDG Target 17.4.

794 The text to note 664 states SDG Target 17.5.

795 The text to note 734 specifies SDG Target 17.6.

796 The text to note 736 states SDG Target 17.7.

797 The text to note 754 specifies SDG Target 17.8.

798 The text to note 769 states SDG Target 17.10.

799 The text to note 665 specifies SDG Target 17.12.

800 The text to note 778 states SDG Target 17.18.

801 The text to note 593 specifies SDG 17.

> support the achievement of the Sustainable Development Goals in all countries, in particular developing countries[.] 17.17 Encourage and promote effective public, public-private and civil society partnerships, building on the experience and resourcing strategies of partnerships[.] … 17.19 By 2030, build on existing initiatives to develop measures of progress on sustainable development that complement gross domestic product, and support statistical capacity-building in developing countries[.][802]

Regarding SDG Target 17.1: (i) government revenue worldwide accounted for about 30% of GDP in 2018, remaining stable but with broad variation among countries, (ii) the average overall 'tax burden' – i.e., revenue in the form of tax inflows – was 25% of GDP among developed countries, and 17% of GDP among developing and emerging market economies, and (iii) the overall average percentage of government expenditure that is funded by taxes was approximately 65% among advanced economies, and 60% among emerging market economies.[803] In respect of SDG Target 17.2: (i) net ODA flows from member countries of the OECD Development Assistance Committee[804] totalled USD 147.4 billion in 2019, which was very similar to the amount of such flows in 2018 but with a greater share going to the poorest countries,[805] (ii) net bilateral ODA to LDCs in 2019 increased in real terms by 2.6% on the 2018 total,[806] and (iii) net bilateral ODA to Africa in 2019 rose in real terms by 1.3% on the 2018 total.[807]

As regards SDG Target 17.3: *FDI* (i) global FDI to developing countries increased by 2% from its level in 2017 to USD 706 billion in 2018, but with noteworthy differences among regions, (ii) developing countries in Asia registered a rise in FDI inflows of 4% to USD 512 billion in 2018 – with increases happening in all Asia's sub-regions, (iii) FDI inflows to Africa rose by 11% to USD 46 billion in 2018, which was below the annual average of the immediately-preceding ten years of approximately USD 50 billion, and (iv) FDI inflows to Latin America and the Caribbean fell by 6%

---

802 Resolution 70/1 adopted by the General Assembly on 25 September 2015, Transforming our world: the 2030 Agenda for Sustainable Development, 26-27.

803 Progress towards the Sustainable Development Goals: Report of the Secretary-General, E/2020/xxx, 22.

804 Note 969 of Chapter Three lists the members of the OECD Development Assistance Committee. Note 963 of Chapter Three states the OECD Development Assistance Committee's overarching aim from 2018 to 2022.

805 Progress towards the Sustainable Development Goals: Report of the Secretary-General, E/2020/xxx, 22; The Sustainable Development Goals Report 2020, 58.

806 The Sustainable Development Goals Report 2020, 58.

807 The Sustainable Development Goals Report 2020, 58.

on their total in 2017 to USD 147 billion in 2018 – although FDI inflows to this region in 2017 were higher than in 2016.[808] Also concerning SDG Target 17.3: *Remittances* (i) remittance flows to low-income and middle-income countries are estimated to be USD 554 billion in 2019, and (ii) these flows increased 4.7% from 2018 to 2019, compared with a rise of 8.6% from 2017 to 2018.[809]

With respect to SDG Target 17.9, total ODA for capacity-building and national planning was USD 33.5 billion in 2017, which represented 14% of total sector-allocable aid – a stable proportion.[810] The principal sectors assisted were the energy sector, the financial sector, and public administration, which together received USD 13.0 billion.[811]

Regarding SDG Target 17.11: (i) the share of LDC exports in worldwide merchandise trade was marginally above 1% in 2018, which is a slight rise from 2017 but at approximately the same level as ten years previously – thereby missing the objective within this SDG Target of doubling the LDCs' share of global exports by 2020,[812] (ii) the share of worldwide exports in services of LDCs rose from 0.7% in 2017 to 0.8% in 2018 – although most LDCs outside Asia contributed little to these exports,[813] and (iii) developing countries' share of both goods exports and service exports has been almost constant from 2012 to 2018, at approximately 45% of global goods exports and 30% of worldwide services exports, respectively.[814] Global merchandise trade is predicted to fall by between 13% and 32% in 2020, due to the COVID-19 pandemic.[815]

---

[808] The Sustainable Development Goals Report 2020, 58.

[809] Progress towards the Sustainable Development Goals: Report of the Secretary-General, E/2020/xxx, 22; The Sustainable Development Goals Report 2020, 58.

[810] Progress towards the Sustainable Development Goals: Report of the Secretary-General, E/2020/xxx, 23.

[811] Progress towards the Sustainable Development Goals: Report of the Secretary-General, E/2020/xxx, 23.

[812] Progress towards the Sustainable Development Goals: Report of the Secretary-General, E/2020/xxx, 23; The Sustainable Development Goals Report 2020, 59. The text to note 802 states SDG Target 17.11 – including this objective.

[813] The Sustainable Development Goals Report 2020, 59.

[814] The Sustainable Development Goals Report 2020, 59.

[815] The Sustainable Development Goals Report 2020, 59. The WHO classified the outbreak and spread of COVID-19 as a pandemic on 11th March 2020 (note 53 of Chapter Two).

Will SDG 17 be achieved punctually?

The data in the immediately-preceding subsection, together with those concerning SDG Targets 17.4,[816] 17.5,[817] 17.6,[818] 17.7,[819] 17.8,[820] 17.10,[821] 17.12[822] and 17.18,[823] tend to support the view that, whilst SDG 17[824] will probably not be met punctually in its entirety, this SDG is likely to be partly fulfilled by 31st December 2030.[825] SDG 17 comprises two objectives within its wording: (i) to 'strengthen the means of implementation of the Global Partnership for Sustainable Development', and (ii) to 'revitalize the Global Partnership for Sustainable Development'. It is submitted that objective (i) has progressed better than objective (ii), in particular because worldwide access to information and communication technologies is improving – which assists in the accomplishment of objective (i), but the prevalence of COVID-19 is dampening enthusiasm for sustainable development amongst advanced economies – who consequently have problems in their own jurisdictions that did not exist in September 2015, i.e., when the SDGs came into effect.[826]

Conclusion

The 'Continuation Microstudy' – Chapter Two – concludes that SDG 1 will not be met punctually.[827] The 'Continuation Macrostudy' – the current

---

816 Table 4.2. The text to note 636 states SDG Target 17.4.

817 Text to notes 669-677. The text to note 664 specifies SDG Target 17.5.

818 Text to notes 739-744. The text to note 734 states SDG Target 17.6.

819 Whilst no data is currently available on SDG Target 17.7 (text to note 749), the application of a literal interpretation to the *prima facie* requirements of SDG Target 17.7 tends to support a reasonable likelihood of its punctual achievement (text to note 753). The text to note 736 specifies SDG Target 17.7.

820 Text to notes 759 and 761. The text to note 754 states SDG Target 17.8.

821 Text to notes 771, 772 and 774. The text to note 769 specifies SDG Target 17.10.

822 Table 4.3. The text to note 665 states SDG Target 17.12.

823 Text to notes 781, 783, 784 and 785. The text to note 778 specifies SDG Target 17.18.

824 The text to note 593 states SDG 17.

825 The target date for the SDGs to be realized is 31st December 2030 (note 930 of Chapter Three and accompanying text).

826 The UN General Assembly adopted the SDGs and their targets in Resolution 70/1, which is dated 25th September 2015 (text to note 35 of Chapter One; note 37 of Chapter One and accompanying text).

827 Text to note 413 of Chapter Two.

Chapter – finds that: (i) SDG 2 will not be achieved punctually,[828] (ii) the progress that has been made towards realizing the targets of SDG 3 is insufficient to make it probable that SDG 3 will be fulfilled punctually,[829] (iii) it is unlikely that SDG 4 will be satisfied punctually,[830] (iv) it is improbable that SDG 5 will be accomplished punctually,[831] (v) SDG 6 is unlikely to be attained punctually,[832] (vi) SDG 14 will not be met punctually, because not all its targets will have been achieved by 31st December 2030,[833] (vii) it is unlikely that either all targets of SDG 15 or every aim within the title of SDG 15 will be realized punctually,[834] and (viii) SDG 17 will probably not be attained punctually in its entirety, but is likely to be partly accomplished by 31st December 2030.[835] It is submitted that this outcome constitutes a fairly disappointing prediction as to the likelihood of punctual achievement of the nine SDGs that Table 1.4 categorizes as proceeding from the MDGs. This conclusion completes the examination of these 'Continuation' SDGs as to the likelihood of their fulfilment by 31st December 2030.

The next Chapter is the 'New Ground Macrostudy', which extends the 'micro' analysis in Chapter Three of the probability of meeting SDG 10 punctually to the other SDGs that Table 1.4 classifies as being new Goals, i.e., SDGs 7, 8, 9, 11, 12, 13 and 16. Like the appraisal of SDGs 2, 3, 4, 5, 6, 14, 15 and 17 in the present Chapter, the work in Chapter Five comprises a 'macro' analysis, which uses the content of published reports as its basis.

---

828 Text to note 95.
829 Text to note 226.
830 Text to note 281.
831 Text to note 332.
832 Text to note 442.
833 Text to note 504. The target date for the SDGs to be attained is 31st December 2030 (note 930 of Chapter Three and accompanying text).
834 Text to note 590.
835 Text to note 825.

CHAPTER FIVE

NEW GROUND MACROSTUDY: PROGRESS TOWARDS FULFILLING THE SUSTAINABLE DEVELOPMENT GOALS WHOSE SCOPE IS BEYOND THAT OF THE MILLENNIUM DEVELOPMENT GOALS

Introduction

Chapter Three – the 'New Ground Microstudy' – systematically considers the targets and indicators for SDG 10, in assessing whether those targets are likely to be achieved punctually – and, ultimately, whether this SDG is to be so attained. In the current Chapter, this method is summarily applied to the other SDGs that Table 1.4 classifies as new Goals – i.e., SDGs 7, 8, 9, 11, 12, 13 and 16, using the content of published reports as the basis for analysis. One section is allocated to the scrutiny of each of these SDGs. The final section concludes both this Chapter and the book as a whole.

Before this 'New Ground Macrostudy' is carried out, a look is taken of the extent of connection of the SDGs that Table 1.4 categorizes as new Goals, with the MDGs. Table 5.1 reproduces that part of Table 1.2 which shows the mappings from MDGs or MDG Targets that are received by these SDGs and their targets.

Table 5.1 shows that there are mappings neither from MDGs to any of SDGs 7, 9, 10, 12, 13 and 16, nor from MDG Targets to any of the targets of these SDGs. Thus, these six SDGs are entirely new Goals. This Chapter does not address SDG 10, as this Goal is the subject of the 'New Ground Microstudy' that is Chapter Three.

Table 5.1 also reveals that there is a mapping of one MDG Target to one target of SDG 8, which is that of MDG Target 1.B to SDG Target 8.5.[1] MDG Target 1.B is to "[a]chieve full and productive employment

[1] Text to notes 100 and 101 of Chapter One.

and decent work for all, including women and young people",[2] which, as Chapter Two notes, has not been achieved[3] and has been updated and re-presented as SDG Target 8.5 – "achieve full and productive employment and decent work for all women and men, including for young people and persons with disabilities, and equal pay for equal work of equal value", by 2030.[4]

Table 5.1: The number of mappings to SDGs 7, 8, 9, 10, 11, 12, 13 and 16 and to their targets

SDG Number	***Number of mappings from MDGs to the relevant SDG***	**Total number of targets of the relevant SDG**	***Number of these SDG Targets to which MDG Targets are mapped***	***Total number of mappings to the targets of the relevant SDG***
7	*0*	5	*0*	*0*
8	*0*	12	*1*	*1*
9	*0*	8	*0*	*0*
10	*0*	10	*0*	*0*
11	*1*	10	*2*	*2*
12	*0*	11	*0*	*0*
13	*0*	5	*0*	*0*
16	*0*	12	*0*	*0*

Table 5.1 additionally shows that: (i) there is a mapping of one MDG to SDG 11, which is that of MDG 7,[5] and (ii) there are two mappings of an MDG Target to an SDG Target, which are not to the same SDG Target. MDG 7 is to "[e]nsure environmental sustainability".[6] SDG 11 is to "[m]ake cities and human settlements inclusive, safe, resilient and sustainable".[7] The connection between MDG 7 and SDG 11 is that human settlements are a part of the environment, and therefore that MDG 7 – as well as SDG 11 – aims to make human settlements sustainable.[8] The two

[2] Note 100 of Chapter One, and text to note 20 of Chapter Two.
[3] Note 21 of Chapter Two and accompanying text.
[4] Note 101 of Chapter One, and text to note 22 of Chapter Two.
[5] Text to notes 132 and 134 of Chapter One.
[6] Note 132 of Chapter One, and text to note 333 of Chapter Four.
[7] Note 134 of Chapter One.
[8] Based on the definition of the word 'ensure', MDG 7 aims to make certain that environmental sustainability will occur (note 377 of Chapter Four). As human

mappings from MDG Targets to targets of SDG 11 are: (i) from MDG Target 7.A to SDG Target 11.3,[9] and (ii) from MDG Target 7.D to SDG Target 11.1.[10]

MDG Target 7.A is to "[i]ntegrate the principles of sustainable development into country policies and programmes and reverse the loss of environmental resources".[11] SDG Target 11.3 is to "enhance inclusive and sustainable urbanization and capacity for participatory, integrated and sustainable human settlement planning and management in all countries", by 2030.[12] SDG Target 11.3 contains two instances of the application of the first part of MDG Target 7.A, i.e., 'integrate the principles of sustainable development into country policies and programmes', which are 'enhance inclusive and sustainable urbanization in all countries' and 'enhance capacity for participatory, integrated and sustainable human settlement planning and management in all countries'.

MDG Target 7.D is "to have achieved a significant improvement in the lives of at least 100 million slum dwellers", by 2020.[13] SDG Target 11.1 is to "ensure access for all to adequate, safe and affordable housing and basic services and upgrade slums", by 2030.[14] The second objective within SDG Target 11.1, i.e., 'upgrade slums', is a concise way of describing the essence of MDG Target 7.D, i.e., 'achieve a significant improvement in the lives of slum dwellers'. Furthermore, SDG Target 11.1 broadens MDG Target 7.D from application to slum dwellers to application to everyone – as the first objective within SDG Target 11.1 is to 'ensure access *for all* to adequate, safe and affordable housing and basic services'.

SDG 7: Ensure Access to Sustainable Energy for All

SDG 7 and its targets

SDG 7 is to "[e]nsure access to affordable, reliable, sustainable and modern energy for all".[15] The targets of SDG 7 are as follows.

---

settlements are a part of the environment, this aim includes making certain that human settlements are sustainable.

[9] Text to notes 137 and 139 of Chapter One.

[10] Text to notes 155 and 156 of Chapter One.

[11] Note 137 of Chapter One, and text to note 336 of Chapter Four.

[12] Note 139 of Chapter One.

[13] Note 155 of Chapter One, and text to note 367 of Chapter Four.

[14] Note 156 of Chapter One.

[15] United Nations, Resolution 70/1 adopted by the General Assembly on 25 September 2015, Transforming our world: the 2030 Agenda for Sustainable Development, 14.

> 7.1 By 2030, ensure universal access to affordable, reliable and modern energy services[.] 7.2 By 2030, increase substantially the share of renewable energy in the global energy mix[.] 7.3 By 2030, double the global rate of improvement in energy efficiency[.] 7.a By 2030, enhance international cooperation to facilitate access to clean energy research and technology, including renewable energy, energy efficiency and advanced and cleaner fossil-fuel technology, and promote investment in energy infrastructure and clean energy technology[.] 7.b By 2030, expand infrastructure and upgrade technology for supplying modern and sustainable energy services for all in developing countries, in particular least developed countries, small island developing States and landlocked developing countries, in accordance with their respective programmes of support[.][16]

Progress to date in the accomplishment of SDG 7

90% of the global population had access to electricity in 2018, which is up from 83% in 2010.[17] Whilst SDG Target 7.1 requires universal access to reliable, affordable and modern energy services by 2030,[18] achieving this goal will be a challenge due to the fact that 53% of the population of Sub-Saharan Africa in 2018 lacked access to electricity.[19] To accomplish SDG Target 7.1 punctually, the annual rate of electrification must rise from the current 0.82% to 0.87% for 2019 to 2030.[20]

The share of renewable energy in total final energy consumption worldwide rose from 16.3% in 2010 to 17.0% in 2015, and thence to 17.3% in 2017.[21] Whilst the greatest increase in the use of renewable energy has been in the electricity sector – driven by expansion of wind and solar power, the share of renewable energy in the heat and transportation sectors – which accounted for 80% of final energy use – fell behind its potential.[22] An acceleration of the use of renewable energy in all these

---

[16] Resolution 70/1 adopted by the General Assembly on 25 September 2015, Transforming our world: the 2030 Agenda for Sustainable Development, 19.

[17] Progress towards the Sustainable Development Goals: Report of the Secretary-General, E/2020/xxx, 11; The Sustainable Development Goals Report 2020, 38.

[18] The text to note 16 states SDG Target 7.1.

[19] Progress towards the Sustainable Development Goals: Report of the Secretary-General, E/2020/xxx, 11; The Sustainable Development Goals Report 2020, 38.

[20] The Sustainable Development Goals Report 2020, 38.

[21] Progress towards the Sustainable Development Goals: Report of the Secretary-General, E/2020/xxx, 12; The Sustainable Development Goals Report 2020, 39.

[22] The Sustainable Development Goals Report 2020, 39.

sectors will be needed to realize SDG Target 7.2[23] punctually, i.e., by 31st December 2030.[24]

In 2017, worldwide primary energy intensity – total energy used per unit of GDP – was 5.0 megajoules per USD, which is a 1.7% improvement on the 2016 level but the smallest annual improvement since 2010.[25] Progress of 2.2% per annum between 2010 and 2017 was more sustained that previously.[26] Preliminary estimates for 2018 and 2019 are for an annual improvement in primary energy intensity of 1.3% and 2.0%, respectively, which would cause the primary energy intensity improvement rate to be about 2.1% between 2010 and 2019.[27] SDG Target 7.3 requires the global rate of improvement in energy efficiency to be doubled by 2030.[28] During the base period – 1990 to 2010 – the annual rate of improvement in worldwide primary energy intensity was 1.3%.[29] Thus, the rate of improvement in global primary energy intensity that SDG Target 7.3 requires is 2 * 1.3% per annum, i.e., 2.6% per annum.[30] Consequently, the current annual rate of improvement in primary energy intensity – 2.1% – is insufficient to attain SDG Target 7.3 punctually, i.e., by 31st December 2030.[31]

Worldwide access to clean cooking fuels and technologies grew from 56% of the global population in 2010 to 60% in 2015, and thence to 63% in 2018.[32] In 2018, about 2.8 billion people remained without access to these fuels and technologies – a number that remained fairly constant for two decades preceding that year.[33] These individuals rely mainly on

---

[23] The text to note 16 specifies SDG Target 7.2.

[24] The target date for the SDGs to be met is 31st December 2030 (note 930 of Chapter Three and accompanying text).

[25] Progress towards the Sustainable Development Goals: Report of the Secretary-General, E/2020/xxx, 12; The Sustainable Development Goals Report 2020, 39.

[26] The Sustainable Development Goals Report 2020, 39.

[27] The Sustainable Development Goals Report 2020, 39.

[28] The text to note 16 states SDG Target 7.3.

[29] The Sustainable Development Goals Report 2020, 39.

[30] The Sustainable Development Goals Report 2020, 39. The Report of the Secretary-General specifies that the annual rate of improvement in global primary energy intensity that SDG Target 7.3 requires, is 2.7% per annum (Progress towards the Sustainable Development Goals: Report of the Secretary-General, E/2020/xxx, 12).

[31] The target date for the SDGs to be achieved is 31st December 2030 (note 930 of Chapter Three and accompanying text).

[32] Progress towards the Sustainable Development Goals: Report of the Secretary-General, E/2020/xxx, 11; The Sustainable Development Goals Report 2020, 38.

[33] The Sustainable Development Goals Report 2020, 38.

inefficient and contaminating cooking systems.[34] In Sub-Saharan Africa, from 2014 to 2018 the population was increasing at a rate that was faster than the rate at which people there were obtaining access to clean cooking fuels and technologies.[35] This situation is fairly unpromising with regard to the chances of achieving SDG Target 7.b[36] punctually, i.e., by 31st December 2030.[37]

Transnational public financial inflows to developing countries in support of clean and renewable energy rose to USD 21.4 billion in 2017, which is 13% up on such inflows in 2016 and double the level of these inflows in 2010.[38] Investment in hydropower projects received 46% of 2017 inflows, whilst investments in solar energy projects, wind energy projects and geothermal energy projects received 19%, 7% and 6% of these inflows, respectively.[39] Only 12% of international public financial inflows to developing countries in 2017 reached the LDCs.[40] It is submitted that this proportion of funds to LDCs would need to increase, in order to raise the likelihood for attaining SDG Target 7.b punctually.

Will SDG 7 be achieved punctually?

On the basis of the information in the immediately-preceding subsection, it is opined that SDG 7[41] is unlikely to be met punctually, i.e., by 31st December 2030.[42] Furthermore, the COVID-19 pandemic[43] will impede efforts towards achieving SDG 7, as disruptions in supply chains may

---

[34] Progress towards the Sustainable Development Goals: Report of the Secretary-General, E/2020/xxx, 11-12.

[35] Progress towards the Sustainable Development Goals: Report of the Secretary-General, E/2020/xxx, 12; The Sustainable Development Goals Report 2020, 38.

[36] The text to note 16 specifies SDG Target 7.b.

[37] The target date for the SDGs to be fulfilled is 31st December 2030 (note 930 of Chapter Three and accompanying text).

[38] Progress towards the Sustainable Development Goals: Report of the Secretary-General, E/2020/xxx, 12; The Sustainable Development Goals Report 2020, 39.

[39] Progress towards the Sustainable Development Goals: Report of the Secretary-General, E/2020/xxx, 12; The Sustainable Development Goals Report 2020, 39.

[40] The Sustainable Development Goals Report 2020, 39.

[41] The text to note 15 states SDG 7.

[42] The target date for the SDGs to be accomplished is 31st December 2030 (note 930 of Chapter Three and accompanying text).

[43] The WHO classified the outbreak and spread of COVID-19 as a pandemic on 11th March 2020 (note 53 of Chapter Two).

devastate energy services, and incomes lowered as a consequence of this crisis could lessen consumers' ability to pay for these facilities.[44]

SDG 8: Promote Economic Growth and Full Employment

SDG 8 and its targets

SDG 8 is to "[p]romote sustained, inclusive and sustainable economic growth, full and productive employment and decent work for all".[45] The targets of SDG 8 are as follows.

> 8.1 Sustain per capita economic growth in accordance with national circumstances and, in particular, at least 7 per cent gross domestic product growth per annum in the least developed countries[.] 8.2 Achieve higher levels of economic productivity through diversification, technological upgrading and innovation, including through a focus on high-value added and labour-intensive sectors[.] 8.3 Promote development-oriented policies that support productive activities, decent job creation, entrepreneurship, creativity and innovation, and encourage the formalization and growth of micro-, small- and medium-sized enterprises, including through access to financial services[.] 8.4 Improve progressively, through 2030, global resource efficiency in consumption and production and endeavour to decouple economic growth from environmental degradation, in accordance with the 10-Year Framework of Programmes on Sustainable Consumption and Production, with developed countries taking the lead[.] 8.5 By 2030, achieve full and productive employment and decent work for all women and men, including for young people and persons with disabilities, and equal pay for work of equal value[.][46] 8.6 By 2020, substantially reduce the proportion of youth not in employment, education or training[.] 8.7 Take immediate and effective measures to eradicate forced labour, end modern slavery and human trafficking and secure the prohibition and elimination of the worst forms of child labour, including recruitment and use of child soldiers, and by 2025 end child labour in all its forms[.] 8.8 Protect labour rights and promote safe and secure working environments for all workers, including migrant workers, in particular women migrants, and those in precarious employment[.] 8.9 By 2030, devise and implement policies to promote sustainable tourism that creates jobs and promotes local culture and products[.] 8.10 Strengthen the capacity of domestic financial institutions to encourage and expand access to banking, insurance and financial services for all[.] 8.a Increase Aid for Trade support for

---

[44] The Sustainable Development Goals Report 2020, 38.

[45] Resolution 70/1 adopted by the General Assembly on 25 September 2015, Transforming our world: the 2030 Agenda for Sustainable Development, 14.

[46] The text to note 4 specifies SDG Target 8.5.

developing countries, in particular least developed countries, including through the Enhanced Integrated Framework for Trade-related Technical Assistance to Least Developed Countries[.] 8.b By 2020, develop and operationalize a global strategy for youth employment and implement the Global Jobs Pact of the International Labour Organization[.][47]

Progress to date in the accomplishment of SDG 8

The worldwide real GDP per capita growth rate was 2.0% per annum in 2018, which is also the average yearly growth rate in global real GDP per capita between 2010 and 2018.[48] In 2019, the worldwide real GDP per capital growth rate fell to 1.5% per annum, and is expected to decline to a negative value in 2020 due to the COVID-19 pandemic[49] and then to rise to a positive value in 2021.[50] The real GDP per capita growth rate for LDCs was 4.5% per annum in 2018, and 4.8% per annum in 2019.[51] These values fall short of the 7% per annum real GDP per capita growth rate that SDG Target 8.1[52] sets for LDCs. Moreover, the annual real GDP per capita growth rate for LDCs is projected to decline to 0.8% per annum in 2020, and thence to rise to 4.6% per annum in 2021.[53]

The worldwide average output per worker – which measures the economic productivity of labour – has steadily grown since 2000, with this growth interrupted briefly in 2009.[54] The global average output per worker rose by 1.6% in 2018, and thence by 1.4% in 2019.[55] The best-performing regions were East and South-East Asia – where the worldwide average output per worker increased by 3.7% in 2018 and thence by 3.9% in 2019,

---

[47] Resolution 70/1 adopted by the General Assembly on 25 September 2015, Transforming our world: the 2030 Agenda for Sustainable Development, 19-20. The Global Jobs Pact's main aim "is to provide an internationally agreed basis for policy-decision making designed to reduce the time lag between economic recovery and a recovery with decent work opportunities." (International Labour Organization, Recovering from the crisis: A Global Jobs Pact – adopted by the International Labour Conference at its Ninety-eighth Session, Geneva, 19 June 2009 (Geneva: International Labour Office, 2019), III).

[48] The Sustainable Development Goals Report 2020, 40.

[49] The WHO categorized the outbreak and spread of COVID-19 as a pandemic on 11th March 2020 (note 53 of Chapter Two).

[50] The Sustainable Development Goals Report 2020, 40.

[51] The Sustainable Development Goals Report 2020, 40.

[52] The text to note 47 states SDG Target 8.1.

[53] The Sustainable Development Goals Report 2020, 40.

[54] The Sustainable Development Goals Report 2020, 40.

[55] The Sustainable Development Goals Report 2020, 40.

and Central and South Asia – where the global output per worker rose by 3.8% in 2018, and thence by 2.4% in 2019.[56] Latin America and the Caribbean was the worst-performing region – worldwide output per worker there decreased by 1.2% in 2018, and thence by 1.7% in 2019.[57] It is submitted that these values provide tepid support for the punctual achievement of SDG Target 8.2[58] – although the global average output per worker is moving in the right direction to meet this SDG Target.

In 2016, 61% of workers worldwide were in informal employment.[59] In that year and globally, 94% of workers in the agricultural sector and 51% of workers in the non-agricultural sector were in informal employment.[60] Regionally, reliance on informal workers was most prevalent in Sub-Saharan Africa (89% in 2016) and Central and South Asia (86% in 2016).[61] The income of informal workers worldwide is estimated to have fallen by 60% in the first months of the COVID-19 pandemic.[62] It is opined that these percentages are not in line with the aim to 'promote development-oriented policies that support decent job creation' – which is a goal within SDG Target 8.3.[63]

In 2019, the global unemployment rate was 5.4% – 13.6% for young workers[64] and 4.0% for other workers.[65] In 40 of the 59 countries with

---

[56] The Sustainable Development Goals Report 2020, 40.

[57] The Sustainable Development Goals Report 2020, 40.

[58] The text to note 47 specifies SDG Target 8.2.

[59] Progress towards the Sustainable Development Goals: Report of the Secretary-General, E/2020/xxx, 12; The Sustainable Development Goals Report 2020, 41. *The Sustainable Goals Report 2020* states: "Typically, informality has a negative impact on earnings, working time, occupational safety and health, and working conditions generally." (The Sustainable Development Goals Report 2020, 41).

[60] The Sustainable Development Goals Report 2020, 41.

[61] Progress towards the Sustainable Development Goals: Report of the Secretary-General, E/2020/xxx, 12; The Sustainable Development Goals Report 2020, 41.

[62] Progress towards the Sustainable Development Goals: Report of the Secretary-General, E/2020/xxx, 12; The Sustainable Development Goals Report 2020, 41. The WHO designated the outbreak and spread of COVID-19 as a pandemic on 11th March 2020 (note 53 of Chapter Two).

[63] The text to note 47 states SDG Target 8.3.

[64] Neither the Report of the Secretary-General nor *The Sustainable Goals Report 2020* states what age range corresponds to the descriptors 'youth' or 'young worker' (Progress towards the Sustainable Development Goals: Report of the Secretary-General, E/2020/xxx, 13; The Sustainable Development Goals Report 2020, 41).

[65] The Sustainable Development Goals Report 2020, 41. The Report of the Secretary-General and *The Sustainable Goals Report 2020* refer to workers that are not young workers as 'adults' (Progress towards the Sustainable Development

recent, comparable data, the unemployment rate was higher for persons with disabilities than the overall unemployment rate there.[66] It is submitted that these statistics are not encouraging with regard to the probability of realizing SDG Target 8.5[67] punctually, i.e., by 31st December 2030.[68] Furthermore, it is opined that the prognosis for realization of SDG Target 8.6[69] by that date is fairly gloomy, due in part to the anticipated adverse impact during 2020 of the COVID-19 pandemic on the worldwide rate of employment.[70] As, in 2019, 22% of the world's young people were neither in employment nor education nor training, and since this level is almost unaltered since 2005,[71] it is submitted that SDG Target 8.6 will not have been fulfilled by its specified target year – which is 2020.

In 9 out of 71 countries that had data available on the matter since 2010, there were more than 10 occupational fatalities per 100,000 workers.[72] These statistics also suggested that migrant workers were exposed to more hazards and risks at work than non-migrant workers.[73] In three-quarters of countries that had recent comparable data, migrant workers had a greater occurrence of work-related injuries than non-migrant workers.[74] It is opined that this information is in accordance with the view that SDG Target 8.8[75] is unlikely to be met punctually, i.e., by 31st December 2030.[76]

Goals: Report of the Secretary-General, E/2020/xxx, 13; The Sustainable Development Goals Report 2020, 41).

66 The Sustainable Development Goals Report 2020, 41.

67 The text to note 4 specifies SDG Target 8.5.

68 The target date for the SDGs to be realized is 31st December 2030 (note 930 of Chapter Three and accompanying text). Like MDG Target 1.B (text to note 2), SDG Target 8.5 requires full employment to be achieved. Full employment is very difficult to accomplish, even in ideal conditions (see the sentence immediately-following the text to note 22 in Chapter Two).

69 The text to note 47 specifies SDG Target 8.6.

70 *The Sustainable Goals Report 2020* states: "Global unemployment may reach an historic high in 2020, depending on the policies adopted. … The eventual increase in global employment over 2020 will depend on how effectively policy measures preserve existing jobs and boost labour demand once the recovery phase begins." (The Sustainable Development Goals Report 2020, 41).

71 Progress towards the Sustainable Development Goals: Report of the Secretary-General, E/2020/xxx, 13.

72 The Sustainable Development Goals Report 2020, 41.

73 The Sustainable Development Goals Report 2020, 41.

74 The Sustainable Development Goals Report 2020, 41.

75 The text to note 47 states SDG Target 8.8.

76 The target date for the SDGs to be attained is 31st December 2030 (note 930 of Chapter Three and accompanying text).

Over the period 2008 to 2018, the contribution of tourism to overall GDP rose in 43 of the 70 countries which reported data.[77] However, tourism is one of the economic sectors to be most-severely hit by the COVID-19 pandemic,[78] due to lockdown measures, travel bans and border closures.[79] Therefore, the punctual attainment of SDG Target 8.9[80] is difficult to achieve under the current conditions. Notwithstanding this, it is opined that there is sufficient time for countries to devise and implement policies to further sustainable tourism in observance of this SDG Target, provided that the global incidence of COVID-19 is considerably reduced soon – and certainly no later than 2025.

In 2018, Aid for Trade commitments remained steady at USD 58 billion (on the basis of current prices), with 37.5% of these funds going to lower-middle-income countries and 36.8% to LDCs.[81] SDG Target 8.a[82] requires Aid for Trade commitments to be increased, especially to LDCs.

Data from 2019 from 102 countries suggest that 98% of these countries had either a strategy for youth employment or a plan to develop one soon.[83] This result indicates that these states are collectively close to meeting the first objective of SDG Target 8.b[84] by its stipulated deadline of 2020. However, it is submitted that the second objective this SDG Target – i.e., 'implement the Global Jobs Pact of the International Organization' – has fallen off the international agenda, as the ILO's website contains no recent reference to its adoption.[85]

---

[77] The Sustainable Development Goals Report 2020, 41.

[78] The WHO classified the outbreak and spread of COVID-19 as a pandemic on 11th March 2020 (note 53 of Chapter Two).

[79] The Sustainable Development Goals Report 2020, 41.

[80] The text to note 47 specifies SDG Target 8.9.

[81] Progress towards the Sustainable Development Goals: Report of the Secretary-General, E/2020/xxx, 13.

[82] The text to note 47 states SDG Target 8.a.

[83] Progress towards the Sustainable Development Goals: Report of the Secretary-General, E/2020/xxx, 13.

[84] The text to note 47 specifies SDG Target 8.b.

[85] The last entry on the 'Pact News' webpage is dated July 2012 ("Pact News", International Labour Organization, accessed September 28, 2020, https://www.ilo.org/jobspact/news/lang--en/index.htm). Note 47 specifies the main objective of the Global Jobs Pact of the ILO. The ILO's website reads: "The [Global Jobs] Pact calls for coordinated global action to maximize the positive impact of policy initiatives on jobs and sustainable enterprises worldwide. Its successful implementation depends on national and international decisions, by governments, business, labour, parliaments, local authorities and civil society, as

Will SDG 8 be achieved punctually?

On the basis of the information that the foregoing subsection provides, it is opined that SDG 8[86] is unlikely to be achieved punctually, i.e., by 31st December 2030.[87] Besides, the immediate global economic outlook is at variance with effective progression towards the accomplishment of this SDG.[88]

SDG 9: Build Infrastructure and Foster Innovation

SDG 9 and its targets

SDG 9 is to "[b]uild resilient infrastructure, promote inclusive and sustainable industrialization and foster innovation".[89] The targets of SDG 9 are as follows.

> 9.1 Develop quality, reliable, sustainable and resilient infrastructure, including regional and transborder infrastructure, to support economic development and human well-being, with a focus on affordable and equitable access for all[.] 9.2 Promote inclusive and sustainable industrialization and, by 2030, significantly raise industry's share of employment and gross domestic product, in line with national circumstances, and double its share in least developed countries[.] 9.3 Increase the access of small-scale industrial and other enterprises, in particular in developing countries, to financial services, including affordable credit, and their integration into value chains and markets[.] 9.4 By 2030, upgrade infrastructure and retrofit[90] industries to make them

---

well as by donors and multilateral institutions." ("About the Pact", International Labour Organization, accessed September 28, 2020, https://www.ilo.org/jobspact/about/lang--en/index.htm).

[86] The text to note 45 states SDG 8.

[87] The target date for the SDGs to be met is 31st December 2030 (note 930 of Chapter Three and accompanying text).

[88] The Report of the Secretary-General comments: "Even before the current crisis, the global economy was growing at a slower rate than in previous years, despite improvements in labour productivity and unemployment. The COVID-19 pandemic has abruptly and profoundly disrupted the global economy, pushing the world into a recession." (Progress towards the Sustainable Development Goals: Report of the Secretary-General, E/2020/xxx, 12).

[89] Resolution 70/1 adopted by the General Assembly on 25 September 2015, Transforming our world: the 2030 Agenda for Sustainable Development, 14.

[90] 'Retrofit' means "add (a component or accessory) to something that did not have it when manufactured; provide (something) with a component or accessory not

sustainable, with increased resource-use efficiency and greater adoption of clean and environmentally sound technologies and industrial processes, with all countries taking action in accordance with their respective capabilities[.] 9.5 Enhance scientific research, upgrade the technological capabilities of industrial sectors in all countries, in particular developing countries, including, by 2030, encouraging innovation and substantially increasing the number of research and development workers per 1 million people and public and private research and development spending[.] 9.a Facilitate sustainable and resilient infrastructure development in developing countries through enhanced financial, technological and technical support to African countries, least developed countries, landlocked developing countries and small island developing States[.] 9.b Support domestic technology development, research and innovation in developing countries, including by ensuring a conducive policy environment for, *inter alia*,[91] industrial diversification and value addition to commodities[.] 9.c Significantly increase access to information and communications technology and strive to provide universal and affordable access to the Internet in least developed countries by 2020[.][92]

Progress to date in the accomplishment of SDG 9

In 2016, the worldwide economic impact – including indirect effects – of air transport was estimated to be USD 2.7 trillion, which equates to 3.6% of global GDP.[93] Due to the COVID-19 pandemic[94] and the restrictions on air travel that governments imposed in response to it, worldwide aeroplane passenger numbers in January to May 2020 were down 51.1% on those in January to May 2019.[95] On 5th June 2020, the International Civil Aviation Organization estimated that the COVID-19 pandemic may cause a global reduction in aeroplane passengers of 2.29 billion people to 3.06 billion aeroplane passengers in 2020, resulting in losses of between USD 302 billion and USD 400 billion in gross operating revenues for airlines relative to business as usual.[96] It is submitted that air travel is a component of transborder infrastructure, which SDG Target 9.1 requires to be

---

fitted to it during manufacture" (Oxford University Press, *The New Oxford Dictionary of English* (Oxford: Oxford University Press, 1998), 1586).

[91] Emphasis added.

[92] Resolution 70/1 adopted by the General Assembly on 25 September 2015, Transforming our world: the 2030 Agenda for Sustainable Development, 20-21.

[93] The Sustainable Development Goals Report 2020, 42.

[94] The WHO categorized the outbreak and spread of COVID-19 as a pandemic on 11th March 2020 (note 53 of Chapter Two).

[95] The Sustainable Development Goals Report 2020, 42.

[96] The Sustainable Development Goals Report 2020, 42.

developed – as long as the infrastructure fits the descriptors 'quality', 'reliable', 'sustainable', and 'resilient'.[97] Thus, it is opined that the recent setback to the aviation industry is also an impediment to the punctual attainment of SDG Target 9.1.

In 2019, manufacturing value added grew by 1.5% from 2018, which is the slowest year-on-year growth rate since 2012.[98] In LDCs, the share of manufacturing in GDP rose from 10.0% in 2010 to 12.4% in 2019.[99] The rate of increase in the share of manufacturing in GDP in LDCs is insufficient to fulfil by 31st December 2030[100] the goal within SDG Target 9.2[101] of doubling the share of industry in LDCs by 2030.[102]

In 2019, 14% of workers globally were employed in manufacturing industries – which is fairly unchanged since 2000.[103] It is submitted that this information supports the view that the objective within SDG Target 9.2 of significantly raising industry's share of employment by 2030 is unlikely to be accomplished punctually, i.e., by 31st December 2030.

Surveys that covered the period 2010 to 2018[104] suggested that: (i) in developing countries, 34.7% of small-scale enterprises – in both the manufacturing and services sectors – are in receipt of loans or lines of credit, (ii) 22.9% of such businesses in Sub-Saharan Africa received loans or lines of credit, and (iii) 48% of these firms in Latin America and the

---

[97] The text to note 92 specifies SDG Target 9.1.

[98] Progress towards the Sustainable Development Goals: Report of the Secretary-General, E/2020/xxx, 13.

[99] Progress towards the Sustainable Development Goals: Report of the Secretary-General, E/2020/xxx, 13; The Sustainable Development Goals Report 2020, 42.

[100] The target date for the SDGs to be achieved is 31st December 2030 (note 930 of Chapter Three and accompanying text).

[101] The text to note 92 states SDG Target 9.2.

[102] Progress towards the Sustainable Development Goals: Report of the Secretary-General, E/2020/xxx, 13; The Sustainable Development Goals Report 2020, 42.

[103] Progress towards the Sustainable Development Goals: Report of the Secretary-General, E/2020/xxx, 14.

[104] The Report of the Secretary General states that these surveys covered "a period from 2010 to the present" (Progress towards the Sustainable Development Goals: Report of the Secretary-General, E/2020/xxx, 14). The title of the relevant figure in *The Sustainable Development Goals Report 2020* reads: "Proportion of small-scale manufacturing enterprises with a loan or line of credit, *according to surveys conducted in 2006-2018* (percentage)" (The Sustainable Development Goals Report 2020, 43; emphasis added). As these two items refer to the same data but with different time periods, the text specifies the time period that is common to both, i.e., 2010 to 2018.

Caribbean benefited from loans or lines of credit.[105] It is submitted that SDG Target 9.3,[106] which requires an increase in the access of small-scale undertakings to financial services including affordable credit, is achievable punctually, i.e., by 31st December 2030,[107] particularly if the problem is addressed regionally as appropriate – such as by the African Union in the case of the shortage of credit for small firms in Sub-Saharan Africa.

After three stable years, worldwide emissions of carbon dioxide from fuel combustion started increasing again in 2017, reaching 32.8 billion tons.[108] The intensity of global emissions of carbon dioxide has fallen by nearly one quarter since 2000, which shows a general decoupling of these discharges from growth in GDP.[109] A corresponding trend was observable for manufacturing industries after 2010, with worldwide manufacturing intensity decreasing at an average annual rate of 3% until 2017.[110] It is opined that these data provide circumstantial evidence of progress towards the punctual realization of SDG Target 9.4,[111] i.e., they tend to indicate – as this SDG Target requires – 'greater adoption of clean and environmentally sound technologies and industrial processes'.

Research and development worldwide has[112] continued to increase, attaining USD 2.2 trillion (PPP) in 2017, which is up from USD 741 billion in 2000 and USD 1.4 trillion in 2010.[113] The percentage of global GDP invested in research and development rose from 1.5% in 2000 to

---

105 Progress towards the Sustainable Development Goals: Report of the Secretary-General, E/2020/xxx, 14; The Sustainable Development Goals Report 2020, 43.

106 The text to note 92 specifies SDG Target 9.3.

107 The target date for the SDGs to be fulfilled is 31st December 2030 (note 930 of Chapter Three and accompanying text).

108 Progress towards the Sustainable Development Goals: Report of the Secretary-General, E/2020/xxx, 14.

109 Progress towards the Sustainable Development Goals: Report of the Secretary-General, E/2020/xxx, 14.

110 Progress towards the Sustainable Development Goals: Report of the Secretary-General, E/2020/xxx, 14.

111 The text to note 92 states SDG Target 9.4.

112 Whilst 'research and development' should take a plural verb according to the rules of construction of the English language, i.e., 'have', the text uses a single verb, i.e., 'has'. This is because 'research and development' – especially in its abbreviated form 'R&D' – is considered to be a single function ("Research and development", WordReference.com, accessed September 29, 2020, https://forum.wordreference.com/threads/research-and-development.524277/).

113 The Sustainable Development Goals Report 2020, 43.

1.62% in 2010, and thence to 1.7% in 2015 and 1.72% in 2017.[114] Regional disparities are enormous, with the proportion of worldwide GDP invested in research and development in (i) Sub-Saharan Africa being 0.36% in 2010 and 0.38% in 2017, (ii) LDCs being 0.21% in 2010 and 0.20% in 2017, and (iii) LLDCs being 0.22% in 2010 and 0.21% in 2017.[115] The number of researchers per million inhabitants worldwide rose from 1,018 in 2010 to 1,198 in 2017.[116] In 2017, there were 99 researchers per million inhabitants in Sub-Saharan Africa.[117] It is submitted that: (i) the spending on research and development and the number of researchers are moving in the right direction for achievement of SDG Target 9.5,[118] but (ii) both these items need to increase considerably in Sub-Saharan Africa – which contains the majority of LDCs[119] – in order for this SDG Target to be realized punctually, i.e., by 31st December 2030.[120]

Total official flows for economic infrastructure in developing countries amounted to USD 61 billion in 2018, which was a rise of 32.6% in real terms from such flows in 2010.[121] The main sectors to which this money was directed were the transport sector – which received USD 22.8 billion, and the energy sector – which was given USD 20.3 billion.[122] Whilst the Report of the Secretary-General does not specify what proportion of these funds were given to Africa, LDCs, LLDCs and SIDS[123] – in accordance

---

[114] Progress towards the Sustainable Development Goals: Report of the Secretary-General, E/2020/xxx, 14; The Sustainable Development Goals Report 2020, 43. The Report of the Secretary General provides the percentages from 2000 and 2015, which it gives to one decimal place. *The Sustainable Development Goals Report 2020* supplies the percentages for 2010 and 2017, which it states to two decimal places.

[115] The Sustainable Development Goals Report 2020, 43.

[116] Progress towards the Sustainable Development Goals: Report of the Secretary-General, E/2020/xxx, 14.

[117] Progress towards the Sustainable Development Goals: Report of the Secretary-General, E/2020/xxx, 14.

[118] The text to note 92 specifies SDG Target 9.5.

[119] Note 130 of Chapter Two lists the LDCs that are located in Sub-Saharan Africa, of which there are 33. Note 125 of Chapter Two lists all 47 LDCs.

[120] The target date for the SDGs to be accomplished is 31st December 2030 (note 930 of Chapter Three and accompanying text).

[121] Progress towards the Sustainable Development Goals: Report of the Secretary-General, E/2020/xxx, 14.

[122] Progress towards the Sustainable Development Goals: Report of the Secretary-General, E/2020/xxx, 14.

[123] Progress towards the Sustainable Development Goals: Report of the Secretary-General, E/2020/xxx, 14.

with SDG Target 9.a[124] which requires facilitation of resilient, sustainable infrastructure development 'through enhanced financial, technological and technical support to African countries, LDCs, LLDCs and SIDS', the rise in these official flows from 2010 to 2018 shows that the 'financial support' objective of SDG Target 9.a is, at least to some extent, being addressed.

The share of medium-high-technology and high-technology goods in global manufacturing production was almost 45% in 2017, with such products accounting for 49% of manufacturing production in developed regions and 9% of manufacturing production in LDCs.[125] It is opined that this low share of advanced goods in the manufacturing production in LDCs is not favourable to the punctual accomplishment of SDG Target 9.b,[126] which aims to 'support domestic technology development, research and innovation in developing countries'.

In 2019, 96.5% of the world's population was covered by at least a 2G mobile cellular network, with 81.8% covered by at least a Long-Term Evolution network.[127] In that year, 93% of the global population lived within reach of a mobile-broadband signal.[128] 79% of the population of LDCs were covered by a mobile-broadband signal in 2019, which is up from 51% in 2015.[129] These percentages suggest that the first part of SDG Target 9.c,[130] i.e., to 'significantly increase access to information and communications technology', will be attained punctually, i.e., by 31st December 2030.[131]

In 2019, 54% of the world's population used the Internet – which included 87% of the population in developed countries working the Internet and 19% of the population in LDCs operating it.[132] As reasons for this difference include the cost of using the Internet (as well as the lack of requisite skills to do so),[133] it is submitted that the second part of Target 9.c, i.e., to 'strive to provide universal *and affordable* access to the Internet in LDCs by 2020', has not been met.

---

124 The text to note 92 states SDG Target 9.a.
125 Progress towards the Sustainable Development Goals: Report of the Secretary-General, E/2020/xxx, 14.
126 The text to note 92 specifies SDG Target 9.b.
127 Progress towards the Sustainable Development Goals: Report of the Secretary-General, E/2020/xxx, 14.
128 The Sustainable Development Goals Report 2020, 43.
129 The Sustainable Development Goals Report 2020, 43.
130 The text to note 92 states SDG Target 9.c.
131 The target date for the SDGs to be realized is 31st December 2030 (note 930 of Chapter Three and accompanying text).
132 The Sustainable Development Goals Report 2020, 43.
133 The Sustainable Development Goals Report 2020, 43.

Will SDG 9 be achieved punctually?

On the basis of the data and comments in the foregoing subsection, it is opined that SDG 9[134] is unlikely to be achieved punctually, i.e., by 31st December 2030.[135] It is submitted that more attention be paid to the application of the targets of SDG 9 to LDCs, in order to create a reasonable chance of fulfilling this SDG in the forseeable future.

SDG 11: Make Human Settlements Safe and Sustainable

SDG 11 and its targets

SDG 11 is to "[m]ake cities and human settlements inclusive, safe, resilient and sustainable".[136] The targets of SDG 11 are as follows.

> 11.1 By 2030, ensure access for all to adequate, safe and affordable housing and basic services and upgrade slums[.][137] 11.2 By 2030, provide access to safe, affordable, accessible and sustainable transport systems for all, improving road safety, notably by expanding public transport, with special attention to the needs of those in vulnerable situations, women children, persons with disabilities and older persons[.] 11.3 By 2030, enhance inclusive and sustainable urbanization and capacity for participatory, integrated and sustainable human settlement planning and management in all countries[.][138] 11.4 Strengthen efforts to protect and safeguard the world's cultural and national heritage[.] 11.5 By 2030, significantly reduce the number of deaths and the number of people affected and substantially decrease the direct economic losses relative to global gross domestic product caused by disasters, including water-related disasters, with a focus on protecting the poor and people in vulnerable situations[.] 11.6 By 2030, reduce the adverse per capita environmental impact of cities, including by paying special attention to air quality and municipal and other waste management[.] 11.7 By 2030, provide universal access to safe, inclusive and accessible, green and public spaces, in particular for women and children, older persons and persons with disabilities[.] 11.a Support positive economic, social and environmental

---

[134] The text to note 89 states SDG 9.

[135] The target date for the SDGs to be attained is 31st December 2030 (note 930 of Chapter Three and accompanying text).

[136] Note 134 of Chapter One, and text to note 7.

[137] The text to note 14 specifies SDG Target 11.1.

[138] The text to note 12 states SDG Target 11.3.

links between urban, peri-urban[139] and rural areas by strengthening national and regional development planning[.] 11.b By 2020, substantially increase the number of cities and human settlements adopting and implementing integrated policies and plans towards inclusion, resource efficiency, mitigation and adaptation to climate change, resilience to disasters, and develop and implement, in line with the Sendai Framework for Disaster Risk Reduction 2015-2030, holistic disaster risk management at all levels[.] 11.c Support least developed countries, including through financial and technical assistance, in building sustainable and resilient buildings utilizing local materials[.][140]

Progress in the accomplishment of SDG 11

The proportion of the world's urban population living in slums fell from 28% in 2000 to 23% in 2014, and then rose to 24% in 2018 – reaching more than one billion people that year.[141] This reversal is at variance with the realization of SDG Target 11.1,[142] which, it is submitted, is unlikely to be fulfilled punctually, i.e. by 31st December 2030.[143]

Data from 2019 involving 610 cities from 95 countries indicated that only 50% of the world's urban population lived within 1,000 metres walking distance of a high-capacity transport system – such as a railway station and/or a ferry terminal, and/or within 500 metres walking distance of a low-capacity transport system – such as a bus stop.[144] It is opined that this datum falls short of the universal access to safe, affordable, accessible and sustainable transport systems that SDG Target 11.2[145] requires.

Data from 2019 from a representative worldwide sample of 755 cities from 95 countries suggest that, over the period 1990 to 2015, the extent of built-up area – defined as the presence of buildings – per person increased

---

[139] 'Peri-urban' means "of or relating to an area immediately surrounding a city or town" ("peri-urban", Merriam-Webster, accessed September 27, 2020, https://www.merriam-webster.com/dictionary/peri-urban).

[140] Resolution 70/1 adopted by the General Assembly on 25 September 2015, Transforming our world: the 2030 Agenda for Sustainable Development, 21-22.

[141] Progress towards the Sustainable Development Goals: Report of the Secretary-General, E/2020/xxx, 16; The Sustainable Development Goals Report 2020, 46.

[142] The text to note 14 specifies SDG Target 11.1.

[143] The target date for the SDGs to be met is 31st December 2030 (note 930 of Chapter Three and accompanying text).

[144] Progress towards the Sustainable Development Goals: Report of the Secretary-General, E/2020/xxx, 16; The Sustainable Development Goals Report 2020, 46.

[145] The text to note 140 states SDG Target 11.2.

in five of seven regions.[146] In some cities, this enlargement evidences unplanned urban sprawl – which renders the delivery of services more inefficient and expensive.[147] These changes are not in accordance with progression towards the accomplishment of SDG Target 11.3,[148] which includes enhancement of sustainable urbanization and of sustainable human settlement planning.

In 2016, nine out of every ten people who lived in urban areas globally were breathing air that did not satisfy the WHO's air quality guidelines for particulate matter.[149] Half the world's urban population suffered a rise in particulate matter and a deterioration of air quality from 2010 to 2016.[150] Ambient air pollution is estimated to have caused 4.2 million early deaths in 2016.[151] These data are at variance with the punctual realization of SDG Target 11.6,[152] which requires a reduction in the unfavourable environmental impact of cities per person – paying special attention to air quality – by 2030.

According to data from 2019 concerning 610 cities in 95 countries: (i) the share of urban land allotted to streets and open public spaces – such as riverfronts and parks – averaged 16% worldwide, (ii) streets accounted for approximately three times as much urban land as open public spaces, and (iii) on average, 46.7% of the population of these cities is within 400 metres walking distance of an open public space along a street network.[153] It is submitted that these data do not support achievement of universal access to safe, inclusive, accessible, green, public spaces by 2030, as SDG Target 11.7[154] requires.

Will SDG 11 be achieved punctually?

On the basis of the limited information in the immediately-preceding subsection, it is submitted that SDG 11[155] will probably not be fulfilled

---

[146] Progress towards the Sustainable Development Goals: Report of the Secretary-General, E/2020/xxx, 16; The Sustainable Development Goals Report 2020, 47.
[147] The Sustainable Development Goals Report 2020, 47.
[148] The text to note 12 specifies SDG Target 11.3.
[149] The Sustainable Development Goals Report 2020, 47.
[150] The Sustainable Development Goals Report 2020, 47.
[151] The Sustainable Development Goals Report 2020, 47.
[152] The Sustainable Development Goals Report 2020, 47.
[153] Progress towards the Sustainable Development Goals: Report of the Secretary-General, E/2020/xxx, 16; The Sustainable Development Goals Report 2020, 47.
[154] The text to note 140 specifies SDG Target 11.7.
[155] The text to notes 7 and 136 each states SDG 11.

punctually, i.e., by 31st December 2030.[156] It is opined that this SDG is particularly difficult to accomplish within a reasonable timescale, because its realization requires structural changes in urban design in order to, for instance, provide good-quality housing with reasonable services, lay down underground rail services in large cities, and increase the density of green spaces within both city centres and suburbs.

SDG 12: Ensure Sustainable Consumption & Production

SDG 12 and its targets

SDG 12 is to "[e]nsure sustainable consumption and production patterns".[157] The targets of SDG 12 are as follows.

> 12.1 Implement the 10-Year Framework of Programmes on Sustainable Consumption and Production Patterns,[158] all countries taking action, with developed countries taking the lead, taking into account the development and capabilities of developing countries[.] 12.2 By 2030, achieve the sustainable management and efficient use of natural resources[.] 12.3 By 2030, halve per capita global food waste at the retail and consumer levels and reduce food losses along production and supply chains, including post-harvest losses[.] 12.4 By 2020, achieve the environmentally sound management of chemicals and all wastes throughout their life cycle, in accordance with agreed international frameworks, and significantly reduce their release to air, water and soil in order to minimize their adverse impacts on human health and the environment[.] 12.5 By 2030, substantially reduce waste generation through prevention, reduction, recycling and reuse[.] 12.6 Encourage companies, especially large and

---

[156] The target date for the SDGs to be achieved is 31st December 2030 (note 930 of Chapter Three and accompanying text).

[157] Resolution 70/1 adopted by the General Assembly on 25 September 2015, Transforming our world: the 2030 Agenda for Sustainable Development, 14.

[158] Adopted at Rio+20 in June 2012, the 10 Year Framework of Programmes on Sustainable Consumption and Production Patterns "is a global framework for action to enhance international cooperation and accelerate the shift towards sustainable consumption and production (SCP) patterns in both developed and developing countries. The framework supports capacity building, and facilitates access to technical and financial assistance for developing countries for this shift." (United Nations, Department of Economic and Social Affairs – Financing for Development Office: The 10 Year Framework of Programmes on Sustainable Consumption and Production Patterns (10YFP) – Interim progress report prepared by the 10YFP Secretariat on behalf of the 10YFP Board for the High-Level Political Forum (New York, 2014), 1).

> transnational companies, to adopt sustainable practices and to integrate sustainability information into their reporting cycle[.] 12.7 Promote public procurement practices that are sustainable, in accordance with national policies and priorities[.] 12.8 By 2030, ensure that people everywhere have the relevant information and awareness for sustainable development and lifestyles in harmony with nature[.] 12.a Support developing countries to strengthen their scientific and technological capacity to move towards more sustainable patterns of consumption and production[.] 12.b Develop and implement tools to monitor sustainable development impacts for sustainable tourism that creates jobs and promotes local culture and products[.] 12.c Rationalize inefficient fossil-fuel subsidies that encourage wasteful consumption by removing market distortions, in accordance with national circumstances, including by restructuring taxation and phasing out those harmful subsidies, where they exist, to reflect their environmental impacts, taking fully into account the specific needs and conditions of developing countries and minimizing the possible adverse impacts on their development in a manner that protects the poor and the affected communities[.][159]

Progress in the accomplishment of SDG 12

From 2017 to 2019, 79 countries and the European Union reported on one or more national policy instruments that contribute to sustainable consumption and production, in their endeavours to implement the 10 Year Framework of Programmes on Sustainable Consumption and Production Patterns.[160] This information shows that at least some states are progressing towards the implementation of the 10 Year Framework on Sustainable Consumption and Production Patterns, which SDG Target 12.1[161] requires them to put into effect.

SDG Target 12.2 requires the sustainable management and efficient use of natural resources by 2030.[162] The material footprint is an indicator of the world's reliance on natural resources; it measures the quantity of primary materials (i.e., metal ores, fossil fuels, biomass and non-metallic minerals) that are required to satisfy the basic human needs for water,

---

[159] Resolution 70/1 adopted by the General Assembly on 25 September 2015, Transforming our world: the 2030 Agenda for Sustainable Development, 22-23.

[160] Progress towards the Sustainable Development Goals: Report of the Secretary-General, E/2020/xxx, 16; The Sustainable Development Goals Report 2020, 49. Note 158 describes the 10 Year Framework on Sustainable Consumption and Production Patterns.

[161] The text to note 159 specifies SDG Target 12.1.

[162] The text to note 159 states SDG Target 12.2.

food, clothing, shelter, infrastructure, and other facets of life.[163] The worldwide material footprint increased from 73.2 billion tonnes in 2010 to 85.9 billion tonnes in 2017, expanding for all types of materials but especially for non-metallic minerals – which accounted for almost half of the global material footprint in both 2010 and 2017.[164] In 2015, the material footprint per person was more than ten times larger in high-income countries than in low-income countries.[165] Moreover, worldwide domestic material consumption per capita increased by 7% from 10.8 tonnes per person in 2010 to 11.7 tonnes per person in 2017.[166] Domestic material consumption per capita in 2017 was 40% higher in Europe and North America than the global average.[167] It is submitted that, on the basis of these data: (i) progress needs to be made to improve the efficiency of use of natural resources in developed states, and (ii) work needs to be done on the sustainable management of such resources, in order to attempt to realize SDG Target 12.2 punctually, i.e., by 31st December 2030.[168]

Whilst it is not yet possible to estimate the proportion of food waste at the retail and consumption levels[169] – SDG Target 12.3[170] requires the worldwide food waste per capita at these levels to be halved by 2030, the global percentage of food lost after harvest and during transport, storage and processing was 13.8% in 2016, which is USD 400 billion per annum.[171] Of the regions, the proportion of food lost in 2016 after harvest and during transport, storage and processing was greatest in Central and South Asia at 20.7%, and least in Australia and New Zealand at 5.8%.[172]

The Montreal Protocol on Substances that Deplete the Ozone Layer has been ratified by 198 parties[173] and, as a result of its implementation, the quantity of ozone-depleting substances in the atmosphere has reduced – and is forecast to return to 1980s values in the 2030s for ozone in mid-

[163] The Sustainable Development Goals Report 2020, 48.
[164] The Sustainable Development Goals Report 2020, 48.
[165] The Sustainable Development Goals Report 2020, 48.
[166] Progress towards the Sustainable Development Goals: Report of the Secretary-General, E/2020/xxx, 16.
[167] Progress towards the Sustainable Development Goals: Report of the Secretary-General, E/2020/xxx, 16.
[168] The target date for the SDGs to be fulfilled is 31st December 2030 (note 930 of Chapter Three and accompanying text).
[169] The Sustainable Development Goals Report 2020, 49.
[170] The text to note 159 specifies SDG Target 12.3.
[171] The Sustainable Development Goals Report 2020, 49.
[172] The Sustainable Development Goals Report 2020, 49.
[173] Text to note 343 of Chapter Four.

latitude locations in the Northern hemisphere.[174] This is in accord with the punctual fulfilment of SDG Target 12.4.[175]

The disposal of e-waste – electronic and electrical equipment – has become a growing problem, which is caused by rising consumption of these products, limited facilities for their repair, and short product life cycles.[176] From 2010 to 2019, global e-waste increased from 5.3 to 7.3 kilograms per person per year.[177] Environmentally sound recycling of worldwide e-waste rose from 0.8 to 1.3 kilograms per person per year over that period.[178] These statistics illustrate that there is progress to be made in order to attain SDG Target 12.5,[179] which requires a substantial reduction in the generation of waste to be achieved by 2030 by means of prevention, reduction, recycling and reuse. The rise of 0.5 kilograms per person per year in environmentally sound recycling of global e-waste over the period 2010 to 2019 only partly makes up for the increase of 2.0 kilograms per person per year of such e-waste through the same period.

Fossil fuel subsidies, i.e., subsidies for coal, gas, oil, and fossil-fuelled electricity, rose from 2010 to 2012, declined from 2012 to 2016, increased from 2016 to 2018 – exceeding USD 400 billion in the latter year, and fell from 2018 to 2019 by about 27% – mainly due to a decrease in the price of fuel.[180] SDG Target 12.c[181] requires 'inefficient fossil-fuel subsidies' to be 'rationalized in accordance with national circumstances', stopping short of demanding their removal – although mentioning their phasing out as a means of this rationalization. It is submitted that, consistent with these data, countries need to do more regarding the reduction of fossil fuel subsidies in order to fulfil SDG Target 12.c punctually, i.e., by 31st December 2030.[182]

---

174 Progress towards the Sustainable Development Goals: Report of the Secretary-General, E/2020/xxx, 17.

175 The text to note 159 states SDG Target 12.4.

176 The Sustainable Development Goals Report 2020, 49.

177 Progress towards the Sustainable Development Goals: Report of the Secretary-General, E/2020/xxx, 17; The Sustainable Development Goals Report 2020, 49.

178 Progress towards the Sustainable Development Goals: Report of the Secretary-General, E/2020/xxx, 17; The Sustainable Development Goals Report 2020, 49.

179 The text to note 159 specifies SDG Target 12.5.

180 The Sustainable Development Goals Report 2020, 49.

181 The text to note 159 states SDG Target 12.c.

182 The target date for the SDGs to be accomplished is 31st December 2030 (note 930 of Chapter Three and accompanying text).

Will SDG 12 be achieved punctually?

On the basis of the statistics and comments in the foregoing subsection, it is opined that SDG 12[183] will probably not be attained punctually, i.e., by 31st December 2030.[184] Nevertheless, this information suggests that progress has been made towards fulfilment of some of the targets of SDG 12.

SDG 13: Take Urgent Action to Combat Climate Change

SDG 13 and its targets

SDG 13 is to "[t]ake urgent action to combat climate change and its impacts".[185] The targets of SDG 13 are as follows.

> 13.1 Strengthen resilience and adaptive capacity to climate-related hazards and natural disasters in all countries[.] 13.2 Integrate climate change measures into national policies, strategies and planning[.] 13.3 Improve education, awareness-raising and human and institutional capacity on climate change mitigation, adaptation, impact reduction and early warning[.] 13.a Implement the commitment undertaken by developed-country parties to the United Nations Framework Convention on Climate Change to a goal of mobilizing jointly $100 billion annually by 2020 from all sources to address the needs of developing countries in the context of meaningful mitigation actions and transparency on implementation and fully operationalize the Green Climate Fund through its capitalization as soon as possible[.] 13.b Promote mechanisms for raising capacity for effective climate change-related planning and management in least developed countries and small island developing States, including focusing on women, youth and local and marginalized communities[.][186]

Progress in the accomplishment of SDG 13

85 countries have reported that they have a national disaster risk reduction strategy in place, which is to some degree aligned to the Sendai

[183] The text to note 157 states SDG 12.
[184] The target date for the SDGs to be realized is 31st December 2030 (note 930 of Chapter Three and accompanying text).
[185] Resolution 70/1 adopted by the General Assembly on 25 September 2015, Transforming our world: the 2030 Agenda for Sustainable Development, 14.
[186] Resolution 70/1 adopted by the General Assembly on 25 September 2015, Transforming our world: the 2030 Agenda for Sustainable Development, 23.

Framework for Disaster Risk Reduction 2015-2030.[187] In 2018, 55 countries reported that at least some of their local authorities have a disaster risk reduction strategy, which aims to augment sustainable development and fortify socioeconomic health and environmental resilience by centring on the eradication of poverty, urban resilience, and adaption to climate change.[188] It is submitted that these actions show some progress from national governments and local authorities towards the punctual fulfilment of SDG Target 13.1.[189]

In 2019, at least 120 of the 153 developing countries had engaged in activities to create and implement national adaptation plans to improve adaptive capacity, strengthen resilience and lower vulnerability to climate change.[190] SDG Target 13.2[191] requires countries to integrate climate change measures into their national planning, policies and strategies.

By 31st March 2020, 186 Parties to the United Nations Framework Convention on Climate Change had published their first nationally-determined contribution, and several Parties to the Convention had transmitted their second or updated nationally-determined contribution.[192] SDG Target 13.a[193] contains a financial commitment relating to the United Nations Convention on Climate Change.

Will SDG 13 be achieved punctually?

Based on the limited information in the immediately-preceding paragraph, it is submitted that states have taken measures towards mitigating climate change which go some way towards satisfying targets of SDG 13.[194] Notwithstanding this, it is opined that this SDG Target will not be met punctually, i.e., by 31st December 2030,[195] because countries – especially developed countries, on which the bulk of the monetary responsibilities

---

[187] Progress towards the Sustainable Development Goals: Report of the Secretary-General, E/2020/xxx, 17. The text to note 378 of Chapter Two states the seven global targets of the Sendai Framework for Disaster Risk Reduction 2015-2030.

[188] Progress towards the Sustainable Development Goals: Report of the Secretary-General, E/2020/xxx, 17.

[189] The text to note 186 specifies SDG Target 13.1.

[190] The Sustainable Development Goals Report 2020, 51.

[191] The text to note 186 states SDG Target 13.2.

[192] Progress towards the Sustainable Development Goals: Report of the Secretary-General, E/2020/xxx, 17.

[193] The text to note 186 states SDG Target 13.a.

[194] The text to note 185 specifies SDG 13.

[195] The target date for the SDGs to be attained is 31st December 2030 (note 930 of Chapter Three and accompanying text).

fall – will not be able to afford the substantial financial commitments that are required of them in order to be able to implement every aspect of this Goal.

SDG 16: Promote Societies for Sustainable Development

SDG 16 and its targets

SDG 16 is to "[p]romote peaceful and inclusive societies for sustainable development, provide access to justice for all and build effective, accountable and inclusive institutions at all levels".[196] The targets of SDG 16 are as follows.

> 16.1 Significantly reduce all forms of violence and related death rates everywhere[.] 16.2 End abuse, exploitation, trafficking and all forms of violence against and torture of children[.] 16.3 Promote the rule of law at the national and international levels and ensure equal access to justice for all[.] 16.4 By 2030, significantly reduce illicit financial and arms flows, strengthen the recovery and return of stolen assets and combat all forms of organized crime[.] 16.5 Substantially reduce corruption and bribery in all their forms[.] 16.6 Develop effective, accountable and transparent institutions at all levels[.] 16.7 Ensure responsive, inclusive, participatory and representative decision-making at all levels[.] 16.8 Broaden and strengthen the participation of developing countries in the institutions of global governance[.] 16.9 By 2030, provide legal identity for all, including birth registration[.] 16.10 Ensure public access to information and protect fundamental freedoms, in accordance with national legislation and international agreements[.] 16.a Strengthen relevant national institutions, including through international cooperation, for building capacity at all levels, in particular in developing countries, to prevent violence and combat terrorism and crime[.] 16.b Promote and enforce non-discriminatory laws and policies for sustainable development[.][197]

Progress in the accomplishment of SDG 16

Whilst there is a duty under international law to safeguard civilians in armed conflicts, the UN recorded at least 106,806 civilian deaths in twelve of the world's worst armed conflicts between 2015 and 2017.[198] This

---

[196] Resolution 70/1 adopted by the General Assembly on 25 September 2015, Transforming our world: the 2030 Agenda for Sustainable Development, 14.
[197] Resolution 70/1 adopted by the General Assembly on 25 September 2015, Transforming our world: the 2030 Agenda for Sustainable Development, 25-26.
[198] The Sustainable Development Goals Report 2020, 56.

number equates to an average of 11.9 civilian deaths per 100,000 population each year.[199] The worldwide murder rate has decreased from 6.8 people per 100,000 population in 2000 to 5.9 people in 2015, and thence to 5.8 people in 2018 – which corresponds to about 440,000 homicide victims globally.[200] To 'significantly reduce all forms of violence' – as SDG Target 16.1[201] requires, stronger efforts are need to reduce the worldwide homicide rate.[202]

Available data from 2012 to 2019 from 69 countries – mostly from low-income and middle-income countries – suggest that almost eight in ten children from one to fourteen years of age were subjected to physical punishment and/or psychological aggression at home in the immediately-preceding month.[203] In 2016, children accounted for nearly one third of detected trafficking victims globally.[204] In a little more than one in four countries with comparable data from 2012 to 2019 – 45 countries in total, at least 5% of women between 18 and 29 years of age reported suffering sexual violence in childhood.[205] It is submitted that, on the basis of these data, SDG Target 16.2[206] will not be realized punctually, i.e., by 31st December 2030.

The 2016 to 2018 data show that the worldwide percentage of prisoners that are held in detention without being sentenced for a crime is 31%, which was the same level as in 2005.[207] Substantial rises in the percentage of prisoners so held were recorded over the last three years in Asia and Oceania.[208] Detention without trial is contrary to the rule of law. Thus, this situation is at variance with SDG Target 16.3,[209] which requires the rule of law to be promoted at both international and national levels.

---

199 The Sustainable Development Goals Report 2020, 56.

200 Progress towards the Sustainable Development Goals: Report of the Secretary-General, E/2020/xxx, 20; The Sustainable Development Goals Report 2020, 56.

201 The text to note 197 states SDG Target 16.1.

202 The Sustainable Development Goals Report 2020, 56.

203 Progress towards the Sustainable Development Goals: Report of the Secretary-General, E/2020/xxx, 20; The Sustainable Development Goals Report 2020, 56.

204 The Sustainable Development Goals Report 2020, 57.

205 Progress towards the Sustainable Development Goals: Report of the Secretary-General, E/2020/xxx, 20; The Sustainable Development Goals Report 2020, 57.

206 The text to note 197 specifies SDG Target 16.2.

207 Progress towards the Sustainable Development Goals: Report of the Secretary-General, E/2020/xxx, 20.

208 Progress towards the Sustainable Development Goals: Report of the Secretary-General, E/2020/xxx, 20.

209 The text to note 197 states SDG Target 16.3.

Data from 38 countries over the last ten years indicate that high-income countries have the lowest prevalence of bribery, whilst lower-income countries bear the greatest burden for bribery when accessing public services.[210] SDG Target 16.5[211] requires states to 'substantially reduce corruption and bribery in all their forms'.

Based on data from 2010 to 2019, the births of approximately one in four children under five years of age globally had never been officially registered as being born.[212] These data suggested that fewer than 44% of all children under five years of age had their births registered.[213] On the basis of these statistics, it is opined that SDG Target 16.9,[214] which requires the provision of legal identity for everyone – specifically mentioning birth registration – by 2030, will not be accomplished punctually , i.e., by 31st December 2030.[215]

The number of countries that have binding laws and policies giving individuals a right to access to information that public authorities hold – the right to information – has continued to rise, reaching 127 in 2019. At least 43 countries adopted such laws and policies in the past decade, 40% of them in Africa.[216] SDG Target 16.10[217] requires countries to make sure that the public have access to information in line with the law, as well as to safeguard fundamental freedoms in accordance with the law. It is submitted that, on the basis of the information in this paragraph, countries are progressing towards punctual attainment of the first of these two objectives of SDG Target 16.10.

Will SDG 16 be achieved punctually?

Based on the information in the foregoing paragraph, it is opined that, whilst progress is being made towards the realization of SDG 16,[218] some

---

[210] Progress towards the Sustainable Development Goals: Report of the Secretary-General, E/2020/xxx, 21.

[211] The text to note 197 specifies SDG Target 16.5.

[212] Progress towards the Sustainable Development Goals: Report of the Secretary-General, E/2020/xxx, 21.

[213] Progress towards the Sustainable Development Goals: Report of the Secretary-General, E/2020/xxx, 21.

[214] The text to note 197 states SDG Target 16.9.

[215] The target date for the SDGs to be met is 31st December 2030 (note 930 of Chapter Three and accompanying text).

[216] Progress towards the Sustainable Development Goals: Report of the Secretary-General, E/2020/xxx, 21.

[217] The text to note 197 specifies SDG Target 16.10.

[218] The text to note 196 states SDG 16.

of its targets will not be achieved on time, i.e., by 31st December 2030, and, therefore, it is probable that this SDG will not be fulfilled punctually. It is submitted that SDG 16 is a particularly significant goal, because it concerns legal rights and legal identity. For instance, an individual has the right not to be assaulted without provocation (SDG Target 16.1), and should be officially recorded as being alive by the possession of a birth certificate (SDG Target 16.9).

Conclusion

The conclusion to the 'New Ground Macrostudy' that constitutes this Chapter is consistent with the conclusion to the 'New Ground Microstudy' which comprises Chapter Three and concerns SDG 10 – namely that the SDGs which Table 1.4 classifies as new Goals are unlikely to be met punctually, i.e., by 31st December 2030,[219] notwithstanding the fact that significant progress is likely to have been made by this date towards the achievement of some of them. Surprisingly, this outcome is a little more positive than that to the 'Continuation Macrostudy' that constitutes Chapter Four,[220] even though the SDGs that Table 1.4 categorizes as proceeding from the MDGs should, to some extent, be familiar ground to those persons whose responsibility it is to supervise implementation of the SDGs and their targets in the relevant jurisdiction.

One stark outcome to the studies within this book is that none of the seventeen SDGs are considered to be on schedule for accomplishment by 31st December 2030. The title of the monograph asks the question: *Achieving the Sustainable Development Goals Punctually: An Impossible Remit?* The text of the monograph provides a resounding answer: *Yes, to achieve the Sustainable Goals punctually is an impossible remit*. Thus, the issue arises that at least some of these Goals should be rescheduled to be met on a slower timescale. How could this be arranged? Here is one proposition.

1. *Check the language of all the SDGs and all the SDG Targets. If any of them appear to be impossible to fulfil, then rephrase these using gentler wording*. For example, SDG Target 8.5 is one such item. This target states: "By 2030, achieve full and productive employment and decent work for all women and men, including

[219] The target date for the SDGs to be achieved is 31st December 2030 (note 930 of Chapter Three and accompanying text).

[220] Text to note 835 of Chapter Four, and the sentence that immediately follows that text.

for young people and persons with disabilities, and equal pay for work of equal value."[221] In Chapter Two, it was claimed: "full employment is very difficult to achieve even in ideal conditions; for instance, some workers need to translocate when their jobs terminate, and others move in order to seek promotion and/or better work conditions".[222] It is opined, therefore, that SDG Target 8.5 could be more realistically phrased as follows: 'Achieve *substantial* and productive employment for *both* women and men, including young persons and persons with disabilities, and equal pay for work of equal value.' This re-phrasing lowers the ideal standard that is the current version of SDG Target 8.5 to an attainable standard – which, as is familiar from the field of cost accounting,[223] is motivational for persons attempting to reach it because the standard is high but realizable. Note also, the omission of a deadline to the rephrased version of SDG Target 8.5 – as this should be open to renegotiation.

2. *Strike off all SDG Targets that all interested parties agree have already been fulfilled.* There are 17 SDGs[224] and 169 SDG Targets.[225] Any reasonable simplification is welcome.
3. *For all SDG Targets that include the phrase 'By 2030', check to see whether or not each of these is on schedule to be met by 31st December 2030. Rephrase those are not, from 'By 2030' to 'By 2040', and set the deadline for these targets as 31st December 2040.* For example, consider SDG Target 3.1 – which states: "By 2030, reduce the global maternal mortality ratio to less than 70 per

[221] Text to note 46; text to note 22 of Chapter Two.

[222] The sentence that follows the text to note 22 of Chapter Two contains this statement.

[223] In cost accounting, an attainable standard is: (i) "based upon efficient (but not perfect) operating conditions", (ii) inclusive of "allowances for normal material losses", (iii) "the most frequently encountered type of standard", and (iv) motivational for employees, because it "provide[s] a realistic but challenging target"; by contrast, an ideal standard is: (i) "based upon perfect operating conditions", (ii) exclusive of provision for inefficiencies, and (iii) associated with the possibility of having "an adverse motivational impact[,] since employees may feel that the standard is impossible to achieve" (Kaplan Financial Knowledge Bank, "Standard costing", accessed November 7, 2020, https://kfknowledgebank.kaplan.co.uk/management-accounting/costing/standard-costing).

[224] Text to note 35 of Chapter One. The text to note 36 of Chapter One lists the 17 SDGs.

[225] Text to note 37 of Chapter One.

100,000 live births".[226] The assessment in Chapter Four concludes that "it is improbable that SDG Target 3.1 will be attained punctually, i.e., by 31st December 2030".[227] If this view is widely accepted, then SDG Target 3.1 should be rephrased as follows: "*By 2040*, reduce the global maternal mortality ratio to less than 70 per 100,000 live births.".

4. *For all the remaining SDG Targets, allocate a deadline to them, which should be no earlier than 31st December 2030, and no later than 31st December 2050.* If some of the SDG Targets are moved to 2050, then there may be time to address them – as, if steps 1. to 3. are followed, there will be some SDG Targets that are due to be met by 2030 (i.e., 31st December 2030), and others that are scheduled to be attained by 2040 (i.e., 31st December 2040).
5. *Recheck all the SDGs and SDG Targets, to ensure that a reasonable balance is accomplished between those that are scheduled to be achieved in 2030, those that are due to be realized in 2040, and those that are planned to be fulfilled in 2050.*

Another issue not addressed in depth here is that a huge amount of financing – several trillion USD on current estimates – is needed to support the effort that is considered to be required to punctually achieve the SDGs. It is submitted that this money will not be forthcoming for a timetable of completion of all the SDGs by 31st December 2030. Funds are even less likely to be offered as a result of the COVID-19 pandemic,[228] because countries which are most blighted are spending the money on domestic schemes that assist with containment of this virus, and those which attempt to stem the flow of job losses in sectors that are most affected by the crisis. From this financial perspective, it is better to reschedule some or all of the SDGs and their targets to a slower timescale than the present one.

As recognized in *The Sustainable Goals Report 2020* and the Report of the Secretary-General of the UN, the COVID-19 pandemic is a setback to progress on many of the SDG Targets, such as those relating to health and to education. The deep and widespread effect of COVID-19 and its stipulated precautions is a third reason to postpone the target date of some or all of the SDGs.

Notwithstanding these comments, the SDGs are a good thing – because they focus the UN and all its partners in sustainable development

---

[226] Note 120 of Chapter One.

[227] Text to note 123 of Chapter Four.

[228] The WHO classified the outbreak and spread of COVID-19 as a pandemic on 11th March 2020 (note 53 of Chapter Two).

endeavours on continuing to improve living standards and the environment. These are worthy goals, to which everyone should be benignly inclined. In some respects, the world today is a better place than it was in the 20th Century, with its devastating major wars and subsequent east-west split – the 'Cold War' – as well as disasters, such as the 1980s famine in Ethiopia. But it is not good enough yet. In this, I agree with the founders of the SDGs – Paula Caballero[229] and Patti Londoño.[230] It is submitted, however, that a realistic timescale towards lasting economic, social and environmental progress should be adopted – which is both longer than that currently in place and also in need of acceptance that the sacrifices required by developed countries to assist LDCs, SIDS, LLDCs, Sub-Saharan Africa and other less prosperous countries and regions to substantially improve their quality of life should be cherished as gift, rather than being taken as of right.

---

[229] Note 10 Chapter One and accompanying text.
[230] Note 12 of Chapter One and accompanying text.

LIST OF ABBREVIATIONS

AfDB	African Development Bank
AIDS	Acquired Immunodeficiency Syndrome
AsDB	Asian Development Bank
CFS	Committee on World Food Security
CPI	Consumer Price Index
ECOSOC	Economic and Social Council of the United Nations
EUR	Euro(s)
FAO	Food and Agriculture Organization of the United Nations
FDI	Foreign Direct Investment
FSB	Financial Stability Board
GDP	Gross Domestic Product
GHG	Greenhouse Gas
GNI	Gross National Income
HIV	Human Immunodeficiency Virus
IADB	Inter-American Development Bank
IBRD	International Bank for Reconstruction and Development
ICJ	International Court of Justice
IFAD	International Fund for Agricultural Development
IFC	International Finance Corporation
IFFIm	International Finance Facility for Immunisation
ILO	International Labour Organization
IMF	International Monetary Fund
IOM	International Organization for Migration
KNOMAD	Global Knowledge Partnership on Migration and Development
LDC	Least Developed Country
LLDC	Landlocked Developing Country
MDB	Multilateral Development Bank
MDG	Millennium Development Goal
MPI	Multidimensional Poverty Index
MSME	Micro, Small and Medium-sized Enterprise

n/a	Not Applicable
NGO	Non-Governmental Organization
OCHA	United Nations Office for the Coordination of Humanitarian Affairs
ODA	Overseas Development Assistance
OECD	Organisation for Economic Co-operation and Development
OHCHR	Office of the United Nations High Commissioner for Human Rights
PPP	Purchasing Power Parity
Rio+20	United Nations Conference on Sustainable Development
SDG	Sustainable Development Goal
SIDS	Small Island Developing States
SME	Small and Medium-sized Enterprise
UDHR	Universal Declaration of Human Rights
UK	United Kingdom of Great Britain and Northern Ireland
UN	United Nations
UN Charter	Charter of the United Nations
UNCTAD	United Nations Conference on Trade and Development
UNDP	United Nations Development Programme
UNEP	United Nations Environment Programme
UN-Habitat	United Nations Human Settlements Programme
UNHCR	Office of the United Nations High Commissioner for Refugees
UNICEF	United Nations Children's Fund
UNDRR	United Nations Office for Disaster Risk Reduction
UNSC	United Nations Security Council
UNStC	United Nations Statistical Commission
UN System	United Nations System
USA	United States of America
USD	United States Dollar(s)
WFP	World Food Programme
WHO	World Health Organization
WTO	World Trade Organization

BIBLIOGRAPHY

Arab.org. "League of Arab States." Accessed June 23, 2020. https://arab.org/directory/league-of-arab-states/.

A-Z Animals. "Animal Classification." Accessed September 12, 2020. https://a-z-animals.com/reference/animal-classification/.

Baber, Graeme. *Essays on International Law*. Newcastle-upon-Tyne: Cambridge Scholars Publishing, 2017.

Baber, Graeme. *International Financial Law: Quo Vadis?* New York: Nova Science Publishers, Inc, 2017.

Baber, Graeme. *Preferential Trade Agreements and International Law*. Abingdon and New York: Routledge, 2019.

Baber, Graeme. *The United Nations System: A Synopsis*. Newcastle-upon-Tyne: Cambridge Scholars Publishing, 2019.

Bauer, Armin, Rana Hasan, Rhoda Magsombol, and Guanghua Wan. "The World Bank's New Poverty Data: Implications for the Asian Development Bank." *ADB Sustainable Development Working Paper Series*, No. 2, November 2008.

Caballero, Paula. *A Short History of the SDGs*. Available at https://web.archive.org/web/20171118221940/http://deliver2030.org/wp%2Dcontent/uploads/2016/04/A%2Dshort%2Dhistory%2Dof%2Dthe%2DSDGs%2DPaula%2DCaballero.pdf. Accessed January 13, 2020.

Cepei. "Patti Londoño." Accessed January 13, 2020. http://cepei.org/unds_staff/patti-londono-2/.

Čirjak, Antonia. "The Countries That Make Up Latin America." *WorldAtlas*, June 5, 2020. Accessed June 24, 2020. https://www.worldatlas.com/articles/the-countries-that-make-up-latin-america.html.

Commitment to Equity Institute. "About CEQ." Accessed May 2, 2020. http://commitmentoequity.org/about/.

Commitment to Equity Institute. *Commitment to Equity Handbook: Estimating the Impact of Fiscal Policy on Inequality and Poverty*. Edited by Nora Lustig. Washington, D.C.: Brookings Institution Press, 2018.

Committee on World Food Security. Thirty-seventh session, Rome, 17-22 October 2011, Item V: Policy Roundtable – Gender, Food Security and Nutrition, CFS: 2011/5, September 2011. Rome, 2011.

Countrymeters. "Kosovo Population." Accessed May 15, 2020. https://countrymeters.info/en/Kosovo.

Development Finance International. "About DFI." Accessed June 16, 2020. https://www.dfintl.com/our-approach/.

Devex. "Development Finance International, Inc." Accessed June 16, 2020. https://www.devex.com/organizations/development-finance-international-dfi-18748.

Emas, Rachel. "The Concept of Sustainable Development: Definition and Defining Principles." *Brief for Global Sustainable Development Report 2015*, 1-3.

Encyclopaedia Britannica. "Abraham Maslow: American Psychologist." Accessed January 10, 2020. https://www.britannica.com/biography/Abraham-H-Maslow.

Encyclopaedia Britannica. "Arab League." Accessed June 23, 2020. https://www.britannica.com/topic/Arab-League.

Encyclopaedia Britannica. "Armenian people." Accessed July 2, 2020. https://www.britannica.com/topic/Armenian-people.

Encyclopaedia Britannica. "Azerbaijan." Accessed July 2, 2020. https://www.britannica.com/place/Azerbaijan.

Encyclopaedia Britannica. "Georgia." Accessed July 2, 2020. https://www.britannica.com/place/Georgia.

Encyclopaedia Britannica. "Russia." Accessed July 2, 2020. https://www.britannica.com/place/Russia.

Encyclopaedia Britannica. "List of countries in Latin America." Accessed June 24, 2020. https://www.britannica.com/topic/list-of-countries-in-Latin-America-2061416.

Encyclopaedia Britannica. "Turkey." Accessed June 30, 2020. https://www.britannica.com/place/Turkey.

Eurostat. Sustainable development in the European Union: Monitoring report on progress towards the SDGs in an EU context: 2020 edition. Luxembourg: Publications Office of the European Union, 2020.

Ferreira, Francis, Shaohua Chen, Andrew Dabalen, Yuri Dikhanov, Nada Hamadeh, Dean Jolliffe, Ambar Narayan, Espen Prydz, Ana Revenga, Prem Sangraula, Umar Serajuddin, and Nobuo Yoshida. "A global count of the extreme poor in 2012: data issues, methodology and initial results." *Journal of Economic Inequality*, 14 (2016): 141-172.

Financial Stability Board. "About the FSB." Accessed July 20, 2020. https://www.fsb.org/about/.

FocusEconomics. "Italy Economic Outlook: March 3, 2020." Accessed March 16, 2020. https://www.focus-economics.com/countries/italy#.

Food and Agriculture Organization of the United Nations. "Agreement on Port State Measures (PSMA)." Accessed September 14, 2020. http://www.fao.org/port-state-measures/en/.

Food and Agriculture Organization of the United Nations. "Agreement on Port State Measures (PSMA): Parties to the PSMA." Accessed September 14, 2020. http://www.fao.org/port-state-measures/background/parties-psma/en/.

Food and Agriculture Organization of the United Nations. Agreement on Port State Measures to Prevent, Deter and Eliminate Illegal, Unreported and Unregulated Fishing. Rome, 2009.

Food and Agriculture Organization of the United Nations. "Global Forest Resources Assessment 2000 – Chapter 21. West Asia." Accessed June 23, 2020, http://www.fao.org/3/y1997e/y1997e0q.htm.

Food and Agriculture Organization of the United Nations. "Sustainable Forest Management (SFM) Toolbox: Forest Certification – Basic Knowledge." Accessed September 16, 2020. http://www.fao.org/sustainable-forest-management/toolbox/modules/forest-certification/basic-knowledge/en/.

Global Knowledge Partnership on Migration and Development. "KNOMAD-ILO Migration and Recruitment Costs Surveys." Accessed August 21, 2020. https://www.knomad.org/data/recruitment-costs.

Global Knowledge Partnership on Migration and Development. "Overview." Accessed August 21, 2020. https://www.knomad.org/about-us.

Gosepath, Stefan. "Equality." In *The Stanford Encyclopedia of Philosophy*, Spring 2011. Edited by Edward Zalta. Accessed May 10, 2020. https://plato.stanford.edu/archives/spr2011/entries/equality/.

Greenwich 2000 Limited. "GMT-12 Offset: Countries and Regions." Accessed March 16, 2020. https://greenwichmeantime.com/time-zone/gmt-12/.

Greenwich 2000 Limited. "GMT+14 Offset: Countries and Regions." Accessed March 16, 2020. https://greenwichmeantime.com/time-zone/gmt-plus-14/.

Huddleston, Joseph. "Can John Bolton Thaw Western Sahara's Long-Frozen Conflict?" *Foreign Policy*, May 9, 2019. Accessed June 30, 2020. https://foreignpolicy.com/2019/05/09/can-john-bolton-thaw-western-saharas-long-frozen-conflict-morocco-western-sahara-polisario-minurso-sahrawi-republic/.

International Court of Justice. *Accordance with International Law of the Unilateral Declaration of Independence in Respect of Kosovo,*

Advisory Opinion, Advisory Opinion of 22 July 2010. *I.C.J. Reports 2010*, 403-453.

International Finance Facility for Immunisation. "About IFFIm." Accessed January 28, 2020. https://iffim.org/about-iffim.

International Institute for Sustainable Development. "Technology Bank Inaugurated in Turkey, Work Under Way in 16 LDCs: 7 June 2018." Accessed September 23, 2020. http://sdg.iisd.org/news/technology-bank-inaugurated-in-turkey-work-under-way-in-16-ldcs/.

International Institute for Sustainable Development. "UN Secretary-General Releases 2020 SDG Progress Report." Accessed September 18, 2020. https://sdg.iisd.org/news/un-secretary-general-releases-2020-sdg-progress-report/.

International Labour Organization. "About the Pact." Accessed September 28, 2020. https://www.ilo.org/jobspact/about/lang--en/index.htm.

International Labour Organization. "ILOSTAT: 1.1.1 Working poverty rate." Accessed March 25, 2020. https://www.ilo.org/ilostat/faces/oracle/webcenter/portalapp/pagehierarchy/Page33.jspx;ILOSTATCOOKIE=4iYG0WpxcNKkwq_7OKV65n0AL_7kXm8QDqnc6720zRNb0WXMYQo2!-1102363596?locale=EN&MBI_ID=530&_afrLoop=9945026141909335&_afrWindowMode=0&_afrWindowId=null#!%40%40%3F_afrWindowId%3Dnull%26locale%3DEN%26_afrLoop%3D994502614190933 5%26MBI_ID%3D530%26_afrWindowMode%3D0%26_adf.ctrl-state%3Dk8au5er2e_4.

International Labour Organization. "ILOSTAT explorer: Dataset SDG indicator 10.4.1 – Labour income share as a percent of GDP (%) – Annual." Accessed June 20, 2020. https://www.ilo.org/shinyapps/bulkexplorer20/?lang=en&segment=&id=SDG_1041_NOC_RT_A.

International Labour Organization. "Pact News." Accessed September 28, 2020. https://www.ilo.org/jobspact/news/lang--en/index.htm.

International Labour Organization. Recovering from the crisis: A Global Jobs Pact – adopted by the International Labour Conference at its Ninety-eighth Session, Geneva, 19 June 2009. Geneva: International Labour Office, 2009.

International Labour Organization. World Employment and Social Outlook – Trends 2020. Geneva, 2020.

International Labour Organization. World Social Protection Report 2017-19: Universal social protection to achieve the Sustainable Development Goals. Geneva, 2017.

International Monetary Fund. "List of Members." Last updated April 15, 2020. Accessed July 14, 2020. https://www.imf.org/external/np/sec/memdir/memdate.htm.

International Organization for Migration. "Download Missing Migrants Project data." Accessed July 24, 2020. https://missingmigrants.iom.int/downloads.

International Organization for Migration. "Methodology." Accessed July 24, 2020. https://missingmigrants.iom.int/methodology.

International Organization for Migration. "Migration Governance Indicators." Accessed August 5, 2020. https://gmdac.iom.int/migration-governance-indicators.

International Organization for Migration. "Regional classifications." Accessed July 25, 2020. https://missingmigrants.iom.int/regional-classifications.

International Telecommunications Union. "Goals, targets and indicators." Accessed February 16 and 17, 2020. http://www.itu.int/ITU-D/ict/mdg/goals.html#fa.

International Trade Centre. "About ITC." Accessed August 23, 2020. https://www.intracen.org/itc/about/.

International Tribunal for the Law of the Sea. "States Parties." Accessed September 14, 2020. https://www.itlos.org/the-tribunal/states-parties/.

International Union for Conservation of Nature and Natural Resources "Red List Index." Accessed September 17, 2020. https://www.iucnredlist.org/assessment/red-list-index.

Investopedia. "Green bond." Accessed January 28, 2020. https://www.investopedia.com/terms/g/green-bond.asp.

Jenkins, Stephen, and Philippe Van Kerm. "The Measurement of Economic Inequality." In *The Oxford Handbook of Economic Inequality*, edited by Weimer Salverda, Brian Nolan, and Timothy Smeeding, 40-67. Oxford: Oxford University Press, 2009.

Kamau, Macharia, Pamela Chasek, and David O'Connor. *Transforming Multilateral Diplomacy: The Inside Story of the Sustainable Development Goals*. Abingdon: Routledge, 2018.

Kamm, Frances. "In Memoriam: Ronald Dworkin." *Harvard Law Review*, 127(2) (2013): 498-499.

Kaplan Financial Knowledge Bank. "Standard costing." Accessed November 7, 2020. https://kfknowledgebank.kaplan.co.uk/management-accounting/costing/standard-costing.

Kiprop, Joseph. "Is Turkey in Europe or Asia?" *WorldAtlas*, April 25, 2017. Accessed June 30, 2020. https://www.worldatlas.com/articles/is-turkey-in-europe-or-asia.html.

Kiyak, Tunga. "Turkey." *Encyclopedia of the Nations*. Accessed June 30, 2020. https://www.nationsencyclopedia.com/economies/Asia-and-the-Pacific/Turkey.html.

Lexico. "Sustainable development." Accessed January 9, 2020. https://www.lexico.com/definition/sustainable_development.

Lustig, Nora, Chiara Mariotti, and Carolina Sánchez-Páramo. "The redistributive impact of fiscal policy indicator: A new global standard for assessing government effectiveness in tackling inequality within the SDG framework." *World Bank Data Blog*, June 11, 2020. Accessed June 16, 2020. https://blogs.worldbank.org/opendata/redistributive-impact-fiscal-policy-indicator-new-global-standard-assessing-government.

Manhattan College "Pamela Chasek." Accessed February 21, 2020. https://manhattan.edu/campus-directory/pamela.chasek.

Maslow, Abraham. "A Theory of Human Motivation." *Psychological Review*, 1943, 50(4), 370-396.

McFarlane, Gavin. *The Layman's Dictionary of English Law*. London: Waterlow Publishers Limited, 1984.

MDG Monitor. "MDG 1: Eradicate extreme poverty and hunger." Accessed February 29, 2020. https://www.mdgmonitor.org/mdg-1-eradicate-poverty-hunger/.

Merriam-Webster. "peri-urban." Accessed September 27, 2020. https://www.merriam-webster.com/dictionary/peri-urban.

Merriam-Webster. "rifampin." Accessed September 7, 2020. https://www.merriam-webster.com/dictionary/rifampin.

Ministry of Foreign Affairs in the Government of Kenya. "Ambassador Kamau Macharia." Accessed January 14, 2020. http://www.mfa.go.ke/?page_id=2224.

Nahmias, Petra, and Natalia Baal. "Including forced displacement in the SDGs: a new refugee indicator." *UNHCR Blogs*, December 2, 2019. Accessed July 21, 2020. https://www.unhcr.org/blogs/including-forced-displacement-in-the-sdgs-a-new-refugee-indicator/.

Nations Online Project. "Reference Map of Melanesia." Accessed August 14, 2020. https://www.nationsonline.org/oneworld/map/melanesia_map.htm.

Office of the United Nations High Commissioner for Human Rights. E-mail of Mr. Francisco Guerreiro to Dr. Graeme Baber, 15 June 2020.

Office of the United Nations High Commissioner for Human Rights. Guidance Note for Implementation of Survey Module on SDG Indicator 16.b.1 & 10.3.1 (Discrimination). Geneva, 2020.

Office of the United Nations High Commissioner for Refugees. Indicator Proposal Summary Template: Proportion of population who are refugees by country of origin. New York, 2019.

Office of the United Nations High Commissioner for Refugees. Report on UNHCR's global strategic priorities, EC/71/SC/CRP.13/Rev.1, 6 July 2020. Geneva, 2020.

Organisation for Economic Co-operation and Development. "Country programmable aid (CPA)." Accessed September 20, 2020. http://www.oecd.org/dac/financing-sustainable-development/development-finance-standards/cpa.htm.

Organisation for Economic Co-operation and Development. DAC List of ODA Recipients: Effective for reporting on 2014, 2015, 2016 and 2017 flows. Paris 2017.

Organisation for Economic Co-operation and Development. DAC List of ODA Recipients: Effective for reporting on 2020 flows. Paris, 2019.

Organisation for Economic Co-operation and Development. DAC List of ODA Recipients. Effective for reporting on aid in 2018 and 2019. Paris, 2019.

Organisation for Economic Co-operation and Development. Development aid in 2015 continues to grow despite costs for in-donor refugees, 13 April 2016. Paris, 2016.

Organisation for Economic Co-operation and Development. "Development Assistance Committee (DAC)." Accessed September 7, 2020. http://www.oecd.org/dac/development-assistance-committee/.

Organisation for Economic Co-operation and Development. "Development finance standards." Accessed May 1, 2020. http://www.oecd.org/dac/financing-sustainable-development/development-finance-standards/.

Organisation for Economic Co-operation and Development. "Frequently Asked Questions." Accessed September 14, 2020. https://www.oecd.org/dac/stats/faq.htm.

Organisation for Economic Co-operation and Development. "Official development assistance – definition and coverage." Accessed August 27, 2020. https://www.oecd.org/development/financing-sustainable-development/development-finance-standards/officialdevelopmentassistancedefinitionandcoverage.htm.

Organisation for Economic Co-operation and Development. "The Development Assistance Committee's Mandate." Accessed August 27,

2020. http://www.oecd.org/dac/thedevelopmentassistancecommitteesmandate.htm.

Our World in Data. "Debt service of exports of goods and services." Accessed September 21, 2020. https://ourworldindata.org/grapher/debt-service-of-exports-of-goods-services?tab=table&time=2015.

Oxford University Press. *The New Oxford Dictionary of English*. Oxford: Oxford University Press, 1998.

Rare. "We are Rare." Accessed January 13, 2020. https://rare.org/we-are-rare/.

Roemer, John. "Equality: Its Justification, Nature and Domain." In *The Oxford Handbook of Economic Inequality*, edited by Weimer Salverda, Brian Nolan, and Timothy Smeeding, 23-39. Oxford: Oxford University Press, 2009.

Rutgers School of Public Affairs and Administration. "Rachel Emas, PhD." Accessed January 11, 2020. https://spaa.newark.rutgers.edu/rachel-emas.

Scott, Russell, and Emma Howard. "Even after a global ban, pangolins are still legally traded." *Unearthed (Greenpeace UK)*, July 23, 2020. Accessed September 18, 2020. https://unearthed.greenpeace.org/2020/07/23/pangolin-ban-legal-trade-cites-china-us/.

SDG Tracker. "Sustainable Development Goal 17: Revitalize the global partnership for sustainable development." Accessed September 24, 2020. https://sdg-tracker.org/global-partnerships.

Secretariat of the Convention on Biological Diversity. "About the Nagoya Protocol." Accessed September 18, 2020. https://www.cbd.int/abs/about/default.shtml/.

Secretariat of the Convention on Biological Diversity. Living in harmony with nature: Strategic Plan for Biodiversity 2011-2020. Montreal, 2010.

Secretariat of the Convention on Biological Diversity. Strategic Plan for Biodiversity 2011-2020 and the Aichi Targets. Montreal, 2010.

Secretariat of the Convention on Biological Diversity. Sustaining life on Earth: How the Convention on Biological Diversity promotes nature and human well-being, April 2000. Montreal, 2000.

Serajuddin, Umar, and Espen Prydz. "SDG indicator 10.2.1." Presentation to the 8th meeting of the Inter-Agency and Expert Group on SDG Indicators, Stockholm, 5th-9th November 2018. Washington, D.C.: World Bank, 2018.

The Jerusalem Bible: Popular Edition. London: Darton, Longman & Todd Ltd., 1974.

Time and Date AS. "Time Zone in American Samoa." Accessed March 16, 2020. https://www.timeanddate.com/time/zone/american-samoa.

Times Books. *The Times Concise Atlas of the World*, Thirteenth edition. London: Times Books, 2016.

Turkish Statistical Institute. "Main Statistics." Accessed June 30, 2020. http://www.turkstat.gov.tr/UstMenu.do?metod=temelist.

United Nations. Beijing Declaration and Platform for Action, The Fourth World Conference on Women, 4-15 September 1994. Beijing, 1995.

United Nations. "Conferences, Meetings and Events: Millennium Summit (6-8 September 2000)." Accessed February 24, 2020. https://www.un.org/en/events/pastevents/millennium_summit.shtml.

United Nations. Decision 67/555 of the General Assembly dated 22 January 2013.

United Nations. Declaration from the Addis Ababa Civil Society Forum on Financing for Development. Addis Ababa, 2015.

United Nations Children's Fund/Save the Children. Indicator Proposal Summary Template: Pro-poor public social spending. New York, 2019.

United Nations. Department of Economic and Social Affairs – Financing for Development Office: The 10 Year Framework of Programmes on Sustainable Consumption and Production Patterns (10YFP) – Interim progress report prepared by the 10YFP Secretariat on behalf of the 10YFP Board for the High-Level Political Forum. New York, 2014.

United Nations. Department of Economic and Social Affairs – Statistics Division: Metadata for Target 1.1 – Indicator 1.1.1: ILO – Last updated: March 2019. New York, 2019.

United Nations. Department of Economic and Social Affairs – Statistics Division: Metadata for Target 1.2 – Indicator 1.2.1: World Bank – Last updated: 24 January 2017. New York, 2017.

United Nations. Department of Economic and Social Affairs – Statistics Division: Metadata for Target 1.2 – Indicator 1.2.2: Last updated: 1st December 2018. New York, 2018.

United Nations. Department of Economic and Social Affairs – Statistics Division: Metadata for Target 1.3 – Indicator 1.3.1: ILO – Last updated: 8th June 2018. New York, 2018.

United Nations. Department of Economic and Social Affairs – Statistics Division: Metadata for Target 1.4 – Indicator 1.4.1: United Nations Human Settlements Programme – Last updated: 16th October 2018. New York, 2018.

United Nations. Department of Economic and Social Affairs – Statistics Division: Metadata for Target 1.4 – Indicator 1.4.2: United Nations Human Settlements Programme and World Bank – Last updated: 12th February 2018. New York, 2018.

United Nations. Department of Economic and Social Affairs – Statistics Division: Metadata for Target 1.5 – Indicator 1.5.1: United Nations Office for Disaster Reduction – Last updated: March 2018. New York, 2018.

United Nations. Department of Economic and Social Affairs – Statistics Division: Metadata for Target 1.5 – Indicator 1.5.2: United Nations Office for Disaster Reduction – Last updated: March 2018. New York, 2018.

United Nations. Department of Economic and Social Affairs – Statistics Division: Metadata for Target 1.5 – Indicator 1.5.3: United Nations Office for Disaster Reduction – Last updated: 7th July 2017. New York, 2017.

United Nations. Department of Economic and Social Affairs – Statistics Division: Metadata for Target 1.5 – Indicator 1.5.4: United Nations Office for Disaster Reduction – Last updated: February 2018. New York, 2018.

United Nations. Department of Economic and Social Affairs – Statistics Division: Metadata for Target 1.a – Indicator 1.a.2: Last updated: 1st December 2018. New York, 2018.

United Nations. Department of Economic and Social Affairs – Statistics Division: Metadata for Target 10.1 – Indicator 10.1.1: World Bank – Last updated: 19th July 2016. New York, 2016.

United Nations. Department of Economic and Social Affairs – Statistics Division: Metadata for Target 10.2 – Indicator 10.2.1: World Bank – Last updated: November 2018. New York, 2018.

United Nations. Department of Economic and Social Affairs – Statistics Division: Metadata for Target 10.3 – Indicator 10.3.1: OHCHR – Last updated: 3rd December 2018. New York, 2018.

United Nations. Department of Economic and Social Affairs – Statistics Division: Metadata for Target 10.4 – Indicator 10.4.1: ILO – Last updated: March 2019. New York, 2019.

United Nations. Department of Economic and Social Affairs – Statistics Division: Metadata for Target 10.5 – Indicator 10.5.1: IMF – Last updated: 3rd December 2018. New York, 2018.

United Nations. Department of Economic and Social Affairs – Statistics Division: Metadata for Target 10.6 – Indicator 10.6.1: Financing for

Development Office at the Department of Economic and Social Affairs – Last updated: 19th July 2016. New York, 2016.

United Nations, Department of Economic and Social Affairs – Statistics Division: Metadata for Target 10.7 – Indicator 10.7.1: ILO and World Bank – Last updated: November 2018. New York, 2018.

United Nations. Department of Economic and Social Affairs – Statistics Division: Metadata for Target 10.7 – Indicator 10.7.2: Department of Economic and Social Affairs and IOM – Last updated: September 2019. New York, 2019.

United Nations. Department of Economic and Social Affairs – Statistics Division: Metadata for Target 10.7 – Indicator 10.7.3: IOM – Last updated: 5th July 2020. New York, 2020.

United Nations. Department of Economic and Social Affairs – Statistics Division: Metadata for Target 10.a – Indicator 10.a.1: International Trade Centre, UNCTAD and WTO – Last updated: 19th July 2016. New York, 2016.

United Nations. Department of Economic and Social Affairs – Statistics Division: Metadata for Target 10.b – Indicator 10.b.1: OECD – Last updated: 19th July 2016. New York, 2016.

United Nations. Department of Economic and Social Affairs – Statistics Division: Metadata for Target 10.c – Indicator 10.c.1: World Bank – Last updated: 2nd February 2018. New York, 2018.

United Nations. Department of Economic and Social Affairs – Statistics Division: Reference metadata template for data reported on the Sustainable Development Goals (SDGs) – Target 1.a – Indicator 1.a.3: Last updated: 30th July 2018. New York, 2018.

United Nations. Department of Economic and Social Affairs – Statistics Division: Reference metadata template for data reported on the Sustainable Development Goals (SDGs) – Target 16.3 – Indicator 16.3.3: Last updated: 3rd December 2018. New York, 2018.

United Nations. Department of Economic and Social Affairs: World Economic and Social Survey 2012 – In Search of New Development Finance, E/2012/50/Rev.1, ST/ESA/341. New York, 2012.

United Nations. Department of Field Support – Cartographic Section: West Africa – Map No. 4533, October 2014.

United Nations. Economic and Social Council: High-level political forum on sustainable development, convened under the auspices of the Economic and Social Council – Progress towards the Sustainable Development Goals: Report of the Secretary-General, E/2020/xxx. New York, 2020.

United Nations. Economic and Social Council: High-level political forum on sustainable development, convened under the auspices of the Economic and Social Council – Special edition: progress towards the Sustainable Development Goals: Report of the Secretary-General, E/2019/68, 8 May 2019. New York, 2019.

United Nations. ECOSOC Development Cooperation Forum: Promoting Sustainable Development through Triangular Cooperation, DCF Policy Briefs, September 2017, No. 19. New York, 2017.

United Nations. E-mail of the Statistics Division at the Department of Economic and Social Affairs to Dr. Graeme Baber, 24 April 2020.

United Nations. "Fundamental Principles of National Official Statistics." Accessed September 25, 2020. https://unstats.un.org/unsd/dnss/gp/fundprinciples.aspx.

United Nations. Global indicator framework for the Sustainable Development Goals and targets of the 2030 Agenda for Sustainable Development, A/RES/71/313, E/CN.3/2018/2, E/CN.3/2019/2, E/CN.3/2020/2. New York, 2020.

United Nations. "IAEG-SDGs: 2020 Comprehensive Review Process." Accessed April 12, 2020. https://unstats.un.org/sdgs/iaeg-sdgs/2020-comp-rev/.

United Nations. International Business Forum: Third International Conference on Financing for Development. Addis Ababa, 2015.

United Nations. "Member States." Accessed June 3, 2020, and July 15, 2020, https://www.un.org/en/member-states/.

United Nations. "Member States." Accessed June 3, 2020, and July 15, 2020, https://www.un.org/en/sections/member-states/.

United Nations. "Methodology: Standard country or area codes for statistical use (M49) – Countries or areas / geographical regions." Accessed July 12, 2020. https://unstats.un.org/unsd/methodology/m49/.

United Nations. "Methodology: Standard country or area codes for statistical use (M49) – Developed Regions." Accessed July 9, 2020. https://unstats.un.org/unsd/methodology/m49/#developed.

United Nations. "Methodology: Standard country or area codes for statistical use (M49) – Developing Regions." Accessed July 9, 2020. https://unstats.un.org/unsd/methodology/m49/#developing.

United Nations. "Non-member States." Accessed August 6, 2020. https://www.un.org/en/sections/member-states/non-member-states/index.html.

United Nations. Oceans and the law of the sea: Report of the Secretary-General, A/75/50, 16 March 2020. New York, 2020.

United Nations. "Office of the High Representative for the Least Developed Countries, Landlocked Developing Countries and Small Island Developing States: List of LLDCs." Accessed June 21, 2020. https://www.un.org/ohrlls/content/list-lldcs.

United Nations. Open Working Group Proposal for Sustainable Development Goals. New York, 2014.

United Nations. Paris Agreement. Paris, 2015.

United Nations. "Paris Agreement – Status of Ratification." Accessed May 4, 2020. https://unfccc.int/process/the-paris-agreement/status-of-ratification.

United Nations. Report of the Committee on Information from Non-Self-Governing Territories, General Assembly Official Records: Eighteenth Session, Supplement No. 14, A/5514. New York, 1963.

United Nations. Report of the International Conference on Population and Development, Cairo, 5-13 September 1994. New York, 1995.

United Nations. Resolution 55/2 adopted by the General Assembly on 8 September 2000

United Nations. Resolution 66/288 adopted by the General Assembly on 27 July 2012.

United Nations. Resolution 67/19 adopted by the General Assembly on 29 November 2012.

United Nations. Resolution 67/290 adopted by the General Assembly on 9 July 2013.

United Nations. Resolution 68/261 adopted by the General Assembly on 29 January 2014.

United Nations. Resolution 69/313 adopted by the General Assembly on 27 July 2015.

United Nations. Resolution 70/1 adopted by the General Assembly on 25 September 2015.

United Nations. Resolution 71/313 adopted by the General Assembly on 6 July 2017.

United Nations. Resolution 74/4 adopted by the General Assembly on 15 October 2019.

United Nations. Resolution 74/97 adopted by the General Assembly on 13 December 2019.

United Nations. Resolution 8(I) of the Economic and Social Council of 16 February 1946 on the Establishment of a Statistical Commission.

United Nations. Resolution 8(II) of the Economic and Social Council adopted 21 June 1946 on the Statistical Commission.

United Nations. "SDG Indicators: Global indicator framework for the Sustainable Development Goals and targets of the 2030 Agenda for Sustainable Development." Accessed April 12, 2020. https://unstats.un.org/sdgs/indicators/indicators-list/.

United Nations. "SDG indicators: United Nations Global SDG Database." Accessed June 20, 2020, July 5 and 9, 2020, August 5, 20 and 22, 2020, and September 22 and 24, 2020. https://unstats.un.org/sdgs/indicators/database/.

United Nations. Secretary-General: Paris Agreement – Depositary Notification C.N.735.2016.TREATIES-XXVII.7.d, 5 October 2016. New York, 2016.

United Nations. Sixty-eighth session of the General Assembly: Agenda items 14, 19(a) and 118, A/68/970, 12 August 2014 – Report of the Open Working Group of the General Assembly on Sustainable Development Goals. New York, 2014.

United Nations. Statistical Commission: Report on the fifty-first session (3-6 March 2020), Economic and Social Council Official Records, 2020, Supplement No. 4, E/2020/24-E/CN.3/2020/37. New York, 2020.

United Nations. "Sustainable Development Goals." Accessed January 27 and 29, 2020. https://www.un.org/sustainabledevelopment/summit/.

United Nations. The Millennium Development Goals Report 2015. New York, 2015.

United Nations. The Sustainable Development Goals Report 2020. New York, 2020.

United Nations. "The United Nations and Decolonization: Non-Self-Governing Territories." Accessed June 30, 2020. https://www.un.org/dppa/decolonization/en/nsgt.

United Nations. "The United Nations and Decolonization: Non-Self-Governing Territories – Western Sahara." Accessed June 30, 2020. https://www.un.org/dppa/decolonization/en/nsgt/western-sahara.

United Nations. "Third International Conference: Financing for Development." Accessed January 27, 2020. https://www.un.org/esa/ffd/ffd3/index.html.

United Nations. "Trade Knowledgebase: Tariff Line." Accessed August 23, 2020. https://unstats.un.org/unsd/tradekb/Knowledgebase/50291/Tariff-Line.

United Nations. United Nations Committee for Development Policy: List of Least Developed Countries (as of December 2018). New York, 2018.

United Nations. United Nations Convention on the Law of the Sea. Montego Bay, 1982.

United Nations. Universal Declaration of Human Rights. Paris, 1948.

United Nations. "We can end poverty: Millennium Development Goals and Beyond 2015 – Goal 1: Eradicate extreme poverty & hunger." Accessed February 24, 2020, and September 3, 2020. https://www.un.org/millenniumgoals/poverty.shtml.

United Nations. "We can end poverty: Millennium Development Goals and Beyond 2015 – Goal 8: Develop a global partnership for development." Accessed September 19, 2020. https://www.un.org/millenniumgoals/global.shtml.

United Nations Conference on Trade and Development. World Investment Report, 2019: Special Economic Zones – Key Messages and Overview. Geneva: United Nations, 2019.

United Nations Development Programme. "Human Development Reports: The 2019 Global Multidimensional Poverty Index (MPI)." Accessed April 20, 21 and 23, 2020. http://hdr.undp.org/en//2018-MPI.

United Nations Development Programme. Human Development Indices and Indicators: 2018 Statistical Update. New York, 2018.

United Nations Office for Disaster Risk Reduction. Technical Guidance for Monitoring and Reporting on Progress in Achieving the Global Targets of the Sendai Framework for Disaster Risk Reduction: Collection of Technical Notes on Data and Methodology: December 2017. Geneva, 2017.

United Nations Office for Disaster Risk Reduction. UNDRR Work Programme 2020-2021 in support of the Sendai Framework for Disaster Risk Reduction. Geneva, 2019.

United Nations Sustainable Development 2015. "Open Working Group on Sustainable Development." Accessed January 15 and 16, 2020. https://www.sustainabledevelopment2015.org/index.php/intergovernmental-processes/sustainable-development-goals/open-working-group/.

United Nations Sustainable Development Knowledge Platform. "First session of the Open Working Group on Sustainable Development Goals." Accessed January 14, 2020. https://sustainabledevelopment.un.org/owg1.html.

United Nations Sustainable Development Knowledge Platform. "Open Working Group on Sustainable Development Goals." Accessed January 14, 2020. https://sustainabledevelopment.un.org/owg.html.

United Nations Sustainable Development Knowledge Platform. "Open Working Group on Sustainable Development Goals (reference #203333)." Accessed January 15, 2020.

https://sustainabledevelopment.un.org/account.php?page=view&nr=751&type=12&msg=203333&menu=1457.

United Nations Sustainable Development Knowledge Platform. "Small Island Developing States." Accessed June 20, 2020. https://sustainabledevelopment.un.org/topics/sids/list.

United Nations Sustainable Development Knowledge Platform. "Sustainable Development Goal 1: End poverty in all its forms everywhere – Targets & Indicators." Accessed March 24, 2020. https://sustainabledevelopment.un.org/sdg1#targets.

United Nations Treaty Collection. "Chapter XXVII Environment: 2. a Montreal Protocol on Substances that Deplete the Ozone Layer." Accessed September 11, 2020. https://treaties.un.org/pages/ViewDetails.aspx?src=TREATY&mtdsg_no=XXVII-2-a&chapter=27&lang=en.

United Nations Water. "Indicator 6.6.1 – Water-related ecosystems." Accessed September 13, 2020. https://sdg6data.org/indicator/6.6.1.

University of Central Florida. "Countries & Regions: Melanesia." Accessed August 14, 2020. https://guides.ucf.edu/countries/melanesia.

University of Central Florida. "Countries & Regions: Micronesia." Accessed August 14, 2020. https://guides.ucf.edu/countries/micronesia.

University of Central Florida. "Countries & Regions: Polynesia." Accessed August 14, 2020. https://guides.ucf.edu/countries/polynesia.

Vienna Energy Forum. "Csaba Kőrösi." Accessed January 14, 2020. https://www.viennaenergyforum.org/content/csaba-k%C5%91r%C3%B6si.

Weiser, Christina. Methodology for computing the indicator on Shared Prosperity for the Global Database of Shared Prosperity (GDSP) circa 2007-2012: Global Poverty Working Group, October 2015. Washington, D.C.: World Bank, 2015.

Wenar, Leif. "John Rawls." In *The Stanford Encyclopedia of Philosophy*, Spring 2017. Edited by Edward Zalta. Accessed May 10, 2020. https://plato.stanford.edu/archives/spr2017/entries/rawls.

Wikipedia. "Cycad." Accessed September 12, 2020. https://en.wikipedia.org/wiki/Cycad.

Wikipedia. "Cycadales." Accessed September 12, 2020. https://en.wikipedia.org/wiki/Cycadales.

Wikipedia. "Scleractinia." Accessed September 12, 2020. https://en.wikipedia.org/wiki/Scleractinia.

Willan, Philip. "45 killed as boat capsizes." *The Times*, August 21, 2020, No. 73244, 9.

Willan, Philip. "Rome offers Tunis €11m to stop flow of migrants." *The Times*, August 18, 2020, No. 73241, 31.

WordReference.com. "Research and development." Accessed September 29, 2020. https://forum.wordreference.com/threads/research-and-development.524277/.

World Bank. "Carbon Pricing Dashboard: What is Carbon Pricing?" Accessed January 28, 2020. https://carbonpricingdashboard.worldbank.org/what-carbon-pricing.

World Bank. "DataBank: Poverty and Equity." Accessed April 15, 2020. https://databank.worldbank.org/source/poverty-and-equity.

World Bank. "DataBank: World Development Indicators." Accessed June 7 and 16, 2020. https://databank.worldbank.org/source/world-development-indicators.

World Bank, "Data Updates and Errata." Accessed June 6, 2020. https://datahelpdesk.worldbank.org/knowledgebase/articles/906522-data-updates-and-errata.

World Bank. "FAQs: Global Poverty Line Update." Accessed February 28, 2020. https://www.worldbank.org/en/topic/poverty/brief/global-poverty-line-faq.

World Bank. Getting SmaRT about remittance price monitoring: Methodology for the Smart Remitter Target (SmaRT): a new approach to measuring the progress towards the global objectives of reducing the cost of international remittances, Payment Systems Development Group, June 2016. Washington, D.C., 2016.

World Bank. Global Database of Shared Prosperity and Median/Income Consumption, circa 2012-2017, as of 17th March 2020.

World Bank. "International Comparison Programme (ICP): Overview." Accessed March 28, 2020. https://www.worldbank.org/en/programs/icp#1.

World Bank. Migration and Remittances: Recent Developments and Outlook – Migration and Development Brief 29, April 2018. Washington, D.C., 2018.

World Bank. "PovcalNet: Choose economies/aggregates." Accessed March 26, 28, 29, and 30, 2020, and April 1, 2, 3, 4, 5, 7 and 8, 2020. http://iresearch.worldbank.org/PovcalNet/povOnDemand.aspx.

World Bank: "PovcalNet: Methodology." Accessed March 27 and 28, 2020. http://iresearch.worldbank.org/PovcalNet/methodology.aspx.

World Bank. "PovcalNet: What is new", Accessed March 28 and 29, 2020. http://iresearch.worldbank.org/PovcalNet/WhatIsNew.aspx.

World Bank. Poverty and Shared Prosperity 2018: Piecing Together the Poverty Puzzle. Washington, D.C., 2018.

World Bank. "Remittance Prices Worldwide: About Us." Accessed August 30, 2020. https://remittanceprices.worldbank.org/en/about-remittance-prices-worldwide.

World Bank. World Development Report 1990: Poverty – World Development Indicators, PUB8507. Oxford: Oxford University Press, 1990.

World Commission on Environment and Development. Report: Our Common Future. New York, 1987.

World Health Organization. "About the WHO Framework Convention on Tobacco Control." Accessed September 8, 2020. https://www.who.int/fctc/about/en/.

World Health Organization. International Health Regulations 2005, Second edition. Geneva, 2008.

World Health Organization. The WHO Framework on Tobacco Control: an overview, January 2015. Geneva, 2015.

World Health Organization. "WHO Director-General's opening remarks at the media briefing on COVID-19." Accessed March 16, 2020. https://www.who.int/dg/speeches/detail/who-director-general-s-opening-remarks-at-the-media-briefing-on-covid-19---11-march-2020.

Worldometer. "7 continents." Accessed June 27, 2020. https://www.worldometers.info/geography/7-continents/.

Worldometer. "Argentina Population (LIVE)." Accessed May 15, 2020. https://www.worldometers.info/world-population/argentina-population/.

Worldometer. "Countries in the world by population (2020)." Accessed April 15, 2020, May 15, 2020, and June 10, 2020. https://www.worldometers.info/world-population/population-by-country/.

Worldometer. "GDP per Capita." Accessed July 2, 2020. https://www.worldometers.info/gdp/gdp-per-capita/.

Worldometer. "How many Countries in Europe?" Accessed August 14, 2020. https://www.worldometers.info/geography/how-many-countries-in-europe/.

Worldometer. "Italy: Coronavirus Cases." Accessed March 16, 2020. https://www.worldometers.info/coronavirus/country/italy/.

Worldometer. "Population of Eastern Asia (2019 and historical)." Accessed June 29, 2020. https://www.worldometers.info/world-population/eastern-asia-population/.

Worldometer. "Population of Nigeria (2020 and historical)." Accessed July 1, 2020. https://www.worldometers.info/world-population/nigeria-population/.

Worldometer. "Population of South-Eastern Asia (2019 and historical)." Accessed June 29, 2020. https://www.worldometers.info/world-population/south-eastern-asia-population/.

Worldometer. "World Population (2020 and historical)." Accessed June 10, 2020. https://www.worldometers.info/world-population/.

Worldometer. "World Population by Year." Accessed June 3, 2020. https://www.worldometers.info/world-population/world-population-by-year/.

World Population Review. "Antarctica Population 2020." Accessed June 13, 2020. https://worldpopulationreview.com/continents/antarctica-population/.

World Population Review. "Continent and Region Populations 2020." Accessed June 13, 2020. https://worldpopulationreview.com/continents/.

World Population Review. "Total Population by Country 2020." Accessed June 21 and 22, 2020. https://worldpopulationreview.com/countries/.

World Resources Institute. "David O'Connor: Sustainable Economist." Accessed February 21, 2020. https://www.wri.org/profile/david-oconnor.

World Trade Organization. "Appellate Body." Accessed September 25, 2020. https://www.wto.org/english/tratop_e/dispu_e/appellate_body_e.htm.

World Trade Organization. "Appellate Body Members." Accessed September 25, 2020. https://www.wto.org/english/tratop_e/dispu_e/ab_members_descrp_e.htm.

World Trade Organization. "Roberto Azevêdo, WTO Director-General, 2013 to 2020." Accessed September 25, 2020. https://www.wto.org/english/thewto_e/dg_e/ra_e.htm.

World Trade Organization. "The Doha Round texts – introduction." Accessed September 25, 2020. https://www.wto.org/english/tratop_e/dda_e/texts_intro_e.htm.

Wright, Tom. *Luke for Everyone*. London: Society for Promoting Christian Knowledge, 2004.

INDEX